D1294511

THE UNIVERSITIES OF EUROPE
IN THE MIDDLE AGES

RASHDALL

𝕷𝔬𝔫𝔡𝔬𝔫

HENRY FROWDE

OXFORD UNIVERSITY PRESS WAREHOUSE
AMEN CORNER, E.C.

𝕹𝔢𝔴 𝖄𝔬𝔯𝔨

MACMILLAN & CO., 66 FIFTH AVENUE

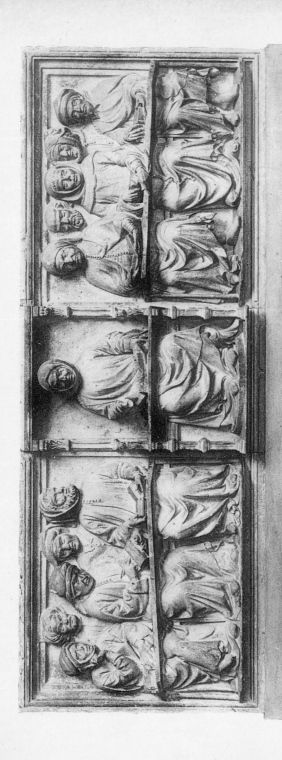

LORENZO PINI JUN. LETTORE DI DECRETALI

MORI IL 18 AGOSTO 1542 E FU SEPOLTO IN SAN PIETRO

TOMB OF A BOLOGNA DOCTOR

THE

UNIVERSITIES OF EUROPE

IN THE

MIDDLE AGES

BY

HASTINGS RASHDALL, M.A.

FELLOW AND LECTURER OF HERTFORD COLLEGE, OXFORD

IN TWO VOLUMES

Volume I

SALERNO — BOLOGNA — PARIS

OXFORD

AT THE CLARENDON PRESS

M DCCC XCV

378.4
R183
V.1

TO

MY FRIENDS AND LATE COLLEAGUES

IN THE UNIVERSITY OF DURHAM

ARCHIBALD ROBERTSON, D.D.

AND

FRANK BYRON JEVONS, D. LITT.

PREFACE

THE writing of this book is a task in which I became involved through winning the Chancellor's Prize at Oxford for an English Essay in 1883. I entered upon it with no intention of undertaking anything more than such a revision and expansion of my Essay as would justify its publication in book form. The Essay was, of course, written in less than a year: the revision has occupied more than eleven. Twelve years will seem none too much to any one acquainted with the extent and the difficulties of the subject: but it is fair to myself to state that I have been throughout pretty fully occupied in teaching subjects quite unconnected with medieval history.

Part of the difficulty has been occasioned by the rapidity with which materials and literature have of late poured from the press. When I began to work at the medieval Universities, no really critical book had appeared on the subject as a whole or on any large section of it. Much labour was therefore expended in discovering for myself the non-existence of the University of Paris during the greater part of that period of its history which it has taken Du Boullai two bulky folios to chronicle. The publication of Father Denifle's great work, *Die Entstehung der Universitäten des Mittelalters*, in 1885, disclosed to me masses of fresh authorities

1417

for which I should probably have hunted in vain for myself. Later on, the publication of new documents in the successive volumes of Denifle and Chatelain's magnificent *Chartularium Universitatis Parisiensis* (1889, 1891), when I thought that my work was nearly at an end, involved much revision of the Paris chapter, and the addition of references to my citations from already published documents. The third volume came into my hands when most of the sheets had been already printed off. The Bologna octo-centenary of 1888 produced a crop of new literature relating to that University, and in particular Malagola's edition of the Statutes, only partially published before. Fournier's great collection of documents for the French Universities (the three volumes of which were published in 1890, 1891, and 1892 respectively) involved the re-writing of the chapter on the French Universities other than Paris. Statute-books, Matriculation books, Chartularia, and histories of particular Universities have also appeared in rapid succession. Since I began to write, the amount of printed matter demanding notice must have about doubled itself. There are now few Universities of which we have not at least the Statutes in print, while in very many cases all the extant documents have been edited with a completeness which leaves nothing to be desired. Unfortunately this cannot be said with regard to our own Universities.

With this growing mass of printed material before me, I felt that it would be unnecessary to occupy myself to any great extent with MS. sources. To have done so with any thoroughness, I should have had to bury myself for years in foreign libraries and muniment rooms: and even so most of the material would have been printed before my book could have appeared. I have made exceptions to this rule in respect of

Oxford, Cambridge, S. Andrews, and (to a very limited extent) Paris. At Paris I have not attempted to deal with original documents beyond a slight study of some MS. Registers: the *Chartularium* has now made this unnecessary for the greater portion of the period embraced within this volume: I have, however, read through the important MS. histories of that University preserved in the Bibliothèque Nationale (see below, vol. I. p. 271). With regard to the British Universities, I have, I believe, made myself acquainted with all the unpublished MS. material which was likely to throw any light upon their history, or upon that of the Colleges so far as the history of the latter is dealt with in these volumes. With regard to Oxford the mass of MS. material is very large indeed. My task has been much facilitated by the transcripts of those indefatigable antiquaries Robert Hare and Bryan Twyne (see below, vol. II. p. 322): but after all I feel the truth of Mark Pattison's remark, 'History cannot be written from MSS.' This is particularly the case with masses of official documents which require to be seen together and to be arranged in chronological order for their full significance to be easily appreciated. It is to be hoped that Oxford will soon cease to be almost the only important University in the world (exclusive, perhaps, of the Spanish Peninsula) whose earlier history cannot be studied in a tolerably complete series of published documents. The work can only be done by the University itself. It is too extensive for private Societies, and in England there is no political capital to be made out of Government aid to scientific undertakings. At Cambridge the amount of unpublished material is smaller, though still considerable.

The plan of this book is to describe with tolerable fulness the three great archetypal Universities,—

Bologna, Paris, Oxford,—and to give short notices of the foundation, constitution, and history of the others, arranged in national groups. Even of the three great Universities, however, I do not profess to have written a history. Exception may possibly be taken to the place assigned to particular Universities. Many of them were, of course, situated in territories which did not then strictly belong to any of the larger divisions of the existing map of Europe, or belonged at one time to one of them, at another time to another. In these cases I have simply endeavoured to assign each University to the group to which it seemed on the whole most naturally to belong.

In endeavouring to cover so large an extent of ground in a work of moderate compass, it was inevitable that many aspects of University history should be dealt with slightly or not at all. The point of view from which I have approached the subject has been primarily that of constitutional history; but I could hardly have hoped to interest any but a few specialists in my subject had I not endeavoured to give some account of the intellectual history of the period. I have, however, touched upon the growth of the Scholastic Philosophy and Theology and the development of legal and medical Science just sufficiently to make intelligible my account of the educational organization of the Middle Ages, and to suggest its historical significance. The condensed treatment of seventy-three Universities in 316 pages has, of course, rendered that part of my work of little interest except for purposes of reference : but to have ignored all but the most famous Studia would have left the reader with a very inadequate impression of the extent and variety of the medieval University system, and of the importance of the part which it played in the making of civilized Europe. Moreover, it would have been impossible to write satisfactorily the history of even one University without an acquaintance with the documents of all the rest. The great defect of University histories has been the non-application of the comparative method. As matters stand, even students will probably skip the greater part of vol. II, part i. The 'general reader' will perhaps find most that will interest him in vol. II, part ii.

Nobody can be better aware than myself of the great deficiencies of my work. Many years more might well have been spent in removing them. I could, of course, indicate point after point which demands further investigation. But I felt that the time had come when the book must be published, if I were not prepared to make it the work of a life-time. Ten or twenty years hence it will perhaps be possible to base a history of the medieval Universities upon an almost complete collection of printed materials. Meanwhile, I hope my Essay will be of some use to the now considerable number of students who are at work on portions of the subject.

It is needless to say that such a work as the present owes a great deal to the researches of others. My obligations to the historians of particular Universities are expressed in the bibliographical notices. But I am particularly anxious to state accurately the extent of my debt to Father Denifle, the only modern writer on the subject as a whole to whom I am under important obligations. If I had not had Father Denifle as a predecessor, my work might have possessed more novelty and originality than it can now claim, since there were large masses of traditional error and misconception which must have been dispelled by the first serious modern student who should take up the subject: but it would assuredly have been very much more incomplete and inadequate than it actually is. At the same time, in justice to myself, I may perhaps point out the following facts:

(1) I had already reached for myself the most important of the corrections which Father Denifle has made in the hitherto received version of the early history of Paris. Some of them were just indicated or implied in a very slight article on Universities which I contributed to the *Dictionary of English History* in 1884.

(2) The amount of my indebtedness naturally varies with the extent to which Father Denifle has been an original worker. In some cases the history of a minor University has been re-written or discovered for the first time by Father Denifle's researches in the Vatican or other archives. In such cases I could do no more than epitomize his results. But where his work is based on the researches of others or on published documents, I have endeavoured to make an independent use of them. I believe I have read every published document relating to any medieval University which I could succeed in getting hold of; and I have, of course, verified (wherever possible) all citations which I owe to other writers. I am, however, everywhere indebted to Father Denifle for bibliographical information, by no means the least difficult or important part of his work.

(3) Father Denifle's *Entstehung* is only the first of a series which is to extend to five volumes. It deals only with the 'origines' of the Universities founded up to 1400. It does not describe in detail their mature constitution, organization, or history. Here, therefore, I have been without the advantage of Father Denifle's guidance, as also in all that relates to the Universities founded after 1400.

(4) To Oxford Father Denifle devotes only twenty pages, and he does not profess to add anything to our

knowledge of that University. The view I have taken of its origin and early history is entirely independent of his work.

(5) The whole plan and arrangement of my book is different from Father Denifle's.

The English Universities form the only part of the subject in which Father Denifle has left scope for much originality to his successors, so far at least as the all-important question of 'origines' is concerned. On details I have sometimes ventured to differ from him. But, as he has been severely criticized and unjustly disparaged by several writers on the same subject, I feel it a duty to give expression to the admiration with which a careful comparison of his book with the authorities upon which it is based has filled me, not merely for the immensity of his learning and for the thoroughness of his work, but for the general soundness of his conclusions. In particular, I think it right to add that, though Father Denifle is a Dominican and Under-Archivist of the Holy See, I have hardly ever discovered any ground for the insinuation of an ultramontane bias.

Throughout the work I have received an amount of help from my friends which I have been almost ashamed to accept, and which it is difficult for me adequately to acknowledge. My greatest debt is perhaps to the constant advice and assistance of Mr. Reginald Lane Poole, Ph.D., Lecturer in Jesus College, Oxford, whose great learning in everything that relates to the Middle Ages has always been accessible to me, and who has kindly read through nearly the whole of my proofs. My proofs have also been read by Mr. T. Tout, Professor of History in Owens College, Manchester, whose wide knowledge of general history has constantly supplied the deficiencies in mine, and by Mr. C. H. Turner, Fellow of Magdalen College, Oxford, who has generously devoted an immense amount of labour to the final correction for the press of a book on a subject quite remote from his own studies. These volumes owe more than I can easily explain to the accuracy and diligence of his revision. My thanks are also due for kind assistance with portions of the revision to my colleague, Mr. S. G. Hamilton, Fellow of Hertford, to Mr. C. W. C. Oman, Fellow of All Souls, and to the Rev. Andrew Clark, late Fellow of Lincoln, who has often helped me with his unrivalled knowledge of the materials for Oxford history.

The nature of my task has necessarily compelled me to touch upon many subjects with which I could not aspire to more than a very second-hand acquaintance. If I have escaped serious error in dealing with the history of medieval Law and Medicine, I owe it largely to the kindness of Professor Maitland, of Cambridge, and of Dr. J. F. Payne, late Fellow of Magdalen College, Oxford, Physician of S. Thomas' Hospital, who were good enough to read through the portions of my proofs relating to their respective subjects. I have also to thank Lord Acton for several valuable suggestions in regard to chap. v, § 6. I have to acknowledge the great assistance which I have at all times received from all the authorities of the Bodleian Library, especially from Mr. F. Madan, Sub-Librarian, and Fellow of Brasenose, to whose help in matters bibliographical and palæo-graphical I am under great obligations. I am indebted to the Society of Antiquaries for access to the Smith MSS. in their Library. I must acknowledge the never-failing courtesy with which the Rev. T. Vere Bayne, Student of Christ Church and Keeper of the Archives at Oxford, has met my, I fear, somewhat troublesome applications for the use of documents under his charge. I must also express my gratitude for similar assistance to the late Rev. Dr. Luard, formerly Registrary of the University of Cambridge, and to his successor, Mr. J. W. Clark ; to Mr. E. J. H. Jenkinson, Librarian of the University of Cambridge ; to his Grace the Archbishop of Canterbury and his Librarian, Mr. Kershaw ; to the Lord Bishop of Lincoln and his Secretary, Mr. S. S. Smith; to the Lord Bishop of Ely and his Registrar, Mr. W. J. Evans; to the Venerable Archdeacon Chapman, of Ely; to the Rev. C. Leeke, Chancellor of Lincoln Cathedral; and to Mr. J. M. Anderson, Registrar and Librarian of the University of S. Andrews, who was kind enough to facilitate my researches by allowing me to make free use of the transcripts which he had made for his work on that University. For the invariable courtesy which I have met with from the Librarians and other authorities of Colleges at Oxford and Cambridge to whom I have applied for access to MSS. or for information on various points, I must ask them to be kind enough to accept this general acknowledgement. Some of these obligations are mentioned in the notes or bibliographical notices. I must not, however, omit to thank Father Denifle and Monsieur Chatelain, Librarian of the Sorbonne, for their kindness in answering enquiries which I have occasionally ventured to address to them.

To my friend and former pupil the Rev. S. Holmes I owe a large part of the Index.

The lists of authorities which are prefixed to each University do not pretend to anything like bibliographical completeness.

H. RASHDALL.

OXFORD :
June 24, 1895.

CONTENTS OF VOLUME I.

———••———

CHAPTER I.

WHAT IS A UNIVERSITY?

CHAPTER II.

ABELARD AND THE RENAISSANCE OF THE TWELFTH CENTURY.

CHAPTER III.

SALERNO.

CHAPTER IV.

BOLOGNA.

§ 1. IRNERIUS AND THE CIVIL LAW REVIVAL.

§ 2. GRATIAN AND THE CANON LAW.

CHAPTER V.

PARIS.

§ 1. THE ORIGINS OF THE UNIVERSITY.

I. The Rise of the University.

§ 4. The Studies of Paris.

§ 5. The Colleges of Paris.

ILLUSTRATIONS.

ERRATA.

VOL. I.

P. 120, n. 2, col. 2, l. 4, *for* Bulgarius *read* Bulgarus
p. 287, *for* Puling *read* Pulling
p. 329 (margin), *for* 1280 *read* 1256 (as in text)
p. 333 (margin), *for* Faculties *read* Faculty
p. 400, n. 1, l. 3, *for* Crivier *read* Crevier
p. 402, n. 3, *for* de Mathu *read* de Matha
p. 442, notes, col. 1, *for* Scholarium *read* Scholarum
p. 508, l. 29, *for* pleine exercise *read* plein exercice
p. 514.   List of Colleges.   *After* C. du Chardonnet *insert* C. des Bons
Enfants de S. Victor, *ante* 1248 (cf. above, p. 486).

VOL. II.   PART I.

P. 14, n. 1, l. 2, *for* Zacharia *read* Zaccaria
p. 92, *for* In 1354 *read* In 1359

PART II.

P. 479, n. 4, *add* See Mr. Hutton's Art. on S. John's College in *The Colleges
of Oxford.*

TABLE OF UNIVERSITIES (*with references*).

		ITALY.	FRANCE, &c.	GREAT BRITAIN.	SPAIN AND PORTUGAL.	GERMANY, BOHEMIA, AND THE LOW COUNTRIES.	OTHER COUNTRIES.
Studia Generalia before or without Bulls.	12th Century.	SALERNO, i. 75. BOLOGNA, i. 89, ii. 6. Reggio, 1188*, ii. 6.	PARIS, i. 271. Montpellier (?). ii. 113.	OXFORD, 1167-8 (?). ii. 319.			
Studia Generalia before or without Bulls.	13th Century.	Vicenza, 1204*, ii. 7. Arezzo, 1215*, ii. 8. Padua, 1222*, ii. 10. Vercelli, 1228*, ii. 26. Siena (1246: I. in 1357)*, ii. 31. Naples, 1224, I. ii. 22. Curia Romana, 1244-5. P. ii. 27. Piacenza, 1248, P. ii. 35.	Orleans, *ante* 1231. ii. 136. Angers*, ii. 148. Toulouse, 1229, 1233 P. ii. 157.	Cambridge, 1209*, ii. 543. (P. in 1318.)	(?) Valladolid, c. 1250 (P. in 1346). ii. 82. Palencia, 1212-1214, R. ii. 66. Salamanca, *ante* 1239, R. ii. 139. Seville, 1254, R.: P. in 1260 (Latin and Arabic). ii. 81. Lisbon-Coimbra, 1290, P. ii. 101.		
Studia Generalia founded by Papal or Imperial Bull (or in Spain by Royal Charter).	14th Century.	Rome (Studium Urbis), 1303, P. ii. 38. Perugia, 1308, P. ii. 40. Treviso, 1318, I. ii. 43. Pisa, 1343, P. ii. 44. Florence, 1349, P. ii. 46. Pavia, 1361, I. ii. 53. Ferrara, 1391, P. ii. 55.	Avignon, 1303, P. ii. 170. Cahors, 1332, P. ii. 179. Grenoble, 1339, P. ii. 181. Orange, 1365, I. ii. 182.		Lerida, 1300, R. ii. 86. Perpignan, 1349, P. ii. 90. Huesca, 1359, R. ii. 92.	Prague, 1347-8, P. I ii. 211. Vienna, 1365, P. ii. 232. Erfurt, 1379, 1392, P. ii. 242. Heidelberg, 1385, P. ii. 247. Cologne, 1388, P. ii. 251.	Cracow (Poland), 1364, 1397, P. ii. 283. Fünfkirchen (Hungary), 1367, P. ii. 286. Buda (Hungary), 1389, P. ii. 288.
Studia Generalia founded by Papal or Imperial Bull (or in Spain by Royal Charter).	15th Century.	Turin, 1405, ii. 56. Catania, 1444, P. ii. 58.	Aix, 1409, P. ii. 184. Dole, 1422, P. ii. 187. Poitiers, 1431, P*. ii. 191. Caen, 1437, P. ii. 194. Bordeaux, 1441, P. ii. 198. Valence, 1459, P. ii. 200. Nantes, 1460, P. ii. 201. Bourges, 1464, P. ii. 204. [Besançon, 1485, P. ii.205.]	St. Andrews, 1413, P. ii. 295. Glasgow, 1451, P. ii. 304. Aberdeen, 1494, P. ii. 309.	Barcelona, 1450, P. ii. 94. Saragossa, 1474 (Arts), P. ii. 95. Palma (Majorca), 1483, R. ii. 96. [(?) Avila, 1482, R.] ii. 96. Siguenza, 1489, P. ii. 97. Alcalá, 1499, P. ii. 99. Valencia, 1500, P. ii. 99.	Würzburg, ii. 253. Leipsic, 1409, P*. ii. 254. Rostock, 1419, P. ii. 256. Louvain, 1425, P. ii. 259. Tréves, 1454, 1473, P. ii. 263. Greifswald, 1428*, 1455 P* ii. 264. Freiburg-im-Breisgau, 1455-6, P. ii. 268. Bâle, 1459, P. ii. 269. Ingolstadt, 1459, 1472, P. ii. 270. Mainz, 1476, P. ii. 272. Tübingen, 1476-7, P. ii. 273.	Poszony or Pressburg (Hungary), 1465-7, P. ii. 289. Upsala (Sweden), 1477, P. ii. 290. Copenhagen (Denmark), 1477, P. ii. 291.

* Known to have been founded by or in connexion with a Migration from some other University.   R. = founded by Royal Charter.
P. = founded by Papal Bull.   I. = founded by Imperial Bull.

CHAPTER I.

WHAT IS A UNIVERSITY?

65

THE MEDIEVAL UNIVERSITIES

---◆◆---

CHAPTER I.

WHAT IS A UNIVERSITY?

Of the older works on Universities in general the most important are— CONRINGIUS, *De Antiquitatibus Academicis Dissertationes Septem* (ed. Heumannus, with HEUMANNI *Bibliotheca Historica Academica*. Gottingæ, 1739 ; and *Opera*. Brunsvigæ, 1730. T.V.). MIDDENDORPIUS, *Academiarum Orbis Christiani Libri duo*. Coloniæ, 1567 (*Libri iv*, Coloniæ, 1594 : *Libri viii*, Coloniæ Agrippinæ, 1602). LAUNOIUS, *De Scholis Celebrioribus*, Lutetiæ Parisiorum, 1672.

The following may also be mentioned—HAGELGANS, *Orbis Literatus Germanico-Europæus*. In Saxo Edigii, 1737. ITTERUS, *De Honoribus Academicis Liber*. Francofurti, 1685.

MEINERS, *Geschichte der Entstehung und Entwicklung der hohen Schulen* (Göttingen, 1802-1805), long remained the only modern work on this subject as a whole, and that a completely uncritical one. SAVIGNY began the scientific investigation of the subject, in his *Geschichte des römischen Rechts im Mittelalter* (Heidelberg, 2. Aufl. 1834, &c.) ; but he is only valuable for the Italian Universities and the legal Faculties. MALDEN, *On the Origin of Universities* (London, 1835) remains almost the only English book on the subject, and is full of blunders ; but more valuable contributions to University History were made by Sir William HAMILTON in his polemical articles in the *Edinburgh Review* (1831-1834), reprinted in *Discussions on Philosophy and Literature, Education, and University Reform* (London, 1852). VALLET DE VIRIVILLE, *Histoire de l'instruction publique en Europe* (Paris, 1849) is an exceedingly interesting work of a popular kind, but hardly pretends to be a serious history of the Universities. Equally popular is Miss DRANE's pleasantly written *Christian Schools and Scholars* (ed. ii., London, 1881). The subject has naturally been the theme of many Academical addresses, pamphlets, &c., but it will be enough to mention DÖLLINGER, *Die Universitäten sonst und jetzt* (München, 1867 ; *The Universities New and Old*. Translated by APPLETON. Oxford, 1867).

The subject remained practically *terra incognita* till the appearance of DENIFLE's great work, *Die Entstehung der Universitäten des Mittelalters bis 1400* (Berlin, 1885), the first volume of a colossal undertaking which is to extend to five volumes (cited as Denifle I.). I have expressed my sense of the value of this great work in the Preface.

B 2

Of the critics of Denifle the most important is Georg KAUFMANN. The first (and only published) volume of his *Geschichte der Deutschen Universitäten* (Stuttgart, 1888) forms an interesting, well-written, and not unimportant contribution to the history of medieval Universities in general, and promises well for his treatment of his proper subject. The controversy between him and DENIFLE (which has been unfortunately violent) has been conducted by KAUFMANN in *Göttingische Gelehrte Anzeigen* (1886. p. 97 *sq.*), *Zeitschrift d. Savigny-Stiftung* (VII. Germ. Abth. Heft i. p. 124 *sq.*), *Historisches Jahrbuch* (ed. Grauert. X. München, 1888. pp. 349-360), *Deutschen Zeitschrift für Geschichtswissenschaft* (Freiburg i. B., 1889. Band I. Heft i. p. 118 *sq.*) ; and by DENIFLE in *Hist. Jahrbuch* (X. pp. 72-98; 361-375), *Archiv für Litteratur- und Kirchengeschichte des Mittelalters* (II. p. 398 *sq.*).

LAURIE, *Lectures on the Rise and Early Constitution of Universities* (London, 1886) is a brilliantly written little book, but is unfortunately full of inaccuracies and misconceptions, old and new. MULLINGER's Article on *Universities* in the *Encyclopædia Britannica* deserves mention as the first tolerably correct (though very brief) account of the subject which has appeared in English.

Import-
ance of
subject.

Sacerdotium, Imperium, Studium are brought together by a medieval writer [1] as the three mysterious powers or 'virtues,' by whose harmonious co-operation the life and health of Christendom are sustained. This ' Studium ' did not to him, any more than the ' Sacerdotium ' or the ' Imperium' with which it is associated, represent a mere abstraction. As all priestly power had its visible head and source in the city of the Seven Hills, as all secular authority was ultimately held of the Holy Roman Empire, so could all the streams of knowledge by which the Universal Church was watered and fertilised, be ultimately traced as to their fountain-head to the great Universities, especially to the University of Paris. The history of an institution which held such a place in the imagination of a medieval historian, is no mere subject of antiquarian curiosity ; its origin, its development, its decay, or rather the transition to its modern form, are worthy of the same serious investigation which has been abundantly bestowed upon the Papacy and the Empire.

Like the Papacy and the Empire, the University is an

---

[1] ' His siquidem tribus, scilicet Sacerdotio Imperio et Studio, tanquam tribus uirtutibus uidelicet naturali uitali et scientiali, catholica ecclesia spiritualiter mirificatur, augmentatur et regitur. His itaque tribus, tanquam fundamento, pariete et tecto, eadem ecclesia tanquam materialiter proficit.' Jordanus, *Chronica*, ap. Schardius, *De Jurisdictione Imperiali*, Basileæ, 1566, p. 307.

institution which owes not merely its primitive form and
traditions, but, in a sense, its very existence to a combination of accidental circumstances ; and its origin can only
be understood by reference to those circumstances. But
the subsequent development of each of these institutions was determined by, and reveals to us, the whole
bent and spiritual character of the age to whose life it
became organic. The University, no less than the Roman
Church and the feudal Hierarchy headed by the Roman
Emperor, represents an attempt to realise in concrete form
an ideal of life in one of its aspects. Ideals pass into great
historic forces by embodying themselves in institutions.
The power of embodying its ideals in institutions was the
peculiar genius of the medieval mind, as its most conspicuous defect lay in the corresponding tendency to
materialise them. The institutions which the Middle Age
has bequeathed to us are of greater and more imperishable
value even than its Cathedrals. And the University is
distinctly a medieval institution—as much so as constitutional Kingship, or Parliaments, or Trial by Jury. The
Universities and the immediate products of their activity
may be said to constitute the great achievement of the
Middle Ages in the intellectual sphere. Their organisation and their traditions, their studies and their exercises
affected the progress and intellectual development of
Europe more powerfully, or (perhaps it should be said)
more exclusively, than any schools in all likelihood will
ever do again. A complete history of the Universities of
the Middle Ages would be in fact a history of medieval
thought—of the fortunes, during four centuries, of literary
culture, of the whole of the Scholastic Philosophy and
Scholastic Theology, of the revived study of the Civil Law,
of the formation and development of the Canon Law,
of the faint, murky, cloud-wrapped dawn of modern Mathematics, modern Science, and modern Medicine. Hardly
more than a glance can be given at many of these subjects
in the present work. Its paramount object will be to study
the growth of the University as an institution, to trace the

CHAP. I. origin of the various Universities, and to sketch the most important changes which passed over their form and their spirit during the period before us. Our attention will be for the most part confined to the parent or typical Universities ; no more than a slight sketch will be attempted of their derivatives or descendants. Even so, our subject is in some respects an inconveniently extended one. But if this diffusion of interest involves some sacrifice of that thoroughness in research, of that concentration of view, and that vividness of local colouring which might have been possible in a monograph on a single University, something will be gained if it becomes clear, as we compare Bologna with Paris, and Paris with Oxford or Prague, that the Universities of all countries and all ages are in reality adaptations under various conditions of one and the same institution ;—that if we would completely understand the meaning of offices, titles, ceremonies, organisations preserved in the most modern, most practical, most unpicturesque of the institutions which now bear the name of 'University,' we must go back to the earliest days of the earliest Universities that ever existed, and trace the history of their chief successors through the seven centuries that intervene between the rise of Bologna or Paris, and the foundation of the new University of Strassburg in Germany or of the Victoria University in England.

Meaning of Universitas.

The word *Universitas* is one to which a false explanation is often assigned for polemical purposes by controversial writers, while the true explanation of it at once supplies us with a clue to the nature and historical origin of the institution itself. The notion that a University means a *Universitas Facultatum*—a School in which all the Faculties or branches of knowledge are represented—has, indeed, long since disappeared from the pages of professed historians ; but it is still persistently foisted upon the public by writers with whom history is subordinate to what may be called intellectual edification. However imposing and stimulating may be the conception of an institution for the teaching or for the cultivation of universal knowledge, however imperative the necessity of such an institution in modern times, it is one which can gain little support from the facts of history. A glance into any collection of medieval documents reveals the fact that the word ' University' means merely a number, a plurality, an aggregate of persons. *Universitas vestra*, in a letter addressed to a body of persons, means merely ' the whole of you '; in a more technical sense it denotes a legal corporation [1] or juristic person; in Roman Law (though in strictness a wider term) it is for most purposes practically the equivalent of *collegium*. At the end of the twelfth and beginning of the thirteenth centuries, we find the word applied to corporations either of Masters or of students; but it long continues to be applied to other corporations as well, particularly to the then newly formed Guilds and to the Municipalities of towns; while as applied to scholastic Guilds it is at first used interchangeably with such words as ' Community' or ' College.' In the earliest period it is never used absolutely. The phrase is always ' University of Scholars,' ' University of Masters and Scholars,' ' University of Study,' or the like. It is a mere accident that the term has gradually come to be restricted to a particular kind of Guild or Corporation, just as the terms ' Convent,' ' Corps,' ' Congregation,' ' College,' have been similarly restricted to certain specific kinds of association. It is particularly important to notice that the term was generally in the Middle Ages used distinctly of the scholastic body whether of teachers or scholars, not of the place in which such a body was established, or even of its collective Schools. The word used to denote the academic institution in the abstract—the Schools or the town which held them—was *Studium* rather than *Universitas*. To be a resident in a University would be *in studio degere* or *in scholis militare*. The term which most nearly corresponds to the vague and indefinite English notion of a University

---

[1] Long after the rise of the scholastic Universities, *Universitas* is used (absolutely) of the town corporations or guilds. Thus Boniface VIII writes 'Universitatibus et populo dicti Regni' [Franciae]. Even so vague a body as ' all faithful Christian people ' is often addressed as ' Universitas Vestra.'

as distinguished from a mere School, Seminary, or private educational establishment, is not *Universitas*, but *Studium Generale*; and *Studium Generale* means, not a place where all subjects are studied, but a place where students from all parts are received. As a matter of fact, very few medieval *Studia* possessed all the Faculties. Even Paris in the days of her highest renown possessed no Faculty of Civil Law; while throughout the thirteenth century graduation in Theology was in practice the almost exclusive privilege of Paris and the English Universities [1].

The term Studium Generale does not become common till the beginning of the thirteenth Century [2]. At that time the

---

[1] Though nominally shared by Naples, Toulouse, and the University of the Roman Court. Bulls for the erection of Studia Generalia usually specified the Faculties in which the *Facultas ubique docendi* was granted; or it was 'in quavis licita facultate.'

[2] 'Universale,' and more rarely 'commune,' are common synonyms for 'generale.' The allusion in Guibertus de Novigento (†1124), *De Vita Sua*, l. i. c. 4 (Migne, T. 156, c. 844), to sleeping 'in cubiculo . . . in quo totius oppidi generale studium regebatur,' is clearly a non-technical use of the word. The earliest instance of the technical expression that I have noticed is in the Chronicle of Emo in relation to Oxford, c. 1190 (Pertz, *Monumenta Germaniæ Historica*, T. XXIII. p. 467; below, vol. II. chap. xii. § 1), where the word is 'commune.' *Studium solempne* is sometimes used as a synonym for *generale*, but occasionally it seems to be distinguished from it, meaning an important or frequented school which was not technically 'general.' See Denifle and Chatelain, *Chartul. Univ. Paris*, 1889, &c., T. II. No. 1015 'in nullo conventu, ubi non est studium generale aut aliud studium

solempne'). See the definition in the Siete Partidas of Alfonso X of Castile, below, vol. II. chap. vii. § 2. The Canonist 'Hostiensis' (Henricus de Segusio), writing at about the same time (†1271) discusses the limits of the privilege of dispensation from residence for the purpose of study, and lays it down: 'Hoc autem arg. potest hinc elici, quod istud intelligatur de generali, non de particulari. Et dicitur generale, quando triuium et quadriuium, Theologia et sacri canones ibidem leguntur. Sed certe et hoc putamus ad arbitrium boni judicis redigendum,' &c. Hostiensis, *in Decretalium Libros*, II. Venetiis, 1581. f. 13. The requirement that Theology should be taught is curious, since Bologna could only satisfy the test by its Friar Doctors, who did not graduate at Bologna. He goes on to ask: 'Nunquid enim si propter guerram non audent ad presens ad scholas Bononie accedere, licebit eis citra montes etiam in castris si competentem magistrum habeant studere?' A gloss declares that the Laws may be read anywhere: 'talis tamen locus non habebit priuilegium studii generalis, nisi ei concedatur a principe, vel consuetudine immemoriali, ut not.

term was a perfectly vague one, as vague and indefinable as the English term Public School or the German *Hochschule*. In the main, however, the term seems to have implied three characteristics, (1) That the School attracted or at least invited students from all parts, not merely those of a particular country or district, (2) That it was a place of higher education; that is to say, that one at least of the higher Faculties—Theology, Law, Medicine—was taught there[1], (3) That such subjects were taught by a considerable number—at least by a plurality—of Masters. Of these ideas the first was the primary and fundamental one: a Studium Generale meant a School of general resort, but in its origin the expression was a wholly popular and extra-legal one. The question whether a particular school was or was not a Studium Generale was one settled by custom or usage, not by authority. There were, however, at the beginning of the thirteenth Century three Studia to which the term was preeminently applied and which enjoyed a unique and transcendent prestige: they were Paris for Theology and Arts, Bologna for Law, and Salerno for Medicine. A Master who had taught and been admitted to the Magisterial Guild in one of those places was certain of obtaining immediate recognition and permission to teach in all other inferior Studia, while these Studia themselves would not receive Masters from other schools without fresh examination. Thus to the original conception of a Studium Generale there was gradually added a vague notion of a certain ecumenical validity for the Mastership which it conferred. But at the same time there was nothing to prevent any School which thought itself entitled to the

---

Bat.' &c. It was no doubt largely the necessity of defining a Studium Generale for the purpose of dispensation from residence on account of study which led to a definite and precise meaning being given to the term.

[1] There are at least two instances of a Studium Generale in Arts only:—
(1) Saragossa, which Denifle some-

what arbitrarily excludes from the category of Universities—see below, chap. vii. § 8. (2) Erfurt, which we learn from a document of 1362 was 'populari sermone' spoken of as a Studium Generale. Since the recognition is in this case equivocal, I have considered Erfurt as founded by the Bull of 1379. See below, vol. II. chap. ix. § 3.

CHAP. I. designation from assuming it.   In the thirteenth Century many Schools besides Bologna and Paris claimed the rank of Studium Generale : it was in fact—at least in Italy where the term was most in use—assumed by any School which wanted to intimate that it gave an education equal to that of Bologna or Paris [1].   And the extension of this usage was facilitated by the fact that most of these early Schools were founded by Masters who had actually taught at one of these places.

The *jus ubique docendi.*

In the latter half of the thirteenth Century this unrestricted liberty of founding Studia Generalia gradually ceased ; and the cessation brought with it an important change in the meaning of the term.   It so happened that at about the same time the two great 'world-powers' of Europe conceived the idea of creating a School which was to be placed by an exercise of authority on a level with the great European centres of education.   In 1224 the Emperor Frederick II founded a Studium Generale at Naples ; in 1229 Gregory IX did the same at Toulouse ; while in 1244 or 1245 Innocent IV established a Studium Generale in the Pontifical Court itself. These foundations would appear to have suggested the idea that the erection of new Studia Generalia was one of the Papal and Imperial prerogatives, like the power of creating Notaries Public.   Moreover, in order to give the graduates of Toulouse (in so far as parchment and wax could secure it) the same prestige and recognition which were enjoyed by the graduates of Paris and Bologna, a Bull was issued (in 1233) which declared that any one admitted to the Mastership in that University should be freely allowed to teach in all other Studia without any further examination.   In the

[1] There were many such schools in Italy during the thirteenth century, but most of them early died out. Where they maintained their ground, the later and more technical ideas about Studia Generalia were naturally applied to them, since the change in the meaning was gradual and unconscious.   Out of Italy there were no doubt many Schools which *de facto* were as much Studia Generalia as Arezzo or Vercelli, but the name does not happen to have been applied to them : hence when the technical interpretation of *Studium Generale* gained ground, they lost their claims to the privileges which it conferred.   Such Schools were Lyons and Reims, for whose inclusion Kaufmann is urgent.

course of the century other cities anxious to place their
Schools on a level with these privileged Universities applied
for and obtained from Pope or Emperor Bulls constituting
them Studia Generalia. The earlier of these Bulls simply
confer the position of Studium Generale without further
definition or confer the privileges of some specified University such as Paris or Bologna. The most prominent practical purpose of such Bulls seems at first to have been to
give beneficed ecclesiastics the right of studying in them
while continuing to receive the fruits of their benefices [1]—
a privilege limited by Canonical Law or custom to Studia
reputed 'General[2].' But gradually the special privilege
of the *jus ubique docendi* came to be regarded as the principal object of Papal or Imperial creation. It was usually,
but not quite invariably, conferred in express terms by the
original foundation-bulls ; and was apparently understood to
be involved in the mere act of erection even in the rare cases

---

[1] The first Bull for a Studium not
actually created to forward some
special purpose of Pope or Emperor
was that for Piacenza in 1248, which
conferred the privileges of Paris and
other Studia Generalia. The Bull
for Rome (Studium Urbis) in 1303
confers the right to receive fruits and
other privileges, but no express *jus
ubique*; those for Pamiers (1295)
and Perugia (1308) simply create a
Studium Generale. On the other
hand, Montpellier (1289) and Avignon (1303) received the *jus ubique
docendi*, which gradually became the
usual form.

[2] Honorius III in 1219 (Decretal.
Greg. IX. Tit. v. c. 5) provided that
teachers *of Theology* as long as they
were teaching, or students for five
years, might receive their fruits, and
prelates and chapters were required
to send 'docibiles' (i.e. Canons) to
study Theology. There was no express limitation to Studia Generalia ;
but by Decretal. Greg. IX. Tit. iii.
c. 12, *Tuæ fraternitatis*, the privilege

is forbidden to those who ' se transferunt ad villas vel castella, in quibus
nullum est vel minus competens studium literarum,' which was usually
interpreted to mean Studia which
were not general. (See the comment
of Hostiensis, above, p. 8, n. 2.)

Later, particular Universities often
obtained special Bulls confirming the
dispensation from residence, and the
right to receive all fruits except the
' daily distribution.' Where this was
not granted, it was generally understood that a beneficed clergyman had
a right to ask for five years' leave of
absence from his Ordinary to study
Theology or Canon Law, though in
some cases (especially in England) it
appears to have been usually granted
for shorter periods only. By Sext.
Decretal. L. i. Tit. vi. c. 34, a Bishop
might dispense a Rector from
proceeding beyond Sub-deacon's
orders for seven years' study,
though the Council of Lyons had
required Rectors to take Priest's
Orders.

where it is not expressly conceded. In 1292 even the old archetypal Universities themselves—Bologna and Paris— were formally invested with the same privilege by Bulls of Nicholas IV. From this time the notion gradually gained ground that the *jus ubique docendi* was of the essence of a Studium Generale, and that no School which did not possess this privilege could obtain it without a Bull from Emperor or Pope[1]. At the same time there were some of the older Studia[2]—such as Oxford and Padua—which, without having been founded by Pope or Emperor and without having procured a subsequent recognition of their *jus ubique docendi*, had obtained a position as *Studia Generalia* too secure to be successfully attacked. Hence, with their habitual respect for established facts, the fourteenth-century Jurists, to whom is chiefly due the formulation of the medieval ideas about Universities, declared that such Schools were *Studia Generalia* 'by custom' (*ex consuetudine*)[3].

Studia Generalia respectu regni.
The view of the fourteenth-century Italian Jurists no doubt on the whole represents the dominant medieval theory on the subject. At the same time it is only natural to find that these ideas were less rapidly and less firmly established in countries which recognised the

[1] The Bull for Paris is given in *Chartul. Univ. Paris.* T. II. No. 578 (in Bulaeus, III. p. 449, wrongly ascribed to Nicholas III) ; the Bologna Bull by Sarti, *De claris Archigymnasii Bononiensis Professoribus*, T. I. P. ii. Bononiae, 1772, p. 59, renewed by Clement V in 1310, *Reg. Clem. V,* Romae, 1885, &c., No. 5275. In the latter case the privilege extended only to the two legal Faculties. Bologna never obtained this privilege for her Faculty of Medicine or Arts, yet this made no difference in practice to the estimation of the degrees—an illustration of the anomalies with which the matter abounds.

[2] Denifle holds (I. p. 777) that no Studium Generale arose without a

Bull after the middle of the thirteenth Century. There are one or two cases where this is doubtful : they are discussed in vol. II.

[3] In some cases these prescriptive *Studia Generalia* assumed the right of conferring the *licentia docendi hic et ubique*. This appears to have been done by Reggio as early as 1276 (see the diploma in Tacoli, *Memorie storiche d. Reggio,* III. p. 215), a circumstance which would suggest that the formula was used at Bologna before the grant of the Papal Bull. In other cases, however, no such change appears to have taken place, e. g. at Oxford, if we may trust the evidence of the extant *formulæ*. Padua eventually (in 1346) obtained a Bull. (See below, vol. II. chap. vi. § 4.)

supremacy of the Holy Roman Empire at most in some shadowy and honorary way, and where the national Churches possessed most independence. Thus we find the Spanish kings erecting *Studia Generalia* without consulting Pope or Emperor. They do not, indeed, claim to confer a *jus ubique docendi*, which would be an absurd pretension on the part of a merely local Sovereign. The Jurists conceded to such Universities all that they could possibly claim when they held them to be *Studia Generalia respectu regni.* If (as is insisted by Kaufmann)[1] there are instances of

---

[1] Kaufmann (*Die Gesch. d. Deutschen Universitäten*, I. pp. 371-409) labours to show that the Papal or Imperial brief was not necessary to the legitimacy of a Studium Generale according to medieval notions— that the essential thing was recognition by the Sovereign of the place. This theory is put forward in opposition to Denifle's view which I have, in the main, adopted. Upon Kaufmann's arguments I remark: (1) That the discussions by Baldus and Bartolus in the extracts which he gives (I. pp. 383, 384) turn not upon the question what constitutes a Studium Generale, but upon the question whether the teaching of the Civil Law was still restricted, as the Constitution *Omnem* (Digesta, ed. Mommsen, Berolini, 1872, I. p. xvi) provided, to *Civitates Regiae*, and what constituted a *civitas regia*. No doubt this constitution, and the claims which Bologna based upon it, powerfully contributed to the growth of the custom of applying for Papal and Imperial Bulls of erection and to the eventual belief in their necessity. But to say that the Laws might be taught ' ex permissione ejus tacita vel expressa qui est princeps ' is not the same thing as to say that any 'princeps' could create a *Studium Generale* (in the full sense, not merely ' respectu regni'). There were scores

of Italian cities (as Denifle has shown over and over again) in which Law was taught by a number of State-authorized teachers which never pretended to be Studia Generalia. (2) That all passages and instances taken from the thirteenth-century writers or documents are not *ad rem*. It is admitted that at this time no Bull or Brief was thought to be necessary. But then so far *Studium Generale* meant merely ' a place of higher education of European or more than local repute.' And equally little is there any general notion (though such a view is undoubtedly expressed by the *Siete Partidas*) that a *Studium Generale* required a Charter from King or Sovereign - City. Undoubtedly it might have been held that it required the Sovereign's ' permissio tacita,' though this might have been denied by a Hildebrandine churchman. There was no more general agreement as to the limits of the authority of Church and State than there is at the present moment between Father Denifle and Prof. Kaufmann. The fact is that this whole discussion as to the educational right of ' the State ' in the Middle Ages involves something of an anachronism. I am bound to say that Kaufmann's treatment of the subject is far more vitiated by an infusion of ideas

attempts on the part of a City Republic to erect a Studium
Generale without Papal or Imperial permission, if in one or
two cases we even have diplomas granted by such bodies
purporting to confer the *licentia ubique docendi*[1], these are

suggested by the *Kulturkampf*, than
Denifle's is distorted by any desire to
find support for those of the Syllabus.

(3) It is useless to quote documents in which a King or town pur-
ports to erect a Studium Generale
without express allusion to Emperor
or Pope, unless it is shown (*a*)
that no Bull was actually applied for,
and (*b*) that a School actually came
into existence without such Bull
which was looked upon as a *Studium
Generale*. Royal charters for the
erection of a University are usually
expressed in this form even where a
Bull was applied for or already
granted. It would be as reasonable
to quote a written agreement between two persons to enter into
marriage as evidence that they
thought marriage would be legal
without the intervention of Priest or
Registrar. Even Denifle does not
contend that it was considered lawful, or at all events possible, for the
Pope to erect a University without
consulting the local Sovereign.

(4) The case of the Spanish Universities is no exception to Denifle's
view, since it is admitted that they
were *Studia Generalia respectu regni*.

(5) Even if it could be shown that
in isolated instances a city did purport
to erect a Studium Generale without a
Bull (after 1300), this would only show
that they used the word in its older
and less technical sense. In this older
sense it is impossible to decide dog-
matically what was a *Studium
Generale* and what was not. It is
therefore better to confine the word
(in dealing with the period 1300–
1500) to its technical sense of a *Studium* which possessed the *jus ubique
docendi* at least *respectu regni*—even
if this sense of the word was not universally accepted. As to the impos-
sibility of a mere city (even if really
Sovereign) granting such a right, I
have said enough. The case of the
Parmese diploma merely proves the
arrogance or ignorance of the scribe
who copied it from some diploma or
form-book of a real University, even if
it was not intended to apply for a Bull.

(6) The only evidence that may
possibly require some modification
of Denifle's view is the language
used by the *Imperial* Bull (the Papacy at this time always assumes
the necessity of a Bull) in the foundation of Siena (1357), where the
Emperor treats the Studium Generale
of that place as already existing.
But if its position as Studium Generale was established before 1250,
Denifle would admit it to be *Studium
Generale ex consuetudine*. Although
Denifle does not admit this to have
been the case, the correction involves no change of principle. See
below, chap. vi. § 9.

(7) It must be conceded to Kaufmann that when Denifle, while fully
admitting the Imperial prerogative
of founding Universities, insinuates (i.
p. 384) that 'Allein gerade dieses letz-
tere Recht war theilweise durch das
Gutdünken des Papstes bedingt,' the
Vatican Archivist does for once get
the better of the historian. For
Denifle's view of the whole question,
see esp. *Die Entstehung*, &c., pp. 763–
791, and for his controversy with
Kaufmann, the Articles mentioned
above, p. 2.

[1] As to Reggio and Parma, see below, chap. vi. § 1 and App. ii.

merely the exceptions which prove the rule. A claim on the part of officials or corporations chartered by a mere local authority to confer rights of teaching in Universities which lay beyond their jurisdiction is too extravagant to have been seriously made, much less to have obtained general recognition.

The fluctuations of meaning which the term Studium Generale underwent in the course of the Middle Age make it no easy task in all cases to adjudicate upon the claims of particular Schools to that title. In the thirteenth Century we are obliged to include in the category of ' Universities ' all bodies which we find expressly styled Studia Generalia in medieval writers, though there were no doubt many Schools (especially in parts of Europe where the term was less current) which had in point of fact quite as good claims to ' generality,' in the sense in which it was then understood, as some of those to which the term is actually applied ; and some of them may have been actually so called, though evidence of the fact does not happen to have come down to us [1]. But from the beginning of the fourteenth Century I accept the juristic definition, and exclude from the category of Universities all bodies which were not founded by Pope or Emperor. *Studia Generalia respectu regni* are, however, included, but these in nearly every case sooner or later strengthened their position by a Papal Bull.

A wrong impression would, however, be given of the whole matter if it were supposed that, even when the *jus ubique docendi* was most indisputably assured by Papal or

---

[1] Such as Lyons, Reims, Erfurt, &c. It is highly probable—and this must be conceded to Kaufmann—that in the 13th century these Schools were sometimes or always called Studia Generalia. A Paris Statute of 1279 (Bulaeus, III. p. 447; Denifle and Chatelain, *Chartul.* T. I. P. i. No. 485) requires candidates for the License in Arts to have determined either at Paris or in some other Studium Generale where there were not less than twelve Regents : this points to the existence of many small Studia Generalia. But if we begin to include in our enumeration Schools which are not expressly described as Studia Generalia or created such by Bull, it would be impossible to know where to draw the line.

Imperial authority, it really received the respect which juristic theories claimed for it. The great primeval Universities perhaps never recognised the Doctorates conferred by the younger bodies[1]. At Paris, even Oxford degrees failed to command incorporation without fresh examination and license, and Oxford repaid the compliment by refusing admission to Parisian Doctors, the Papal Bull notwithstanding[2]. Even in less illustrious Universities the Statutes provide for some preliminary test before the reception of a graduate from another University which can hardly be distinguished from the 'Examination' which the Papal Bulls forbade[3], since it is always implied that the University reserved the right of refusing permission to lecture and exercise other magisterial rights to any foreign graduate of whose competence it was not satisfied[4]. It should be added that in proportion as the real privileges of the Mastership

[1] When Paris complained of the rights given to the graduates of Toulouse, Gregory IX himself explained that the privileges of the new University were not intended to interfere with those of Paris. *Chartul. Univ. Paris*, T. I. P. i. No. 101. In granting the *jus ubique docendi* to Salamanca, Alexander II expressly excepted Paris and Bologna. See below, chap. vii. § 2.

[2] 'Qui Parisius vel alibi ubi Oxonienses a resumptione malitiose excluduntur, nec ipsi Oxoniæ admittantur' (*Munimenta Academica*, ed. Anstey, p. 446), and Paris complains to the Pope that her *jus ubique docendi* is not respected everywhere 'ut in Anglia et apud Montem Pessulanum.' *Chartularium Univ. Paris*, T. II. No. 728. Attempts were made in 1296 and 1317 to procure the *jus ubique docendi* by Papal Bull. Documents in Lincoln Register (Bishop Sutton's *Memoranda* f. 141 b); Wood, *Hist. and Antiq. of Oxford*, ed. Gutch, I. 155; *Chartul. Univ. Paris*. T. II. No. 756. As the attempt was not

made at a later date, we may perhaps assume that Oxford was satisfied with its position as a Studium Generale *ex consuetudine*; yet Oxford never actually conferred the *licentia ubique docendi*, nor (of course) did she confer degrees 'Apostolica auctoritate.' At Bologna we find the personal intervention of Charles II of Naples necessary to obtain recognition for Jacobus de Belvisio, who had graduated at Naples in 1298 or 1299; and even then he appears to have gone through the ceremony of promotion *de novo*. Savigny, cap. xlix.

[3] See e. g. *Mun. Acad.* p. 446; Kink, *Gesch. der Univ. Wien*, II. p. 167. At Angers, it is expressly provided that no graduates from another University shall lecture before 'per scholasticum et doctores examinentur diligenter,' but 'si repetant alia examinatione non indigent.' Rangeard, *Hist. de l'Un. d'Angers*, II. p. 221.

[4] In 1321 Orleans enacted 'quod nullus doctor extrinsecus veniens,

were restricted (as was eventually more or less the case in CHAP. I.
the majority of Universities) to a limited body of salaried
Doctors, the ecumenical rights conferred by graduation in a
Studium Generale came to possess a purely honorary value.
The Mastership was reduced to a universally recognised
honour, but nothing more [1].

It remains to point out the relation of the term 'Studium
Generale' to the term 'Universitas.' There was originally
no necessary connexion between the institution denoted by
the term Universitas and that denoted by the term Studium
Generale. Societies of Masters or Clubs of Students were Universi-
formed before the term Studium Generale came into habitual tas and
Studium
use; and in a few instances such Societies are known to have Generale;
existed in Schools which never became Studia Generalia [2]. originally
The University was originally a scholastic Guild whether afterwards
of Masters or Students. Such Guilds sprang into existence, synony-
like other Guilds, without any express authorisation of mous.
King, Pope, Prince, or Prelate. They were spontaneous

---

ad actum regendi ordinarie ... in
nostra Universitate admittatur, vel
ad alios actus doctorales, nisi per
collationem doctorum, ut moris est,
fuerit approbatus, et hic insignia re-
ceperit doctoratus'—Fournier, *Stat. et
Privilèges des Univ. Françaises* (Paris,
1890) T. I. No. 78. It is true that there
is a 'salvo honore . . sancte sedis
apostolice.' In 1463 (ib. No. 320) we
find the Pope interfering to prevent
a 'doctor bullatus,' i. e. made by the
Pope, from assuming the rights of a
Regent at Orleans. Cf. *Chartul.
Univ. Paris.* T. II. No. 1174.

[1] Kaufmann (I. p. 366 *sq.*) has the
merit of first pointing out the very
limited respect which was actually
paid to these Papal Bulls.

[2] Thus at Cremona it is provided
by the town-statutes of 1387 'quod
duo rectores possint elligi per scholares legum vel unus, secundum quod
placuerit dictis scholaribus' (*Statuta
Civ. Crem.*, Cremonae, 1678, p. 135),

and the privileges accorded by the
town are as ample as those enjoyed
by Masters and Scholars in *Studia
Generalia*. So at Perugia and at Pisa
(see below, chap. vi. §§ 11, 12) before
they became *Studia Generalia*. It
should be added that a Studium
Privilegiatum — even with Papal
privileges—was not necessarily a
Studium Generale, unless the Bull
expressly created it such. Thus in
1247 the Pope gave 'doctoribus et
scholaribus universis Narbonne in
studio commorantibus' the privilege
of absence from benefices, as though
they were scholars in a *Studium
Generale. Reg. Innocent IV*, ed.
Berger, Paris, 1884, &c., No. 2717.
Fournier prints a Bull of 1329
exempting the Studium of Arts
at Gaillac from the control of the
Bishop of Albi and 'rectoris et
magistrorum studii Albiensis' (l. c.
No. 1573). As to Valencia, see
below, chap. vi. § 11.

CHAP. I. products of that instinct of association which swept like a great wave over the towns of Europe in the course of the eleventh and twelfth centuries[1]. But in two places especially—Bologna and Paris—the scholastic Guilds obtained a development and importance which they possessed nowhere else. And, as we shall see, nearly all the secondary Studia Generalia which arose spontaneously without Papal or Imperial Charter, were established by secessions of Masters or students from Paris or Bologna. The seceders carried with them the customs and institutions of their Alma Mater. Even in the few cases where the germs of a University or College of Doctors may have originated independently of the influence of Paris and Bologna, their subsequent development was due to more or less direct and conscious imitation of the scholastic guilds of these two great schools. Thus it came about that a Universitas, whether of Masters or of Students, became in practice the inseparable accompaniment of the Studium Generale—and a Universitas of a particular and definite type formed more or less ón the model of one of these great archetypal Universities[2]. Thus in the later Middle Ages the term Studium Generale came practi-

---

[1] Among general historians, no one has so fully appreciated this essential fact as the learned, if unsympathetic, Church-historian Mosheim: ‘They who had satisfied all the demands of this academical law, and gone through the formidable trial with applause, were solemnly invested with the dignity of professors, and were saluted masters with a certain round of ceremonies, that were used in the societies of illiterate tradesmen, when their company was augmented by a new candidate. This vulgar custom had been introduced, in the preceding century, by the professors of law in the academy of Bologna; and in this century it was transmitted to that of Paris, where it was first practised by the divinity colleges, and after-

wards by the professors of physic and the liberal arts.’ [This last distinction is unfounded.] *Ecclesiastical History*, trans. by Maclaine, 1826, vol. iii. p. 137.

[2] It is clear that graduation in its stricter sense could only exist where there was a Universitas. A *licentia docendi* of purely local validity might of course have continued to be given by Studia which were not general, but gradually the *licentia docendi* seems usually to have disappeared with the growing employment of University graduates to teach in the smaller Studia. This seems to me a truer mode of statement than to say (with Denifle, I. p. 21) that Studia Particularia could only enjoy the ‘Promotionsrecht’ by special Papal privilege or special custom.

cally to denote not merely a school with the *jus ubique docendi* (though this remained its legal and technical differentia), but a scholastic organisation of a particular type and endowed with more or less uniform privileges. By the fifteenth Century the original distinction between the two terms was pretty generally lost; and Universitas gradually became a mere synonym for Studium Generale[1]. In the following pages the term University will be used in this comprehensive sense except where it is necessary expressly to distinguish the Studium from the Universitas proper.

Paris and Bologna are the two archetypal — it might almost be said the only *original* Universities: Paris supplied the model for the Universities of Masters, Bologna for the Universities of Students. Every later University from that day to this is in its developed form a more or less close imitation of one or the other of these two types, though in some few cases[2] the basis of the organisation may be independent. In the case of the earlier Universities the imitation was, with whatever adaptation to local circumstances, conscious and deliberate; while the most purely utilitarian of new Universities retains constitutional features or usages which are only explained by the customs and institutions either of the Bologna students or of the Parisian Masters at the end of the twelfth or the beginning of the thirteenth centuries. It is clear therefore that a somewhat minute study of these two typical bodies is essential to a proper understanding of the University as an institution.

Paris and Bologna the two archetypes.

The two great parent Universities arose at about the same time—during the last thirty years of the twelfth century. They arose out of different sides of that wonderful deepening and broadening of the stream of human culture which may be called the Renaissance of the twelfth century. In Italy

Order of treatment.

[1] The way for the identification was prepared by the intermediate term *Universitas Studii*, which was used at first distinctly of the Society, as at Perugia in 1316, afterwards more loosely.

[2] Chiefly some of the older French Universities, such as Angers and Orleans. See below, vol. II. chap. viii. Denifle will not admit this except in the case of Oxford, where the contention is doubtful.

CHAP. I. this Renaissance found its expression most conspicuously in a revival of the study of the Roman Law, which started from Bologna ; in France it took the form of a great outburst of dialectical and theological speculation which found its ultimate, though not its earliest, home in Paris. The Bologna University of students, though perhaps later than the first rudimentary germ of the Parisian Society of Masters, completed its organisation earlier. And though each type of constitution was affected in its development by the influence of the other, Bologna in all probability exerted more influence over Paris than Paris over Bologna. Bologna therefore shall be dealt with first. With regard to the derivative Universities, it might seem natural to divide them into two great classes, and to deal first with the Universities of students, and then with the Universities of Masters. When, however, we come to examine the various constitutions in detail, it will be found that it is not always possible, without a very arbitrary treatment, to assign a given University definitively either to the Bolognese or the Parisian group. Many Universities were influenced both by Paris and by Bologna. For it must be remembered that, though at Bologna the Student-Guild eventually established complete supremacy over the Magisterial body, the Masters always had a College of their own, to which alone belonged the right of admitting new Masters or (in the modern phrase) 'granting degrees.' There might, therefore, be, and in fact there were, great variations in the distribution of academic power between the Magisterial College and the Student-Guild. Moreover, this distribution might vary at different times ; so that some Studia approximate at one period of their history to the Bolognese, at another to the Parisian type. Hence, though a classification into Student-Universities and Master-Universities would bring into prominence the curious fact that the French Universities are mostly children of Bologna rather than of Paris, and that the Scotch Universities are in certain points more closely affiliated to Bologna than to Paris or Oxford, I have deemed it best on the whole (after dealing with the

great Model-Universities) to group together the Universities of each country in Europe, which naturally have
certain features in common, though the differences between
these national varieties are often far smaller than the fundamental distinction between the Student and the Magisterial
type. Our own Universities shall be reserved to the last,
because, though belonging wholly to the Magisterial type,
and originally modelled on Paris, they exhibit from the
first such marked constitutional peculiarities as almost to
constitute a separate natural order of Universities, distinct
alike from the Bologna and the Parisian groups.

There is, however, one great Studium Generale, older Salerno.
in a sense than either Paris or Bologna, which stands
absolutely by itself. Its original constitution, of which,
indeed, not much is known, appears to have had little
resemblance to that of any other ; and it never enjoyed
that reproductive power which is so remarkable a characteristic of Bologna and Paris. The Medical School of
Salerno did not (so far as it is known) influence the constitution even of the Medical Universities or the Medical
Faculties. Such treatment as can be given to it must
precede our account of Bologna. But, before entering upon
the Universities in detail, it will be convenient to give
some general sketch of the great intellectual movement
out of which in a sense all the Universities, though pre-
eminently that of Paris, arose, and, as an introduction
to it, of the state of European education, especially in
France, before the rise of the Universities proper.

Before closing this preliminary survey of our subject, it The
may be well to point out that the three titles, Master, Doctor, synonyms
Professor, were in the Middle Ages absolutely synonymous. *Master,*
At Paris and its derivative Universities we find *Magister* *Doctor,*
the prevailing title in the Faculties of Theology, Medicine *Professor.*
and Arts ; the title *Professor* is however pretty frequently,
that of *Doctor* more rarely, employed[1]. The teachers of
Law at Bologna, however, specially affected the title

---

[1] That is, after the rise of the University. At an earlier period it had
been common. — *Hist. Lit. de la
France,* IX. p. 81.

CHAP. I. *Doctor*; they were also called *Professores* and *Domini*, but not as a rule *Magistri*. The same usage was transferred to Paris. In the Acts of the Faculty of Canon Law, we find the term *Doctor* habitually used. Thus, when letters are addressed 'Rectori, Magistris, *Doctoribus* et Scolaribus Universitatis Parisiensis,' the order makes it plain that the theological teachers are included in the Magistri, while the teachers of Canon Law are specially designated by the Doctores. The same distinction was observed at Oxford: but in the fifteenth century—at least in the English Universities—the practice gradually arose of appropriating the title *Doctor* to all the superior Faculties and reserving that of *Magister* for the inferior Faculties of Arts and Grammar. In Italy the term Doctor soon spread from the Faculty of Law to all the other Faculties. The same was eventually the case in Germany, where the Master of Arts is still styled Doctor of Philosophy. The purely accidental character of the distinction is strikingly illustrated by the fact that in the English Universities the Doctor of Music, who in spite of his gorgeous plumage is not a member of Convocation and only ranks above the modest Bachelor of Arts, enjoys that imposing prefix of *Doctor*, while his superior, the teacher of Arts, is confined to the (in popular estimation) humbler style of *Master*. German diplomas often confer the style 'Doctor of Philosophy and Master of Arts.' It is much to be regretted that not only that constitutional monstrosity, the University of London, but the ancient University of Cambridge, should have committed the historical solecism of conferring a Doctorate and a Mastership in the same Faculty, the more so when medieval precedent (still followed in France) would have supplied the intermediate degree of Licentiate, the meaning of which must be explained more fully hereafter [1].

[1] In the above chapter, I am under exceptional obligations to Denifle, and have with some reserves adopted his position; but I have put the matter in my own way, and do not hold myself responsible for his views except so far as I have actually reproduced them. Denifle hardly recognizes sufficiently the prominence of the dispensation from residence in the earlier conception of a Studium Generale. See the Bull for Rome, cited below, chap. vi. § 8, and above, p. 8, n. 2.

CHAPTER II.

ABELARD

AND THE RENAISSANCE OF THE TWELFTH CENTURY.

CHAPTER II.

ABELARD AND THE RENAISSANCE OF THE TWELFTH CENTURY.

For the general literary and educational history of the period with which this Chapter deals, the most important authorities are the immense mass of material collected by BULAEUS in Vols. I. and II. of his *Historia Universitatis Parisiensis*, Parisiis, 1665; the *Histoire Littéraire de la France* par les Bénédictins de Saint-Maur, 1733, &c.[1]; JOLY, *Traité Historique des Écoles Épiscopales et Ecclésiastiques*, Paris, 1678; OZANAM, *La Civilisation Chrétienne chez les Francs*, Paris, 1849; AMPÈRE, *Histoire Littéraire de la France avant le douzième siècle*, Paris, 1839; MAITLAND, *The Dark Ages*, London, 1844; MAÎTRE (Léon), *Les Écoles Épiscopales et Monastiques de l'Occident*, Paris, 1866; MULLINGER, *The Schools of Charles the Great*, London, 1877 (also the Introduction to his *University of Cambridge to* 1535, Cambridge, 1873); POOLE (R. L.), *Illustrations of the History of Medieval Thought*, London, 1884; COUSIN, *Ouvrages Inédits d'Abélard*, Paris, 1836, and *Petri Abaelardi Opera*, Parisiis, 1849; SCHAARSCHMIDT, *Johannes Saresberiensis*, Leipzig, 1862; DE RÉMUSAT, *Abélard*, Paris, ed. 2, 1855; COMPARETTI, *Virgilio nel Medio Evo*, Livorno, 1872; John of Salisbury, Peter the Lombard, S. Bernard, etc., are cited from the editions of Migne, *Patrologiæ Cursus Completus Lat.*, Paris, 1839, &c. Among the more recent writers my greatest acknowledgments are perhaps due to Mr. Poole. I am also considerably indebted to Mr. Mullinger.

For the history of the Scholastic Philosophy and Theology in the Middle Ages, I have used chiefly BAUR, *Die christliche Lehre von der Dreieinigkeit und Menschwerdung Gottes*, Theil 2, Tübingen, 1842; DEUTSCH (S. M.), *Peter Abälard*, Leipzig, 1883; ERDMANN, *Grundriss der Geschichte der Philosophie*, Berlin, 1866 (Eng. Trans. by Hough, London, 1890, &c.); HAGENBACH, *Lehrbuch der Dogmengeschichte*, Leipzig, 1840 (E.T., ed. Buch, Edinburgh, 1846-7); HAMPDEN, *The Scholastic Philosophy considered in its relation to Christian Theology*, Oxford, 1833; HAURÉAU, *Histoire de la Philosophie Scolastique*, Paris, P. I. 1872, P. II. 1880; JOURDAIN (Amable), *Recherches critiques sur l'âge et l'origine des traductions latines d'Aristote*, Paris, 1843; JOURDAIN (Charles Bréchillet), *La Philosophie de Saint Thomas d'Aquin*, Paris, 1858; MAURICE, *Moral and Metaphysical Philosophy*, vol. III. ed. 2, 1857; MORIN, *Dictionnaire de Philosophie et de Théologie Scolastique*, Paris, 1856; MUNK, *Mélanges de Philosophie Juive et Arabe*, Paris, 1857; PRANTL, *Geschichte*

---

[1] This work, with its continuation 'by members of the Institute,' may here be mentioned, once for all, as an authority for many parts of my subject.

CHAP. II.   *der Logik im Abendlande*, Leipzig, 1870; ROUSSELOT, *Études sur la Philo-*
            sophie dans le Moyen-Âge, Paris, 1840-42; RENAN, *Averroès et l'Averroisme*,
            Paris, 1866; WERNER, *Die Scholastik des späteren Mittelalters*, Wien, 1881-3.
            Among these works I am most indebted to Hauréau, Erdmann, and Renan;
            Prof. SETH's Art. on *Scholasticism* in the *Encyclopædia Britannica* is an
            excellent summary. Among general ecclesiastical historians, I need only
            mention my obligations to GIESELER, *Lehrbuch der Kirchengeschichte*, Bonn,
            1827-57 (E.T., from 4th ed., Edinburgh, 1853-4).

The Bene-
dictine
Age.

THE period which intervenes between the time of Charles
the Great and the eleventh century has been called the
Benedictine Age. The phrase exactly expresses its position in the history of education: it was the age, and the
only age, during which European education was in the
hands of Monks. With the progress of the barbarian
invasions, the old Imperial and municipal Schools had
everywhere disappeared: their place had been taken by
the episcopal and monastic Schools which the imperative
needs of the Church had called into existence. In transalpine Europe, at all events, the old educational system
was completely swept away, though some of its traditions
for a time survived in the Christian Schools by which it was
supplanted.

Attitude of
the Church
towards
Education.

It is generally acknowledged that the age which immediately followed the completion of the barbarian conquests
is the darkest age in the intellectual history of Europe.
Whatever view may be taken of the part played by Christian Theology in bringing about that rapid evanescence
of intellectual light which culminated in the almost total
night of the seventh century, it is at least certain that
so much of the culture of the old Roman world as survived
into medieval Europe survived by virtue of its association
with Christianity. The truth is that the hostility of
Christian theologians to secular culture was to a very great
extent merely the reflection within the sphere of Theology
of the political and social conditions of the time. If Gregory the Great interpreted the advance of the barbarian
hosts, the slaughter and pillage which they brought in their
train, as sure signs of the coming end, the events themselves were sufficiently calculated to discourage study and

education apart altogether from any theological interpretation which might be put upon them. All culture that was
not obviously and immediately useful was doomed to extinction. Christianity at least considerably widened the
limits assigned to utility. The Christianised barbarian
recognised the spiritual, if he did not recognise the intellectual, needs of humanity: and some measure of intellectual cultivation was made necessary to the satisfaction of
those spiritual needs by the narrowest interpretation of
a religion whose principles had to be gathered from books,
and whose services formed a small literature by themselves.
Narrow as may have been the Churchman's educational
ideal, it was only among Churchmen that an educational
ideal maintained itself at all. The tendency of the Church's
teaching was undoubtedly to depreciate secular, and especially literary, education—at least for the only class which
still possessed education of any sort: but the grossest
ignorance of the Dark Ages was not due to the strength
of the ecclesiastical system but to its weakness. The
improvement of education formed a prominent object
with every zealous Churchman and every ecclesiastical
reformer from the days of Gregory the Great to the days
when the darkness passed away under the influence of the
ecclesiastical revival of the eleventh and twelfth centuries.
If the monastic system of Cassian retained something of
the ascetic and obscurantist traditions of the Egyptian
desert, the Benedictine Monasticism which superseded it
created almost the only homes of learning and education
and constituted by far the most powerful civilising agency
in Europe until it was superseded as an educational instrument by the growth of the Universities.

The ecclesiastical character of medieval education was
in the first instance due solely to the fact that, in the
general extinction of Roman civilisation, the clergy were
almost the only class which possessed or desired to
possess even the rudiments of knowledge[1]. The intimate

[1] These generalizations apply in their full extent to Northern Europe
only. As to Italy see below, chap. iv.

CHAP. II. connexion between the Church and the School was stereotyped by the legislation of Charles the Great. A revival
of education formed a prominent part of the wise and far-
reaching scheme of ecclesiastical reform which originated
with that monarch. The centre of the Carolingian edu-
The Palace cational system was the Palace School, whose head, the
School. famous Alcuin, was a sort of Minister of education as well
as the actual teacher of the young courtier-nobles and even
of the great Monarch himself. But this school hardly
constitutes an exception to the ecclesiastical character of
the system : it was primarily intended as a nursery for the
future Bishops and Abbots of the Frankish Empire : it was
perhaps in its origin an outgrowth of the royal chapel [1].
Revival But though under Alcuin in the days of Charles the Great
of Epi-
scopal and and again under Erigena in the days of Charles the Bald,
Monastic the Palace School took the lead and served as a sort of
Schools. normal school to the whole Empire, a more permanently
influential part of the Carolingian Reform lay in the
enactment that every Monastery and every Cathedral should
have a school for the education of young clerks [2]. Of these
two classes of schools by far the most important were the
schools of the Monasteries which now, for the first time,
opened their doors to non-monastic students. Nearly all
the schools which possessed more than a local importance
were monastic. From the beginning of the ninth century
all the more famous monasteries had two distinct schools

---

[1] Lay nobles may have been encouraged to attend the Palace School,
but I see no evidence for Ozanam's
view (*Civil. Chrét.* p. 457) that the
Monastic Schools were intended for
the laity.

[2] The Capitularies on the subjects
issued in 787 and 789 are printed in
Pertz, *Mon. Germ. Hist., Leges*, T.
I. (Hannoveræ, 1885), pp. 52, 65.
At times it was attempted to extend the educational system to
every parish. Thus Theodulfus,
Bishop of Orleans (c. 808–821),
orders that ' Presbyteri per villas

et vicos scholas habeant, et si
quilibet fidelium suos parvulos ad
discendas litteras eis commendare
vult, eos suscipere et docere non
renuant. . . . Nihil ab eis pretii pro
hac re exigant, . . . excepto quod eis
parentes . . . sua voluntate obtule-
rint.'—Migne, T. 105, c. 196. Cf.
Concil. Gall. III (1629), p. 623. In the
Edict of Louis the Pious, however,
(Pertz, *Legg.* i. 231), ' parochia '
should not be translated ' parish ' (as
by Mr. Mullinger, *Schools of Charles
the Great*, p. 135), but ' diocese.' Cf.
also below, chap. v. § 1.

—one of its own *oblati*, the other for outsiders [1]. All the enlightened ecclesiastics of the time were educated in Monasteries, and most of them were Monks: it was from the Monasteries that the episcopal Schools derived their teachers. On the other hand, it was, as we shall see, from the Cathedral Schools that the Universities were at length developed when the intellectual enthusiasm of the Middle Age began to flow in a distinct channel from its religious enthusiasm. The Cathedral Schools were of course as ecclesiastical in their character and aims as the monastic; and this ecclesiastical character of the pre-University education should be remembered as the first of the conditions which determined, at least in Northern Europe, the form of the intellectual movement out of which the Universities grew and the shape of the University-system itself. In Italy and Southern Europe generally, neither the education of the pre-University era nor the movement which gave rise to the Universities was so predominantly ecclesiastical as was the case beyond the Alps. For the present, however, we shall confine ourselves to the countries whose educational system was most powerfully and permanently affected by the traditions of the School of Alcuin and his successors, and especially to the original home of European Scholasticism, Northern France.

Thanks to Charles the Great and the little group of learned ecclesiastics promoted by him, Europe was never again plunged into intellectual darkness quite as profound as that of the Merovingian epoch. But, as in the political, so in the intellectual world, the bright auguries which might have been drawn from the enlightened administration of the

Retrogression after Charles.

---

[1] For the evidence, see Joly, p. 144 *sq.*; Mullinger, *Schools of Charles the Great*, p. 130. Sometimes this distinction between the external and internal school extended to the Cathedrals. Thus at Reims; ' Praefatus denique praesul honorabilis Fulco . . . duas scholas Remis, canonicorum scilicet loci atque ruralium clericorum, jam pene delapsas restituit, et evocato Remigio Autissiodorensi magistro, liberalium artium studiis adolescentes clericos exerceri fecit, ipseque cum eis lectioni ac meditationi sapientiæ operam dedit.' —Flodoardus, *Chron.*, lib. iv. c. 9 (Migne, T. 135, c. 289).

great barbarian were not destined to immediate fulfilment. The revival of intellectual life which might have been expected as the outcome of the Carolingian schools was thrown back for nearly two centuries by the political confusion consequent upon the break-up of the Frankish Empire, by the renewal of Scandinavian devastations in the North, and by the Saracen invasions in the South. But though the general level of education among the clergy throughout large parts of Europe may have sunk in the tenth century to very nearly the eighth-century level, there were always at least a few Monasteries or Cathedrals which kept alive a succession of comparatively well-educated ecclesiastics. It may be broadly stated that whatever knowledge was possessed by Alcuin, was never allowed entirely to die out. The torch was handed on from one generation to another: the seeds of a new order of things had been sown, though it was not till the beginning of the eleventh century that even the first-fruits of harvest were reaped.

The new birth of Europe in the eleventh century.
The change which began to pass over the schools of France in the eleventh century and culminated in the great intellectual Renaissance of the following age, was but one effect of that general revivification of the human spirit which should be recognised as constituting an epoch in the history of European civilisation not less momentous than the Reformation or the French Revolution. It is, indeed, only the absence of any clearly marked breach of political or ecclesiastical continuity that can excuse the designation by a common name of two periods so utterly dissimilar in their social, intellectual and religious conditions, as the period before the eleventh century and the period after it. It is only the first of these periods that can with any propriety be called the Dark Age of European History: it would conduce to stamp the distinction between the two periods in the popular mind if the term 'Middle Age' were reserved for the latter.

The Millenial Year.
The eleventh century forms the transition between one of the darkest and what was in many respects the brightest of

all the centuries generally included in 'the Middle Age': Chap. II.
but in the main it belongs to the second—to the period of
progress, not to the period of stagnation or retrogression.
It cannot be too emphatically stated that there is no historical evidence for the theory which connects the new birth
of Europe with the passing away of the fateful millennial
year and with it of the awful dread of a coming end of all
things [1]. Yet, although there was no breach of historical
continuity at the year 1000, the date will serve as well as
any other that could be assigned to represent the turning-
point of European history, separating an age of religious
terror and theological pessimism from an age of hope and
vigour and active religious enthusiasm. Monasticism renewed its life in the Cluniac and a century later in the
Cistercian Reforms. A revival of Architecture heralded,
as it usually does, a wider revival of Art. The schools of
Christendom became thronged as they were never thronged
before. A passion for enquiry took the place of the old
routine. The Crusades brought different parts of Europe
into contact with one another and into contact with the
new world of the East—with a new Religion and a new
Philosophy, with the Arabic Aristotle, with the Arabic
commentators on Aristotle, and eventually even with
Aristotle in the original Greek.

Of the complex causes of this astonishing new birth of Pre-exist-
ing causes
Europe, some were no doubt in operation before the of the Re-
mysterious thousandth year of grace. The conversion of the naissance.
Scandinavian pirates into Christian and civilised Normans
was one of them. In Germany, under the enlightened rule
of the Ottos, the symptoms of a better order of things may
already be traced before the middle of the tenth century. To
the Ottos, too, was due the regeneration of the Papacy. In
Italy the very necessity of fortifying the towns against the
Saracenic and Hungarian raids, had begun to develope that
civic life which there played so large a part in the intellec-

---

[1] This view is expressed for instance in a very exaggerated way
by Mullinger, *Cambridge*, p. 45.

For the disproof, see Orsi's Art.
in *Rivist Storica Italiana*, T. IV,
1887.

CHAP. II. tual revival.   All these causes contributed to that restoration of political order, of ecclesiastical discipline, and of social tranquillity which began with the close of the tenth century.   Order and peace, leisure and security are the most indispensable conditions of intellectual activity [1], and after all it is for the most part the conditions only, and not the originating causes of great spiritual movements, which admit of analysis at the hands of the Historian.

Influence of the Dark-age Curriculum.

Whatever the causes of the change, the beginning of the eleventh century represents, as nearly as it is possible to fix it, the turning-point in the intellectual history of Europe. But it must not be supposed that the change at once manifested itself in any great ' movement' or discovery.   The fact that the tide has turned, reveals itself solely in the increased efficiency and wider diffusion of an education such as the Church schools had never wholly ceased to impart, at least since the time of Alcuin ; in the increasing vigour of the theological controversies in which the Dark Ages had expended whatever intellectual activity they possessed ; in the increased volume and more vigorous movement of that stream of theological literature which had never entirely ceased to flow.   It was not, however, till the very end of the eleventh or the beginning of the following century that the improvement becomes rapid [2] and surprising ; it is not till then that we trace the first beginnings of that great Scholastic movement out of which grew the Northern University-system.   To enable the reader to appreciate the causes and

[1] I do not ignore the stimulating intellectual effects of political revolutions and social upheavals; but this will not apply to such devastation as was wrought by Danes or Saracens. When an Abbey was in constant danger of pillage by Danes or robber-nobles, the monks were not likely to think much about Logic or Verse-making, though a modern war may interfere but little with professorial studies.

[2] How rapid may be judged from the change which Guibert of Nogent

notices as having taken place within his own lifetime. 'Erat paulo ante id temporis, et adhuc partim sub meo tempore, tanta grammaticorum charitas, ut in oppidis pene nullus, in urbibus vix aliquis reperiri potuisset, et quos inveniri contigerat, eorum scientia tenuis erat, nec etiam moderni temporis clericulis vagantibus comparari poterat.' *De Vita Sua*, l. i. c. iv. (Migne, T. 156. c. 844). He wrote in the first half of the 12th Century.

the character of that movement, it is essential to give some
account of the educational system which it eventually transformed. The revival of educational activity in the course
of the eleventh century was, as has been said, but one side of
a far wider movement—of the re-awakening of the European
mind from the torpor of centuries, of the triumph of order
and civilisation over disorder and barbarism. But the particular direction which was taken by the re-awakened
intellectual energies of Europe was completely determined
by the character of the traditional education which it had
inherited from the past.

Of the ecclesiastical character and objects of this education enough has already been said. The end and object
which the teacher set before himself was to enable the future
ecclesiastic to understand and expound the Canonical Scriptures, the Fathers and other ecclesiastical writings. But
beyond the elementary instruction in the Psalter and Church
Music, we hear little of any systematic training in Theology.
In truth Theology at this time had not yet become a system.
The object of an ecclesiastical education was to enable the
Priest or Monk to read and meditate upon the Bible and
Fathers for himself: the theological writings of the times
are for the most part either refutations of prevalent errors
or abridgments of the patristic commentaries or treatises.
What regular theological teaching there was, assumed of
course a similarly positive and traditional character. But
for the proper understanding of these sacred writings a
certain amount of secular culture was considered to be
necessary[1]. The maximum secular knowledge which the
ordinary Schools imparted is represented by that celebrated
division of the ' Seven Arts '[2] into the elementary *Trivium*

*Theo-
logical
Education.*

*The Tri-
vium and
Quadri-
vium.*

---

[1] The theory finds expression in
the Capitulary of Charles the Great:
' Cum autem in sacris paginis sche-
mata, tropi, et cætera his similia
inserta inveniantur, nulli dubium est
quod ea unusquisque legens tanto
citius spiritualiter intelligit, quanto
prius in litterarum magisterio plenius

instructus fuerit.' — Pertz, *Leges*, I.
pp. 52, 53.

[2] The idea of the *Seven* Liberal Arts
dates, according to Ozanam (*La Civilization Chrétienne*, p. 389) from Philo,
De Congressu (ed. Mangey, IV. Erlan-
gæ, 1788, p. 148, *sq.*) But in any case
it owed its popularity mainly to the *De*

CHAP. II. and the more advanced *Quadrivium*. The *Trivium* consisted of Grammar, Rhetoric, and Dialectic : the *Quadrivium* of Music, Arithmetic, Geometry, and Astronomy. What was known of these Arts may be estimated from the contents of the ordinary text-books of the age—the work of three writers who, living in the dim twilight which intervened between the daylight of ancient culture and the total night of barbarism, had occupied themselves with reducing to compendiums so much as they could save or so much as they could appreciate of the intellectual treasures destined otherwise to be buried for centuries or lost for ever. These three writers were Boethius, the popularity of whose works was largely increased by his supposititious fame as a Theologian and Christian martyr[1], the Christian Cassiodorus,

The text books.

Nuptiis Philologiae et Mercurii of Martianus Capella, in which the Seven Arts appear as the attendant Virgins of Philology upon her marriage with Mercury. The scope of some of the Arts was wider than is indicated by modern usage. Rhetoric included the elements of Law as well as prose and verse composition (see below, ch. iv. § 1); so 'Geometria est ars disciplinata quae omnium herbarum graminumque experimentum enuntiat : unde et medicos hac fretos geometres vocamus, id est, expertos herbarum.' Virgilius Maro (the Toulouse Grammarian of the sixth Century), *Epistole*, IV, ed. Huemer, Lipsiæ, 1886, p. 22. The origin of the idea of Seven Arts has recently received an elaborate investigation from Mr. H. Parker (*Eng. Hist. Review*, 1890, p. 417–461), who shows good reason for believing that Martianus based his book upon a treatise on the *novem disciplinae* by Varro, omitting Architecture and Medicine, which he did not propose to deal with. Mr. Parker somewhat underrates the wide extension given to some of the Arts in the Middle Ages (e. g. he considers Poetry as excluded, whereas it was always in-

cluded in Rhetoric) ; and he overrates the importance of the Seven Arts in the Universities (see below, ch. v. § 4; ch. xii. § 5), where, by the way, the supremacy of Theology was by no means so overwhelming as he represents. He confounds the University era with the 'Dark Ages.'

[1] M. Charles Jourdain (*Excursions historiques à travers le Moyen Âge*, Paris, 1888, p. 19 *sq.*), has suggested an exceedingly plausible explanation of the attribution of the theological works to Boethius, in a confusion with an African Bishop of the same name, who lived as an exile in Sardinia in 504–522—a blunder perpetuated by the Lombard King Luitprand, who constructed a tomb in S. Peter's, Pavia, over the remains of the Bishop, which he found in Sardinia, and mistook for those of his more famous namesake. Mr. H. F. Stewart, in an excellent and learned monograph (*Boethius*, Edinburgh, 1891) is much more successful in showing that Boethius may possibly have been a Christian than in defending his theological authorship. He does not do justice to Jourdain's theory.

and the half-pagan Martianus Capella [1]. Of the Quadrivium even Boethius gives but a meagre outline, the other two but the scantiest smattering [2]. In the Dark Ages Arithmetic and Astronomy found their way into the educational curriculum chiefly because they taught the means of finding Easter. Music included little but a half-mystical doctrine of numbers and the rules of plain-song: under Geometry Boethius gives little but a selection of propositions from Euclid without the demonstrations. Historically speaking, the Quadrivium is chiefly important as supplying the skeleton outline of a wider course of study which was afterwards filled up by the discoveries or rediscoveries of the twelfth-century Renaissance. The real secular education of the Dark Ages was the Trivium—Grammar, Rhetoric, and Dialectic. Under Grammar had long been included, not merely the technical rules of Grammar as formulated by Priscian and Donatus, but all that we should include in the studies known as classical or philological— the systematic study and interpretation of the Classical writers of ancient Rome. Before the age of Charles the Great, whatever secular culture survived the wreck of ancient civilisation had, in spite of the frowns of the severer Christian teachers, been based upon the Latin Classics. Alcuin, though certainly himself well acquainted with the principal

[1] For an account of his strange treatise *De Nuptiis Philologiae et Mercurii* (ed. Eyssenhardt, Lipsiæ, 1866), see Mullinger, *Cambridge*, p. 23 *sq.* Mr. H. Parker, in the learned article already mentioned, has made it probable that this treatise (based upon Varro) was not written, as commonly supposed, c. 470 A.D., but before the building of Constantinople (i.e. before 330). He accounts for the barbarity of the style by the fact that the author was (as he professes to be) an African farmer.

[2] Another still more meagre compilation, the *Etymologiarum Libri XX* (Migne, T. 81, *sq.*) of Isidorus of Seville (570–638) is chiefly based upon the *De Artibus ac Disciplinis Liberalium Litterarum* (Migne, T. 70) of Cassiodorus († ? 562), but its author is now better remembered as the earliest of Canonists, the author of the *De Officiis Ecclesiasticis*, and of the *Collectio Canonum* of which the celebrated forged Decretals purported to be a completion. What Mr. Mullinger calls the 'School History of the Middle Ages,' the *Historiarum Adversus Paganos Libri VII* of the fifth-century Presbyter Orosius (Migne, T. 31), being 'a kind of abstract of the *De Civitate*,' belongs rather to the theological than to the secular literature of the age.

Roman poets, in later life condemned the teaching of Pagan
poetry to the Christian youth : and the tendency of the age
which he inaugurates was on the whole in the same direction, though the more enlightened teachers of the Dark Ages
took a more liberal view, and it is probable that in practice
boys continued to be taught grammatical Latin by reading
a classical author, such as Virgil or Ovid [1] : and in the best
schools, notably at Ferrières, under Alcuin's pupil, the Abbot
Servatus Lupus, a wider study of Classical literature was
pursued with some enthusiasm [2].   Under the head of Rhetoric the treatises of Cicero, such as the Topics (with the
Commentary of Boethius), the *De Oratore* and the Pseudo-
Ciceronian *ad Herennium*, were largely read.   The elements
of Roman Law were often added, and all schoolboys were
exercised in writing prose and what passed for verse.   But
the heart and centre of the secular education of the time in

Promi-
nence of
Logic.
Northern Europe was the study of Dialectic or Logic.   Here
the teacher was untrammelled by the lurking uneasiness of
conscience which haunted the medieval Monk who loved his
Virgil : there was nothing pagan about syllogisms : the
rules of right reasoning were the same for Christian and for
pagan alike, and were (as was thought) essential for the right
comprehension and inculcation of Christian truth.   Under
cover of this idea teacher and pupil alike were enabled in
the study of Dialectic, and perhaps in Dialectic only, to
enjoy something of the pleasure of knowledge for its own
sake. ' The mysteries of Logic were indeed intrinsically
better calculated to fascinate the intellect of the half-
civilised barbarian than the elegancies of classical Poetry
and Oratory.   At all events, in this department a richer

---

[1] See *Vita Alcuini* (Migne, T. 100,
c. 101), where a story is told of Alcuin
(when Abbot of Tours) detecting his
Scholasticus Sigulfus secretly teaching Virgil to his pupils (cf. Ep.
clxix, *l. c.*, c. 441), while in Lupus,
Abbot of Ferrières, we find as keen
a devotee of Classical Literature and
collector of MSS. as any Italian
scholar of the Renaissance. See his

letters, *passim* (Migne, T. 119). For
the toleration of Classics, cf. Rabanus
Maurus, *De Clericorum Institutione*,
Migne, T. 107, c. 396.

[2] Lupus Ferrarensis, *Epp.* lxii, ciii.
(Migne, T. 119, cc. 526, 579.) The
passages are interesting, as showing
that Quintilian, though little known,
was not so entirely lost as is sometimes supposed.

material, meagre as even that undoubtedly seems to us, CHAP. II.
was placed at his disposal than in most other branches of
secular knowledge. Boethius (475–525) had translated the Know-
ledge of
Aristotle.
De Interpretatione and the *Categoriæ* as well as the *Isagoge*
of Porphyry, but in the time of Alcuin only the translations
of Porphyry and the *De Interpretatione* (with the commentary of Boethius) were generally known, together with an
abridgement of the Categories falsely ascribed to S.
Augustine [1], and some logical writings of Boethius. Such
were the chief sources of the scholar's secular inspiration
down to the eleventh century. Even Abelard knew only the
Categoriæ and the *De Interpretatione* in actual translations :
the rest of the *Organon* he knew only from the Boethian
*De Syllogismis Categoricis, De Syllogismis Hypothecis, De
Differentiis Topicis* and *De Divisionibus.*

Though in a sense the authority of Aristotle was Influence
of Plato.
supreme throughout this as well as the later medieval
period, in the formation of the Scholastic Philosophy the
influence of Plato upon medieval thought counted for at
least as much as that of the Stagirite. The authority of
Aristotle was in the first instance due to his position as a
Logician, and Plato was the author of no logical system that
could rival that of Aristotle : while the later Middle Ages
had before them in the writings of Aristotle a whole Encyclopedia of subjects upon which Plato had written nothing.
Of Plato's own writings none were known at any period of
the Middle Ages, except the *Timæus* in the translation by
Chalcidius, the *Phædo* and the *Meno* [3], and even of these the
circulation was not very wide—certainly not in the seed-time

---

[1] Hauréau, Pt. i. p. 95 *sq.* : Jourdain
(*Recherches*, p. 379) treats this work as
an actual translation. Some knowledge of the Physics and Metaphysics
was also obtainable through a collection of Axioms ascribed to Bede
(Jourdain, p. 21).

[2] The *Consolatio Philosophiæ* was
throughout the Middle Ages perhaps
the most popular work in circulation.
It belongs, however, rather to Litera-

ture than to technical Philosophy.

[3] Hauréau, Pt. i. p. 92. M. Cousin
discovered a MS. of the *Phædo* of
the thirteenth century ; but the translation (with the *Meno*) is now known
to have been made c. 1160. See
App. vi. The *Timæus* was probably
known before this ; but the Timæus
expounds just the most unorthodox
part of Plato's system. Plato was
never the subject of medieval Lectures.

of the Scholastic Philosophy. The immense influence which Plato exercised upon medieval thought was mainly derived from mere fragments or reproductions of his teaching in Macrobius or Augustine, or from the mere record of his opinions by Aristotle himself. Little in short was known of Plato besides his doctrine of Ideas: but the controversy between Aristotle and Plato upon this matter supplied the Middle Ages with the great central subject— in the earlier period of its development the sole subject— of its metaphysical controversies. The concentration of intellectual interest upon a single topic of ancient Philosophy originated the never-ending controversy over the reality of Universals.

Origin of the Scholastic Philosophy.

Thus the whole scholastic training of the pre-University era paved the way for the absorption of the intellectual energies of entire generations by this highly speculative question. The one stimulating and interesting morsel which the monastic teacher could place before the hungry intellect of the enquiring student, was a morsel of Logic. Logic was the one treasure snatched from the intellectual wreckage of a by-gone civilization which he was encouraged to appropriate. The one fragment of 'the Philosopher' (as Aristotle was called in the Middle Ages) was a fragment of his Logic. And at the very threshold of Logic the student was encountered by this question of the reality of Universals—on the face of it (as it is apt to appear to the modern mind) a dry, abstract, uninviting topic—a topic which at first sight might seem to belong rather to the theory of Grammar than to Logic or Metaphysic. Yet no sooner does he approach it than the student finds himself led by imperceptible steps from Logic into Physics, and from Physics into Metaphysics, and from Metaphysics into Theology. Indeed, the solution of the most momentous questions to which the human intellect can address itself is inextricably bound up with the solution of a question which 'common-sense' will undertake to clear up in five minutes, or which it will indignantly pronounce too trifling to be asked or answered. Yet he who has given his answer to it, has implicitly constructed CHAP. II. his theory of the Universe.

In the introduction to the Logic of Aristotle which was The Scholastic problem. in the hands of every student even in the Dark Ages, the *Isagoge* of Porphyry, the question was explicitly raised in a very distinct and emphatic manner. The words in which this writer states, without resolving, the problem of the Scholastic Philosophy, have played perhaps a more momentous part in the history of Thought than any other passage of equal length in all literature outside the Canonical Scriptures. They are worth quoting at length :— ' Next, concerning genera and species, the question indeed whether they have a substantial existence, or whether they consist in bare intellectual concepts only, or whether if they have a substantial existence they are corporeal or incorporeal, and whether they are separable from the sensible properties of the things (or particulars of sense), or are only in those properties and subsisting about them, I shall forbear to determine. For a question of this kind is a very deep one and one that requires a longer investigation [1].'

Such was the central question of the Scholastic Philo- The Scholastic Philosophy before Roscellinus. sophy. At what period are we to say that the great debate was opened? In a sense the history of the Scholastic Philosophy begins with the revival of Aristotelian Dialectic in the Carolingian Schools, but its characteristic question about the reality of Universals did not come into great prominence till the far-reaching issues of the conflict were brought out by the teaching of the Realist Johannes Scotus Erigena in the second half of the ninth century. From this time onwards there is a succession of dialecticians by whom the question is more or less distinctly raised. But the hottest battles of the long campaign do not open until we come to that great intellectual revival of the eleventh and twelfth centuries

---

[1] ' Mox de generibus et speciebus illud quidem sive subsistant sive in solis nudis intellectibus posita sint, sive subsistentia corporalia sint an incorporalia, et utrum separata a sensibilibus an in sensibilibus posita et circa hæc consistentia, dicere recusabo : altissimum enim negotium est hujusmodi et majoris egens inquisitionis ' (In trans. Boethii.)

with which we are chiefly concerned. The second and by far the most brilliant period in the history of Scholasticism is opened up by the teaching of the Nominalist Roscellinus at the end of the eleventh and beginning of the twelfth centuries. With Roscellinus we enter upon the most important period of the Scholastic *Philosophy*, while the Scholastic *Theology* can hardly be said to begin before this epoch. There had been indeed a growing tendency to apply the weapons of Dialectic to the discussion of theological questions before this period. Johannes Scotus had pushed the Realist argument very near to the borders of Pantheism, but he had not directly either assailed or defended the truths of revealed Religion. He was rather a somewhat unorthodox Christian Platonist or a belated Gnostic than a dialectical Theologian. A nearer anticipation of the Scholastic conflicts is the controversy which broke out in the middle of the eleventh century—just before the period from which we have seen reason to date the intellectual new birth of Europe—in consequence of Berengar's attack upon the doctrine of the Real Presence of Christ in the Eucharist : but this controversy was in the main conducted upon the basis of authority—at least in the hands of the chief defender or (since the dogma had not yet been authoritatively defined) the chief formulator of the orthodox doctrine, Lanfranc, the famous teacher of the great monastic School of Bec. It was not till the time of Lanfranc's greater successor, Anselm of Aosta, that a marked change took place in the character of the theological teaching and the theological controversies of the Church's Schools.

The Scholastic Theology. The Scholastic Theology grew out of the concentration upon theological study of minds whose only or chief secular culture was supplied by Dialectic. In the intellectual torpor of the Dark Ages young ecclesiastics might be taught to think or to argue by the teacher of Dialectic, and to repeat doctrinal formulæ or mystical interpretations of Scripture by the teacher of Theology without feeling the temptation to apply to the subject-matter of the one school the weapons which they had learned to use in the other. But when once real intellectual activity was roused, this state of things could not last much longer. And as soon as the combustible materials which had long lain side by side without mixing were brought into contact, an explosion was inevitable. Intellectual activity stimulated by Dialectic, intellectual curiosity aroused by the glimpses of old-world Philosophy which were afforded by the traditional education of the age, had no material on which to expend themselves, except what was supplied by the Scriptures, the Fathers, and the doctrinal system of the Church. To investigate and to interpret, to attack or defend what was found there, was the natural impulse of the cloister-bred ecclesiastic of Northern Europe. At about the same period this tendency found marked expression in the writings of two great teachers—the orthodox Anselm and the heretical Roscellinus. In Anselm we are perhaps met for the first time with the spectacle of an orthodox teacher expending his utmost intellectual ingenuity in first raising and then meeting objections to the doctrine which he himself unhesitatingly accepted. With Anselm, author of the famous *Credo ut intelligam*, this effort was made entirely for the instruction of the believer: his object was to add knowledge to a pre-existing Faith: Reason was entirely subordinated to Authority. In Roscellinus Reason undertook the task of criticising and (where it seemed needful) modifying the doctrines of the received Theology [1].

From Roscellinus the speculative impulse was com- Abelard. municated to Abelard, in whose hands the Scholastic treatment of Theology attained its full development. Anselm and Roscellinus were the precursors, Abelard

---

[1] A complete account of the growth of Scholasticism would have to take into consideration the influence of John of Damascus, in the eighth century, who already exhibits the two changes introduced (at different periods) into Western Theology by Scholasticism, viz. (1) the introduction of dialectical processes, and (2) the prominence of the Aristotelian Philosophy. He originates Scholasticism in the Eastern Church, and was by no means without influence in the West.

was the true founder of the Scholastic Theology. With Abelard the great Scholastic movement reaches a point at which it begins to identify itself with what we may call the University movement. Most emphatically it must be asserted that Universities, even in their most rudimentary form, did not exist till at least a generation after Abelard. But Abelard inaugurated the intellectual movement out of which they eventually sprang. The method of enquiry and of teaching of which he was the originator, was the method which essentially characterised the teaching of the medieval Universities—a method transferred by Abelard from Philosophy to Theology, and afterwards (in a greater or less degree) to the whole cycle of medieval studies. Even from the point of view of external organisation Abelard may in a sense be said to inaugurate the University movement. Anselm was the last of the great monastic teachers. A generation later the Monasteries began to shut their doors upon secular students ; and their educational activity was taken up by the Cathedrals and their more independent secular teachers. It was the Cathedral School in which Abelard had taught—the Cathedral School of Paris— which eventually developed into the earliest and greatest University of Northern Europe. Abelard, though not in any strict sense the founder, was at least the intellectual progenitor of the University of Paris.

The monastic Schools superseded by Cathedrals.

Relations of Philosophy to Theology. A slight sketch of the life and teaching of this extraordinary man will be the best introduction to the investigation of our main subject. But to appreciate Abelard's position in the history of medieval thought, it will be well to start with some clear ideas as to the relations between the old speculative problems which in the age of Abelard were being debated with a fury hitherto unknown in the history of Philosophy and the new problems of the Scholastic Theology. We have defined the Scholastic Theology as the result of an attempt to apply dialectical methods to the discussion of theological problems. But it was not only philosophical methods, but philosophical conclusions, that were now imported into the schools of Theology. At this period it was in the main the question of the reality of Universals that troubled the traditional repose of the theological Schools : at a later date, as we shall see, the whole of the Aristotelian philosophy was reimported into the Schools of Europe, and demanded that its relations with Theology should be adjusted. At present we need only deal with the theological bearings of the great problem raised by the earlier Scholasticism. The modification of theological doctrine by ancient Philosophy was, indeed, no new thing in the history of Christian thought. Philosophy had just begun to colour the expression of Christian doctrine before the close of the New Testament Canon : in the hands of the Fathers it entered into its substance. It was, indeed, largely the discrepancies between the traditional Augustinian Theology based upon a Platonic Philosophy and the conclusions to which more independent thinkers were led by the study of Aristotle that created many of the problems with which the Scholastic Theologian was confronted. But none of the recognised answers to the great Scholastic problem was without its theological difficulties. Without an appreciation of the theological bearing of the questions at issue between medieval Realism and medieval Nominalism, the inner history of the movement of which the Universities were originally the outgrowth and afterwards became the organs, nay, it is no exaggeration to say the whole ecclesiastical history of the Middle Ages, will be unintelligible. Unless we see Theo-clearly the theological rocks on which the combatants logical difficulties on either side were alternately in danger of being wrecked, of different we shall be unable to understand either the alarm with philosophical which the rise of the Scholastic Theology in the twelfth positions. century was regarded by old-fashioned and conservative Churchmen, or the way in which now one, now another, metaphysical position was proscribed in the interests of Orthodoxy.

In the first place, the dialectician who maintained (with Realism. Scotus) that reality belonged only to the idea or universal while the particulars are mere phantasms, was liable to

CHAP. II. be confronted with this line of argument. If the reality which the class-name 'Table' stands for is the immaterial self-subsistent idea of a table, the same principle must clearly be applied to the class-name 'Man.' The real thing in man must then be the humanity which is shared alike by Socrates, by Plato and by every other individual man: individuality thus belongs merely to the phenomenal world, to the seeming and the transitory. What then, the Realist was liable to be asked, becomes of the immortality of the Soul? One step more and the personality of God disappears with the personality of man. If the reality of the individual is constituted merely by its participation in the essence of the species, must not the reality of the species in like manner be absorbed into that of the genus, and the reality of the genus into that of the more comprehensive genus in which it is embraced, and so on? The *summum genus* would thus appear to be ultimately the only reality: all substances become mere forms or modes of the being of the one substance: all material things and all individual minds must be regarded as essentially and fundamentally one: mind and matter alike are reduced to modes of the One, the Absolute Being. There are, of course, innumerable ways of evading the consequences of the Realistic premisses: one dialectician or another might stop here or there in the chain of argument. But in proportion as his mind was logical, in proportion to the clearness and fearlessness of his intellect, Pantheistic tendencies were sure to become apparent. All Realism *which starts with denying the reality of the particular* is essentially (as M. Hauréau has said of more than one Scholastic system) an 'undeveloped Spinozism [1].'

Nominal-
ism.

On the other hand the opposite extreme of Nominalism, the theory which declared that Universals are mere sounds (*meræ voces*) and that predication has to do with nothing

[1] In attributing this tendency to Realism in general, M. Hauréau (who writes from a strongly Nominalist point of view) omits what seems to me to be the necessary qualification. There is a Realism which does not deny that the particular is real, though it may be there is no such thing as a particular apart from universal relations.

but names, is a doctrine whose sceptical tendency lies upon
the surface. In Roscellinus the heretical tendency of the
doctrine became immediately evident. Starting with the
assumption that only the individual was real and that
intellectual relations had no existence, he required the
Theologian to choose between an absolute Unitarianism
and the admission that the Persons of the Holy Trinity
are 'tres res,' himself inclining to the Tritheistic alternative. The same rigorous Logic was applied to the doctrine of the Real Presence. But, even apart from its
application to particular dogmas, the destructive tendency
of a doctrine which declared the particular, the isolated
unrelated atom to be the only reality was sufficient to
alarm the medieval Theologian at first sight : his instinct
was right in rejecting a doctrine of which the sensation-
alistic scepticism of Hume or the crudest modern materialism is but an illogical attenuation. Strange as it may
appear, Nominalism was to have its fleeting triumph
even within the pale of the Church : but when it was first
broached, it was heresy.

It might seem that the cautious Dialectician who wished
to keep on good terms with the Bishops and the Theologians must fall back upon the peripatetic view which
acknowledged the reality of the universals while it denied
that the universal had any reality apart from the particulars. And the logical position of the most orthodox
dialecticians who immediately followed Scotus was in the
main of a peripatetic cast, while they fenced themselves off
against the attacks of the ever-watchful Theologian by
drawing a sharp line between the province of Theology
and that of Philosophy. But tendencies were at work
which by the time of Abelard had resulted in making
Realism the orthodox philosophy of the Church's Schools.
The Pantheistic tone of Erigena's own writings was, indeed,
too obvious to escape notice. Nevertheless this same
Erigena contributed largely by his translation of the
Pseudo-Dionysian treatises *De hierarchiâ coelesti* and *De
nominibus divinis* to a modification in the philosophical

CHAP. II. attitude of the orthodox Theology. The mingled mysticism and sacerdotalism of these works, further recommended in France by the identification of their author with S. Denys of Paris, was so attractive to the medieval mind that the current Theology became largely coloured by the Neo-Platonic ideas which had given so much offence in the original writings of their translator. Moreover, since the time of Erigena a change had passed over the Sacramental teaching of the Church, which was destined eventually to make some form of Realism almost essential to the Dialectician who aimed at giving a philosophical explanation of the doctrines which he accepted as a Theologian.

Realism and Sacramentalism. First revealed perhaps by a chance word or two of the Platonist Justin, the belief in a physical though mysterious and vaguely conceived change in the consecrated elements in the Eucharist had found some support among later Fathers, though a more spiritual view was upheld by Theologians of as great or greater authority, such as S. Augustine and Pope Gelasius. Both in the popular and in the clerical mind the growth of the belief kept pace with the decay of education, the advance of sacerdotal pretension, the deepening Paganism of popular Religion. The belief in an actual transformation of the consecrated elements into the very body and blood of Christ was perhaps for the first time fully and formally promulgated in the writings of Paschasius Radbertus (†853) about the middle of the ninth century. Though strongly opposed by Rabanus, Ratramnus, and others, the dogma now took firm hold of the popular imagination. In the darkness of the succeeding age of ignorance it became the very central truth of popular Orthodoxy. The first indication of the re-awakening of the European mind after its long slumber is the denial of the popular superstition by Berengar of Tours. When conservative Theologians like Lanfranc attempted a scientific defence of the popular creed, the necessity of more accurate definition was felt. Berengar's attack rested upon a Nominalistic basis : with Lanfranc began the attempt to defend and at the same time to sublimate the

coarse materialism of the current doctrine[1] by introducing
the realistic distinction between the substance—the impal-
pable universal which was held to inhere in every particular
included under it—and the accidents or sensible properties
which came into existence when the pure Form clothed
itself in Matter. Thus was gradually built up the fully-
developed doctrine of *Transubstantiation*[2]. The substances
of the bread and wine were changed, it was held, by the act
of the priest into the substance of the body and blood of
Christ, while the accidents remained the same. Thus
Realism bespoke the favour of the Theologian by supplying a
much-needed philosophical dress for his cherished doctrine.
However jealously he might defend the claims of Authority
against Reason, in his exposition of theological doctrine
Anselm leant to the same side. In fact, from this time
forward, though reactionary Theologians declaimed against
all Philosophy, the tendency to introduce dialectical distinctions and methods of argument into Theology became
more and more irresistible : and in whatever proportion this
was done, the Philosophy which was made use of among the
orthodox was sure to be of a more or less realistic cast.

The outburst of pure, unadulterated, extravagant Roscel-
Nominalism in Roscellinus was the first wholly new linus.
idea which had moved upon the surface of philosophic
thought since the time of Johannes Scotus, afterwards
known as Erigena. But Scotus is a solitary genius
emerging from the dead level of traditional education
and passing away without founding a school or inspiring
a successor. Roscellinus supplied that powerful shock

---

[1] Thus Berengar was compelled
at a Synod of Rome in 1059 A. D. to
declare that the body and blood of
Christ ' *sensualiter,* non solum sacra-
mento, sed in veritate manibus sacer-
dotum tractari et frangi et fidelium
dentibus atteri.' (Mansi, *SS. Con-
ciliorum Ampliss. Collectio,* T. XIX,
Venetiis, 1774, c. 900.)

It will be seen that the doctrine of
Transubstantiation was originally a
refinement upon a stronger and
coarser identification of the Euchar-
istic elements with the body and
blood of Christ.

[2] According to Gieseler, the *word*
Transubstantiation first occurs in
Damian (†1072), *Expositio canonis
Missae* (Migne, T. 145. c. 883).

to established beliefs and modes of thought in which
great speculative movements usually have their origin.
His teaching awoke the Schools of Europe to a consciousness of the speculative issues of the logical question which
they had been languidly discussing since the time of Alcuin,
as well as to the speculative possibilities of the dialectical
weapons whose use they had long made it their chief business
to teach. In Abelard—at once the pupil, the successor, and
the antagonist of Roscellinus—this consciousness of the
power of thought, which now began to take the place of
the timid Dialectic and conventional Theology of the
Dark Ages, found its fullest and most brilliant exponent.

Life of
Abelard.

Like Roscellinus, Peter Abelard was a Breton, born at
the village of Palais near Nantes in 1079. It is a sign of
the change which was coming over the face of Europe that
the eldest son of a Seigneur, himself destined to the profession of arms, should be given the education of a clerk.
The boy soon discovered so ardent a zeal for knowledge
that he was content to be disinherited rather than abandon
his studious life. After the fashion of the age, he wandered
from one School to another [1], and it was in the course of
these early wanderings that he was for a time the pupil of the
great Nominalist Roscellinus [2]. At last, at about the age of
twenty, he was attracted by the fame of William of Cham-

Collision
with
William
of Cham-
peaux.

peaux to the Cathedral School of Paris. His new Master
had done more than any one else to formulate that Realistic
doctrine which was more and more assuming the position
of an orthodox or official Philosophy. His teaching was
the very quintessence of crude, uncompromising Realism.
He maintained that the whole thing, i. e. the idea repre-

---

[1] 'Proinde diversas disputando
perambulans provincias, ubicunque
hujus artis (sc. Dialecticæ) vigere
studium audieram, Peripateticorum
æmulator factus sum.' Ep. i. c. 2.
For the facts of Abelard's life I
may refer to this autobiography or
Historia Calamitatum which stands
as the first of his letters, and to
Rémusat's most interesting Life.

[2] The fact, though stated by Otto
of Freisingen (*De Gestis Frid.* i. cap.
47, ap. Muratori, *Rerum Italicarum
Scriptores*, Mediolani, 1723, &c. T. VI.
p. 678), was formerly doubted, but
is now put beyond dispute by the
Letter from Roscellinus to his pupil
published by Cousin, *Opp.* II. 794 *sq.*
Cf. Poole, p. 362 *sq.*

sented by each specific or generic name, was 'essentially' present in each individual of the genus or species. His brilliant pupil, imbued with at least the critical side of Roscellinus' doctrine, ventured, with a presumption which shocked an age disposed to apply the principles of feudal loyalty to the warfare of the Schools, openly to combat the principles of his teacher [1]. At what was then accounted an unusually early age, long before the completion of the ordinary period of study, the ambitious and self-confident youth became anxious to set up as an independent teacher. But in France, education was the monopoly of the Church. No one could teach, at least in the neighbourhood of any re-cognised School, without the permission of its duly appointed Head: and William was naturally not disposed to admit so presumptuous a pupil to a participation in his privileges. At Paris Abelard could not venture to defy the established custom : he succeeded however in establishing himself as a Master at Melun without opposition, if not with the assent of the ecclesiastical authorities of the place. As his fame spread, he ventured to move nearer Paris, to Corbeil. An illness compelled him to retire for some years to his native Brittany, whither he was followed by many of his enthusiastic disciples. Disgusted at the success of his conceited pupil, the old Master became more than ever convinced of the vanity of secular knowledge [2]—a suspicion which often haunted the teacher of the old school even while he was spending his life in imparting it. When Abelard returned to Paris, he found that the famous Archdeacon of Paris, the 'Column of the Doctors' as he was called, had retired from his pre-ferment to the little chapel of S. Victor which grew into the famous Abbey of that name [3]. But the passion for

---

[1] 'Primo ei acceptus, postmodum gravissimus extiti, cum nonnullas .. ejus sententias refellere conarer, et ratiocinari contra eum saepius aggrederer et nonnunquam su-perior in disputando viderer.' Ep. i. cap. 2.

[2] Abelard as usual assigns a more

sinister motive : ' ut quo religiosior crederetur, ad majorem praelationis gradum promoveretur, sicut in proximo contigit.' *Ib.*

[3] As to the early history of this House, cf. Rémusat, p. 18, *note*; Robertus de Monte, ap. Pertz, SS. VI. p. 484.

CHAP. II. Dialectic had invaded even this new retreat of mystical and
sanctified learning, and William was persuaded to resume
his lectures for the benefit of the Canons of his House as
well as of outsiders.   Professing a desire to learn Rhetoric,
but more probably thirsting for fresh laurels, Abelard placed
himself again under the instruction of his former Master.
The old conflicts were resumed.   Abelard contended that
if the whole 'thing,' i. e. the whole of the Universal, were
'essentially' present in each individual of the genus or
species, none of it was left to be present in any other individual at the same time.   So conclusive was this argument, if we may trust to its author's account of the matter,
that the Master was obliged to retract and amend his formula
by substituting the vaguer 'indifferently'[1] for the more
definite 'essentially.'   This retractation gave the death-
blow to what was left of the older Schoolman's reputation.
The distinction which Abelard gained by the encounter
was such that William's successor in the Schools of Notre
Dame offered to resign in his favour and to sit at the feet
of the young Master.   Abelard was, therefore, duly installed
in the Cathedral School[2].   But the cowl had not made
a genuine 'religious' of the ex-Archdeacon, and he succeeded in procuring the removal of the Master who had
lent Abelard his chair, and the substitution of a jealous
rival in his place.   Abelard was thus obliged to retire once
more to Melun.   But now William also retired for a time
with his disciples into the country—as Abelard suggests, to
convince sceptical critics of the reality of his 'conversion.'
Abelard at Abelard thereupon ventured to set up his chair, not
Ste. Gene-
viève.   indeed within the walls of the city, but in the precincts of
Ste. Geneviève on the southern bank of the Seine.   The
immunities of this Church, at that time in the hands of a

[1] Such is no doubt the right reading. (See Cousin, *Opera*, l. c. : *Œuvres
Inéd.* p. cxvii.)   The old reading is
'individualiter,' which is hardly intelligible.   But cf. Deutsch, p. 103,
note 2.

[2] There is not the slightest reason

(with Rémusat and Poole) for making
Abelard a Canon of Notre Dame.
Would it not have been undignified
for a Canon to live as a boarder in
the house of another Canon of the
same Church ?

Chapter of secular Canons, enabled it to offer an asylum CHAP. II.
to Masters who were excluded from teaching by the
Cathedral authorities: and henceforth the 'Mountain' of
Ste. Geneviève became and long remained the headquarters
of philosophical teaching in Paris.

Abelard had hitherto been a teacher of Dialectic and Studies
Grammar, or, as we should express it, of Logic and Classics. Theology
under
But no sooner had the promotion of William of Champeaux Anselm of
to the See of Châlons (in 1113) left him without a rival in Laon.
this field than he became ambitious of attaining distinction
as a Theologian. With this view he put himself under the
instruction of the most famous theological Master of his
day—Anselm of Laon [1]. The great Philosopher was not,
however, long content to be a student in his new faculty
under an aged Master of whose powers he appears to have
formed the lowest possible estimate [2]. He soon ceased to
attend lectures regularly, and at length, in the course of
conversation with some of his fellow-students, freely expressed his surprise that educated men should not be
able to study the scriptures for themselves without any
other aid than the text and the gloss. The unheard-
of doctrine was received with derision, and Abelard was
jestingly challenged to make the attempt. He took the
students at their word, and offered, if they would provide
him with one of the usual commentaries, to begin lecturing
on the most difficult book of the Bible that they might
choose, the very next day. They pitched upon the book
of Ezekiel. Abelard fulfilled his promise. The attempt
was at first regarded as a mere piece of braggadocio, but

---

[1] To him is due the amended form
of the *Glossa Ordinaria*, originally
the work of Walanfrid Strabo (†849),
which with further improvements
by Gilbert de la Porrée formed
the authorised commentary of the
Middle Ages. See Poole, *Med.
Thought*, p. 135 *n.*; and for an
account of the gloss, Farrar,
Hist. of Interpretation (London,
1886), p. 251 *sq.*, who however does

not mention the share of Anselm
and Gilbert.

[2] 'Accessi igitur ad hunc senem,
cui magis longævus usus quam ingenium vel memoria nomen com-
paraverat. Ad quem si quis de
aliqua quæstione pulsandum ac-
cederet incertus, redibat incertior.'
Abelardi Ep. i. cap. 3. He afterwards compares him to the barren
fig-tree of the Gospel.

CHAP. II.   after a few lectures, the reports of those who came attracted a large audience, and Abelard became almost as formidable a rival to Anselm as he had been to William of Champeaux. Abelard had, however, 'incepted' or begun to teach in defiance of all established custom without any authorisation : and he was compelled to give up lecturing in Laon.

Abelard at Paris.

He returned to Paris, and was now allowed to lecture without interruption as a duly authorised Master in the Schools of Notre Dame : and his fame as a Theologian soon equalled that which he had won in earlier days as a Philosopher. Abelard had reached the zenith of his glory : and now began his rapid and terrible downfall—a moral downfall which prepared the way for his undeserved persecutions, and gave some colour to the arguments of men to whom that spirit of Rationalism which Abelard represented seemed a direct inspiration of the Evil One. It is, however, surprising how little his treacherous crime seems to have shocked the men who professed such a holy horror of his theological enormities. The tragic story of Abelard—of his connection with his pupil Heloissa and the terrible revenge by which it was terminated—is too well known to need repetition, and does not directly concern us here. Nor need we follow the pathetic story of the quarrels with his Abbot as a monk of S. Denys,—where the whole convent was roused to fury against him by his denial of their founder's identity with Dionysius the companion of S. Paul,—of his hermit life near Nogent at the oratory of the Paraclete built for him with their own hands by his faithful disciples, of his troubled career as Abbot of the poor, remote and unruly Breton monastery of S. Gildas de Rhuys, of his half-imprisonment, half-retirement at Cluny. This part of his life belongs rather to the general ecclesiastical history of the time than to the history of Universities. All through his later years S. Bernard was preaching a crusade against him : he was almost as much done to death by S. Bernard as if he had died at the stake [1].

---

[1] But see Denifle in *Archiv*, I. p. 595, *note* 1. It is probable that in   Ep. 189 the Saint does not hesitate to incur the 'venial sin' of lying to

It is unnecessary for us to estimate the exact extent of Abelard's heresy. As has been already pointed out, Nominalism had become associated in Berengar with the denial of Transubstantiation, and in Roscellinus with heretical views of the Holy Trinity. As to the Eucharist, Abelard's position amounted to a somewhat mystical form of Transubstantiation[1] : but comparatively little was made of this point against him. From the Tritheism of Roscellinus he most emphatically dissociated himself : Roscellinus, indeed, was one of his accusers at the Council of Soissons. His teaching on the Trinity is not essentially different from the doctrine of the Master of the Sentences solemnly affirmed by a General Council : in its general tone and spirit it is substantially (certain metaphysical technicalities apart) the teaching of S. Thomas Aquinas[2]. One of the passages to which most exception was taken at Soissons turned out, on further inspection, to be a citation from S. Augustine himself. The charge of Sabellianism at one Council is sufficiently refuted by the charge of Arianism founded upon precisely the same expressions at another. What may perhaps be thought his most indefensible heresy, the doctrine known as Nihilianism, which may be construed into an obscuration of the real humanity of Christ, was shared by his disciple

---

accomplish the object of his pious zeal, by representing that the appeal to the Holy See was made after his condemnation ; whereas from his own statement it appears that it was before. Cf. Rémusat, I. p. 223.

[1] If we may trust the so-called *Epitome Theologiæ Christianæ* as containing Abelard's teaching, though probably not his work (*Opera*, ed. Cousin, T. II. p. 578). See also the 'Capitula errorum' in Bernard (Migne, T. 182, c. 1052). Large extracts from Walter of S. Victor's polemic against Abelard are printed by Bulæus (II. 404).

[2] The explanation of the 'tres personae' as 'tres proprietates,' i. e. Potentia, Sapientia, and Bonitas or

(as Aquinas said) Amor, which together form the one 'substantia' or 'essentia' of God. The main distinction of Aquinas' position is that he makes 'tres substantiæ' or even 'tres res' (for which poor Roscellinus suffered so much), though adhering to the one 'essentia,' and admitting that substantia may be used in the sense of 'essentia.' Yet Innocent III in the Lateran Council of 1215 issued a decree, permanently embodied in the Canon Law (i. Decret. Greg. IX. tit. i. c. 2), in favour of Peter the Lombard's doctrine (attacked by the Abbot Joachim) that the three Persons form 'una substantia, essentia, seu natura divina,' and even 'una res.'

Peter the Lombard, the 'Master of the Sentences,' the author of the accredited medieval text-book of Theology [1]. His view of redemption, one of his most damnable heresies in the eyes of S. Bernard, was partly shared by no less a person than S. Anselm [2]. Twice Abelard was condemned ; the first time in 1121 at the Synod of Soissons [3], afterwards by the Prelates of France,—aroused against him by his indefatigable enemy S. Bernard,—at Sens in 1141 [4]. On the first occasion Abelard had to submit to the humiliation of burning his book with his own hands, and was imprisoned in a monastery : on the second, after the condemnation had been confirmed by the Pope, he was again sentenced to imprisonment in a monastery, though upon the intercession

[1] Alexander III directed the Archbishop of Sens to condemn certain propositions of the Lombard, among others the doctrine of *Nihilianismus*, i. e. the 'quod Christus secundum quod est homo non est aliquid' (Bulæus, II. 403 ; *Chartul. Univ. Paris*, Introd. No. 3. Cf. Sententiarum lib. iii. dist. 10). Again, in 1177 the Archbishop of Reims is directed to condemn the doctrine, 'convocatis magistris scolarum Parisiensium et Remensium et aliarum circumpositarum civitatum' (*Chartul.* Introd. No. 9). The Pope had once taught the doctrine himself (Denifle, *Archiv*, I. p. 617). The historical explanation of Nihilianism is that it was a reaction from the 'Adoptionism' of a preceding age. Though the medieval Church formally repudiated the Lombard's teaching, the Christology of both medieval and modern Churches received from this time an Apollinarian taint from which they have never completely emancipated themselves. This was, however, due far more to the turn given to the doctrine by the Lombard than to the much more rational form which it assumes in Abelard. See the valuable chapter

in Dorner, *Hist. of the development of the doct. of the Person of Christ*, Eng. Trans. by Simons, div. 2. vol. i. p. 309 *sq.*

[2] His denial that the death of Christ was a price paid to the Devil for the redemption of man from his just dominion (though Anselm held a theory of satisfaction which Abelard rejects). Cf. Anselm, *Cur Deus Homo*, i. cap. vii. (Migne, T. 158. c. 367 *sq.*), with Bernard, ap. Migne, T. 182. c. 1063 *sq.* For the theological teaching of Abelard, see Deutsch, p. 192 *sq.*

[3] The actual work condemned on this occasion, the *Tractatus de unitate et trinitate divina*, has recently been discovered and edited by Dr. Remigius Stölzle of Würzburg (Freiburg im Breisgau, 1891) ; the *Theologia Christiana* is now seen to be a revised form of this treatise with a few highly significant omissions and much amplification, especially in the way of apology.

[4] Not 1140, as has been shown by Deutsch in his pamphlet *Die Synode von Sens 1141*. Berlin, 1880, p. 50 *sq.* : though Vacandard still defends 1140 (*Rev. des Ques. hist.* vol. 50, 1891, p. 235).

of Peter the Venerable, the good Abbot of Cluny, he was Chap. II.
allowed a more honourable retirement in that illustrious
House.

In the estimation of men like Bernard and Norbert, His
the real grievance against Abelard was not this or that Rational-
particular error, but the whole tone, spirit and method cause of
of his theological teaching[1]. He had presumed to endea- offence.
vour to understand, to explain the mystery of the Trinity:
he had dared to bring all things in heaven and earth to the
test of Reason[2]. For his conservative opponents that was
heresy enough : to accept the doctrines of the Church
because they were rational was hardly less offensive than
to reject them as irrational. The well-known story of the
proceedings at Sens, when drowsy Bishops woke up from
their slumbers at each pause of the reader's voice to mutter
' 'namus,' ' 'namus '[3] against theological positions which they
were incapable of understanding, has become the typical
illustration of the methods by which an intolerant ecclesiastical imbecility has sometimes endeavoured to stifle
theological enquiry. But the Council of Sens was no
fair representative even of the Church of the twelfth
century. It is evident that the intellect of the age was
with Abelard ; and the heresy of one generation became
the orthodoxy of the next.

It is from one point of view little more than an accident

---

[1] Cf. the words of S. Bernard :
'Irridetur simplicium fides, evisce-
rantur arcana Dei, quæstiones de
altissimis rebus temerarie ventilantur,
insultatur Patribus, quod eas magis
sopiendas quam solvendas cen-
suerint.' (Ep. 188, Migne, T. 182.
c. 353). And again : ' Nihil videt per
speculum in ænigmate, sed facie ad
faciem omnia intuetur.' (Ep. 192,
ib. c. 358.)

[2] Bernardi *Opera*, ap. Migne, T.
182. cc. 359 *sq.*, 539 *sq.*

[3] ' Inter hæc sonat lector, stertit
auditor. Alius cubito innititur, ut
det oculis suis somnum, alius super

molle cervical dormitionem palpebris
suis molitur, alius super genua caput
reclinans dormitat. Cum itaque lector in Petri satis [? scriptis] aliquod
reperiret spinetum, surdis exclamabat
auribus Pontificum: *Damnatis?* Tunc
quidam vix ad extremam syllabam
expergefacti, somnolenta voce, capite
pendulo, *Damnamus,* aiebant. Alii
vero damnantium tumultu excitati,
decapitata prima syllaba, *namus*
inquiunt.' Berengarius Scholasticus, *Apologeticus pro magistro,* ap.
Bulæum, II. p. 183; Abæl. *Opp.* II.
pp. 773, 774. The writer is of course
a partisan.

that the odour of heresy still cleaves to the name of Abelard, while Peter the Lombard lived to be Bishop of Paris, to be consulted by a Pope on a question of Theology, and to see his 'Sentences' already becoming the very Canon of Orthodoxy for all succeeding ages. Not only had the Lombard shared Abelard's most serious deviation from Catholic teaching: he had adopted from his persecuted Master that dialectical treatment of Theology—that system of fully and freely stating difficulties before attempting their solution—which had given so much umbrage to Bernard and the obscurantists. By opponents of the next generation, such as Walter of S. Victor, Peter the Lombard is classed with Abelard and two other victims of Bernard's theological malice among the 'sophists' and enemies of the Faith—the four 'Labyrinths' of France [1]. So far, it was the principle soon to be embodied in the University of Paris which was condemned at Soissons and which triumphed when the new University became recognised as the first School of the Church and its most illustrious teachers as Saints and accredited 'Doctors of the Church.' From another point of view we must pronounce that the estimate which orthodox opinion has formed of the relative position of Abelard and the Lombard is amply justified. From this point of view Abelard was a Confessor in a losing cause. In Abelard we must recognise incomparably the greatest intellect of the Middle Ages, one of the great minds which mark a period in the world's intellectual history: in the Lombard we descend from the mountain to the plain. Not only did the Nominalism of which Abelard was the champion long remain under the ban of the Church, but the spirit of free enquiry, for the moment associated with Nominalism, was crushed with it. Abelard, a Christian thinker to the very heart's

---

[1] Walter of S. Victor wrote a treatise 'Contra manifestas et damnatas etiam in conciliis hæreses, quas Sophistæ Abelardus, Lombardus, Petrus Pictavinus et Gilbertus Porretanus libris Sententiarum suarum acuunt, limant, roborant'; in which he declares them, 'dum ineffabilia Trinitatis et Incarnationis scholastica levitate tractarent, multas hæreses olim vomuisse.' Bulæus, II. p. 402. Cf. p. 200.

core (however irredeemable the selfishness and overweening vanity of his youth), was at the same time the representative of the principle of free, though reverent, enquiry in matters of Religion and individual loyalty to Truth. To say that Abelard anticipated the spirit of Protestant Theology would be scant praise. He was not of course altogether exempt from the traditionalism of his age : still at times a note of criticism may be discerned in his methods of exegetical and historical discussion [1]. And on such subjects as the Holy Trinity, the Atonement [2], and the doctrine of Grace, we should have to come down to very recent times indeed for more enlightened attempts at the philosophical presentation of Christian doctrine.

Peter the Lombard inherited the form but not the spirit of Abelard's theological methods. The attempt to appeal from recent tradition to the ancient Fathers, and from the ancient Fathers to Scripture and to Reason, is abandoned. With the Master of the Sentences Scholasticism ceases to wear the aspect of a revolt against Authority. There remains, indeed, a deep conviction of the necessity for a rationalisation of Christian doctrine, and the method of boldly stating and attempting to answer the most formidable objections to received opinions : but, with the Lombard, Theology returns to her earlier habit of unquestioning submission to Patristic and Ecclesiastical authority when once the balance of authority has been determined. It is the object of the 'Sententiæ' to collect and harmonise the opinions of the Fathers upon every point of Christian Theology, and to extract from their

---

[1] The whole principle of sixteenth-century Protestantism is contained in the declaration that the ' ecclesiastici doctores' are to be read 'non cum credendi necessitate, sed cum judicandi libertate,'—a principle which he does not extend to the Canonical Scriptures, though even there he recognises (with Jerome) the possibility that 'aut codex mendosus est, aut interpres erravit.' *Sic et Non (Œuv. Inéd.* p. 14).

[2] I cannot forbear to quote one of the 'blasphemies' against which Bernard exhausts the resources of his pious scurrility : ' Puto ergo quod consilium et causa incarnationis fuit, ut mundum luce suæ sapientiæ illuminaret, et ad amorem suum accenderet.' Bernardi *Opera* (Migne, T. 182. cc. 1050, 1051). For the Saint's reply, see *ib.* c. 1062, *sq.*

CHAP. II. scattered and sometimes conflicting *dicta* a precise and explicit answer to every question which the dialectical activity of the age had suggested. Of the Scholastic Theology which henceforth expressed itself chiefly in the form of lectures and comments upon the Sentences, Abelard is unquestionably the father: but the child only partially reproduced the intellectual characteristics of its parent. It was from Abelard's 'Theologia' that the Lombard derived the idea of reducing Theology from a chaotic literature to a philosophical system: it was in Abelard's audacious 'Sic et Non' that he found a precedent for the marshalling of argument against argument and authority against authority: but in the 'Sentences' the critical attitude of Abelard is exchanged for the more modest attempt to harmonise the apparently conflicting authorities by the aid of subtle distinction and ingenious inference. If (as was undoubtedly the case [1]) the Lombard's object was to appease the raging sea of theological speculation and disputation on which his lot was cast, he succeeded singularly ill: but the publication of the 'Sentences' did largely tend to that gradual limitation of the controversial area which accompanied the eventual triumph of the Scholastic method throughout the Western Church. In the generation after Abelard, and still more emphatically in the thirteenth century, the Philosophy and philosophical Theology against which Bernard had arrayed all the ecclesiastical chivalry of Europe, finally triumphed over the mystical or positive teaching of the Monasteries. Were S. Bernard at this moment to revisit the banks of the Seine, he would be nearly as much shocked at the 'solvuntur objecta' of S. Sulpice as he would be at the philosophical speculations of the now secularised Sorbonne [2]. But the triumph of Scho-

[1] See the Prologue to the *Sententiæ*.

[2] How offensive the new Theology still seemed to old-fashioned Churchmen up to the very end of the twelfth century may be judged from the letters of Stephen, Bishop of Tournay, who complains that nowadays 'discipuli solis novitatibus applaudunt, et magistri glorie potius invigilant quam doctrine, novas recentioresque summulas et commentaria firmantia super theologia passim conscribunt, quibus auditores suos demulceant,

lasticism was a 'Cadmeian victory': it cost the vanquished
hardly more than the victors. If the University of Paris
was born of the spirit of which Abelard is the foremost
representative, every increase of her material splendour and
ecclesiastical importance was bought by some fresh departure from that principle of free enquiry which it is the
highest function of a University to enshrine[1].

The career of Abelard at Paris just coincided with the
first steps in the rapid rise to commercial and political importance of the ancient stronghold of the Counts of Paris.
The military strength of the Island-city was the principal
instrument in the rapid aggrandisement of the descendants
of Hugh Capet. The increasing importance of the place
had already (as we have seen) lent fame to its Schools
before the wandering Breton scholar of twenty appeared
for the first time in the cloisters of Notre Dame. The
renown of Abelard drew crowds of students from the
remotest parts of Europe[2]: it is said that twenty of his

Growth of
the Parisian
Schools.

detineant, decipiant, quasi nondum
suffecerint sanctorum opuscula patrum, quos eodem spiritu sacram
scripturam legimus exposuisse, quo
eam composuisse credimus apostolos
et prophetas ... Disputatur publice
contra sacras constitutiones de in-
comprehensibili deitate, de incarnatione verbi verbosa caro et sanguis
irreverenter litigat. Individua Trinitas
et in triviis secatur et discrepitur,
[? discerpitur] ut tot jam sint errores
quot doctores, tot scandala quot
auditoria, tot blasphemie quot platee.'
Migne, T. 211. p. 517; *Chartul. Univ.
Paris*, Introd. No. 48. Such is the way
in which orthodox and conservative
Churchmen greeted the introduction
of the Theology now taught in every
Roman Catholic seminary. Even
Gregory IX in 1228 writes in
much the same strain to warn the
Theologians of Paris 'ne ad
mundanam scientiam declinent
nec verbum Dei philosophorum
figmentis adulterent.' Bulæus, III.

129; *Chartul. Univ. Paris.*, T. I. P. i.
No. 59.

[1] S. Bernard puts his case against
Abelard in a nutshell when he says,
' Ita omnia usurpat sibi humanum
ingenium fidei nihil reservans ... et
quidquid sibi non invenit pervium id
putat nihilum, credere dedignatur.
Ep. 188 (Migne, T. 182. c. 353). In
judging of Bernard's attitude towards
Abelard, we must remember that, as
Otto of Freisingen has it, the good
man was ' tam ex Christianæ religionis fervore zelotypus, quam ex
habitudinali mansuetudine quodam-
modo credulus.' (*Gest. Frid.* i. 47,
ap. Pertz, SS. XX. p. 376.)

[2] ' Roma suos tibi docendos trans-
mittebat alumnos: . . . Anglorum
turbam juvenum mare ... non ter-
rebat ... Remota Brittania [probably
Brittany] sua animalia erudienda
destinabat. Andegavenses eorum
edomita feritate tibi famulabantur in
suis. Pictavi, Vuascones et Hiberi;
Normania, Flandria, Theutonicus et

CHAP. II.
—•+•— pupils became Cardinals and more than fifty of them Bishops[1]. He attracted to himself all the new-born enthusiasm for learning which was everywhere springing up, and which itself resulted from the operation of vaster forces than the genius of the greatest of its representatives. Though crowds of enthusiastic disciples followed their persecuted Master from one retreat to another—even when he sought to bury himself like an anchorite in the desert—it was at Paris that his teaching began and at Paris that his largest audiences were gathered. The stream of pilgrim scholars which set in towards Paris in the days of Abelard flowed continuously for at least a century and a half, when its volume began to be somewhat abated by the growth of daughter-Universities in other parts of Europe. Had Paris been no more than a mere ecclesiastical city clustering round some ancient sanctuary, the fame which Abelard had won for its schools might have passed away like the scholastic fame of Tours or of Chartres. But the process was already beginning by which the successors of the Counts of Paris were to become the real Kings of France : and one of the effects of this movement was to make Paris incomparably the greatest and most important city of Transalpine Europe. This increase of political and commercial importance had a decisive influence in constituting the city the permanent head-quarters of the movement which Abelard had inaugurated. The University, the corporation of Masters (as we have so often to remark), existed as yet hardly even in germ : but from the days of Abelard Paris was as decidedly the centre of European thought and culture as Athens in the days of Pericles, or Florence in the days of Lorenzo de Medici.

Character of the twelfth century Renaissance.　　In order to understand the character of that mighty stirring of the human spirit which Abelard represents, it is essential to form as accurate a conception as possible of the nature and subject-matter of the teaching which

---

Suevus tuum calere ingenium, laudare et prædicare assidue studebat.' Ep. Fulconis Diogillensis ad Abæ-

lardum, Abelard. *Opp.* I. pp. 703, 704 (for ' calere ' read ' colere ').

[1] *Hist. Lit.* Tom. IX. p. 85.

awakened so much enthusiasm. There is the broadest distinction between the culture of the twelfth century and the culture of the thirteenth century. Though the former period was the epoch of the highest or at all events of the most varied intellectual activity which the schools of the Middle Ages ever knew, the greater part of the books which were to absorb all the energies of the Universities for the three following centuries were not yet known in Western Christendom. The Renaissance of the twelfth century began, like the more brilliant but not more real Renaissance of the fifteenth, with a revived interest in a literature which had never passed into total oblivion : like that later Renaissance, it culminated in the rediscovery of a literature which had been practically lost, or at least buried, for centuries. Abelard belongs to the first half of this movement. Of the works of Aristotle he knew little if anything but what had been known to Alcuin or Erigena[1]. It was not till the generation after Abelard that the hitherto unknown books of the Organon, newly translated by James of Venice, came into circulation in Northern Europe[2]. Abelard's older contemporary Gilbert de la Porrée is the first writer who can with certainty be shown to have made use of them[3]. By the time of his pupil, John of Salisbury, the New Logic (as it was called) took the foremost place among the acknowledged text-books of the schools. Abelard concentrated his attention upon the old question of the schools—the question of the reality of Universals. And on this subject he did little more than continue with more moderation and more common-sense

Abelard's logical position.

---

[1] Schaarschmidt (pp. 70, 120) maintains that his knowledge of Aristotle was limited to the *Categories* and *De Interpretatione.* So Cousin, *Œuv. Inéd.* p. liii : Prantl (vol. II. 100-4) includes also the *Prior Analytics.* Jourdain (p. 29) makes him cite the *Sophistici Elenchi* and the *Topics* in addition to the Old Logic. But at all events during the earlier part of his life he was dependent upon the Old Logic only.

[2] 'Jacobus clericus de Venecia transtulit de greco in latinum quosdam libros Aristotelis et commentatus est, scilicet Topica, Anal. priores et posteriores et Elencos, quamvis antiquior translatio super eosdem libros haberetur.' Robertus de Monte, *Chronica,* an. 1128, ap. Pertz, SS. VI. p. 489.

[3] Erdmann, E. T. I. p. 327.

CHAP. II. the polemic inaugurated by Roscellinus against the crudities
of a Realism which understood the Aristotelian doctrine of
the priority of the Universal as a priority in order of time[1].
He may be said to have almost formulated the position
which in modern times would be described as Concep-
tualism, though in the Middle Ages this position was
always looked upon as a form of Nominalism. This
teaching had the stimulating effect of all teaching which
clears away time-honoured cobwebs, however little the
reformer may discern the truth which lies buried beneath
the rubbish. And with the cobwebs in which the older
dialecticians had been immeshed there disappeared also
the caution and timidity which, since the time of Erigena,
had characterised their attitude towards Theology. The
weapon of Dialectic was now freely applied to the problem
of Revealed as well as of Natural Religion : the boundaries
which had hitherto divided Philosophy and Theology were
broken down : the sovereignty of Reason was proclaimed.

His many-
sidedness.
But it was not only as the clear-headed Logician, the bold
and independent Moral Philosopher[2], and the daring Theologian that Abelard cast such a spell over the student of his
generation. Anticipating the sixteenth century in his
advocacy of the rights of private judgment, Abelard (though
less than some of his contemporaries) anticipated it also in
his enthusiasm for the study of classical literature. He was
at least one, if not the most prominent, of the little band
of scholars who imparted fresh vigour to the teaching of

---

[1] His logical position is fairly expressed by the following sentences :
'Clarum itaque ex supradictis arbi-
tror esse, res aliquas non esse ea,
quæ a propositionibus dicuntur . . .
Non itaque propositiones res aliquas
designant simpliciter quemadmodum
nomina. Imo qualiter sese ad in-
vicem habeant, utrum scilicet sibi
conveniant annon, proponunt . . . ; et
est profecto ita in re, sicut dicit vera
propositio, sed non est res aliqua,
quod dicit ; unde quasi quidam rerum modus habendi se per proposi-

tiones exprimitur, non res aliquæ
designantur' (*Dialect.* ap. *Œuv. Inéd.*
p. 245). 'Aliud enim in nomine
Socratis quam in nomine hominis
vel cæteris intelligitur ; sed non
est alia res unius nominis quod
Socrati inhæret quam alterius'
(*Ib.* p. 248).

[2] The *Scito te ipsum* is an original
treatise on Moral Philosophy, more
valuable and interesting perhaps
than anything which the Middle Ages
produced after the recovery of the
Nicomachean Ethics.

Grammar as well as to Philosophy and Theology. Though he was not (as has sometimes been supposed) a Greek scholar, Virgil and Ovid, Seneca and parts of Cicero were as familiar to him as Boethius and Augustine: and even the great Classical Law-texts were included among the subjects which divided the attention of this many-sided teacher[1]. Abelard was an orator and a stylist as well as a logician and dialectical Theologian: and, even on the subjects of the old traditional curriculum, his lectures no doubt owed their popularity as much to the attractiveness of the manner[2] as to the novelty of the matter.

There was no one among Abelard's immediate successors who united the same variety of gifts to the same extraordinary charm of voice and manner; but there is hardly any period in the history of the Schools of France when so many famous Masters were teaching at the same time, and certainly no period in which their teaching extended over so varied a field as in the middle of the twelfth century. The subsequent predominance of an all-absorbing Scholasticism has almost thrown into oblivion the fact that for about half a

Breadth of twelfth century studies.

---

[1] When and where Abelard appeared in the character of a teacher of Law we do not know, but the traditional story about him in this capacity by Odofredus is, except in the different sequel of the boast, so exactly parallel to the story of his relations to Anselm of Laon that it may conveniently be given here. Odofredus remarks, *Com. in Cod.* iii. tit. 39, l. 5 (Lugd. 1550, III. f. 184 b): ‘In lege ista ... fuit deceptus quidam qui magnus philosophus putabatur: et dicitur quod fuit quidam qui vocabatur magister Petrus Baiardi ... et valde deridebat legistas, et iactabat se quod nulla lex esset in corpore iure (*sic*) quantumcunque esset difficilis in litera quin in ea poneret casum et de ea traheret sanum intellectum. Unde una die fuit sibi ostensa a quodam ista lex, et tunc ipse dixit: Nescio quid velit dicere ista lex, unde derisus fuit.’ I owe the reference to Chiapelli, *Lo Studio Bolognese*, p. 82.

[2] Cf. the words of Heloissa: ‘Duo autem .. tibi specialiter inerant, quibus feminarum quarumlibet animos allicere poteras; dictandi videlicet et cantandi gratia; quae cæteros minime philosophos assecutos esse novimus.’ Abæl. Ep. 2. *Opera*, I. p. 76. Abelard's Latin hymns are printed in *l. c.* p. 295 and have no particular charm: but he appears also to have composed vernacular songs. Another side of Abelard as a Lecturer is brought out by Otto of Freisingen: ‘Inde magistrum induens Parisius venit, plurimum in inventionum subtilitate non solum ad philosophiam necessariarum, sed et pro commovendis ad iocos hominum animis utilium valens.’ *De Gestis Frid.* i. 47. (Pertz, SS. XX. p. 377.)

century Classical Latin was taught—not merely to young boys, but to advanced students—with almost as much thoroughness in at least one school of medieval France, as it was afterwards taught in the Universities of the Reformation, or in the Jesuit Colleges of the Counter-reformation.

Studies of John of Salisbury. The Englishman, John of Salisbury, has left us a full and complete account of his education in France between 1137 and 1149 [1]. He is indeed the typical scholar of the period. In those days there was no regular curriculum of studies. Scholars wandered from school to school, and from subject to subject at their pleasure. They were no more bound to spend a fixed number of years upon any one branch of knowledge than the students at Rhodes or at Athens in the days of Cicero. John of Salisbury's studies extended over a period of twelve years, though during part of the time he was engaged in teaching privately as well as in attending the public lectures of eminent Masters. First he went to Paris, and applied himself to the study of Logic. Abelard had just managed to escape from his uncongenial retreat at S. Gildas, and had resumed his lectures at Ste. Geneviève, where for a short time John was able to sit at his feet. The departure of Abelard (S. Bernard was no doubt upon his track) compelled him to fall back upon the teaching of the orthodox Realistic dialecticians, Alberic of Reims and Robert of Melun, the last an Englishman and afterwards Bishop of Hereford. After two years he left Paris, and spent three years under the famous 'Grammarian' William of Conches, at Chartres. At Chartres too he went on to the *Quadrivium* under the learned Richard l'Evêque, and (at a later date) studied both Dialectic and Theology under Gilbert de la Porrée, the first logician of the day, afterwards Bishop of Poitiers, 'the one man whom saint Bernard of Clairvaux unsuccessfully charged with heresy [2].' Afterwards he returned to Paris, and heard Theology under Robert Pulleyn and Simon of Poissy. The order and varieties of these studies present the strongest contrast to the fashions of the next century, with its strict

---

[1] *Metalogicus,* II. x. (Migne, T. 199. c. 867.)   [2] Poole, p. 133.

distinction of 'Faculties' and invariable succession of CHAP. II. studies, which reduced 'Grammar' to a mere schoolboy preparation for Dialectic, and practically compelled the student to abandon for ever each subject in the course when he had heard the regulation lectures upon it.

Among these varied studies what really interested our author most were the Classical, or, as they were then called, Grammatical lectures. He has left us a very full and highly interesting account of the teaching of William of Conches [1]. This teacher followed a method invented by his Master, Bernard of Chartres, and based on the recommendations of Quintilian, a method which bears a striking resemblance to that most thorough-going application of the principle of Classical education which gained such a marvellous popularity in later days for the Schools of the Jesuits. The lectures (or at least the course of reading recommended) covered pretty well the whole field of Classical Latin [2]. After questions on parsing, scansion, construction, and the grammatical figures or 'oratorical tropes' illustrated in the passage read, the Lecturer noticed the 'varieties of phraseology' occurring therein, and pointed

Twelfth century Humanism : Method of Bernard of Chartres.

---

[1] *Metalogicus,* I. c. xxiv. (Migne, T. 199. c. 853.)

[2] Petrus Blesensis, Archdeacon of Bath, John of Salisbury's pupil, tells us that he read 'præter cæteros libros qui celebres sunt in Scholis', Trogus Pompeius, Josephus (translated), Suetonius, Egisippus (*sic*), Q. Curtius, Cornelius Tacitus, and T. Livius, besides the Latin poets. (Ep. 101. Migne, T. 207. c. 314 : *Chartul. Univ. Paris.* T. I. pt. i. No. 25. This list, however, seems to be taken from John of Salisbury, *Polycraticus,* viii. 18, Migne, T. 199. c. 788, who does not explicitly say that he had read them, and must be looked upon with some suspicion, since John makes Suetonius and Tranquillus into two distinct authors.) The only modern author whom John's pupils were encouraged to read was Hilde-

bert ... afterwards Archbishop of Tours († 1134). 'Profuit mihi quod Epistolas Hildeberti Cenomanensis Episcopi styli elegantia et suavi urbanitate præcipuas firmare et corde tenus reddere adolescentulus compellebar.' Petrus Blesensis, *l.c.* The compliment seems to be well merited and supplies another illustration of the classical taste of Abelard's generation. (See his *Epp.* ap. Migne, T. 171. c. 141 *sq.*) The same writer (Petrus Blesensis) in remonstrating with a correspondent (circa 1155, *l.c.* c. 18) for spending all his time on profane authors, says, 'Priscianus et Tullius, Lucanus et Persius, isti sunt Dii vestri.' Sismondi (*Hist. des Français,* Paris, 1823, T. V. p. 67) remarks on the stilted and laboured imitation of classical models by the inferior writers of the time.

CHAP. II. out the 'different ways in which this or that may be expressed,'—in short subjected the whole diction of the author
to an elaborate and exhaustive analysis with the view of
stamping it upon the memory of his audience. He then
proceeded to comment on or explain the subject-matter,
enlarging upon any incidental allusions to physical Science
or any ethical questions touched on by the author [1]. The
next morning the pupils were required, under the severest
penalties, to repeat what they had been taught on the preceding day [2]; and there was daily practice in Latin prose
and verse composition in imitation of specified Classical
models, and frequent conversation or discussion among the
pupils on a given subject, with a view to the acquisition of
fluency and elegance of diction [3].

---

[1] 'Auctores excutiat, et sine intuen-
tium risu eos plenius spoliet, quas (ad
modum corniculæ) ex variis disciplinis, ut color aptior sit, suis operibus
indiderunt. . . . Excute Virgilium,
aut Lucanum, et ibi, cujuscunque
philosophiæ professor sis, ejusdem
invenies condituram.' Even mathematics are included among the subjects which might be introduced *obiter*
in the course of a classical lecture !

[2] 'Et quoniam memoria exercitio
firmatur, ingeniumque acuitur ad
imitandum ea quæ audiebant, alios
flagellis et pœnis urgebat. Coge-
bantur exsolvere singuli die sequenti
aliquid eorum, quæ præcedenti audierant, alii plus, alii minus ; erat
enim apud eos præcedentis discipulus
sequens dies.'

Then follows a passage about a
certain 'Evening exercise,' the
exact nature of which I confess to
being unable to make out. 'Vesper-
tinum exercitium, quod declinatio
dicebatur, tanta copiositate grammaticæ refertum erat, ut si quis in eo
per annum integrum versaretur, rationem oquendi et scribendi, si non
esset hebetior, haberet ad manum, et

significationem sermonum, qui in
communi usu versantur, ignorare non
posset. Sed quia nec scholam, nec
diem aliquem decet esse religionis
expertem, ea proponebatur materia,
quæ fidem ædificaret, et mores, et
unde qui convenerant, quasi collatione
quadam, animarentur ad bonum.
Novissimus autem hujus declina-
tionis, immo philosophicæ collationis,
articulus, pietatis vestigia præferebat:
et animas defunctorum commendabat,
devota oblatione psalmi, qui in
pœnitentialibus sextus est, et in
oratione Dominica, Redemptori suo.'
For ' declinatio,' cf. Cicero, *de Orat.*
III. c. 54.

[3] 'Prosas, et poemata quotidie
scriptitabant, et se mutuis exercebant
collationibus, quo quidem exercitio
nihil utilius ad eloquentiam, nihil
expeditius ad scientiam, et plurimum
confert ad vitam, si . . . in profectu
literario servetur humilitas.' The
whole chapter throws a most interesting light on the Schools of the period
—would that we had an equally full
and graphic account of the Schools
of any later period in the Middle
Ages !

The Latinity of the great writers of this intermediate
period—of Abelard's letters, and still more of Hildebert
of Tours and John of Salisbury—though Latin was to
them too much of a living language to permit of a
dilettante Ciceronianism, was often more classical than the
Latinity of the African Fathers. A revival of serious study
had raised their style out of the barbarism of ignorance;
and even in their theological and philosophical writings it was as yet but little disfigured by the barbarism
of the new Scholastic terminology. A combination of
circumstances narrowed the culture and the education of
the succeeding age. Even in the hey-day of the twelfth
century Renaissance, the Humanists (if one may so call
them) were in a minority, just as they were in the days of
Erasmus and Reuchlin. John of Salisbury's *Metalogicus*
was largely written to vindicate the claims of 'Grammar'
or Philology. His writings are full of lamentation over the
prevailing passion for frivolous, subtle, and sophistical disputation. Fully as he appreciated the value of Logic as an
instrument of education, he recognised, as his contemporaries for the most part did not recognise, the intellectual
barrenness of logical training for minds ignorant of everything besides Logic[1]. All his reflections on education—
which may be almost said to amount to a treatise on the
subject—imply that he is the advocate of a losing cause.
The Humanists of the sixteenth century had a battle to
fight, but the opposing cause was then no longer intellectually formidable ; the world was sick of syllogisms. In
the twelfth century the Scholastic Philosophy was in its
vigorous youth; a majority of the best intellects of the
age were devoted to its pursuit; the Humanists themselves were Philosophers too. The revived Classicism of
that day was not crushed by an opposing Obscurantism
such as vainly attempted to resist the Humanism of the

---

[1] 'Expertus itaque sum quod liquido colligi potest, quia sicut Dialectica alias expedit disciplinas, jacet ex-sanguis et sterilis, nec ad fructum philosophiæ fœcundat animam, si aliunde non concipit.' *Metalogicus,* ii. c. 10. (Migne, T. 199. c. 869.)

CHAP. II.

The new Aristotle.

Reformation period; it was simply crowded out in the 'conflict of studies.'

By the beginning of the thirteenth century, in consequence of the opening up of communications with the East —through intercourse with the Moors in Spain, through the conquest of Constantinople, through the Crusades, through the travels of enterprising scholars—the whole of the works of Aristotle were gradually making their way into the Western world. Some became known in translations direct from the Greek: more in Latin versions of older Syriac or Arabic translations. And now the authority which Aristotle had long enjoyed as a Logician—nay, it may almost be said the authority of Logic itself—communicated itself in a manner to all that he wrote. Aristotle was accepted as a well-nigh final authority upon Metaphysics, upon Moral Philosophy, and with far more disastrous results upon Natural Science. The awakened intellect of Europe busied itself with expounding, analysing and debating the new treasures unfolded before its eyes, and the Classics dropped again, for the mass of students whose reading was bounded by the prescribed curriculum of the Universities, into the obscurity from which they had for a brief period emerged. Not only did bad translations of a writer whom the best translator would perhaps have found it impossible to clothe in a dress of elegant Latinity take the foremost place in education,

Decadence of Classical Studies.

but the eagerness to drink of what seemed the fountain of all wisdom, and to reach the more and more coveted honours of the Mastership in Arts or Philosophy, reduced to a minimum the time that could be bestowed upon the mere acquisition of the language. As soon as the student had learnt the rules of Grammar and the vocabulary of the conversational Latin in ordinary use, he hastened to acquire the subtle but unliterary jargon which would enable him to hold his own in the arena of the Schools[1]. The Humanists

---

[1] 'Sufficiebat ad victoriam verbosus clamor, et qui undecunque aliquid inferebat, ad propositi perveniebat metam. Poetæ, historiographi, habebantur infames, et si quis incumbebat laboribus antiquo-

who wrote towards the close of the twelfth century are full of complaints at the increasing neglect of grammatical and historical training and the undisciplined rawness of the young Philosophers. At times, indeed, their chief grievance is that the study of Law is destroying all liberal education. This last tendency the discovery of the new Aristotle at the beginning of the thirteenth century did something to arrest, but the fresh vigour thus imparted to speculation only added to the growing contempt for Classical study and for all literature as such. For the attainment of the Mastership in the Liberal Arts, Logic and Philosophy were the essential requisites : and at that early period in the history of the examination-system it was soon found that the establishment of a prescribed curriculum of studies and the offer of a premium to those who pursue it is fatal to all subjects excluded therefrom.

While the main explanation of the rapid decline of Humanism towards the close of the twelfth century must be sought in the tendencies of the age and the influence of the new Aristotle, one of the contributory causes was due to a merely accidental circumstance. It has been commonly assumed that the whole of the scholastic career of John of Salisbury was passed at Paris : but more careful

Influence of Chartres overshadowed by Paris.

---

rum, notabatur, et non modo asello Arcadiæ tardior, sed obtusior plumbo, vel lapide, omnibus erat in risum. Suis enim, aut magistri sui, quisque incumbebat inventis. Nec hoc tamen diu licitum : cum ipsi auditores in brevi coerrantium impetu urgerentur, ut et ipsi, spretis his, quæ a doctoribus suis audierant, cuderent, et conderent novas sectas. Fiebant ergo summi repente Philosophi : nam qui illiteratus accesserat, fere non morabatur in scholis ulterius, quam eo curriculo temporis, quo avium pulli plumescunt. Itaque recentes magistri e scholis . . . sicut pari tempore morabantur, sic pariter avolabant. . . . Solam convenientiam sive rationem

loquebantur. . . . Impossibile credebatur convenienter et ad rationis normam quicquam dicere aut facere, nisi convenientis et rationis mentio expressim esset inserta. Sed nec argumentum fieri licitum, nisi præmisso nomine argumenti. Ex arte et de arte agere idem erat.' Jo. Saresberiensis, *Metalogicus*, lib. i. c. 3 *sq.* (Migne, T. 199. c. 829.) Cf. the extremely interesting preface to the *Speculum Ecclesiæ* of Giraldus Cambrensis (written circa 1220, in old age) ed. Brewer, IV. 1873, p. 3 *sq.*), and Wood's account of the unmutilated passage (*Hist. and Antiq. Univ. Oxon.* I. p. 56).

investigation has revealed the fact that his classical teacher, William of Conches, like his more celebrated predecessor Bernard Sylvester, taught not at Paris but at Chartres[1]. Chartres rather than Paris was the centre of the Classical Renaissance. At Paris on the other hand Dialectic and Theology were the prominent subjects. The founder of the scholastic fame of Paris, William of Champeaux, was a Dialectician and nothing else; though not without Classical learning, it was chiefly as a Logician and a Theologian that Abelard appealed to his own age. As has been already pointed out, the increasing tendency towards a centralisation of intellectual and scholastic activity in Paris was to a large extent independent of the fame of any single teacher: but the superlative vogue of the Parisian Schools carried with it as one of its incidental effects the collapse of the weaker if more solid and more promising movement which had found a home in Chartres, and the direction of all intellectual activity into the speculative groove marked out for it by the controversies of William and of Abelard. Possibly, probably, the dialectical passion of the age was too strong to be resisted: but the fortunes of European civilization might have been considerably altered had William of Champeaux taught in provincial Chartres and Bernard Sylvester in metropolitan Paris. Had the new Aristotle fallen into the hands of scholars trained in the school of Chartres, instead of into the hands of dialecticians versed in the debates of the Quartier Latin, the approxi-

---

[1] The correction of this error is due to C. Schaarschmidt (*Johannes Saresberiensis*, 1862, p. 22 *sq.*). The first English writer who has rewritten the life of John of Salisbury and of the School of Chartres in the light of this correction is Mr. Poole, *Illustrations*, &c. (p. 109 *sq.*, p. 201 *sq.* : Art. in *Dict. Nat. Biog.*). Budinszky (*Die Univ. Paris und die Fremden an derselben in Mittelalter*, p. 92) still makes John study at Paris for twelve years, though he knows of Schaarschmidt's work. The classical traditions of Chartres may possibly be traced back to direct contact with the old Rhetorical Schools of the Roman world. About the year 570 a young Roman (according to an early biographer) 'litteris . . . decentissime eruditus' went to Chartres, 'tantoque honore institutus, ut doctor divinarum litterarum et magister totius civitatis diceretur.' He eventually became Bishop of that See.— A.SS. 2 Aug. vol. I. p. 170.

mation which the great twelfth century writers exhibit CHAP. II.
to the intellectual tone and level of the sixteenth
might have been indefinitely more close than it actually
was [1].

As a matter of fact the new Aristotle proved simply so The new
Aristotle :
much additional fuel thrown upon the all-consuming dia- gain and
lectical fire of the philosophical Schools. While it enorm- loss.
ously widened the range of study, it did nothing to improve
its method. The Psychology, the Metaphysic, and the
Theology which the enlarged Aristotle of the thirteenth
century made possible was certainly a more nutritious
intellectual diet than the mere endless, purposeless logic-
chopping which John of Salisbury had denounced. It
must not be too hastily assumed that Europe would have
gained more from an earlier Renaissance than it gained
from the Scholasticism of the thirteenth and fourteenth
centuries. But advance in one direction had to be bought
by retrogression in another. Freshness, originality, style,
culture, solidity—such as we find in the great writers of
the twelfth century—all these were crushed beneath the
dead weight of a semi-authoritative literature of barbaric
translations. A comparison of John of Salisbury's account
of his education in the first half of the twelfth century with
the earliest University Statute at the beginning of the next
century enables us to trace the startling rapidity of this
decline in literary culture [2]. Grammar is prescribed as one
of the subjects of Examination, but Grammar is represented
solely by the works of Priscian and Donatus. Rhetoric
receives hardly more than a complimentary recognition :
the Classics are not taken up at all. The student's whole
attention is concentrated upon Logic and Aristotle. Boys
in Grammar Schools might still learn their Grammar by

---

[1] 'Le plus grand étonnement de
ceux qui étudient de près l'histoire du
moyen âge est que le protestantisme
ne soit pas produit trois cents ans
plus tôt. Toutes les causes d'une
révolution religieuse existaient au
xiii° siècle ; toutes furent étouffées.'
Renan, *Nouvelles Études d' Hist. Religieuse*, Paris, 1884, p. 301. The
dictum is at least as applicable to
the age of Abelard as to the thirteenth
century.

[2] Bulæus, III. p. 82 ; *Chartul.*
T. I. P. i. No. 20.

construing Ovid or 'Cato'[1], but henceforth the poets, the historians, the orators of ancient Rome were considered unworthy of the attention of ripe students of fourteen or sixteen in the University Schools.

[1] The work commonly styled 'Dionysii Catonis Disticha de moribus ad filium,' a work of un- known origin which served as the universal Delectus of the Middle Ages.

CHAPTER III.

SALERNO.

CHAPTER III.

SALERNO.

The first considerable account of the School is that given by NAPOLI-SIGNORELLI, *Vicende della Coltura nelle due Sicilie*, Napoli, 1784, T. II. pp. 147 *sq.* 257 *sq.* Cf. also MURATORI, *Antiq, Italicæ*, Mediolani, 1740, T. III. c. 935 *sq.* The School receives more systematic treatment in ACKERMANN, *Regimen Sanitatis Salerni*, Stendaliæ, 1790 [1], and *Institutiones Historiæ Medicinæ*, Norimbergæ, 1792 ; and from TIRABOSCHI, *Storia della Letteratura Italiana*, Milano, 1822, &c., T. III. pp. 576–590. But the most important authority is the *Collectio Salernitana* (including the medical treatises discovered by HENSCHEL, the *Regimen Sanitatis Salerni*), &c., of DE RENZI, Napoli, 1852, who has also published a *Storia documentata della Scuola Medica di Salerno* ed. 2. Napoli, 1857. I have also consulted MEAUX, *L'École de Salerne* (an edition and translation of the *Regimen Sanitatis* with Introduction by DAREMBERG), Paris, 1880 ; HAESER, *Lehrbuch der Geschichte der Medicin*, Jena, ed. 3. 1875, I. p. 645 *sq.*), and *Grundriss der Gesch. d. M.*, Jena, 1884, p. 114 *sq.* ; LECLERC, *Histoire de la Médecine Arabe*, Paris, 1876 ; POUCHET, *Histoire des Sciences Naturelles au Moyen Âge*, Paris, 1853 ; the Article *Médecine (Histoire de la)* in the *Dict. Encycl. des Sciences Méd.* (Sér. ii. T. 16. Paris, 1877) by BEAUGRAND (which see for a very full bibliography), and the very interesting and learned article on the same subject by Dr. J. F. PAYNE in the *Encyclopædia Britannica.* PUSCHMANN, *Geschichte des medicinischen Unterrichts*, Leipzig, 1889 (E. T. by E. H. Hare, London, 1891) contains nothing new.

CONSIDERATIONS of chronological sequence make it desirable to introduce in this place a short notice of the School of Salerno. For more than two centuries Salerno as a School of Medicine stood fully on a level in point of academic fame with Bologna as a School of Law, and Paris as the head-quarters of Scholasticism. The

The revival of Medicine.

---

[1] I am indebted for the use of a copy of this rare work to the Library of the Royal College of Surgeons.

Chap. III.　eleventh century was marked by a revival of Medicine
as well as by a revival of legal, theological, and dialectical
study. And in point of time the medical revival seems
to have been the earliest phase of the movement. At all
events, the unique fame of Salerno as a School of Medicine
was fully established long before the dialectical movement
centred in Paris or the legal in Bologna. The subject of
medieval Medicine is so obscure and technical that the
reader will not expect any detailed history of its rise and
progress : while so little is known of the origin and development of the School as an educational institution that we
are absolved from taking more than a passing notice of its
place in the academic system of medieval Europe.

Date of
Medical
School at
Salerno.
　　The origin of the School of Salerno is veiled in im-
penetrable obscurity. There are some traces of the study
or at least the practice of Medicine here as early as the
ninth century[1], but of course the fact that the town possessed a Physician does not show the existence of a Medical
School. In the tenth century the place was certainly
famous for the skill of its Physicians[2] ; while in the first

---

[1] The name of a Salerno Physician
occurs in a charter of 848 (Renzi,
Storia Documentata, No. 22), but the
names in Renzi's list do not become
frequent till after 1050 (*Coll. Salern.*
II. p. 797). Perhaps the earliest indication of a repute for medical skill
occurs towards the middle of the
tenth century (before 946), when a
French Bishop 'in arte Medicinæ peri-
tissimus,' and 'quidam Salernitanus
medicus,' met at the court of Louis IV.
It is noticeable that while the Bishop
was 'litterarum artibus eruditus,'
the Salerno practitioner 'licet nulla
litterarum scientia præditus, tamen ex
ingenio naturæ multam in rebus ex-
perientiam habebat.' (Richerus, *Hist.*
ap. Pertz, *Mon. Germ. Hist. SS.* III.
p. 600.) It would thus seem that the
earliest Salerno physicians were
empiric rather than scientific. For

other early notices of the School
see de Renzi, *Coll. Salern.* I. p. 121
sq., and the signatures collected from
the *Codex Diplomaticus Cavensis* (Nea-
poli, 1873) by Gloria, *Monumenti della
Università di Padova* (1222-1318) p. 91.

[2] In 984 Adalbert Bp. of Verdun
went to Salerno to be cured—probably of the stone. The Chronicler's expression 'cum ... a *medicis* curari non
posset' (D'Achery's *Spicilegium* T. II.
p. 238) seems to show that he was
not merely attracted by the fame of a
single physician. It is unnecessary
to refer to the mythical theory which
of course attributes the origin of the
school to Charles the Great, while
the uncritically destructive view of
Conringius and others who refer it
to Constantinus Africanus is inconsistent with the facts mentioned in
the text.

half of the twelfth century the School is described by CHAP. III. Ordericus Vitalis as 'existing from ancient times[1].' Its European celebrity dates at least from the middle of the eleventh century—about half a century before the teaching of Irnerius and the earliest dawn of the scholastic fame of Paris.

The early revival of Medical Science at Salerno is the Its origin. more remarkable inasmuch as (with this exception) South-ern Italy took hardly any part in the great intellectual movements of the Middle Age. Salerno was purely a Medical School; and in the other Faculties Southern Italy never possessed a University of more than the third rank. It is no doubt at first sight tempting to trace the medical knowledge and skill of Salerno to contact with the Saracens of Southern Italy or Sicily: but it appears to be well established by the researches of Henschel, Daremberg, and de Renzi, that no external cause can be assigned to the be-ginnings of the movement, any more than to the somewhat later revival of dialectical and literary culture north of the Alps, or to the revival of the Civil Law in the Lombard cities. The medical traditions of the old Roman world lingered on amidst the material civilisation of Magna Græcia, just as

---

[1] 'Physicæ quoque scientiam tam copiose habuit ut in urbe Psaler-nitana, ubi maximæ medicorum scolæ ab antiquo tempore habentur, neminem in medicinali arte, præter quamdam sapientem matronam, sibi parem inveniret.' *Hist. Eccles.* P. ii. l. iii., 11. (Migne, T. 188. c. 260). The statement relates to one Rodulfus Mala-Corona, *sub anno* 1059. In about 1173 Benjamin of Tudela, speaks of Salerno as 'the College of the Physicians of the Sons of Edom' (*Itinerary* trans. by Asher, 1840, T. I. p. 43, 'the principal university of Christendom,' but there is, I believe, nothing corresponding to 'principal' in the original). He speaks of there being 600 Jews in the place, but the above expression shows that the School was purely Christian. There is a panegyric upon this ' Fons physi-cæ, pugil eucrasiæ, cultrix medicinæ,' in the medical poem of the Paris phy-sician Ægidius Corboliensis, c. 1198, who evidently learned his medicine there. (Leyser, *Historia Poetarum et Poematum Medii Ævi*, Halæ Magdeb. 1721, p. 593 ; cf. pp. 538, 539.) Another allusion occurs in the *Archipoetae carmen de itinere Salernitano* (J. Grimm, *Gedichte des Mittel. auf König Fried. I.*, ap. Klein, *Schriften*, T. III. Berlin, 1866, p. 68) :
' Laudibus eternum nullum negat esse Salernum,
Illuc pro morbis totus circumfluit orbis,
Nec debet sperni, fateor, doctrina Salerni.'

the traditions of legal culture lingered in the freer and more political atmosphere of Northern Italy.   The theory which attributes the rise of the School of Salerno to the introduction of Arabic writings by Constantinus Africanus, towards the end of the eleventh century, is a legend of the same order as the legend (to which we shall have to return hereafter) about the discovery of the Roman Law at the capture of Amalfi, and is as completely inconsistent with facts and dates as the theory which assumes the Northern Renaissance of the eleventh century to begin with the introduction of Arabic translations of Aristotle.   Hippocrates, Galen and the other Greek physicians had been translated into Latin as early as the sixth century [1] : and, though these early traditions are said to have disappeared, the Græco-Latin medical tradition was no more extinguished by the ages of darkness which followed than Roman Law was extinguished in the North by the barbarian invasions.   We possess works of the medical writers of Salerno from the early part of the eleventh century.   The most important of these early writers is Gariopontus, who wrote *circa* 1040.   Their writings exhibit not the slightest trace of Arabic influence. Their Medicine is Neo-latin, but the dominant influence is not that of Galen, but the equally ancient though less enlightened system known as 'Methodism,' of which Cælius Aurelianus is the chief representative.   After the middle of the eleventh century, however, there are evidences of a more direct acquaintance with the writings of Hippocrates and Galen, and from this time the system known as Humorism becomes the established doctrine of the School.   It is from this period—the middle of the eleventh century, a generation at least before Constantinus, and a generation at least before the Renaissance of the Roman Law at Bologna—that we must date the first medical Renaissance.   The Græco-Roman medical classics may not have been entirely unknown to the earlier Salerno Doctors, any more than Justinian had been unknown in Northern Italy before Irnerius.   But it

---

[1] Cassiodorus, *De Instit. divin. litt.*, cap. xxxi. (Migne, T. 70. c 1146).

was at this period that they began to be studied energeti- Chap. III.
cally and scientifically, and their teaching to be applied
with greater fidelity than heretofore. The smouldering
sparks of scientific culture which had survived from the
old-world illumination, were fanned into a flame by the
first breath of that mysterious new spirit which at this time
began to move upon the face of European civilization.

How shall we explain the concentration of this revival of Survival of
Medical Science in the city of Salerno, or (if that be too Græco-
Latin
particular a question to be answered upon *a priori* or Medicine in
general grounds) why did it find its home in this part of Southern
Italy.
Italy? The main cause must perhaps be sought in Roman
times. It would seem that, after the full development of
the Schools, it was in Latin translations that the works of
Hippocrates were habitually studied in what was henceforth
styled the *Civitas Hippocratica*. But it cannot be doubted
that the revival of Medical Science in the eleventh century
was not unconnected with the survival[1] of the Greek language Survival of
in this part of Italy, and the presumption is strengthened by Greek
language.
the fact that the decline of the School after about the middle
of the thirteenth century kept pace with the decline of the
language. It should be remembered, moreover, that in
the tenth century the Counts of Salerno usually acknowledged the Eastern Emperors, and that this part of Italy
was in constant communication with Constantinople,
the head-quarters alike of Greek culture and of Greek
authority[2].

An incident in the life of the traveller Adelard of Bath Adelard of
confirms the view that the medical studies of the place were Bath at
Salerno.
at least in part promoted by their contact with the Greek
medical writers. Adelard in the course of his travels came
to Salerno, and afterwards describes himself as listening
(not, indeed, in Salerno, but in its immediate neighbourhood) to a 'Greek philosopher' discoursing upon 'Medicine and the nature of things.' Among the subjects of the

---

[1] I.e. from the time of the
Byzantine re-conquest under Justinian.

[2] Giesebrecht, *Gesch. d. Deutschen
Kaiserzeit*, Braunschweig, ed. 5,
1881, I. 374 *sq.*

Philosopher's enquiries was the cause of magnetic attraction, which Adelard is the first Western writer to mention[1].

Salerno a
health-
resort.

If we ask why it was at Salerno rather than elsewhere in Southern Italy that the medical revival centred, the answer may possibly be found in its renown as a health-resort, chiefly due to the mildness of the climate, but partly also perhaps to the mineral waters of the neighbourhood. As to the theory which connects the rise of the School with the Benedictine monastery of Monte Casino, it is sufficient to say that Salerno is eighty miles from Monte Casino, and that the theory has not a particle of historical foundation[2].

But whatever theory we adopt as to the origin of the Medical School, one thing is absolutely established by the researches which began with the discovery of a volume of Salerno *Codices* by Henschel at Breslau in 1837, and that is that the School was in its origin, and long continued to be, entirely independent of Oriental influences. No traces of such influences are to be found before the last quarter of the eleventh century, and then they are long confined almost entirely to the use of new Latin translations of Greek authors made through the Arabic. The study of Avicenna and the other independent Arabic writers hardly began before the middle of the thirteenth century[3]. It is, however,

[1] The following is from the unedited *de eodem et diverso*: 'Et ego . . . a Salerno veniens in Grecia maiore, quedam (*sic*) philosophum Grecum qui pre ceteris artem medicine naturasque rerum disserebat . . . causam scilicet querens qua vi et natura magnetes ad se ferrum trahat ejus que super hac re ceterisque similibus solutiones audita (*sic*).' Bibl. Nat. Cod. Lat. 2389, *ad fin.* (ap. Libri, *Hist. des Sciences Mathématiques en Italie*, Paris, 1838, II. p. 62). The book was written before 1116 A.D. (Jourdain, *Recherches sur des traduc. d'Aristote*, p. 258).

[2] If additional evidence is wanted, it may be worth pointing out that the poem in praise of Monte Casino, written by Alphanus, who became Abp. of Salerno in 1085, contains no hint of any such connection. The poem is published by Ozanam, *Doc. inédits pour l'hist. litt. de l'Italie*, p. 261. After all, Benedictine monks were not 'University Extension Lecturers.' De Renzi (I. p. 128) remarks that most of the writers who have derived the School of Salerno from Monte Casino did not know the distance of Monte Casino from Salerno: the former did not belong to the principality of Salerno but was under the jurisdiction of the Counts of Capua.

[3] In support of these conclusions, I may refer generally to the works of Daremberg and Renzi (*Coll. Saler.* esp. I. pp. 116-118), mentioned

the reintroduction to Western Europe of hitherto unknown Classical Greek Physicians that forms the chief
contribution of the Arabs to medical progress. In Medicine,
as in Philosophy and Mathematics, they are more important
as transmitters than as originators.

The first introduction of the Arabic influence at Salerno
is traditionally associated with the name of Constantinus
Africanus, one of those misty characters in the history of
medieval culture whom a reputation for profound knowledge
and Oriental travel has surrounded with a halo of half-
legendary romance. It is unnecessary to repeat the story [1]
of his wanderings in the East, his settlement at his native
Carthage, his enforced flight to Salerno, just before the
advent of the Norman Robert Guiscard, and his eventual
retirement from the world into the illustrious Benedictine
Abbey of Monte Casino, where, under the patronage of
the famous Abbot Desiderius, afterwards Pope Victor III,
he occupied himself for the remainder of his life in making
Latin translations or compilations from Arabic or Greek
medical writers. Whatever uncertainty may remain about
the details of his history, there is no doubt that Constantinus' translation from the Arabic of the Aphorisms of Hippocrates was produced at Monte Casino about the year 1080
A. D. [2], and that it long retained its place in the Medical
Schools. As with the early versions of Aristotle, the extreme badness of this translation is frequently commented
upon by the more discerning medieval writers ; but though
better ones appeared, they long failed to drive out Constan-

above, which are accepted by all the
historians of medicine whom I have
consulted. Against this consensus
of experts, the opinion of laymen like
Prof. Laurie and Mr. Mullinger, who
do not profess to have studied the
Salerno physicians, cannot have much
weight when they allege no definite
historical facts in support of their
contentions. See correspondence in
The Academy, Nos. 764, 765-769,
in which the view which I then took

was supported by the high authority
of Dr. J. F. Payne.

[1] The half-legendary story of Con-
stantinus is told by Petrus Diaconus,
Chron. Casin. III. 35, ap. Pertz, SS.
VII. p. 728.

[2] Jourdain, however, seems to
place his work somewhat earlier in
the century. *Recherches*, p. 96. Constantinus also translated other works
of Hippocrates and the Commentaries of Galen.

CHAP. III. tinus [1]. The zenith of the medical reputation of Salerno is marked by the visit of Robert Duke of Normandy, who came to the place to be cured of his wound after the Crusade of 1099, and there received the news of the death of his brother, William II of England. The celebrated metrical treatise on Medicine or Hygienics, styled *Flos Medicinæ Scholæ Salernitanæ*, or *Regimen Sanitatis Salerni* [2], was dedicated to him as ' King of the English ' on this occasion.

The Regimen Sanitatis Salerni, 1100.

Organization.

The opening of this work [3] makes it plain that something like an organized School or College of Doctors at this time existed at Salerno. Beyond that, we can really say next to nothing as to the government or institutions of the School. Somewhat later it had a *Præpositus* at its head, afterwards called a *Prior* [4]. Nothing approaching a regular University ever existed there. Certainly there was no University of students: while a mere College of Doctors in one Faculty could present but a distant resemblance to the magisterial or Parisian type of University organization. Salerno in fact remains a completely isolated factor in the

---

[1] Tiraboschi, III. p. 581.

[2] Of this curious production there had been (up to 1852) thirty-three translations (or new editions of translations) into German, fourteen into French, nine into English, nine into Italian, one into Czech, one into Polish, and one into Dutch. (De Renzi, *Coll. Salernitana*, I. p. 431.) Most of these belong to the sixteenth and seventeenth centuries, when the work was evidently still regarded in a serious light, but it seems to be still popular in some quarters. A new English translation appeared at Philadelphia in 1870, a translation into Italian verse at Pavia in 1835, and the French translation of M. Daremberg as recently as 1880. Many still current pieces of proverbial medicine may be traced to this source (sometimes slightly altered) : e.g.

' Sex horis dormire sat est juvenique senique

Septem vix pigro, nulli concedimus octo ': and

' Post cœnam stabis aut passus mille meabis.'

It is printed in de Renzi's *Coll. Salernitana*, I. p. 445; and there is an important edition by Sir Alexander Croke (Oxford, 1830).

[3] ' Anglorum Regi scribit Schola tota Salerni.' It is attributed to a John of Milan. An earlier Medical treatise of Gariopontus bears the title *Gariopontus Salernitanus ejusque Socii*, which shows at least a habit of co-operation among the Salernese Physicians though not necessarily a regular College (de Renzi, *l. c.* I. p. 115). It should be observed that the *Scola Salernitana* continued to receive additions down to the time of Arnauld de Villeneuve who played the part of Pisistratus to this Medical Homer.

[4] De Renzi, *l. c.* I. pp. 226, 269, 274.

academic polity of the Middle Ages. While its position
as a School of Medicine was, for two centuries at least, as
unique as that of Paris in Theology and that of Bologna in
Law, while throughout the Middle Ages no School of Medicine except Montpellier rivalled its fame, it remained without influence in the development of academic institutions :
the constitution and organization even of the Medical
Faculties in other Universities appear to have been quite
uninfluenced by the traditions of this earliest home of
medieval Medicine.

It was not (so far as appears) till 1231 that Salerno obtained any official recognition, whether from Church or
State. In that year Frederick II, as King of Sicily, forbade
either the practice or teaching of Medicine within his dominions without the Royal License, which was to be given
after examination in the King's Court by the Masters of
Salerno and certain other Royal officers[1]. These provisions show how far the Faculty of Medicine at Salerno
was from enjoying the position and privileges of the
Medical Faculties elsewhere. In pursuance of the same
paternal system the Emperor proceeded to issue an ordinance enforcing a period of medical study as well as a preliminary course of Arts, and regulating a number of matters
relating to the study and practice of Medicine, elsewhere
left to the free disposition of the Faculties or the Univer-

---

[1] 'Nisi Salerni primitus in conventu publico magistrorum judicio
comprobatus, cum testimonialibus
literis de fide et sufficienti scientia
tam magistrorum *quam ordinatorum
nostrorum, ad presentiam nostram*
vel, nobis a regno absentibus, ad
illius presentiam qui vice nostra in
regno remanserit, [ordinatus accedat]
et *a nobis vel ab eo* medendi licentiam
consequatur.' — Huillard - Bréholles,
Hist. Diplomatica Fred. II. T. IV.
Parisiis, 1855, p. 150. The examination of those who wanted to
teach was also to be conducted ' in
presentia nostrorum officialium et
magistrorum artis ejusdem' (*ib.* p.
151). The provisions and the form
of the *licentia medendi* given by
Huillard-Bréholles (which does not
even mention the Masters of Salerno)
show that these licenses have nothing in common with the licenses
granted by the Universities themselves. Characteristically medieval
is the provision that druggists should
be sworn to make their medicines
'juxta artes et hominum qualitates '
(*l. c.*). By an earlier Ordinance the
intending physician had merely to
present himself 'officialibus nostris et
judicibus.' (*ib.* p. 149.)

sities[1].   Among the most astounding of these provisions is one requiring druggists (*confectionarii*) to sell their drugs at so much the ounce without reference to the nature and composition of the preparation, except in the case of those which required long keeping.

Mode of graduation.   As to the methods of graduation in use at Salerno in the earliest period we have no evidence, though we may presume that the College of Doctors conducted both the License and Inception of candidates for the Mastership according to the system practised in the earliest days of Bologna.   After the above-mentioned edict of Frederick II in 1231, the candidate for a degree appeared in the Royal Court, produced letters testimonial from some of the Doctors under whom he had studied, and was then examined in the presence of the Court, which, in the event of his success, drew up a *License* or warrant to his own Doctor to conduct his *Conventio* or Inception by tradition of the book in the presence of his colleagues[2], as in other Universities.   Further explanation of this custom will be found in the chapters on Paris and Bologna[3].

Rival University of Naples, 1224.   In the year 1224 the Emperor Frederick II opened a University at Naples[4], and endeavoured to force all his subjects to study therein[5].   A Faculty of Medicine was at first included in the new University, but in 1231 this was

---

[1] The student was required to study three years 'in scientia logicali' (since 'nunquam sciri potest scientia medicine nisi de logica aliquid presciatur'), and five years in medicine, attending lectures on Hippocrates and Galen. He was also to practise for a year (like Bachelors in other Universities) 'cum consilio experti medici.' The physician was required to give advice *gratis* to the poor : to visit his patients '*ad minus* bis in die, et ad requisitionem infirmi semel in nocte.' He was not allowed to sell his own drugs ('nec ipse etiam habebit propriam stationem'). Huillard-Bréholles, T. IV. pp. 235–6.

[2] See the diplomas in de Renzi, *Storia Doc.*, p. xcviii *sq.*

[3] See below, pp. 286 *sq.*, 223 *sq.*, 452 *sq.*

[4] See below, vol. II. chap. vi. § 6.

[5] If the Charter of Frederick II (Huillard-Bréholles, T. II. 450) be literally interpreted, even Salerno would have been included in the prohibition to study or teach anywhere else : but the Professors mentioned in the Charter are Professors of Civil Law only, and it seems improbable that Salerno was really affected. Ackermann (*Institutiones*, p. 349) says, 'ita tamen, ut Salerno medicinæ docendæ facultas maneret.'

implicitly suppressed (if it ever obtained a substantial ex- Chap. III.
istence) by the already-quoted decree which confined the
right of examining in Medicine to the Salerno Doctors [1].
In spite of the monopoly which it enjoyed, the University
of Naples [2] never was a success : and in 1253 the attempt
to galvanize it into life was abandoned and an effort made
to transfer all its Faculties from Naples to Salerno, and to
unite them with the old School of Medicine in that place [3].
By 1258 this experiment also had failed, and the *status quo*
was re-established. The other Faculties moved back to
Naples, and Salerno remained a School of Medicine only.
By this time, however, the European importance of the
School of Salerno was passing away. So far from the rise
of the fame of Salerno having been due to Oriental influences, it was these influences which brought about its
fall. It was the increasing popularity of the Arabic Medicine in the thirteenth century, combined with the growth of
Medical Faculties elsewhere—especially of the Medical
Schools at Montpellier and Bologna—which destroyed the
popularity of the more conservative *Civitas Hippocratica* [4].

By the beginning of the fourteenth century the decline of The
Salerno was complete, and the Arabic Medicine everywhere in Arabic
Medicine.
full possession of the Medical Faculties. It is, however, quite
a mistake to assume (as is very frequently done) that this
new influence indicates a great advance. The Medicine of
medieval Islam was based upon that of the Greek physicians
as much as that of medieval Christendom : and what was
added to this traditional system by the Arabs themselves or
the Physicians who practised in Arabic countries—for Arabic
Medicine was largely in the hands of Jews—was by no
means equal in importance to what they had received from
the Greeks. The most valuable Arabic contributions to
Medicine were chiefly in the region of Medical Botany.

[1] It should be noticed, however, that there is no mention of Salerno in the Greek version.

[2] See below, vol. II. chap. vi. § 6.

[3] Huillard-Bréholles, T. II. p. 447–453 : Denifle, I. 236–7.

[4] De Renzi, I. 280 : Haeser, *Lehrbuch*, I. p. 651. Leclerc speaks of the Arabs (always transmitters rather than originators) as intro-ducing Indian Medicine into the West.

CHAP. III. The Arabs added some new remedies to the medieval Pharmacopeia, but against their services in this respect must be set their extensive introduction of Astrological and Alchemistic fancies into the theory and practice of Medicine. On the whole, the thirteenth century represents a retrogression in medical theory, though an advance in the region of Surgery and Anatomy. But of this advance Salerno was not the centre.

Women Doctors.

Before taking leave of the School of Salerno, there is one curious fact connected with its history which possesses a peculiar interest for the nineteenth century reader. Among the medical practitioners, teachers, and writers of its palmiest days were several women [1]. Haeser relies upon this circumstance as proof positive of the peculiar lay character of the School : but Denifle rejoins by capping Haeser's argument with an account of one Mangold, a married theological Professor of Paris in the second half of the eleventh century, whose daughters taught Theology [2]. The question of the clerical or lay origin of the School is left by Denifle in suspense : but the theory of a 'clerical' School at Salerno is really part and parcel of the theory that the School owes its existence in some mysterious way to the distant Benedictine Monastery of Monte Casino ; and this theory again is a survival from the traditional error which ascribes its origin to Constantinus Africanus [3].

---

[1] Daremberg, *L'École de Sal.* p. 18 sq. Of these the most eminent was Trotula (fl. *circa* 1059), who wrote especially but not exclusively upon the diseases of women.

[2] Denifle, I. 233—*Hist. Lit.* IX. 281. It is probable, however, that this was a mere eccentricity : there is no proof that the young ladies were recognised teachers. At Sa-

lerno lady Doctors were a recognised institution. It should be remembered that Mangold may have been and probably was a widower : and his connection with Paris is more than doubtful. As to marriage of Masters, see below, vol. II. chap. xiv.

[3] The University of Salerno was suppressed by a decree of Napoleon I in 1811, Haeser, l. c. p. 652.

CHAPTER IV.

BOLOGNA.

CHAPTER IV.

BOLOGNA.

§ 1. IRNERIUS AND THE CIVIL LAW REVIVAL.

The work of DIPLOVATACCIUS (fl. c. 1510), *De claris Jurisconsultis*, &c., has remained in MS., only extracts having been published by Sarti (see below) and others. He was followed by ALIDOSI, *Li Dottori Bolognesi di legge canon. e civile*, Bologna, 1620, and *Li dott. Bol. d. teol. filos. med. e d' arti liberali*, Bologna, 1623, and PANCIROLUS, *De Claris Legum Interpretibus*, Venetiis, 1627 (republished with Jo. Fichardus, *Vitæ Recentiorum Jurisconsultorum*, and Marcus Mantua, *Epitome Virorum illustrium qui vel docuerunt in scholis Juris prudentiam* &c., Lipsiæ, 1721), but both were superseded by the learned and critical work of SARTI (continued by FATTORINI), *De claris Archigymnasii Bononiensis Professoribus*, Bononiæ, T. I. P. i. 1769, P. ii. 1772. Of the new edition published at Bologna by Cæsar Albicinius Forloviensis there have appeared only T. I. P. i. in 1888, T. I. P. ii. in 1889. (T. I. P. i. and ii, correspond to T. I. P. i. of the original edition ; wherever I have cited T. I. P. ii. of that edition I have added the date 1772. All other references are to the new edition.) Sarti may occasionally be supplemented by OR-LANDI, *Notizie degli Scrittori Bolognesi*, Bologna, 1714, and FANTUZZI, *Notizie degli Scrittori Bolognesi*, Bologna, 1781. In spite of this wealth of Bolognese literary history, no systematic history of the University has appeared except the slight work of SCARABELLI, *Delle Constituzione Discipline e Riforme dell' antico Studio Bolognese*, Piacenza, 1876. An earlier but valueless work by FORMAGLIARI († 1769) remains in MS. at Bologna (Bibl. Mun. No. 5935), and other MS. collections are mentioned in FRATI's very careful bibliographical work, *Opera della Bibliografia Bolognese*, Bologna, 1888. The want of such a history is, however, nearly supplied by the notices and documents in Sarti, by the notices in TIRABOSCHI, *Storia della Letteratura Italiana*, Milano, 1822, T. III, IV, V, VI, and by the full treatment which the University receives in SAVIGNY, *Geschichte des röm. Rechts im Mittelalter*, cap. xxi, supplemented and corrected (as to the earliest period) by the researches of DENIFLE, *Die Entstehung der Universitäten des Mittelalters bis* 1400 (Berlin, 1885, p. 132).

The following books on the history of the City contain frequent notices of the University—SIGONIUS, *Historia de rebus Bononiensibus.* Francofurti, 1604: GHIRARDACCI, *Della historia di Bologna.* Bologna, pt. i. 1596; pt. ii. 1669: SAVIOLI, *Annali Bolognesi.* Bassano, 1784-1795. The Statutes of the City have been edited by FRATI, ap. *Monumenti istorici pertinenti alle provincie della Romagna.* Ser. I. *Statuti,* Vol. I–III, Bologna, 1869-80. The little tract of GAGGI, *Collegii Bononiensis Doctorum Origo et dotes* (Bononiæ, 1710; unpaged) is chiefly valuable for its information as to the customs of the author's own time.

The Jurist Statutes of 1432 were printed in 1561 (*Statuta et privilegia almæ universitatis Juristarum Gymnasii Bononiensis,* Bononiæ); those of the Artists (*Philosophiæ ac medicinæ scholarium Bononiensis gymnasii statuta,* Bononiæ) in 1609. The Statutes of 1432 were the earliest then known to exist; but in 1887 DENIFLE published in the *Archiv für Literatur- und Kirchengeschichte* III. p. 195 *sq.* a large portion of the Statutes of 1317, with additions up to 1347, from a MS. discovered by him in the Chapter Library of Pressburg in Hungary. These, together with the earliest extant Statutes of the other Universities and of the Doctoral Colleges (hitherto unpublished), are printed in the magnificent volume edited by MALAGOLA, *Statuti delle università e dei collegi dello studio bolognese* (Bologna, 1888). The Statutes and Registers of the German Nation are published in *Acta Nationis Germanicæ Univ. Bonon.* Berolini, 1887; other documents in DALLARI, *I rotuli dei Lettori Legisti e Artisti dello Studio bolognese dal* 1384 *al* 1799, Bologna, 1888-91.

A number of monographs were published in connection with the Octo-centenary of 1888. Of these, FORNASINI, *Lo Studio Bolognese* (Firenze, 1887), is little better than a guide-book, and LEONHARD, *Die Universität Bologna im Mittelalter* (Leipzig, 1888), only professes to be a magazine article : CASSANI, *Dell' Antico Studio di Bologna e sua origine* (Bologna, 1888) is especially valuable in relation to the early history of Canon Law studies at Bologna : CHIAPELLI, *Lo Studio Bolognese* (Pistoia, 1888), contains some original and valuable researches as to the Pre-Irnerian Jurisprudence : but the work to which I am most indebted is FITTING, *Die Anfänge der Rechtsschule zu Bologna,* Berlin u. Leipzig, 1888 : RICCI, *I primordi dello Studio di Bologna* (2ª Ed. Bologna, 1888), prints the documents relating to Irnerius with some useful researches as to the origines of Bologna and Ravenna : MALAGOLA, *Monografie Storiche sullo Studio Bolognese* (Bologna, 1888), contains interesting essays on detached points.

The study of the Italian Universities in general was begun by MURATORI, *Antiquitates Italicæ medii ævi* T. III. (Milano, 1740), Diss. xliv, and carried on by Tiraboschi and Savigny in the works already named. Since then no work specially devoted to this subject has appeared which calls for notice except COPPI, *Le Università Italiane nel Medio Evo* (Ed. 3, Firenze, 1886), which is, however, an unsatisfactory piece of work.

For the history of the Roman Law in the Middle Ages SAVIGNY (*op. cit.*) is the primary authority. Among his predecessors, I may mention Arthur DUCK, *De Usu et Authoritate Juris Civilis Romanorum,* Londini, 1653, and BERRIAT-SAINT-PRIX, *Histoire du Droit Romain,* Paris, 1821, and among his

successors FICKER, *Forschungen zur Reichs- und Rechtsgeschichte Italiens,* CHAP. IV,
1868–73; FITTING in *Zeitschrift der Savigny-Stiftung für Rechtsgeschichte,* § 1.
vol. VI. Röm. Abth. (1885), p. 94 *sq.,* and vol. VII. Röm. Abth., Heft 2. p. 1,
and *Juristische Schriften des früheren Mittelalters,* Halle, 1876; FLACH, *Études
critiques sur l'histoire du droit Romain au moyen âge,* Paris, 1890; MUTHER,
Zur Geschichte der Rechtswissenschaft und der Universitäten, Jena, 1876; CON-
RAT, *Die Quellen und Literatur des Römischen Rechts im früheren Mittelalter,*
Leipzig, 1889.

For the history of Literature and Culture in medieval Italy and Europe
generally (besides Tiraboschi and the works mentioned above, p. 25),
I am indebted to LIBRI, *Histoire des Sciences Mathématiques en Italie depuis la
Renaissance des lettres,* Paris, 1838–41 (ed. 2, 1865); GIESEBRECHT, *De litterarum studiis apud Italos,* Berolini, 1845; OZANAM, *Documents inédits pour
servir à l'histoire littéraire de l'Italie,* Paris, 1850; POUCHET, *Histoire des
Sciences Naturelles au Moyen Âge,* Paris, 1853; BALL (W. W. R.), *A short
account of the History of Mathematics,* London, 1888.

THE original impetus which imparted new life to the Contrast between the eleventh century was, in its essence, the same spiritual force which manifested itself North of the Alps in the teaching of Roscellinus and Abelard. But in Northern Italy that strange new birth of the world's energies took place under a totally different set of conditions and consequently gave rise to a movement in a totally different direction. In France the overthrow of Roman civilization by the barbarian conquest, followed by the ecclesiastical legislation of Charles the Great, had indissolubly associated Education with the Monasteries and the Cathedrals. In Italy Education was never as completely extinguished as had been the case in continental Europe North of the Alps. It was from the Italian Deacon Peter of Pisa that Charles himself took his first lessons; it was from Italy that he obtained the first teachers whom he imported into Gaul[1]. Some of these teachers were undoubtedly ecclesiastics; for it was the ecclesiastical Education of the North that Charles had especially set himself to reform. But it would appear that in Italy the educational tradi-

Contrast between the Trans- alpine and Cisalpine Renais- sance.

---

[1] Pertz, *Mon. Germ. Hist.* SS. II. p. 456; Tiraboschi, *Storia della Lett. Ital.* III. 228 *sq.* This author even suggests that Alcuin himself obtained his learning in Italy, but this is mere patriotism. In the Carolingian age Learning survived beyond the seas as well as beyond the Alps.

tions of the old Roman world were by no means entirely broken off. The Carolingian enactments respecting the Cathedral and monastic Schools no doubt extended to Italy; but here they seem to constitute no conspicuous landmark in the history of education[1]. Church Schools of course existed[2], and many of the famous Italian teachers of the dark ages were ecclesiastics. But here the Church Schools enjoyed no monopoly. In the cities of Northern Italy the race of lay teachers seems never to have quite died out: and it is certain that when the revival came, its most conspicuous effects were seen not in the Church Schools but in the Schools of independent lay Masters. In Italy we find no trace of the theory which looked upon Masters and scholars as *ipso facto* members of the ecclesiastical order, nor were they subject in any greater degree than other laymen to ecclesiastical supervision or jurisdiction. Many teachers might receive the tonsure to secure the valuable ecclesiastical immunities; but in the City-republics of North Italy there were ecclesiastical disabilities as well as ecclesiastical immunities; there were civil careers

Lay Education in Italy.

[1] Roger Bacon says as to his own time : 'Atque domini legum Bononiæ et per totam Italiam volunt vocari magistri vel clerici, nec coronam sicut clerici habent. Uxores ducunt,' &c.—*Opera Ined.* ed. Brewer, p. 419. 'Nolunt' should probably be read for 'volunt.'

[2] Indeed, the system of ecclesiastical education adopted by Charles the Great seems to have been borrowed from Italy (Giesebrecht, p. 9). Later, in 826, Eugenius II ordered 'in universis episcopiis subjectisque plebibus (i. e. the Archipresbyteral Churches) et aliis locis, in quibus necessitas occurrerit, omnis cura et diligentia adhibeatur ut magistri et doctores constituantur, qui studia literarum liberaliumque artium habentes, dogmata assidue doceantur' (Giesebrecht reads 'doceant'). Pertz, *Mon. Germ. Hist.* LL. II. add. p. 17.

Only a year before, schools—not apparently ecclesiastical — had been established in eight principal cities of Lombardy by Lothair, the smaller cities being each assigned to one of these centres. Pertz, LL. I. p. 249. Attempts were made to compel even the ordinary Parish Priests to establish schools in their parishes. Atto of Vercelli in the tenth century ordered that 'Presbyteri etiam per villas et vicos scholas habeant.' *Capitulare*, cap. 61 (Migne, T. 134. c. 40). Ratherius Bishop of Verona declares that he will not ordain any one who has not been educated 'aut in civitate nostra, aut in aliquo monasterio, vel apud quemlibet sapientem.' *Synodica*, 15 (Migne, T. 136. c. 564). The last clause indicates a freedom of private education hardly recognised in the North.

open to the ambitious citizen for which the ecclesiastical Chap. IV,
§ 1. status would have been a disqualification[1]. Corresponding to the difference in the status of the teacher, there was a difference no less marked in the class from which scholars were drawn. It was customary for the Lombard nobility to give their sons a literary education at a time when the Knights and Barons of France or Germany were inclined to look upon reading and writing as unmanly and almost degrading accomplishments fit only for Priests or Monks, and especially for Priests or Monks not too well-born.

Connected with the wider diffusion of education South *Its subject-* of the Alps was a certain difference in its subject- *matter.* matter. In Italy as in France or Britain all education was held to be comprised in the seven liberal Arts, and the ground covered by the seven liberal Arts was much the same in all parts of Europe. But the relative importance of the different elements in this apparently comprehensive though really very meagre programme varied widely in accordance with the different bent and genius of North and South[2]. North of the Alps it was upon Dialectic—and especially upon Dialectic in its metaphysical and theological applications—that attention was concentrated. The famous teachers of the North from Scotus to Abelard, though most of them no doubt taught the whole of the narrow Encyclopedia of their time, were known chiefly as dialecticians. And when the revival of intellectual activity came, it showed itself at once in a revival of dialectical activity, of speculation, of theological controversy. In

[1] Thus while few of the civilians were *clerici*, the humbler class of teachers often took the tonsure to escape taxation. A City Statute at Bologna (Frati, II. p. 102) directs the Podestà to enquire ' omnes et singulos magistros qui sunt de civitate vel comitatu bon. qui doceant pueros et omnes illos qui dicunt se clericos vel conversos esse . . . . et non habeant clericam (*sic*) vel tonsuram, et faciant extimare bona eorum.' The

same statutes exclude ' clerici ' from the office of Notary or ' Tabellio.' Ib. p. 190.

[2] It is an indication of this difference that Charles the Great ' in discenda *grammatica* Petrum Pisanum, diaconum, senem audivit, in *cæteris disciplinis* Albinum cognomento Alcoinum, item diaconem, de Britannia,' &c.—Einhardi *Vita Karoli M.* (Pertz, SS. II. p. 456).

Italy on the contrary Grammar and Rhetoric absorbed a large part of the attention almost monopolised in the North by Theology and Logic. Ozanam is right in declaring that people have exaggerated the abyss which separates the Middle Age and the Renaissance[1]. Throughout the Middle Ages the 'literary Paganism' which seems to cling to the very soil of Italy always kept alive in the scholar's breast an attachment to the myths and poetry of Antiquity, which occasionally assumed a character as really Anti-Christian as the Paganism of the fifteenth century and more avowedly so[2]. Moreover, in the Dark Ages Grammar and Rhetoric had a practical as well as a literary side. In Italy these Arts were studied as aids to the composition of legal documents, as a preparation for the work of the notary and the pleader, rather than as the indispensable preliminary to the study of Scripture and the Fathers. Even Logic was regarded rather as a sharpener of the wits and a discipline for the word-battles of the Law-court than as the key to the mysteries of Theology : while Rhetoric was considered to include not merely instruction in the Art of persuasion and of literary composition but at least a preliminary initiation into the Science of positive Law. The Scholastic Philosophy and Theology of the later Middle Ages were the natural fruits of the seed sown in Northern

---

[1] 'On a poussé trop loin le contraste, on a trop élargi l'abîme entre le moyen âge et la renaissance. Il ne fallait pas méconnaître ce qu'il y eut de paganisme littéraire dans ces temps où l'on attribue à la foi chrétienne l'empire absolu des esprits et des consciences.' *Doc. inédits*, p. 28.

[2] Rodulphus Glaber relates an outburst of heresy under the year 1000 at Ravenna which seems to have amounted to an actual recrudescence of Paganism, excited by one 'Vilgardus dictus, studio artis grammaticae magis assiduus quam frequens, *sicut italicis mos semper fuit* artes negli-gere ceteras, illam sectari.' Virgil, Horace and Juvenal, or demons in the form of these poets, appeared to him in dreams and promised him a share of their glory, in consequence of which he 'cepit multa turgide docere fidei sacre contraria, dictaque poetarum per omnia credenda esse asserebat' (ed. Prou. Paris, 1886, p. 50). The heresy was only suppressed by much burning. As to the prominence of Grammar in Italy, see Giesebrecht *passim* : the only point on which his admirable monograph seems to need correction is his assertion (p. 22) that the Italians neglected Rhetoric.

France, England, and Germany by the Dialecticians of the Dark Ages. The revival of legal Science which is associated with the name of Irnerius was the natural outcome of the educational traditions which the cities of North Italy had inherited from that old Roman world to which alike in spirit and in constitutional theory they had never wholly ceased to belong.

In truth, the differences between the two educational *The con-* systems, if such they can be called, are all explained by *trast ex-*
plained by the one great contrast which is presented by the social and *the social* political conditions of the two regions. In Northern *condition*
of France France [1] all intellectual life was confined to the cloister *and Italy* or to schools which were merely dependencies of the *respec-*
tively. cloister, because the governing class itself was composed of but two great orders—the military and the clerical—in the latter of which alone was there any demand for learning. In Italy, in place of a régime of pure feudalism tempered only by ecclesiastical influence, there had survived all through the darkest ages [2] at least the memory of the old Roman municipal system, and with it at least the germ and the possibility of a free and vigorous municipal life. Hence, in Italy it was in the political sphere that the new eleventh-century activity first manifested itself; while the consequent or concomitant revival of culture took a correspondingly secular turn.

If the continued existence of the Roman Empire is the *Continuity* key to the history of medieval Europe at large, the con- *of Muni-*
cipal Life tinued existence (amid all social and political changes) of the *in N. Italy* Roman Law is the key to the history of the Lombard Cities and the Lombard Schools. Beneath all changes of external government, the continuity of city life was never quite destroyed. Successive waves of conquest—Roman, West-

---

[1] M. Thurot (*L'Organisation de l'Enseignement dans l'Un. de Paris*, p. 3) remarks that the contrast ought strictly to be drawn between the countries North of the Loire on the one hand and Southern France and Italy on the other. This is to a great extent true, though, as we shall see, the educational system of Southern France stands in some respects midway between the Italian and the Northern system.

[2] For authorities to supplement and correct Savigny, see App. v.

Gothic, East-Gothic, Lombard, Frank—had swept over
them without destroying their limited Autonomy. The
Goths had appropriated a share of the land, the Lombards
a share of the produce: the castles of the invading hordes
spread over the country. But within the walls of the towns
at least the forms and the names of the Roman legal
system maintained an unbroken continuity. It is true
that Savigny exaggerated the extent of this continuity,
and underestimated the transformation which the whole
political and judicial system underwent at the hands first
of the Lombard, then of the Frankish, invaders. But it is
probable that the details of internal administration, and
certain that the private relations of the native citizens,
continued to be regulated by Roman law or Roman tradition. Whatever changes were made in the Magistracies,
the Roman was still supposed to be judged according to
Roman Law, the Lombard according to Lombard Law. In
the period immediately after the barbarian invasions this
state of things was more or less common to all parts of
the Roman world. Eventually, however, the two races
were everywhere fused. Where the barbarians formed a
majority of the population, where the oppression and
dispossession of the old inhabitants had been carried
furthest, the Law of the invaders prevailed, or rather the
place of Roman and national Law alike was taken by a
multitude of varying local customs which had absorbed
varying proportions of both the conflicting systems. Where
the Roman element predominated, where the barbarian
yoke was lighter and the Roman civilization more firmly
established, there Roman Law sooner or later asserted itself[1].
To a certain extent this was the case in Southern Europe
generally : the conditions of Burgundy and of the so-called
pays de droit écrit partly resembled those of Northern Italy.
But in some respects the position of the Lombard towns
was peculiar to themselves. In the first place the cities
were here more numerous, more populous and prosperous as

---

[1] Savigny, cap. ii. and iii. §§ 49, 50.

well as more independent than in any other part of Europe [1]; CHAP. IV, the Lombard invasion was a conquest rather than an immi- § 1. gration. Here the old municipal life died only to rise again with renewed vitality: the Romanised City-communities proved strong enough gradually to absorb a large part of the Germanic population, which passed into the position of a civic, instead of a feudal, Aristocracy. And here eventually the towns were able with more or less of Imperial assistance to throw off the yoke of the Lombard Counts, except where the milder rule of their own elective Bishops formed the stepping-stone to entire independence.

Several distinct chains of external circumstances com- Causes bined with the social condition of the cities and the in- which herent vitality of their civic life to facilitate the develop- fostered ment of the Lombard towns from mere municipalities autonomy. into practically independent Republics. The first of these was the absorption of the Lombardic kingship into the Holy Roman Empire, and the gradual transformation of that Empire into a Germanic Monarchy whose possessors —except during an actual occupation of Italy by armed hosts—were without the power of permanently enforcing their high-sounding prerogatives. Thus when the cities were once emancipated from the rule of their Counts, they found themselves practically without a political superior. The attempt of the Hohenstaufen to convert their nominal Italian monarchy into a real one was finally frustrated by

---

[1] To account for their position we must go back to the early distinction between Italy and the Provinces. The Italians were the *socii* of Rome: their *Municipia* retained their autonomy and continued to elect their own magistrates. The provinces were conquered dependencies. Autonomy was at first granted to a few provincial cities as a rare and exceptional privilege: though eventually such privileges were widely extended in Southern France and Spain—the countries whose civic life (and consequently whose uni-

versities) approximated most closely to those of North Italy. Gallia Cisalpina ceased to be a *provincia* after B.C. 43. Some limitations were, indeed, placed upon the autonomy of the cities, but these were afterwards extended to other Italian cities. As to Southern Italy, the absence of political life in the few large cities, the use of the Greek language, and above all the Norman and Saracen invasions, are the chief causes which explain its slight participation in the Revival of Roman Law.

the victory of the Lombard League at Legnano in 1176 : the Treaty of Constance in 1183 secured the practical freedom of the cities. Another favourable circumstance was the long contest between the Emperors and the Popes. The co-operation of the Italian cities was of vast importance to both the contending parties, each of which was able to give some kind of constitutional sanction to any usurpation on the part of its allies which it might find it expedient to tolerate. By engaging on one side or other of this great struggle the cities succeeded on the whole in maintaining an Autonomy which often amounted to practical Sovereignty.

Political character of the intellectual Revival.

The intellectual Renaissance of the twelfth century found the Italian cities just entering upon this struggle for independence : the intellectual Renaissance was indeed only another side of a political Renaissance. As the Lombard cities awoke to a consciousness of their recovered liberty, their energies were absorbed by a political life as engrossing, as interesting and dignified, as it had been in the cities of ancient Hellas. And thus a career was opening itself to men who were neither Churchmen nor soldiers. In such communities it cannot be a matter of surprise that the revival of intellectual activity took a political, or at least a civil, direction. Just as the demand of the cloisters North of the Alps for speculative knowledge—for knowledge for its own sake, knowledge apart from all relation to social life, manifested itself in a revival of metaphysical and theological speculation and was ultimately met by the rediscovery of the forgotten Aristotle ; so in the commercial and political society of the Italian cities there arose a demand for fruitful knowledge, for Science applied to the regulation of social life—for *civilization* in the strictest sense of the word. And this demand was met by a revived study of the long-neglected, but never wholly forgotten, monuments of Roman Jurisprudence. It is only in such communities that in the heart of the Middle Ages the purely mundane Science of Law could have awakened the enthusiasm—the genuine intellectual enthusiasm—which attended its study in the early days of the School of

Bologna: it is only in such communities that so democratic, so unhierarchical an institution as an autonomous
University of Students could have sprung into existence.

It must not be supposed, indeed, that the intellectual
movement in Northern Italy had no spiritual side, or that
because men's minds were here little absorbed with metaphysical problems, their interests were purely material and
utilitarian. On the contrary the struggle between the
Empire and the Papacy was essentially a battle of ideas.
But the questions at issue assumed the form of constitutional questions. Both sides appealed in support of their
claims to antiquity and to authority rather than to abstract
Reason; both sides derived large elements in their respective ideals as well as the weapons with which they
fought for them in the legal literature of ancient Rome.

The old account of the revival of the Roman Law represents that the Pisans, upon the capture of Amalfi in 1135,
discovered a MS. of the Digest or Pandects of Justinian,
whereupon the Emperor Lothair II, with an intuitive recognition of the value of the 'find,' forthwith directed its
contents to be taught in the schools and enforced in the
tribunals. Since the time of Savigny at least[1] the baselessness of this story has been generally recognised. It
is nearly certain that the celebrated MS. in connexion
with which it is told, and which was removed to Florence
after the capture of Pisa, had been in that city long
before this event—according to the thirteenth-century
jurist Odofredus, since the time of Justinian, when it
was brought there from Constantinople[2]. The story, as

[1] The fact was known to scholars long before. See e. g. Sarti, I. P. i. p. 3. The story finds a place in Gibbon's narrative (*Decline and Fall of the Rom. Emp.* chap. xliv), though he recognised that it was 'unknown to the twelfth century, embellished by ignorant ages, and suspected by rigid criticism.'

[2] The story of course breaks down with the explosion of the theory that the Pandects were unknown in North Italy till the twelfth century. Moreover, it is inconsistent with the probable date of Irnerius' teaching. Nor is there any evidence whatever of the existence of the law of Lothair II enforcing the use of the Roman Law: the Bologna text of the Pandects shows the influence of other sources than the Pisan MS.; finally, the story about the seizure

commonly told, is one of those which are not merely not
literally true, but which possess what may be called
the higher kind of historical falsity. It misrepresents
the whole nature of the revival which we are studying,
assuming as it does that the Roman Law, or at least the
Pandects, had been hitherto as unknown in medieval
Europe as the Laws of Manu. As a matter of fact, it may
be broadly asserted that the Roman Law never ceased
through what are called the Dark Ages of European
History to be (subject of course to changes incident to the
altered political status of the Roman citizens) the law of the
conquered races ; while it powerfully affected and entered
into the composition of the laws of the conquering tribes.

Continuous
use of
Roman
Law in
Italy.
Most conspicuously, as might be expected from the
political and social conditions, did the Roman Law maintain its authority in the Lombard towns of Northern
Italy. Elsewhere later compilations (of which the most
important was the *Breviarium*) were more frequently
appealed to than the compilations of Justinian : in Italy
the *Breviarium* was not introduced till Carolingian times,
and even then it by no means superseded either the use
or the authority of the Institutes and the Code[1]. There
is abundant proof that these works were never entirely
unknown from the fall of the Western Empire to the
day of the alleged 'discovery[2].' They were known of
course only in the sense in which books are known in an
illiterate age ; that is to say, there were learned men here
and there whose writings exhibit an acquaintance with
them. It does not of course follow that the whole of the
learned class or the whole of the lawyer-class were familiar
with the original sources, or that every Lombard town

at Amalfi rests on the statement of
two chroniclers of the fourteenth
century. Savigny, cap. xviii. §
35 *sq.* The Pisa MS. is now in the
Laurentian Library at Florence. It
forms the basis of the text of the
Pandects.

[1] The *Breviarium* has been pub-

lished by Hänel under the title of
Lex Romana Visigothorum (Lipsiæ,
1848). The Theodosian Code was
also largely used.

[2] Savigny, cap. xiv. I have
thought it unnecessary to reproduce
the evidence for facts which are
hardly disputed.

possessed a complete library of texts. The Pandects were, indeed, unknown or unstudied during the greater part of this period, but their recovery dates from at least half a century before the capture of Amalfi. Still, the Roman Law was in all the Lombard towns at least in part the recognised Law of the Tribunals : and some knowledge of it was required for the exercise of public functions. This knowledge was obtained in two ways. To a large extent no doubt the Lawyer-class — the *Judices*, the *Advocati*, and the *Notarii*—acquired their knowledge of Law, not by attendance at Professorial lectures but (like our English lawyers) by tradition and practice [1]. But Law was also taught in the Schools. When we remember the enormous proportion of the intellectual energy of Europe which had been concentrated on the study of Law during the latter days of the Roman Empire, it would have been antecedently probable that, wherever any education at all survived, some elementary instruction in Law would have formed part of that education. And as a matter of fact there are many distinct traces of the continuance of legal instruction in the Schools of the Dark Ages throughout Europe. In spite of the rigid attachment of the English to their ancestral customs, Roman Law (no doubt in some extremely rudimentary form) is said to have formed part of the curriculum of the School of York in the days of Alcuin [2]. Even in the cloisters of saintly Bec it seems probable that Law was among the subjects taught by Lanfranc, who afterwards

---

[1] Savigny (cap. ix. § 42), though aware that Roman Law was taught in the Schools, laid most stress on the traditional mode of transmission : Fitting, while rightly emphasizing the extent and importance of the School teaching, declares (*Die Rechtsschule zu Bol.* p. 33) that Savigny's statement that Law was learned by practice, would be no more true of the early medieval period than of our own. The evidence hardly warrants the assertion that the Italian lawyer of the tenth or eleventh century learned his law in the Schools to the same extent as the German lawyer of the present day. Indeed, Fitting himself insists much on the literary and introductory character of the School Law-teaching.

[2] For the rather slight evidence, see Savigny, cap. vi. § 135.

CHAP. IV,
§ 1.

played so important a part in Romanising the Law of the English Church[1]; and it may have been at Bec that the Abbot Theobald acquired that enthusiasm for the Roman Law which led him as Archbishop of Canterbury to promote the study of the Roman Law-texts, hitherto comparatively little known in England, among the clerks of his own household. But all that has been said as to the political and social condition of Italy would prepare us to find that it was especially here that Law held its ground in the Schools. That Irnerius was not in any sense whatever the first teacher of Law in the medieval Schools of Italy was strongly insisted upon by Savigny: he quotes for instance the statement of Lanfranc's biographer that the future Archbishop studied at Pavia 'in the Schools of the Liberal Arts and of the secular laws according to the custom of his country[2].' Our conception of the extent and importance of this pre-Irnerian Law-teaching as also of the pre-Irnerian Law-literature has been considerably widened by later researches. The universality of this practice of learning Law at School can be adequately

Law a part of Rhetoric.

---

[1] This is an inference from Lanfranc's fame as a lawyer and the fact that the celebrated Canonist Ivo of Chartres was his pupil. Robertus de Monte (Pertz, SS. VI. p. 485) merely says that Ivo heard him 'de secularibus et divinis literis tractantem,' and associates Lanfranc and Irnerius as joint discoverers of the Roman Law-books : ' Lanfrancus Papiensis et Garnerius socius eius, repertis apud Bononiam legibus Romanis, quas Justinianus imperator Romanorum anno ab incarnatione Domini 530 abbreviatas emendaverat, his inquam repertis operam dederunt eas legere et aliis exponere; sed Garnerius in hoc perseveravit, Lanfrancus vero disciplinas liberales et litteras divinas in Galliis multos edocens tandem Beccum venit et ibi monachus factus

est.' Ib. p. 478 (an. 1032). The passage, in spite of the confusion of dates, is valuable as testifying to Lanfranc's high legal reputation. The opinions of Lanfranc are often cited by the Commentators of the *Papiensis* (Pertz, LL. iv. pp. xcv, xcvi).

[2] ' Nobilis ortus parentela, ab annis puerilibus eruditus est in scholis liberalium artium et legum sæcularium ad suæ morem patriæ. Adolescens orator veteranos adversantes in actionibus causarum frequenter revicit torrente facundiæ accurate dicendo. In ipsa ætate sententias depromere sapuit, quas gratanter iuris periti aut iudices vel prætores civitatis acceptabant. Meminit horum Papia.' Milonis Crispini *Vita Lanfranci,* cap. v. (Migne, T. 150, c. 39).

illustrated only by the accumulation of passages, quoted by Savigny, Giesebrecht, Ozanam, Fitting, and others[1]. If the evidence is not more abundant than it is, it is on account of the complete amalgamation of Law-studies with the ordinary educational curriculum. At least some rudiments of Law were everywhere taught in the 'Schools of the Liberal Arts' and by the Masters of these Arts. The old division of Rhetoric into the three branches, 'demonstrative,' 'deliberative,' and 'judicial' allowed the introduction of Law-studies under the last-mentioned category without requiring the addition of a new Art to the sacred Seven[2]. The characteristics of this scholastic Law-teaching may be inferred from its position as an element in the ordinary literary education. It must be remembered that the Law-texts were written in what was becoming more and more a dead language even to Italians. Hence the close association of this Law-instruction with Grammar[3] as well as with Rhetoric. Some linguistic culture was required to enable a Lombard youth to read the text of the Institutes, and more to enable him to draw a Latin deed; and if to the reading and writing of Law Latin we add the explanation of the technical terms arising in the text-books, some rhetorical rules of pleading, and practice in their appli-

---

[1] Some of these are given in Appendix iii.

[2] 'Tria sunt genera causarum, quæ recipere debet orator: demonstrativum, deliberativum, iudiciale.' *Auctor ad Herennium*, II. i. The metrical biographer of Adelbert VI, Archbishop of Mainz (1137–1141), adopts this distinction in speaking of his hero's studies at Paris including Rhetoric:—

'iudiciale genus causæ, quod abhorret egenus,
quod tunc tractatur, cum iudex ius meditatur.'

Bibl. Rer. Germ. ed. Jaffé, vol. III. p. 590.

[3] Thus the *Vocabulista* (*circa* 1060

A.D.) of Papias (Venet. 1496, fol.) explains a large number of technical terms both legal and logical. Cf. the lines of Theodulf, Bishop of Orleans (circa 798–821):—

' Rhetorica atque foro dextram protensa sedebat,
Turritæ atque urbis fabrica stabat ei,
Jura quod eloquio peragit civilia magno
Litibus et populi dedere frena solet.'

Dümmler, *Mon. Germ. Poet. Lat. æv. Carolini* I. (Berolini, 1881), p. 545. Cf. Alcuin, *Dial. de arte rhetorica* (Halm, *Rhetores lat. minores*, p. 525 *sq.*).

cation by means of imaginary cases, we shall perhaps
obtain a fair idea of what was involved in the ordinary gram-
matico-legal education of the Schools before the time of
Irnerius.

Legal
literature
before
Irnerius.

When we turn from the Schools to the literary remains
of this period, we enter upon a more debatable region.
By making the most of such scanty abridgements or
epitomes as have come down to us and by assigning early
dates in doubtful cases, Fitting and others have attempted
to demonstrate the existence of a considerable Jurisprudence [1], not only in the age immediately preceding Irnerius
but throughout the Dark Ages [2]. Most minds unbiassed by
enthusiasm for an *a priori* ' law of continuity ' will probably
be disposed to acquiesce in the conclusion of Flach, viz.
that the earlier treatises and glosses [3] brought in evidence

---

[1] Fitting, *d. Rechtssch. zu Bol.* p.
51, &c.; Chiapelli, *Lo Studio Bol.* p.
45 *sq.*, 98 *sq.*, 125, and his edition of
the celebrated Pistoian gloss (*La
Glossa pistoiese al Codice Giustinianeo*,
Torino, 1885 (*Mem. della R. Acad.
di Scienze di Torino*, Ser. ii. T. 37 :
Conrat, *Epitome exactis regibus*
(Berlin, 1884). The last writer,
however, unlike Fitting, contends
for a revolution in legal Science
at the beginning of the eleventh
century.

[2] In the Irnerian glosses we find
such expressions as ' quidam dicunt,'
' solutio antiqua,' ' veteres præcep-
tores dicebant,' ' secundum quosdam.'
See the passages in Chiapelli, pp.
45, 46, 55. There occur also allusions to an ' antiqua littera ' which
seem to point to a current text
earlier than that bequeathed to the
School of Bologna by Irnerius and
his immediate successors (*ib.* p. 47).
Chiapelli also collects initials or
abbreviations appended to glosses
which cannot be identified with
any known Jurist, and which may
therefore with some probability be

ascribed to unknown predecessors
of Irnerius. He is, however, hardly
justified in his assumption (p. 45)
that pre-Irnerian law-teachers or
law - writers alluded to by later
Bolognese doctors must have lived
at Bologna wherever their habitat is
not specified. The idea that Irnerius was the first of the Glossators
dates from the time of Odofredus
(† 1265), who says : ' Sed dominus
Yr. . . . fuit primus illuminator scientie nostre, et quia primus fuit qui
fecit glosas in libris nostris, vocamus
eum lucernam iuris.' In Dig. Vet.
de just. et jure L. jus civile (Lugd.
1550, T. I. f. 7 *a*). The statement is
accepted by Savigny, cap. xxiv. §
207.

[3] Flach, *Études Critiques*, pp. 50,
102. I am much indebted to Prof.
Flach's criticisms on Fitting and his
School, which I have in the main
accepted. He perhaps slightly under-
estimates the work which they have
done in showing (1) the gradualness,
(2) the pre-Irnerian, and even pre-
Bolognese date of the legal Renaissance.

by the new School, where they do not date from the age of Chap. IV,
Justinian or a little later, are after all inconsiderable both § 1.
in quantity and quality. They go to confirm Savigny's
view of a continuous knowledge and practice of some parts
of the Roman Law throughout the Middle Ages, but they
do little to remove a prevailing impression of the general
ignorance of the earlier half of this period. On the other
hand, the more important of these writings, such as the *Exceptiones Petri* [1] and the *Brachylogus* [2] cannot be shown to
be earlier than the twelfth or at the earliest the end of the
eleventh century—that is to say to the first dawn of the
legal Renaissance. And here it may be admitted that the
new School has done something to confirm and emphasise
the important fact that the revival dates from considerably
before the time of Irnerius; and though Fitting and his
followers are disposed to exaggerate the 'scientific' character of the earliest products of the legal Renaissance, it
is true also that Bologna was not the very earliest seat of
this revival. In fact the Law revival, in its commencement and its subsequent progress, exactly kept pace with
the revival of dialectical activity North of the Alps ; and
the rise of the School of Bologna synchronises almost
exactly with the rise to pre-eminent importance of the
Schools of Paris. The Scholastic movement did not begin
in Paris and the Civil Law movement did not begin in

[1] This Epitome or Introduction to
the study of Roman Law, known as
the *Exceptiones legum Romanarum*,
printed by Savigny in an Appendix to
his *Gesch. d. Röm. Rechts*, is referred
by Fitting (in the form in which it
appears in the Tübingen MS.) to
the School of Pavia and to *circa* 1063,
but he regards it as a redaction of
an early work belonging to the first
half of the eleventh century. He
identifies its author with Petrus de
Ravenna, who appears with the
title *Scholasticus, Scholasticissimus* or
Disertissimus in various documents
of 1021-1037. Fitting, *d. Rechtssch.*

zu Bol. p. 60 ; *Ztschr. d. Sav.-Stift.*
T. VII. Röm. Abth. Heft 2, pp. 42,
61 *sq.* Cf also Chiapelli, p. 78 *sq.*

[2] The *Brachylogus* according to
Fitting was compiled at Orleans at
the end of the eleventh or the beginning of the twelfth century. See
Fitting, *d. Rechtssch. zu Bol.* pp.
47, 67 ; and *Über die Heimat und
das Alter des sog. Brach.* (Berlin,
1880). Its value is attested to by
the twenty-three editions published
between 1548 and 1829. For other
pre-Irnerian Law-books see Fitting,
l. c. pp. 59 *sq.*

Bologna ; but though the movement may have been somewhat more gradual, and its earlier stages somewhat more
important than has been commonly supposed, the latest
researches do not detract very seriously from the epoch-
making importance hitherto attached to the rise of the
Bologna School.

Three places in Italy have been especially claimed
as pre-Bolognese Schools of Law : Rome, Pavia, and
Ravenna.

ROME.

To the city of Rome, indeed, the term School can be
applied only in a somewhat vague and general sense. There
is no real evidence of any systematic or professorial teaching of Law at Rome during the dark ages over and above
the elementary school-teaching customary throughout Italy[1].
Odofredus represents the Studium of Law as having been
transferred from Rome to Ravenna in consequence of 'the
wars in the March'—that is presumably after the great
burning of Rome by the Normans in 1084. Elsewhere he
tells us that it was at this time that 'the books' of Law
were transferred from the city of Rome to Ravenna[2].
Odofredus is not a very valuable authority for the events of
the eleventh century, but we may probably recognise a
certain element of truth in the general statement that at
about this time Rome was superseded by Ravenna as the
centre of the best knowledge and teaching of the Roman
Law which then existed in Italy.

PAVIA.

The School of Pavia was famous from at least the beginning of the eleventh century. It was primarily a School
of Lombard Law : but Roman Law was studied with much
earnestness by the Lombard lawyers as a kind of universal
code which might be called in to supplement and elu-
cidate the municipal law of a particular nation[3].　The

[1] Fitting contends for a continued
existence of the School founded
by Justinian down to the time of
Gregory VII.

[2] In Infortiatum, *ad L. Falcidiam*
(Lugduni, 1650, T. II. f. 83). Cf.
below, p. 112, n. 1.)

[3] Fitting, *d. Rechtssch. zu Bol.* p. 40.
The fullest account of the School of
Pavia is given by Merkel, *Gesch. des
Langobardenrechts*, Berlin, 1850. Cf.
also Boretius, præf. ad Libr. Papi-
ensem (*Mon. Germ. Hist.* LL. iv. p.
xcliii *sq.*).

prominence of Roman Law at Pavia is shown by the fact that the School was resorted to by foreigners who could have had no object in studying the legal system of the Lombards[1]. But after the decline of the School of Rome (in whatever sense such a School existed) Ravenna was unquestionably *the* School *par excellence* of Roman Law in Italy[2]. There are faint traces of some kind of systematic organisation from at least the seventh century[3]. The School no doubt declined for a time with the extinction of the Exarchate, but in the ninth and tenth centuries many notices of its Masters occur: and it was at its highest celebrity in the second half of the eleventh century[4]. Though it is contended that the School of Pavia and the scientific study of the Law-texts practised by the Lombard

---

[1] In 1065 a Monk of Marseilles writes a letter to his Abbot in which he apologises for having betaken himself to the study of Law by alleging 'per totam fere Italiam scholares et maxime Provinciales necnon ipsius ordinis, de quo sum, quia plures [*lege* quamplures] legibus catervatim studium adhibentes incessanter aspicio.' Martène and Durand, *Ampl. Coll.* I. c. 470. He adds that he intends hereafter to go to Pisa 'ad exercendum ibi studium.' Later (1119-1124) a French scholar is represented in a Form-book as writing 'me exulem Papie studio legum— *vel* dialectice—alacrem.' Cf. Fitting, *Zeitschr. d. Sav.-Stift.* VII. Röm. Abth. Heft 2. p. 66.

[2] Here the poet Venantius Fortunatus studied in the sixth century. 'Ravennæ nutritus et doctus in arte Gramatica sive Rethorica seu etiam metrica clarissimus extitit.' Paul. Diacon. *De Gestis Long.* Lib. ii. c. 13. (ed. Waitz, Hannov. 1878, p. 79).

[3] A document of the Byzantine period speaks of a *Primicerius Scholæ Forensium Civitatis Ravennensis*. Marini, *Papiri*, No. 110. lin. 38. But *schola* need not imply education.

Other notices of Masters (*Magister, Scholasticus*) at Ravenna occur as witnesses in Fantuzzi, *Monum. Ravenn.*, Venezia, 1801, I. 215 an. 984; I. 229 an. 1002; II. 60 an. 1036. They appear associated with *tabelliones, judices*, &c., never with ecclesiastics. It should be observed that Scholasticus = a learned man, not necessarily a teacher (as is shown by the superlative *scholasticissimus*). This may be the case even with Magister.

[4] See the account by Petrus Damianus of his disputation in 1045 with the Ravenna jurists who took the anti-Church side on the question of the prohibited degrees, *De Parentelæ gradibus*, Opusc. viii. (Migne, T. 145. c. 191 *sq.*). Fitting considers that their opposition provoked the decree of the Lateran Council in 1063 (*Die Rechtss. zu Bol.* p. 39). In 1080 the Ravennese Petrus Crassus addressed a legal disquisition in defence of the Emperor against Gregory VII which is highly esteemed by Fitting (p. 40), to Henry IV for use at the Council of Brixen. It is printed by Ficker, *Forschungen z. Reichs- u. Rechtsgesch. Ital.* &c., Innsbruck, 1868, IV. p. 106.

lawyers had much influence on the early Bolognese
jurists, it is on the whole the School of Ravenna that we
must look upon as the immediate predecessor of Bologna
in the history of Roman Jurisprudence, as in some sense
the Mother of the School which proudly styles itself the
Alma Mater Studiorum[1].

Ravenna a
point of
contact
between
old Rome
and Lom-
bard City-
life.

At Ravenna the old traditions of Roman jurisprudence had been kept alive alike by its earlier connexion
with the new Rome and by its later connexion with
the Holy Roman Empire[2]. At Bologna—the point of
junction between the Exarchate and the Lombard terri-
tory—these traditions came into contact with the new-
born political life of the Lombard cities and with that
development both of professional and of scholastic Law-
studies which was one of the outcomes of the Lombard
political activity[3]. To a large extent the revival of legal
Science was common to all parts of Northern Italy. But
in the Lombard cities the Roman Law had to contend for
supremacy in the Schools as well as in the Courts with a
rival Lombard Jurisprudence: it was not unnatural that
the Roman Law should achieve its decisive victory in the
most Roman of the Lombard towns.

Position of
Irnerius.

Enough has been said to show the baselessness of the
theory that Irnerius was the first teacher of the Roman
Law in medieval Italy. The traditional ideas of intellectual history seem to admit of no epochs or new
departures except in immediate connexion with a great

[1] A slight monograph on the
Origini dello Studio Ravennate is
published by Ricci, *Primordi dello
St. d. Bol.* p. 201 *sq.* Its scientific
relations to Bologna are discussed by
Tarlazzi, *Scuole d. dir. rom. in Rav.
ed in Bol.* in *Atti e Mem. della Dep. d.
Sto. Pat. per la prov. di Romagna*,
Ser. III. v. 4. p. 29 ; Fitting, *op. cit.*
p. 38 *sq.*; Chiapelli, p. 38 *sq.*; Ficker,
op. cit. vol. I. Abth. i, p. 104 *sq.*

[2] 'De Ottone, incertum Ine an
II, constat palatium imperiale ab eo
conditum Ravennæ, ut ex placito

Joannis Archiepiscopi placentini
apud MURATORI, *Antiq.med.œvi,*diss.
xxix. De Conrado etiam Salico
narrat Wippo Ravennam illum in-
trasse et cum magna potestate ibi
regnasse. WIPPO in *Vita Conradi*
ap. PISTOR. *Rer. Germanic. Script.*
t. iii. p. 471.' Sarti, T. I. pt. i. p. 4.

[3] Chiapelli, p. 132 *sq.* Ficker (II.
Abth. i. p. 139) traces the rise of the
School of Bologna to an 'Anwen-
dung der longobardischen Methode
auf die Behandlung der römischen
Rechtsquellen.'

discovery or a great name. As a matter of fact, Irnerius
'discovered' nothing at all. 'Revival' is a term more
applicable to the life-work of Irnerius. But his true position is rather at the culmination than at the beginning of
the revival. So far his position in the great movement
with which his name is associated may be compared to
that of Abelard in the speculative movement North of the
Alps. But the pre-eminence of Irnerius in historic fame
over his predecessors, his contemporaries, and his immediate followers is perhaps less due to the personal greatness
of the man than was the case with Abelard. What was the
exact position of Irnerius in the development of medieval
Jurisprudence, we shall be better able to examine when we
have collected together what is known of his immediate
predecessors and of his own biography. We have seen
that there was a medieval Jurisprudence before the rise of
the School of Bologna : it remains to show that there was
a Law-school at Bologna before Irnerius.

At this point it becomes important to bear in mind what
has already been said as to the close connexion subsisting
in the early medieval Schools between legal Science and
general literary culture. The earliest scholastic fame of
Bologna was that of a School of the Liberal Arts; and it
is very probable that in that School what may be called
the juristic side of Rhetoric early began to occupy the
most prominent place. At all events, by the year 1000 A. D.
Bologna was already sufficiently famous as a Studium of Arts
to attract Guido, afterwards Bishop of Acqui (1035–1070)
to its Schools from a region as distant as the neighbourhood
of Genoa[1]. In about the third quarter of the same century
we hear of another future Bishop going to Bologna as a
student of the Liberal Arts[2]. Even after the career of

---

[1] 'Ab ineunte igitur ætate Guido memoratus . . . . studiorum causa Bononiam contendit. Ubi aliquot annis non minus sanctis moribus quam litterarum disciplinis incumbens socios et æmulatores sui in utroque studii honore devicit.' *Acta Sanctorum*, Jun., T. I. p. 229.

[2] S. Bruno, Bishop of Segni († 1123). 'Voluntate parentum se Bononiam transferens, liberalium artium doctrinæ vigilem curam exhibuit.' It is added that he studied both *trivium* and *quadrivium*, and afterwards, still apparently at Bologna, 'divinæ paginæ propensius operam

Irnerius had closed, Bologna was still famous primarily as a School of Literature: Law was only one, though here no doubt the main, element in general Education.

John of
Salisbury's
allusions to
Bologna.
Nothing can more strikingly illustrate the importance of Bologna as a School of the Liberal Arts than the fact that a famous teacher of Paris should have thought it worth while to go to Bologna to study Dialectic. Yet such appears to have been the case. In one of those auto-biographical fragments which give so peculiar an interest to his writings, John of Salisbury tells us that he studied Dialectic for two years in 'the Mount' of Ste. Geneviève under Alberic and Robert of Melun (1136–8). Later on, one of these teachers went to Bologna and 'unlearned what he had taught,' after which he went back to Paris and 'untaught' the same to his pupils [1]. Though the Dia-lectic of Bologna may well have been of a more practical and legal kind than the speculative Dialectic of Paris, John of Salisbury does not seem to be conscious that they were two distinct Sciences. How slowly the development of technical Jurisprudence threw into the shade the ancient repute of Bologna as a School of the Liberal Arts may also be illustrated by the fact that even in 1158 Frederick I speaks of scholars of 'various Arts' being attracted to the Lombard Schools from all parts [2].

Bologna
famous for
Dictamen.
In the older Law-Schools of the medieval world, and particularly at Bologna, the gulf which according to our ideas separates technical and legal from general education

dedit.' A. S. S., Jul. (Tom. IV. p. 479). He had already been in-structed ' singularibus disciplinis ' in a Monastery.

[1] Deinde . . . adhæsi magistro Alberico, qui inter ceteros opinatis-simus dialecticus enitebat . . . Sic ferme toto biennio conversatus in Monte, artis huius præceptoribus usus sum Alberico et magistro Ro-berto Meludensi . . Postea unus eorum profectus Bononiam dedidicit quod docuerat, siquidem et reversus

dedocuit; an melius, iudicent qui ante et postea audierunt.' *Metalogi-cus,* lib. ii. c. 10.

[2] See below, p. 145. As late as 1162 Bolognese Law is still looked on as a department of general 'lite-rary studies'; 'Pollebat equidem tunc Bononia in litteralibus studiis pre cunctis Ytalie civitatibus quatuor legum columpnis inter ceteros magni-fice radiantibus.' Acerbi Morenæ *Continuatio,* &c. (Pertz, SS. XVIII. p. 639).

was bridged over by the existence of the rather curious Art known as *Dictamen*. *Dictamen* may be comprehensively described as the Art of Composition. The poetical branch of the Art had of course no special relation to legal pursuits[1]: but the *Dictamen prosaicum*, besides teaching general principles of literary composition, was specially occupied with the Art of letter-writing, and included not only rules for private epistolary correspondence, but also more technical rules for the compilation of official briefs or bulls and other legal documents. In an age wherein reading and writing were the accomplishments of the few, while all business transactions of any solemnity or importance were carried on in a dead language, it is obvious that the connexion between Grammar and Law was indefinitely closer than it is according to modern ideas[2]. Dictamen may be described at pleasure as a branch of Grammar or as a branch of Law. For this Art of Dictamen Bologna possessed a special notoriety; the School of Dictamen was the cradle of the special School of Law. Irnerius himself wrote a Notarial Form-book (*Formularium Tabellionum*)[3]. We also possess a work entitled *Rationes dictandi* written by the Bolognese Canon Hugo *circa* 1123[4]. But the most famous Bolognese Master of Rhetoric and Dictamen was Boncompagni, who lived as late as the beginning of the thirteenth century. The fact that in 1215 his *Rhetorica Antiqua* was solemnly read before the professors and students of Canon and Civil Law[5] shows at

---

[1] Yet the two branches were often professed by the same person. Thus the Englishman Gaufridus wrote at Bologna, *circa* 1224, (*a*) a book on prosody or versification called *Poetria Nova*; (*b*) an *Ars Dictaminis*, sc. Prosaici. Sarti, I. Pt. ii. p. 601.

[2] By the Bologna City-statutes the 'Consules artis tabellionatus' are to examine candidates for the office of Notary 'qualiter (sciunt) latinare et dictare.' Frati, II. pp. 185, 188.

[3] Sarti, I. pt. ii. p. 505.

[4] Edited by Rockinger in *Quellen zur bayerischen und deutschen Geschichte*, Bd. IX. Abth. i. p. 53 *sq.* It is noteworthy that in the specimen letters which are given by the writer there are allusions to the scholastic fame of Bologna for Philosophy, Medicine, and Dictamen, none to the special teaching of Law.

[5] Sarti, I. pt. ii. p. 602; Rockinger, *Die Ars Dictandi in Italia* (*Sitzungsberichte d. bayerischen Akad. zu*

once the importance attached to the Art and the close
connexion which still subsisted between this branch of the
old comprehensive Rhetoric and the rising professional
School of Law.

Pepo pre-
decessor of
Irnerius.
The principal source of the once universally accepted
view of Irnerius as the sole originator of the Law-revival at
Bologna, is a celebrated passage of Odofredus in which
he speaks of Irnerius as the 'first who taught in that city.'
Yet Odofredus himself has preserved to us the name of
one of Irnerius' predecessors, Pepo, adding however that
'whatever his knowledge may have been, he was a man
of no name[1].' This contemptuous judgment of Odofredus
is, however, hardly borne out by the scanty additional
notices of Pepo which have come down to us[2]. One of

München, 1861, p. 134 *sq.*). The
Cedrus and the treatise on *Notaria*
are printed by Rockinger in *Quellen*
&c., vol. IX. pp. 121 *sq.* It is observable as we look through these
treatises that they become increasingly technical in the later Middle
Ages. Before the middle of the
thirteenth century Notaria had become a distinct Art or Faculty:
Rolandinus, whose *Summa Notariæ*
became the text-book of the Art,
successfully asserted the monopoly
of Bologna citizens to the right of
teaching it in 1284. According to
Sarti (I. pt. ii. pp. 505-6), there
were regular graduations in *Notaria*.
The Notaries formed a Corpus or
Guild in the days of Odofredus.
Sarti, I. pt. ii. p. 506. Instruction in
Notaria included the Elements of
Law, e. g. the Institutes. Sarti, l. c.

[1] 'Signori, Dominus Yrnerius qui
fuit apud nos lucerna juris, id est
primus qui docuit in civitate ista,
nam primo cepit studium esse in
civitate ista in artibus : et cum
studium esset destructum Rome,
libri legales fuerunt deportati ad
civitatem Ravenne, et de Ravenna

ad civitatem istam. Quidam Dominus
Pepo cepit auctoritate sua legere in
legibus ; tamen quidquid fuerit de
scientia sua, nullius nominis fuit.
Sed Dominus Yr., dum doceret
in artibus in civitate ista, cum
fuerunt deportati libri legales, cepit
per se studere in libris nostris, et
studendo cepit docere in legibus, et
ipse fuit maximi nominis ; et fuit
primus illuminator scientie nostre ;
et quod primus fuit qui fecit glossas
in libris nostris, vocamus eum lucernam juris.' Odofredus, in l. *Jus
Civile*, Dig. Vet. *De justitia et jure*
(1550, T. I. f. 7).

[2] His name occurs in a Placitum
of the Countess Matilda in 1072.
'Ibi eorum presentia venit Maurus
Habas de Ecclesia Sancti Salvatoris
de Monte Amiata, una cum Pepo Avo-
cato suo, et retulit,' &c. Document
in Muratori, *Ant. It.* II. c. 955, and
Ricci, No. II. Again in a similar
document of 1078 : 'Ibique in eo
iudicio veniens Gerardus abbas sancti
Salvatoris sito monte Amiate simul
cum Pepo advocatore suo.' Ficker,
Forschungen, iv. p. 103 ; Ricci,
No. V.

the documents in which he appears as a 'legis doctor' Chap. IV,
§ 1.
and Assessor to a feudal Court[1] is said to exhibit as
compared with others of the same or earlier dates a very
superior legal skill and knowledge[2]. It is said that this is the
earliest medieval document (1076 A. D.) in which the
Digest is expressly cited as the ground of a legal decision[3], His use of
and, if that be the case, it may reasonably be inferred that the Digest.
the revived study of the Digest which characterised the
Bologna School dates not from Irnerius but from Pepo.
Pepo is the only Doctor of Law who can be positively
proved to have been taught at Bologna, though allusions
to other 'legis doctores' in Bolognese documents of about
the same period may, or may not, be interpreted of actual
teachers[4].

The above cited passage and one or two digressions in Life of
the garrulous Odofredus, together with a few allusions in Irnerius.
documents or chronicles, constitute the whole of our authorities for the life and work of Irnerius. The one fact about
his personal history which Odofredus tells us is that he was

---

[1] 'In presentia Nordilli missi domine beatricis ductricis et marchio-
nissæ et iohannis uice comitis . . .
in iudicio cum eis residentibus guil-
lielmo iudice et pepone legis doctore,' &c. Savioli, vol. I. pt. ii. p.
123 : Ficker, *op. cit.* IV. p. 99 : Ricci,
No. iii. : Muratori, *Ant. It.* III. c.
889. Cf. Fitting, *Die Rechtssch. zu
Bol.* p. 84.

[2] What strikes the lay reader is the
superiority of the Latinity to that of
some other of the documents published by Ricci, which (if properly
transcribed) are full of outrageous
grammatical blunders such as are
quite unparalleled in any legal documents of the later Middle Age which
are known to me—another illustration of the fact that the 'revival of
Roman Law' was merely one side
of a revival of general education and
culture.

[3] 'His peractis supradictus Nor-
dillus, predicte domine Beatricis
missus, lege digestorum libris inserta
considerata per quam copiam magistratus non habentibus restitutionem
in integrum pretor pollicetur, restituit in integrum ecclesiam et monas-
terium sancti Michaelis,' &c.

[4] The earliest published by Ricci
is a deed of 1067, witnessed by
'Albertus legis doctor' (Ricci, No.
i). An 'Iginulfus legis doctor' occurs in *op. cit.* No. iv. But Savigny
(cap. vi. § 136) warns us against inferring the existence of a Law
School from the mention of *legis
doctores*, an expression which is
sometimes a mere synonym of *iudex*
or *causidicus*. This principle, not
always sufficiently borne in mind by
later enquirers, is unquestionably
true of the earlier period, but it is
not quite so clear of this period.

CHAP. IV,
§ I.

a Master of the Liberal Arts[1], and this is completely in accordance with all that we know of the character of his teaching and of the state of legal education at the time[2]. Odofredus goes on to tell us that ' when the books of Law were brought from Ravenna, he began to study in them by himself, and by studying to teach the Laws, and he was a man of the greatest renown.' The literal truth of this account is quite out of the question. It is impossible to suppose that there were no Law-texts at Bologna before the time of Irnerius. Indeed, Odofredus refutes himself, for he admits that before Irnerius a ' certain dominus Pepo began by his own authority to lecture in the Laws.' If therefore there be any truth in this story of the importation of Law-books from Ravenna, it must have taken place in the time of Pepo and not in that of Irnerius ; and it is quite possible that the Digest at least may have been first introduced into Bologna from Ravenna in the time of Pepo[3].

Extent of
Irnerius'
originality.

There is great probability in Odofredus' view that Irnerius was to a certain extent self-taught. It cannot, indeed, for a moment be supposed that Irnerius derived no assistance from any of those earlier law books or glosses of which we have already spoken. In the scanty Irnerian glosses which

---

[1] ' Et debetis scire vos, domini, sicut nos fuimus instructi a nostris maioribus, quod dominus Yr. fuit primus qui fuit ausus dirigere cor suum ad L. istam. Nam dominus Yr. erat magister in artibus, et studium fuit Ravenne, et collapsa ea fuit studium Bononie. Et dominus Yr. studuit per se sicut potuit ; postea cepit docere in iure civili et ipse fecit primum formularium, i. e. librum omnium instrumentorum : scripsit instrumentum emphyteuticum.' Odofred. in Codicem, *De SS. Eccl.* Auth. *Qui res* (T. III. f. 17).

[2] I do not know what authority Coppi (p. 54) has for making him ' maestro di grammatica a Ravenna.'

[3] It has indeed been established by the critical investigations of Mommsen that the texts of the Digest which were current in the Schools of Bologna were all derived from a single original—the celebrated Pisan MS. which the later tradition supposed to have been captured at Amalfi, corrected from independent and sometimes better codices (*Digestorum Libri*, Præf., Berolini, 1870, p. lxiv. *sq.*). There is no reason why Odofredus' story of the importation of ' the books ' from Ravenna may not to this extent be true. It is also worth noticing that this particular MS. of the Digest has no glosses ; and this is no doubt the origin of the idea of Irnerius as the first of the Glossators.

have come down to us occur distinct allusions to the
opinions previously expressed and to standing questions
habitually discussed by his predecessors or contemporaries.
If he had not heard of these discussions in the Schools, he
must have met them in books. The literary or grammatical
character of the glosses ascribed to Irnerius makes it quite
probable that his legal knowledge was originally the acquisition of a scholar without practical training or legal
education beyond what was obtained by every young
Italian of his time in the Schools of the Liberal Arts[1];
the notion that he was as much without predecessors and
without assistance in his legal studies as the Western
Scholar dealing with a newly discovered language, is only
a part of the general misconception of an uncritical generation to which the history even of its own School before
Irnerius was rapidly becoming a blank relieved only by a
few flashes of confused and incoherent tradition.

When all deductions are made from the exaggerated Reasons for
position accorded by a later age to the traditional founder growth of
Bolognese
of the Bolognese School, there can be no doubt of the School.
importance of the epoch which is associated with his name.
Unquestionably it was his lectures that first raised Bologna
to European fame. Can we in any way explain this sudden
emergence of Bologna into the position not merely of a
great School of Law but of *the* School of Law *par excellence*?
We have already dwelt upon the political and intellectual
conditions which account for a great revival of the study of

[1] This is illustrated by the historically worthless story that Irnerius
was led to the study of the Civil
Law by a dispute as to the meaning
of the word *as*. 'Nonne duo
passeres asse veneunt? propter
quod verbum venit Bonon. studium
civile, sicut audivi a domino meo.'
Hostiensis (Henricus de Segusio)
Comment. in Decretalium libros,
Venet. 1581. *De Testamentis*, III.
fol. 73. Cf. also the remark of
Odofredus : 'Or, segnori, plura non

essent dicenda super lege ista,
Dominus tamen Ir., qui laicus
fuit, et magister fuit in civitate
ista in artibus, antequam doceret in legibus, fecit unam glosam
sophisticam, que est obscurior
quam sit textus.' *In Codicem* l. ult.
de in int. rest. min. (Lugduni,
1650, T. III. f. 101 *b*). So Odofredus
in Dig. Vet. *De justitia et jure*, L.
Manumissiones: 'hic glossat dominus
Yr. elegantissimis verbis.' (T. I. f.
7 *a*).

Roman Law in Northern Italy; can we account for its concentration in the city of Bologna? Much influence must of course be accorded to the genius of the man. The less it is admitted that there was any new departure involved in the subject or the method of his lectures, the more must they have owed their attractiveness to their own intrinsic merits. The more emphatically it is denied that his undoubtedly valuable glosses mark an entirely new beginning in the development of medieval Law-literature, the more evident is it that Irnerius must have possessed powers as a teacher of which these scanty remains fail to give us any adequate idea. But the greatest of teachers is unable to raise a School even to temporary, much less to permanent, renown unless he appears at the right place and at the right moment—unless a concurrence of favourable circumstances second the personal attraction of the individual intellect. Even the career of Abelard was, as we have seen, only one of the causes which concurred to make Paris the intellectual centre of Northern Europe; and Irnerius, on the most favourable estimate, does not belong to the same intellectual rank as Abelard. A passage of the chronicler, Richard of Ursperg, supplies us with an important clue towards the solution of the problem. After speaking of the work of Gratian, he tells us that ' at the same time dominus Irnerius at the request of the Countess Matilda renewed the books of the Laws, which had long been neglected, and, in accordance with the manner in which they had been compiled by the Emperor Justinian of divine memory, arranged them in divisions, adding perchance between the lines a few words here and there[1].'

Patronage of Matilda.

The value to be assigned to a tradition of this kind, revealed to us nearly a century after the death of the persons

---

[1] ' Eisdem quoque temporibus dominus Wernerius libros legum, qui dudum neglecti fuerant nec quisquam in eis studuerat, ad petitionem Mathildae comitissae renovavit: et secundum quod olim a divae recordationis imperatore Iustiniano compilati fuerant, paucis forte verbis alicubi interpositis, eos distinxit, in quibus continentur instituta,' &c. *Abb. Ursperg. Chron.* (Pertz, SS. XXIII. p. 342.)

to whom it relates, must depend entirely upon its accordance or non-accordance with the probabilities of the case and the facts known to us on more reliable evidence. Here there is considerable probability in favour of the chronicler's statement. The notion that Matilda founded the School of Bologna in the sense in which later Emperors or Kings founded Universities, is of course on the face of it untenable. It has grown largely no doubt out of this passage, but it is not really supported by its contents. There is nothing improbable in the statement that Matilda encouraged a Bologna Master, already of some repute as a scholar and a teacher of the Liberal Arts, to apply himself to the study and editing of the Roman Law-texts. And there were political reasons which sufficiently account for Matilda's wish to establish or foster a Law-school at Bologna. Hitherto, as we have seen, Ravenna had been the centre of Italian Jurisprudence: Ravennese Jurists appear from the documents to have been constantly employed as advocates or assessors in the Italian law-courts. It is just after the accession of Matilda in 1075 that we first begin to meet the names of Bolognese Doctors in Tuscan deeds : and after 1113 the Ravennese names disappear altogether [1]. Ravenna, the seat of the Imperial jurisprudence, the inheritor of so many Imperial traditions, warmly embraced the side of Henry IV in the great conflict with the Papacy; when a Council was assembled at Brescia in 1080 for the election of an anti-Pope, it was in the Archbishop of Ravenna that the required anti-papal ecclesiastic was found. Hence it is easy to conceive that Matilda was anxious to enlist in her service a body of lawyers less unfavourable to the Papal claims than the *causidici* of Ravenna; and the cause of Matilda was the cause of Italian liberty. The ultimate result of the anti-papal and anti-national attitude of Ravenna in this encounter was the ruin of its School of Law. At that moment Bologna was ready to step into the vacant place ;

---

[1] Fitting, *d. Rechtssch. zu Bol.* p. 99 *sq.*

though the Bolognese Doctors were not permanently
faithful to the Papal cause. If any further explanation
is wanted for the supersession of Ravenna by Bologna as
the headquarters of Italian Jurisprudence, it may be found
in the final extinction of any Schools there may have
been at Rome by the Norman conquest of 1084, in the
neighbourhood of Bologna to Ravenna, and its immense
superiority in accessibility and position to the isolated and
marsh-girt city on the Adriatic coastland. Bologna lay,
as a forged University Charter correctly states, 'at the
intersection of four provinces—Lombardy, the March of
Verona, the Romandiola, and Tuscany[1].' To this day it
is the point at which converge all the great lines of communication between the Northern entrances to Italy and
its centre : in that age there was no place better situated
for a meeting-place between the students of Italy and
students from beyond the Alps.

Date of
Irnerius'
teaching.
The facts and dates of Irnerius' life are all quite in accordance with the chronicler's statement as to his connexion with Matilda. Though the name (variously spelt
as Irnerius, Yrnerius, Gernerius, Warnerius, Wernerius,
Varnerius, Guarnerius or Garnerius[2]) is Teutonic, there is
no reason to doubt the common account that he was a
Bolognese citizen by birth[3]. His name first occurs among
the *causidici* in a *placitum* of the Countess Matilda relating
to property at Ferrara in 1113[4], and as a *judex* in various
documents of the same kind under the Emperor Henry V
ranging from 1116 to 1125. It was argued by Savigny
that since Irnerius was in the Imperial service from 1116
up to the time at which his name disappears from the
documents, his work as a teacher must have been over
before the beginning of that period. This contention can

---

[1] Muratori, *Ant. It.* III. c. 22.

[2] Fitting, *Die Rechtssch. zu Bol.*
p. 89 ; documents in Ricci.

[3] This is expressly stated. He is
habitually described as 'de Bononia'
or 'Bononiensis.'

[4] 'Causidici quoque Varnerius de
Bononia, Lambertus, et Albertus
seu (*sic*) amicus.' Document in
Savioli, vol. I. pt. ii. p. 151 ; Ricci,
No. xvii ; see also Ricci, Nos. xx--
xxv, xxvii, xxviii, xxxi, xxxiv.

hardly be admitted, since it assumes that the position of a CHAP. IV,
teacher was inconsistent with occasional employment of § 1.
a judicial character [1]. A more important reason for throwing back the teaching of Irnerius to the very beginning of
the twelfth century or the end of the eleventh is the early
occurrence of the epithet 'learned' as applied to Bologna
and its Law School. Thus in 1119 an anonymous poet
writes on the capture of Como :—

> Docta suas secum duxit Bononia leges [2].

Again, with reference to the year 1127 the same poet has
the line :—

> Docta Bononia venit et huc cum legibus una [3].

It should be observed, however, that there is here no
allusion to professorial teaching, but only to a reputation for
legal learning : and it is certain that whether or not they
were teachers, whether or not they had attended lectures
on Law, the reputation of the Bologna lawyers was not in
the first instance created by Irnerius. While it is probable
that he had begun his work before the beginning of the
century, even this is not certain : still less is there any
positive evidence for placing the beginning of his career as
a Law teacher as early as 1088—the year assumed by the
recent Octo-centenary celebration at Bologna. If, however, the University had been content to accept Pepo as its
pious founder instead of Irnerius, Bologna would have
been justified in fixing her Octo-centenary at a still earlier
date.

It should also be mentioned that though the name of
Irnerius does not occur in the documents after 1125, it is
probable that he lived, and perhaps taught, to a somewhat

---

[1] Even non-legal teachers were
often in request as assistants in
legal business: e. g. 'Albertus grama-
ticus de sancto marino' is associated
with the *Causidici* in 1113 (Ricci, No.
xviii).

[2] Muratori, *Ital. SS.* V. p. 418,
l. 211.

[3] Ib. p. 453, l. 1848. Early Bo-
logna coins have the legend BONONIA
MATER STUDIORUM, and somewhat
later BONONIA DOCET: the ancient
Seal of the City has the words
PETRUS UBIQUE PATER LEGUMQUE
BONONIA MATER. Sarti (1888), T. I.
pt. i. p. 10.

later date. The Ursperg Chronicle speaks of him under the reign of Lothair II (1125–1138)[1]. But the most weighty reason for supposing that the scholastic career of Irnerius did not close when he entered the service of the Emperor is that only on that supposition can the 'Four Doctors' who come next to Irnerius in the succession of great Bologna jurists have been his actual pupils, as they are stated to have been by the chroniclers of the next generation[2]. On the whole, then, it would appear that the teaching of Irnerius may be assigned roughly to the period 1100–1130.

Irnerius
at Rome.

So far we have still left unmentioned the most striking incident in the life of Irnerius which has come down to us. On the election of Gelasius II in 1118 we find 'Master Irnerius of Bologna and many lawyers' taking a prominent part in the election of the Anti-pope Gregory VIII. They are represented by a contemporary chronicler as 'summoning the Roman people to the election of a Pope,' while 'a certain reader in the pulpit of S. Peter's by a prolix lecture expounded the decrees relating to the substitution of a Pope'[3]. This is the one piece of contemporary

[1] Pertz, SS. l. c. The *Chron.* of Burchard of Ursperg († 1226) is believed to rest on the earlier work of John of Cremona (Fitting, *l. c.* p. 96). Gervase of Canterbury similarly associates Irnerius and Gratian. (II ed. Stubbs, 1880, p. 385.) On the other hand, Robertus de Monte speaks of 'Lanfrancus Papiensis et Garnerius socius eius' ad an. 1032! (Pertz, SS. VI. p. 478.) But so gross a blunder can hardly count for much.

[2] Ricobaldus Ferrarensis (*circa* 1298), *Vita di Federigo I.* (Muratori, SS. T. ix. c. 371): Otto Morena ad a. 1158 (Pertz, SS. XVIII. p. 607). The probabilities of the case are a weightier argument than the Chroniclers' statement. Irnerius' fame would be hard to account for if he did not form a single teacher of

repute and if those who brought the School to the zenith of its fame owed him nothing. Of the illustrious 'four,' Bulgarius died in 1166, Martinus before 1166, Jacobus in 1178, Hugo *circa* 1168. Fitting, *l. c.* p. 103. Gloria (*Monumenti d. Un. di Padova, 1222–1318,* pp. 107–8) identifies with our Irnerius the 'Warnerius missus domini imperatoris, delegatus ab ipso principe in iudicio iudiciarie Montis silicis,' in the document of 1100 (Ricci, No. xi): but this is clearly the 'Guarnerius de Montesilicis' or 'comes Guarnerius' of Ricci xii, and therefore not the Jurist, unless (as Gloria suggests) the 'comes' is the blunder of the scribe.

[3] 'Magister Guarnerius de Bononia, et plures legis periti populum Romanum ad eligendum Papam convenit, et quidam expeditus lector

testimony which really justifies the personal importance traditionally ascribed to the reputed Founder of the School of Bologna. Whatever was the exact nature of his connexion with the Countess Matilda, this notice testifies to the completeness of his conversion to the Imperial cause. It would be vain to speculate as to the relative shares which the ideas embodied in the Imperial jurisprudence and the prizes of the Imperial service had exercised upon the mind of the Jurists. Certain it is that the early Bologna Doctors were all staunch Imperialists; and the patronage of the Emperors was at least an element in promoting the growth and prosperity of the School. If such patronage may not have done much to increase the prestige of the School in Italy, it may well have had its influence in attracting that swarm of German students who had the largest share in raising Bologna from the position of an Italian to that of a European or cosmopolitan seat of learning [1].

We are now perhaps in a position to estimate the nature of the epoch in the history of medieval Jurisprudence and of medieval education which is represented by the name of Irnerius. Most of the titles to fame traditionally claimed for him rest, as we have seen, upon no historical basis. He was not the re-discoverer of the Roman Law, not even of the Pandects. He was not the first medieval teacher of Law, even at Bologna. He was not the first of the Glossators, probably not the first even of the Bolognese Glossators. There is, indeed, hardly any one respect in which Irnerius marks an absolute new departure.

How then does the rise of the Bologna School constitute

---

in pulpito S. Petri per prolixam lectionem decreta Pontificum de substituendo Papa explicavit. Quibus perlectis et explicatis totus populus elegit in Papam quendam Episcopum Hispaniæ qui ibi aderat cum Imperatore.' Landulfus jun., *Hist. Mediolan.* c. 32 (Muratori, *SS.* T. V. p. 502).

[1] Before the close of the thirteenth century (*circa* 1298) we find a chronicler speaking of ' lo Studio Bolognese, poco avanti in quella città per Henrico instituito.' Ricobald. Ferrar. (Muratori, SS. T. IX. p. 371). There is probably a confusion between Henry IV and Henry V.

Study of
Digest.

an epoch? In attempting to answer the question it must be premised that some of the changes which the Irnerian epoch introduced began a generation before Irnerius himself, and some were probably not completed till at least a generation after him.

(1) In the first place the rise of the School of Bologna is marked by an increased prominence of the Digest—that is to say, of far the bulkiest, most elaborate and most important section of the Corpus Juris. The Digest was practically unknown before the time of Pepo [1]. Pepo was certainly acquainted with the ' Old Digest,' but we do not know that the whole of that work was known at Bologna in his time ; and the peculiar division of the Pandects into the Old and the New Digest with the detached parts known as the *Infortiatum* and the *Tres Partes* make it tolerably certain that they must have been introduced into the Schools of Bologna in successive instalments [2]. It is quite probable therefore that the remaining parts of the Digest may have been first introduced by Irnerius [3]. The reputed founder of the

---

[1] Thus it appears that so eminent a canonist as Ivo of Chartres derived his extracts from the Pandects only from an epitome, published by Conrat from a British Museum MS. (*Der Pandekten- und Institutionenauszug der brittischen Dekretalensammlung Quelle des Ivo.* Berlin, 1887). Fitting (*l. c.* p. 57) refers to Mommsen's Preface to the Digest (Berolini, 1868) as evidence of the existence of ' Vorbolognesischen Glossen' on the Digest : but Mommsen himself (p. lxviii) places these glosses (which appear to consist entirely in various readings), ' aut decimo aut quod magis crediderim undecimo sæculo ætate Irneriana.' The evidence which Fitting produces to show that the Digest was not unknown between the time of Gregory the Great and the middle of the eleventh century is of a very slender description. (See

his Art. in *Zeitschrift der Savigny-Stiftung*, T. VI. Röm. Abth. pp. 112, 113.)

[2] As Odofredus declares, In Infort. *ad L. Falcidiam* (T. II. f. 83).

[3] Fitting (*Die Rechtssch. zu Bol.* pp. 94, 95) thinks ' dass sich Irnerius einzelne Stücke der Justinianischen Gesetzgebung, wie etwa das Infortiatum, erst aus Ravenna verschafft hat, und dass so vielleicht in der Erzählung des Odofredus doch ein Körnchen Wahrheit steckt.' Chiapelli (pp. 40-56) collects allusions to earlier comments on the Codex, Dig. Vetus and Dig. Nov., but there is only one not very convincing instance from the Dig. Vetus (p. 54), and the passages cited in the Dig. Nov. do not really prove the existence of pre-Irnerian glosses. He also notices (p. 96) that the *Notulæ* — short expository, grammatical or critical remarks—of the primitive

Bologna School may therefore have been the first Lecturer upon the *whole* Digest, and he may even have been the first Glossator on any portion of it. What this change implies will be understood when it is remembered that the Institutes were a mere introductory text-book and the Code a compilation of Imperial edicts — for the most part late Imperial edicts—while the Digest was composed of the *responsa* of the Jurists, and chiefly of the great Classical Jurists who made Roman Law what it was. Without the Digest the study of Roman Law was in a worse position than the study of Aristotle when he was known only from the Organon, or of Plato when he was known only from the *Phaedo* and the *Timaeus.* The Digest alone adequately revealed the *spirit* of Roman Law.

(2) The emphasis now laid upon the Digest is only a detail in a more important change introduced into the spirit of medieval Jurisprudence by the Bologna school. We have already insisted upon the literary character of the earlier legal literature. From another point of view it might be styled philosophical. In many of the countries in which Roman Law was studied, it must be remembered that its enactments were merely called in to fill up gaps left by local laws or customs, to explain and to supplement in a more scientific and philosophical manner the inadequate provisions of the non-Roman or half-Roman codes or customs of the barbarian kingdoms [1]. At times, indeed, the Roman Law-texts were studied almost purely as a literary exercise. Even where, as among the Romanised inhabitants of the Italian cities, the old Roman Law was still theoretically current in its integrity, it was looked upon to a large extent as a kind of higher natural Law which owed its authority as much to its intrinsic reasonableness as to its express enactment. The very conflict of Laws

A close, more technical and more professional study of Texts.

---

type embedded in the Accursian gloss are found more frequently in the Institutes and Code than in the Pandects, and more frequently in the Dig. Vet. than in the Dig. Nov.

[1] A Visigothic Law (cited by Fitting) declares: 'Alienæ gentis legibus ad exercitium utilitatis et permittimus et optamus ; ad negociorum vero discussionem et resultamus et prohibemus.' (Bouquet, IV. p. 294.)

which in the Dark Ages prevailed among the mixed popula-
tions of the Lombard towns (where every one was supposed
to be judged according to the law of his own race), tended
to bestow this universal character upon the Law which, by
virtue largely of its intrinsic superiority, was gradually
asserting its supremacy over all rival systems. Hence it
was natural that the Law-writers and Law-teachers should
be more anxious to extract from the texts before them a
principle which seemed to accord with their ideas of equity
and natural justice than to interpret, in the spirit of the
exegete or the mere practitioner, the actual letter of the
texts : the Doctors of the early Middle Age often wrote
rather as Publicists, Jurists, legislators than as mere
lawyers : or, if they wrote as lawyers, they wrote in the
spirit of the old Jurisconsults of the time when the *Responsa
prudentum* were looked upon as actual sources of Law. At
times they venture explicitly to criticise the provisions of
the code before them, and to substitute rules of their own,
as though fully on a level in point of authority with the
rule which they so superciliously set aside. From the
point of view of the Jurist, the Irnerian epoch represents
the beginning of a more close, critical and textual[1]—and at
the same time more professional—study of the original
sources of the Law.

Organiza-
tion of
legal
Study.
(3) From the point of view of the historian of education,
the epoch introduced by Irnerius marks the beginning of
the systematic study of the whole Corpus Juris Civilis as
the regular curriculum of an ordinary legal education.
Hitherto the ordinary text-books had been in parts of
Europe the West-Gothic Breviarium, elsewhere the Institutes, together with the compilations or introductions
composed by the older medieval teachers. It was at
Bologna in all probability for the first time that lectures

[1] This return to the letter of the
Imperial decrees no doubt tended to
bring into prominence the source of
their authority and so to emphasize
the legislative prerogatives of the
Roman Emperor, whether we regard this attachment of the Bologna
School to the *littera scripta* as the
cause or the effect of its Imperialist proclivities.

were delivered on all parts of the Corpus, and that attendance at such a complete course of lectures became the indispensable equipment of a properly trained Civilian. The sections into which the Law-texts are still divided are expressly ascribed to Irnerius by Odofredus[1]. How far the system of legal education—the division of lectures into ordinary and extraordinary, the 'Repetitions,' the disputations, and the examinations—which we find in operation in the later University of Bologna may be traced back to the age of Irnerius, we have no materials for estimating. The examinations and the ceremonial of graduation are in all probability not earlier than the generation of Irnerius' disciples. But at all events we may safely declare that the organization of legal education which extended itself in time to all the Universities of Europe and which has to a large extent descended to modern Universities, is the work of the early School of Bologna and th atthis work of organization was begun by Irnerius.

(4) We are merely describing another side of the same change when we trace back to Irnerius and his immediate followers the differentiation of Law-studies and Law-students from the Faculty of the Liberal Arts.

If the whole Corpus Juris was to be taught, it required the undivided attention of its students ; henceforth the student of Law had no leisure for other studies, and the student of Arts no longer ventured to meddle with so vast and so technical a subject until mere school-education was over. There may, indeed, have been special Schools at which Law was taught by distinct teachers at such places as Pavia and Ravenna before the rise of the Bologna School. But from this time the distinction of the teachers and the students of Law from other teachers and students came to be much more sharply drawn and extended itself to all Universities and Schools at which Law was taught at all. The change was not indeed quite complete in the time of Irnerius. In his day *Dictamen* was still a prominent element in a legal education, and *Dictamen* included the

Separation of Law from general Education.

---

[1] See above, p. 116 n., and below, p. 208.

art of literary composition as well as the technical art of the Notary.　Even the notes of the ‘Glossators’ who followed Irnerius still retained something of the grammatical or literary character which marked the expositions of the Founder of their School.　But in the main it is true that from the time of Irnerius Law ceases to be a branch of Rhetoric and therefore an element in a liberal education; it becomes a purely professional study for a special class of professional students.

A new
class of
Students.
　(5) One consequence of this change—though we have little direct evidence on the subject—was no doubt the growth of a class of students older and more independent than the students of the earlier Middle Age.　In this fact—when taken in connexion with the lay character and higher social position already characteristic of the Italian student—we may trace the germ of that most characteristic institution of Bologna, the Student-University.　It was from the age of Irnerius, or at least very early in the century ushered in by his teaching, that men of mature age—men of good birth and good position—beneficed and dignified ecclesiastics [1] or sons of nobles—flocked from the remotest parts of Europe to the lecture-rooms of Bologna.　Con-

---

[1] See for instance the *Acta Nationis Germanicæ*, where on an average about half the students matriculated are beneficed ecclesiastics, the great majority of them being Dignitaries or Canons.　It must, however, be remembered that by Canon Law a boy of fourteen might be a Canon of a Cathedral Church.　Exceptional instances are mentioned of very young Bolognese students, such as Baldus who held a *repetitio* at 15 (Savigny, cap. lv. § 66): parallels to which might be found in the Oxford of the last generation.　Phillpotts, afterwards Bishop of Exeter, entered as a Scholar of Corpus at 13, and Bethell (afterwards Lord Westbury) at Wadham at 14 in spite of the Warden's objection that they ‘did not receive children.’　The Statutes of Florence exclude from the right of voting students under 18.　On the whole it appears that a majority of law-students in Italy were not younger than modern undergraduates, while the proportion of men considerably older was very much larger.　It is curious, however, that the minimum age for the Doctorate was lower than that at Paris.　The Paris M. A. was required to be 20 (see below, p. 453); while in Italy (though the Statutes are silent) Petrus Anchoranus (ap. Middendorp., *Acad. Celebr.* Col. Agrippinæ, 1602, p. 141) lays it down that a Doctor must be at least 17 and of legitimate birth.

nected with this change in the position of the Law-students was the rise of the Law-Doctor in Southern Europe to a position of marked superiority to that of all other Masters. Legal knowledge possessed then, as it still possesses, a political and commercial value to which no purely speculative knowledge can pretend. No teachers perhaps in the whole history of Education had hitherto occupied quite so high a position in public estimation as the early Doctors of Bologna ; their rise to this position marks an epoch not only in the evolution of the University system but in the development of the legal profession.

§ 2.　Gratian and the Canon Law.

Chap. IV,
§ 2.

On the Origines of the Canon Law I have consulted chiefly Maassen, *Geschichte der Quellen und der Literatur des canonischen Rechts*, T. I. Gratz, 1870; Schulte, *Geschichte d. Quellen u. Literatur des Canonischen Rechts*, Stuttgart, T. I. 1875, T. II. 1877, T. III. 1880; Friedberg, *Corpus Iuris Canonici*, Lipsiæ, P. I. 1878, P. II. 1881; Sarti, *De claris Archigymnasii Bononiensis Professoribus*, 1889, T. I. P. ii. p. 317 *sq.*

The forged Decretals.

THE movement which is associated with the name of Gratian played as large a part in the development of the University system as the Irnerian revival of the Civil Law, and was destined to exercise perhaps an even more powerful influence over the course of European affairs. Twice in the course of its onward march the Papal Absolutism received a powerful impulse from literature: first from the publication of the pseudo-Isidorian Decretals in the ninth century, and now again in the middle of the twelfth from the publication of the *Decretum* of Gratian. By this comparison it is not intended to place the compiler of the *Decretum* on the moral level of the Isidorian forger. Though incorporating the pseudo-Isidorian and many other spurious documents, the *Decretum* was a perfectly *bona fide* compilation. From a very early period attempts had been made to codify the mass of Conciliar Canons, Papal rescripts, patristic *dicta*, and enactments of Christian Emperors, from which the Law of the Church had to be gleaned [1]. And in the eleventh and twelfth centuries the improved method and completeness of these compilations had fully kept pace with the advance of secular Jurisprudence. Among the more important predecessors of Gratian's work

Gradual Codification of the Canon Law

---

[1] An account of those which survive is given by Savigny (cap. xv. § 100 *sq.*); Schulte, vol. I. p. 29 *sq.*; Friedberg, I. p. xlii. *sq.* The earlier compilations consist simply of extracts from Canons or Rescripts arranged in chronological order: but as early as the ninth century they begin to be arranged under the order of subjects, and these show the influence of the Civil Law in their arrangement, and also contain numerous extracts from the Institutes, &c. Cf. Maassen, p. 798 *sq.*

may be mentioned the *Decretum* of Burchard of Worms (1012–1023), the *Collectio Canonum* of Anselm of Lucca († 1086), and the work bearing the same title by Cardinal Deusdedit (1086–1087)[1]. But the most complete of all these earlier Collections were the two compilations, known respectively as the *Panormia* and the *Decretum,* ascribed to Ivo, a pupil of Lanfranc at Bec and afterwards Bishop of Chartres[2] (1115), a city famous for its school of classical literature almost before the dawn of Parisian Science. In fact, the *Decretum* of Gratian, which by its superior completeness and arrangement rapidly supplanted all rivals, is little more than a re-editing of the materials collected by a succession of Canonists.

The *Decretum* is one of those great text-books which, appearing just at the right time and in the right place, take the world by storm. For in form it must be remembered that the *Decretum* is a text-book and not a code. Its title is a *Concordantia discordantium Canonum.* While its arrangement is more distinctly juridical than the half-theological, half-legal compilations which had preceded it, its method (unlike theirs) is distinctly Scholastic: and so far it may be considered as an attempt to do for Canon Law what Peter the Lombard did a little later[3] for Theology proper by the publication of the Sentences. Both works are only fresh applications of the method inaugurated by Abelard. The mighty influence of the *Sic et Non* is as palpable in the *Decretum* as in the Sentences. Gratian's method is to present the reader with all the authorities alleged on both

The *Decretum* of Gratian.

Its scholastic method.

---

[1] The two earliest collections of importance are (1) an anonymous *Collectio Anselmo dedicata* (883–897) and (2) the *libri duo de synodalibus causis et disciplinis ecclesiasticis* (c. 906) by Regino, Abbot of Prüm. Friedberg, I. cc. xlii, xliii.

[2] The *Panormia* has been edited: (1) Basil. 1499, 4to. (2) Lovan. 1557, 8vo. (3) Lovan. 1561. fol. The *Decretum Ivonis* was printed at Louvain in 1561 and is included in Ivo's *Œuvres complètes,* Paris, 1647. Both are reprinted by Migne, tom. 161. The *Panormia* is unquestionably the work of Ivo; of the *Decretum* the authorship is more doubtful. Sarti, I. P. ii. p. 318.

[3] So Friedberg (I. p. lxxiv), though Schulte makes Gratian use the Sentences. Denifle dates the Lombard's work 1145–1150 (*Archiv,* I. p. 611).

sides of every disputed question in Ecclesiastical Law. The most exaggerated statements of views the most opposed to those of the compiler are produced with all the freedom and ostensible impartiality employed by Scholastic Theologians in stating the arguments of the *advocatus diaboli*. Citations from Laws or writers whose authority the compiler would have disputed are given no less than rulings of the most unquestionable validity: it is even maintained that Gratian did not feel bound to exclude documents which he knew to be forged; his object being simply to present the reader with the evidence actually alleged by the conflicting parties. The compiler's object is to extract from the conflict of opinions the doctrine which from its superior authority, its more recent date, or its intrinsic reasonableness, may be taken to be the ascertained Law of the Church. Sometimes the writer's opinion is indicated in express words at the beginning or end of the citations, at others (when the case is clear) the authorities are left to speak for themselves[1].

A Text-book, not a Code.
Almost from its first publication the *Decretum* sprang into the position of a recognised text-book both in the Schools and in the Ecclesiastical Courts. But a text-book the *Decretum* always remained. The authority due to the opinion of Gratian himself is the authority which in our own Courts is ascribed to Bracton or Coke: his own comments—the *context* as they are technically called—are appealed to in the Ecclesiastical Courts, either as a witness to the Common Law or traditional practice of the Church or as the opinion of an eminent Jurist, not as itself a binding authority. The several Canons or other extracts which form the substance of the book derive no authority from their insertion in the *Decretum* or their adoption by its compiler that they would not have possessed independently of such insertion

---

[1] The *Decretum* is divided into two parts. In the first the main outlines of the Law are collected. The second is occupied with the discussion of *causæ* or imaginary cases, each of which gives rise to a number of *quæstiones* which are discussed in a thoroughly Scholastic manner.

or adoption. Nevertheless it must be remembered that the authority of a text-book was in the Middle Ages something of which we have very little conception. To the medieval Doctor the *littera scripta* was an end of all strife not only on matters of faith but on matters of Science or speculation. The authority of Aristotle in Philosophy and of Hippocrates in Medicine was not less than that of S. Paul or S. Augustine in matters of Theology. In a world habituated to this reliance on authority, it is obvious what an accretion of strength was brought to the cause which its compiler represented by the appearance and universal reception of such a text-book on what had hitherto been the chaotic and ill-defined field of Ecclesiastical Law. That cause was, it need hardly be said, the cause of Papalism against Imperialism, and what in that age was practically the same thing (at least in Italy), the cause of ecclesiastical immunity against civil authority. Wherever Canon Law was studied at all, it had henceforth to be studied in a work which placed the decrees of the Roman Pontiffs practically on a level in point of authority with the Canons of General Councils or the consensus of the most venerable Fathers. Individual Doctors might differ from the views of Gratian, particular States or even particular Churches might refuse to accord to the decrees of the Roman Pontiff the reception which was given to them in the Courts of Rome or the Schools of Bologna, but nevertheless the eventual triumph of the *Decretum* is a monument of the victory, at least within the bosom of the Church, of the ideas for which Hildebrand contended against the Emperor Henry IV and S. Thomas against our own Henry II. The ideas of national independence and Royal prerogative such as had animated so many of the English Bishops in their opposition to Anselm and Becket, disappeared from the minds of a generation of churchmen whose education had been based upon the *Decretum* of Gratian.

Of Gratian himself and his life almost nothing is known. Life of Gratian. He was a monk in the Camaldunensian Monastery of

S. Felix in Bologna[1]. Lest mistaken inferences should be drawn from this fact, it may be added that there is not the slightest trace of any School of Theology or of Canon Law in connexion with that or any other Monastery at Bologna[2]. Although commonly styled Magister, Gratian was not, so far as is known, a teacher at all, but a solitary penman. It is natural to conjecture that he may have been among the pupils of Irnerius, but

Date of
Decretum.
of this we know nothing. The *Decretum* is traditionally stated to have been published in the year 1151, but from examination of other works which appeared before that date, it seems to be generally agreed that the *Decretum* was completed at least as early as 1142[3].

Oppor-
tuneness of
its appear-
ance,
We have said that the *Decretum* owed no small part of its success to its appearance at the right time and in the right place. In point of time it came about twenty years after the settlement of the long feud between the Papacy and the Empire in the matter of Investitures by the Concordat of Worms in 1122. It was this conflict—a conflict of antagonistic ideals of human society no less than of opposing armies—which gave so great an impetus, which imparted such intense interest and actuality, to the legal and canonical studies of the Irnerian epoch. The outcome of that conflict was—for the present at least—a modified victory to the Church party. In theory, though not always in practice, the principle of the Concordat of Worms remained the accepted principle as to the relations between Church and State on this fundamental point throughout the Middle Ages. Thanks to Gratian's

---

[1] Sarti, I. P. i. p. 331. There are some traces of an earlier residence at Classe (Ravenna), *Ib.* 332. The Canonist Huguccio, the Master of Innocent III, was also a monk of S. Felix, according to Sarti (I. i. p. 372), but his evidence does not seem to prove the statement.

[2] How far the Schools of Canon Law, before their definitive differentiation from Theology, were connected with the Cathedral, it is more difficult to say. Bishop Lambert in 1065 gives an endowment to the Church in which occur the words ' Idcirco nostros canonicos in studiis intentos esse decrevimus.' Doc. ap. Sarti, T. I. pt. i. p. 6.

[3] Schulte, I. p. 48. Cassani (p. 192) says before 1141. The traditional 1151 rests upon the authority of a gloss. Sarti, I. P. ii. p. 336.

method of antagonistic citation, the whole history of the controversy, as well as its eventual settlement, could be studied by the medieval Churchman in a single work. To prove that the *Decretum* appeared at the right place, it is only necessary to say that it appeared at Bologna. Bologna was the centre of the Investiture controversy in so far as it represents an intellectual and not a merely physical antagonism. It was in the Bologna Jurists that both parties found their intellectual champions. Irnerius' application to the Civil Law seems to have been partially inspired by the need which the Countess Matilda experienced of learned defenders for the cause of the Church and of testamentary freedom : afterwards Irnerius and other Bologna Jurists are found playing a leading part on the Imperialist side. At the Diet of Worms the solution ultimately arrived at was chiefly the work of Lambert of Fagnano, citizen and Archdeacon of Bologna, afterwards Pope under the title of Honorius II [1]. Another great champion of the Church's cause was teaching Theology—in which Canon Law was then included—in the Schools of Bologna while Gratian was working in defence of the same cause in his laborious cloister, Roland Bandinelli, afterwards Pope Alexander III, whose *Summa* of Canon Law still survives [2]. Little as we know of the Bologna Schools of this epoch, there can be no doubt that these momentous questions of Constitutional Law in Church and State did much, both by the intellectual stimulus which they supplied and by the practical demand for trained lawyers which they created, to raise the Law-schools of Bologna to their proud pre-eminence. It is easy to understand how welcome such a composition as the *Decretum* would be to the defenders of the Papal cause ; and, once accepted as the recognized text-book by Bologna, the prestige of the School secured the ecumenical reception of Gratian's work.

[1] The importance of Lambert in this controversy is pointed out by Cassani, p. 41 *sq.*: cf. Sarti, I. ii. pp. 636-7.

Lucius II was also a Bolognese.

[2] Edited by Thaner, *Die Summa Magistri Rolandi*, Innsbruck, 1874.

CHAP. IV,
§ 2.

Relation of
Canon to
Civil Law.

(1) The
Civil a
source of
the Canon
Law.

The connexion of the Canon with the Civil Law is almost too vast a question to be touched upon here: but a few words as to the relation between the movement represented by Irnerius and the movement represented by Gratian are imperatively called for, to explain the position which these studies occupied in relation to each other and in relation to other University Faculties at Bologna and elsewhere. The connexion between the formation of the Corpus Juris Canonici and the old Imperial Jurisprudence of Rome may be regarded from three main points of view. In the first place the Civil Law may be regarded as one of the actual sources of the Canon Law. The Civil Law of Rome had entered into the composition of the law of the Christian Church at every stage of its formation. Its subtle and unrecognized influence upon the forms, institutions and organization of the Christian Church—nay, in the West, even upon the very content of her Theology—dates from the earliest days of Gentile Christianity. Every growth of systematic Theology—at least in the Latin half of Christendom—deepened its influence. Then, in proportion as ecclesiastical bodies acquired property and became involved in complicated secular relations with one another and with non-ecclesiastical property-owners, a knowledge of Law became increasingly necessary to ecclesiastical persons. The conversion of Constantine imparted of course an immense impetus to this tendency[1]. The laws of the Christian Emperors became laws at once of the Church and of the State; the sanction of Christian Emperors gave the force of coercive jurisdiction to the rules of the Christian Society: the increasingly legal character of the Church's internal discipline tended to introduce the forms and procedure of the secular tribunals into the administration of the Christian Society and even into the relations of the individual conscience towards God. The extension of ecclesiastical jurisdiction to large classes of civil cases tended in the same direction. The barbarian conquests

---

[1] 'Der Begriff eines Kirchenrechts entstand in dem Momente, wo kirch-liche Normen staatliche Anerken-nung fanden.' Schulte, I. p. 32.

promoted still further the fusion of Law and Theology. In an ignorant age the Bishops and clergy became, if not the sole, certainly the most learned, depositaries of Roman Jurisprudence. On the principle of personal Law recognized by the barbarian rulers, the clergy in Italy were as Roman citizens entitled to claim the privilege of trial by Roman Law; and, throughout the Middle Ages, the Roman Law was recognized as more or less applicable to the transactions and property of ecclesiastics and ecclesiastical corporations in proportion as the immunity of ecclesiastics from the jurisdiction of the Civil Courts was recognized at all[1]. The combined result of all these causes was that even before the appearance of the *Decretum*, the Roman Law, whether by actual embodiment in Canons or by practical recognition, already governed the forms and procedure of the ecclesiastical Courts and supplied the principles of action wherever property or civil rights were concerned. In fact it may broadly be asserted that everything in the Canon Law was Roman which was not of directly Christian or of Jewish origin.

From another point of view the Canon Law, as embodied in the *Decretum* of Gratian, may be looked upon as an imitation of the Civil Law. It was the systematic study of the compilations of Justinian in the Schools of Bologna which inspired the Curialist monk with the ambition to create for the Church a code no less complete, no less imposing, and no less scientific than the code of the State: and this object could only be effected by means of a still further infusion of Roman Law into the disciplinary system of the Western Church. Every fresh step in the development of the Canon Law after Gratian brought with it a still further infiltration of legal ideas, so that ere long a study of the Civil Law became an indispensable preliminary to the education of the Canonist, who became in conse- *(2) The Canon Law an imitation of the Civil.*

[1] By Savigny (cap. iii. § 40; and cap. xv. § 95) these qualifications are omitted. If, as seems to be the case, Savigny refers to the 'Germanic States' in the pre-Irnerian period, England at all events must be excepted; cf. Brunner, *Deutsche Rechtsgesch.*, Leipzig, 1887, I. p. 269.

CHAP. IV, quence less and less of a Theologian, and more and more
§ 2. of a lawyer.

(3) The   From a third point of view the *Decretum* may be said
Canon Law
as a reac- to represent a reaction against the ideas associated with
tion against the Civil Law. The influence of the revived study of the
the Civil.
Imperial Codes in promoting the growth of Imperialist
ideas in Italy may no doubt be exaggerated: but there
can be no question about the reality of that influence,
at least in the eleventh and twelfth centuries: we have
already noticed the part played both by the Ravennese
and the Bolognese Doctors in opposition to the claims
of the Papacy. The advantage which the Empire derived
from its possession of a venerable system of Law whose
continuity was everywhere more or less completely admitted and in which the Emperor was recognized as the
fountain-head of all authority, suggested to the partisans
of the Papacy the idea of setting up an opposing system
of ecclesiastical polity in which the Pope should take
the place accorded by the Civil Code to the Holy
Roman Emperor. By the labours of successive compilers
culminating in the final work of Gratian, the Canon Law
was for the first time erected into a system distinct from
Theology on the one hand and from the Civil Law on
the other.

Differentia-   The importance of this change in the development of
tion of
Canon   the University system at Bologna needs no comment.
Law from   We have seen how Irnerius marks an epoch in the history
Theology.
of education by the differentiation which he effected between the study of Law and the study of the Liberal
Arts. With the name of Gratian must in like manner
be associated the differentiation of Canon Law from general Theology, of which it had been hitherto but an ill-
defined department. There is abundant evidence that in
the time of Gratian the study of Theology was carried on
with as much vigour and in the same spirit at Bologna
as at Paris. The enemies of Abelard complained bitterly
that Abelard's books had flown across the Alps. The
earliest Bologna Canonists were, as has been made more

than ever evident by recent researches of Father Denifle, Theologians as well. Rolandus, Omnibonus, and Gandulph composed books of Theological Sentences [1], as well as books on Canon Law: and the two last were, as Theologians, avowed disciples of Abelard. Even Gratian himself (as we have seen) owed his method to the Abelardian influence. The Civil Law was hardly regarded as a proper study for ecclesiastical persons [2]. But after the time of Gratian all this was changed. The study of the *Decretum* called into existence a class of teachers and students distinct alike from the Theologians on the one hand and from the Civilians on the other, but ultimately in much closer relation with the latter than with the former [3]. In the middle of the twelfth century the study of Theology was (it would seem) more or less closely connected with the Cathedral. But by the following century a College of Doctors in Decrees has been developed side by side with the College of Civil Law, and no less independent of the Cathedral and the Bishop. The Cathedral chair of Theology no doubt remained, but from this period the study of Theology proper ceased to have any special importance at Bologna. In the thirteenth century the theological instruction was here practically confined to the Schools of the Mendicant Friars and had no organic connexion with the Universities

---

[1] All three collections exist in MSS. discovered or first described by Denifle. See his interesting Articles, in which ample extracts are given: *Archiv*, I. pp. 402 *sq*., 584 *sq. Die Sentenzen Rolands* are now edited by Gietl (Freiburg im Breisgau, 1892).

[2] See Ep. VIII of Petrus Blesensis (Migne, T. 207. c. 22) 'ad quemdam Priorem,' apologizing because in an address to his convent 'quaedam interserui, quae potius philosophum et ethnicum, sicut asseris, sapiebant, quam Christianae fidei professorem.' The same writer, who had studied the Civil Law of Bologna, tries to defend himself by showing that 'Je-

remias propheta quasi in jure civili fuerit eruditus.' Yet he confesses that 'res plena discriminis est in clericis usus legum.' (Ep. xxvi, *ib.* c. 91). As to the later prohibition of the study to *Priests*, beneficed clergy, and monks, see Appendix xi. It was rendered entirely inoperative by wholesale dispensations.

[3] It was only gradually that the Canon and Civil Law came to be studied by the same persons. Pascipoverus (fl. *circa* 1240-1250) is said to have been the first 'Utriusque juris professor': he wrote a 'Concordia juris canonici cum civili.' Sarti, I. pt. i. p. 173.

or Doctoral Colleges. Even the erection of a theological Faculty at a later date, of which I shall speak hereafter, made practically little change in the academical system. The intellectual movement which culminated in the rise of the Bologna School of Law was felt as powerfully by the Church as by the laity. Indeed, even in Italy, there were perhaps nearly as many clerks as laymen studying in the Universities: but after the age of Gratian the studies even of ecclesiastics took a predominantly legal turn; speculative Theology was abandoned in favour of the Canon and even the Civil Law: while the estrangement of the Canon Law from Theology kept pace with the increasing closeness of its union with the Faculty of Civil Law[1].

The Canon Law and the 'lay spirit' of Bologna. The contrast between the lay, democratic, Student-Universities of Italy and the hierarchically governed Church-schools of Paris and Oxford has been dwelt upon often enough. At times, however, a greater importance is given to the contrast than is warranted by the facts of the case. From a merely constitutional point of view, nothing can be more important than a correct apprehension of this fundamental distinction. But at times this constitutional difference is supposed to be a comprehensive key to the spirit of the respective Universities. The spirit of Bologna is represented as free, enlightened, anti-Papal, anti-clerical, revolutionary. Paris is regarded as the home of narrow bigotry, theological conservatism, and ecclesiastical despotism. Such a representation arises from the importation of modern ideas into a period in which they were quite unknown. Bologna owed its fame as much to the Canon Law as to the Civil Law: and that School of Canon Law originated, as we have seen, in the triumph of all that is represented by the name of Hildebrand. Even in the Imperialist Civilian of Bologna there was hardly anything in common with the modern anti-clerical. Of the spirit of intellectual revolt, of freedom of thought

---

[1] Ægidius Fuscararius (†1289) is said to have been the first layman who taught Canon Law. Sarti, I. ii. p. 447.

and audacity of speculation, there was far more in the earlier days of Paris than there ever was at Bologna. If we speak of the ' lay spirit ' of Bologna in contrast with the clerical spirit of Paris, we shall be nearer the mark, but it must be distinctly understood that the lay spirit was not necessarily anti-clerical or irreligious, and that the clerical spirit of the North was by no means always ultra-orthodox or submissive, still less Ultramontane. The Bologna Civilian is a representative of the lay spirit if by that is meant that his mind was entirely absorbed in the practical affairs of life to the exclusion of speculative questions ; and hardly less might be said with truth of the Bologna Canonist. In the eleventh and twelfth centuries, Religion exercised at least as powerful an influence upon human affairs in Italy as it did in the North of Europe : but here even religious questions assumed a political shape. Bologna was absorbed with the questions about Investiture, about the relations of Papacy and Empire, Church and State, Feudalism and civic liberty, while the schools of France were distracted by questions about the Unity of Intellect, about Transubstantiation, about the reality of Universals.

The publication of the *Decretum* was merely the basis of a vast superstructure. Its importance is, in fact, largely due to its having suggested to the Papacy a new method of imposing its will upon Christendom. In 1234 a compilation of five books of Decretals, selected for the most part from the previous Decretals or rescripts of himself and his predecessors[1], was published by Gregory IX and despatched to the Universities of Paris and Bologna with the command that they should be taught in the Schools[2]. In 1298 there followed the *Liber Sextus* of Boniface VIII. The *Corpus Juris Canonici* was completed by the addition

The Decretals of Gregory IX.

The Liber Sextus.

---

[1] Though partly (like the *Decretum*) derived from earlier materials— Canons, Fathers, Imperial Laws, and Frankish Capitularies. Friedberg, II. cc. xi–xviii.

[2] Friedberg, II. cc. x. 2. The Code was the work of the Papal Penitentiary Raymund de Peñaforte, and was really made from a number of previous collections.

CHAP. IV,
§ 2.

The Extra-
vagants.

of the *Clementines* prepared by Clement V and published by his successor John XXII in 1317[1], and an unofficial collection of later Decrees extending down to the time of Sixtus IV and known as the *Extravagants*[2]. The Decretals of course occupy a different position in point of authority from the *Decretum*. The *Decretum* was a text-book: the Decretals were a code. But though the Decretals carried with them the full weight of the Papal authority, the extent to which they were practically enforced in the ecclesiastical Courts depended upon the degree of recognition accorded to them by the Synods and Prelates, and still more by the secular Princes, of various nations. Even the Decretals had to be modified in their practical operation by the local custom of the more independent National Churches and by their varying relations to the temporal power[3], while in the Clementines and the Extravagants the exaltation of Papal and ecclesiastical authority was carried to such a pitch that they conflicted with the secular laws of every country in Europe.

The Canon
Law in
England.

It is, indeed, sometimes much too broadly asserted that the Roman Canon Law was only current in England in so far as it was freely received by the Church of England and embodied in her provincial Constitutions[4]. Though there

---

[1] There had been, however, a previous publication by Clement himself, but whether they were transmitted to the Universities before Clement's death in 1314, and how far they were altered afterwards, is disputed. See Ehrle in *Archiv*, IV. p. 361; Friedberg, II. cc. lvii–lxii; Denifle and Chatelain, *Chartularium Univ. Paris*. T. II. No. 708 *et not.*, No. 754.

[2] These are divided into (1) the *Decretales Johannis XXI* (XXII), made soon after the publication of the Clementines, and (2) five books of *Extravagantes communes*. Their arrangement in the form in which they were generally current and were included in the official ' Roman edition' of Gregory XIII, is due

to Jean Chappuis. Friedberg, II. c. lxiv.

[3] The English Courts, for instance, resisted the Canon Law requiring disputes as to rights of Patronage to be decided solely by the Ecclesiastical Courts and the reservation of every Civil suit in which an Ecclesiastic was involved to the Ecclesiastical Courts.

[4] The Bishop of Oxford, for instance, in his most interesting Lectures on the History of the Canon Law in England (Stubbs, *Lectures on Med. and Mod. Hist.* Oxford, 1886, p. 305) goes too far when he says that ' the great compilations are not received as having any authority in England.' Lyndwood's *Provinciale* is

were, no doubt, parts of it which remained practically inoperative, it is not disputed that, according to the law of the English Church (whatever the State might occasionally say to the contrary) an appeal lay from all inferior ecclesiastical tribunals to the Roman Court, where the cases were of course decided by the Canon Law; and the law of a Court of first instance cannot remain permanently and fundamentally different from the law of the appellate Tribunal by whose decision it is bound, even had the acknowledged jurisdiction of Rome been limited to the cognisance of Appeals, which was far from being the case[1]. It was the opposition of Kings and Parliaments and secular Courts rather than any claim to spiritual independence on the part of the Anglican Church herself that put obstacles in the way of the complete realization in England (as in most other countries) of the Curialist ideal.

But, whether recognized or not in the Courts, the whole of this marvellous jurisprudence of spiritual despotism was studied in the Faculties of Canon Law throughout Europe; and the Faculty of Canon Law was a Faculty which every University in Europe possessed. By means of the happy thought of the Bolognese Monk the Popes were enabled to convert the new-born Universities—the offspring of that intellectual new-birth of Europe which might have been so formidable an enemy to Papal pretensions—into so many engines for the propagation of Ultramontane ideas. Even in their earlier days the Universities often showed symptoms of

Influence of the Canon Law.

not (as even the Bishop seems to suggest) 'the authoritative Canon Law of the realm' (*ib.* p. 309), but simply what it professes to be, a codified and annotated edition of the Provincial Constitutions, i. e. of such parts of the Canon Law as were peculiar to the English Church. It would be impossible to decide the simplest cases by the *Provinciale* alone (the important subject *De Jure Patronatus* is disposed of in three titles); and Lyndwood's notes habitually cite all parts of the Canon Law (including the earlier Extravagants) and the continental Canonists as possessing as much authority in England as elsewhere, except where modified by the special custom or Canon of the English Church, such customs or Canons being usually due to lay pressure, e. g. a lay Court is allowed to decide a disputed title to Patronage.

[1] Professor Maitland refers me to Bracton, f. 412, where it is said that the Pope 'in spiritualibus super omnibus habeat ordinariam jurisdictionem.'

an anti-Papal spirit : at a later time they became the very
hot-beds of ecclesiastical revolt.   But it was never in the
ranks of the Canon Lawyers that the Papacy found its
most formidable opponents.   At all periods of the Middle
Age it was the Canonists who filled the most important
sees in Christendom : and herein lay one great cause of
the failure of all Academic attempts at Church Reform.
It was not so much the specific doctrines taught by the
Corpus Juris Canonici that favoured Papal usurpations
and ecclesiastical abuses of all kinds as the habit of mind
which its study created.   In all ages the lawyers, invalu-
able as a conservative force, have been as a body greater
enemies of Reform than the Priests.   The worst corruption
of the Middle Age lay in the transformation of the sacerdotal hierarchy into a hierarchy of lawyers.

*Its effects
on secular
Law.*
And yet there is another side to the question.   It may
not be assumed that if the clergy of the later Middle Age
had not become lawyers, they would have been devout
Theologians or earnest Pastors.   From the point of view of
the Church no doubt the influence of the Canon Law stands
almost wholly condemned to the modern mind : nor does
the superiority of this ecclesiastical jurisprudence to that
administered by the Civil tribunals (wherever the Roman
Law was not in force), or its consequent extension to
large departments of secular life, altogether destroy the
impression that the development of the Canon Law was
a retrograde movement—the most conspicuous triumph of
that ecclesiastical reaction which to so large an extent
managed to enlist the newly-born intellectual forces of the
twelfth century in its service.   It is only when we turn to the
indirect influence of the Canon Law upon the practice and
procedure of the secular Courts, and even upon the substance
of the secular Law in the less romanized parts of Europe,
that we must recognize in the Canon Law one of the great
civilizing and humanizing influences of the later Middle
Ages.   It was chiefly through the Canon Law that the
Civil Law transformed the jurisprudence of nearly the
whole of continental Europe.   Even so, its record is not

wholly favourable: some growth of despotic power in King and Lord, some decay of rude Teutonic liberty, the historian — especially the German historian — has been wont to trace to the influence of Roman Law, steadily increased by the growth of Universities, especially during the fourteenth and fifteenth centuries. We have to take ourselves back to a state of society in which a judicial trial was a tournament and the ordeal an approved substitute for evidence, to realize what civilization owes to the Canon Law and the Canonists with their elaborate system of written Law, their judicial evidence, and their written procedure. Even the very chicanery of the ecclesiastical Courts assisted the transfer of administration and judicature from the uneducated soldier to the highly educated man of peace. From this point of view the development of the Canon Law and its diffusion throughout Europe represent a very important stage in the triumph of mind over brute force.

So far I have spoken of Irnerius, of Gratian, and the School of Bologna ; only by anticipation has there been any reference to the University the foundation of which is traditionally ascribed to Irnerius. This was perhaps the best way of emphasizing the fact that in the days of Irnerius no such thing as a University existed at all. When the University arose, and what in its origin the University was, must be investigated in the next section.

§ 3. The Origines of the Jurist Universities.

The Antiquarian bias.

THE passion for ascribing an immemorial antiquity to the place of one's education, which has hardly yet been killed by the progress of historical criticism, is a passion of very early growth in the history of the human mind. In the Middle Ages, indeed, men found it difficult to believe that an institution which had existed since a time 'whereof the memory of man goeth not to the contrary,' had not existed from the remotest antiquity. When once the Universities had sprung up it was found impossible to picture to the historical imagination a state of things in which there were no Universities. Another inveterate prejudice of the human mind is the disposition to ascribe the origination of a great institution to a great man. Greek cities ascribed their origin to an eponymous hero; and, if tradition did not supply them with a name for him, they invented one. The medieval scholar, accustomed by the later practice to associate the origin of a University with a Charter of Foundation, was driven to postulate such a foundation where history recorded it not, and if the Charter was not to hand, he forged one.

The Theodosian legend.

By the thirteenth century, and probably early in that century [1], this familiar logical process had resulted in

[1] The deeds are printed—one by Ughelli, *Italia Sacra* (1717), II. p. 9, the other by Muratori, *Ant.* III. c. 21. In these documents the authority of the Archdeacon over the Inceptions, first entrusted to that official in 1219 (see below, p. 223), is enforced as though it were still by no means beyond the reach of attack. The growth of this monstrous legend is elaborately traced by Chiapelli (cap.

1). The ἀπαρχή of the Theodosian legend seems to be an older tradition as to the foundation of the *City* by Theodosius I or Theodosius II. In 1306 the Papal Legate Ancaldo was petitioned to confirm the Theodosian privilege: the Legate replied that he must first see the Privilege. Ghirardacci, I. p. 525. The forgeries were then already in existence.

a legend which attributed the foundation of the University of Bologna to Theodosius II and in the concoction of a Charter of Foundation by that monarch bearing date 433 A.D. Unfortunately for the success of this patriotic effort, the zeal of the forgers somewhat overshot the mark. Two distinct Charters were produced, both purporting to be issued by the same Emperor in the same year. Possibly in consequence of this contretemps, the Theodosian legend has never attained the same popularity or acceptance as the legends which make Charles the Great the Founder of Paris and Alfred the Founder of Oxford, the last of which still maintains a kind of underground existence in University Calendars, in second-rate Guide-books, and in popular Histories of England. The early date of the legend is worth noticing as an illustration of the extremely small value which ought to be attached to scholastic traditions of this type even when they are not capable of the same definite historical confutation which is possible in this case. A further discussion of this and other inconsistent legends or traditions as to the origin of the University would be neither interesting nor instructive. All that is really known as to the origin of the School has been placed before the reader in a preceding section. So far there has been not the faintest trace of any even rudimentary organization similar to that of the later University. Irnerius and his contemporaries, so far as we know, were private and unauthorized teachers; neither they nor their scholars belonged to any institution or enjoyed any legal privilege whatever. The first legal Charter in which the School receives even an implicit recognition is a Charter of the Emperor Frederick Barbarossa, known as the Authentic *Habita* and issued in 1158 at the Diet of Roncaglia, in which the Doctors of Bologna played a very prominent part.

This Privilege has often been treated as a kind of Charter, if not as an actual 'foundation,' of the University of Bologna. But though there is no reason to doubt that this legislation was primarily intended for the benefit of the increasingly numerous body of law-students at Bologna, that city is not expressly mentioned in its provisions, and it is perfectly arbitrary to limit its actual scope to the Schools of that place[1]. In any case this document does not recognize the existence of a University whether of Masters or of Students at Bologna or anywhere else. It is a general privilege conferred on the student-class throughout the Lombard Kingdom. This Charter does, however, constitute an important indication of the growing importance and the independent position of the Doctors of Law, and was no doubt procured by the interest of the Bologna Doctors. Its provisions were suggested by the older privilege conferred by Justinian upon the scholars of Berytus[2]. Besides taking the scholars under the especial protection of the Emperor, it provides that in any legal proceedings against a scholar, the defendant is to have the option of being cited before his own Master or before the Bishop[3]. Attempts were made at

[1] As is done by Savigny (cap. xxi. § 63). This limitation is criticised by Denifle (vol. I. p. 49 *sq.*), whose view I have adopted. He there examines a story embodied in a Latin poem (partly printed by Giesebrecht ap. *Sitzungsberichte d. bayer. Akad. d. Wiss.* Histor. Klasse, 1879, II. p. 285), according to which Frederick granted some such privilege to Bologna, on the petition of the Scholars in 1155. He comes to the conclusion that the Charter meant is the Authentic *Habita* itself, some copies of which bear no date, and that the story grew out of the fact of Frederick's having been near Bologna in 1155. It is quite possible that the Privilege was asked for and perhaps granted in 1155, but formally promulgated at the Diet in 1158 (as is suggested by Kaufmann, *Gesch. d. Deutschen Universitäten*, I. p. 164). On the part played by these Bologna Doctors at Roncaglia, see below, p. 259.

[2] The enforcement of the Emperor's regulations is entrusted at Constantinople to the Prefect, at Berytus to the *Præses* of the province, the Bishop and the 'legum professores.'

[3] 'Coram Domino vel Magistro suo, vel ipsius civitatis Episcopo.'—There has been much needless discussion as to the meaning of ' Dominus,' but there can be no doubt that it is a synonym for 'Magister,' though Malagola (*Monografie*, p. 39) still appears to understand it of the Rector. The use of this title (which was affected only by the Law-professors) shows that the Law-students were primarily in view; though the term Magister would include the teachers of other Faculties. Justinian had entrusted a disciplinary jurisdiction over students and copyists at the Law-school of Berytus to the Professors in conjunction with the *Præses* of the province and the Bishop. But it appears doubtful whether this is extended to ordinary criminal and civil proceedings. See the *Proœmium* to the Digest.

times to extend the first of these provisions to the scholars in the other parts of Europe, and in the Italian Universities this pre-University Charter was usually recognized as the basis of all the special privileges conferred on particular Universities by the States in which they were situated. Whatever privileges were afterwards granted to the Universities, whatever jurisdiction was conferred on their Rectors, the jurisdiction of the Bishop and the Professors was usually, at least in theory, maintained. But after the rise of the Universities the scholar was not allowed by their Statutes to decline the jurisdiction of his own Rector. Hence the choice of tribunal practically passed to the plaintiff, and was lost by the defendant scholar[1]. The jurisdiction of the Professors was found difficult to enforce, and that of the Bishop remained only in the case of scholars who were also clerks.

While the Authentic in no way recognizes the corporate existence of a College or Guild of Doctors, it does indirectly make it probable that some such Society must have by this time sprung into existence[2]. In the days of Irnerius the teaching office could (so far as can be gathered) be assumed by any one who could get pupils : he required no license or permission from any authority whatever, ecclesiastical, civil, or academical. We can hardly, however, suppose that the Emperor would have conferred important judicial functions upon an independent body of self-constituted teachers like our modern 'Professors' of Music or of Dancing. It is therefore probable that in Italy as in France at least some recognized course of study was demanded by custom before the pupil could become a Master, and that he was required to obtain the approval of the existing body of Masters and

Indications of a Society of Masters.

---

[1] *Stat.* p. 12.

[2] I cannot understand the ground of Kaufmann's statement that at the time of the Authentic ' Es gab also damals wahrscheinlich schon landsmannschaftliche Verbindungen unter den Scholaren' (*Deutsch. Univ.* I. p. 166: cf. p. 184). These 'Verbindungen' he apparently regards as ' Anfänge von Korporationsbildung ' (I. p. 184). It is quite possible that the beginnings of informal Associations may be as early as 1158, but of this there is no evidence—least of all can it be inferred from the *Habita.*

to enter upon the teaching office by some public, definite ceremonial, such as the later *Conventus* or Inception. We may therefore consider it tolerably certain that at least the idea of a co-opting College or corporation of Doctors dates in some shadowy form from before the year 1158 ; although the Masters may not yet have proceeded to such definite manifestations of corporate existence as the making of written statutes, and the election of common officers. The Guild was already in existence, but was merely, so to speak, a customary Society, which existed in fact, though not on paper. Such an inference is strongly supported by the analogy of Paris, where we have positive evidence of the existence of a customary Guild of Masters, some ten or twenty years later, though it was not till fifty years after that that a single written Statute existed, and not till a still later period that the Guild was sufficiently organized to elect officers or use a common seal. At Bologna the first express evidence of the existence of such a Society of Masters comes in the year 1215, when we hear of Boncompagni's new book being read before the 'University of Professors of the Civil and Canon Law[1]': but the whole system of degrees which is known to have been fully established before 1219 implies the existence of such a Society in a rudimentary form at a much earlier date. Taking the degree of Doctor or Master in its earliest form meant simply the being admitted or made free of the Guild of Teachers by receiving from one of its members[2] the insignia of Mastership.

[1] The *Rhetorica Antiqua* of Boncompagni, who says : 'Recitatus equidem fuit hic liber, approbatus et coronatus lauro Bononiæ apud sanctum Johannem in monte in loco qui dicitur paradisus anno domini 1215 septimo Kal. April. coram universitate professorum iuris canonici et civilis et aliorum doctorum et scolarium multitudine numerosa.' Ap. Rockinger, *Sitzungsberichte der bay. Akad. zu München*, 1861, p. 135.

The same writer, however, says : 'Tunc amici ... ad Majorem Ecclesiam deverunt (*sic*). Et ita fuit Magistrorum et Scholarium Universitas congregata' (ap. Sarti, II. p. 32)— which might be held to indicate that some loose organization of *Masters and Scholars* preceded the formation of the Student-Universities. Cf. below, p. 214.

[2] It is probable that, originally, any Master might admit any other

In the account of Boncompagni's recitation, to which I have already alluded, the Professors of the Civil and Canon Law are described as forming a single Universitas [1]. What were the exact relations between the two classes at this time, we do not know ; eventually there were two wholly distinct Colleges—one of Canon and one of Civil Law, each with a Prior and other Officers, and a code of Statutes of its own. It is probable that the College of Canon Law was a later imitation of the Civilian organization. In most other Universities, however, the Doctors of Civil and Canon Law were united in the same College or Faculty, though the degrees were distinct.

Chap. IV,
§ 3.
Doctors of
Civil and
Canon Law
at first
united.

Two decades later than the Charter of Frederick I, we meet with another official recognition of the Scholars, though it does not distinctly imply the existence of any Academical organization. In 1189 a Bull of Clement III confirms an already existing legatine Ordinance forbidding Masters or scholars to offer to the landlord a higher rent for a house already inhabited by scholars [2]. At a very early date it became customary for the rents to be fixed by arbitrators or taxors, two of them appointed by the scholars, and two by the town. It is difficult to say whether the above-mentioned Bull implies the existence of this system [3], but we find a similar system established

person to the Mastership, but that this right was controlled by the customs of the Profession. It is possible that this state of things lasted longer in the Arts Schools than in the Schools of Law. Cf. the way in which Rolandinus speaks of his graduation in 1221 : 'apud ipsos Bononienses in scientia literali nutritus, in Anno Domini M CC XXI illic a Bonocompagno meo Domino, et Magistro, natione et eloquentia Florentino, licet indignus, recepi officium Magistratus.' *Lib. Chronicorum,* ap. Muratori SS. T. VIII. c. 314.

[1] It is not implied that the mere use of the term *Universitas* proves the existence of a formal Guild : the term *Universitas* might be used quite untechnically of any collection of persons : but the passage seems to imply that the Doctors of Law were a recognized class or official body.

[2] Savioli, II. ii. p. 160. So Decretal. Greg. IX. III. Tit. xviii. c. 1.

[3] It is ordered that 'a te frater episcope et tuo quolibet successore hoc singulis annis in communi audientia Magistrorum atque scholarium recitetur.' This implies that Congregations of some kind were customary, but it also shows a very different relation existing between the Masters and their Scholars from that which we find a century later.

CHAP. IV,
§ 3.

The Magis-
terial Guild
and the
'Conven-
tus.'

in the very infancy of other Universities and it obtained in some schools which never grew into Universities at all.

The University of Bologna has already been described as a University of students. And it is quite true that at Bologna it was the Guild or rather Guilds of students which eventually succeeded in getting into their own hands the real control of the Studium in most of those matters which were at Paris settled by the Masters alone. But it cannot be too clearly understood that the Doctors of Bologna, probably at as early a date as the Masters of Paris, formed a Guild or Guilds of their own, and that it was not till a later period than that with which we are now engaged that the control of strictly Academical matters passed to the Universities of students. It was a mere accident that the term University was appropriated by the Student-guild, while the Doctoral Guilds were known as Colleges. The students did no doubt at last succeed in reducing the Masters to an almost incredible servitude. But there remained one function and one only over which the Doctors to the last retained an exclusive control, and it is of the greatest importance that this should be clearly understood. Even the domineering Student-guilds of Bologna left to the Masters the indefeasible right which every professional Guild possessed of examining into the qualifications of candidates for admission to the Profession. The Doctors examined the Candidate, gave him license to 'incept' or give his public probationary discourse, after which, if this further test was satisfactorily passed, he was received into the Collegium of the Doctors of Civil or Canon Law, as the case might be, being presented by an existing member in the presence of the rest with the insignia of his office. Such in its essence was the idea of the 'Conventus,' 'Principium,' or 'Inceptio'—the simple institution which formed the keystone of the whole University constitution. Unless its nature and meaning are thoroughly understood, the whole organization of medieval education will remain an unintelligible enigma. Postponing to a later date a detailed explanation of this part of the

Academic polity, we must now proceed to trace the origines of the Student-Universities.

The Student-University which originated at Bologna forms a wholly new departure in the history of education; the institution is as distinct from anything which preceded it as it is unlike any of the modern institutions which have nevertheless been developed out of it. It is not, however, difficult to explain the genesis of the new creation, if we bear in mind the character of the environment wherein it grew up. We have already contrasted the state of Society in the Lombard towns with that which prevailed in the feudal Monarchies of Europe. We have seen that traditions of education, and of legal education, survived among the noble families of Italy at a time when the French or Norman nobles were inclined to look upon reading and writing as rather effeminate luxuries, fit only for plebeian clerks. It is probable, if we may draw an inference from the state of things which we find established at a later date, that the teaching of Irnerius attracted somewhat older men and men of much greater wealth and social position than the boys who attended the Arts Schools of Paris. Into the Bologna Lecture-rooms the idea of discipline never entered at all. The associations of the School and of the Cloister were alike absent. The Professor was not originally the officer of any public institution: he was simply a private-adventure Lecturer—like the Sophist of ancient Greece or the Rhetor of ancient Rome—whom a number of independent gentlemen of all ages between seventeen and forty had hired to instruct them. If many of the students were ecclesiastics, they were most of them already beneficed—many of them Archdeacons or dignitaries in Cathedral Churches[1]: and they owed no ecclesiastical obedience to their teachers. But even more important than the age and status of the

[1] The German students were probably more predominantly ecclesiastical than the Italian. In the earlier period laymen predominate even among the Germans, in the latter period ecclesiastics nearly all holding Canonries or other benefices. See the *Acta Nationis Germanicae*, passim.

Chap. IV,
§ 3.
‑‑
Fostered
by the poli-
tical and
social en-
vironment. students was the political condition of the city in which Irnerius and his successors taught. The conception of citizenship prevalent in the Italian Republics was much nearer to the old Greek conception than that which prevails in modern States. Citizenship, which is with us little more than an accident of domicile, was in ancient Athens or medieval Bologna an hereditary possession of priceless value. The citizens of one town had, in the absence of express agreement, no civil rights in another. There was one law for the citizen; another, and a much harsher one, for the alien[1]. Prolonged exile was a serious penalty, to which a body of young men of good position in their own cities, many of them old enough to be entering upon political life, would naturally submit with reluctance. The Student-Universities represent an attempt on the part of such men to create for themselves an artificial citizenship in place of the natural citizenship which they had temporarily renounced in the pursuit of knowledge or advancement; and the great importance of a Studium to the commercial welfare of the city in which it was situated may explain the ultimate willingness of the Municipalities—though the concession was not made without a struggle—to recognize these Student-communities.

---

[1] The Town-Statutes eventually provided 'quod scolares sint cives et tanquam cives ipsi habeantur, et pro civibus reputentur, donec scolares fuerint, et res ipsorum tanquam civium defendantur ... nec possint ipsi tanquam forenses nec eorum res detineri vel molestari occasione represalie concesse contra commune vel civitatem terre vel castri, vel banni dictis terris castris vel civitatibus dati, vel alicuius debiti pecuniarii.' *Stat.* p. 162. It is of course certain that no *political* rights whatever were conferred upon students: the provision that they should be treated as citizens was necessary to secure them the ordinary protection of the law. Scholars who had resided over ten years at Bologna were sometimes granted actual citizenship: but then they lost their rights in the University. Savigny, cap. xxi. § 69, *note*. That the grievances against which the foreign student wanted protection were not merely sentimental, we are reminded by the frequent occurrence of a privilege exempting scholars from torture except in the presence of and with the sanction of the Rectors. See e. g. *Stat. Fiorent.* ed. Gherardi, p. 109. So at Padua, *Stat. Artist.* f. xxxiii. b.

Two other circumstances serve to explain the patience with which Bologna and other towns after her submitted to the erection of an 'Imperium in Imperio' within their own walls, and to confer an extensive civil, and sometimes even criminal, jurisdiction upon the elected officers of a Student-club. The first is the prevalence of the conception of 'Personal Law.' For centuries Lombards and Romans had lived together under different codes of law and different magistrates. At an earlier date it had been quite common for even three or four men to live in the same town and yet to be in matters of private Law members of as many distinct states : and respect for these personal rights had not entirely died out in the thirteenth century[1]. It remained in all its fulness as regards the clergy. This conception made it seem the less unnatural that alien-students should live under the jurisdiction of their own Rectors, just as in Eastern countries where there is a mixture of races foreigners are freely permitted to live under the jurisdiction of their own Consuls or their own Bishops. And then there is a fact which is, indeed, the most important clue to the origin of Universities here and elsewhere. The University, whether of Masters or of Students, was only a particular kind of *Guild*[2]: the rise of the Universities is merely a wave of that great movement towards Association which began to sweep over the cities of Europe in the course of the eleventh century.

And the ruling ideas of the age made the Guild a closer and more powerful association in an Italian city than it could be in a modern state. In the first place, the Roman Law conferred a legal existence upon 'Collegia' or corporations of three persons or more, without any special authorisation of the state. In some of the Italian cities the Guelph and Ghibelin party-clubs (at Bologna known

[1] Savigny, cap. iii, § 30 *sq.*

[2] As late as the middle of the fourteenth century this was still so fully realized in the Italian cities that we find at Florence the Statutes of the *Universitas Scholarium* subjected to the approval of the 'Approbatores Statutorum Artium (trades or crafts) comunis Florentie.' *Stat. Fiorent.* p. 135.

as Lambertazzi and Geremei), overtly aiming at violent changes in the government of the city, were as much recognized legal corporations as the Guilds of merchants or craftsmen[1]. Moreover, while the legal authority of modern Clubs and other Societies over their members is based for a most part upon a mere contract, in the Middle Ages it was based upon oath. And in the Middle Ages an oath meant a great deal more than it does in modern communities. Perjury was a mortal sin : and the oaths of obedience consequently enabled the Guilds to subject disobedient members not only to public 'infamy' and to spiritual penalties at the hands of their confessors but even to proceedings *in salutem animæ* in the Ecclesiastical Courts[2]. The combined force of the social and the spiritual penalties thus wielded by the Guilds was so enormous

---

[1] Ghirardacci, P. I. p. 248.

[2] In the Italian Universities, every offence prohibited by the Statutes is forbidden 'sub pœna periurii.' Thus at Bologna, even absence from Congregation involved perjury unless the offender paid a price of five *solidi* within eight days (*Stat.* p. 129). So at Paris the Rector, 'si dicti Scholares ipsas bursas solvere noluerint, et rebelles extiterint, contra ipsos procedere tenebitur tanquam perjuros et infames (Bulæus, IV. 232). Whether this implied the promotion of an ecclesiastical suit or (as seems probable) simply a public notification of the fact, but such proceedings would have been quite in accordance with Canon Law. The German Nation at Bologna provides that the 'cohercio' of the Bishop of Bologna or his Vicar shall be brought to bear upon 'contradictores,' but with the explanation 'quorum iurisdictioni circa execucionem conservacionis predictorum ordinamentorum ipsa nacio specialiter se subiecit.' *Acta Nat. Germ.* p. 350. Here the right to promote a suit rests upon consent ; but in Gloria, *Mon. della Univ. di*
Padova (1318-1405) II. pp. 223-227, are documents which seem to relate to suits before the Bishop concerning disputes in the College of Arts where the jurisdiction is founded entirely upon the oaths taken by its members. So in London we find that the Bishop's Court 'entertained suits exactly analogous to those of the trades unions at the present day, turning on the question how far it is a breach of oath for the sworn member of the Guild to impart the arts and mysteries of his Guild to outsiders' (Stubbs, *Lectures on Medieval and Modern History,* Oxford, 1886, p. 316). It may be observed that the dependence of University authority upon an oath secured for the Papacy an especial jurisdiction over them, even where (as in Italy) they were not wholly composed of ecclesiastics. As to the ecclesiastical jurisdiction in matters of oath or contract, cf. Fournier, *Les Officialités au Moyen Âge.* Paris, 1880, p. 86 ; and, for its importance in the development of English Equity, Fry, *Specific Performance of Contracts,* London, 1892, p. 8 *sq.*

that in the Italian cities they often became more powerful than the State. At Bologna the Revolution of 1228 gave them an important constitutional position ; their magistrates were almost equal in authority to the magistrates of the Republic and almost independent of their control[1]. In such a state of Society, membership of a Guild was essential to personal security. If the students had not formed themselves into Guilds, if they had not insisted upon legal recognition and privilege for their officers, the position of scholars residing in a foreign city would have been well-nigh intolerable[2].

To the Professors and Students who were citizens of Bologna these considerations of course did not apply. The State was not disposed to abandon any part of its jurisdiction over its own citizens, nor the Universities to receive as citizens of the Academic Commonwealth students who were unable to give it an undivided allegiance. Bolognese students retained their natural citizenship: Bolognese Professors were accorded a high position in the constitution of the Republic[3]. Both alike were excluded from the scholastic Guilds.

Citizens excluded from the Universities.

Thus, by merely attending to the conditions or environment in which the Law-Universities grew up, the peculiar relations which subsisted in them between the students and the Professors, and again between the Bolognese students and those from a distance, receive adequate explanation. Even had we no knowledge of the actual history of the evolutionary process, it would be unnecessary to look upon this constitutional phenomenon, as it has too often been looked upon, with mere stupid astonishment, as a kind of historical *lusus naturæ*. Whatever surprise may be still felt at the appearance upon the page of

The Student-Universities can be explained.

---

[1] The most convenient account of the Bologna constitution is given by Savigny, cap. xx.

[2] M. Thurot well remarks that the University of Paris ' se constitua sous l'empire de cet esprit d'association qui produisait en même temps les villes Lombardes, les communes de France, et les corporations de métiers.' *De l'organisation de l'enseignement dans l'Un. de Paris*, p. 3.

[3] The Constitution of 1245 made them *ex officio* members of the *Credenza* or Council of 600. Savigny, *l.c.*

CHAP. IV,
§ 3.

History of an institution so startling to modern ideas as a Student-University will be removed by an examination of the actual facts, scanty as they are, which have come down to us with respect to the early history of the earliest Student-guilds of Bologna.

The *two* Law Universities.

From about the middle of the thirteenth century[1] the organization of Law-students at Bologna consisted of two closely allied but distinct *Universitates*—a *Universitas Citramontanorum* and a *Universitas Ultramontanorum*, each under a Rector of its own. We have no direct documentary evidence of the state of the Academic organization in the first half of the century. But we have evidence that in the Universities which were established elsewhere by schisms or migrations from Bologna there existed at the beginning of the century not two Universities but four. This was the case at Vicenza, where a colony from Bologna established itself in 1204 A.D., and in Vercelli which was colonised in 1228 from Padua, itself an earlier colony of Bologna. To anyone aware of the servile fidelity with which the institutions of a mother-University were reproduced in its daughters, the mere fact that there were four Universities at Vicenza and Vercelli would be a sufficient proof that at one time there had been four Universities at Bologna also[2]. But we are not left entirely to inference upon this fundamental point of our enquiry into the origin of Student-Universities.

Elsewhere four Universities.

So originally at Bologna.

In 1217 we hear of the ' Scholars from the City ' (i. e. Rome), Campania, and Tuscany as forming either a separate Society or more than one separate Society; but in any case it is clear that they are not embraced in the same organization as the other Italian students. What

---

[1] The earliest evidence of the change is in a city-statute of 1244. Frati, I. p. 367.

[2] Savigny conjectured that originally there were four Universities at Bologna, cap. xxi. § 616. When Kaufmann (I. p. 189) objects to Denifle's inferences from the Bull of 1217, because by 1250 we hear of a single ' Universitas scholarium,' he appears to forget that the term *Universitas* does not necessarily imply a legal corporation, but may be applied to any collection of people. Kaufmann seems to me to exaggerate the solidarity of the Student-body both before and after 1250.

was the exact distribution of the students at Bologna at this time, it is impossible to determine with absolute certainty. But it seems highly probable that originally the four Universities were, (1) Lombards, (2) Ultramontanes, (3) Tuscans, and (4) Romans, in which last University the Campanians may have been included[1]. This view is supported by two facts. First, in the later united Cismontane University there were, as is evident from the Statutes, three original *Nationes*—the Lombards, Tuscans, and Romans, which were subdivided into smaller *Consiliariæ*[2] (bodies electing one or more Councillors), while the Ultramontane University contained a much larger number of Nations—in 1265 fourteen[3]—each of which corresponded with a *Consiliaria* of the Cismontane University. Whether or not the united Ultramontane University arose by

---

[1] Sarti II. (1772) p. 58. If this view be accepted, of course the 'scholares de urbe, Campania et de Tuscia' (notice the omission of the preposition before Campania) will represent *two* separate Guilds, acting on this occasion in conjunction. The fact that a Bull is addressed to the three together does not, as Denifle assumes (I. p. 140), prove that they were embraced in one organization, any more than the existence of Papal Bulls addressed to the Masters and Scholars of Bologna proves that the Masters belonged to the Universities or the students to the Doctoral Colleges, or the fact that Bulls were often addressed to the Doctors of Civil and Canon Law at Bologna proves that there was a single College for both Faculties. Moreover, the earliest Statutes of the United Universities *prove* the original distinctness of the Lombardi: 'De Citramontanis vero iuxta morem antiquum nacio Romanorum habeat sex (consiliarios), Tuschorum alios sex, reliquos habeat nacio Lombardorum, quos per consciliarias sic dividimus, sicut *nacionis statutis est descriptum.* (*Stat.* p. 16.)

Denifle further assumes from the language of the Bull that this Guild of the Romans, Campanians, and Tuscans had only just been formed (I. 140), and hence infers that the *Universitas* originated with the Ultramontani. The fact is not improbable, but the language of the Bull seems to me to establish nothing as to the length of time (when the question is between one year and twenty-five) during which the Guild or Guilds had been formed. Honorius III speaks of the original motive of their formation, but so does the University of Paris fifty years after its first institution. See below, p. 303 n. 1. The amalgamation-theory is supported by the employment of the term Rector, which was especially used to denote the Head of a federation of Guilds. See below, p. 164.

[2] *Stat.* pp. 16, 68.

[3] Gallici, Picardi, Burgundionenses, Pictavienses, Turonenses et Cenomanenses, Normanni, Catelani, Ungari, Poloni, Theotonici, Yspani, Provinciales, Anglici, Vascones. Sarti, I. ii. (1772), p. 61.

CHAP. IV, amalgamation from these smaller Nationes, its later consti-
§ 3.   tution bears no trace of having at any earlier period
consisted of two or three separate Universities or Nations,
whereas this is distinctly the case with the Cismontane
University[1]. The second reason for supposing that the
four Universities were originally constituted as above, is
that the University of Medicine and Arts was to the
last sub-divided into four Nationes only—Ultramontane,
Lombard, Tuscan, and Roman[2].

The various Universities probably arose at distinct periods.
The fact that there were originally four distinct Universities and that we find one or more of them acting in
independence of the rest, makes it probable that they
originated at distinct periods; and it is highly probable
that the final emergence of two closely united Universities
is but the last stage of a process of amalgamation by
which the three Societies of Cismontanes and the numerous
small Ultramontane Nations had reduced themselves to
four large Societies[3]. The very distinct organization and
exceptional privileges of the German nation[4] find their

[1] See above, p. 157, n. 1.

[2] *Stat.* p. 215. Denifle (I. p. 139)
argues that since at Vicenza, Vercelli, and Padua, we find *one* University embracing all the Italians,
while at Bologna there was certainly
more than one Italian University,
there must once have been more than
four Universities at Bologna. I fail
to follow the argument. The different
distribution of Nationalities in these
offshoots of Bologna may have been
due to the composition of the seceding
bodies of students. In the migrations,
both from Bologna and from other
Universities, the *number* of Nations
(four) was always preserved, but
their composition varied. His suggestion (*l. c.*) that the larger Universities may have arisen by amalgamation from smaller Nationes which
after their union remained as sub-
divisions of the larger body, seems
to me probable as regards the Ultra-

montane Nations only. Throughout,
Denifle fails to recognize the marked
distinction between the Ultramontane
Nationes and the Cismontane *Consiliariæ*.

[3] For the similar federation of Guilds
in London, see Brentano, Pref. to
Toulmin Smith's *English Gilds* (E.
Eng. Text Soc. 1870), p. xlix; but
Mr. Gross (*The Gild Merchant,* I. p. 61
sq.) has now shown that it is a mistake
to identify the Merchant Guild with
the Municipality.

[4] In 1273 it is already claimed as
an ancient privilege ' quod nobiles
de Alamania non teneantur jurare
rectori' (*Acta Nat. Germ.* p. 349).
The accounts of 1305 allude to
written privileges (*ib.* p. 58), while
a ' privilegium quod nobiles Almanni
non tenentur iurare rectori' is included in an inventory taken in 1442
(*ib.* p. 189). The Statutes speak
generally of privileges granted by

most natural explanation in the supposition that it was
the earliest of these national clubs and formed the nucleus
round which other and younger bodies grouped themselves. Even in the fully developed Academic constitution,
the Nations of the *Ultramontani* retained a much larger
measure of individual corporate existence than either
the three original Nations of the *Citramontani* or the
smaller *Conciliariæ* into which they were sub-divided[1].

But whatever uncertainty there may be as to the early
history of these Student-Guilds, the one fact about them
which is certain is fortunately the one fact which it is of
fundamental importance to grasp. They originated with
non-Bolognese students; and this circumstance is by itself
a sufficient clue to their *raison d'être*. It is probable,
indeed, that it was the German students who first felt
the need of mutual protection and co-operation[2]; but
at all events the Guilds were formed by non-Bolognese
students. The fact has been slightly obscured by the
circumstance that the Universities eventually succeeded
in asserting *some* authority even over the Bolognese
scholars, though to the last they remained exempt from
the oath of obedience to the Rector, without a vote in
the University Congregations, and ineligible for University
offices. To the last they were not in the strict sense
members of those Corporations; originally they must have
been wholly exempt from their authority[3]. The reason

The Universities were Guilds of foreign Scholars.

---

the Emperor (*ib.* p. 13): but no actual Charter appears to be preserved
of earlier date than 1530, when
Charles V wholly exempted the
German nation from the Rectorial
jurisdiction, and subjected them to
that of their own Masters. At the
same time the latter were created
ex officio Counts of the Lateran, and
granted the power of making Notaries and legitimating bastards (*ib.*
p. 19 *sq.*). The nation retained its
existence as a Student-organization
till the Revolution terminated its
existence just, it would appear, as

it was about to die by the less noble
method of Bankruptcy. (Malagola,
Monografie, p. 286.)

[1] *Stat.* p. 139.

[2] Cf. the words of Honorius III
to the Tuscans and Campanians:
'Etsi multam honestatem, imo ne-
cessitatem, sicut asseritis, causa
contineat, que vos ad contrahendam
societatem induxit.' Sarti, II. (1772)
p. 58. This 'necessity' would be
likely to be still earlier experienced
by the Germans.

[3] The earliest Bologna Statutes
assert the jurisdiction of the Rector

CHAP. IV,
§ 3.

of the exclusion is obvious. The Bolognese student no more wanted to be protected by a University than a young Englishman reading for the bar in London requires to be protected by a Consul. The very existence of the University was due to the want of political status on the part of its members. In exactly the same way we find foreign merchants [1] and other strangers in an Italian town forming themselves into Guilds for the prevention of quarrels among themselves and the promotion of their common interests.

Exclusion of Professors.

In the same fact is found the explanation of the other characteristic peculiarity in the organization of the Universities of the Italian type—the exclusion of the Professors from membership. The earliest Bolognese Professors were citizens of Bologna. Unlike Paris, whose political and commercial importance attracted student and teacher alike from distant lands, Bologna owed her scholastic fame to the accident (if it was an accident) that Irnerius and his first successors happened to live, and therefore to teach, at Bologna [2]. Had the earliest teachers been foreigners, they might have occupied important positions in the University:

over the Bononiensis (*Stat.* p. 12); cf. the Stat. of Lerida formed on the model of Bologna in 1300 : 'cum te dicas civem Ilerdae, jurare non cogeris universitatis statuta, licet dum in hoc studio fueris ad eorum observantiam tenearis.' Villanueva, *Viage Literario*, XVI. p. 229. So at Pisa and Florence the Rector must be 'forensis.' Citizens were forbidden to take the oath to the Rector on pain of confiscation and the ban by a Town-statute of 1245 (Frati, II. p. 29). Afterwards, a special oath merely binding them not to injure the University, &c. was imposed on the Bolognese student (*Bononiensis vel diocesanus*) and his name inserted in a 'matricula specialis.' *Stat.* p. 128 (cf. p. 132 : 'Compaternitatem cum bononiensi cive vel diocesano nullus scolaris contrahat, nisi prius petita

licentia et obtenta a Rectore suo'). So they paid modified dues to the University officials on taking their degree, *ib.* p. 145.

[1] Especially German merchants. Denifle, I. p. 136; Simonsfeld, *Der Fondaco dei Tedeschi in Venedig*, Stuttgart, 1887. So there were *Universitates Judæorum*, e. g. at Catania in Sicily before 128⅔ (*Documenti per servire alla Storia di Sicilia*, Palermo, vol. VI. p. 28); so at Messina (*ib.* p. 63), Syracuse (*ib.* p. 78), Trapani (*ib.* p. 89), &c.

[2] Thus the Bull of Honorius III in 1220 reminds the town 'quod ipsi gratuito ad studendum vestram preelegerint civitatem, que cum prius esset humilis, per eos ibidem congregatis divitiis fere supergressa est civitates Provinciæ universas.' Sarti, T. II. (1772). p. 57.

as it was, the students had to choose their office-bearers
from their own number. At first the Professors were
excluded not so much because they were Professors as
because they were citizens. But at a very early period in
the development of the Universities, we shall find the
Bolognese Doctors allying themselves with the City against
the students in the selfish effort to exclude from the
substantial privileges of the Doctorate all but their own
fellow-citizens. The antagonism of interest thus created
between the Doctors and their pupils has much to do with
the growth of the student domination. The Doctors, as
citizens and as laymen, were connected with the City in
a way wholly foreign to the traditions of northern Schools.
It was through identifying themselves in the pursuit of
a common pecuniary interest with the City rather than
with the scholars that the Doctors of Bologna sank into
their strange and undignified servitude to their own pupils.

How entirely parallel to those of the non-scholastic The origi-
Guilds were the original purpose and organization of the nal purpose
of the Uni-
Student-Universities is best illustrated by the Statutes of versity
the German Nation[1] which have fortunately come down to illustrated
by Statutes
us. The original idea of the Universities became more of German
or less obscured by the Academical power which they Nation.
eventually acquired. The smaller National Associations
naturally retained the more homely character of Clubs for
mutual protection, assistance, and recreation, and for the
performance of those religious functions which in the
Middle Ages supplied the sanction for every social bond
and the excuse for every convivial gathering. In these
Statutes the object of the Guild is declared to be the
cultivation of 'fraternal charity, mutual association and
amity, the consolation of the sick and support of the
needy, the conduct of funerals and the extirpation of
rancour and quarrels, the attendance and escort of our
Doctorandi to and from the place of examination, and the
spiritual advantage of members[2].' The Statutes of any

[1] For the position of these sub-   below, p. 184 *sq.*
divisions of the University, see   [2] 'Hec nostra congregatio, utili-

ordinary religious Guild or Confraternity would define its objects in precisely similar language. The Statutes before us go on to provide that the two Proctors of the Society shall visit sick members and (if necessary) make a special collection for their benefit, or apply the general funds of the Guild to that purpose, or, if they are not in need of assistance, at least alleviate their sufferings by their 'cheerful presence[1].' The same officials are also required to adjust quarrels and to take measures, in the interest of other members, for compelling students who had left Bologna to satisfy their creditors[2]. But the liveliest picture of the ordinary purposes of the Guild is supplied by its accounts from the year 1292—one of the earliest and completest series of University documents of the kind which have come down to us[3]. The receipts are derived from entrance-payments varying, according to means, from five to sixty *solidi* or more, from fines, and from the occasional presents of a newly-mitred alumnus. The payments are chiefly devoted to convivial and religious purposes, wine and spices upon the great feasts either for the consumption of members[4] or the payment of the officiating clergy[5] and singers, candles for processions, charities to the poor, and other pious uses, such as an occasional vestment or ornament for the Conventual Church of S. Firmian habitually used by the Guild. Sometimes, however, a larger drain is made upon the resources of the Society by the expenses attending the rescue of a comrade lying fettered in the Bishop's prison[6]. These interesting

---

tatis tamen et publice et private nequaquam expers credenda, presertim ex qua fraterna caritas, societatis amicitieque communicatio, infirmorum consolatio et egenorum subsidium, funerum deductio et rancoris simultatumque extirpatio, tum doctorandorum nostrorum in locum et ex loco examinis comitiva atque constipacio, bona spiritualia resultarent.' *Acta Nat. Germ.* p. 4.

[1] *Ib.* p. 6.   [2] *Ib.* p. 7.

[3] *Ib.* p. 36 *sq.*

[4] The juxtaposition of the following is significant: 'Item, pro malvasia (Malmsey) libras III. Item, pro vitris fractis,' &c. *Ib.* p. 133.

[5] 'Item pro vino propinando presbitero, qui nobis die illo missam cantavit ibidem, II solidos.' *Ib.* p. 36.

[6] *Ib.* p. 83. It was no doubt on some similar occasions that it was necessary to spend sixteen *denarii* in gratifications to the Bishop's Chap-

records enable us to realise the original purposes of the Chap. IV,
§ 3. larger Universities of which the smaller National Unions were either the prototypes or the imitations[1], though the former may have been too large for the frequent convivialities and fraternal intercourse of the smaller Societies.

To appreciate the fact that the University was in its origin nothing more than a Guild of foreign students is the key to the real origin and nature of the institution. It is also the starting-point for an enquiry into the date at which these Societies began to be formed. It was not till towards the end of the twelfth century that Guilds of any kind, Colleges of Arms and of Arts (as they were called), came into existence in the Italian cities. In the city of Bologna itself, for instance, the first allusion to the existence of a Guild occurs in 1174[2], when we hear of a Lombard 'Societas armorum.' The probabilities of the case would suggest that some little interval would elapse between the formation of the Guilds of Arms and Arts and the imitation of them by the scholars. The only direct evidence available is derived from the silence of documents and other authorities—particularly of the Civilians who in their commentaries on the title *De Collegiis* might be expected to allude to the existence of a kind of Association the legitimacy or illegitimacy of which was a matter of considerable personal importance to themselves. Now the first of the long series of Jurists who comment upon the anomalous character of the *Universitas Scholarium* is Bassianus, who, towards the close of the twelfth century[3], disputes the right of the scholars to elect a Rector. Thus the evidence all points to the conclusion that the earliest

Date of the first Student-Universities.

lains or other domestics to get an audience ('pro copia episcopi'). *Ib.* p. 76.

[1] Denifle (I. p. 153) makes the Scholastic Guilds originate with the Germans. This would to a large extent explain the exceptional privileges of the German Nation: but the question turns in part upon the larger and very difficult question whether the Guild was originally of Teutonic origin or a direct descendant of the Roman Collegia. On this question I do not feel competent to enter.

[2] Denifle, I. p. 159.

[3] As to the date of his life or writings nothing appears to be known except that he was a pupil of Bulgarus. Sarti, I. pt. i. p. 89.

Universitas of students originated with the foreign students of Bologna in the course of the last quarter of the twelfth century. Further than this it is hardly possible to push the enquiry; though there is probability in Denifle's opinion that the last decade of the century saw the birth of the first University of students [1].

Their evolution spontaneous and gradual.

When, however, the spontaneous character of these Student-societies is taken into consideration it will become evident that the process of growth may have spread over a considerable time. Such Societies at first neither sought nor obtained charters, privileges, or incorporation from King, Bishop, or Municipality, any more than such permission is required for the establishment of a debating-society or a cricket-club among modern students. The University may, indeed, have originated in a definite meeting of the students from a particular country at a particular date: but it may equally have grown out of informal gatherings or indignation-meetings to concert measures for the release of an imprisoned comrade or for the punishment of an extortionate landlord. But we have no data for tracing the earlier stages of a process which may be considered to have been completed when the Society proceeded to elect its first permanent Rector. As to the date at which this fundamental step was taken, we can only say that it was before the close of the twelfth century.

Origin of the Rectorship.

The title of Rector was one which only began to be applied to various civic Magistrates and officers of Guilds after the revival of Roman Law-studies in the twelfth century. It was a term commonly used as the Latin equivalent of the Italian *Podestà*, to denote the elected Chief Magistrate or Dictator of a Lombard town [2]. It was also used of the Head of the whole federation of Guilds in a town, or of the Head of a single Guild [3]. In the Guilds

---

[1] Denifle, I. p. 160. Cf. Savigny, cap. xxi. § 65.

[2] Denifle, I. p. 147. Under the Empire *Rector* had been one of the regular terms for the Civil Governor

or *Judex Ordinarius* of a Province after Diocletian. Savigny, cap. ii. § 25.

[3] Thus at Bologna we hear of a *Rector Societatum* in 1194. (Savioli,

the term Rector is especially employed where the Society
was placed under the government of a single Head, instead
of (as was frequently the case) under a plurality of *Consules*
or other officers[1]. All the associations of the word suggest
a concentration of corporate power in the hands of a single
individual. From the Guilds the expression was borrowed
by the Universities, as it had been borrowed by the Guilds
from the constitutions of the towns. The same was the
case with the University *Consiliarii*, who are first heard of
in 1224[2]. In fact, the whole organization of the University
was exactly parallel to that of the Guilds, of which it
formed merely a particular variety : while the organization
of the Guilds themselves was in Italy largely a reproduction of the municipal organization of the cities. The
Guild, whether of scholars or of the members of a political
party or a particular trade, was a civic state in miniature,
a *civitas in civitate.*

The jurisdiction of the Rector was in the main derived
from the Statutes voluntarily enacted by the members,
and from that formidable oath of obedience to them and
to himself, on the significance of which we have already
commented. At the same time the Rectorship was from
the first looked upon as something more than the mere
presidency of a private Society. According to the idea of
the Roman Law (at least as understood in the Middle
Ages), every trade or profession had a kind of intrinsic
right to form a *collegium* and elect Magistrates of its own[3] :

Nature of Rectorial jurisdiction

II. Pt. 2, p. 177); at Perugia in
1223 of 'Bailivi, Rectores vel Priores
fraternitatum, societatum, familiarum
seu quarumlibet artium (Theiner,
Cod. Dipl. dom. temp. s. sedis, I. 77);
at Verona ' Prohibebo, quod nullum misterium (ministerium) de
civitate seu districtu Veronae habeat
vel habere possit gastaldionem vel
rectorem, nisi qui sit de suo misterio,
&c.' (*Liber juris civilis urbis Veronæ
script. 1228*, ed. Campagnola, 1728,
p. 147). The last mentioned Stat.

probably originated in the twelfth
century (see Denifle's note, I. p. 146).

[1] So Denifle, I. p. 146. But Accursius has a gloss on the passage of
the Code quoted below : ' Pone in
Campsoribus Bon. qui suos habent
consules sive rectores ' (ed. Contius,
Parisiis, 1576, c. 559).

[2] Savioli, III. pt. ii. p. 56.

[3] See the passage in the Code (III.
Tit. xiii.) : 'Periniquum et temerarium
esse perspicimus, eos qui professiones
aliquas seu negotiationes exercere

and the jurisdiction of these Magistrates over its members in matters relating to the profession or trade was recognized by the Town-governments even without any Charter or express enactment as a legal, and not a merely consensual, jurisdiction. And the scholars, in setting up a *Universitas* and electing a Rector, undoubtedly claimed for themselves what were considered the natural or intrinsic privileges attaching to all recognized trades or professions. In general there seems to have been no unwillingness on the part of the Lombard towns to recognize to the full the jurisdiction of these Student-guilds and their Rectors, except on the

Opposition of the Professors.

part of one particular class. These were naturally the Professors of Law themselves. A *Universitas* of students at once offended their legal susceptibilities and infringed upon what they considered their professional prerogatives. They did not dispute the right of a profession or trade to be under the jurisdiction of a Rector : but the students, they urged, did not form an independent trade or class by themselves. They were merely the pupils of the Doctors of Law. The right to elect a Rector and to frame Statutes binding at once upon the full members and the students of the profession belonged *de jure* to themselves, as it did *de facto* to their more fortunate brethren at Paris and elsewhere. The pupils of the Doctors had no more right to form a *collegium* and elect Magistrates than the apprentices of the smiths or the skinners [1]. The protests of the Jurists, however, failed to check the growth of the institution. The University of students once formed was stronger than the handful of Professors. Townsmen and

noscuntur, iudicum ad quos earum professionum seu negotiationum cura pertinet, jurisdictionem et praeceptionem declinare conari.'

[1] See for instance the words of Azo, Lecture in Cod. ad L. fin. C. *de jurisdict.* (III. 13): ap. Denifle, I. p. 170: 'Ergo scolares, quia non exercent professionem sed sub exercentibus sunt discipuli, non possunt eligere consules, sicut nec discipuli pellipariorum. Magistri ergo possunt eligere consules, quia ipsi exercent professiones. Savigny (cap. xxi. § 65) continues the quotation : ' Sic et faciunt fabri, in terra ista, et alia corpora quia eligunt ministeriales suos sub quibus possunt conveniri.' This opinion is embodied in the Accursian gloss. Other instances are given by Denifle, I. p. 170 *sq.*

Professors alike stood in awe of a body which by the simple expedient of migration could destroy the trade of the former and the incomes of the latter. The Jurists from the first recognize the *de facto* existence of the Rectorial jurisdiction ; and, after the fourteenth century, men who had grown up as students under the Rectorial *régime* even attempted a theoretical justification of the anomaly [1].

It must not be supposed that opposition to the Professors formed any part of the original *raison d'être* of the Universities. At first the Universities no more claimed authority over the Doctors or the control of strictly Academical matters than the Union Societies of Oxford and Cambridge, or the militant and beer-drinking corps of a German University. The Universities were formed for purposes of mutual protection and self-government, and had nothing to do with the *Studium*, which was managed by the *Collegia Doctorum* as much as at Paris. The jealousy of the Professors arose simply (so far as appears) from the fact that the students were attempting to do for themselves what the Professors (on the analogy of the relations ordinarily subsisting between Masters and their apprentices) claimed to do for them. But in process of time the Universities did gradually acquire a complete control over the Professors ; and to a large extent usurped the powers elsewhere exercised by the Professorial body. By means of the terrible power of 'boycotting,' which they could bring into play against an offending Professor or a student who adhered to a 'boycotted' Professor, the student-clubs were masters of the situation [2]. And when the Professors began

The Universities originally claimed no Academic authority.

---

[1] Cinus (ad *l. cit.*) after giving his own opinion against the scholars, says : 'Quidam moderni dicunt contrarium, quia scolares exercent professionem, ut in Aut. Habita, et quia eorum universitas est licita, et sic possunt dare jurisdictionem, ut ff. [*i. e.* Digest] *quod cujusque universitatis.*' (Venet. 1493.) So the earlier

Odofredus (†1265) admits 'tamen per legem municipalem hujus civitatis scholares creant rectores.' In Cod. ad *l. cit.* (T. III. f. 148 *a*).

[2] The Statutes of the Student-universities sometimes prescribe the measures to be taken against a contumacious professor. Thus at Parma penalties are provided against a

to accept *salaria* from the Universities themselves or from the towns which stood in awe of the Universities in lieu of collecting fees from their scholars, they passed still more completely under the authority of the Universities and their Rectors. By these means the Universities were able to compel the Professors to take the oath of obedience to the Rectors, which gave a certain legal sanction to their subjection. This subjection was well established by the end of the thirteenth century, as is evident from the Statutes of Lerida : though the Doctors still continued to assert their theoretical superiority to the Universities[1].

It must be remembered, indeed, that in the Student-statutes we have merely the students' estimate of their own relations to the Doctors. And we can no more assume that this was identical with the view taken by the Doctors themselves than quotations from the writings of an ancient Bishop can be taken to represent the views as to the limits of Episcopal authority entertained by his Presbyters or by the Church at large. Thus, while it is expressly provided by the Student-statutes that they shall overrule all contradictory provisions in the Statutes of the Doctoral Colleges[2],

---

scholar who attempts to graduate under a deprived Doctor. (*Mem. e doc. per la storia della Un. di Parma*, Parma, 1888, vol. I. p. xxxix.) It should be remembered that 'privatio' meant *social excommunication* as well as mere refusal of official recognition. Thus the above-quoted Statute of Parma provides that 'scholares teneantur eum vitare tanquam privatum omni commodo et honore Universitatis, et nullus Scolaris ipsum admittat in societate nisi ottentum in Universitate fuerit, ut predicitur' (*l. c.*).

[1] 'In universitate ista Bononiensi doctores subsunt rectori ... Modo quæro, num quid Doctores subsint universitati? Breviter dicendum est quod non : *nisi ex prærogativa consuetudinis vel juramento*, quia juraverunt obedire rectori.' Bartolus

(†1357), ad Auth. *Habita*, (quoted by Savigny, cap. xxi. § 70).

[2] 'Cassa et irrita et inania statuta et consuetudines decernimus que doctorum collegium habuerit vel observaverit seu habiturum servatum vel facturum de novo fuerit contra statuta universitatis nostre et scolasticam libertatem.' *Stat.* p. 144. On the other hand, after the table of degree-fees, appears a clause respecting the Statutes of the Colleges. (*Ib.* p. 151.) The City enacted that their own Statutes should prevail over those of the Colleges, but the College-statutes over those of the Universities. (*Stat.* p. 156.) In one place in the University-statutes we find a clause 'secundum quod in statutis ipsius Collegii determinatum invenimus.'

the Town-statutes enact precisely the opposite. Moreover, it should be noticed that when the students seem to be most clearly usurping the functions of the Doctoral body in defining the conditions precedent to degrees, their enactments are in the main identical with those found in the Doctoral Statutes: just as many of the provisions by which the students seem to be legislating for the City and its Magistrates are mere embodiments of privileges conferred by the latter[1]. At the same time there can be no doubt that the real supremacy rested with the students; and the Statutes of the Colleges themselves in general adopted a sufficiently humble tone in their attitude towards the Student-Universities.

In so far as the claims of the Student-corporations rested on anything more than usurpation and their undoubted right to pursue their studies elsewhere in the event of disagreement with the town-authorities[2], their legal and constitutional basis would be found in the Papal Bulls which from time to time confirmed the Statutes of the Universities, and subjected the impugners of them to ecclesiastical censures[3]. But little use seems practically to have been made of this Papal Privilege except as a weapon against the City in the earliest days of the University. The students seldom or never appealed, like the Masters of Paris, to ecclesiastical authority for assistance in enforcing their own internal discipline.

There was, as we have seen, nothing in the University as an institution to arouse the jealousy or hostility of the

---

[1] *e. g.* in the Statute *De domibus in quibus habitant scolares non destruendis* (pp. 126, 153). The whole of the Fourth Book of University Statutes is a reproduction of Town-statutes.

[2] Cf. the Stat. of Florence as late as 1472 in *Stat. Fiorent.* p. 24. The Rector is to insist on payment of the *salaria* by the City, 'Alias interdicat studium.'

[3] The first general confirmation dates from 1253. The bull was addressed to the Archdeacon of Bologna and a Dominican Friar. Sarti, T. II. (1772) p.124. Other ecclesiastics were from time to time appointed Conservators of the privileges of the University, but their jurisdiction does not seem to have become so extensive as at Paris (Ghirardacci, T. I. p. 539; T. II. pp. 27, 66). Savigny, by the way, makes the *Arch*bishop (!) of Bologna Conservator in 1326. Cf. below, chap. v. § 3.

Magistrates or City of Bologna. That the students should have a *collegium* and be governed by a Rector was completely in accordance with the political ideas of the time. The *Universitates* met with no systematic opposition from the municipalities of the kind which we shall find the Parisian University of Masters experiencing at the hands of the Bishop, Chancellor, and Church of Paris. The Bolognese government was quite content to concede to the Universities of Students what it conceded to other Guilds. But in certain respects the Universities demanded more than the City conceded to other Guilds. The Guilds were composed of citizens, who never thought of disputing the authority of the city-government, and who could not put themselves beyond its jurisdiction without losing both property and status. The Universities were composed of aliens, who refused to recognize the authority of the State in which they lived when it conflicted with the allegiance which they had sworn to their own artificial commonwealth [1]. One matter was pre-eminently a subject of contention between the City and University. The power of secession was cherished by the University as its great instrument of warfare against all manner of enemies. The City naturally wished to deprive it of this unfair advantage in its controversies with itself and to render its own prosperity independent of the good-will of an alien corporation.

The first Migrations originate with Professors.

In the first collisions between Town and Gown at Bologna it was, however, the Professors who were directly involved. Long before the close of the twelfth century we find a tendency in the Bolognese Professors to wander

---

[1] It was not merely in its relations with the City, as a whole, but in quarrels with individual citizens that the University could bring its powerful organization into play. Thus the Paduan *Statuta Artistarum* (fol. xxxiii. b) denounce the punishment of 'interdictio' (i. e. from intercourse with scholars) against anyone who cites a scholar before the City Magistrates—the sentence to extend to the third generation of the offender's posterity. The same Statutes (fol. xxxii. b) enact that if a householder refuses to execute repairs after fifteen days' notice, the tenant is to repair, and deduct the expense from the rent.

abroad, whether in consequence of disputes with the town-authorities or allured by prospects of more liberal remuneration elsewhere. Thus Placentinus had left Bologna to establish schools first at Mantua, afterwards at Montpellier, in the third or fourth quarter of the twelfth century. And most of the numerous Law-schools which we find established in the Italian towns by the beginning of the thirteenth century, had apparently been founded by similar secessions of Doctors or students or both. The City was at last forced to bring to bear against the vagrant Doctors the usual medieval method of prevention—making the suspected party swear that he would not commit the apprehended crime[1]. The first time that this measure was adopted was in the case of Pillius. Getting wind of a negotiation with the neighbouring town of Modena for the purchase of the Doctor's services, the Magistrates assembled all the Professors of the School and compelled them to swear not to teach out of Bologna for the next two years. In spite of his oath, however, Pillius could not resist the renewed offers of Modena gold[2]. After this time such oaths appear to have been habitually exacted of the Doctors[3]; and from 1227 to 1312 the oath was regularly enforced by the Town-statutes upon all Doctors who intended to teach at Bologna[4]. At the beginning of the thirteenth century, however, the City found itself threatened with a much more formidable danger. Not merely individual Professors, but whole bodies of students, dissatisfied with their treatment at Bologna, entered into negotiations with other towns for the transference of the *Studium* to them. In 1204, after a secession of this kind to Vicenza, the City passed a Statute prohibiting citizens

The Student-migration to

---

[1] Sarti, I. pt. i. pp. 77, 78. Savigny (cap. xxi. § 81) gives a list of the Doctors who took the oath. Cf. Savioli, II. pt. ii. p. 465.

[2] See extracts from Pillius in Sarti, I. pt. i. p. 84. Savioli gives 1188 as the date of Pillius' flight, but he appears to be established in Modena before 1182. Savigny, cap. xxii.

[3] Sarti, I. pt. i. pp. 84, 85.

[4] Frati, II. p. 23. In 1312 the oath was abolished, but penalties for Doctors absconding during the time of their contract reappear in 1334. Savigny, cap. xxi. § 81 : Ghirardacci, T. I. pp. 560, 561 ; T. II. pp. 11, 117.

CHAP. IV,
§ 3.

Vicenza,
1204.

Secession
to Arezzo
in 1215 pro-
vokes fresh
quarrels.

from following the seceding scholars or from aiding and abetting similar secessions in future [1]. After the secession to Arezzo in 1215, in consequence of a great quarrel between the Lombards and the Tuscans [2], or possibly in consequence of the measures which the city had adopted for the suppression of the tumults, the penalties of banishment and confiscation of goods were denounced against any scholar who should administer an oath to another binding him to leave the city if commanded to do so by him [3]. The Podestà required the Universities to incorporate the Town-statute with their own, by which means every student would be compelled to swear obedience to it. The 'scholars' especially aimed at were of course the Rectors [4], who must have been empowered either by a permanent Statute or by some extraordinary resolution to demand such an oath as a means of securing a prompt and universal secession in the event of a request being refused or an injury going unpunished. One at least of the Universities, if not all, appealed to the Pope, who, in accordance with what became the universal policy of the Holy See, warmly espoused the cause of the scholars; and in 1217 a Bull was issued by the new Pontiff Honorius III —formerly Archdeacon of Bologna—urging or commanding the revocation of the obnoxious law, while the scholars were exhorted to leave the city rather than violate their

[1] Frati, II. p. 23. In 1211 we find a Statute passed, which, without directly naming the scholastic Universities, may possibly be directed against them, since in it citizens as well as strangers are forbidden to give a promise or oath 'de adiuvando unus alium;' the Societies of Arms and Arts being alone exempted from its provisions. Savioli, II. pt. ii. p. 464. At this time a clause was inserted into the Doctors' oath pledging them not to aid and abet secessions of scholars. Sarti, I. pt. ii. pp. 70, 71.

[2] 'Ideo ego Rofredus Beneven-

tanus juris civilis professor ad preces et instantias sociorum meorum, nobilium de partibus Tusciæ, cum essem in civitate scilicet arretina,' &c.—ap. Sarti, I. pt. i. p. 139. Cf. *ib.* pp. 133, 134.

[3] 'Si quis scolaris vel alius aliquem scolarem aliquo modo vel ingenio astrinxerit ut ei possit precipere de ducendo de civitate ista causa studii banniatur,' &c. Frati, II. p. 25. Cf. Denifle, I. pp. 161–162; Savigny, cap. xxi. § 65.

[4] Explicitly mentioned in the Bull of 1220. See below, p. 173.

oaths[1]. It would appear from subsequent documents that the Papal intervention was unsuccessful, that the suppression of the Rectorship took effect, and that the scholars, for non-compliance with the demands of the citizens, were placed under the ban of the city, by which they became 'infamous,' lost their civil rights and were liable to the confiscation of all their goods. In fact it is probable that from 1217 to 1220, or at least for some time before the last-mentioned year[2], there was a more or less complete dispersion of the *Studium*. In 1220 a fresh Papal remonstrance[3] induced the Town to yield so far as to repeal the penal enactments against the scholars and their Rectors, but it required that upon their accession to office the Rectors should swear not to entertain any project for the removal of the *Studium* from Bologna. The truce, if such it was, was of short duration, and in 1222 a great migration to Padua took place[4]. But in 1224 another Migration to Padua, 1222. Papal Bull[5]; combined with the efforts of the Emperor Frederick II to destroy the *Studium*[6], seems practically to have resulted in the abandonment of the attempt to exact the suicidal oath from the Rectors, though the Statute requiring it remained on the City Statute-book till 1288[7]; though in the City-statutes, printed as a supplement to the University-statute of 1432, we still find the penalty of death denounced against any person whatever, whether citizen or stranger, who shall enter into a conspiracy for transferring the *Studium*, as also against any citizen-doctor over the age of fifty who shall without permission of the city magistrates leave Bologna for the purpose of lecturing elsewhere. If the offender were

---

[1] Sarti, II. (1772), pp. 57, 58.

[2] Savioli records these events under 1220, but the documents do not indicate that any fresh measures were taken in this year.

[3] Savioli, II. pt. ii. p. 466. Cf. II. pt. i. p. 395.

[4] See below, chap. vi. § 4.

[5] Savioli, III. pt. ii. p. 56.

[6] See the Bull of Honorius III in 1227, requiring the Emperor to revoke his edicts against the Lombard league, 'et specialiter constitutionem factam de Studio et Studentibus Bononie.' Sarti, I. pt. ii. (1772) pp. 72-74.

[7] Denifle, I. 176.

a younger and therefore a less valuable Professor, the milder penalty of 200 ducats is substituted[1].

A full account of the relations between the University and the City of Bologna in the thirteenth century would form one of the most interesting chapters in the history of Universities. Unfortunately, the fragmentary and scattered details which have been given are all which can be collected. It seems that a fairly satisfactory *modus vivendi* was effected between the two bodies at about the middle of the thirteenth century, after a great collision provoked by the execution of a scholar, and also by the efforts of the Bolognese Doctors to convert their office into a lucrative monopoly[2]. Again the Rectorate was threatened; again the counter-threat of secession eventually prevailed. The Statutes of 1245, while taking precautions against the transference of the *Studium* and still continuing to prohibit oaths pledging the scholars to obey a Rectorial order for secession, fully recognize the right of the scholars to elect Rectors, though forbidding citizens to swear obedience to them. Students are accorded the private or *civil* (though of course not the *political*) rights of citizens; they are to be allowed to make a will or receive property under a will, to give evidence, and to do other 'legitimate acts[3].' The Statutes of 1289 confer still further privileges upon scholars: exceptional steps are taken for the protection of their person and property, and the Podestà is even directed to enforce the Rectorial sentences in civil disputes between scholars[4]. At some time before 1432 the University appears to have succeeded in imposing upon the Podestà a special oath to respect and enforce the Statutes of the University: at all events the Rectors are required by the Statutes of the University to demand such an oath[5].

---

[1] *Stat.* p. 157.

[2] Savioli, III. pt. i. p. 332.

[3] Frati, II. pp. 25–29.

[4] *Stat.* p. 163.

[5] *Stat.* p. 64. The Statute was introduced later than 1347. The

Town-Statutes of 1244 required the Podestà to swear obedience to all the Town's provisions in favour of the Studium. Frati, I. p. 369. The later Town-Statutes are not published.

CHAP. IV,
§ 3.

Migration
of 1321 :
Peace be-
tweenTown
and Gown.

The last important collision between Town and Gown at Bologna took place in 1321, when, in consequence of the execution of a scholar for the abduction of a rich citizen's daughter, the majority of the students, together with many Professors, seceded to Siena[1]. In the following year a reconciliation was effected; the City compelled its Podestà to receive discipline in the Dominican Church, and a chapel or church was built for the University by the grateful townsmen in memory of the event. The building was styled 'The Church of S. Mary of the Scholars in the Borgo of S. Mamolo,' though spoken of in the Statutes as the University Chapel[2]. The fact testifies to the vital importance of the University to the City[3], and the consequent power wielded by the former.

Even for tracing the internal development of the University the materials are singularly scanty compared with those which we possess for the history of Paris. We know that a body of Statutes received the Papal approval in 1253. But the earliest collection of Statutes available until quite recently dates only from 1432. Enough might even then have been gathered by inference from the Statutes of daughter-Universities to demolish the rash assumption of Savigny[4] that the bulk of these Statutes had come down unaltered from the earliest days of the University. Father Denifle has, however, recently dis-

---

[1] Ghirardacci, II. pp. 5, 6.

Melloni, *Elenco delle Chiese della Città e Diocesi di Bologna compilato nel MCCCLXVI* (Bologna, 1779, p. 18), and *Stat.* pp. 14, 61 *notes.* After 1529 the Church was styled S. Maria delle Grazie: it is now suppressed.

[3] The *Acta Nationis Germanicæ* bear curious testimony to the frequency of Secessions or Migrations in the period immediately preceding this approximately permanent settlement. Under the year 1309 occur the words 'Nota, quod hic vacaverat natio tribus annis, quibus non fuit

studium' (p. 59), and among the accounts of 1308 (*l. c.*) is an entry 'pro sacco, in quo portabantur res nacionis in discordia, II solidos.' Under 1312 (p. 65) is a payment 'pro instrumento cautionis, quam fecimus nacioni dum timore novitatum cederemus de Bononia.' There is a similar entry in 1316 (p. 72); while under 1321 and 1322 there are payments connected with the secession to Imola (pp. 79-80). On this last see Banchi, *Giornale Storico degli Archivi Toscani,* Anno V. 1861, p. 237.

[4] Cap. xxi. § 61.

covered in the Chapter Library of Pressburg in Hungary,
an earlier redaction of about half of this Statute-book.
From the information supplied by these Statutes themselves, it appears that they were originally drafted by
the celebrated Canonist Johannes Andreæ, and published
by the University in the year 1317. Additions were made
to them in the years 1326, 1336, and 1346, and in the
last-mentioned year they were subjected to a complete
revision. The Pressburg MS. contains the form which
was given to them in the academical year 1346–1347.

Statutes
of 1317.

But a comparison of these Statutes with those of
various Universities formed on the Bologna model in the
period between 1317 and 1347 makes it clear that the
changes introduced in 1347 were but slight. The re-
editing consisted chiefly of additions, deciding moot points
that had arisen in the interval, and which can generally be
recognized by their interrupting the alphabetical arrangement of the original Statutes. When, however, we turn to
the only extant collection of University Statutes believed
to be copied from those of Bologna at an earlier date than
1317, we find little verbal coincidence with the collection of
1317. The University constitution in its main outlines—
the Rectorial jurisdiction, the Nations and Consiliarii, the
Student-supremacy over the Professors[1] and other institutions to be more fully described in our next chapter—
are all found faithfully anticipated in the Statutes made for
the University of Lerida in the year 1300[2]. But the actual
Statutes are expressed in a different style and language, and
are very much less bulky and detailed than the Bologna
Code of 1317. It is from this epoch then that we must
date the Code of Laws which continued with few modifications to govern the University of Bologna throughout
our period.

[1] This supremacy was virtually
recognized by Honorius III as early
as 1224, where he speaks of the
Doctors 'qui . . . stare ut tenebantur sententiæ rectorum con-

tempserunt.'—Savioli, III. pt. ii.,
p. 56.

[2] Published by Villanueva in *Viage
Literario à las Iglesias de España*,
T. XVI. p. 207.

In the following Section I shall content myself with giving a sketch of the University system as it is presented to us by the first collection of Statutes which we possess in their integrity—the Code of 1432. But the discovery of Denifle enables us to add that the account will in the main be applicable to the whole period between 1317 and 1432 [1].

It may be convenient here to explain that there was at Bologna a wholly distinct University of Students in Medicine and Arts, and a wholly distinct College of Doctors in those Faculties, which will be dealt with in detail hereafter. In the next two sections I am concerned only with the Jurist organization.

[1] See below, § 6.

§ 4. The Constitution of the Student-Universities.

Chap. IV,
§ 4.
—•—
Close
union of
the two
Universi-
ties.
It will be noticed at once on comparing the extant Statutes with the state of things disclosed by the isolated documents of earlier times that a great change has taken place in the mutual relations of the separate Universities. At the beginning of the thirteenth century the four Universities of Jurists appear as distinct as a number of separate trade-guilds. Though the city legislation against the administration of oaths pledging scholars to leave Bologna under certain circumstances was directed against all the Universities, it was (so far as appears) only by the non-Italian Societies that it was resisted : and other instances occur of independent action on the part of particular Universities. By the fourteenth century the Universities of Jurists (now amalgamated into the two Ultramontane and Cismontane Universities) though remaining theoretically distinct bodies, are practically almost fused into one. They have a common code of Statutes; they hold common Congregations; the Rector of either University is empowered, in the absence or default of his colleague, to act on his behalf[1]; they have even (it would seem) one common seal[2]. Though they have no common Head, the two Universities have become practically as much one body as the four Nations of Paris[3].

The jurisdiction of the Rector was originally based upon

---

[1] *Stat.* p. 63 *et passim.*

[2] *Stat.* p. 127.

[3] It would seem that this state of things came into existence at about the close of the thirteenth century. In 1273 the Ultramontanes in their separate Congregation discuss a proposed alteration in their permanent Statutes (*Acta Nat. Germ.* p. 349). In 1301 we read of a ' liber statutorum scholarium ultramontanorum et citramontanorum ' (*ib.* p. 350). In 1306 the Ultramontanes are said ' statuere et declarare *ad hoc*' (*ib.* p. 352), but its resolution related merely to an internal dispute between its constituent nations and does not seem to have involved any alteration in its permanent Statutes. Except where the contrary appears from the context, I shall employ the term University to denote the combined Universities of Jurists.

the Statutes of the University and derived its sanction from the penalties which the University as a private society had in its power to inflict on its own members, including the spiritual penalties in which transgressors were involved by their oaths of obedience. In accordance, however, with the prevalent ideas as to the authority of *collegia* and the inherent power of their members to elect Consuls or Rectors, the Republic recognized the authority of the Rectors over their students and directed its own Magistrates to enforce their sentences. This applied, however, only in the first instance to causes in which both parties were members or public servants of the Universities. But the Universities claimed more than this. They claimed for the Rectors an exclusive jurisdiction in all cases in which a scholar was involved either as plaintiff or defendant [1]. Such a demand the Republic naturally resented, and there remained a permanent contradiction upon this point between the Statutes of the University and those of the City [2]. Citizens may at times have elected to cite a Scholar before the Rector : but it is improbable that the Rectors ever succeeded in getting their jurisdiction *in invitos* acknowledged where a citizen was defendant. The Statutes of 1432 require the Rector to demand of the Podestà an oath to respect the privileges of the University and to enforce the Rectorial sentences [3], but in the practical ap-

---

[1] Sometimes, but not always, the Italian University Statutes admit the household (*familiares*) of scholars to their privileges, e. g. at Florence *Stat.* p. 22. So apparently at Bologna, *Stat.* p. 163.

[2] Cf. *Stat.* p. 57 with the Extract from the Town-statutes, *ib.* p. 163. Such collisions between the Town-statutes and those of the Scholars could probably be found in most Italian Universities. Sometimes the Universities expressly claim to override those of the town. Thus at Florence the Rector is to bear arms 'non obstantibus .. Statutis vel re-

formationibus Populi et comunis Florentie in contrarium loquentibus' (*Stat. Fiorent.* p. 28). In 1366 we find the Rectorial jurisdiction sanctioned by the City Statutes with the express exception of the right to bear arms or 'ire de nocte' (*ib.* p. 149). In 1403, however, licenses to bear arms might be granted to the *familiares* of the Rector (*ib.* p. 181.) At Ferrara the Rector's House is to be a sanctuary for criminals (Borsetti, I. p. 379).

[3] 'Item mandabit sententias Rectorum vel alterius ipsorum esecutioni.' *Stat.* p. 183.

CHAP. IV,
§ 4.

plication of this enactment there remained no doubt the old diversity of interpretation between the imponent and the taker of the oath ; though, from the variations observable on this point in other University Statutes, it is probable that at Bologna itself there may have been fluctuations in the practical limits of the Academical jurisdiction at different times.

The Rector bound to exact penalties.

So completely was the Rector's jurisdiction dependent upon the Statutes that his functions were, in many cases, almost purely executive. When the Statutes denounced deprivation or expulsion upon Professor or student, the Rectors had no discretion in inflicting it. The power of restoring a deprived Doctor was reserved to the University itself[1]. Similarly when the amount of a fine was fixed by Statute, it was regarded as a debt to the University incurred *ipso facto*. If the Rector failed to collect it, he became himself indebted to the Society to the same amount, and at the scrutiny held at the end of his term of office was required by the Syndics appointed for that purpose to make good the deficiency[2]. All students—with a peculiar exception in favour of Bishops and high dignitaries—were bound to give information if any breach of the Statutes came under their notice[3]. At the *Syndicatus* on the expiration of his office complaints might be made against the Rector by Professors or Scholars, and the Rector was personally liable in damages to individuals whom he had annoyed by excessive zeal just as he was liable to the Society for his omissions[4].

No criminal jurisdiction.

Criminal jurisdiction even over its own members—still less over citizens—the Universities do not seem to have secured[5] until the fifteenth century, when it was conceded

---

[1] *Stat.* p. 110.

[2] *Stat.* pp. 60, 67 *sq.*, 149. This is one of the innumerable adaptations from Italian civic practice. The same method was adopted with the Podestà.

[3] *Ib.*

[4] For a most curious record of

such a syndicatus, see *Statut. Fiorent.*, pp. 425–438.

[5] ' Jurisdictionem ordinariam Rectores habeant in scolares in causis civilibus ' (*Stat.* p. 56). In a later addition (p. 181) there is an elaborate scale of fines for various forms of injury to the person or dignity of the

where both parties were scholars. In the late additions to the Statutes of 1432 we find, moreover, a provision that a student shall not be arrested (except for treason) without the permission of the Rector, that he shall not be dragged through the streets, and that he shall be admitted to bail when accused of carrying arms [1].

There was, indeed, a large class of citizens on whom the Statutes did impose penalties. By a judicious employ-ment of the mighty power of interdict or 'boycotting [2],' the University had acquired jurisdiction over the landlords of Students' houses in matters affecting their relations with the students [3], and over all classes of tradesmen or work-men engaged in the production of books [4]. With these

Interdict.

Rector, culminating in the provision that any one who assaults that official 'cum armis et sanguinis effu-sione citra mortem vel mortale vulnus pœnam manus et centum lib. bonon. incurrat.' But from the context it ap-pears that the University was merely 'puniri curare et usque ad finem prosequi' before the City Magi-strates. In 1411 the Rector's criminal jurisdiction over scholars is recognised by the city (*ib.* p. 168). So later (*ib.* p. 195) : 'Et talis gerens se pro Bidello trudetur carceribus domini Potestatis per spacium trium dierum per Rectores Universitatis nostræ.' A Privilege of Paul III in 1544 gave the Rectors jurisdiction in all non-capital criminal cases in which a scholar was involved. *Stat. Jur. Bon.* pp. 97, 98. Savigny (cap. xxi. § 74) says that the right of the Rectors to punish small offences was never contested, but gives no proof of such a right being recognized except in the case of offences against the Statutes, which do not provide for the punishment of offences against the ordinary Law.

[1] *Stat.* p. 184.

[2] At Padua a person who violates the privilege of the University

'per scholas publicetur et comertio scholarium interdicatur.' *Stat. Artis-tarum*, f. xxxvi. The penalty of 'Privatio' sometimes extended to the fifth generation. *Stat. Univ. Jur. Patavini Gymn.* 1550, f. 51.

[3] The town recognizes the system of joint-taxation (*Stat.* p. 160), but it denies the University's right of Interdictio, at least in certain cases (p. 161), while the University Statutes denounce it against the 'hospites' of houses near which an outrage on a scholar is committed, even if the owner was not personally responsible (p. 124). Under the Papal Bull authorizing the taxation (see above, p. 149) disputes about lodgings might be taken before the Spiritual Courts, but the University denounces perpetual interdiction against an interdicted landlord invoking their help (*Stat.* p. 125).

[4] 'Scriptores, miniatores, cor-rectores èt miniorum repositores atque rasores librorum, ligatores, cartolarii et qui vivunt pro universi-tate scolarium.' *Stat.* p. 59. The town-statutes require that disputes between scholars and *scriptores* shall be settled by the Podestà (*Stat.* p. 162).

exceptions the jurisdiction of the Rector was confined to the members of the University ; and even over Students this jurisdiction was very strictly limited and defined by Statute. The penalties which he could inflict consisted in ordinary cases of fines, or in serious cases of expulsion or 'privation,' together with the power of pronouncing a Student perjured. In the last two cases, the assent of a majority of the Council was required. In the enforcement of his civil penalties, the Rector was dependent upon the assistance of the Podestà and his officers [1].

The Professorial Jurisdiction. As has been already said, the jurisdiction conferred by the Authentic *Habita* upon the Professors was always legally recognized, however much out of harmony with the later relations in other respects between the Professors and their domineering pupils. By the decree of Frederick I this jurisdiction extended apparently both to criminal and civil matters. This interpretation of the law was, however, much disputed by the citizens : and a great feud between the Lombards and the Tuscans early in the thirteenth century, when (according to the Jurist Odofredus) there were 10,000 students at Bologna, compelled them for a time to renounce a criminal jurisdiction which they found themselves incapable of enforcing. This jurisdiction had been, however, nominally resumed in the time of Odofredus († 1265 A.D.), though it is probable that it was very much of a dead letter [2]. At all events the Professors

---

[1] Cf. *Stat. Fiorent.* p. 430, where a student complains that the Rector ' misit pro familia domini Potestatis, uno mane, dum esset dominus Andreas in scolis ad audiendum, et eum de Studio ignominiose et vituperose capi fecit et duci ad Palatium et in carceribus detrudi,' &c., for which excess of zeal the Rector was heavily fined by the Syndics.

[2] 'Sed per scholares et doctores renunciatum est Bononiæ quantum ad criminales, et sic servatur exceptis clericis qui suo non potuerunt privilegio renuntiare.' Accursius in

Cod. iv. tit. 13 *Habita* Verb. *si litem* (ed. Contius, Parisiis, 1576, c. 750). 'Or, segnori, videtur quod hec constitutio quantum ad verba loquatur in civili et in criminali, nam vidi hoc in civitate ista tempore Domini Azonis quod scholares poterant declinare forum in causa criminali, et erant hic tunc temporis bene x. millia scholarium. Sed scholares renuntiaverunt huic privilegio tempore Domini Azonis et fuit renuntiatum tali ratione, quia inter Lombardos et Tuscos fuit maxima discordia et maximum bellum, ita quod domini doctores non pote-

would be entirely dependent upon the co-operation of the Town authorities for the enforcement of any sentences that they might venture to pronounce. The right secured by the *Habita* of citing a scholar before the Bishop was no doubt intended primarily for clerks, though originally the alternative appears to have been always open to a plaintiff-student; but in practice it was seldom claimed except by ecclesiastics. And at no time was either clerk or layman allowed to decline the Rector's jurisdiction if cited before him by the other party [1]. As, however, the Canon Law forbade the exercise of any jurisdiction by a layman over a clerk, the University Statute provided that the Rector should be himself a clerk [2]. We shall have occasion again to speak of the medieval conception of *clericatus*, which is, indeed, of great importance in the appreciation of the relations between the Universities and the Church. Here it will be sufficient to say that any student could become a clerk and so acquire the immunities of an ecclesiastic by merely receiving the tonsure from a Bishop,

---

rant se intromittere in puniendo eos; ... sed in civili bene habent adhuc suum hodie privilegium. Sed hodie reversum est ad pristinum statum: tamen deus velit quod non faciant sibi male adinvicem, nam'per dominos doctores male puniuntur illa maleficia.' Odofredus, *Super Codicem* (T. III. f. 204). Auth. *Habita*. He adds that the privilege applies only to *scholares qui studiorum causa peregrinantur*, hence not to *Bononienses*. Accursius (*c.* 1220) treats even the Bishop's jurisdiction as obsolete ' quantum ad delicta,' *Authenticorum Collatio* III. tit. 4 (Parisiis, 1576, c. 133), though this must be understood with an exception in favour of clerici. Odofredus *ad Dig. Vetus* Const. *Omnem* (T. I. f. 4) assumes that even a lay scholar may still be cited before the Bishop. The clerical privilege is enforced by Bull in 1252 (*Archiv f. Kirchengesch.* IV. p. 245).

[1] *Stat.* p. 57.

[2] The above explanation of the proviso is clearly given by the jurist Baldus and adopted by Denifle, I. 87. Savigny (c. xxi. §72), who never could understand what a *clericus* meant in the Middle Ages, rejects it, and says that *clericus* must mean merely 'scholar.' But compare the following Statute of Ferrara (Borsetti, I. 367): ' Et si fieri posset, sit (Rector) qui promotus sit ad primos ordines ecclesiasticos, scilicet ad primam tonsuram et quatuor Ordines Minores et hoc quo convenitur (*lege* convenienter) Judex competens Scholaribus fieri queat.' For the importance attached to the tonsure and clerical habit, cf. *Stat. Fiorent.* p. 437, where it is pleaded in the Archbishop's Court that ' non potuit nec potest dictus magister Ieronimus gaudere aliquo privilegio clericali, et maxime quia jam diu ivit sine habitu et tonsura clericali.'

adopting the clerical dress, and remaining celibate. The Rector of a University of students was usually a beneficed ecclesiastic—a Dean or Archdeacon or Canon for instance[1]. In such cases he would have to be at least in minor orders : but he might be a *clericus* without being even in minor orders.

The Nations.

We have already alluded to the subdivision of the two Universities into Nations. In the earliest Statutes we find the Citramontani divided into three nations only, the Romans, the Tuscans, and the Lombards : but these are further subdivided into *Consiliariæ*, or smaller local divisions, each of which elected one or two Councillors[2]. By 1432, however, these *Consiliariæ*, seventeen in number, are occasionally spoken of as distinct Nations, though traces of the earlier arrangement still remained in the Statute book[3]. As early as 1265 the Ultramontani were divided into fourteen Nations[4]. In 1432 there were sixteen Ultramontane Na-

[1] Thus, at the time of the Reformation of the Statutes in 1432 we find that both Rectors are scholars in Canon Law, one being Dean of Troyes, the other Provost of a collegiate Church (*Stat.* p. 47). At Florence, in 1487, we find the *minimum* age reduced to nineteen (*Stat. Fiorent.* p. 15).

[2] 'Statuimus quod consiliarii sint numero triginta octo, scilicet decem et novem ultramontani, et totidem citramontani. De ultramontanis autem quod solitum est servetur. De citramontanis vero iuxta morem antiquum nacio Romanorum habeat sex, Thuscorum alios sex, reliquos habeat nacio Lombardorum, quos per consiliarias sic dividimus, sicut nacionis statutis est descriptum.' *Stat.* p. 16.

[3] The above-cited words are repeated nearly *verbatim*, except that the allusion to the Statutes of the Nation disappears and the Councillors are redistributed as follows : ' Natio Romanorum habeat octo, Tuscorum

sex, et natio Lombardorum quinque. Quas nationes per consiliarias sic dividimus, videlicet: Nationes vero sunt decem et septem, sex Romanorum, sex Tuscorum et quinque Lombardorum. Romana continet sub se has nationes : Nationem Romanorum, nationem Abrucii et terre laboris, apulie et calabrie, marchie inferioris, marchie superioris, item totius insule Sicilie. Natio Tuscorum habet sub se sex nationes, scilicet Florentinam, pisanam et lucanam, senensem, ducatum, ravenatem et venetorum. Natio lombardorum quinque nationes, cum vocibus contentis sub illis, scilicet ianuensium, mediolanensium, tessalonicam, longobardam et celestinam' (*Stat.* p. 68). Rome and Sicily have each two councillors. So in *Stat.* p. 50 the Ultramontane Consiliariæ are distinguished from the Cismontane Nationes.

[4] See doc. in *Acta Nationis Germ.* p. 347. The Nations are Gaul, Picardy, Burgundy, Poitou, Touraine and Maine, Normandy, Catalonia,

tions [1], each electing one, or in a few cases two *Consiliarii* [2]. In early times these Nations (which we have seen reason to believe were in reality earlier than the two great Federations into which they were ultimately merged), were, like the Nations of Paris, distinct corporations with Statutes, officers, and meetings of their own. But (except in the case of the specially privileged German Nation) they here appear to have lost much of their importance and autonomy, though they must have held Congregations of their own for the election of *Consiliarii* [3].

It is obvious that so enormous a body as the whole body of Law-students could not meet so frequently as the Parisian University of Masters. Many matters therefore which were at Paris dealt with by the University itself were at Bologna left to the Rectors and *Consiliarii*, who jointly formed the ordinary executive body of the University. The consent of one Rector and a majority of the Councillors was necessary to the calling of a congregation [4] —a provision which of course gave them the initiative in all University legislation. Upon the requisition of two Councillors, the votes were taken by ballot [5]. The concur-

The Consiliarii.

Hungary, Poland, Germany (Teothonici), Spain, Provence, England, Gascony. Poitou and Gascony were merged and assigned two councillors by the agreement made in this year (*ib.* p. 348).

[1] The names are now (*Stat.* pp. 70, 71): (1) Gaul, (2) Portugal and the Algarve, (3) Provence, (4) England, (5) Burgundy, (6) Savoy, (7) Gascony and Auvergne, (8) Berry, (9) Touraine, (10) Aragon and Catalonia with Valencia and the Majorcas (two councillors), (11) Navarre, (12) Germany (two councillors), (13) Hungary, (14) Poland, (15) Bohemia, (16) Flanders. The Statute speaks of nineteen ultramontane councillors, but only eighteen are accounted for.

[2] From the expressions 'habeat unam vocem et unum conciliarium,' 'habeat duas voces,' &c. (*Stat.* p. 68),

it would seem as if the voting was by Nations as at Paris (below, p. 405 *sq.*), but the Statute *De modo partiti ponendi in Universitate* proves the contrary (*Stat.* p. 130). Possibly the expression may be a survival.

[3] The Statutes of 1432 limit the 'festivitates Nationum que non sunt descripte inter festa universitatis' and abolish the 'officia prepositorum seu priorum Nationum seu consiliariorum ultramontanorum per que etiam Rectorum iurisdictio per tempora extitit multum impedita' (*Stat.* p. 139). We know from the *Acta Nat. Germ.* that the independent existence of the specially privileged German Nation was quite unaffected by this Statute: how it affected other nations we do not know.

[4] *Stat.* p. 60.

[5] *Stat.* p. 57.

CHAP. IV, rence of a majority of the Council was, as has been said,
§ 4. necessary before the Rector could pronounce the sentence
of deprivation, or declare a Doctor or scholar perjured [1].

Election of The Rector was chosen biennially by that method of
Rector. indirect election which bore so prominent a part in the
constitutions of Italian Republics. The electors were the
ex-Rectors, the newly-elected Councillors, and an equal
number of special delegates. The voting was by ballot,
a Dominican Priest acting as returning-officer [2]. The
Rector was required to be a 'secular clerk, unmarried,
wearing the clerical habit [3],' of five years standing in the
study of law, and at least twenty-four years of age [4]. The
Rector took precedence over all Archbishops and Bishops
(except the Bishop of Bologna) and even over Cardinals [5].

Rectorial The expenses of the office must have been in pro-
expenses. portion to its dignity, the only salary attached to it
being a moiety of the fines exacted by its occupant [6].
The Rector was expected to live with a certain amount of
state; he was bound, for instance, by Statute to keep at
least two liveried servants [7]. But the most serious expense was incurred in connexion with the festivities of the
Installation-day. If we may transfer to Bologna the custom of Padua, the ceremony took place in the Cathedral,
where, in presence of the assembled University, the Rector-
elect was solemnly invested with the Rectorial hood by

---

[1] *Stat.* p. 50.

[2] *Stat.* pp. 49–51.

[3] 'Clericus non coniugatus, habitum deferens clericalem, ac nullius religionis appareat.' *Stat.* p. 49.

[4] 'Qui ... vigesimum quintum sue etatis attigerit' (*Stat.* p. 49). Savigny wrongly gives the minimum age as twenty-five (cap. xxi. § 72).

[5] *Stat. Jur. Bon.* p. 90. The Legate and the Vexilifer Justicie are also placed above the Rectors. Cf. Ghirardacci, II. p. 424.

[6] *Stat.* p. 60. It appears that it had been at one time customary for the University to grant a *subventio*

towards the Rector's expenses. This is forbidden by the Statutes of 1432 (pp. 53, 54), unless the insufficiency of the Rector's purse is proved. But later it appears that it was customary to elect the Rectors to Student-chairs of 100 *libræ* — a salary which was doubled when the two Rectorships were amalgamated, and largely increased in the sixteenth century. Malagola, *Monografie*, pp. 52, 53: *Stat.* p. 181.

[7] *Stat.* p. 256: the title *Rector Magnificus* does not begin to be used till the end of the fifteenth century. Malagola, *Monografie*, p. 47.

one of the Doctors : after which he was escorted in triumph by the whole body of students to his house ; where a banquet, or at least wine and spices, awaited the constituents to whom he owed his exalted office [1]. It is worth mentioning as an illustration of the continuity of Academic custom that this 'deductio' with the subsequent 'wine and spices' was prescribed not only by the Statutes of Universities which directly copied those of Bologna, but by the ancient customs both of Paris and of Oxford [2]. At the latter it is observed in a somewhat shrunken form at the inauguration of the Vice-Chancellor, and of the Proctors. But in the Italian Universities the festivities at the Rectorial Inauguration were on a much vaster scale than anything that could have been provided by a poor Master of Arts in a Master-University. At Padua a tilt or tournament was held at which the new Rector was required to provide two hundred spears and two hundred pairs of gloves for the use of combatants. The Statutes of the Bologna University of Arts and Medicine forbade the Rector to feast those who escort him home, to give a banquet to more than twelve persons on the day of his election, or to 'dance or make to dance with trumpets or without' for a month after that event [3]. In the terms of this prohibition we may probably read a picture of the rejoicings which were permitted in the case of the wealthier University of Jurists. A still more curious and no less expensive feature of the entertainment as conducted in the sixteenth century was the custom of setting upon the newly-elected Rector, tearing his clothes off his back, and then requiring him to re-

---

[1] *Statuta Universitatis Juristarum Patavini Gymnasii,* 1550, f. 11.

[2] Facciolati, *Syntagmata,* p. 17 *sq. Stat. Jur. Pat. l. c.*

[3] 'Tripudiare aut tripudiari facere cum trombis vel sine vel cum aliis instrumentis, de nocte, cum dopleriis vel sine, directe vel indirecte.' *Stat.* p. 221. What is to dance ' in-

directly'? The Artists' Statutes of 1486 at Padua (*Stat. Artistarum Achademiæ Patavinæ,* fol. 3 b, 4 a) require the Rector to provide a *collatio* for the whole University, and to find at least 800 spears for the tournament, at which he awarded prizes compulsorily given by himself and the *Doctores legentes.*

CHAP. IV,
§ 4.

deem the fragments at an exorbitant rate. The Statute of 1552, which was passed to restrain 'the too horrid and petulant mirth' of these occasions, does not venture to abolish the time-honoured 'vestium laceratio[1].' These are a few examples of the extortions to which the newly-elected Rector was exposed. The Statutes of the various Universities abound with regulations as to the number of servants that the Rector shall keep, the value of his liveries[2], the quality of the wine that he should provide at his Installation banquet, and the like. Altogether, there is little cause for surprise that students eventually became as anxious to avoid the Rectorship as English country gentlemen are to escape the burdensome honour of the Shrievalty. The acceptance of the office by students of sufficient means was made compulsory, and elaborate precautions had to be taken to prevent those who had this unwelcome greatness thrust upon them from absconding before the expiration of their year of office. The Rector was, therefore, not allowed to leave the city without the permission of his Council, or without giving sufficient security for his return[3].

Accept-
ance com-
pulsory.

Decay of
the Rec-
torship.

In the middle of the fourteenth century we already find an instance of the two Jurist-rectorships being held by a single individual. Towards the end of the fifteenth century this arrangement became the rule instead of the exception. In the sixteenth century the difficulty of obtaining candidates able to perform such expensive duties, together with the growing hostility of governments to Student-rectorships, led either to a great reduction in the

---

[1] 'Vestem quoque abripi atque etiam lacerari non prohibemus dummodo sciant hi qui lacerarunt nihil hinc exigi posse, &c. Qui vero integram detulerunt, contenti discedant pecunia eis danda per rectorem que non sit minoris summe scutorum sex in totum.' *Stat. Jur. Bon.* (1561) p. 103.

[2] So at Ferrara, where he is also to keep a horse 'vel mulam honora-

bilem.' Borsetti, I. p. 376. He is also to provide a 'collationem laudabilem' to appease the 'altercationes' that were wont to arise at Rectorial elections, but it may be doubted whether the 'vinum dulce optimum' was the best means of securing that end.

[3] *Stat.* p. 65. Cf. the elaborate Statute *De excusatione electi,* p. 53.

splendour and dignity of the office, or to its permanent CHAP. IV, discharge by deputies—often Professors—who were not § 4. expected to maintain the state invariably associated with the actual Rectorship. At Bologna several instances of the appointment of a Vice-Rector occur in the later me- dieval period, and after 1580 this arrangement became per- manent. After 1609 the Rectorial duties were discharged by a deputy known as Prior, elected by the students for a single month only[1]. In 1742 the Rectorship was revived, but only to be conferred upon the Cardinal-legate of Bologna. This arrangement is a sufficient indication of the practical extinction of the student-liberties : still in this their earliest home the whole Student-constitution lasted in a shadowy form down to the Revolution[2]. In the Univer- sity as in the State the sixteenth century everywhere (except to some extent in England) broke down the old medieval liberties as well as the medieval licenses which those liber- ties had too often sheltered : but the last vestiges of them often lived on till they were swept away—only too ruth- lessly—by that mightier Revolution which was to bring back in a more advanced form the liberty which they had once enshrined.

The supreme governing body of the Society was the Congre- Congregation of the two Universities, i. e. the whole body gation. of students with the exception of poor men who lived ' at others' expense[3].' The Universities in their earliest days had no buildings of their own, and the fact is one which is of primary importance for the appreciation of the genius and history of the institution. Their power depended wholly upon the facility with which they could move from town to town : and when a University or a large section of it had decamped from the place, there were no effects left

---

[1] Malagola, *Monografie,* pp. 34, 133 *sq.* There was an isolated revival of the Rectorship in 1604. *Ib.* pp. 60, 205.

[2] *Ib.* pp. 72, 205 *sq* . After many vicissitudes (*ib.* pp. 75–81), the Rectorship is now re-established, but the Rector is of course no longer elected by the Students.

[3] ' Viventes sumptibus alienis . . . ut sunt socii doctorum bononiensium et scolarium bonon., repetitores et similes.' *Stat.* p. 147.

behind for the authorities to attach. In the earliest days of the Universities, the lecture-room or school was simply a hired apartment, or the private house of the Doctor[1]. None of these schools of course were large enough to hold the entire body of students. For great solemnities, such as Doctoral Inceptions, the Cathedral was used. For ordinary Congregations a Convent or a Church had to be borrowed. At Bologna the usual place of meeting was the great convent of S. Dominic (the burial-place of the Saint), in the sacristy of which the common chest and seal of the University were kept[2]. Attendance at these Congregations was compulsory. When a question was laid before the Assembly by the Rectors, every member had the right of speaking, but the Rectors had the power of 'closure,' and might 'impose silence on too prolix speakers[3].' The votes were taken by ballot with black and white beans[4].

Permanence of the Statutes.

It must not be supposed that University legislation was to the students of Bologna the weekly employment that it has become to the resident M.A.s of Oxford and Cambridge. As in the old Greek and medieval Italian Republics, the Constitution provided most effectual checks against hasty or over-frequent legislation of a permanent

---

[1] The will of Bonrecuperus Porrus († 1278) contains a clause : 'Et si decederet sine liberis legitimis masculis voluit et jussit ut domus ipsius testatoris in qua ipse moratur sic existat separata per murum a domo alia testatoris in qua morantur scholares et sunt schole,' ap. Sarti, I. pt. i. p. 215. So Sarti tells us that Odofredus ' Scholas habuit peramplas in suis aedibus, quarum aliquando mentionem ingerit in commentariis ad Pandectas.' *Ib.* p. 166.

[2] *Stat.* pp. 127, 189 : Ghirardacci (I. 525) says the usual place was 'al luogho de S. Dominico.' Was this the Church or the Piazza outside ? No room in the Convent would have been large enough. The only approach to a University building

which existed in medieval times was a ' Statio Universitatis ' in which the Rector sat and the Notary had his office, but there is no evidence that it was actually the property of the University. *Stat.* pp. 81, 83. The Rector held his Court in the ' Statio bidellorum generalium ' — probably the same place. *Ib.* p. 85.

[3] ' Possint tamen Rectores nimium prolixis in sermone silentium imponere.' *Stat.* p. 61.

[4] ' Priusquam ad fabas albas et nigras perveniatur.' *Stat.* p. 61. Cf. p. 130. At the beginning of every Congregation four Consiliarii were chosen who with the Rectors determined the form in which the question should be put ('forma partiti'). *Stat.* p. 60.

character. The Statutes could only be altered once every twenty years, when eight *Statutarii* were appointed to conduct the revision and to publish the new Code, which passed into law without any further confirmation by the University. In the intervals between these revisions, changes could only be made by the unanimous consent of the University upon a proposal already approved, first by the Rectors and Councillors, and then by a body of twenty-four members of the University named by them. A still more self-denying ordinance was the provision that in this case the consent of the Doctors was also necessary[1].

One of the most curious parts of the University system was the institution of *Peciarii*[2]. The Peciarii were six in number. Their duty was to supervise the *Stationarii* or keepers of book-stalls. The Stationer was compelled periodically to submit his MSS. to the inspection of this board, and the Stationer was liable to a fine of five Bologna *solidi* for every incorrect copy which he produced. Students who might detect clerical errors in their books were bound on pain of perjury to give information against the Stationer : and both Doctors and Students were bound at all times to lend their books to the Peciarii for the purpose of collation. The actual correction of the MSS. was carried out by the *Correctores peciarum.* The Stationer's primary business was to let out books on hire to scholars, the rate of hire being determined by the University Statutes[3]. So far the regulations are mainly applicable to books produced by the writers in the Stationers' employment. But a very large proportion of the book-trade in the Middle Ages was a second-hand trade. Books were dearer, but much more durable, than at the present day. In the sale of second-hand books, however, the Stationer was not allowed to reap the enormous profits made possible by the modern

---

[1] *Stat.* pp. 76–78.

[2] The following regulations are from *Stat.* pp. 75, 76.

[3] Six *denarii* were paid for the loan of a *quaestio* (for how long does not appear), and the Stationer might demand a 'pignus' of twice the value. (*Stat.* p. 76). A list of prices for the hire of books is given in *Stat.* p. 91, *sq.* A complete Digest costs 32 *solidi,* the Institutes 2*s.*

CHAP. IV, system.   He occupied the position not so much of a trader
§ 4.   as of an agent acting on behalf of the owner, and was
          remunerated by a fixed commission which was defrayed
          half by the buyer and half by the seller[1].   In the sale of
          new books he likewise, it would appear, served as a middle-
          man between the buyer and the writers.   A continual
          supply of fresh scholastic literature was ensured by the
          provision that every Doctor, after holding a 'disputatio'
          or 'repetitio' should, on pain of a fine of ten golden ducats,
          write out his argument and deliver it to the General Bedel
          of the University, by whom it was transmitted to the
          Stationers for publication[2].   Some similar regulation in
          our own Universities might be found a more effectual
          stimulus to research than much 'endowment' and many
          'visitatorial boards.'   The *Stationarii* were subject to a
          number of other minute regulations, most of which we shall
          find substantially reproduced at Paris, with a view of
          securing an adequate supply and keeping down the prices.
          Paternal government was in this matter carried so far that
          books above a certain value might only be sold in presence
          of the University notary[3].

Taxors.   Of the remaining University officials the most important
(*Taxatores* were the Taxors, who, jointly with arbitrators appointed
Hospici- by the city, fixed the rents of houses used by scholars.
orum.)   Five years' 'interdiction to scholars' was the penalty of
          refusal to abide by the decision of the arbitrators or any
          other infringement of the regulations of the University[4].
          This system of taxation was, as has been seen, very early
          recognized by Papal authority.   Traces of it are found in
          other places even before the rise of the Universities, and it
          soon became universal in all University towns whether of
          the Parisian or of the Bologna type.   Landlords were not

---

[1] Six *denarii* on each *libra* up to
60, afterwards four.   *Stat.* p. 89.
[2] *Stat.* p. 109.
[3] *Stat.* p. 87.   In Fournier, *Stat.
et Priv. des Univ. Françaises*, I. No.
150. is a contract for the sale of a
book as elaborate as a conveyance

of a landed estate.
[4] *Stat.* pp. 121 *sq.*, 160.   Four
proxenetæ were also appointed by the
Universities to assist students in
finding lodgings and the employment
of other intermediaries was forbidden.   *Ib.* p. 123.

the only class of citizens against whose exactions the Universities sought to protect their members. Both the University and the Town Statutes provide for the appointment by the University of four licensed Merchants or money-lenders or (as they might be no less correctly termed) pawnbrokers, who were privileged to lend money to students [1].

The other officials employed by the University but not selected from the student-body were the two *Massarii* or Treasurers [2], the *Notarius* [3], the *Syndicus* or common Advocate (a lawyer who also acted as legal assessor to the Rectors [4]) and the Bidelli Generales [5] (one for each University). The functions of the first three pretty well explain themselves. The duties of the Bedels were fairly analogous to those of the venerable and picturesque functionaries who bear the same name in our own Universities, except that they performed some of the duties now entrusted to the Clerk of the Schools and others which have fallen into desuetude. Thus, besides preceding the Rectors on public occasions, collecting the votes in Congregation, and so on, the Bedels went the round of the schools, to read Statutes and decrees of Congregation, announcements of lectures by students, lists of books which the *Stationarii* or individual students had on sale and other matters of general interest. He was remunerated by a special *collecta* to which all students were required to contribute the customary amount.

The Bedelship is among the most ancient of Academical offices—perhaps as ancient as the Rectorship. It is found

---

[1] *Stat.* p. 64, *De electione mercatorum.* The nature of their functions is explained in the Town-statute (*Stat.* p. 161), which exempts from military service ' quatuor mercatores vel feneratores qui mutuent eis pecuniam.' So at Florence, a *Fænerator* is to be elected ' cum quo paciscatur de salario usurarum ; qui Scholaribus mutuet sub usuris, pro minori quantitate lucri quam alii feneratores mutuent, tempore opportuno.' *Stat. Fior.* p. 34. Scholars were here forbidden to borrow from other money-lenders.

[2] *Stat.* pp. 19, 20.

[3] *Stat.* p. 79 *sq.* He kept the Matricula, and recorded the acts of the University.

[4] *Stat.* p. 79.

[5] *Stat.* p. 84 *et passim.*

CHAP. IV,
§ 4.

in all medieval Universities without exception. In fact, an allusion to a *bidellus*[1] is in general (though not invariably) a sufficiently trustworthy indication that a School is really a University or Studium Generale. It is interesting to observe that in spite of the decay of most that is medieval in the continental Universities the Bedels of Bologna and the other Italian Universities still appear upon public occasions with the ponderous maces which they have borne from medieval times, and which retain almost exactly the form familiar to Oxonian or Cantabrigian eyes.

Special Bedels.

Besides the General or University Bedels, each Doctor had a 'special Bedel' of his own, who looked after his school, opened and shut the door, swept it out twice a month, strewed the floor with straw in winter and carried his Doctor's books to the school. He was remunerated by a *collecta* from his Master's pupils. Both the special and general Bedels preceded the Rectors at funerals or other University processions[2].

Few disciplinary Statutes.

The Statutes of the Student-Universities naturally do not regulate the private life of students with the same detail as the College-statutes or even the later University-statutes of Paris and Oxford. The students of Bologna lived in their own houses and entirely after their own fashion. The usual practice was not to take lodgings in a citizen's house like the modern extra-collegiate student, but for parties of students (*socii*) to hire the whole house together and make their own arrangements as to servants, furniture[3] and the like[4]. To live in a townsman's house (*ad contubernia* or *ad*

---

[1] Often spelt *pedellus*, whence the *Pedel* of the German Universities. It is derived of course from *pedum* (a stick).

[2] *Stat.* pp. 84, 85. Cf. *Stat. Fiorent.* pp. 68, 81, 96.

[3] What this furniture was may be gathered from a Statute of the College of Spain at Bologna : 'Cameram quoque unusquisque predictorum fulcitam habeat expensu collegii lectisternio uno, matalatio uel cultra,

cooptorio plumari et linteaminibus de tela grossa, archobanco, studio (a desk) et paleis pro lecto necessariis.' He is allowed to buy additional furniture at his own expense. MS. *Stat.* f. 13 b. (See below, p. 200, n. 4).

[4] At Lerida the Bedel is required to introduce the new-comer to a suitable *Societas*. *Stat.* ap. Villanueva, *Viage Literario*, XVI. p. 223. So at Bologna a student 'going

cameram) was the exception[1]. The principal disciplinary regulations which we do find relate to two subjects—the wearing of arms and the practice of gambling : quarrelling and gambling were no doubt the most prevalent, or at all events the most troublesome, vices among Italian students. The wearing of arms at Congregation is prohibited : but, mindful that without them the life of a student would not always be safe, the Statutes allow any one who fears his enemy's stiletto privately to inform the Rector and so obtain leave of absence[2]. The Statutes against gambling are extremely strict. 'With a view of obviating the loss of money' attendant upon the practice, it is made an offence even to watch a game of dice played in public. Students are forbidden to enter or to keep gaming-houses, and the latter prohibition is expressly extended to Doctors[3]. There is also a very curious provision that a student was not even to play in his own house during the three months before 'going down' for good or (as it was technically styled) 'going home a wise man,' or again for one month after taking his degree[4]. Was the legislator anxious to provide against the exceptional temptations to frivolity and dissipation which the close of an Academic career brought with it, or was he influenced by a merely prudential desire to protect the remaining students against irrecoverable debts of honour? In the Student-University of Lerida scholars are forbidden to entertain or be entertained by actors or pro-

---

down' is required to deliver his key not to the landlord but to his 'socii.' *Stat.* p. 125.

[1] *Statuta Juristarum Patavini Gymnasii*, 1550, f. 119. If the analogy of Paris may be trusted it was customary only with the poorest students. (Cf. below, p. 475.)

[2] *Stat.* pp. 130, 131.

[3] *Stat.* p. 133 (*De ludo taxillorum*). There is, however, an exception in favour of playing 'ad scacos (chess) vel ad tabulas causa recreationis.' (What was the principle of the dis-

tinction between 'taxilli' and 'tabulæ'?) The provisions against professorial gambling were not uncalled for : 'Joannes Bassianus . . . nonnumquam pannis exutus, nudus remanebat in alea.'—Guil. de Pastrengo ap. Sarti, I. pt. i. p. 90.

[4] 'Adjicientes quod nullus doctorari volens, vel sapiens recedere infra duos menses ante suum recessum vel conventum audeat ludum in hospitio suo tenere, vel aliis ludentibus consentire nec etiam post doctoratum per mensem.'—*Stat.* p. 133.

fessional jesters, except at Christmas, Easter and Whitsun-tide, or at the Inceptions[1] : even at these times they might only provide them with food, but not with money, in return for their professional services. The thrifty students of Lerida are also forbidden to ride to the schools or to keep a horse, though a mule is allowed. The Statutes even prescribe the number of courses to which they might entertain their friends, and the maximum price of their clothes[2]. At Bologna the regulations, so far as extant, were less inquisitorial.

Academical dress.

The Statutes relating to costume must be regarded more in the light of sumptuary regulations than as a requirement of 'academical dress.' The 'Cappa' or other outer garment was required to be of ' statutable or black' stuff[3], the penalty for the violation of this Statute being much higher than the ineffectual Oxford five shillings. Hoods were not limited to graduates, but a miniver hood was the especial distinction of Rectors and Professors. The former were

---

[1] ' Mimis, joculatoribus, istrionibus, militibus qui dicuntur salvatges, cœterisque truffatoribus, &c.' Villanueva, *Viage Literario*, XVI. p. 230. The clause as to the Rectorial and Doctorial inaugurations was repealed in the following year, *l. c.* p. 233.

[2] *Ib.* pp. 233, 234.

[3] ' Damnosis scolarium sumptibus providere cupientes, statuimus quod nullus scolaris . . . emat per se vel per alium pannum alium quam qui vulgariter vocatur pannus de statuto vel de panno coloris nigri, quem pannum pro habitu superiori, cappa, tabardo vel gabano vel consimili veste consueta pro tunc longiore veste inferiori et clausa a lateribus ac etiam fibulata seu maspillata anterius circa collum portare teneantur infra civitatem sub pœna trium librarum bonon.' (*Stat.* pp. 132, 133.) It is difficult to explain the contradiction between the insistence in this

Statute upon *black,* and the fact that in the medieval illumination reproduced in *Acta Nationis Germanicæ* the majority of the Students are represented as coming to the Proctor to be sworn attired in long *red* gowns. Was this a privilege of the German Nation or of nobles? The Statute at Florence simply requires ' omnes de uno eodemque colore panni.' (*Stat. Fior.* p. 97.) The form of both the Doctoral and Student *Cappa* may be seen in the beautiful tombs of the Doctors which form the most characteristic feature of the Bologna Churches. There is usually a recumbent effigy of the Doctor above, while below he is represented as lecturing (seated) to his students sitting at slightly sloping desks or narrow tables, very much like those of a modern lecture-room. Some of the College Statutes, even in Italy, insist on the ' clericalem habitum.' (Facciolati, *Fasti,* p. xx.)

required to wear their hoods whenever they appeared in public, but in summer were allowed to exchange them for cooler hoods of silk [1]. On state occasions at least, the Doctors of all Faculties wore robes of purple and miniver, while the Rectors were robed in scarlet or scarlet and gold.

If the discipline which the free and independent students of Bologna imposed upon themselves exhibits few indications of extraordinary strictness, the same cannot be said of the discipline which they imposed upon their subjects—the Professors. Whatever view, as a matter of constitutional theory, the Doctors might take of their relations with the students, it is certain that while the latter were in no way bound to obedience to the Prior or College of the Doctors, the Doctors were compelled, under pain of a ban which would have deprived them of pupils and income, to swear obedience to the Students' Rector [2], and to obey any other regulations which the Universities might think fit to impose upon them. While not entitled to a vote in the University Congregation, the Professor was liable to 'privatio' or expulsion from a Society to whose privileges he had never been admitted [3]. At any moment his lectures might be interrupted by the entrance of the Bedel to serve a summons on the Professor to appear before the Rector, or to read a Rectorial proclamation to the students or a new Statute of the Student-University to which his consent had not been asked but to which his obedience was none the less required. A scholar was, indeed, obliged as the con-

Bondage of the Professors.

[1] *Stat.* p. 55. At Padua the Rector of the Artists is to wear a robe of scarlet silk in summer, and a scarlet robe of some thicker material (*de grana*) in winter (*Stat. Artist. Pat.* f. iii, *b.* iv. *a*), while the Rector of the Jurists wears robes embroidered with gold as well as fur. (Colle, *Storia dello Studio di Padova*, I. p. 104 : Malagola, *Monografie*, p. 87). Later we hear of a Rectorial hood of gold brocade. *Ib.* p. 62. In the time of Gaggi, Doctors of Divinity wore the *Almutium violaceum*

(a tippet) and Doctors of the other Faculties had the privilege 'uti Varris (ermine) et torque aurea.' In processions of the College, the Bedels carried gold maces before them.

[2] *Stat.* p. 99. A Doctor, neglecting to take the oath, 'non possit eo anno facere collectam suam et ultra hoc Rectorum arbitrio puniatur.' *Ib.* p. 100.

[3] A ban which sometimes extended even to the descendants of the offender.

dition of enjoying the privileges of 'scholarity' to attend lecture at least three times a week : but a Professor requiring leave of absence even for a single day was compelled to obtain it first from his own pupils and then from the Rectors and *Consiliarii* : and if he proposed to leave the town, he was required to deposit a sum of money by way of security for his return [1].   He is expressly forbidden 'to create holidays at his pleasure [2]'; and his scholars are bound on pain of perjury to give information against a truant Doctor [3].   By the City-regulations, moreover, for each day on which he failed to secure an audience of five for an ordinary lecture, or three for an extraordinary one, he was treated as absent and incurred the appointed fine accordingly [4].

Punctuality enforced upon Professors.

Punctuality is enforced with extreme rigour.   The Professor was obliged to begin his lecture when the bell of S. Peter's began to ring for mass, under a penalty of 20 *solidi* for each offence [5], though he has the privilege of beginning at an earlier hour if he pleases ; while he is forbidden to continue his lecture one minute after the bell has begun to ring for tierce.   To secure the observance of this Statute a more effectual means is adopted even than that of fining the Doctor : his pupils are required under a penalty of 10 *solidi* each to leave the Lecture-room as soon as the bell begins.

Mode of lecturing prescribed by Statute.

Even in the actual conduct of his lectures the Doctor is regulated with the precision of a soldier on parade or a reader in a French public library.   He is fined if he skips a Chapter or Decretal: he is forbidden to postpone a difficulty to the end of the Lecture lest such a liberty should be abused as a pretext for evading it altogether. In medieval as in modern times Lecturers had a tendency

---

[1] *Stat.* p. 109.

[2] 'Nec festa pro libito faciant.' A penalty of 40s. is provided 'pena periurii non obstante.' *Ib.* p. 101.

[3] *Ib.* p. 110.

[4] 'Punctetur perinde ac si eo die non legisset.' Dallari, I. p. xxii.

[5] 'Nec audea[n]t tardare ad veniendum post pulsationem dicte campane ad scolas pena XX solidorum.' *Stat.* p. 105.

to spend a disproportionate time over the earlier portions Chap. IV,
§ 4. of a book, and so leave none for the rest. With a view of checking this practice, an expedient was adopted at Bologna which became universal in the Law-Universities of Southern Europe[1]. The Law-texts were divided into portions known as *puncta*; and the Doctor was required *Compelled* to have reached each *punctum* by a specified date. At *servare puncta.* the beginning of the academical year he was bound to deposit the sum of 10 Bologna pounds with a banker, who promised to deliver it up at the demand of the Rectors : for every day that the Doctor was behind time, a certain sum was deducted from his deposit by order of these officials. With a view of enforcing obedience to this and other Statutes on the part of the Doctors, a Committee of students (*Denunciatores Doctorum*) was appointed by the Rectors to observe their conduct, and report their irregularities to the Rector[2].

The Colleges which played so large a part in the *Colleges.* development of the Northern Universities were comparatively unimportant in Bologna and the other Italian Universities. They were as a rule smaller foundations than the Colleges of Paris and Oxford, and they remained to the last (what all Colleges were originally intended to be) eleemosynary institutions for the help of poor students, boarding-houses and not places of education. A small *Coll. of* College of Avignon was founded in Bologna in 1267 by *Avignon, 1267.* Zoen Tencararius, Bishop of Avignon, for eight students, three of whom were to be Canons of his Cathedral[3]; but it does not seem clear whether its members originally lived

---

[1] This provision occurs only in the earlier Statutes (p. 42), but the institution is implied in the later Statutes (pp. 78, 79). The meaning of the expression ' ut puncta per eos bene serventur ' has to be inferred from the Statutes of other Universities.

[2] *Stat.* pp. 23, 78, 79. The stakeholder was known as the *Depositarius*

(Dallari, I. p. xxiv). The students profess to be actuated by anxiety for their masters' spiritual welfare. The Statute begins ' Christiano cuique sed precipue sacre legis doctoribus periculosum noscentes esse periurium' (*Stat.* p. 78).

[3] Sarti, I. pt. ii. (1888), p. 416 ; I. pt. ii. (1772), pp. 118-123.

in community, or merely received pensions : in any case the property of the scholars was held in trust for them by the Bishop of Avignon. The College of Brescia was founded by Guglielmo de Brescia, Archdeacon of Bologna, in 1326 [1], and the College of Reggio by the Physician, Guido Bagnoli

di Reggio, in 1362 [2]. But the first College, on a scale at all approaching that with which we are familiar in the English Universities, was the College of Spain, founded by the will of the great Spanish Cardinal, Egidio Albornoz, (once Archbishop of Toledo, but compelled to fly from the tyranny of Peter the Cruel, and afterwards Papal legate at Bologna), who died in 1367 [3]. This College appears to have been the model of many others in Italy and Spain. In the sixteenth century we may infer from the privileges which the University conferred upon its Rector, that it had acquired some faint shadow of the prestige enjoyed by the Sorbonne and the College of Navarre at Paris or at Oxford by the foundations of Wykeham and Wolsey. The College of Spain may be taken as a type of the College-constitution in Universities of the Bologna type [4]. A short account of its organization and arrangement may therefore be worth giving.

In the Statutes as revised by Papal delegates in 1377 it is provided that the College shall consist of thirty scholars —eight in Theology, eighteen in Canon Law, and four in Medicine. The scholars held their places for seven years, except in the case of a Theologian or Medical student who

---

[1] Sarti, I. pt. ii. p. 523 : Orlandi, p. 89. It was afterwards merged in the Collegium Gregorianum founded by Gregory XI in 1371. Cf. Ghirardacci (II. 302, 307), who prints the Statutes. They provide for thirty Scholars of Law and six Chaplains. The lecture-fees of Scholars are to be paid out of the foundation—a rather unusual provision in the North.

[2] Malagola, Pref. to *Stat.* p. xiii.

[3] Ghirardacci, T. II. p. 285 ff. Savigny in his list mentions this College twice over under different names (cap. xxi. § 72).

[4] The printed Statutes are of the sixteenth century; no earlier Statutes were known to be extant. In 1889, however, I found that the statutes of 1377 were contained in MS. No. 5383 of the Phillipps Library at Cheltenham (catalogued as ' Statuta Bononiensia '). Their provisions are materially different from the printed edition.

wished to stay up and lecture as a Doctor. The scholarships were divided among the numerous Spanish dioceses
in which the founder had held preferment. The patronage
was vested in the Bishops and Chapters of those dioceses
together with two members of the Albornoz family, i. e.
the head of the house and any member of it who was a
prelate, or if more than one were prelates, then the superior
or senior prelate. The qualification for election was
poverty [1], and competent grounding, 'at least in Grammar.'
In the case of the Theologians and Medical students,
Logic was also required, and if they had not heard Philosophy before, their first three years of residence were to be
devoted mainly to that Faculty [2]. An entrance examination was held, and the College was at liberty to reject
nominees who failed to satisfy these requirements. Every
scholar received daily a pound of moderate beef or veal or
other good meat with some 'competent dish,' the larger
part at dinner, the smaller at supper [3]. Wine, salt, and bread
were at discretion ; but the wine was to be watered in
accordance with the Rector's orders [4]. A portion of the
allowance for meat might be applied by the Rector to the
purchase of salt meat or fruit. We may charitably hope
that the College availed itself of this provision on Feast-
days and on the Sunday before Lent, when the above mentioned 'portions' of meat were doubled. On Fast-days the
ordinary allowance was to be spent on fish and eggs. At
a 'congruous time' (not further defined) after dinner and
supper respectively, the College re-assembled for 'collation,'
when drink was 'competently' administered to every one [5].

---

[1] i. e. his income (unless he were Rector) must not be 'ultra summam quinquaginta florenorum auri Bono-niensium'. *MS. Stat.* f. 5 b.

[2] The printed Statutes add that the Scholars must be 'Ancient Chris-tians'—a provision redolent of the Moorish wars and the fanaticism which they engendered.

[3] 'Carmium castratinarum uel uitilinarum mediocrum uel aliarum

bonarum ... cum aliquo ferculo com-petenti. ' *MS. Stat.* f. 12 b.

[4] 'De uino autem Rectoris arbi-trio temperato, panem, et sal habeant in prandio et in cena quantum uo-luerint et conueniat honestati,' *l. c.*

[5] 'Post prandium uero et post cenam quolibet die hora congrua signo campane in modum cibali ad iussum Rectoris uel eius uices gerentis pulsato, ad collacionem

Besides commons, each scholar received every autumn a new scholastic 'cappa, sufficiently furred with sheep-skin,' and another without fur, and with a hood of the same stuff and colour as the cope[1], at the beginning of May; and there was an annual allowance of twelve Bologna pounds for candles, breeches, shoes, and other necessaries. Poor scholars of the founder's kin have a peremptory claim to a vacant scholarship; while any scholar of the Albornoz family residing in Bologna becomes the 'Protector' of the College with certain visitatorial powers, and the right to a seat in the College 'Chapter.' If he is twenty years of age, these powers are to be exercised on his own responsibility: if under twenty, he is to act by the advice of his tutor, but may none the less be present at College meetings to gain experience.

Demo-
cratic con-
stitution
of the
College.

So far the regulations of the College of Spain are of very much the same character as those of medieval College-statutes in our own magisterially-ruled Universities. When we come, however, to those respecting the mode of internal government, all is changed. The Bologna College is governed as democratically as the Bologna University. Scholars under eighteen years of age are, indeed (as was the case in many Universities), to have no vote, though they might be present at Chapters. But the Rector is to be elected annually by ballot; like the Rector of the University he is to be at least twenty-four years of age and a clerk.

conueniant et prebeatur potus cuilibet competenter.' *MS. Stat.* f. 13 a.

[1] ' Una capa scolastica et noua et foderata suficienter pellibus pecudis, ut studentes Bononienses habere communiter consueuerint': the other to be 'sine foderatura de panno statuti coloris eiusdem et capuceum de competenti panno eiusdem eciam coloris, ualoris quinque solidorum.' (f. 13 a.) The printed Statutes (Bonon. 1558, f. xviii.) order that Scholars 'utentur veste ex panno nigro ... talaris sit et manicata, qua forma nunc doctores, olim cum hoc primum in Collegio fuit institutum etiam scholastici Bononienses uti videbantur, et focali quod dicitur caputeus ex hyacinthino panno qui morellus vulgo nuncupatur ...quibus vestibus et focali semper uti debeant, quocumque sive ad scholas sive per urbem iuerint et quacunque hora diei.' It is obvious that the form of the dress has considerably altered since the fourteenth century. A black gown with a cherry-coloured silk scarf (by way of 'focale') is still worn by students of the College on state occasions.

He is assisted by *Consiliarii* elected in the same way : but in important matters such as the alienation of property, the consent of the whole College is necessary. In fact the constitution of the College is the University constitution in miniature. But though establishing this system of popular government, the Cardinal-founder was not of opinion that democracy necessarily meant weak government or no government at all. The discipline prescribed by the Strict Statutes is decidedly stricter than that contemplated discipline. by the Oxonian or Parisian Statutes of the same period. There was a Chapel served by four Chaplains ; two masses were to be said daily, one before and one after the 'Ordinary' lecture, and presence at one or other of these was to be compulsory, besides attendance at Matins and Vespers on holidays and at Vespers on Vigils. Daily attendance at lecture is enforced by fines. The monastic silence and Bible-reading are observed in Hall[1]. Lateness in returning to College at night is visited by a day's 'penitence on bread and water,' a second offence by three days' bread and water, and a third offence entails expulsion. A Chaplain who stays out of College for a night loses half his year's salary, besides being condemned to three days' bread and water. A nocturnal exodus by the window involves immediate expulsion. For an assault on a brother-scholar, the penalty was no less than five days in the stocks and one day's penance on bread and water to be eaten sitting on the floor of the Hall[2]. For an assault resulting in effusion of blood or for assisting in the quarrels of others, the penalty was doubled. The punishment of the stocks is not mentioned in English or Parisian Colleges till the sixteenth century, though these Colleges contained boys much younger than were usually to be found in the College of Spain. It may be added that women are warned off the premises — including even the Chapel — in language as

---

[1] It is, however, expressly provided that Scholars may be either *clerici* or *laici*.

[2] 'Quinque diebus stent in cipo ligneo saltem cum uno pede et die qua extrahentur in pane et aqua coram omnibus in terra peniteant.' (*MS. Stat.* f. 27 a.)

The Col-
lege sur-
vives.

ferociously ungallant as could be culled from the Statutes of the rudest northern disciplinarian [1].

The College of Spain still flourishes upon its ancient site in sumptuously adorned buildings of the sixteenth century, whose quadrangle, Chapel, Hall, and students' rooms still testify to the continuance on a small scale (there are only five or six students) of the College life with which we are familiar in the English Universities. Indeed, the College of Spain reproduces the medieval type far more faithfully than any English College : for all its members are graduates in Arts, none of them teachers, but all students in Law. The College is now under the control of the Spanish Government, which sends to it candidates for the diplomatic service who have taken the B.A. degree in a Spanish University.

Later
Colleges.

The Colleges continued to be exceptionally few at Bologna—fewer even than in other Italian Universities—throughout the medieval period. The names of only two others are recorded as founded before 1500 [2]—the *Collegium Gregorianum* founded by Gregory XI in 1371, and the *Collegium Ancaranum* founded by Pietro d'Ancarano, Doctor of Decrees, in 1414 [3]. It was only in the fervour of the Catholic Reaction that Bologna began to be a City of Colleges. One explanation of the paucity of the Bologna Colleges is no doubt to be found in the selfish policy pursued by the Bologna Government towards foreign students who were here deprived of all chance of a career as teachers. One of the numerous seventeenth century Colleges—the little house founded by John Jacobs for Flemish students in 1650 [4]—still survives to assist the more magnificent

---

[1] ' Et quia mulier est caput peccati, arma diaboli, expulsio paradisi et corrupcio legis antique et propterea omnis eius conuersacio sit diligencius euictanda, interdicimus,' &c. (*MS. Stat.* f. 20 a.) Dancing is forbidden ' quia secundum sanctorum patrum sentenciam in coreis diabolus facilius illaqueat homines' (*l. c.* 27 b).

[2] See the Statutes in Ghirardacci,

II. p. 308 *sq.* Here also we find the Students' Lecture-fees paid out of the foundation.

[3] Orlandi, *Notizia*, p. 89. Cf. Ghirardacci, II. p. 603 : *Stat.* p. 200.

[4] *Statuta servanda a Juvenibus Belgis qui admissi fuerint in Collegium Jacobs Bononiæ fundatum an.* 1650 *sub titulis SS. Trin. Reformata*, A. D. 1829, &c.

College of Spain in bearing testimony to the cosmo-
politanism of the old medieval Universities. Thus at
Bologna, all but alone among continental Universities, in
one of the two great original homes of University life, there
survive specimens of the true medieval College, reduced to
smaller dimensions than of old, but retaining more completely the old form and purpose of a medieval College
than the more famous but more altered foundations which
form the especial glory of our English Universities.

§ 5. The Organization of the Studium.

Chap. IV,
§ 5.
The Guild
of Doctors
acquires a
monopoly.

We have seen reason to believe that the Guilds of Doctors were in their origin somewhat more ancient than the Guilds of foreign students. By some process which we are quite unable to trace the old liberty of unlicensed lay teaching, in which the School of Bologna originated, came to an end. In the teaching profession, as in so many others, trades-unionism ultimately triumphed over liberty of contract, and the right of teaching became practically, if not theoretically, restricted to those who had been made free of the teaching Guild[1]. This restriction was the foundation of the system of Academical degrees. The degree was in its origin nothing more than a qualification to teach. But when, in consequence of the general advance of civilization and enlightenment which marked the twelfth century, the services of learned men came to be in general request, it was natural that this certificate of competency should be valued for other than teaching purposes. In the course of the twelfth century the style of Master came to be regarded as a title of honour which it was not beneath the dignity of a Bishop or a Cardinal to prefix to his name.

If we may judge from the number of persons who enjoyed this designation in the second half of the century, we may infer that it had already become pretty common for a 'degree' to be taken—to use the modern expression—by persons who had no intention of devoting themselves, or at least of permanently devoting themselves, to the work of teaching. We may presume that this was the case at Bologna as well as at Paris, though the Masters of the

---

[1] The liberty of private teachers may perhaps be considered to have been legally terminated by the Bull of Honorius III, in 1219. See below, p. 223.

Civil or Canon Law were never so numerous as the Parisian Masters of Arts. But at Bologna the distinction between simple 'graduates,' who had no intention of permanently devoting themselves to the teacher's office, and actually teaching Doctors, was from an early period much more sharply drawn than at Paris and Oxford. The number of actual teachers of Law at Bologna was always comparatively small : enormous crowds attended the lectures of a single Professor ;· the teacher's chair was here a coveted and lucrative prize. At Paris, in consequence of the multiplication of Masters of Arts, the remuneration that could be got by teaching was small, and a difficulty was experienced in getting a sufficient supply of teachers. Hence it was left open to anyone to teach who chose, and it was even necessary to compel graduates to reside and teach for a time to ensure a sufficient number of lecturers. At Bologna, on the contrary, the distinction between the *Magistri* or *Doctores legentes* and the *Non-legentes* was fundamental. The teaching Doctors of Bologna very Teaching confined to an inner circle of Doctors. soon passed into something like the position of a modern Professoriate, and the rights of the Doctor or Master as such fell more and more into abeyance. The various steps of this process must now be investigated, so far as the scanty data at our disposal admit. As to the use of these alternative titles, it may be observed that at Bologna the title most affected was Doctor, rather than Professor or Master. At first the title Master was used by other Faculties than the legal, but eventually the term Doctor became universal. The Doctors of Law were also frequently called 'Domini.' A scholar would speak of his Master as 'Dominus meus'; but the mere use of the term 'Dominus' does not imply a Master : in Italy it is often applied to mere students. It is characteristic of the different relations in which the Master stood to his class at Bologna that the Parisian term 'Regens' is here rarely used.

Before, however, the successive changes in the position of 'Ordinary' the teaching body can be understood, it is absolutely necessary to explain a distinction between two classes of lectures 'Ordinary' and 'Extraordinary' Lectures.

which originated at Bologna, and which afterwards spread, with more or less modification, to all the Universities of Europe. The lectures were divided into 'Ordinary' and 'Extraordinary.' Ordinary lectures were those given in the morning: Extraordinary lectures in the afternoon. Originally this distinction of time corresponded with a distinction between what were considered the more essential and the less essential of the Law-texts. The Ordinary books of the Civil Law were the first part of the Pandects technically known as the *Digestum Vetus* and the Code: the extraordinary books were the two remaining parts of the Pandects known respectively as the *Infortiatum*[1] and the *Digestum Novum*, together with the collection of smaller text-books known as the *Volumen* or *Volumen Parvum*, which included the *Institutiones* and the *Authentica* (i.e. the Latin translation of Justinian's Novels), the Lombard *Liber Feudorum*, and a detached fragment of the Code known as the *Tres Libri*.

Origin of this distinction.

This distinction between the various parts of the Digest is purely arbitrary. The *Infortiatum*, though its ending corresponds with a natural transition in the subject-matter, begins in the middle of a book. It is obvious on the face of it that the division must have originated in an accidental separation of some archetypal MS.—probably of the original Bologna copy of the great Pisan codex. According to a tradition which has already been alluded to, Irnerius began his work as a teacher by lecturing on a MS. of the Old Digest, which was the first to arrive from Ravenna ; while the *Infortiatum* came to Bologna later and the *Digestum Novum* (we may presume) last of all[2]. The

---

[1] The *Dig. Vetus* extends from the beginning to the end of Lib. XXIV. tit. ii, the *Infortiatum* thence to the end of Lib. XXXVIII. tit. iii, the rest of the Pandects being the *Dig. Nov.* There is an extremely arbitrary section known as the *Tres Partes* (beginning in the middle of a paragraph), so called from its commencement at the words *Tres Partes* in *L. Quere-* *batur.* 82. D. *ad L. Falcidiam.* The *Tres Partes* is sometimes treated as part of the *Infortiatum*, sometimes as a distinct portion.

[2] See above, pp. 112, 122. Of the various explanations of 'Infortiatum' Mommsen accepts the view 'Id est auctum'; he sanctions the above explanation of the division. *Digest. Libri*, 1866. I. Præf. p. lxxii.

distinction must in any case have originated in some accidental circumstance of the kind : and the matter is only
noticed here because it seems probable that the distinction
between Ordinary and Extraordinary books originated
in the same historical fact. The Ordinary are not intrinsically more important than the Extraordinary, but they
must have formed the main or exclusive subject of the
Doctoral lectures in the early days of the School, the
Infortiatum and the *Digestum Novum* being successively
introduced at a later period. In the Schools of the Canon
Law the Ordinary books were the *Decretum* and the Five
Books of Decretals published by Gregory IX, the Clementines and Extravagants being Extraordinary [1].

Ordinary lectures were reserved to Doctors, but Extraordinary lectures on certain limited portions of the Law-
texts might be given also by Scholars of a certain standing,
after being 'admitted to read' such lectures by the
Rector. By delivering such a course of lectures a Scholar
became a Bachelor. The term was at first probably a
popular term applied to any senior student who was shortly
intending to proceed to the Doctorate : eventually it obtained the more definite and technical meaning already
mentioned [2].

---

[1] *Stat.* p. 159. At Paris only the *Decretum* was ordinary, which was no doubt once the case at Bologna. See below, chap. v. § 4. Kaufmann (I. p. 213), on the authority of Odofredus (' licet insolitum sit quærere a dominis sive doctoribus in mane de eo quod legant in mane, peto veniam'), holds that questions might be asked at ex-traordinary and not at ordinary lectures. This is not impossible, but I do not feel sure that the distinc-tion is not one between the lectures proper and the afternoon *repetitiones* on the morning lecture. The lectures of Odofredus on the *Infortiatum* certainly show no difference in style or manner from those on the *Dig. Vet.*

Hugolinus makes it the duty of the student ' socium quærentem pati cum benignitate' (ap. Savigny, *l. c.*).

[2] Many absurd definitions of the word *Baccalaurius* or (according to the earlier spelling) *Baccalarius* have been given. The actual etymology of the word seems to be doubtful; but there can be no doubt that the general meaning of the word *Bache-lier* at the time when it came to be applied—first in common usage, and eventually as a formal designation— to students authorized to teach by way of preparation for the master-ship, was 'a young man,' with the special sense of apprentice or as-sistant (e. g. the landless man who worked for a *colonus*). ' En réa-

We are now in a position to trace the process by which the simple Doctorate was gradually shorn of its prerogatives and degraded from an office—carrying with it the full rights of teaching, of membership in the Doctoral College, and of control over the extension of those rights to others —into a mere honorary distinction or 'degree.' This revolution was the effect of three distinct changes :—

Doctors originally dependent upon fees.

(1) We know in reality very little of the teaching system of the University—or indeed of any other parts of its organization—in the thirteenth century. But enough evidence has come down to us to make it clear that the teacher was absolutely dependent for support upon his *collecta*, i. e. the fees paid to him by his pupils[1]. The ordinary practice was for a Professor to employ a couple of scholars to negotiate with the other students as to how much each was to pay : but at times a large body of students would make their own terms with the Professor, and divide the cost among themselves. The amount of the honoraria was not even approximately fixed by custom, and at times we find learned Professors of the highest reputation haggling with their scholars over these payments in a highly sophist-like and undignified manner[2].

lité,' says M. Thurot (*L'Organisation de l'enseignement dans l'Un. de Paris,* p. 137), ' ce terme signifiait apprentissage.' We everywhere meet with the institution of the Baccalaureate or pupil-teachership before the name occurs in formal documents. It probably arose as a slang term : cf. the list of students ' qui legunt extraordinarie et *vulgariter Bachalarii vocantur,*' in a document of 1297, ap. Sarti, I. ii. (1772) p. 105. At Paris we likewise find the *institution* before the name. See below, p. 443.

[1] Ghirardacci (I. p. 77) speaks of 'molti Dottore da publico stipendiati' in 1150, but produces no evidence.

[2] ' Anno MCCLXIX die Jovis XIII exeunt. April. Albertus qu. (*sc.* quæstor) dn. Odofredi doct. leg. fuit confessus recepisse a dn. Viviano . . . scholare bonon. quinquaginta libras bonon. quas in solidum cum mag. Gorlano suo fratre ei dare tenebatur ex instrumento manu Ugolini qu. Ugolini Presbiteri notar. Item xxxvi libr. bonon. pro parte sua et dicto suo fratri contingente de debito quadringentarum libr. bonon. quas in solidum cum pluribus scholaribus dicto dn. Odofredo dare tenebantur ratione collectae ex instrum. Mich. Vineiguerrae notar. *Ex Memor. Com. Bonon.* ap. Sarti, I. pt. i. p. 166. ' Bene scitis quod cum doctores faciunt collectam, doctor non quærit a scholaribus, sed eligid duos scholares, ut scrutentur voluntates scholarium : promittunt scholares per illos. Mali scholares nolunt solvere quia dicunt, quod per procuratorem

Thus, for instance, we find the eminent Jurist Odofredus CHAP. IV,
announcing at the termination of a course of lectures, that § 5.
next year he would give no afternoon lectures at all, because
he had not found the scholars good pay-masters : 'they want
to profit,' he pathetically explains, 'but not to pay. All want
to profit, but no one will pay the price[1].' The introduction Fees
of the system of *Salaria* paid by the State seems to have partially
superseded
arisen elsewhere than in Bologna. The neighbouring towns by *Salaria*.
in their eagerness to rival the Academical fame of Bologna,
would make overtures to a Bologna Doctor, and invite him
to come and lecture in their midst: and afterwards, when
the great scholastic migrations began, the Universities
through their Rectors would make a contract with the

non quæritur actio domino.' Odofredus in l. *Si procuratori* : Dig. *De
verb. obligat.* ap. Sarti, I. pt. i. p. 167.
And the Doctor is much concerned
to prove that he has a right of action
against 'bad scholars' who would
not pay. Franciscus Accursius obtained absolution for himself and his
late father for having lent money to
students in hopes of obtaining 'majores collectas', Sarti, I. pt. ii. (1772)
and from the words of Odofredus—
'contra doctores qui mutuant pecunias scholaribus ut audiant eos'—it
would seem that this was a frequent practice (ad L. *Omnia omnino crimina* Dig. *de off præf. urbis,*
T. I. f. 27 b). So another Doctor
leaves a sum of money to the poor
'ex questu, quem feci in Scholis, quia
multis et variis modis peccatur in Scholaribus habendis' (Sarti, I. pt. ii. 1772,
p. 76). We find Doctors (not of Law)
subletting their 'Schools and Scholars' in a very curious fashion (Sarti, I.
(1769) pt. i. p. 245; pt. ii. pp. 110,131).
Franciscus Accursius gives two Cha-
lices to a Minorite Church on behalf
of the souls of the Scholars, 'a quibus aliquid iniuste percepit tam Lai-
corum quam Clericorum dantium
de bonis eorum propriis eidem non
secundum dictum.' Sarti, I. pt. ii.

(1772) p. 95. Sometimes there is
a contract for board and lodging as
well as instruction: 'An. MCCLXVIII
Mag. Gerardus de Cremona Doctor
Grammaticæ promittit Adamaro Te-
baldi de Villa S. Attredii docere eum in
scientia Grammaticæ et dare sibi libros
quos legerit in Scholis et victum in
duodena secundum quod alii Scholares
habuerint et dare cameram a festo
S. Michaelis ad omnem annum pro
pretio libr. xxiii. Bonon. de quibus
habuit lib. x.' Ex *Memor. Com.
Bonon.* ap. Sarti (1769), I. i. p. 511.
So 'aliquem ex Scholaribus intrin-
secus abitantibus in dictis Scholis cum
dicto Mag. Petro,' *l. c.* pt. ii. p. 110.

[1] Odofredus in *Dig. Vet.* (ad L.
fin. D. *de divortiis*), T. II. f. 192,
'Et dico vobis quod in anno sequenti intendo docere ordinarie bene
et legaliter, sicut unquam feci ; extraordinarie non credo legere ; quia
scholares non sunt boni pagatores ;
quia volunt scire, sed nolunt solvere,
juxta illud ; "Scire volunt omnes :
mercedem solvere nemo." Non habeo
vobis plura dicere : eatis cum benedictione Domini.' In the preceding
sentences Odofredus alludes to the
custom of attending a Mass of the
Holy Ghost after the completion of
every 'Book' in lecture.

town selected, in which, together with facilities for the hiring of houses, exemptions from taxation, immunities from the ordinary Courts and the like, the payment of certain *stipendia* to the Professors was stipulated for. Eventually the Bolognese Republic found it necessary to imitate the liberality of its neighbours. The first recorded instance of such a payment occurs in 1280, when the Spanish Canonist Garsias agreed to lecture for one year at a salary of 150 *libræ*[1]. The contract was originally made by the students, but at their petition the Republic undertook the payment, and in 1289 two permanent chairs were endowed with salaries of 150 and 100 *libræ* respectively *per annum*[2]. The election of the Professor was annual and was left to the students, which must have been, at all events, an excellent system for keeping the teacher up to the mark.

Appointment to salaried chairs.

The chairs were at first few in number, poorly endowed, and conferred only on strangers (*forenses*), no such measures being necessary to keep Bologna citizens from straying abroad in search of higher pay. Gradually, however, the number and amount of the *salaria* were increased : and as the power of the purse thus passed from the students to the City, the control of the former over the elections was gradually withdrawn, and the nomination appropriated by the State[3]. In 1381 we find as many as twenty-three salaried

[1] Sarti I. i. p. 481. The first Civis who received a Stipendium—a small one of fifty *libræ*—was Joannes Passavantius, in 1289. *l. c.* p. 498.

[2] The first Doctors elected were the Canonist Altigradus de Lendinaria and the better-known Civilian Dinus. Sarti, I. pp. 255, 491. In 1297 Guildinus de Patralata is offered 500 *libræ*. *Ib.* p. 495. In 1305 the number salaried has risen to seven besides six (in various Faculties) appointed by the Council. Ghirardacci, I. p. 504.

[3] At first it seems clear that the *Salaria* did not supersede the *collectæ* (Sarti, I. pt. i. p. 256); afterwards the practice seems to have varied.

The Canonist Hostiensis (*Summa in decretal.* tit. *de magistris*, n. 7, Lugduni, 1597, f. 288 b) raises the question 'utrum a scholaribus collectam facere vel levare possit ?' and answers, 'quod sic, si non percipiat salarium de publico,' or if the Master is poor. On the other hand we find a Bolognese Student, Wardus de Clusio, in 1324-5, paying 'Domino meo Ray. Doctori pro suo salario . . . unum florenum. Item dedi Domino Belvisi ' (evidently a Bachelor) ' pro bancis et domo . . . decem solidos.' Clossius, *Codicum MSS. Dig. vet. descriptio.* Vimariæ (1818), 8. pp. 16–18 (Savigny, xxi. § 94). The contracts with Garsias certainly allowed

Doctors of Law, receiving payments varying from 100 to 620
libræ[1], the total grant for all Faculties amounting to 63,670
libræ. At this time the fact that one of the twenty-one
salaried Law Professors had been elected by the University
is mentioned as something exceptional[2]. The appointment
of the Doctors and the general management of the Studium
in its relations to the State were eventually entrusted to
a board known as the ' Reformatores Studii[3].' In the
course of the fourteenth and fifteenth centuries such a body
(under that or some similar name[4]) was established by the
City Government or Prince in all Italian Universities, and
the real control of the University more and more passed to

him ' collectas facere ' (Sarti, I. pt. ii.
(1772) p. 131). At Padua, by the
Town statute of 1283 (Facciolati, *Fasti*,
p. vi), salaried Doctors are forbidden
to charge anything except ' pro
ædium pensione '; but we hear of a
collecta in the later Statutes f. 15 b.
At Lerida in 1300 A. D. the payment
to the salaried Decretist is ' ad
minus tempore collectæ viginti turonenses argenti ' (*Stat.* ap. Villanueva,
Viage Literario, xvi. pp. 220, 221). At
Florence there were some ' Doctores
ordinarie legentes ' who received a
collecta limited to one florin a head
per annum; others were forbidden
to take anything. (*Stat. Fior.* pp. 65,
66.) So at Perugia (*Doc. per la
storia dell' Univ. di P.*, p. 52),
though here *cives* were exempted
from the *collecta*. At Bologna a non-
doctor 'extraordinarie legens' is forbidden to demand fees (*Stat.* p. 111),
which may be thought to imply that
Doctors might receive them, but possibly not the salaried Doctors. In
1437 Eugenius IV assigned a particular tax—the ' datum gabellæ
grossæ mercantiarum '—to the payment of the Salaria (Bull of Pius V.
ap. Gaggi). Kaufmann's inference
from the passage of Odofredus
(quoted above, p. 211, *n.* 1), that ' die

Scholaren hatten die ausserordent-
liche Vorlesung eines Professors
frei, dessen ordinaria sie hörten und
bezahlten ' (I. p. 209), is unwarranted.
Odofredus merely states that he did
not find his afternoon lectures pay
sufficiently to make it worth his
while to continue them.

[1] Ghirardacci, II. pp. 389, 390.
The year before the University had
itself attracted the Civilian Guido
Suzarino by the offer of 300 *libræ*,
Sarti, I. pt. i. p. 185.

[2] Ghirardacci, T. II. p. 389. The
Canonists and Medicals still retained
a larger share in the elections. The
Statutes of the College of Spain
provide : ' Hec autem in canonistis
et medicis qui solent per suas uniuer-
sitates eligi locum uolumus obtinere.'
MS. Stat. f. 6 b.

[3] Dallari, I. p. xix. Earlier we find
the elections made ' per dominos
Antianos . . . et per collegia domino-
rum Confaloniorum et Massariorum
artium civitatis Bononie.'

[4] Such as ' Gubernatores Studii '
or ' Tractatores Studii.' In the
smaller Studia the Universities were
from the first more closely dependent on the State, of which they
were the creatures, than at Bologna
or Padua.

CHAP. IV,   this body of external Governors, which by the sixteenth or
§ 5.   seventeenth century succeeded in destroying the Student
autonomy or reducing it to a shadow.   After the full establishment of the Papal domination in Bologna a supreme
control was exercised over the University by the Legate
and the ' Sixteen[1].'

Restriction   (2) The 'right of promotion,' i.e. of taking part in the
of Right of   admission of other Doctors, which had originally no doubt
Promotion.
(if we may trust the analogy of Paris and the probabilities
of the case) been enjoyed by all Doctors, came to be restricted to a small inner circle, who were limited in number
and who filled up the vacancies in their body by co-optation[2].
By the earliest extant Statutes of the Civil Law College
(published in 1397) their number is fixed at sixteen[3],
together with three supernumeraries who possessed the
right of voting in all matters except graduations (in which
they could only participate during the absence of any of
the sixteen), and who succeeded to vacancies as they
occurred.   The College of Canon Law in 1460 consisted
of twelve members, to which three supernumeraries were
added in 1466[4].

Restriction   (3) Membership of the College and admission to the
to Bolog-   most valuable salaried Chairs were alike restricted to
nese Citi-
zens.   Bologna citizens[5].   Both these restrictions probably had

[1] The consent of the Legate was
required for an additional holiday.
l.c. p. xxiii. An official was appointed
to keep an eye on the Professors, and
inform the Reformers as to their attendance, &c.

[2] The process by which this
change was effected is far from
clear; but it would seem as if at
first the attempt was made to exclude even from the honorary Doctorate all Bolognese citizens except
relatives of Doctors. Sarti, I. pt. i.
pp. 291, 300. At all times the
number of Bolognese citizens who
might be promoted was limited.
Stat. p. 386. In part the exclusion
was perhaps accounted for by the

efforts of the dominant political party
to exclude their opponents. Cf.
Ghirardacci, T. I. p. 327. It is clear
that by 1304 the College was already
limited to Bolognese, since in that
year the City and University united
to force it to admit new members.
Ghirardacci, T. I. p. 464.   It would
appear that at present *all* Bolognese
Doctors became *ipso facto* members of
the College.

[3] *Stat.* pp. 370, 371.

[4] *Stat.* pp. 336, 353.

[5] 'Vere et naturaliter cives civitatis Bononie origine propria, paterna
et avita'—Stat. of Civil Law College
in 1397 (*Stat.* p.370, cf. p. 391).

their origin in the fact that Irnerius and the other Doctors
who made the fame of the School were citizens of Bologna,
and this original nucleus of Bolognese Professors was assisted
by all the resources at the disposal of the Republic in the
patriotic effort to reserve for their own countrymen the
substantial emoluments, while they freely distributed to
strangers the honorary distinctions, of their world-famous
Studium. Attempts to narrow the teaching body had
been made before the year 1259, but in that year the
Doctors were compelled to swear (no doubt under pressure
from the students) that they would not prevent external
Doctors duly elected by the Universities from filling a chair
at Bologna[1]. Eventually, however, the City enacted that
Ordinary lectures on Ordinary books should be reserved
to Bolognese citizens[2]: and also that admission to the
Colleges should be similarly restricted[3].

So long as the Doctors limited their efforts to creating
a monopoly for the Bolognese, their interests were identical
with those of the City and were accordingly supported by
the Municipal authorities. It appears, however, that from
the first the ultimate object of the Professorial clique was to
reserve the substantial endowments of the Studium to members of their own families. The preferential right of sons
of Doctors to succeed to vacant chairs is expressly claimed
by the Jurist Accursius[4]. In 1295, however, we find the City
interfering to prevent the Faculty promoting their own sons
or nephews[5]: and similar interpositions compelled the

Efforts to make the Profes- soriate hereditary.

---

[1] 'E si decretò finalmente, che a
qualsivoglia straniero invitato per
via legittima degli studenti sarebbe
libero il presentarsi, ed ascendere
col favo loro le Cattedre,' Savioli, III.
pt. i. p. 333. They also swore 'non
ricevessero degli Alunni compenso
alcuno per dichiararli capaci del
Magistero' (*ib.*).

[2] *Stat.* p. 159 (cf. p. 391). In
Canon Law the restriction was extended to extraordinary books if read
at ordinary hours, *Stat.* p. 337. There
were, however, as late as 1347, four

Chairs—two ordinary and two extraordinary—to which the Universities
elected; and to two of these (one
ordinary and one extraordinary)
'forenses' alone might be nominated,
Stat. pp. 36, 37. This Statute disappears before 1432.

[3] *Stat.* pp. 336, 370.

[4] In Codicem L. 4. *de adv. div.
judic.* (ed. Contius, cc. 353, 354).

[5] At this time it appears to have
been necessary for the Faculty to
obtain leave from the city authorities
before carrying out a promotion of

Doctors to admit outsiders in 1299[1] and 1304[2]. At the date of the earliest Statutes of the Civil Law College (1397) the privileges of Doctoral families are found to be much restricted. As a general rule, only one Bolognese citizen might be promoted to the Doctorate in any one year: but sons, brothers and nephews of Doctors are exempted from this provision[3]. On the whole then it appears that the actual monopoly of the Doctoral families was destroyed, but there can be no doubt that from about the middle of the thirteenth century the Professoriate of Bologna became largely hereditary. The effects of this restriction upon the prosperity of the School we shall see hereafter: but the most fervent believer in hereditary institutions will hardly augur well of the experiment of an hereditary Professoriate.

Collegia in other Universities.

From the nature of the case this limitation to citizens could not be imitated in new and struggling Universities. The object of Bologna was to reap the full pecuniary benefit of an established prestige; towns which had a reputation to create, were anxious to entice Doctors from other cities. All the Universities organized on the Bologna model had a limited College or 'Faculty of Promotion,' but it was not always restricted to citizens[4], while in some cases citizens were actually excluded from the salaried Chairs[5].

The Student Chairs.

A very peculiar and anomalous feature of the Bologna constitution as it is presented to us in the Statutes of 1432 now demands a word of explanation. This anomalous

---

Bologna citizens: on this occasion leave was granted on condition that the new Doctors should be 'della parte della Chiesa, e de' Gieremei di Bologna ... ò non fossero figliuoli, fratelli, ò nepoti di detti Dottori.' Ghirardacci, I. p. 327. Not all the Professors were on the Guelf side. When the city imposed differential taxes upon the Lambertazzi party, the descendants of the Accursii were specially exempted on petition of the Universities—Sarti, T. I. p. ii. (1772) p. 76.

[1] Alidosi, pp. 223, 224.

[2] Fantuzzi, *Scritt. Bologn.* II. pp. 48, 49, 331.

[3] *Stat.* p. 386. There is no similar provision in the Statutes of the Decretist College published in 1460. The earlier canonists were unmarried ecclesiastics.

[4] At Florence this restriction at one time existed, but was modified in 1404 and repealed in 1417, *Stat. Fiorent.* pp. 182, 195.

[5] e.g. at Florence in 1392, *ib.* p. 172.

feature is the existence of six salaried Chairs for which only students or Bachelors were eligible. Its origin must be sought in the events of the year 1338. In that year, Bologna, having expelled the Legate, had fallen under the power of Taddeo Pepolo. Its tyrant siding with the Ghibelines, the City was laid under an interdict, a sentence which forbad the legal continuance of the Studium. A body of the students, however, seceded to Castro Pietro and there elected six of their own number to take the place of the silent or scattered Professors[1]. Upon the return of the seceders, the City found it advisable to allow the chairs to continue, perhaps as a solatium for the loss of the University's right to elect to the regular Professor-ships[2]. In the course of time, however, it was found that these elections led to serious encounters in the streets be-tween armed supporters of the rival candidates, to infinite perjury, and to the election of undeserving and illiterate can-didates, perhaps popular athletes or the like. Henceforth the lot was substituted for election[3], a remedy which might have been considered worse than the disease, had not the chance of delivering one of these lectures been looked upon as more valuable than the privilege of listening to them[4].

I must now try to give the reader some connected account of the career of a Law-student at Bologna, from the time of his Matriculation to his graduation. 'Matri-culation' it should be observed, i. e. the placing the name of the student upon the 'Matricula' or list of members of the University, was originally peculiar to the Student-universities; because only in them was the student a full member of the University. At Paris and Oxford only the

The Stu-dent's career: Ma-triculation.

---

[1] 'De mense Aprilis Dominus Ray-nerius de Forlivio Doctor Legum, et sex Scholares electi ad legendum et tenendum Studium in Castro S. Petri propter interdictum Studii, iverunt ad dictum Castrum, dicta occasione, et multi Scholares iverunt ad intran-dum ibi.' (Matt. de Griffonibus, *Me-moriale Historicum*, ap. Muratori, SS. XVIII. c. 163.) Cf. *Stat.* p. 95.

[2] The origin of these chairs ex-plains the fact that one of them, though held by a student, was 'or-dinary.' *Stat.* p. 95 *sq.*

[3] *Stat.* p. 188 *sq.*

[4] By the city-regulations of 1475 students are required to 'prove their poverty' by two witnesses before becoming candidates. Dallari, I. p. xxiii.

CHAP. IV,
§ 5.

Masters were really members of the Corporation: consequently there was no Matricula of students. At
Matriculation, the student took his oath of obedience to
the Rector[1] and at the same time (it goes without saying)
paid a fee—at Bologna amounting to twelve *solidi*[2].

Hours of
Lecture.

It is difficult to reproduce the time-table of a medieval
institution, since the time of day was more frequently indicated by the hour at which the bells rang for such a service
at such a Church than by the clock or the sun-dial. At
Bologna there appear to have been three Lecture-hours
daily. The first and most important Lecture of the day—
the 'Ordinary' lecture—began at the hour of the 'morning
bell' for mass at S. Peter's and lasted till the bell began to
ring for tierce (presumably about 9 a.m.). It must therefore
have lasted at least two hours and possibly longer[3]. In the
afternoon, there might be two lectures of two hours and one-
and-a-half hours respectively, the time being 2–4[4] p.m. and
4–5.30 in winter, 1.30–3 p.m. and 3.30–5 p.m. in summer.

The period from tierce till 1.30 or 2 p.m. was thus left
vacant for dinner and siesta: but it is probable that Extraordinary lectures might be given after tierce. Other University Statutes provide for a lecture at this time in addition
to the two hours or two-and-a-half hours' lecture in the morning[5]. It should be observed that there was this difference
between the two legal Faculties as to the distinction between Ordinary and Extraordinary lectures. In Civil Law
the Ordinary books were reserved for the Ordinary hours:
in Canon Law, since the bulk of the Ordinary books far
exceeded that of the Extraordinary, Extraordinary lectures
might be given on Ordinary books. The books were

---

[1] *Stat.* p. 128.

[2] *Stat.* p. 73.

[3] By the city-regulations of 1475
the Salaried Doctors are required to
lecture for one or two hours 'secundum quod disponunt statuta Universitatis predicte.' Dallari, I. p. xxii. At
Padua the Doctor must lecture for
two hours (*Stat. Jur. Pat.* f. 76 b).

Students are forbidden 'bancas pul-
sare' to enforce an earlier termination.

[4] ' In hora vigesima intrent scolas,
et in eis legendo stent usque ad
vigesimamsecundam horam.' *Stat.*
p. 105.

[5] *e. g.* at Ferrara. Borsetti, *Hist.
Gym. Ferrar.* I. p. 434.

divided among the Doctors in such a way that all the texts Chap. IV,
§ 5.
should be lectured on annually (if the Studium had sufficient Doctors) or at least once in two or four years [1].

The place of the lectures was originally the private house Lecture-
rooms.
of the Doctor, or a School rented for that purpose. In the
case of an exceptionally popular Professor whose audiences
could not be crowded into any ordinary room, a public
building or an open space in the City is said to have been
borrowed for the purpose. There is a tradition that Irnerius himself lectured from the open-air pulpit in the corner
of the great square in front of the venerable Basilica of
S. Stephen [2] : and Albericus is recorded to have lectured
in the Palazzo Pubblico [3]. It was not till the fifteenth
century that the Universities generally began to build or
acquire handsome and permanent buildings of their own,
instead of leaving their Professors to lecture in their private
houses or hired Schools. The existing Archiginnasio of
Bologna dates only from the sixteenth century [4].

A good idea of the nature of a Bolognese Law-lecture—
or indeed (allowing for the difference of subject-matter) of
a lecture in any Faculty in any medieval University—is
given by the following account of the plan of a course of
lectures by Odofredus, which is quoted by Savigny [5] :—

‘ First, I shall give you summaries of each title before Manner of
Lecturing.
I proceed to the text ; secondly, I shall give you as
clear and explicit a statement as I can of the purport of
each Law (included in the title) ; thirdly, I shall read the
text with a view to correcting it ; fourthly, I shall briefly
repeat the contents of the Law ; fifthly, I shall solve appa-

---

[1] *Stat.* p. 104 *sq.* Cf. Borsetti,
I. 433. Fabroni, *Acad. Pisan. Hist.*
I. p. 122.

[2] The tradition perhaps arose from
the statement of Odofredus ad L. *Si
duas*, Dig. *De excusat.* (ap. Sarti,
I. pt. I. p. 86) that ‘ Scholares voluerunt quod dominus Azo legeret in
platea S. Stephani.’

[3] The tradition is preserved by
Odofredus in Dig. vetus L. 2 *de*

fide instrum. (Lugd. 1557, T. II.
f. 165 b).

[4] In the fifteenth century we find
salaries voted to Doctors of Arts
‘ dummodo legat in scholis consuetis
artistarum ’ (Dallari, I. p. 46). But I
can find nothing else about these
Schools.

[5] Cap. xxiii. § 204. This *Proœmium* does not appear in the printed
edition of Odofredus.

CHAP. IV,
§ 5.

rent contradictions, adding any general principles of Law (to be extracted from the passage), commonly called ' Brocardica [1],' and any distinctions or subtle and useful problems (*quæstiones*) arising out of the Law with their solutions, as far as the Divine Providence shall enable me. And if any Law shall seem deserving, by reason of its celebrity or difficulty, of a Repetition, I shall reserve it for an evening Repetition.'

Glosses.

In the above account there is, however, no mention of a very important feature of all medieval lectures—the reading of the 'glosses.' By the Bologna Statutes the Doctor is required to read the ' glosses' immediately after the text [2]. The 'dictation' of lectures in the 'Ordinary' hours was strictly forbidden [3] : and the extant lectures of Bologna Doctors are thoroughly familiar and conversational in style. The ' repetitiones' alluded to by Odofredus consisted in a more detailed and elaborate discussion of some particular question arising out of a recent lecture. Any Doctor might give a Repetition in extraordinary hours whenever he pleased : but the salaried Doctors were required to arrange by rotation among themselves for a Repetition every week on some day on which no Ordinary lectures were given [4]. In Lent Repetitions were suspended and disputations took their place [5]. At these disputations, the Doctor maintained a thesis against all comers. The Rectors presided and determined the order of precedence when two rose at once. The precedence was settled by degree or standing, but nobles who sat on the front bench at lecture took precedence over all but Doctors [6]. The Students' disputations, which were presided over by a Doctor, took place on holidays [7].

Repetitions.

Disputations.

---

[1] Sarti explains the word by ' generales regulæ quasi loci communes.'

[2] *Stat.* p. 105.

[3] *Ib.* At Padua the Doctor 'post horam lectionis teneatur summarium lectionis, vel questionis disputate, dictare' (*Stat. Jur. Patav.* ff. 79, 80), also to answer questions handed to him in writing (f. 77); and in 1474

he is required 'ad se reducendum post lectionem ad conferendum et ad circulos more artistarum' (*ib.* ff. 78, 79). These ' circuli' seem to have been informal disputations or discussions among the students presided over by a Doctor.

[4] *Stat.* p. 106.   [5] *Stat.* p. 107.

[6] *Stat.* p. 108.

[7] Dallari, I. p. xxiii.

Holidays were of frequent occurrence. To obviate the CHAP. IV, inconveniences arising from the caprices of the ecclesiastical § 5. Calendar, it was prudently provided that there should be Holidays. a holiday on every Thursday when no Festival recognized by the University occurred during the week : but on such days Repetitions and disputations might be held. While Doctors were peremptorily forbidden to lecture on Saints' days, students, whose lectures there was of course no moral or legal obligation to attend, were allowed to lecture whenever they would. The scholastic year opened with a Mass of the Holy Ghost[1] in the Dominican Church on the morrow of St. Luke, i. e. October 19th, while the Long Vacation, unlike the luxurious recess of Oxford and Paris, did not begin till September 7th[2]. There was a Vacation of ten days at Christmas, a fortnight at Easter, and three days at the Carnival, which was afterwards extended to three weeks[3]. Bologna also enjoyed two days' holiday at Whitsuntide, in place of the short vacation allowed at the beginning of May in other Italian Universities for medical purposes[4].

After five years' study a student of Civil Law might be Bachelor- admitted by the Rector[5] to lecture on a single title of the ship.

---

[1] Which the Friars were required to say 'sine nota prolixa.' *Stat.* p. 101.

[2] In the time of Odofredus the Long Vacation seems to have begun earlier and to have lasted a little longer. Savigny, cap. xxi. § 92.

[3] *Stat. Jur. Bon.* p. 106.

[4] Borsetti, *Hist. Gym. Ferrar.* I. 418, 419. Fabroni, *Hist. Acad. Pisan.* I. 446. At Ferrara the May Vacation is described as 'pro potionibus sumendis more solito'; at Pisa it is more bluntly styled 'vacatio Purgationum.' At Pisa there was also a week at Midsummer.

[5] Elsewhere the admission to Bachelors' degrees belonged to the Masters, very rarely to the Chancellor. So at Vienna, 'Ordinamus

quod ad solos Doctores et non ad alios spectet . . . Baccalarios creare.' Kink, *Gesch. d. k. Univ. zu Wien,* II. p. 136. The candidate having held a 'repetition,' and responded to opponents, was solemnly admitted by a Doctor (*ib.* p. 146).

This was probably the original custom at Bologna, where an early city Statute provides that no one 'sinatur regimen inchoare (i. e. to become a Doctor), nec aliquis Doctor legum *det ei librum suum*, nisi primo juret,' &c. ap. Sarti, I. ii. (1772) p. 222. A Bachelor was originally simply a student allowed to teach in a Master's School—a pupil teacher. Thus it is said of S. Richard, Bishop of Chichester, who studied at Bologna in the early years of the thirteenth century,

Civil or Canon Law, or on a whole book after six years. A Canonist could similarly lecture on a single title after four years of 'hearing,' or on a whole Decretal after five years. The License of the Rector to 'read' a title or book or rather the completion of such a course of lectures made a man a Bachelor. Bachelors admitted to read a whole Book or Decretal might give a Repetition [1]. They might lecture twice a week [2]. Before presenting himself for admission to the Doctorate, a Bachelor must have given a course of lectures or at least a Repetition, must have completed eight [3] or at least seven years of study in Civil Law or six years for the degree in Canon Law. But time spent in the study of one Law was accepted in reduction of the time necessary for graduation in the other, and it was possible to become a Doctor of both Civil and Canon Law (*Doctor utriusque iuris*) in ten years [4]. Bachelor-lectures were apparently looked upon rather in the light of academical exercises for the Lecturers than as means of instruction for the pupils. It was sometimes necessary for an ambitious student who was anxious to have an audience to bribe scholars to come and sit under him by gifts or loans of money [5]. No examination or formal test was ever required at Bologna for the Baccalaureate, which was altogether much less of a distinct 'degree' and of much less importance than it eventually became in the Academical system of Paris or Oxford [6].

In the earliest period the Masters of Bologna had en-

---

that 'mellea Canonum fluenta sic hausit, quod Magister suus, infirmitate detentus, ad lectiones suas vice sua continuandas, præ omnibus discipulis suis dictum Richardum elegit.' A. S. Ap. 3. T. I. p. 278.

[1] *Stat.* p. 111.   [2] *Stat.* p. 112.

[3] So by the Civil Law College Statutes, p. 382. The University Stat. of 1432 adds 'vel ad minus per septem annos' (p. 113).

[4] According to the Stat. of 1432 (p. 113).

[5] Sarti, I. i. p. 231.

[6] On this point Kaufmann (I. p. 361 *sq.*) has some good remarks. When he makes the Bachelorship more of a distinct degree at Oxford than at Paris, the remark is only true in respect of the Bachelorship of Arts, which perhaps gained additional importance from the fact that here alone was it conferred by the Chancellor. As to the explanation of this peculiarity of Oxford, see below, chap. xiv. § 1.

joyed the same freedom as any other professional Guild in Chap. IV,
admitting or rejecting candidates for membership. They § 5.
alone conducted the Examinations, and conferred in their License
own name the license to teach: and the student thus Doctorate.
licensed became an actual Doctor by receiving the 'book,'
the symbol of his office, from an existing member of the
Guild. This unfettered liberty of the Bologna Doctors was,
however, out of harmony with hierarchical ideas : it was contrary to the general principle of Canon Law which claimed—
though in Italy it had scarcely succeeded in securing—for
the Church a certain control over education : and it was
contrary to the analogy of the Schools North of the Alps,
particularly of the great University of Paris, where the
licentia docendi had always been obtained from the Chancellor of the Cathedral Church. Accordingly, in 1219 Honorius
Honorius III, himself a former Archdeacon of Bologna, III intro-
duces au-
enjoined that no promotion to the Doctorate should take thority of
place without the consent of the Archdeacon of Bologna [1], the Arch-
deacon,
who was probably the Head of the Chapter School [2] as well 1219.
as of the Chapter itself. The innovation was accepted without opposition, perhaps on account of the accident that the
Archdeacon's stall was at the time filled by a distinguished
Bolognese Canonist, Gratia Aretinus [3]. In 1270 an attempt
was made on the part of the Doctors to throw off the yoke [4].
but, with this exception, the relations between the Arch-

---

[1] Doc. in Sarti, I. ii. (1772) p. 59. At
the same time the Archdeacon received a faculty for absolving scholars
excommunicated for assaults on
clerks. *Ib.*

[2] It would seem that the Archdeacon was occasionally called ' Cancellarius,' and already exercised a
kind of honorary and informal presidency over the Studium. Cf. the
words of Buoncompagni, who, in
1214, read his *Rhetorica novissima* 'in
præsentia venerabilis fratris Henrici
Bononiensium episcopi, magistri
Tancredi archidiaconi *et cancellarii*,
capituli et cleri, et in presentia doc-

torum et scolarium,' &c. (ap. Rockinger in *Sitzungsberichte d. bay. Akad.
zu München*, 1861, p. 136). In the
Church of Bologna the Archdeacon
ranked next to the Bishop. See
Stat. p. 417.

[3] Savigny (cap. XXI. § 83) thinks
that the right was meant to be a
personal concession to the then
Archdeacon, but the document does
not prove this.

[4] See the ' compromise' referring
the dispute (which had led, as usual,
to a scene in church) to the arbitration of the Bishop, in Sarti, I. ii.
(1772) 106; Savioli, T. III. ii. p. 433.

CHAP. IV,
§ 5.

deacon on the one hand, and the Doctors and the University on the other, present a striking contrast to the chronic hostility which prevailed between the Chancellor and University at Paris. The comparatively wealthy students of Bologna were less disposed to resent the pecuniary exactions of the Archdeacon, and enforced them by their Statutes. The Archdeacon on the other hand, content with an accession of dignity and an enormous increase of income, does not appear after 1270 to have seriously attempted to interfere with the actual conduct of the Examinations over which he presided.

Importance of the change.

It is hardly necessary to comment on the importance of the Bull of Honorius III in the history of the University system throughout Europe. By that Bull and the imitation of its provisions in favour of other Schools the Universities throughout Europe were, so to speak, brought within the ecclesiastical system. Graduation ceased to imply the mere admission into a private Society of teachers, and bestowed a definite legal status in the eyes of Church and State alike. The gulf which had hitherto separated the free lay system of education in Italy from the ecclesiastical system of Northern Europe was to some extent (more, it is true, in form than in substance) bridged over. By the assimilation of the degree-system in the two great Schools of Europe, an archetypal organization was established which supplied a norm for all younger Universities. It came to be a recognized requirement of every University organization that it should have an official duly commissioned by public authority to confer the license. And a further step was taken in the same direction in 1292, when a Bull of Nicholas IV conferred on all Doctors licensed by the Archdeacon of Bologna the right to teach not only in Bologna but throughout the whole world[1]. Henceforth the Universities passed from

---

[1] The Bull is also noticeable as recognizing the Doctorate as a permanent rank which a man retained even when he had ceased to teach : ' ut quicumque ex Universitate vestra apud Civitatem predictam per Archidiaconum Bononien., vel ejus Vicarium, prout est ibidem hactenus observatum, examinatus et approbatus fuerit, et docendi ab eo licentiam obtinuerit in Jure Canonico, vel Civili, ex tunc absque examinatione,

merely local into ecumenical organizations : the Doctor- CHAP. IV,
ate became an order of intellectual nobility with as distinct §5.
and definite a place in the hierarchical system of medieval
Christendom as the Priesthood or the Knighthood. The The Arch-
Archdeacon henceforth occupied the same relation to the deacon
eventually
University of Bologna that the Chancellor of the Cathedral styled
occupied towards the University of Paris : and in course of Chancellor.
time it became usual to speak of the Archdeacon of Bologna
and the officials charged with similar functions elsewhere
as Chancellors of their respective Universities : in a Bull of
1464 this phraseology even receives the sanction of Papal
authority[1]. By this time the term ' Universitas ' or rather
' Universitas studii ' was coming to be usual as a synonym
of Studium or Studium Generale. But originally it should
be remembered that the Archdeacon or Chancellor was not
an official, or even *ex officio* a member, of either the University of students or the Doctoral Colleges[2]. He was rather
an external representative of the Church's authority over
the Studium. The only jurisdiction which he exercised in
connexion with the school besides that of presiding over
the promotions, was that of absolving for assaults on clerks,
an offence for which absolution was by Canon Law reserved
to the Holy See. The faculty for this purpose was conferred upon the Archdeacon by a Bull of Honorius III at
the same time as the right of promotion[3].

The account which must now be given of the graduation Process of
ceremony at Bologna relates to the period in which it was Graduation.

vel approbatione publica, vel privata,
aliquo vel alio novo privilegio regendi atque docendi ubique locorum
extra Civitatem Bononien. predictam
liberam habeat facultatem, nec a quo-
quam valeat prohiberi, et sive velit
legere sive non, in facultatibus preli-
batis, pro Doctore nihilominus habeatur.' Sarti, I. ii.(1772) pp. 59,60. The
privilege was confined to the Faculties
of Canon and Civil Law, yet it was
never disputed that Bologna was a
Studium Generale in Arts and Medicine also.

[1] ' Universitatem Studii Bononie,
cui archidiaconatum ipsum pro tempore obtinens, ut illius maior Cancellarius, preesse dignoscitur.' (*Stat.*
p. 417.) In the same Bull he is styled
' caput et Cancellarius Universitatis
dicti studii.'

[2] If a Doctor of the College of
Canon Law received this appointment he ceased to be a member of
it, unless dispensed by a unanimous
vote. *Stat.* p. 343.

[3] Doc. in Sarti, I. ii. (1772)
p. 59.

presided over by the Archdeacon. Of the earlier procedure we know nothing : but in all probability the main outlines of the ceremony were already established before the introduction of the Archidiaconal presidency. The process of graduation consisted of two parts, (1) The private Examination, (2) The public Examination or Conventus.

The Private Examination. The private Examination was the real test of competence, the so-called public Examination being in practice a mere ceremony. Before admission to each of these tests the candidate was presented by the Consiliarius of his Nation to the Rector for permission to enter it, and swore that he had complied with all the statutable conditions, that he would give no more than the statutable fees or entertainments to the Rector himself, the Doctor or his fellow-students, and that he would obey the Rector. Within a period of eight days before the Examination the candidate was presented by ' his own ' Doctor or by some other Doctor or by two Doctors to the Archdeacon, the presenting Doctor being required to have satisfied himself by private examination of his presentee's fitness. Early on the morning of the examination, after attending a Mass of the Holy Ghost, the candidate appeared before the assembled College and was assigned by one of the Doctors present two passages (*puncta*) in the Civil or Canon Law as the case might be[1]. He then retired to his house to study

---

[1] It will not be necessary to give a separate reference for every detail of the above account : I may refer generally to the University Statutes, pp. 116–119, and those of the Colleges, pp. 344–346, 383–386, and Gaggi. For the elucidation of the somewhat perplexing Statute *De punctis in privata examinatione*, the Statutes of Montpellier (*Cartulaire*, I. p. 314 *sq.*, cf. also p. 389 *sq.*) and other Universities, are almost indispensable, e. g. the *Stat. Varia Civ. Placentiæ*, pp. 565–8; Fabroni, *Acad. Pisan. Hist.* I. pp. 431, 457, which show the universality of this system

of *punctorum assignatio*. At Bologna it dates from before 1289. See the doc. in Sarti, I. ii. (1772) p. 106. It also obtained in the Medical School of Montpellier, Astruc. p. 86, and in the Law Faculty at Vienna. Kink, *Gesch. d. k. Univ. zu Wien*, II. p. 147. So at Cologne, where the candidate was allowed eight hours' study and to give his lecture in the evening. Bianco, *Die alte Un. Köln* I. *Anl.* p. 53. Something like a survival of this system is said to be found at Salamanca (see Graux, *Notices Bibliographiques*, Paris, 1884, p. 335), and Coimbra, where candidates are re-

the passages, in doing which it would appear that he had the assistance of the presenting Doctor [1].   Later in the day the Doctors were summoned to the Cathedral or some other public building [2] by the Archdeacon, who presided over but took no active part in the ensuing examination. The candidate was then introduced to the Archdeacon and Doctors by the presenting Doctor or Promotor as he was styled. The Prior of the College then administered a number of oaths in which the candidate promised respect to that body and solemnly renounced all the rights of which the College had succeeded in robbing all Doctors not included in its ranks. The candidate then gave a lecture or exposition of the two prepared passages : after which he was examined upon them by two of the Doctors appointed by the College [3]. Other Doctors might ask supplementary questions of Law (which they were required to swear that they had not previously communicated to the candidate) arising more indirectly out of the passages selected, or might suggest objections to the answers [4]. With a tender regard for the feelings of their comrades at this 'rigorous and tremendous Examination' (as they style it) the students by their Statutes required the Examiner to treat the examinee 'as his own son.'   The Examination concluded, the votes of

---

quired to lecture on three questions chosen by lot from a large number, and to meet objections, answer questions, &c., three hours' preparation being allowed.

[1] 'Et die extimationis [*leg.* examinationis] ipsius scholaris teneatur dictus doctor presentans ire ad domum dicti scholaris et eum iterum examinare et ipsum audire super legibus eidem in punctis assignatis.' *Stat.* p. 384. In the time of Gaggi, the candidate was still further assisted by knowing that one of a limited number of *puncta* was sure to be set, and was coached in the preparation of his apparently written exposition.

[2] The Statutes seem to contem-

plate that the ceremony took place in the Cathedral : Gaggi, however, speaks of an examination 'in Palatio DD. Antianorum,' and of a *doctoratio* 'in Palatio ipsius Gubernatoris.'

[3] By the Statutes of Padua (*Stat. Jur. Patav.* f. 94), the 'puncta' were to be taken from the first 'utilis materia' which occurred after the place at which the book was casually opened.

[4] The function of the Examining Doctors is only distinguished from that of the rest by the University Statutes.   In the College Statutes of 1387 all the Doctors in turn are to argue with the candidate (*Stat.* p. 385).

CHAP. IV,
§ 5.

the Doctors present were taken by ballot and the candidate's fate determined by the majority, the decision being announced by the Archdeacon.

Relation of License to Doctorate.

A candidate who had passed the private, and had been admitted to the public Examination, became a Licentiate. Normally and naturally the Licentiate proceeded to the ceremony which made him a full Doctor after a very short interval: but the expense of this step sometimes compelled candidates to postpone it, while others (in spite of statutory prohibition) went off and took it at a cheaper University [1].

Public Examination.

On the day of the *Conventus*, or public Examination [2], the love of pageantry characteristic of the medieval and especially of the Italian mind was allowed the amplest gratification. Shortly before the day appointed the candidate had ridden round the city to invite public officials or private friends to the ceremony or to the ensuing banquet, preceded by the Bedels of the Archdeacon and of the Promotor or Pro-

---

[1] The Paduan Statutes allow a Licentiate of Bologna to receive the insignia at Padua. *Stat. Jur. Patav.* f. 95 b. In the 16th century, however, when Padua had far surpassed Bologna in scientific prestige, the Paduan charges were higher than Bologna. Ferrara was much cheaper. A student of this period, George Wagner, thus writes: ' Laurea, seu doctoratus gradus, ut vocant, Patavii sine maximo sumptu suscipi non potest: nam collegio Doctorum amplius 43 sc. numerantur et subductis aliis impensis sumptus fere ad 50 sc. excurrunt. Bononiæ paulo minus numeratur, Senis circiter 34 sc., Ferrariæ vix ultra 28, sed hæc urbs, nec literis nec studiosorum frequentia celebris, vulgo miserorum refugium vocatur, qui suæ inscitiæ conscii alibi alliam rigorosi examinis, ut dicunt, subire non audent. Qui Patavii et Bononiæ insigniuntur, apud Italos in precio, sed nec contemnuntur Doctores Senonenses ob Academiæ quondam florentissimæ et professorum qui eam

illustrarunt auctoritatem.'—ap. *Nuovi Documenti reguardanti la Nazione Alemanna nello Studio di Bologna*, ed. Luschin von Ebengreuth, Modena, 1884. There are two important Articles by the same writer on the German students at Bologna in *Sitzungsberichte d. Kais. Akad. d. Wissenschaften.* Ph-Hist. Cl. B. 118, 124.

[2] Kaufmann (I. p. 364) well points out that there was a certain difference between the License of Paris and that of Bologna. At Bologna the License conferred at the *Privata* was merely a License to proceed to the *Publica*; at Paris it was the actual *Licentia docendi*, which at Bologna was only given in the *Publica*. Consequently the Archdeacon presided at both functions: whereas at Paris the Chancellor (except in the Faculty of Theology) took no part in the Inception. It should be added that the *Publica* is occasionally described as a *Principium* in Universities of the Bologna type.

motors. The Statutes, indeed, forbade on this occasion the
blowing of trumpets or other instruments, but on the actual
day of the Conventus no such sumptuary limitation was
imposed. On that day the candidate was accompanied to the
Cathedral by the presenting Doctor, and by his 'socii' or
fellow-students lodging in the same house with him. The
idea of the 'Conventus,' or 'Public Examination,' was essentially the same as that of the ceremony known as the
'Principium' or 'Inceptio' in the Northern Universities. That
idea was derived from the principle of the Roman Law
according to which a man was invested with the *de facto*
possession of his office by an actual and solemn performance of its functions. At the same time and by the same
act the new Doctor was recognized by his colleagues and
received into the teaching Guild or brotherhood, though at
Bologna (as has been explained), by the period with which
we are dealing, that admission had ceased to carry with
it a practical right to the full exercise of the Doctor's
teaching functions.

Arrived at the Cathedral, the Licentiate delivered a The Cere-
speech and read a thesis on some point of Law, which he monial.
defended against opponents who were selected from among
the students, the candidates thus playing for the first time
the part of a Doctor in a University disputation. He was
then presented by his Promotor to the Archdeacon, who
made a complimentary oration, and concluded by solemnly
conferring the license to teach the Civil, Canon, or both
Laws as the case might be, by the authority of the Pope
and in the name of the Holy Trinity. In pursuance of the
license thus conferred, he was then invested by the Promotor with the *insignia* of the teaching office, each no doubt
with some appropriate formula. He was seated in the
Magisterial chair or *cathedra*. He was handed the open
book—one of the Law texts which it was his function to
expound. A gold ring was placed upon his finger, whether
in token of his espousal to Science or in indication of the
Doctor's claim to be the equal of Knights, and the Magisterial *biretta* placed upon his head : after which the Pro-

CHAP. IV,
§ 5.

motor left him with a paternal embrace, a kiss, and a benediction [1]. The ceremony concluded, both Universities were
required to escort him in triumph through the town, surrounded no doubt by a mounted cavalcade of personal
friends or wealthier students, and preceded by the three
University pipers and the four University trumpeters [2].

New
Guildsmen
required to
pay their
footing.

A fuller knowledge of the customs and ritual of the
Italian guilds would perhaps reveal a tolerably close analogy
between these ceremonies of the Conventus and those by
which other Guilds of merchants, professional men or craftsmen received a new member into their brotherhood. In
obedience to an inveterate instinct of human nature, members so admitted, while welcomed with effusive cordiality,
were also expected to pay their footing. The earliest custom was no doubt to send presents of robes to the Doctors,

---

[1] 'Cum paterna benedictione conferri pacis osculum consuetum ; in
nomine Patris et Filii et Spiritus
Sancti, amen.' *Stat. Fiorent.* p. 439,
where the ring is explained, 'in
signum desponsationis utriusque scientie, canonice scilicet et civilis.' At
Padua we find the ring described as
'signaculum fidei quam debent sacris jussionibus professores.' Gloria,
Mem. di Padova, 1318–1405, II. p.
267. In the Medical Faculty at Montpellier the Doctor was also invested
with a golden girdle. Astruc, *Mém.
de la Fac. de Méd. à Mont.* p. 88. At
Valladolid, the Doctorand 'gradum
sibi conferri humiliter deprecetur,
et Patrinus ipsum Cancellarium
oratione quadam ad illud faciendum,
et dandum sibi facultatem ac potestatem insignia tribuendi, exoret,
et mox Cancellarius conferat gradum,
quo dato novus Doctor Thronum
conscendat,' &c. See *Estatutos, &c.
de Valladolid*, 1651, p. 33, where
the whole ceremony is minutely
described. Here the new Doctor
kisses the Chancellor and every
Doctor present. The ceremony in
Spain included investiture with

gloves, a golden cincture and
golden spurs ('non tantum in signum nobilitatis equestris, sed ut
magis ac magis per assiduum studium continuumque laborem ad
honorem conservandum exciteris'),
and finally with the sword ('ut . . .
officium et munus tibi concessum
tuendi Regem, Legem, et Patriam
accurate adimpleas'). See the formulæ in use at Alcalá, ap. de la
Fuente, *Hist. de las Universidades en
España*, II. p. 620. Cf. *Cartulaire de
l'Un. de Montpellier*, I. p. 373: 'dicunt
quod unus doctor non potest ince-
dere comode sine uno scutifero.'
Charles V conferred on the College
at Bologna the right of conferring
actual knighthood upon Doctors,
while the Doctors of the College
were themselves *ipso facto* knights
and counts of the Lateran. At the
same time the College received the
widely diffused Imperial privilege
of legitimating bastards. Gaggi,
ad init.

[2] In the case of poorer students it
would seem that these ceremonies
were dispensed with. See the Stat.
de recipiente librum in secreto (p. 119).

Bedels, and other officials taking part in the ceremony :
but by the date of our Statutes these presents were com-
muted into money payments, though a fixed quantity of
cloth of a certain specified colour might still be substituted
for some of them ; and in addition to the regular fees there
were also some customary presents,—a cap, gloves, and a present of sweetmeats to each of the Doctors and to the Archdeacon, while the Prior of the College claimed a ring[1]. But
the greatest expense of all was the banquet which the new
Doctor was expected to give to his colleagues and University friends. Even more magnificent entertainments, such
as tilts or tournaments, were at times provided by wealthier
students[2]. At some of the Spanish Universities the incepting Doctors were required to provide a bull-fight for
the amusement of the University. The immense scale on

---

[1] So at Pisa, the candidate is required to send each Doctor a box
full of comfits, of 1 lb. weight (*Sca-
tulam unam refertam Libra una con-
fectorum*). Fabroni, *Acad. Pisan.
Hist.* I. p. 477. At Bologna the
Archdeacon received 12 *lib.* 10*s.*
from each candidate at each Examination (*Stat.* p. 150), the University 30*s.*, each Doctor 40*s.* at the
private and 20*s.* at the Public Examination, the presenting Doctors
10 or 12 ducats. A host of minor
officials of the Universities, the Doctors, and the Archdeacon, had also
to be remembered. One poor student annually received the Doctorate
gratis (pp. 181, 348). There were
also certain exemptions for sons
or brothers of Doctors; and for
all citizens the fees were much
lower. *Stat.* p. 145. Many of these
expenses depended partly upon the
inclinations of the owner. Thus the
Statutes of the Spanish College forbid the provision of refreshments for
the Examiners: 'Panis uero uel
uinum in dicto priuato examine uel
in disputacionibus uel repeticionibus

per eos fiendis . . . de bonis Collegii
alicui nullatenus errogetur : ymo
eciam de proprio facere reprobamus,
quia tales uanitates et pompe nedum
in pauperibus scolaribus set eciam in
diuiditibus (*sic*) sunt per sapientes
et uiros laudabiles reprobate et per
statuta uniuersalia (?) studii bonoñ.
prohibite.' *MS. Stat.* f. 6 *b*. A
Statute of Toulouse, on the other
hand, makes compulsory a payment
of 8 *grossi* to the Capitouls' jesters
or mummers (' quatuor mymis domi-
norum de capitulo eadem die, si dicti
domini veniant ad aulam '); besides
a payment to the three ordinary
' *mimi*.' Fournier, *Stat. des Univ.
Franç.* I. No. 772.

[2] These are forbidden by the
Statutes: 'Nullus autem scolaris, in
alicuius civis vel forensis scolaris
publica, se pro chorea vel brigata
seu hastiludio faciendis vestire audeat vel tunc eques hastiludere ';
and the Doctorand is to swear
' quod die qua equitat invitando
pro publica recipienda non faciat
hastiludere seu brigardare.' (*Stat.*
p. 116.)

CHAP. IV,
§ 5.

which these Inception-rejoicings were carried out may best be estimated from the fact that the Council of Vienne in 1311 passed a Canon limiting the expense of such entertainments to ' 3000 pounds Tournois[1].' It should be added that besides the legitimate expenses of graduation, bribery was by no means unknown in the Bologna Examinations[2].

Survival of
Inception-
ceremo-
nies.

In our English Universities, conservative as they are in many things, every trace of the ceremony of Inception has at length unhappily disappeared ; only the preliminary ceremonial of the License survives. Fragments of the old ritual survive in different parts of Europe. In the Scotch Universities Doctors are created by *birettatio* : at Bologna honorary Doctors are still invested with the *anulus*. Still more of the full medieval ceremonial survives in the Spanish Peninsula, and at Coimbra Doctors of Law or Medicine are said even now to enter upon their office with the full medieval pageantry of book and ring, *cathedra, biretta*, and *osculum pacis*[3].

---

[1] 'Tria millia Turonensium argenteorum' or ' circa 500 libræ Bononienses.' Clem. 2. *de magistris.* See Savigny's note, cap. xxi. § 82.

[2] The Jurist Francis Accursius took the precaution to' get a Papal absolution for the ' munera ' which he and his father had received from L. Faminando. Sarti, I. pt. ii. p. 96.

[3] Some of these ceremonies survive (I am informed) in Spain, but not the kiss ; as to Coimbra, see *Notice Historique de l'Un. d. C.* p. 172. Oxford still retained the creation of Doctors, by the cap, ring, kiss, &c., in 1654. *Diary of John Evelyn*, ed. Bray, I. p. 290. The ceremonial has also been revived at Louvain, see below, chap. ix. § 9.

§ 6. THE UNIVERSITIES OF MEDICINE, ARTS, AND
THEOLOGY.

One of the most striking differences between the
Academical system of Bologna and that of the Northern
Universities lies in the mutual relations of the various
Faculties.   In the organization which originated under the
very peculiar circumstances of Paris, but which has eventually spread over Europe, the Doctors and Students of
all Faculties are embraced in a single body and subject
to a common Head and a common government.   In
ancient Bologna there was absolutely no constitutional
connexion between the Faculty of Law on the one hand
and that of Arts and Medicine on the other, except the
fact that the students of each Faculty obtained their
degrees from the same Chancellor, the Archdeacon of
Bologna.   The Student Universities with which we have
been hitherto engaged were composed of Law-students
only, the Colleges composed solely of Doctors of Civil
and Canon Law.   The organization of the Law-Students
and the Law-Professors attained a developed form far
earlier than that of the Students and Doctors of Medicine
or the Liberal Arts.   The Doctors of Arts were no doubt
from an early period sufficiently organized to conduct graduations very much after the same fashion as the Doctors
of Law.   But the Students long remained without any
recognized organization of their own.   In the thirteenth
century, indeed, if we may trust to the analogies of Padua
and Lerida, the Jurist Rectors with characteristic insolence
claimed jurisdiction over the students of other Faculties [1].

*Entire se-
paration of
Law from
Arts and
Medicine.*

*Students
of Arts
and Medi-
cine origin-
ally subject
to Law
Universi-
ties.*

---

[1] As to Padua see below, chap. vi.
§ 4. At Lerida, the Statutes (1300 A.D.)
provide that 'quamvis scolares cives
civitatis istius, necnon phisici et
artistæ, et alii multi non sint de
stricto corpore universitatis studii

nostri quantum ad ordinationes sive
statuta condenda, debent tamen Rectoris subesse judicio et universitatis
statuta servare.' Villanueva, *Viage
Literario*, T. XVI. p. 226.

The necessities of the struggle by which the latter eventually won their independence may partly account for the curious fact that the Medical Students were members of the same University as the Students of the liberal Arts, including even the mere school-boy Grammarians. But since there was a similar relation between the Doctors of the two Faculties, the explanation must also be sought in the close relations of the two branches of study which obtained in Italy.

Rhetoric and Grammar important but preparatory.

We have seen that the Law-School of Bologna was itself only an outgrowth of a more ancient and very famous school of Rhetoric and Grammar. Rhetoric and Grammar always remained important subjects of instruction in Italy; throughout the Middle Ages they were far better and more thoroughly taught than in Northern Europe, where the new Aristotle and its attendant Scholasticism threw all literary studies into the shade. But after the rise of the Law-school at Bologna, Rhetoric and Grammar came to be looked upon mainly as a school-boy preparation for the higher professional studies; and the importance of their Professors who, unlike the lawyers, were entirely dependent upon teaching for an income, was proportionately diminished. Logic was also regarded as a useful discipline for the future lawyer: but the new Aristotle—

Unimportance of Philosophy.

the study of Physics, Metaphysics and Moral Philosophy— was in no way an essential or usual preliminary to a legal education: nor were these speculative studies or the degrees to which they led ever able in Italy to attain anything approaching the importance which they occupied in the less materially-minded Universities of Northern

Except as a preparation for Medicine.

Europe. But there was another study whose practical value commended it not less strongly to the utilitarian sympathies of Italian citizens than the study of Law: and that was the study of Medicine. Its development in Northern Italy was somewhat later than the Law-revival: and its practice, though almost as lucrative, never led to the same political or ecclesiastical distinction as a legal career. The status of the Medical Doctors and the Medical Universities of

Bologna always remained inferior to that of the Jurists. Nevertheless Bologna occupies a very important place in the history of medieval Medicine—a position second only to that of Salerno and Montpellier. And the study of Medicine according to medieval notions was closely bound up with the study of the Aristotelian Physiology, and consequently with the whole of the Aristotelian Philosophy. Aristotle, regarded in Northern Europe chiefly as the basis of speculative Philosophy and as the indispensable propædeutic for the Scholastic Theologian, was in Italy studied largely as constituting the scientific basis of Medicine. Hence the intimate connexion in all Italian Universities between Medicine and Arts.

The names of Physicians are of frequent occurrence in Bologna documents from the beginning of the eleventh Century, and from about the end of it some of these bear the title of *Magister*[1]. At the beginning of the thirteenth Century we hear of a *Medicus Vulnerum*, Hugh of Lucca being induced by an offer of 600 *libræ* to come to Bologna as a Public Surgeon—a sort of Military Surgeon and Police Surgeon combined[2]; his son Theodoric and many other members of his family were also eminent Surgeons[3]. Some of the early Physicians were ecclesiastics[4], others laymen.

Growth of Medical School at Bologna.

---

[1] The first recorded Medicus styled Magister is said to be Jacobus Britonoriensis. Sarti, I. pt. ii. p. 527.

[2] In 1214. Sarti, I. pt. ii. p. 531; II. p. 146. Cf. the City Statute in Frati, I. p. 47, which provides that in cases of violence 'a magistro dentisalvi medico [a dentist] vel a magistro ugone de lucha vel ab aliquo alio medico plagarum quesitum fuerit,' &c. Ozanam (*Docs. inédits*, p. 5) notices the numerous lay physicians mentioned in the Archives of Lucca (Brunetti, *Codice dipl. Toscano*, No. 68 *sq.*) between the eighth and eleventh centuries. Lucca no doubt received the Arabic medicine from Spain or Southern France. Brunus

came from Calabria (Raige-Delorme and Dechambre, *Dict. Encyc. des Sciences Méd.* Art. Bruno), another channel of communication with the East. All the early Bologna Physicians and Surgeons came from other towns.

[3] Sarti, I. pt. ii. p. 537 *sq.*

[4] The prohibition of the study to the Priests, Monks, and beneficed Clergy addressed by Honorius III to the Bishop of Bologna in 1219 (see Appendix xi) shows its growing importance, but did little to check the practice denounced, since dispensations were freely granted. Theodoric, though a Friar, was allowed to make a fortune by the

But at first the profession seems to have had little connexion with the regular Academical Schools. It is not
till the second half of the century that teachers of Medicine
assumed the title of Doctor or Professor [1], that graduations
can be shown to have taken place [2] and the School to have
been organized after the fashion already established in the
schools of Law and Arts. It was, it would appear, at
about this time that the study of Medicine, hitherto pursued
at Bologna empirically and traditionally, began to be under-
taken by men philosophically trained in the Schools of the
Liberal Arts and to be based upon the writings of the
classical Physicians and their Arabian imitators or cor-
rupters. The foundation of a scientific School of Medicine
at Bologna is generally associated with the name of
Thaddeus of Florence who began to teach in that city
about the year 1260 [3].

exercise of his Art, which he appears
to have practised even after becoming
a Bishop. *Ib.* pp. 537–541.

[1] From 1222 we begin to find a
class styled *Medici Physici*—a title
used apparently to distinguish the
scientific Physicians alike from the
ordinary empirical practitioners and
from the *Medici Vulnerum* or Surgeons (Sarti, I. pt. ii. pp. 520, 555):
the title *Medicinæ* or *Physicæ Professor*
or *Doctor* begins to be used about
the middle of the century (*ib.* pp. 463,
464) and implies a distinct imitation
of the titles assumed by the *Doctores
Legum.* In the *Rationes dictandi* of
Hugo Bononiensis is a letter from a
Master to his Scholars in which he
wishes them 'Ypocratis prudentiam
et tullianam eloquentiam.' Rockinger, *Quellen zur bayer. u. deutschen
Gesch.* Vol. IX. Abth. i. p. 63.

[2] One of the first academically
trained physicians who taught at
Bologna was Nicolaus de Farnham,
who, after teaching at Paris and Oxford in Arts, professed Medicine
(*rexerat*) at Bologna (Mat. Paris,

Chron. Maj. ed. Luard, IV. p. 86;
Sarti, I. pt. i. p. 535), and became
Bp. of Durham in 1241. It does not
follow that there was a separate
graduation in Medicine. As to Graduation in Arts, see above, p. 148.

[3] 'Hæc potissima Thaddæi laus
fuit quod primus ex nostris Medicinam
cum Philosophia arctissimo fœdere
conjunxisse visus sit.' (Sarti, I. ii.
p. 555.) Marvellous stories are
told of his wealth and professional
exactions. He received 3000 *libræ*
to attend a patient at Modena (see
the contract in Sarti, II. 1772, p. 153):
and would not go to Rome to attend
the Pope for less than 100 golden
ducats *per diem* (Villani, *Vite d' uomini
illustri Fiorentini,* Firenze, 1826, p. 24).
His bequests of books (Sarti, I. ii.
p. 559: I. ii. 1772, p. 158) suggest
that this teaching was largely based
on Avicenna, but he at times con-
sults the original Greek as well as
the Arabic versions of the Greek
physicians; he is even said to have
made a translation of the Nicomachean Ethics into Tuscan—a trans-

It was no doubt in consequence of this revolution that CHAP. IV,
the College of Doctors in Medicine and Arts, and the § 6.
University of students in the same Faculties, began to Graduation in Arts and
acquire a fresh importance, if not their first definite organ- Medicine.
ization. Graduation in Arts was certainly practised before
1221 [1], that is to say regular Inceptions took place, and
so at least in a rudimentary form some Guild or College
of Doctors must have existed. But we have no proof of
the existence of a distinct Medical graduation till the days
of Thaddeus [2], though in each case the custom of Inception
probably dates in some form or other from a much earlier
period. The first evidence of the existence of an organized The Col-
joint-College of Doctors of Medicine and Arts and of a lege of Arts and
joint-University of students is supplied (as is so often the Medicine.
case in University history) by a daughter-University—that
of Padua, where Rolandinus read his book before the
assembled Masters and students in 1262 [3]. Whether the The Stu-
Medical University of Bologna at this time had no Rector dent University and
at all or whether the Medical Rector was subject (as was Rector.
certainly the case at Padua) to the over-lordship of the
Jurist Rectors, it is certain that the Medical University
did not at first enjoy the same legal recognition and
privilege as the Universities and Rectors of the Jurists.
In 1295 we find the Jurists successfully opposing the pretensions of the Medical University to elect an independent
Rector like themselves, and it was not till 1306 that the

---

lation which is severely criticised
by Dante (*Convito*, Tratt. I. cap.
10). Special privileges were
granted to his scholars by the
City in 1283. Sarti, I. ii. p. 557.
It is difficult to know what Coppi
can mean by saying (p. 82) that
'fino dal secolo XIII la scuola
bolognese fu esclusivamente giuri-
dica.'

[1] See the passage quoted above,
p. 148.

[2] Gulielmus Brixiensis 'a Padua
recedens conventum suscepit in
Medicinis Bononiæ sub Magistro

Tatheo, Medico præcipuo tunc ibidem.' Engelbertus Abbas, ap. Pez,
Thes. Anecd. Nov. 1721, I. c. 430.

[3] *Chron.* xii. 19 ap Muratori, SS.
VIII. c. 360 (cf. below, chap. vi.
§ 4). The first express mention of
the *Collegium Magistrorum* (of Arts
and Medicine) at Bologna appears
to occur in 1292. Sarti, I. pt. ii.
p. 558; I. pt. ii. (1772), p. 155.
The gift of the translated Arabic and
Greek Philosophers and Mathemati-
cians by Frederick II would imply a
tolerably definite organization. Doc.
in Sarti, I. ii. (1772), p. 163. But the

CHAP. IV,
§ 6.

Constitu-
tion like
that of
Jurist Col-
lege and
University.

independent jurisdiction of the Medical Rector was recognized by the City and the rival Jurist-corporations[1].

The Medical College and University, when once their
constitution was developed, were mere imitations of the
corresponding institutions among the Jurists. The exact
parallelism which exists between the two organizations
will make it unnecessary to do more than notice a
few points on which the account already given of the
Jurist organization is inapplicable. The Medical University claimed to embrace every student in Medicine,
Surgery, ' Notaria,' Philosophy, Astrology, Logic, Rhetoric
or Grammar residing in the City of Bologna, and to exercise jurisdiction over the teachers of all those Faculties.
It is, indeed, obvious from the language of the Statutes, as
well as probable from the nature of the case, that there
were many more or less irregular Schoolmasters who with
their pupils neglected to take the oaths to the Rector and
get themselves put upon the Matricula. But the constitutional right of the University to control the humbler order
of Masters and scholars does not appear to have been
contested. It imposed few restrictions and conferred important privileges.

Only the
Medical
Students
had votes
in Congre-
gation.

Although scholars in all the above-mentioned subjects
were subject to the Rectorial jurisdiction and the University
Statutes, and entitled to University privileges and protection, only the students of Medicine were full citizens of the
Academical Republic : they alone were ' Scholars of the
University' and entitled to vote in Congregation : the rest
were only *subditi* or subjects of the University[2]. But
students of a certain standing in any Faculty were allowed
to take part with those of the superior Faculties who had
passed through the inferior in the election of their own
Professors, except in the case of students of Grammar.

letter is also attributed to Manfred.
See below, p. 359, *note.*

[1] Ghirardacci. I. pp. 329, 588.

[2] *Stat.* pp. 287, 288. At Florence
a curious and invidious distinction
is drawn between the Medical stu-

dent and the Artist. The former's
oath in a civil dispute is to be
taken ' usque ad quantitatem unius
floreni auri' : the Artist's only
to a smaller amount. *Stat. Fiorent.*
p. 23.

Moreover, all above the Grammarians were qualified to Chap. IV, vote in the Rectorial elections except the students of § 6. Rhetoric, who were only allowed to elect twelve represen- tatives to vote with the students of Medicine and the higher Arts[1].

The relations between the Professors and the students Relation of are exactly the same as those contemplated by the Jurist Students and Doc- Statutes.   Even the schoolboys possessed, it would seem, tors. at least theoretically, the same rights against their School- masters as the students of Medicine or Philosophy, except that the Statutes which conferred them were made by their older brethren, the students of Medicine.   But the power of the Medical Student-University does not seem quite so entirely beyond question as the power of the Universities of Jurists.   The Statutes occasionally admit that they are not always implicitly obeyed, and complain somewhat querulously of the 'arrogance' of Masters who defied the University and the extreme penalty which it had the power to inflict, i.e. 'privation[2].'   The only way in which the University could enforce its privation upon a non-salaried Doctor was by threatening his scholars with a like penalty if they refused to leave their deprived in- structor; but since the scholars of Arts had not the full privileges of membership in the Guild, it is clear that the hardship of exclusion must have been rather sentimental than substantial.

The Medical Statutes claim for the students the right Students to elect to all chairs salaried by the Municipality, though elect Pro- here they are directly contradicted by the counter-claim fessors.

---

[1] *Stat.* pp. 305, 306. In 1378 a distinction was drawn between Medical students who lived at their own expense and those who lived at the expense of others, (i.e. on charity or as dependents or servants). But by an agreement arrived at in 1379 an elaborate system of indirect election to the Rectorship is pre- scribed, so as to give a preponderat- ing weight to the students of indepen- dent means. Ghirardacci, II. 377. It is curious that the statute of 1378 should be so early disturbed. At Padua 'nullus nisi qui pervenerit ad quartum decimum ætatis suæ annum' was allowed to vote. Priests, Re- gulars, and 'famuli' or 'mercenarii' were also excluded. *Stat. Artist. Patav.* fol. 1 b.

[2] *Stat.* p. 256.

of the Magisterial College. So far as historical records go, the students succeeded in enforcing their pretensions[1]. Salaries appear to have been first extended to other Faculties than Law in 1305, when they were bestowed upon Doctors in Grammar, Physics and 'Notaria[2].' In 1321 we hear of Antonio de Virgilio being appointed with a 'large salary' to lecture upon Virgil, Statius, Lucan, and Ovid, an indication of the enormously higher position occupied by Classical studies in the Italian as compared with the Northern Universities; and at about the same time a salaried Professor of Rhetoric lectured on Cicero[3]. Soon afterwards salaries of 100 *libræ* were voted to Professors of Philosophy, of Astrology, of Medical Practice, of Natural Philosophy[4]. At a later time the Salaries, as in the case of the legal Faculties, increased in number and amount; but it would appear that here also the appointment to the majority of them was eventually lost by the students[5]. The highest Salaries paid in Medicine were nearly, but not quite, equal to the Salaries enjoyed by eminent Doctors of Law; and were generally higher than the salaries for Arts. The fees payable to Doctors of the various Faculties, whether salaried or otherwise, were limited by Statute. The Lecturer in Logic might charge anything up to 40 *solidi Bononienses*, the Doctor of Grammar up to 30. The latter, however, might add to his profits by taking boarders; though there was no obligation for the Grammarian any more than for any other scholar to reside in a house kept by a Master[6]. The fee for the medical lecture was, strange to say, lower than that for the lecture on Grammar, being limited to 20 *solidi*[7], probably because the Medical Doctor addressed a large audience, while the Grammar-boy required 'individual at-

---

[1] See above, p. 213, *note* 2.

[2] Ghirardacci, I. p. 504.

[3] *Ib.* II. pp. 17, 18, 19.

[4] *Ib.* II. p. 56.

[5] In 1383 it is specially mentioned that two of the twenty chairs in Medicine and Arts were filled by student-election. *Ib.* II. p. 398: Dallari, I. p. 45.

[6] *Stat.* pp. 248, 249.

[7] *Stat.* p. 253. For reserved seats ('si fuerit scholaris in bancha Rectoris vel in banchis anterioribus') a florin might be charged.

tention.' In Philosophy, the fees were fixed not by the year but by the course, varying from 40 *solidi* for the *De Animalibus* to five for the *Œconomica*[1].

Next to the entire separation of the legal Faculty on the one hand from the Faculties of Arts and Medicine on the other, the most distinctive peculiarity of the Italian University-system was the relation in which the Professors of the various Sciences represented by the Medical University stood towards each other. In the Northern Universities Medicine ranked with Theology and Law (though the lowest of the three) as a ' Superior Faculty'; all Masters of Arts, whether they actually taught Philosophy or Logic or Grammar, possessed equal rights as members of the Faculty of Arts. Grammar was hardly a Faculty at all. Some of the Universities claimed authority over the Grammar Schools; in some there was even a ceremony of graduation in Grammar[2]. But the Master of Grammar had no rights in the University. At Bologna a much more complicated system prevailed. There was a Collegium, composed—like the Colleges of Canon and Civil Law—of a limited number of Bolognese citizens, which possessed an exclusive right of examining candidates for the Doctorate in all the Faculties embraced in the Medical University[3]. This College consisted, it would appear, only of Doctors in Medicine or full Doctors in Arts, i. e. those who had graduated in all the liberal Arts[4]; though those who were Masters of Arts only, of course, took no part in the Medical Examinations, and had not the full rights of the Medical Doctors. But besides this complete graduation in all the liberal Arts, it was possible

---

[1] *Stat.* p. 252 (for extraordinary Lectures only).

[2] See below, vol. II. chap. xiv.

[3] See the Statutes of the College (dated 1378), *Stat.* p. 425 *sq.*

[4] *Stat.* pp. 257, 445. The Medici and the Artistæ are spoken of as the two ' membra ' of the College : the Doctors of Arts are apparently in-

cluded in the number above given, but the relation between the two bodies is somewhat obscure. In the lists of the Paduan College (Gloria, *Monumenti della Univ. di Padova, 1318–1405*, T. I. p. 78 *sq.*), there are Doctors of Medicine only, Doctors of Medicine and Arts, and a few of Arts only.

Chap. IV,   at Bologna to graduate in, and obtain authority to teach,
§ 6.   some of the subjects embraced in the Arts' curriculum with-
—•+—   out taking up or being examined in the rest. We thus
hear of Doctors of Philosophy, of Astrology, of Logic, of
Rhetoric, and of Grammar, the Faculties being enumerated
in what appears to have been considered their relative
dignity[1].

Graduation   It should be added that, though graduation in the lower
not essen-   Arts was recognized, it was not essential.   Though the
tial for
teaching   University claimed to extend both its privileges and its
inferior   control to the humblest Schoolmaster in the City, the
Arts.   monopoly of graduates extended only to the higher
Faculties and Arts ; the teacher of Grammar or Surgery
was not required to have graduated in the University,
but merely to have put his name upon its Matricula[2].

Scientific   Two of the subordinate subjects which fell within the
side of the jurisdiction of the Medical University demand special
twelfth-
century   notice—Astrology and Surgery.   The scientific side of the
Renais-   twelfth century Renaissance has often been too much
sance.   ignored ; it is the peculiarity of scientific writing that it
is doomed to almost complete oblivion the moment it
is superseded, even when the theories which it contains
are permanently accepted—still more so when they are
exploded.   Nevertheless, modern Science has its roots in
the intellectual revival of the twelfth century as much as
modern culture and modern Learning and modern Philosophy : and of the scientific side of this revival Italy was
the centre.   This branch of the movement began, indeed,
before the twelfth century.   It was in Italy that the Latin
world first came into contact with the half-forgotten treasures of Greek wisdom, with the wisdom which the Arabs
had borrowed from the Greeks and with original products
of the remoter East.   Of the Medical School of Salerno
we have already spoken.   It was probably in Italy and
through the Arabic that the Englishman Adelard of

---

[1] *Stat.* pp. 287, 488, 489, &c. Ac-   appear from the Statutes, though we
cording to Sarti, actual degrees were   hear of scholars in that Art.
given in ' Notaria,' but this does not   [2] *Stat.* p. 254.

Bath translated Euclid into Latin during the first half of the eleventh century[1]. At about the same time modern musical notation originated with the discoveries of the Camaldunensian Monk Guido of Arezzo[2]. In the first years of the following century the Algebra and the Arithmetic which the Arabs had borrowed from the Hindoos[3] were introduced into Italy by the Pisan merchant, Leonardo Fibonacci[4]; and this learned intercourse between East and West was still further promoted by the Imperial sceptic, Frederick II. It was to this Arabo-Greek influence that Bologna owed its very important School of Medicine and Mathematics—two subjects more closely connected then than now through their common relationship to Astrology[5].

[1] Libri, II. p. 48. The same writer remarks (II. p. 203), 'il faut se borner à constater ce fait peu connu, qu'il y a eu au quatorzième siècle, en Italie, un nombre tel de personnes qui ont écrit sur les diverses branches des mathématiques, qu'il serait difficile de croire que ce nombre ait jamais été surpassé dans aucun autre siècle. ... On pourrait retrouver encore les titres de plusieurs centaines d'ouvrages de mathématiques écrits au quatorzième siècle par les Italiens.'

[2] See Angeloni, *Sopra Guido d'Arezzo*, Parigi, 1811, p. 62, &c. His works are edited by Gerbert, *Scriptores Ecclesiastici de Musica*, Typis San-Blasianis, 1784. T. II. p. 1 *sq.*

[3] The Arabs appear to have added little in substance to Greek Geometry and Indian Arithmetic and Algebra. It is worth noticing that the Indian contribution to Mathematics was made by the Aryan conquerors within the first two or three centuries after the conquest. (Ball, *Hist. of Mathematics*, pp. 141, 142.) Even the Jews, with all their capacity for absorbing Aryan Mathematics, Medicine, and Philosophy, *originated*

little or nothing in the purely intellectual sphere.

[4] Libri, II. p. 20 *sq.* The preface of his *liber Abbaci* is given in Appendix viii. Ball remarks (*Hist. of Mathematics*, p. 153): 'In all these early works [of the Arab School] there is no clear distinction between arithmetic and algebra, and we find the account and explanation of arithmetical processes mixed up with algebra, and treated as part of it ... This arithmetic was long known as *algorism*, or the art of Alkarismi [an Arab Mathematician, who wrote *c.* 830 A.D.], which served to distinguish it from the arithmetic of Boethius; and this name remained in use till the eighteenth century.'

[5] How important was the constitutional connexion between the Arts Schools (including Mathematics) and Medicine, we are reminded by the fact that Galileo began life as a Medical student at Pisa. Libri, IV. p. 171. On the Mathematical School of Bologna, Libri (IV. p. 98) remarks: 'On ne saurait se dispenser de faire remarquer ici combien l'école de Bologne a été utile aux progrès de l'algèbre; c'est là que sont sortis Ferro, Ferrari, Bombelli et Cataldi,

Bologna did not become important as a School of Medicine till the close of the thirteenth century, when the power of Salerno had begun to decline, and the popularity of the Arabic medical writers was at its height. The effect of the new influence—in so far as it was really Arabic and not a revival of Greek Medicine and Surgery in an Arabic dress —was on the whole distinctly detrimental to the progress of Medical Science. It contaminated the quasi-scientific Medicine of Hippocrates and Galen with a mass of astrological superstition : it was considered necessary for the Physician to ascertain what would be his patient's critical days and to modify his treatment according to the aspect of the heavens[1]. We have already seen that Astrology was one of the regular Faculties of Bologna : there was a salaried Professor of Astrology, one of whose duties was to supply 'judgments' *gratis* for the benefit of enquiring students[2]. The position of an astrological Professor in a medieval University must have been a delicate one ; for the scientific prediction of future events which might be practised and taught by ecclesiastic or layman under the patronage of the Church shaded off into the Necromancy and the materialistic Fatalism on which the Church had no mercy. The most distinguished occupant of the Astrologer's chair at Bologna—the Prince of medieval Astrologers—Cecco d' Ascoli, ended his days at the stake in 1327, a victim of the Florentine Inquisition[3].

qui tous ont enrichi cette science de quelque notable découverte. Malheureusement leurs concitoyens semblent les avoir tout-à-fait dédaignés. Leur nom est à peine enregistré dans les bibliographies les plus étendues.'

[1] 'Oportet Medicum de necessitate scire ac considerare naturas stellarum et earum conjunctiones, ad hoc ut diversarum ægritudinum et dierum creticorum habeat notiones quoniam alterabilis est equidem ipsa natura secundum aspectus et conjunctiones corporum superiorum. . . . Medicus sine Astrologia est quasi oculus, qui non est in potentia ad operationem.' Ciccus Asculanus *in prœem. Astrolog.* ap. Sarti, I. pt. ii. p. 523.

[2] *Stat.* p. 264.

[3] Gio. Villani, *Hist. Fiorent.* ap. Muratori, XIII. c. 625. His encyclopædic Italian poem *L' Acerba* was printed at Venice in 1481, &c. There is nothing in the Statutes to support Libri's assertion (II. p. 193) that there were at Bologna two distinct chairs of Astronomy and Astrology. Libri (*l. c.*) has an interesting account of Cecco's really considerable knowledge of Physical Science.

Although the astrological bias of Bologna was not an improvement from a medical point of view, we must not despise the illusions through and by means of which all truth has to be reached. It was at Bologna, it would appear, that Copernicus, though a student of Canon Law, began the calculations which founded modern Astronomy[1], and the University had already produced in Copernicus' Master, the Cardinal Nicolas of Cusa[2], one of those anticipators who herald the approach of every great scientific revolution. In the department of Medicine it was only or chiefly on account of its increased attention to Surgery that the fourteenth century represents a period of progress: and in the history of medieval Surgery Bologna holds an important and very distinguished place. There were surgical writers at Bologna as early as the second half of the thirteenth century whose works continued in sufficient circulation to be included among the earliest productions of the Venetian press and to be often reprinted up to the middle of the seventeenth century[3]. The theoretical part of these books

---

[1] See the interesting monograph of Malagola (*Monografie*, p. 367 *sq.*).

[2] He became a Scholar of Law in 1437 and afterwards expounded an Astronomical system according to which the sun moved. *Ib.* p. 431. According to Libri (III. p. 99) Novara and a Neapolitan Jurisconsult discovered independently the change in the axis of the earth's rotation. He makes Novara Copernicus' Master.

[3] Among these were the above mentioned Theodoric of Lucca, whose work was, however, largely based upon the earlier Paduan teacher Brunus, and the more important Gulielmus de Saliceto (fl. *c.* 1270). Gui de Chauliac, the famous fourteenth-century surgeon of Montpellier, speaks of these two Surgeons as the chief representatives of the school ' qui indifferenter omnia vulnera cum vino exsiccabant,' a treatment based upon the Galenian doctrine that ' siccum vero sano est propinquius, humidum vero non sano.' There were, however, at Bologna representatives of the older Salerno school, which treated wounds on the principle that ' Laxa bona, cruda vero mala' (a Hippocratic maxim); of these the most important was Roland of Parma (a pupil of the Salernitan Roger), who was the first Bolognese writer on Surgery. (Sarti, I. pt. ii. p. 536 *sq.*: Raige Delorme et Dechambre, *Dict. Encycl. des Sciences Méd.* Art. Bruno.) The ' Chirurgia Magna' of Brunus and the ' Chirurgia' of Theodoric and of Roland were published with the 'Chirurgia' of Gui de Chauliac at Venice, in 1497, &c. It is a curious fact that the Bishop-Physician Theodoric paid special attention to Veterinary Surgery: he wrote a *Mulomedicina* and a *de cura Accipitrum*. (Sarti, I. pt. ii. p. 544.)

was based upon the Arabic authors who derived them for the most part from the late Greek writer Paul of Ægina: but it is the especial glory of the Bolognese Medical School that it was the earliest home of real anatomical enquiry. It was one of the first schools at which the old religious prejudice against dissection succumbed to the advance of Dissection. the scientific spirit [1]. Dissection was practised at Bologna at least as early as the time of Thaddeus; and the later Statutes make provision for somewhat more frequent 'Anatomies' than were customary in other Universities Mundinus. even in the South of Europe [2]. Mundinus, the Father of Modern Anatomy, was one of the earliest teachers of Surgery at Bologna, and his 'Anatomia' remained the standard text-book on the subject for more than two centuries. It was the ordinary practice in the Italian Universities for a Medical Doctor to read the relative parts of this treatise while the Professor of Surgery performed the dissection and another Doctor pointed out to the students the various bones or muscles as they were named by the reader [3]. By the Statutes of Florence food and wine and spices were to be provided to keep up the spirits of Professors and Students during this unwonted ordeal [4]. The importance of Surgery in Italy as compared

---

[1] Not, however, without a struggle: 'Ante hunc (Mundinum) obsoleta quasi erat secandorum humanorum cadaverum consuetudo nimirum contra Græcorum barbaram immanemque feritatem atque audaciam publico supplicio condemnatos avide impetrantium, ut in seditionem quasi concitatis, lex tandem injuncta infamiæ pæna vetavit, ne quis exuviis denudata cadavera imposterum ferro scindere et ut exta videret, auserit aperire.' Gulielminus, *De claris Bononiæ Anatomicis Oratio*, Bononiæ, 1737. For further information, see the elaborate work of Medici, *Compendio storico della Scuola Anatom. di Bol.* (Bologna, 1857) p. 8 *sq.*

[2] It was arranged that every Medical student of over two years' standing should be able to attend an 'Anatomy' once a year, twenty students being admitted to see the anatomy of each man, thirty of each woman. *Stat.* p. 289. Some other Universities had to be content with the body of a single criminal *per annum* for the whole body of Students.

[3] *e. g.* at Padua (Facciolati, *Fasti*, p. xlviii: *Stat. Artist.* f. xxvii *b*). The method is described in some University Statutes, and depicted in the woodcuts prefixed to many early editions of the old Medical writers.

[4] *Stat. Fiorent.* p. 74.

with its neglect in the Northern Universities is indicated by the different position occupied by its teachers. Not only was Surgery taught by Doctors of Medicine, but the latter were allowed to engage in surgical practice, an employment which was looked upon by the Doctors of Paris as a degrading manual craft, entirely beneath the dignity of a sage learned in all the wisdom of Aristotle and Galen[1]. At the same time the mere Surgeon who was not also a Physician was in an inferior position. Examinations in Surgery were held by the Medical Faculty, and licences to practise granted to those who passed them: but such qualified Surgeons did not apparently rank as Doctors of Surgery[2].

The subjects in which the Medical student was examined for his degree were simply the 'Liber Tegni' (i. e. τέχνη ἰατρική) of Galen and the Aphorisms of Hippocrates, on each of which the candidate was required to give one 'lectio[3].' The custom dates perhaps from a period previous to the introduction of the Arabian Medicine; it may be presumed that in the ensuing discussion the candidate might be required to show a knowledge of the other books lectured on in the Schools. Among these the 'Canon' of Avicenna had the first place; but they included also other works of Galen and Hippocrates

The Medical Curriculum.

---

[1] *Stat.* p. 444.

[2] *Stat.* pp. 442, 443. What was the exact position of the 'Doctor Cirurgiæ' is not at all clear. In the College Statutes of 1378 (p. 443) we hear of 'promoveri ad examen Cirurgiæ' as if it was possible to take a degree in Surgery only : on the other hand in the College Statutes of 1395 (p. 471) it is ordered 'quod nullus possit audeat vel presumat legere in scientia medicine Bononie, tam in physica quam in cirusia, nisi fuerit doctoratus in eadem scientia medicine, videlicet in physica.' The Student-Statutes (p. 254), after laying it down that no one who is not 'conventuatus' may teach at Bologna, adds 'salvo

quod legentes in gramatica vel Cyrurgia non teneantur ad predicta, nisi esset pro utilitate Universitatis scholarium.' In Gloria, *Mon. d. Padova,* 1318-1405 (II. p. 289) is a diploma conferring 'auctoritatem ubique legendi . . in eadem facultate cyrugie.' It is clear, therefore, that there were degrees in Surgery only, but that at Bologna the *Doctor legens* in Surgery was required to be also M. D. At Padua, no one was allowed to practise Surgery who was not either *Doctor Cyrugiæ,* or a student of three years' standing who had 'seen' a Doctor practising for one year. *Stat. Art. Patav.* f. xxvii *b.*

[3] *Stat.* p. 439.

besides those above mentioned, and a medical treatise
of Averroes[1]. The two *lectiones* of candidates for the
Examination in Surgery were upon a part of Avicenna and
upon the 'Surgery' of Brunus[2]. Among the books lectured
on appear also the 'Surgery' of Galen and the seventh
book of the 'Almansor' of Rhazes[3].

For the degree of Doctor in Medicine, the candidate was
required to be twenty years of age, of five years' standing
in the study of Medicine, and 'sufficient in Arts.' If he
had been licensed in Arts, four years' study of Medicine
sufficed. He must also have lectured on some medical
'tractate or book' as a Bachelor, and have responded or
disputed at least twice in the Schools[4]. The Medical
Statutes of some Universities further require that as a
Bachelor he should practise for a year under the supervision
of 'some famous Doctor[5].'

Course in
Philoso-
phy.
The subject-matter of the Arts course was so exactly the
same as that of Paris that it will be best to treat in detail
of the medieval philosophical curriculum when we come to
deal with the University which was its head-quarters. It
will be enough to say here that in the Italian Universities
parts only of the Aristotelian treatises[6] were lectured on

---

[1] 'Legatur de libro *coliget* [*i. e.*
Kitâb al Kollijât or Universalis de
Medicina] primo prohemium,' &c.
Stat. p. 275 *et not.*

[2] ' Pro prima lectione super tercia
parte fen quarti canonis Avicenne,
et pro secunda parte cirugie Bruni.'
Stat. p. 443.

[3] *Stat.* p. 247. It may be presumed that the 'Cirugia Avicenne'
is the same as the portion of the
Canon mentioned above.

[4] *Stat.* p. 433.

[5] *e. g.* at Padua, *Stat. Artistarum*,
f. xxix *a* : cf. a Statute of Angers,
'Nullus non graduatus præsumat
ordinare seu administrare quamcun-
que medicinam digestivam, laxativam
seu etiam confortativam, nec alias
quovis modo infirmum visitare, causa

curæ, excepta prima vice, nisi cum
Doctore vel Licentiato, si aliqui
fuerint præsentes.' *Statuts des Quatre
Facultés de l'Un. d'Angers*, Angers,
1878, p. 38. Here the Bachelor was
either non-existent or not reckoned
a 'Graduate.'

[6] *Stat.* p. 274. The Paduan Artist-
statutes of 1486 (*Stat. Art.* f. xxxiii *bis*)
introduce a number of Text-books
by recent writers, mostly Paduan
teachers : 'deputati ad sophistariam
teneantur legere logicam pauli ueneti
questiones strodi cum dubiis pauli
pergulensis et pro tertia lectione regu-
las seu sophismata tisberi.' Radulphus Strodus is said to have been a
Scotch Fellow of Merton, afterwards
a Dominican, who travelled through
France, Italy, and the Holy Land

instead of the whole: while the actual examination was
limited to still smaller portions[1]. Moreover, the course
seems to have been got through in a much shorter time—
four years instead of a real or nominal seven. But, while
the Italian Universities never rivalled the Scholastic fame
of Paris, Rhetoric, Mathematics, and Astrology flourished
more vigorously in the Italian Universities than in the
North. In the former subject the text-books at Bologna
were the *De Inventione* of Cicero and the treatise *Ad Herennium* then attributed to the same writer[2], or the compendium of it compiled by the Friar Guidotto of Bologna.

Astrology was so interpreted as to include Mathematics[3]. Astrology
The subjects prescribed were :— and Mathe-
matics.

(1) A work on Arithmetic or Algebra, styled *Algorismi
de minutis et integris* [? of Gerard of Cremona].

(*circa* 1370) 'contra Wiclefi dogmata acriter disputans' (Fabricius, *ad
voc.* ; Brodrick, *Memorials of Merton
Coll.* p. 214). He is mentioned as a
poet by Chaucer ('the philosophicall
Strode,' *Troilus*, l. 1869): and his
poem 'Pearl' is edited by Gollancz
(London, 1891). Paul of Pergolæ
was a Venetian philosopher contemporary with Paul of Venice. M.
Hauréau, *Dict. des Sciences Phil.*, *ad
voc.*, questions whether the 'Dubia'
ascribed to Paul of Pergolæ is not
really the work of the better-known
Paul of Venice. The above allusion
seems to show the doubt to be unnecessary. Tisberus is the Oxonian
Heytisbury, as to whom see Poole
in *Dict. of Nat. Biogr.* XXVI. p. 327,
Wood's *City of Oxford*, ed. Clark, I.
p. 346 *note*. At this time it is observable that both in the Theological
and the Philosophical Faculties (as
in so many German Universities),
there were separate sets of Lectures
for Thomists and Scotists; the Paduan
Statute (*l.c.*) provides : 'Volumus
quod deputati ad legendum theologiam unus legat secundum uiam
sancti thomæ alter secundum uiam

scoti. Et similiter deputati ad metha-
phisicam.' Scotus was himself much
influenced by the Averroistic Philosophy.

[1] ' Qui examinari voluerit in artibus omnibus simul, ordine servato
supradicti statuti, prima die recipiat
poncta pro prima lectione in libro
metaphysice et pro 2ª lectione in
matematicis in libro sp[h]ere ; in
2ª vero die pro prima lectione in
loyca in libro posteriorum, pro secunda lectione in gramatica in pri-
siano minori.' *Stat.* p. 489. At
Florence the whole of the Organon
is read, to which was added the
Tractatus and *Fallaciæ* of Thomas
Aquinas (*Stat. Fior.* p. 65).

[2] The former was styled the *Retorica vetus*, the latter the *Retorica
nova*. *Stat.* p. 488 *et not.*

[3] There was a chair of Arithmetic
whose occupant was required ' omnem mensuram terre et muri et
generaliter cuiuslibet laborerii communis Bononie mensurare et agri-
mensare, et etiam omnes rationes
communis Bononie male visas et
chalculatas revidere et refformare.'
Dallari, I. p. 5.

(2) Euclid, with the Commentary of the thirteenth-century Geometrician, Johannes Campanus de Novara.

(3) The tables of Alfonso X, King of Castile, with the 'Canons' [of Giovanni di Sassonia].

(4) The *Theorica Planetarum* [? of Gerard of Cremona, or Campanus de Novara's free translation of Ptolemy's *Almagesta*].

(5) The *Canones super tabulis de lineriis*, i.e. rules for the use of astronomical tables to determine the motions of the heavenly bodies, by John of Linières or Lignières of Amiens (fl. 1330 A.D.).

(6) The *Tractatus astrolabii* of Messahala or Maschallah [a Jewish Astrologer of the ninth century].

(7) Alchabicius [fl. *c.* 850 A.D.: probably his *Isagoge* to judicial Astrology, translated by Gerard of Cremona].

(8) The *Quadripartitum* and the *Centiloquium* of Ptolemy with the Commentary of Haly, which were works upon judicial Astrology.

(9) A certain *Tractatus Quadrantis*. [On the use of the Quadrant.]

(10) A work on Astrological Medicine or Medical Astrology, which bore the title, very characteristic of the Arabs and their followers, *de urina non visa* [by Gulielmus Anglicus or Grisauntus][1].

(11) Portions of the *Canon* of Avicenna[2].

Repetitions and Repetitores. Characteristic of the Arts' course at Bologna was the prominence of the *Repetitiones*. A *Repetitio* in Medicine and Arts was apparently somewhat different from the exercise so called in the Law-schools. It was, as a rule, not given by the Master himself but by a 'Repetitor' who attended the lecture and then repeated it to the students afterwards and

---

[1] Said to have been the father of Urban V. (fl. 1350) Fabricius *ad voc.*
[2] *Stat.* p. 276. I am indebted to Malagola for some of the above explanations. According to Boncompagni (*Della vita e delle op. di Gherardo Cremona*, Roma, 1851) the

Theorica planetarum is the work of Gerardus Cremonensis of Sabbionetta (thirteenth cent.), not of the earlier Gerardus Cremonensis or Carmonensis [of Carmoni in Spain], the translator of the medical works of Avicenna, &c.

catechized them upon it[1].   Every Doctor teaching Logic
was obliged to have a 'Repetitor generalis' attached to
his chair[2]; besides these official 'Repetitores' there were
'Repetitores speciales' who may be considered the private
Tutors or 'coaches' of the period[3].   The 'Repetitores' at
Bologna occupied to some extent the position of the
Bachelors in the Northern Universities[4].   Although students
of a certain standing in all Faculties could be admitted to
give extraordinary lectures by the Rector, and by so doing
become Bachelors[5], the Bachelorship possessed much less
importance in the Bolognese Schools of Arts and Medicine,
than in the Schools of Paris or even in the Law-School of
Bologna.

The last peculiarity of the Italian Universities which has
to be noticed was the absence, in their earliest days, of a
Theological Faculty.   Ecclesiastics attended the Universities as much in Italy as in France; but in Italy, after
the rise of the Canon Law, the study of Theology proper
was completely overshadowed by the practical studies of
Law and Medicine.   Many of the greatest Schoolmen
were Italians by birth; but Theology rarely flourished on
Italian soil.   Just as among secular studies the practical and
the literary prevailed over the speculative, so in Italy ecclesiastical studies flourished chiefly in their practical, their

Theology in thirteenth century left to Friars.

---

[1] 'Teneatur etiam repetere lectiones, scilicet de mane et in nonis
usque ad pascha, et examinare de
sero.' *Stat.* p. 253.

[2] *Stat.* p. 251.

[3] *Stat.* p. 253.

[4] But the Repetitores were more
decidedly attached to the particular
Master than Bachelors: they were
in fact in the position of Assistant-
Masters in the School of their chief.
See the curious deed of scholastic
partnership in Sarti, I. ii. (1772) p. 11.

[5] *Stat.* p. 272.   Nothing seems to
be said of 'Responsions,' or any
preliminary Examination in the
Statutes, but at Padua we find a

student supplicating 'quod possit
acedere ad examen—absque respon-
sione questionum et lecturis librorum,
Gloria, *Mon. d. Padova* (1318–1405)
II. p. 267.   So *ib.* p. 273, and the
Statuta Artistarum of 1465 (fol.
xxviii) provide 'Rector autem in
Baccalariis ab ipso creandis ex auctoritate qua fungitur antequam illi
gradum Baccalariatus conferat in
eius presentia super duobus punctis
sibi asignatis, per duos idoneos
Doctores Legentes quos ipse Rector
elegerit, diligenter examinari faciat,
quibus si approbatus fuerit illi gradum
Bacallariatus conferat, et privelegium
per notarium nostrum fieri mandet.'

social, their political applications.　For secular Churchmen Canon Law took the place of Theology.　Pure Theology was abandoned to the Regulars, that is, for the most part, to the Mendicant Friars, who taught and studied not, as in France, in Universities where they had to hold their own against scholastically trained seculars, but in purely conventual Schools.　Here too it may be said that the practical interest was predominant; unlike the speculative secular Doctors of Paris and Oxford, the Friars studied as a preparation for the work of the preacher and the confessor.　While the seculars were fighting for the rights of the Church against the Empire or the Municipalities, the Friar alone sought to bring other weapons to bear upon the souls of men than those of Excommunication and Interdict.

No Theological Faculty till 1352.

Throughout the thirteenth and the first half of the fourteenth century, the Italian Schools of Theology had no official relations with the Universities of the Studia in which they were placed[1].　The policy of the Popes preserved for Paris and the English Universities their practical monopoly of Theological graduation.　Friars might prepare themselves for their Theological degrees wholly or partially in other convent Schools, but they had to go to Paris to graduate[2].　Bologna obtained its Theological Faculty from Innocent VI, in 1352[3].　A little later, the Schism altered the relations between Paris and the Papacy; and the Roman Popes sought to weaken the great School of the Avignon obedience by granting Bulls to authorize theological graduation both in the existing and in the newly created Universities; while after the Schism the same policy was continued by the Pontiffs of reunited Christen-

---

[1] They were no doubt open to such secular Students as chose to attend them: but these were probably few.　We hear that S. Richard, Bp. of Chichester, *circa* 1241 ' ad Theologiam se contulit Aurelianis in domo Fratrum Prædicatorum addiscendam.'　*Vita*, ap. A. S. Ap. 3.

T. I. p. 279.　For another case at Padua, see Pez, *Thes. Anecd. Noviss.* I. c. 43.　See above, p. 8, n. 1.

[2] Papal bulls were frequently granted to exempt Friars from all or part of the requisite residence and exercises.

[3] Doc. in Ghirardacci, II. p. 262.

dom who had discovered at Pisa, at Constance, and at Basle, that Paris was now a rival rather than a supporter of the Papal Autocracy. But the establishment of these Faculties of Theology in Southern Europe made little real change in the constitution of the Studia. Theology was still taught and studied almost exclusively by the Mendicants[1]. The few secular students of Theology continued, it would appear, to be members of one of the already existing Universities[2], but the latter never attempted to extend their despotic sway over the Professors of Theology. The College of Theological Doctors was wholly independent alike of the Student-Universities and of the other Colleges. On the other hand its Doctors naturally stood in a closer relation to the Chancellor, who was in this case the Bishop of Bologna[3]. The Archdeacon had nothing to do with the licensing of Theological Doctors.

In the following Chapter we shall see how important in their effect upon the history of Italian culture were the purely constitutional relations of the various Faculties to one another—the predominance of law-studies, the separation of Theology from the secular Arts-schools, the close alliance between the Faculties of Arts and Medicine. Rather perhaps we ought to say that these constitutional arrangements are but the external counterpart and concomitant of deeply seated tendencies of the North-Italian genius.

---

[1] Ghirardacci, II. p. 278, &c. That a secular, however, could become a Doctor and teacher at Bologna is shown by the provisions of the Statutes of the College of Spain (*MS. Stat.* f. 6 *b*). The printed Statutes of 1536 provide for a permanent chair of Theology in the College (ff. xxi *b*, xxii *a*).

[2] It is usually stated that they belonged to the University of Arts. The student in Theology would often be already a member of that University, but it appears that he might be in the Jurist-University. A Privilege (ap. Malagola, *Monografie*, p. 257) granted in 1741, enabled the German Nation to present a poor scholar from its own members for gratuitous graduation in Theology.

[3] At Padua, the Dean and College of Theology could not make Statutes without the consent of the Bishop. Gloria, *Mon. di Padova, 1318–1405*, I. p. 83 : so the Bishop admits to the Bachelorship ('ad lecturam libri sententiarum'). Gloria, *l.c.* II. p. 151.

§ 7. The Place of Bologna in the History of Culture.

Chap. IV,
§ 7.
—٭—
The great
age of
medieval
Jurispru-
dence.

In many respects the work of the School of Bologna represents the most brilliant achievement of the intellect of medieval Europe[1]. The medieval mind had, indeed, a certain natural affinity for the study and development of an already existing body of Law. The limitations of its knowledge of the past and of the material Universe, were not, to any appreciable extent, a bar to the mastery of a Science which concerns itself simply with the business and the relations of every-day life. The Jurist received his Justinian on authority as the Theologian received the Canonical and Patristic writings, or the Philosopher his Aristotle, while he had the advantage of receiving it in the original language. It had only to be understood, to be interpreted, developed, and applied. The very tendencies which led men of immense natural powers so far astray in the spheres of Theology, of Philosophy, and still more of Natural Science, gave a right direction to the interpretation of authoritatively prescribed codes of law. An almost superstitious reverence for the *littera scripta*; a disposition to push a principle to its extreme logical consequences, and an equally strong disposition to harmonize it at all costs with a seemingly contradictory principle ; a passion for classification, for definition and minute distinction, a genius for subtlety—these, when associated with good sense and ordinary knowledge of affairs, are at least some of the characteristics of a great legal intellect. Moreover, the exercises which were of such doubtful utility in other branches of knowledge formed an excellent course of legal

---

[1] In the following account of the medieval Jurists I rely mainly on Savigny, though I have tried to correct and supplement him by later authorities (see above, pp. 90, 91).

education. The practice of incessant disputation pro- Chap. IV,
§ 7.
duced a dexterity in devising or meeting arguments and a
readiness in applying acquired knowledge, of comparatively
little value to the student of History or Physical Science,
but indispensable to the Advocate and even to the Judge.
While it fostered an indifference to the truth of things fatal
to progress in Theology or Philosophy, it gave the pleader
the indispensable faculty of supporting a bad case with
good, and a good case with the best possible, arguments[1].

In estimating the place of the Civil Law in the history The Glos-
sators.
of medieval culture, we must carefully distinguish between
its cultivation as a science and its pursuit as a profession.
During the most brilliant period of its cultivation as a
science its Professors were almost all congregated in
Bologna itself. That period embraces the century and a
half after its revival by Irnerius. It was in the hands of
the 'Glossators'—of Irnerius, of the famous 'Four Doctors'
of whom we shall have more to say hereafter, of Rogerius,
Placentinus, Azo and Hugolinus—that the most real progress was made. The works of these men are, perhaps,
the only productions of medieval learning to which the
modern Professor of any science whatever may turn, not
merely for the sake of their historical interest, not merely
in the hope of finding ideas of a suggestive value, but with
some possibility of finding a solution of the doubts, difficulties and problems which still beset the modern student.

One important part of the work of the School of the Textual
criticism.
Glossators was the formation of a sound text. In no other
department of knowledge did the medieval mind show
itself capable of judicious textual criticism. The Jurists of
Bologna made frequent pilgrimages to Pisa to consult the
celebrated 'Florentine' Codex[2] of the Pandects. By diligent
collation of this and other MSS. there was gradually formed
what was known as the *Textus Ordinarius* or Vulgate of

---

[1] It is interesting to observe that
the old 'Moots' or arguments by
Students under the presidency of
a Bencher have recently been revived in the English Inns of Court.

[2] So called since its removal to
Florence, after the Florentine conquest of Pisa.

the Civil Law, the text which was henceforth so jealously guarded by the 'Peciarii' of the Universities and which has formed the basis of all subsequent editions down to quite modern times.

Democratic
Revolu-
tion: De-
cline of the
School.
Good sense and knowledge of affairs were, it has been said, conditions of progress in the study of law. It was just during the period when the Jurists of Bologna were most conspicuous as statesmen in a free Republic that their labours produced really valuable results. Before the middle of the thirteenth century there occurred at Bologna, as in most of the other Lombard republics, a great democratic Revolution. The chief power in the State passed out of the hands of the aristocracies into the hands of the people[1]; and in the popular governments the Jurists enjoyed a less commanding position[2]. The Doctors more and more degenerated as teachers into mere legal schoolmen, as Jurisconsults into mere practitioners. The use or abuse of the forms of Dialectic, the imitation of the subtleties, the intricacies, the interminable elaboration of the Philosophers exercised a malign influence upon their work. Jurisprudence—like every other department of human knowledge (including even Grammar and Medicine[3])—became Scholastic: while the formation of a semi-hereditary Professoriate tended to the extinction of originality and genius in the School of Bologna. And to these causes of the decline of the Science ought perhaps to be added the innate tendency of medieval learning to a sort of crystallization. Reverence for authority was harmless when the only authorities were the original sources of law. When the same reverence was extended to the glosses as had before been bestowed on the text, progress was at an end. The gloss of Accursius exercised upon the Civil Law the same narrowing in-

The
Accursian
Gloss.

---

[1] i. e. as in ancient Athens, the citizens, not the actual population. See Symonds' *The Age of the Despots*, London, 1875, p. 131.

[2] Thus Odofredus complains that 'Quando plebeii hujus civitatis volunt facere sua statuta non plus vocarent prudentes quam tot asinos et ideo ipsi faciunt talia statuta que nec habent Latinum nec sententiam.' Ad. leg. *Lex est*, Dig., *de orig. jur.* (T. I. f. 10).

[3] Well pointed out by Kaufmann, *Gesch. d. Deutschen Un.* pp. 25, 73 *sq.*

fluence which the 'Sentences' of Peter the Lombard had on Theology. This gloss was a selection, and as we are assured by Savigny not altogether an intelligent selection, of the glosses of previous writers. Yet a century later the Professors had come to busy themselves more with this Gloss than with the text. Instead of trying really to develope the meaning of the text, they aimed at a tediously exhaustive recapitulation and criticism of all the Glosses and comments they could collect. In short, they lost sight of the end and aim of their work, which consequently became more and more stagnant and pedantic [1].

The mere mass of matter accumulated by his predecessors must have weighed upon the unfortunate Professor of a later age, crushed his originality, and narrowed the sphere within which originality could be exercised. The truth is that the exigencies of Academic lecturing upon text-books tend of themselves to produce a vast quantity of unnecessary commentation [2]. Where much has been well said, it is hard to say anything fresh that is both original and important : comments must perforce be either unoriginal or superfluous. No doubt comments, analyses, paraphrases, illustrations, applications, which are of no permanent value, may be useful simply as a means of impressing the substance of an author upon the mind of pupils. Lectures of this character are not commonly, in modern times, given to the world. In the Middle Ages, however, when it was possible to pro-duce a dozen copies of a book at the same proportionate

Multiplica-tion of Comment-aries.

---

[1] A fifteenth-century writer com-plains : 'Scribunt nostri doctores mo-derni lecturas novas, in quibus non glossant glossas, sed glossarum glos-sas. Et hodie in lecturis suis trans-ponuntur jam dicta. Quod enim unus in una lege ponit, alius ponit in alia per eadem verba, vel paulo distantia.' Ap. Sarti, I. i. p. 155.

[2] Thus the sixteenth century Jurist Alciatus (*Opera*, Francofurti, IV. 1617, c. 866) notices the contrast between the glossators and the fourteenth cen-tury Doctors who ' diffusius omnia attigerunt . . . non usque adeo tamen, ut omnia in unum locum congere-rent : dumtaxat vacationum diebus aliquam legem iterum interpretandam accipiebant quam diffusius disputa-rent, ideoque Repetitiones dixerunt: et hodie omnes repetitiones sunt nihilque plerisque dictum videtur, si quidquam omissum fuerit, quod com-modius in alium locum reservetur. Unde efficitur ut singulis annis pau-cas admodum leges interpretemur.'

cost as to produce a hundred or a thousand, the temptation
to the publication of lectures was greater.   To this cause
we may perhaps owe the publication of large quantities of
matter contrasting unfavourably with the terseness, the
freshness, the good Latinity, the close contact with the
original texts which impress the modern student of the
older medieval Jurists.

The most
famous
Jurists.   It must not be supposed that the estimate which has
been given of the relative importance of the earlier and
the later medieval Jurists corresponds with the reputation
which they enjoyed in the Middle Ages themselves.   The
greatest legal reputations of the Middle Ages were made
in the period which begins with Accursius.   In the estimate
of the later medieval world, the greatest authorities (next
to Accursius himself) were such men as Odofredus, Dinus,
Cinus, Bartolus, Baldus, and Jason [1] : and it is to no small
extent the very success of these men (especially of the
Bartolists) in adapting the Roman Law to the needs and
the customary practice of their own time that diminishes
their value as scientific commentators.   Nor must it be supposed from what has been said as to the altered position of
the Bologna Jurists after the democratic Revolution that
Lawyers and Law-professors no longer played an important
part in public life : but their influence was of a different
kind.   The effect of the study of Roman Law upon the
progress of Imperialistic ideas has sometimes been exag-
Political
influence
of the ear-
liest Jurists.   gerated.   It is chiefly in the earliest period that this
influence can be traced.   In the later Middle Age as many
Civilians were Guelph as Ghibelline.   But it is a fact that
the most famous of the early Glossators were Imperialists,
and in their case it is perhaps no mere fancy to connect
their politics with a bias derived from their special studies.
Irnerius, as has been mentioned, played an important part

---

[1] Savigny's somewhat enthusiastic
admiration of the Glossators may
be qualified by the remarks of Berriat-Saint-Prix (p. 286 *sq.*) who, however, has no higher estimate of their
successors, the Bartolists.   The
great disqualification of all medieval
Interpreters was of course their inadequate knowledge of classical antiquity.

in the Imperial service. The four Doctors, the most celebrated of his immediate successors—Bulgarus, Martinus,
Jacobus, and Hugo—were prominent Imperialist politicians,
and the two former were intimate friends and advisers of
Frederick Barbarossa. It was (according to the common
but uncertain tradition) by the advice of the Four Doctors
that the celebrated attempt was made to reimpose the
neglected 'regalian rights' upon the Lombard towns, at
the Diet of Roncaglia in 1158. The Doctors, if they did
not answer as Roman Lawyers, certainly answered as
lawyers[1]. They earned the undying hatred of their fellow-
citizens as traitors to the liberty of their country.

From this period the position of the great Professors as
Bolognese statesmen was no doubt altered, but Jurists were
still in request both in Bologna and other Italian cities as
Judges and Magistrates, as Assessors or Ambassadors, or
simply as consulting lawyers[2]. A large and very lucrative
part of the business of the great Law-doctors consisted in
giving 'consultations' whether to private enquirers or to
Princes and Cities on matters of public and constitutional
Law. In truth, if the purely scientific and the purely
political greatness of the Bologna School belongs pre-
eminently to its earliest period, it was at a much later
period that its influence was most widely diffused, though
it was an influence now exerted indirectly through a
multitude of daughter-Universities whose Professors often

---

[1] Ghirardacci, I. p. 80 : Sarti, I. pt. i.
(1888), p. 37 : Savigny, cap. 24 and
28, points out that these rights were
founded on Lombard, not on Roman,
Law, and vehemently defends the
counsel of the Doctors. Perhaps,
while disposed to deny altogether
the imperialistic tendency of the
study of the Civil Law, the great
Jurist is really illustrating its effect
upon his own mind.

[2] Study at a University was usually
required by the Italian cities as a
qualification for judicial posts. Cf.
the Stat. of Bologna in 1158 (Frati,

I. p. 119): ' Nullus possit esse Judex
Comunis, nec vocari ad aliquod dandum conscilium, nisi ipse studuerit
in scolis V. annis in legibus.' So in
France, 'Nemo in Gallia admittitur
in Judicem aut Advocatum nisi
in utroque aut altero jure Doctor
aut Licentiatus fuerit, iis solum
Dignitatum porta in Curiis Galliæ
supremis aperta est sicut et apud
reliquas nationes (paucissimis exceptis) soli juris Romani Consulti
Judicum et Advocatorum munera
exercent.' Duck, *De usu Jur. Civ.*
f. 102 *b*.

eclipsed the reputation of their Alma Mater. The great
work of the Universities—in Southern Europe at least—
was the training of educated lawyers: the influence of
Bologna and of the Universities generally meant the influence of the lawyer-class upon social and political life.
To estimate the extent and value of that influence would
lead us too far astray from our immediate subject. We
must be content to state in general terms that wherever
the Civil Law was more or less recognized as the law of the
secular courts—in Italy, Southern France, Spain, Germany,
and (at a later date) Scotland—the men who aimed at being
Advocates and Judges went to the Universities, just as
lawyers and country gentlemen alike went to the London
Inns of Court in the days when the Inns were in fact
what they were sometimes expressly called, a University
of English Law. And the Universities were almost as
much the nurseries of practical lawyers in many countries
governed by customary Law, as for instance in the French
pays de droit coutumier, in which the Civil Law was used
to explain and to supplement a local custom often itself in
part of Roman origin. Even where the Civil Law commanded least respect in the secular courts, its study was still
indispensable to the Canonist. The study of the Civil
Law was indeed forbidden to Priests by Honorius III[1].
The Canonist accordingly who looked forward to an ecclesiastical career usually went through the course of Civil
Law or at least spent some years in its study before taking
Holy Orders and entering upon the proper studies of his
own profession, though it was easy for an individual or
even for a whole University to obtain dispensation from
the prohibition[2]. While the Science of Civil Law rapidly

---

[1] Savigny speaks as if this prohibition was altogether inoperative, at
least at Montpellier. But it was
fully respected at Oxford and Cambridge, as is evident from the provisions as to Orders in the Statutes
of Trinity Hall and New College.
It is possible that Savigny forgets
that in the Middle Ages a Canonry
or a Rectory might often be held
by a Deacon or a Clerk in Minor
Orders.

[2] These bulls were often granted
for a term of years, such a course
being the more remunerative to the
Holy See.

degenerated and the Civilians no longer held the place they had once occupied as Italian statesmen, the importance of the profession of the Canon Law continued to increase, until it reached the zenith of its influence in the days of the Avignon Papacy, though here also the period of scientific progress has ceased. Distinction in Canon Law at the Universities and practice at the Bar of the Ecclesiastical Courts constituted the great avenue to fame and preferment.

In the fifteenth century Roman Law began to attract attention as a branch of Roman literature, and to be studied by Politian and others in its connexion with Roman History and antiquities; but the scientific and historical study of Roman Law made little progress till the time of Alciatus and Cujas. The history of this later revival is a part of the history of the Renaissance. And if in Italy the Renaissance was contemporary with the Middle Age of Northern Europe, it closes the Middle Age of Italy, and we must abstain from entering upon the origins of the mighty movement which was destined, after a long struggle, to extinguish scholasticism beneath a torrent of execration and contempt, and to destroy or transform throughout Europe that medieval University system which it is our present object to sketch. *The study of Law and the Renaissance.*

It was through the Civil and Canon Law that the School of Bologna exercised its most powerful, at least its widest, influence over the course of human affairs. It would, however, be a great mistake to look upon Bologna as purely a School of Law. We have, indeed, seen that from the time when Canon Law became fully differentiated from Theology, no secular Studium of Theology of any importance existed at Bologna. In the Academic organization a Faculty of Theology had no place till 1352. The consequences of this constitutional peculiarity were of the highest importance. From the Schools of Bologna strictly theological speculation was practically banished, and with it all the heresy, all the religious thought, all the religious life to which speculation gives rise. The prominence of *The Canon Law.* *Neglect of Theology.*

legal studies in the South of Europe and of Theology in
the North is a fact of decisive importance in determining
the destinies of the Western Church. In the Middle Ages
Theology was, if not the foe of the Papacy, at least a very
dangerous and suspected ally. The Latin Church received
her laws from Rome, her Theology from Paris and Oxford.
It was only in the hands of the Dominican Friars—and not
quite always even then—that Theology could be reckoned
upon as a safe ally of Papal pretensions. Wherever
Theology was studied by Seculars—in France, in England,
and in Germany—revolt came sooner or later. It was
not by Theology so much as by Law—by her inheritance
of those traditions of Imperial Jurisprudence which had
subtly wound themselves round the common Faith of
Europe—that Rome established her spiritual monarchy.
The Canonist was by his profession a champion of the power
which had created his class. No Canonist (with the doubtful
exception of Cranmer) ever headed a reform-party or inaugurated a religious movement and no religious movement was
ever originated or fostered in an Italian University.

Specula-
tion finds a
refuge in
the Schools
of Medi-
cine.
On the other hand, the speculative thought which at
Paris was cultivated in the Schools both of Theology and
of Philosophy by philosophically trained ecclesiastics, was
in Italy abandoned to Schools of Philosophy taught by
laymen and chiefly attended by future Physicians. In
Italy Medicine was a more distinct and a more flourishing
profession than in Northern Europe; medical men were
not as a rule ecclesiastics; and the Faculties were quite
independent, in so far as any profession was independent,
of ecclesiastical authority. The popularity of the Arabic
Medicine carried with it the popularity of Arabic Astrology and Arabic Philosophy. And the Philosophy of
Averroes, the most famous of the Arabs, was (in a popular if not in a strictly philosophical sense) a system of
Pantheism, and a Pantheism of a materialistic rather than
a spiritualistic complexion. In theological Paris, as we
shall see, Averroism was for a time a source of serious
alarm. But long before the close of the thirteenth century

the triumph of the orthodox Monotheism in the Parisian
Schools was complete. Averroes was remembered chiefly
as the Commentator, and was regarded, indeed (his theological errors duly excepted) as one of the accredited
expositors of the accredited Philosophy of the Church[1].
But Averroes, the champion of the 'Unity of Active
Intellect' and all the heresies and infidelities associated
with that Pantheistic theory, ceased after the thirteenth
century to have any formidable influence over the thought
of Paris. In Italy it was far otherwise. To the Schools of
Arts and Medicine in Italy Averroes was not merely 'the
Commentator.' The authority ascribed to his characteristic
doctrines equalled that attributed throughout Europe to
Aristotle himself: here the Averroistic Aristotle well nigh
superseded not merely the actual Aristotle but the Aristotle
of Albert and of Aquinas. To the Italian mind of the
Middle Ages Averroes presented himself, as he does in
the poetry of Dante and the painting of Orcagna, as the
incarnation of all heresy. Some of the foremost leaders of
Averroistic thought both in and out of Italy were Friars
or Churchmen[2]: some made distinctions and attempted
to minimize the heterodoxy of the Averroistic theses;
others saved themselves, sincerely or insincerely, by the
convenient assumption that what was philosophically true
might be theologically false. And in some cases the
reserve was quite sincerely made. The authority of
Averroes stood almost as high with Savonarola and with

---

[1] See below, p. 368. The Statute there cited must qualify what Renan (*Averroès*, p. 425) says as to the neglect even of the Comments of Averroes in France. At Paris in the fourteenth century Averroistic influences were felt almost exclusively, (1) among the Franciscans, (2) in the English Nation, i.e. not in the dominant School; and even here they produced no irreligious movement.

[2] Two Oxford Doctors, the Carmelite John of Baconthorp, known as *Averroistarum princeps*, and Walter Burleigh, were much influenced by Averroes, but their own influence was much greater in Italy than in England. Renan, *Averroès*, p. 318 *sq.* Two of the leaders of Italian Averroism were Friars, the Servite Urbano of Bologna, and the Augustinian Paul of Venice. The first denied the most dangerous Averroistic doctrine of the Unity of Intellect, the latter maintained it in its most uncompromising form. *Ib.* pp. 343-47.

Cajetan as with the most heterodox of the lay Averroists[1]. But there cannot be the smallest doubt that under the name of Averroism a thinly-veiled materialism which treated the most fundamental doctrines of Christianity with no more respect than the myths of Paganism became fashionable among the cultivated Physicians and so to a large extent in cultivated Italian lay society—and not always in lay society only—particularly in that north-east corner of Italy which included Bologna, the Mother of Italian Science, her twin-sister the Venetian University of Padua, and gorgeous, materialistic, worldly Venice herself. The philosophical scepticism of the Renaissance period was, indeed, very largely due to the working of the old leaven of Averroism which had long been fermenting beneath the superficial orthodoxy of medieval Italy. The new leaven of Humanism and the purer Hellenistic Philosophy which Humanism brought with it encountered a no less strenuous opposition from the lay, sceptical, materialistic Scholasticism of the South than from the clerical, orthodox, metaphysical Scholasticism of the North[2].

We need not go back to the Middle Ages to find that the adherents of a dominant Philosophy—even a negative philosophy—are quite as prone to an immovable conservatism and a bigoted attachment to the tradition of a School as the adherents of a dominant Theology. But it is, indeed, characteristic of the Middle Ages that an unreasonable subservience to authority was carried quite as far among the sceptics as among the orthodox; they differed only in the choice of authorities. To the Italian Physician—sceptical in Religion, but capable of enormous superstition in an astrological direction—Averroes was as infallible whether in Medicine or in Metaphysics as was the Bible in matters of Faith and Aristotle in matters of

---

[1] Renan, *Averroès*, pp. 350, 351.

[2] Petrarch, in particular, maintained a furious polemic against the Averroists and the Physicians. He even refuses to be cured on Arab principles, or by drugs with Arabic names. See his *Contra medicum quendam invect.* (*Opp.* Basileæ, 1559, p. 1093, &c.; Renan, *Averroès*, p. 329 *sq.*)

Philosophy to the Parisian ecclesiastic. But though the deference to authority is now less avowed, it would be easy to illustrate from every period in the history of modern Philosophy the truth of the statement that authority counts for quite as much in the formation of philosophic as it does in the formation of theological opinion.

Indeed, in the Italian Schools of Philosophy, Scholasticism offered a perceptibly more vigorous resistance to the encroachments of Humanism than was the case elsewhere. The reign of Scholasticism lasted longest in the country where the reaction against it first began. In the School of Padua an Averroistic Scholasticism of the driest and most pedantic type lasted in a tolerably vigorous condition far into the seventeenth century[1], even after the reign of Scholasticism had been substantially overthrown in the Schools of Paris, of Germany, and of England, by Ramus, by Descartes, by the Humanists, and by the Reformation[2]. *Persistence of Scholasticism in Italy.*

This curious fact illustrates the extreme tenacity of educational traditions. A Philosophy, a mode of thought, a habit of mind, may live on in the lecture-rooms of Professors for a century after it has been abandoned by the thinkers, the men of letters, and the men of the world. The contrast which we have drawn between the history of Scholasticism in Italy and its history in Northern *Tenacity of educational tradition.*

---

[1] According to Berriat-Saint-Prix (p. 315) exactly the same phenomenon is exhibited by the history of Italian Jurisprudence. The Humanism which had produced the School of Alciatus and Cujas in France, did not extinguish the legal Scholasticism of the Bartolist type till the middle of the seventeenth century or later.

[2] The mode of thought characteristic of the School of Padua, was really in full vogue in the fourteenth century, though the period in which the School stands out with the strongest individuality—because in greater contrast with other Schools —was later. It is usually considered to have been founded by Gaetano of Tiena (1387–1465). (Renan, *Averroès*, p. 347). Renan treats Peter of Abano (writing in 1303) as its real founder. (*Ib.* 326.) In justification of the whole of the preceding paragraph, I must be content to refer generally to the same admirable work, which should be read by anyone who wishes to realize the seething mass of free-speculation which really underlay the smooth surface of medieval orthodoxy. His estimate requires, however, some qualification. See below, p. 342 *sq.*

Europe also illustrates another important truth in the history of Education, i. e. the close connexion between great educational reforms and religious movements. The rapidity with which Humanism conquered in the Schools of Italy and Germany was due to its association with the cause of the Reformation. It was not till the counter-Reformation had raised up a body of educational reformers in Catholic Europe that Humanism triumphed over Scholasticism in the Schools of the laity and considerably limited its dominion in the Schools of the clergy.

Downfall of Scholasticism completed by Positive Science.
One other influence ought to be mentioned as completing the downfall of Scholasticism in its last stronghold ; and that is the progress of positive Science. Italy was not more decidedly the earliest home of Humanism than she was the earliest home of modern Science. And here too—here even more perhaps than on its literary side—the course of the movement was determined by the traditions
Science originates in the medieval Schools of Medicine.
of Italian education in the Middle Ages. It was Astrology-loving Italy that produced Galileo : it was the University of Mundinus that produced Galvani : it was a continuation of a medieval tradition that made Montpellier and Padua the centres of European Medicine in the sixteenth and seventeenth centuries. The Renaissance was no doubt from one point of view a reaction against the ideas and tendencies of the Middle Ages : but the direction which a reaction assumes is determined by the direction of the forces against which it reacts : the reformer is as much indebted to his environment as the conservative. The Renaissance was none the less indebted to the traditions of classical education, of medical and legal study, of student-freedom, of municipal patronage, of lay teaching and lay speculative culture, which we have found to be characteristic of the Italian University-system, because it was a reaction against many of the traditions of which the Universities, even in Italy, were the depositaries.

Influence of Renaissance : continuity of
The Renaissance undoubtedly made its influence felt in the Schools long before the period which has been chosen as a *terminus ad quem* ; but it was not till the sixteenth

—even if we should not say the seventeenth—century that it succeeded in revolutionizing that medieval system of education which it has been our business to study. The Renaissance lies beyond our province. It will be enough to have pointed out to what a large extent the peculiarities of the Italian system contributed to pave the way for that movement and to make Italy its earliest home. Enough has already been said to show how decided, all through the medieval period, was the predominance in Italian education of human and practical, of linguistic and literary interests as compared with the theological and speculative tendencies of Parisian and Teutonic culture. In the Arts Schools of Italy the study of antiquity, the half-regretful looking back to antiquity, never quite died out. The Schools of Italy could no more escape from the traditions of the old Roman culture than the architects of her Churches and her Palaces could avoid the unconscious influence of Classical Art even when most vehemently striving after the ideals of the ruder but more vigorous North. The revival of Roman Law studies in the eleventh century was itself but one phase of the return to antiquity which I have ventured to call the first Renaissance : and throughout the Middle Ages the Schools of Roman Law, in spite of their invasion by the methods and traditions of Scholasticism, were training the Italian mind for that second return to antiquity which is known as the Renaissance *par excellence.* The more deeply the history of the Italian Middle Age is studied, the more shall we discover to justify the striking saying of Ozanam that in Italy the night which intervened between the intellectual daylight of antiquity and the dawn of the Renaissance was but 'une de ces nuits lumineuses où les dernières clartés du soir se prolongent jusqu'aux premières blancheurs du matin [1].'

For the limits which I have imposed upon myself there is a double justification. In the first place, although in Italy the earlier phases of the movement lie within our Reasons for stopping at Renaissance.

---

[1] *Doc. inédits,* p. 78.

chronological limits, it would be unsatisfactory to attempt
to trace its beginnings and suddenly to break off at some
arbitrarily selected date: it is best to deal with the history
of the Italian Universities in the fourteenth and fifteenth
centuries only in so far as they still belonged to the
medieval world. In the second place, although the progress of the Renaissance may be traced in the foundation
or increased importance of Chairs for Rhetoric or Poetry
or Dante or Classical Literature in the Universities of Arts,
yet in the main Humanism was not primarily in Italy
a University movement. Its earliest home was rather
in Courts or princely Houses, in cultivated social circles or
dilettante 'Academies' than in the Schools—in Tuscany
rather than in Lombardy—in artistic, dreamy, Platonic
Florence than in stately, scientific, scholastic Bologna [1].

---

[1] I should have made more use in
this section than I have been able
to do of Flack's most interesting
brochure, Cujas, les Glossateurs et les
Bartolistes, Paris, 1883, had it come
into my hands earlier. He sup-
ports Savigny's high estimate of the
Glossators.

CHAPTER V.

PARIS.

CHAPTER V.

PARIS.

§ 1. The Origins of the University.

The earliest historical account of the University of Paris is a little black-letter quarto by Robertus GOULET (*Compendium recenter editum de multiplici Paris. Univ. magnificentia*, Parisiis, 1517), which is more valuable as a contemporary sketch of the University than for its historical information. BELLE-FOREST (*La Cosmographie Universelle.* Paris, 1675, T. I. p. 187 *sq.*) gives a somewhat fuller historical sketch of the University and Colleges. PASQUIER made valuable critical researches into the early history of the University, rejecting the Carolingian myth, but mistakenly dating the existence of the University from the Charter of Philip Augustus in 1200. (*Les Recherches de la France*, Paris, 1596, &c.) The first systematic historian of the University is HEMERÆUS (*De Academia Parisiensi*, Lutetiæ, 1637), who gives a fairly correct account of the evolution of the University out of the Episcopal School. Cæsar Egassius BULÆUS (du Boulay), in his six enormous folio volumes, *Historia Universitatis Parisiensis a Carolo M. ad nostra tempora*, 1665–1673, gathered together an immense mass of material for its history, but his own view of its origin is as completely mythical as anything in the first decade of Livy : while his inaccuracies and inconsistencies are only equalled by his tedious prolixity. He was perhaps the stupidest man that ever wrote a valuable book. (He also published an *Abrégé de l'histoire de l'Univ. de Paris*, no date.) The later historians of the University have done little but copy his conclusions with a little more common-sense, but no original research. The most important are CREVIER (*Histoire de l'Université de Paris, depuis son origine jusqu'en l'année 1660*, Paris, 1761), and DUBARLE (*Histoire de l'Unversité depuis son origine jusqu'à nos jours*, Paris, 1829). RICHOMME, *Histoire de l'Université de Paris* (Paris, 1840), is a slighter work of the same type. The only English book on the subject is an Oxford Prize Essay by T. RALEIGH (*The University of Paris*, 1873).

Meanwhile, the most valuable contribution ever made (till quite recently) to the history of this or any other University had been lying unpublished (on account of its unpatriotic view of the date of the University) and unstudied in the MS. presses of the Sorbonne. This anonymous work is entitled

CHAP. V,   *Universitas Parisiensis eiusque Facultatum quatuor Origo vera,* and is usually
§ 1.   spoken of as the MS. refutation of du Boulay, who is throughout styled the
——♦—   'Fabulator' and attacked with the characteristic bitterness of the seventeenth
          century scholar.   Two copies of it exist, one at the Sorbonne, the other
          in the Bibliothèque Nationale (Cod. Lat. 9949).   I have used the latter.
          There is also in the Bibl. Nat. (Cod. Lat. 9943–9948) a MS. History of the
          University by RICHER, of no particular value, but far more enlightened
          than du Boulay and his adherents.   THUROT's Essay, *De l'organisation de
          l'enseignement dans l'Université de Paris au moyen âge,* Paris and Besançon,
          1850, gave a fairly accurate picture of the educational system in the developed
          University, but hardly touched the question of origins, the critical treat-
          ment of which begins with the appearance of DENIFLE's great work in 1885.
          Ch. Brechillet JOURDAIN had, however, done good service by his *Index
          Chronologicus Chartarum pertinentium ad historiam Universitatis Parisiensis,*
          Parisiis, 1862, which printed in full many important documents omitted by
          Bulæus.   But this collection is now being superseded by the magnificent
          Chartularium Universitatis Parisiensis, edited by DENIFLE and CHATELAIN, of
          which two volumes (to 1350) have as yet appeared (Parisiis, 1889, 1891).

             Notices and documents relating to the University occur in many of the
          older books, of which it will be enough to mention DUBOIS, *Historia Ecclesiæ
          Parisiensis,* Parisiis, 1690–1710 ; SAUVAL, *Histoire et Recherches des Antiquités
          de la Ville de Paris,* Paris, 1724 ; DU BREUL, *Théâtres des Antiquités de Paris,*
          ed. 2, Paris, 1639 (1st ed. 1612) ; FÉLIBIEN, *Histoire de la Ville de Paris,*
          ed. Lobineau, Paris, 1725 ; D'ARGENTRÉ, *Collectio Judiciorum de Novis Erro-
          ribus,* Lutetiæ Parisiorum, 1728–36; GUÉRARD, *Cartulaire de l'Église de Notre-
          Dame de Paris* (in *Docs. inédits pour l'hist. de France*), Paris, 1855, &c.;
          JAILLOT, *Recherches Critiques sur la Ville de Paris,* Paris, 1772–1775.

             Other works bearing on special departments of the subject are LAUNOI,
          De varia Aristotelis in Academia Parisiensi fortuna, Lutetiæ Parisiorum,
          1653, &c., and the tractates of DU BOULAY, *Remarques sur la dignité, rang,
          préséance, autorité, et jurisdiction du Recteur de l'Un. de Paris,* Paris, 1668 ;
          Factum ou Remarques sur l'élection des Officiers de l'Université, Paris,
          1668 ; *Remarques sur les bedeaux de l'Université,* Paris, 1670 ; *Recueil des
          Privilèges de l'Université de Paris,* Paris, 1674 [Anon.] ; *Mémoires his-
          toriques sur les Bénéfices qui sont à la présentation de l'Université de
          Paris,* Paris, 1675 [Anon.]; *Fondation de l'Université de Paris par l'Em-
          pereur Charlemagne, de la propriété et seigneurie du Pré-aux-Clercs,* 1675,
          4to. [this last I have not seen; only one copy is said to exist] ; *De
          patronis quatuor Nationum,* Paris, 1662 ; *Défense des droits de l'Université,*
          Paris, 1657.   The very rare *Mémoire touchant la seigneurie du Pré-aux-Clercs,
          appartenante à l'Université de Paris* (Paris, 1694 and 1737), by POURCHOT, based
          on the above work of du Boulay, has been reprinted by FOURNIER (Marcel)
          in *Variétés Historiques et Littéraires,* Paris, 1856, T. IV. p. 87.   FILESACUS,
          Statutorum Sacræ Facultatis Theologiæ Parisiensis origo prisca, Parisiis, 1620,
          I have not seen.   BUDINSZKY, *Die Universität Paris und die Fremden
          an derselben im Mittelalter,* Berlin, 1876, is a useful piece of work.   So is
          DELALAIN, *Étude sur le Libraire Parisien du xiiie au xve siècle,* Paris, 1891 ;
          HALMAGRAND, *Origine de l'Université,* Paris, 1845, and DESMAZE, *L'Université
          de Paris, 1200–1875,* Paris, 1876, are of no value.   PÉRIES, *La Faculté de Droit
          dans l'ancienne Université de Paris,* Paris, 1890, is a substantial and learned

piece of research; Corlieu, *L'ancienne Faculté de Médecine de Paris*, Paris, 1877, a slight but interesting work, is chiefly concerned with post-medieval times. Spirgatis, *Personalverzeichniss d. Paris. Unv. von 1464*, Leipzig, 1888, is useful on the question of the numbers at Paris. Some paragraphs in the following chapter are reproduced from the author's Art. in the *Eng. Hist. Review*, 1886, p. 69 on *The Origines of the University of Paris*. The Art. by Feret, *Les Origines de l'Université de Paris* in *Rev. des Questions Historiques*, 1892, p. 337 *sq.* is quite uncritical, and ignores all recent research.

For a full bibliography, see Chatelain, *Essai d'une Bibliographie de l'ancienne Université de Paris* in *Revue des Bibliothèques* T. I. (1891); and for books on French education generally, below, vol. II. chap. viii.

I. *The Rise of the University.*

THE myth which attributes the foundation of the University of Paris to Charles the Great is one which ought long since to have ceased to be mentioned by serious historians even for the purpose of refutation. There is not the slightest ground for localizing the Palatine Schools of Charles the Great or Charles the Bald, the School of Alcuin or the School of Scotus, in the city of Lutetia Parisiorum. These Schools were probably migratory and followed the person of the Sovereign, like our ancient Courts of Law, in his progresses through his dominions. In so far as they had any fixed abode we should have to look for it rather at Aachen than at Paris. The assumption of an identity between the Schools of the Palace and the later Church Schools of Paris is in truth only an outgrowth of that inveterate historical misconception, dear to the heart of the French nation, which represents the founder of the Germano-Roman Empire as a French King with his Capital and his Court at Paris[1].

The sole historical connexion between the Palatine Schools of Charles the Great or Charles the Bald[2] and

The Carolingian Palace School not at Paris.

Real effects of the Carolingian Reform in Education.

[1] 'On ne voit pas même que, durant tout le cours de son long règne, ce prince, qui visita tant de villes, habita tant de palais, ait séjourné quelques heures dans la ville de Paris.' Hauréau, *Charlemagne et sa cour*, p. 172.

[2] The bull printed by Bulæus (I. p.

184) in which Nicolas I is represented as speaking of John the Scot as living 'Parisius in Studio cuius Capital jam olim fuisse perhibetur' is obviously interpolated. Part of it (which may be genuine), is given by William of Malmesbury (ed. Hamilton, p. 393), Symeon of Durham (ed.

the later University of Paris is to be found in that revival of
the episcopal and monastic Schools throughout the Frankish
Empire of which enough has already been said. Before
the time of Charles the Great the British Isles could boast
of far more famous Schools than any that were to be found
in continental Europe. The call of Alcuin from York to
the Palace School marks the transference of the primacy
of Letters from Britain to France. And some of the
features which characterized the Parisian University system
may really be traced to the work of Charles. In the first
place there is its intensely ecclesiastical character—the
system of supervision by ecclesiastical authorities and the
complete identification of the scholastic with the clerical
order. Moreover the educational tradition which was
inherited by the School of Paris was one ultimately derived
from the Schools of Alcuin and John the Scot. But this
educational tradition was not transmitted by any single
School. All through the dark ages that intervened between Charles the Great and the twelfth century, there
were at least a few monasteries and perhaps one or two
Cathedrals where the fame of some great teacher drew
students from distant regions, and where some ray of
enthusiasm, some spark of controversial fire, infused a little
life into the dull conglomerate of old-world learning and
traditional Theology which made up the education of this
dismal period. The historians of the University of Paris
have amused themselves with tracing the long scholastic
pedigree of Master and Scholar—the Academical succession, so to speak—which connects Alcuin with Abelard[1].
But it is only in this somewhat imaginative sense that the

Arnold, II. 116), and Hoveden (ed.
Stubbs, I. p. 47, &c.), but without
the allusions to Paris. Cf. Poole,
Illustrations, p. 56, n. 3. Bulæus, in
I. p. 183, gives this version as well as
his own, but includes part of Hoveden's text in the letter. The words
are also omitted in the collection of
Nicholas I's Letters. (Migne, T. 119.

c. 1119). Erdmann is still (1878)
without suspicions as to Erigena's
connexion with Paris (E. T. I.
p. 293).

[1] Thus Rabanus was the pupil of
Alcuin at Tours ; at Fulda Rabanus
taught Servatus Lupus of Ferrières,
whose pupil Heiricus was the Master
of Remigius, &c. (*MS. Refut.* f. 181).

smallest connexion can be established between Charles Chap. V,
and the great French University. In the age of Charles § 1.
the Great or of Charles the Bald nothing whatever is heard
of the Schools of Paris. Tours and Fulda and Reims were
famous places of education before Paris could claim a
single important Master or a single distinguished scholar[1].

The first School at Paris which is actually known to The
history is the School of Remigius at the end of the ninth School of
Remigius
century. But the utmost diligence of an investigator full at Paris.
of the most infatuated belief in the unfathomable antiquity
of his Alma Mater has only succeeded in discovering two
or three names of Masters or scholars recorded to have
taught or studied at Paris in the ninth or tenth centuries— Early
Remigius' pupil, Odo, afterwards Abbot of Cluny[2] (912–942 Scholars
at Paris.

---

[1] These assertions may perhaps surprise the reader who glancing over du Boulay's colossal work finds one folio volume devoted to the history of the University before 1000 A. D., another to the period between 1000 A. D. and 1200 A. D., of which the first 550 pages refer to the first of the two centuries thus embraced, i. e. to the period during which practically nothing is known of the state of the Schools of Paris. But the preliminary dissertation on 'the Academies of the Druids' will have warned the reader not to take du Boulay *au sérieux.* The first writer whom our author can adduce in support of the connexion of the University with Alcuin is Helinandus († 1227 A. D.), who says that Alcuin 'Studium de Roma Parisius transtulit' (Bulæus, I. 110) : but the passage which he quotes must be an insertion, since it does not occur in the printed edition. See Tissier, *Biblioth. Cisterc.* vii. (Paris, 1669) p. 100 : Migne, T. 212. c. 833 *sq.* In the fifteenth century, a Papal legate gravely ascribes the foundation of Schools at Paris to Bede, whom he declares to have stopped there on his way to Rome

(Bulæus, I. 113). A number of similar absurdities are critically examined by Launoi, *De Scholis Celebrioribus,* pp. 1–26.

[2] 'Nono decimo ætatis suæ anno apud beatum Martinum Turonis est tonsus, ibique grammaticæ artis liberalibus studiis educatus. Deinde apud Parisium dialectica musicaque a Remigio doctissimo viro est instructus, et tricesimo ortus sui anno Burgundiam petiit,' &c. *Vita scripta a Joanne monacho ejus discipulo ;* ap. Migne, T. 133. c. 45. 'His diebus abiit Parisius, ibique dialecticam sancti Augustini Deodato filio suo missam perlegit, et Martianum in liberalibus artibus frequenter lectitavit : præceptorem quippe in his omnibus habuit Remigium ; quo peracto Turonicam remeavit,' *ib.* c. 52. Another biographer says, 'His diebus honestus juvenis succensus amore discendi, Parisium [? Parisius] adiit primam sedis regiæ civitatem. Ibi Remigius Autissiodorensis, vir prædicabilis, et thesauros scientiæ tunc temporis plures habens, moderandis et regendis studiis insudabat. Florescebant sub eo studia, quæ obsoluerant jam per tempus, quia tunc primum

A. D.), Abbo, the Scholasticus of Fleury [1] († 1004 A. D.), and one Hucbald of Liège [2] who (some time between 972 and 1008 A. D. taught in the Schools of Ste. Geneviève. Nor do the names become more frequent till after the middle of the following century, when we find the Schools of Paris attracting a few scholars from a distance, such as the Englishman Stephen Harding [3], afterwards Abbot of Citeaux, and the Breton Robertus de Arbrissello [4]. Of course there would be no reason, even had the allusions been fewer than they are, to doubt that there were Schools in the Monasteries of Paris, just as there were in all other Monasteries, at least from the reign of Hugh Capet, when the cessation of the Viking ravages and the substitution of regular Abbots for the lay usurpers of the ' iron age' began to make learned leisure once more

ex ejus magisterio nascerentur.' Migne, T. 133. cc. 89, 90. The anonymous Refuter of Bulæus indeed (f. 179) suggests that the story of Remigius of Auxerre having taught at Paris is due to some confusion between S. Germain of Auxerre, of which Remigius was a monk, and the monastery of S. Germain-des-Prés at Paris : but this is a somewhat hazardous conjecture.

[1] Parisius atque Remis ad eos qui philosophiam profitebantur profectus, aliquantulum quidem in astronomia, sed non quantum cupierat, apud eos profecit. Inde Aurelianis regressus,' &c. *Vita auctore Aimoino Monacho* (his pupil), ap. Migne, T. 139. c. 390.

[2] 'Quid dicam de Hupaldo, qui, dum adolescentulus a scolari disciplina hinc (i. e. from Liège) aufugisset, Parisius venit, canonicis sanctæ Genovefæ virginis adhesit, in brevi multo (*sic*) scholarium instruxit. [Bulæus, I. p. 314, reads 'multarum scholarum institutor fuit': the true reading is perhaps ' multorum scholarium institutor fuit.'] Ubi cum aliquamdiu moraretur, interim videlicet cum a domno Notkero episcopo

nesciretur, tandem canonica episcopalis sententiæ executione compulsus est redire.' Anselmi Leodiensis *Gesta Episcoporum Leodiensium,* ap. Migne, T. 139. c. 1094. Notker was Bishop from 972 to 1008 A.D.

[3] ' Ex Anglia studiorum caussa primum Scotiam, inde in Galliam Parisios transfretaverat.' *A. S.* Ap. 7. T. II. p. 493.

[4] 'Et quoniam Francia tum florebat in scholaribus emolumentis copiosior, fines paternos, tanquam exsul et fugitivus, exivit, Franciam adiit et urbem quæ Parisius dicitur intravit, litterarum disciplinam, quam unice sibi postulaverat, pro voto commodam reperit, ibique assiduus lector insidere cœpit.' *Vita auctore Baldrico* (a contemporary), ap. Migne, T. 162. c. 1047. Of the scores of names massed together by Bulæus in his *Catalogus Illustrium Academicorum* (vol. I. pp. 542-649) this is the only one for whose connexion with Paris he produces a respectable authority. In some few cases a very late writer is cited, in most none at all. Crevier (I. p. 69) mentions a few names as belonging to the eleventh century, but without citing authorities.

a possibility. But it is abundantly clear that Paris was not at this period even one among the great educational centres of Europe; Remigius was the only Master of any note who is recorded to have taught there, and his connexion with Paris, if historical, seems to have been of very short duration. It is not till quite the end of the eleventh century that anything like a stream of scholastic pilgrimage begins to flow towards Paris. The authors of the *Histoire Littéraire de la France* have spoken of the School of Remigius as the 'first cradle of the University of Paris[1].' But the School of Remigius was no doubt connected with a Monastery—probably that of Saint Germain-des-Prés[2]— and the University Schools were essentially secular. The only secular School that we hear of before the end of the eleventh century is the School of Ste. Geneviève, which in the following century passed into the hands of the Canons Regular, and which at first had no organic connexion with the University. The University was an outgrowth of the Cathedral School of Paris[3], and this School did not attain the very smallest repute till towards the close of the eleventh century. The transference of educational activity from the Monks to the secular clergy constituted (as has been remarked) the great educational revolution of that century. In this change we may already discern the germs of the University movement[4]. In this

---

[1] *Hist. Lit.* VI. p. 100.

[2] That it was here that Abbo studied is suggested, but not proved, by a passage in his poem *De Bellis Paris. Urbis*, ap. Pertz, *SS.* II. p. 779 *sq.* In the continuation of Aimoinus (Bouquet, XI. p. 275), Remigius and Abbo are said to have been successive 'Deans' of the Monastery under Count Robert who 'Abbatis nomen assumpsit.'

[3] A curious relic of this connexion was the right of Canons of Paris to teach Theology and Canon Law without the authority of the University. It was not till 1384 that it

was definitely decided that a Canon must be a Doctor of Canon Law before being appointed to one of the Chapter Schools. See Hemeræus, p. 45.

[4] In this change the zeal of Monastic Reformers probably co-operated with the improvement of the Cathedral Schools. Cf. Petrus Damianus, *Opusc.* 36. c. 16, ap. Migne, T. 145. c. 621. The Benedictine Reform of 1337 forbids seculars to be taught with the Monks, and it is evident that there were not at this time any 'exterior schools.' Wilkins, *Concilia*, II. p. 594.

sense we shall be right in finding the cradle of the University, not indeed in the School of Remigius, but in the School of William of Champeaux, the first known Master of the Cathedral School, and the first Parisian teacher who left his mark upon the development of the Scholastic Philosophy. It was not till the time of William that Paris even began to rival the scholastic fame of Bec or of Tours, of Chartres or of Reims. But half a century later Paris had fairly surpassed its rivals. It was the teaching of William's great pupil and opponent Abelard that first attracted students from all parts of Europe and laid the foundation of that unique prestige which the Schools of Paris retained throughout the medieval period.

The Schools of Paris in the time of Abelard.

The less imaginative historians of the University of Paris have generally been contented with tracing its origin to the teaching of Abelard. And it was undoubtedly to the intellectual movement of which Abelard is the most conspicuous representative that the rise of the University must ultimately be ascribed. But there was nothing in the organization of the Schools wherein Abelard taught to distinguish them from any other Cathedral Schools which might for a time be rendered famous by the teaching of some illustrious Master. In the age of Abelard there were three great Churches at Paris more or less famous for their Schools. In the first place there was the Cathedral, whose Schools were presided over by William of Champeaux. Then, on the left bank of the Seine, there was the Collegiate Church of Ste. Geneviève: and there was the Church of the Canons Regular of S. Victor's, where a School for external scholars was started by William after his retirement from the world. S. Victor's became the Head-quarters of the old traditional or positive Theology, and produced the chief opponents of the rising dialectical or 'Scholastic' Theology —mystics like Adam and Hugh and Walter of S. Victor. Hence the School played no part in the development of the University: it had ceased to exist, or ceased to attract secular students, before the first traces of a University

No University at this time.

organization begin to appear[1]. With both the secular
Schools of Paris Abelard was at one time or other connected. It was during the period at which he taught 'the
liberal Arts' at Ste. Geneviève that his teaching attracted
the greatest crowds. For a time the 'Mount' of Ste.
Geneviève became the most famous place of education in
Europe. But the external Schools of Ste. Geneviève appear
to have declined, though not to have totally disappeared,
by the end of the century. In 1147 the Church passed
from its secular Chapter to a body of Canons Regular
imported from S. Victor's and S. Martin-de-champs[2]:
and though there are certainly traces of external Schools
in the 'Mount' after this date, the change was no doubt
calculated to drive away secular Masters. Before the
beginning of the following century the Cathedral seems
to be the only centre of education for seculars in Paris[3]: it
is from the Chancellor of Notre Dame alone that the
Masters obtain their licenses : it is not till the second or
third decade of the century that we again find the Masters
of Arts attempting to cross the river and teach under the
authority of the Abbot of Ste. Geneviève. Denifle's repudia-
tion of the old view that the University arose from a
junction between the Arts Schools of Ste. Geneviève and the
Theological Schools of Notre Dame goes slightly beyond
the evidence, but in the main he is unquestionably right in
contending that it was the Cathedral Schools which eventually developed into the University[4].

---

[1] It had quite disappeared by 1237, *Chartul.* T. I. pt. i. No. 111. At a later date, the House of S. Victor, with a view of obtaining certain fiscal immunities, obtained recognition as a 'College of the University,' *Chartul.* T. II. No. 675 : Bulæus, V. p. 208.

[2] See documents in Bulæus, II. pp. 216, 228–230 : Bouquet, *Rer. Franc. SS.* XIII. pp. 183, 291, XV. pp. 503–505, 449–451 : *A. S.* Ap. 6. T. I. p. 617 *sq.* : Feret, *L'Abbaye de Sainte-Geneviève*, Paris, 1883, I. p. 101 *sq.*

[3] This is strongly supported by

a rhetorical description of Paris in a letter of Guido de Bazoches (1175–1190 A. D.) which declares that ' in hac insula perpetuam sibi mansionem septem pepigere sorores, artes videlicet liberales,' without any reference to the Schools of Ste. Geneviève, though he dwells upon the glories of the ' duo suburbia' on the two banks. *Chartul.,* I. Introd. No. 54.

[4] See Denifle, I. 656 *sq.* He de-
clares that all trace of external or secular Schools at Ste. Geneviève are lost after 1147. But Giraldus Cam-

Certain
scholastic
traditions
date from
Abelard's
time.

It was the fame of Abelard which first drew to the streets of Paris the hordes of Students whose presence involved that multiplication of Masters by whom the University was ultimately formed. In that sense, and in that sense only, the origin of the University of Paris may be connected with the name and age of Abelard. Of a University or a recognized Society of Masters we hear nothing ; nay, the existence of such an institution was impossible at a time when the single Master of the Cloister School seems to have been as a rule the only recognized Master in or around each particular Church. At the same time we do find in the Schools of this period some slight traces of a traditional discipline and organization, of a kind of scholastic common-law which formed the basis of the later Academic polity.

Origin
of the
License.

Education in France since its revival under Charles the Great had been so completely confined in practice to the Cathedrals and Monasteries that no express legislation was needed to establish the necessity of the Church's sanction to the teacher [1]. In the days when a Church

---

brensis (ed. Brewer, I. p. 93) tells us that his old master Willelmus de Monte obtained his name ' quoniam in monte S. Genovefæ Parisius legerat quem etiam archidiaconus tunc noverat.' Now this William died Chancellor of Lincoln in 1213 (Le Neve, *Fasti Eccles. Ang.* Oxford, ed. T. D. Hardy, 1854, II. p. 91) : and Giraldus was born in 1147, so that there must have been secular Schools at Ste. Geneviève at least as late as 1165 or 1170. Nor do the Letters of Stephen of Tournay, Abbot of Ste. Geneviève 1176-1191, seem to me to prove Denifle's case. The Abbot refuses the request of the Archbishop of Lund, who has asked that his nephew should study in the secular Schools : ' Quod autem de ipso nobis per litteras vestras intimastis, vel in monte, vel ad Parisienses secularium scolas et venditores verborum mittendo . . . non admittimus.' (Ep. 80, Migne, T.

211. c. 377 : *Chartul.*, T. I. Introd. No. 42, where the text is corrected.) The nephew was residing in the Convent, and was therefore not allowed to go to secular Schools, but the words distinctly imply that there were secular Schools 'in monte' as well as in the city proper. It is impossible to say whether there were any Schools left at Ste. Geneviève at the beginning of the thirteenth century; but it is plain that at this time the Cathedral 'Parvis' was the centre of such Schools. This is one of the points upon which Denifle has been criticised by Kaufmann, *Zeitschr. der Savigny-Stiftung*, VII. p. 124 f. : but the latter fails to see the substantial truth of Denifle's main contention —that all Paris Masters were originally licensed by the Cathedral Chancellor.

[1] In face of the difficulty which Abelard constantly experienced in

normally possessed no more than one authorized Master, this Master might or might not, it would appear, be a member of the capitular body, according to circumstances. Any member of the Church from the Bishop or Abbot downwards who was capable of teaching would gather other scholars around him. If none of the Canons were competent to teach, they would hire the services of some wandering scholar. From the eleventh century onwards, however, we find a tendency to make the Master of the Schools, as he was called, a regular member of the Cathedral body[1]. This was done in one of two ways. Either the new dignity of *Scholasticus* or *Magister Scholarum*[2] was created, or the duty of presiding over the Schools was annexed to some already existing office—often in Southern Europe to that of Primicerius or Precentor[3], in Northern Europe more frequently to that of Chancellor. The original duties of the Chancellor were analogous to those of a Royal

---

lecturing at Paris, I cannot imagine what Kaufmann (*Deutsch. Univ.* I. p. 246) can mean by saying that the works of Giraldus Cambrensis and Stephen of Tournay show 'dass die Pariser Lehrer in den letzten Jahrzehnten des 12. Jahrhunderts noch in ähnlicher Unabhängigkeit neben einander standen wie zur Zeit Abälards, dass es keine überwachende Behörde und keine bindende Regel gab.' Stephen of Tournay's later complaints of the extreme youth and profane audacity of the Masters (Migne, T. 211. p. 517) do not show that no authority was recognized at this time but only that the authority was not efficient. Kaufmann's whole view of the 'Lehrfreiheit' of the early Middle Ages as regards the North of Europe seems to me opposed to all the evidence, though no doubt there may have been exceptions and irregularities in the application of the general principle of ecclesiastical control.

[1] For instances of such arrangements, see *Hist. Lit.* T. IX. p. 31 *sq.* The Council of Lateran in 1179 required that in every Cathedral 'magistro qui clericos ejusdem ecclesie et scholares pauperes gratis doceat, competens aliquod beneficium prebeatur,' *Chartul.*, T. I. Pars. Introd. No. 12. But it seems probable that by this time the duties of the titular *Magister Scholarum* were limited to supervision and that the benefice was intended for an actual working Master: the matter is, however, an obscure one. Cf. Joli, pp. 173, 174. The Fourth Lateran Council repeats the injunction, adding that every Metropolitan Church should have also a 'Theologus.' (Mansi, XXII. c. 999.)

[2] Instances of both will be found below in the Chapters on the French and Spanish Universities. In Narbonne and Gascony we find the title *Capischola.* Joli, pp. 160, 166.

[3] So also at Metz. *Hist. Lit.* VII. p. 28. For other cases, see vol. II, chap. viii. § 5.

Chancellor, i. e. to keep the Chapter seal and to draw up
the letters and documents which required sealing ; and, as
this function demanded an amount of learning which was
not a matter of course in those days, it was natural enough
that the supervision of the Schools, and again the care of
the Library, should be entrusted to the same functionary [1].
But while a definite ecclesiastical status was thus given to
the Head of the capitular School, a tendency was also at work
which made him less and less of a teacher himself. Wherever
the number of scholars required it, he would naturally
appoint others to teach under his direction. If he still
taught Theology himself, he would delegate the teaching
of Grammar and Dialectic to others [2] : and in the course of
time the elementary instruction of the choir-boys and other
poor Scholars seems usually to have been delegated to a
regular paid Master who taught under the supervision of
the nominal Head of the Schools. But with the rapid
spread of education in the twelfth century there also
grew up round the more famous Churches an increasing
number of Masters anxious to obtain permission to teach

[1] Thus an agreement between the
Chapter of Paris and the Chancellor
drawn up in 1215 (*Chartul.*, T. I.
pt. i. No. 21) contains the following
clause : ' Libros quidem Parisiensis
Ecclesie sine cantu corrigere, ligare
et in bono statu tenebitur conservare,
et talem instituere Magistrum in
Claustro qui sufficiens sit ad Scholarum regimen, et ad officium quod
debet facere in Ecclesia, et ad litteras
capituli, si opus fuerit, faciendas.' Cf.
the very similar statute of S. Paul's,
London. *Registrum Stat. et Con-*
suetud. Eccl. Cath. S. Paul. Lond. ed.
Simpson, 1873, p. 23. At Paris the
supervision of the Schools by the
Chancellor may be traced at least
from 1120. Guérard, I. pp. 28, 142.
As some confusion exists on this
subject in the minds of some English
writers, it may be well to point out
that the Chancellor of the Church is a
quite different officer from the Chancellor of the Diocese, a title applied
by modern English usage to the
Bishop's ' Official.'

[2] Cf. the Statute of the Metropolitan Church of York : 'Cancellarius
(qui antiquitus Magister Scolarum
dicebatur) Magister in Theologia
esse debet, et juxta Ecclesiam actualiter legere, et ad ipsum pertinet
Scholas Grammaticales conferre.
Sed Scholæ Eboracenses, alicui Regenti in artibus ... qui secundum
antiquam consuetudinem Ecclesiæ
ipsas habebit per triennium.' *Brit.*
Mus. Addit. MS. (Cole) 5884, f. 63.
So at London, while the Chancellor appoints the Grammar Master,
he is bound to teach Theology
' per se vel substitutum ab eo
ydoneum.' *Chartul. Univ. Paris.*
T. II. No. 791. Cf. Simpson, *l. c.*
p. 413 *sq.*

Scholars who could afford to pay something for their education.   Hence it became usual for the Scholasticus or Chancellor to grant a formal permission to other Masters to open Schools for their own profit in the neighbourhood of the Church.   In 1138 we find a Council at London forbidding the growing practice of selling such permissions [1].   By a Decretal of Alexander III [2] and a little later at the Third Council of Lateran in 1179 a still more important step was taken.   Not only were the presiding Masters of the Church-Schools forbidden to take any fee or reward for granting the *licentia docendi* (as the permission to teach had come to be called) but they were absolutely required to grant such a license to every properly qualified applicant [3].   The Chancellor thus ceased to be the holder of a lucrative educa-

---

[1] 'Sancimus præterea, ut si magistri scholarum aliis scholas suas locaverint *legendas* pro precio, ecclesiasticæ vindictæ subjaceant' (Mansi, *Concilia*, T. XXI. c. 514). Bulæus reads 'tenendas' (II. 155), but the expression 'tenere scholas' is unusual if not unparalleled: read 'regendas.' Crevier is inaccurate in saying that this Council as well as the Lateran Council of 1179 'ordonnent aux maîtres des Écoles d'accorder la *license* à tous ceux qui en sont dignes' (I. p. 256). It merely forbids the sale of the permission, and it should be noticed that the technical expression *licentia docendi* does not occur till the time of Alexander III. A comparison between the language of the two canons throws much light on the growth of the system.

[2] 'Sub anathematis interminatione hoc inhibere curetis ne qui dignitate illa, si dignitas dici potest, fungentes, pro prestanda licentia docendi alios sub aliquo quidquam amodo exigere audeant vel extorquere ; sed eis districte precipiatis, ut quicumque viri idonei et litterati voluerint regere studia litterarum, sine molestia et exactione qualibet scolas regere

patiantur ne scientia de cetero pretio videatur exponi, que singulis gratis debet impendi.' *Chartul.* Introd. No. 4. The custom of taking fees was, however, so inveterate, that the Chancellor of Paris obtained a Decretal enjoining respect for his vested interests. *Ib.* No. 8. In the Canon of 1074 cited by *Hist. Lit.* IX. p. 82 and Crevier, VII. p. 108, the expression 'docere populum' probably refers to religious, not scholastic, teaching; and the quarrel between the Bishop and Ste. Geneviève mentioned by Bulæus, II. p. 128, has nothing to do with the License.

[3] 'Pro licentia vero docendi, nullus omnino pretium exigat, vel sub obtentu alicujus consuetudinis ab eis qui docent aliquid querat, nec docere quemquam petita licentia, qui sit idoneus, interdicat. Qui autem contra hoc venire presumpserit, ab Ecclesiastico fiat beneficio alienus. Dignum quippe esse videtur, ut in Ecclesia Dei fructum sui laboris non habeat, qui cupiditate animi dum vendit docendi licentiam, ecclesiasticum profectum nititur impedire.' *Chartul.* Introd. No. 12 : Mansi, XXII. c. 228.

tional monopoly, and became merely a judge of the fitness of the candidates for the teaching office or, as we might say, an ecclesiastical Superintendent of Education [1].

Characteristics of the French University system.

The control of the Chancellor on the one hand, and the right of the competent teacher to a gratuitous license on the other, formed the basis of the French educational system. The control of the Chancellor distinguished it from the early Italian system : without the corresponding right, a University of Masters could never have grown up at all.

Masters united by a body of customs formed Guilds.

The right to the license once established, there was nothing to prevent the multiplication of Masters in connexion with any famous Church-School. Wherever Scholars congregated round some famous teacher, the number would increase of those who were ambitious of becoming teachers themselves. And, wherever teachers multiplied, there naturally in that age of Association grew up certain professional customs and unwritten laws which in some cases ere long crystallized into statutes of an organized Guild or University.

Germs of the Inception.

That nobody should set up as a teacher without having

---

[1] Specht lays it down that the authority of the Scholasticus extended to Schools of the whole diocese ; and cites the case of Aschaffenburg (*Gesch. des Unterrichtswesens in Deutschland,* Stuttgart, 1885, pp. 187, 188). This was certainly the case in some places, e.g. at Noyon, *Chartul.* T. I. pt. i. No. 322, and Amiens (Darsy, *Les Écoles et les Collèges du Dioc. d'A.,* Amiens, 1881, pp. 20, 181) : but sometimes it only extended to the City, e.g. in London, where to the Chancellor of S. Paul's 'subsunt scolares in civitate morantes, exceptis scolaribus scolarum de Arcubus et Sancti Martini, qui se privilegiatos in hiis et aliis esse contendunt.' *Registrum S. Paul.,* ed. Simpson, p. 23. It must not be assumed that because a Municipality sometimes supported a School and nominated the Master he could dispense with the Chancellor's License. See *Extracts from Council Reg. of Aberdeen* (Spalding Club), I. pp. 5, 37. The theory of Mr. Mullinger (*Cambridge,* I. p. 78) that the conferment of the License originally rested with the teachers is inconsistent with all our data as to Paris : it is possible that it was the case under the very peculiar circumstances of Oxford and Cambridge. Mr. Mullinger misses what seems to me the keystone of the whole constitutional structure, i. e. the distinction between the License conferred by the Bishop's representative and the *Magisterium* conferred by the University.

been himself for an adequate period taught by some duly authorized Master was almost too obvious a principle to need formal enactment [1]. That he should not enter upon the work of teaching without his former Master's sanction and approval was an almost equally natural piece of professional etiquette. In the time of Abelard we see these principles, if not firmly established, at least on their way towards recognition. We have seen how, when the famous dialectician became ambitious of distinguishing himself as a theologian, it was considered necessary for him to put himself under a Master before he could teach in another Faculty, as it would have been called in later times : and, when after an incomplete period of study he ventured without his master's permission to begin the lectures on Ezekiel, this unauthorized assumption of the magisterial office was treated not merely as a scandalous exhibition of immodesty, but as an actual ecclesiastical offence. He was compelled to leave Laon [2], and at the Council of Soissons his conduct on this occasion was made the subject of a distinct article of charge, the accusation being not that he had taught without the License of the Church —though even this would have been unlawful—but that he had begun to teach ' without a Master [3].' Then too the

---

[1] It seems that a period of five to seven years was expected at an early period. Nigellus, in his *Speculum Stultorum* (*Satirical Poets of the 12th Century*, ed. Wright, 1872, I. pp. 9, 10), speaks of the 'asinus, qui Parisius scholas frequentat . . . quia discedens nomen urbis non poterat retinere in qua moram fecerat septennem.' In the Life (written *c.* 950 A.D.) of Aicadrus, who lived as early as the seventh century, we read 'Quinquennio transacto visum illi fuit magistrum fore et inter primores conscholasticos residere ' (Mabillon, *A. SS. Ord. S. Ben.*, Venetiis, 1733, II. p. 916),—an expression which points to something like an Inception about 950 A.D. It

cannot of course be relied upon as evidence for the seventh century.

[2] For a curiously parallel story, cf. Martène, *Thesaurus Anecdot.* T. III. p. 1714.

[3] ' Quod sine magistro ad magisterium divinæ lectionis accedere præsumpsisset,' Bulæus, II. 66. In the words 'Quod nec Rom. pontificis nec ecclesiæ auctoritate commendatus legere publice præsumpseram ' from Abelard's *Hist. Calam.*, Bulæus (I. 284, II. 67, 669) relies upon a corrupt text. Cousin reads *commendatum* (*sc.* librum) for *commendatus*. The notion that the Chancellor conferred the License in the name of the Pope is much later. See Denifle, I. p. 765. It is tempting to see the

opening of his course on Ezekiel seems to be spoken of as a kind of formal and public inaugural lecture, or what would have been called in later times an 'Inception,' though, since no master presided over it, it was an irregular one. How far the Inception was already accompanied by those ceremonies which were afterwards an essential part of it, we cannot tell. It is possible that some of them may be of great antiquity : it is just possible that some of them may have descended by some vague tradition from the philosophical and rhetorical Schools of the old Roman world. We have already seen the establishment of a very similar institution in Italy, where the sanction of the Masters was the only necessary qualification for the assumption of the Magisterial office. Although in France a previous license from the Head of the Church-Schools was necessary, the idea of the 'Principium' or 'Inceptio' was essentially the same as that of the Italian 'Conventus [1].' A clear understanding of this idea is absolutely essential to appreciate the constitutional theory of the Parisian University. It was out of this custom that the University of Masters ultimately grew.

Idea
of the
Inception.

The idea of the Inception involved two elements. It was, on the one hand, the formal entrance of a newly licensed teacher upon his functions by the actual performance of its duties—a ceremony which, according to the ideas of the Roman Law, was essential to the actual investiture of an official with his office [2]. On the other hand, it was the recognition of the new-comer by his old Master and other members of the Profession—his incorporation into the Society of teachers [3]. The new Master had a cap placed upon

germs of the Baccalaureate in the position occupied by Abelard when he taught in the School of another Master.

[1] The Paris term 'Principium' is often applied to the Bologna 'Conventus' or 'Conventatio'; more rarely the Paris License-examination is styled 'Privatum Examen,' and the Inception 'Publicum Examen.'

[2] For similar customs in the Merchant Guild, see Gross, *The Gild-Merchant*, Oxford, 1890, I. pp. 33, 34.

[3] Compare the reading of the Gospel by the newly ordained Deacon. In the Roman Church the newly ordained Priests stand for the rest of the office in a circle round the altar and are 'concelebrant' with

his head, which is sometimes explained as the old Roman ceremony of manumission or emancipation from the subjection of pupillage. But the biretta[1] was also a badge of the Mastership, which with the other insignia of his office —the ring and the open book—he received from his former Master, who further conferred upon him a kiss and a benediction. Then, seated in the Magisterial Cathedra, he gave an exhibition of his professional capacity by delivering an inaugural lecture or holding an inaugural disputation. The idea that a new comer should 'pay his footing' seems almost a primitive instinct of human nature. It formed an essential part of Inception that the 'Inceptor' should entertain at a banquet the whole or a considerable number of his new colleagues. Presents of gloves or gowns had also to be made ; and gradually contributions in money to the funds of the society were exacted in addition to the presents to its individual members—an exaction which has ever since been the inseparable accompaniment of degree-taking even in those Universities in which all other formalities are most generously dispensed with. The whole affair was originally nothing but a piece of unauthorized buffoonery—hardly more dignified or important perhaps than those sometimes brutal and sometimes silly student

---

the Bishop (cf. Hatch, *Organization of the Early Christian Churches*, London, 1882, pp. 131, 132). A relic of the last usage survives in the neglected Anglican rubric which requires the newly ordained Priests to 'remain in the same place where Hands were laid upon them, until such time as they have received the Communion.' The tradition of the Insignia of the various orders—which in the case of the minor orders constitutes the whole of Ordination—is another point of analogy between the ceremonies of graduation and those of Ordination. On a lower level an excellent illustration of the idea is supplied by the investiture of the Grammar-Master with a birch with which he proceeded to flog a boy. See below, chap. xiv. Another analogy is supplied by the ceremony with which a Scotch Judge takes possession of his office. After presenting his patent to his colleagues, he tries two cases and reports his decision on them before being sworn in as a member of the 'College of Justice.' There was anciently a somewhat similar probation for Serjeants-at-law in England. See Puling, *Order of the Coif*, London, 1884, p. 8.

[1] The 'biretta' was always regarded as the most important of the insignia of the office. Bachelors taught uncovered.

CHAP. V,
§ 1.

The University or Guild of Masters grew out of Inception.

initiations which the Masters of later times tried to stamp out by every possible penalty, and which still linger on in bad schools and in the artistic *ateliers* of modern Paris [1].

Out of this custom, however, the idea of a Guild or corporation of teachers in all probability arose, as perhaps other Guilds may have arisen from similar initiations. Gradually, and, probably by imperceptible steps, the ceremony passed from a mere jollification or exhibition of good-fellowship into the solemn and formal admission of a new Master into an organized and ultimately all-powerful corporation of teachers. And the Trades-union of teachers rapidly succeeded in acquiring a monopoly of the trade. 'Inception' became as necessary to the teacher as the Chancellor's license. The 'Licentiate' was not regarded as a full 'Master' or 'Doctor' till he had 'incepted.'

Analogy of Knighthood.

Another great institution which was a development of the same idea was the institution of Chivalry. The original conception of Knighthood was the solemn reception of the novice into the brotherhood of arms. The blessing of the Priest was required by the Knight Bachelor as the scholastic Bachelor required the License of the Chancellor;

---

[1] It is not impossible that the magisterial initiation was partly copied from the student initiation, which was certainly of great antiquity. See the passages cited by Conringius, *Op.* V. pp. 447, 448. Gregory Nazianzen gives an elaborate account of his τελετή at Athens, which he describes as παιδιὰ σπουδῇ σύμμικτος—*Or.* xliii. ed. Migne, T. 36, cc. 515, 516. Photius, on the authority of Olympiodorus, declares that in the fifth century no one was allowed to teach (εἰς τὸν σοφιστικὸν θρόνον ἀναχθῆναι) at Athens ᾧ μὴ τῶν σοφιστῶν ἡ γνώμη ἐπέτρεπε καὶ αἱ κατὰ τοὺς σοφιστικοὺς νόμους τελεταὶ ἐβεβαίουν τὸ ἀξίωμα. The new Master went to the bath, where he and his friends had to force an entrance against a body of students

who made a στάσις and tried to keep them out. He then came out wearing the τρίβων, was escorted home in solemn procession, δαπάνας σιτιανοὺς φανερὰς εἰς τοὺς τῶν διατριβῶν προστάτας τοὺς λεγομένους Ἀκρωμίτας, Migne, T. 103, p. 269. The parallel to the later Inception is curiously exact. An edict of Justinian forbids practical jokes — an integral part of the τελετή—on freshmen in the law schools (Digest. *Procem.*). In medieval Paris frequent statutes were passed against the exaction of money from *bejauni* (= *becs-jaunes*, yellow-bills), *i. e.* unfledged birds (Bulæus, IV. 266; *Chartul.* T. II, No. 1032). In the sixteenth century the practice of initiating *bejauni* passed into the brutal ceremony of *depositio*, as to which, see below, chap. xiv.

but it was by the touch of the veteran's sword that the candidate received his actual initiation into the brotherhood
of arms, as it was through the veteran Master's act that
the Licentiate became a full member of the brotherhood of
teaching. Both of these great institutions arose from the
transference to the military and the scholastic life respectively of one of the most characteristic social and political
ideas of the age—the idea of a Guild or sworn brotherhood
of persons following a common occupation. In the later
ceremonies attending the bestowing of degrees there are
many traces of the idea that graduation formed a sort of
intellectual knighthood. In some of the Spanish Universities the new Doctor was actually invested with a sword:
in all Universities the ring formed one of the insignia of
the Doctorate, and at Vienna the preliminary bath of the
candidate for knighthood appears to have been imitated by
candidates for degrees [1].

In the age immediately succeeding the years of Abelard's
teaching Paris leapt almost at one bound into a unique
position in the scholastic world.   The Cathedral or Abbey-
schools, however numerous their Students, had owed their
celebrity entirely to one or two illustrious teachers.   Paris
became a city of teachers—the first city of teachers the
medieval world had known.   Here then were the materials
for the formation of a University.   In that age of Guilds,
we may almost say that the formation of a teaching-guild
in some form or other was inevitable.   At what precise
date the body of teachers loosely bound together by a pro-

---

[1] Such at least is the only explanation I can give of the words of the
Statute : ' Quod nullus baccalariorum
aut scolarium finito examine pro
baccalariatu aut magisterio aliquem
inuitet ad balneum ante suam determinationem aut incepcionem preter
examinatores, cum quibus balneetur
in eodem balneo, si saltem pro
tunc sibi placeat balneari, sub pena
retardacionis, &c. . . . quod nullus
licentiatus post suam incepcionem

exponat in balneo ultra 30 denarios
ultra hoc, quod placet sibi pro magistro, qui eum promovit,' &c. (Kink,
Gesch. d. kais. Univ. Wien, I. pt. ii.
p. 55.) It is obvious from these
last words that for internal application some liquid more expensive than
water was provided : and it is just
possible that the ' bath ' was wholly
metaphorical, but the explanation
given in the text is the more
probable.

CHAP. V,
§ 1.

fessional etiquette assumed something like the form of an organized Society we cannot exactly determine. Any precise date that might be given would be essentially misleading. The University was not made but grew. We can only notice the few recorded facts which throw light on the process of development, culminating (as we shall see) at the beginning of the thirteenth century in the reduction of the hitherto unwritten customs of the profession to a code of regular statutes or bye-laws.

A statute of the Bishop and Chapter in 1127[1] ordering that none but members of the Cathedral body should lodge in the cloister seems to mark the beginning of the process by which a Studium Generale was evolved out of the mere cloister-school. Before long we find the teachers too numerous to be accommodated within the cloister or even in the Island round the Cathedral walls. And now we hear of Masters licensed by the Chancellor of Notre Dame teaching in houses built upon the bridges of the Seine[2]. At about the same time—towards the middle of the century—we can trace in the writings of John of Salisbury a multiplication of Masters both round the Cathedral and in the Mount

---

[1] Bulæus, II. p. 666: Guérard, I. p. 339. This regulation was, however, relaxed in the case of young men of royal or illustrious birth, who were frequently admitted to board with the Canons (Bulæus, III. p. 307; *Chartul.* I. pt. i. No. 283). S. Louis was one of the band, as well as his brother Philip, afterwards Archdeacon in the same church. Other instances are given in the *Hist. Lit.* IX. p. 62. At the end of the century the Cathedral Schools were moved from the cloister of the Cathedral or the adjoining Episcopal Palace to the 'Parvis' between the Palace and the Hôtel-Dieu. The special Cathedral School for the Cathedral 'clerks' was of course quite distinct from the Schools which now began to multiply around it. In the time of Bishop

Maurice (1160–1196), a Statute of the Bishop and Chapter ordained 'ne quis canonicorum domos claustrales alicui scolari conduceret aut etiam commodaret'. *Chartul.* T. I. Introd. No. 55.

[2] One of John of Salisbury's Masters was known as Adam de Parvo Ponte, from his School on the Petit-Pont. He was afterwards Bishop of S. Asaph (*Hist. Lit.* IX. p. 62). There were also a Jean de Petit-Pont and an Adam de Grand-Pont who taught at Paris later in the century (*ib.* p. 75) : also a Pierre de Petit-Pont (*ib.* p. 78). A letter of Guido de Bazoches (1175–1190) declares that ' Pons . . Parvus aut pretereuntibus, aut spatiantibus, aut disputantibus logicis dedicatus est.' *Chartularium,* T. I. Introd. No. 54.

of Ste. Geneviève. The absurd story which represents Gra- tian as having deliberately 'invented' Academical degrees and Peter the Lombard as having transferred the system to Paris may be accepted as fixing roughly the period at which the honours of the Master's chair began to be sought by those who had no intention of devoting themselves, or at least of permanently devoting themselves, to the profession of teaching. The consequences of this rising passion for 'degrees' were particularly important to the Faculty of Arts. We have seen how in the days of John of Salisbury 'Grammar' and Rhetoric were taught and studied as earnestly as Theology. The teachers were mature scholars who looked upon teaching as their life's work. The students studied for long periods. After the middle of the century the passion for graduation together with the absorbing enthusiasm for the Scholastic Philosophy and Theology caused the usual course of study in the Latin language to be reduced to a minimum. The Mastership in the philosophical Faculty became the natural goal of every student's ambition and the usual if not essential preliminary to study in the higher Faculties. Hence the enormous multiplication of Masters, and especially of very young Masters, which was one of the immediate causes of the growth of the University[1]. Another indication of the increasing prestige attaching to academical learning and position is afforded by the custom which grew up in the course of this century

---

[1] Cf. *Carmina Burana* (ed. Schmeller, Breslau, 1883), p. 40 :—

'Sed retroactis seculis
vix licuit discipulis
tandem "nonagenarium"
quiescere post studium.

At nunc decennes pueri
decusso iugo liberi
se nunc magistros iactitant,
cęci cęcos pręcipitant.'

So again :—

'Jam fit magister artium
qui nescit quotas partium
de vero fundamento:

habere nomen appetit
rem vero nec curat nec scit,
examine contento.

Jam fiant baccalaurei
pro munere denarii
quam plures idiotæ :
in artibus, ab [? et] aliis
egregiis scientiis
sunt bestiæ promotæ.'

Du Méril, *Poésies Populaires du Moyen Age*, Paris, 1847, p. 153.
But of this poem the date is unfortunately doubtful.

Early
scholastic
privileges.

of prefixing the title of 'Master' as an honourable designation to the names even of Cardinals and Bishops.

In the second half of the century we meet with increasingly frequent recognition of scholars as a distinct and privileged class. The privileges of the scholars in Northern Europe rested upon a somewhat different basis to the privileges bestowed upon students in the Italian Universities. In the Italian towns scholars were recognized as a class distinct alike from the clergy and from the ordinary lay population : their privileges were obtained for the most part by treaty with the citizens. In France, all students and still more all Masters in the Church Schools were assumed as a matter of course to be clerks, and enjoyed—like a host of other persons connected however remotely with the service of the Church—the immunities of clerkship as fully as persons actually in orders. Hence the Parisian scholar's privilege of trial in the ecclesiastical courts originates in no explicit grant of any secular or ecclesiastical authority. It existed long before the rise of the University. After the grant of the special privilege of trial by their own Masters to the students of Bologna by Frederick I, some attempts were, indeed, made to introduce the same principle into France. Thus in the case of a quarrel at Reims, Alexander III ordered that the townspeople should allow scholars to be tried by their own Masters [1], and the earliest Papal statutes of Paris—those of 1215—appear to recognize

---

[1] 'Prohibeatis omnibus ne prefatos scolares contra libertatem eorum in aliquo molestare audeant vel gravare, quandiu coram magistro suo parati sunt justitie stare.' *Chartul.*T.I.Introd. No. 5 : Bulæus, II. p. 501 (here only in part). Two points are to be remarked in this document, (1) that the principle is claimed as an old custom ; (2) that it holds good as against ecclesiastical censure as well as civil justice. The appeal to Rome had arisen in consequence of the conduct of a certain 'J. Presbyter de burgo S. Remigii' who had been derided by certain scholars when publicly dancing on a Sunday. Provoked by this he first assaulted the scholars and broke the windows and doors of their schools, and then (without applying to Archbishop or Official) promulgated sentence of excommunication against them! So at Salisbury, where no University existed, there was a dispute between the Sub dean and the Chancellor in 1278 for ecclesiastical jurisdiction 'in scholasticos in ciuitate Sarisburiensi studiorum causa commorantes.' See Caius, *De Antiq. Cant.* (1574), p. 110.

the same privilege. But the youth, number, and legal in-
experience of the Masters of Arts must have made a system
which eventually broke down even at Bologna wholly un-
workable at Paris, and the Master's jurisdiction was rapidly
superseded by the ordinary ecclesiastical courts and by the
extraordinary academical tribunals which the growth of the
Universities called into existence in the course of the following century [1]. Another remarkable privilege was possibly
granted to the Masters and Scholars of Paris before the
close of the twelfth century. Louis VII is said to have
authorized the Masters to suspend their lectures as a means
of protest in the event of an outrage being committed upon
a Master or scholar as a means of compelling the authorities to grant redress [2]. The text of this privilege, if it ever
assumed a documentary form, is not preserved : but, so far
as appears, there was nothing in it to constitute a recognition of the University or corporation of Masters as such.

So far we have heard nothing of a University in the
strict sense of the word. One passage, and one only, in
all the chronicles and documents of the period supplies us
with positive evidence of the existence of a Guild of Masters at Paris before the beginning of the thirteenth century.
In the life of Johannes de Cella, Abbot of S. Alban's, by his
pupil Matthew Paris, we are told that the subject of the
biography was, as a young man, a student at Paris and was

First
trace of
University,
c. 1170.

---

[1] The bull of Celestine III in
1194 (Bulæus, I. p. 266 : *Chartularium,* T. I. Introd. No. 15), directing
that 'causas seculares,' or (according to another reading) 'pecuniarias'
of 'clerici Parisius commorantes'
should be tried by canon law is
usually quoted as the foundation of
the ecclesiastical privilege of the
scholars. But (1) this privilege
appears to have been covered by the
general principle above explained.
(2) The bull is not specially applicable to scholars. (3) The true explanation of it would seem to lie in
the secular jurisdiction of the Bishop

of Paris. Causes of laymen would
of course be tried by the ordinary
law ; but a doubt would arise as to
the *Law* to be applied to the civil
cases in which ecclesiastics were
either plaintiffs or defendants. This
is made particularly clear by the
concluding words 'nec permittatis
juri scripto consuetudinem preva-
lere.' See Bulæus, II. p. 498:
Denifle, I. p. 679 : *Chartularium,*
T. I. Introd. No. 15 *note.*

[2] This rests on the authority of
Guillelmus Armoricus, *De Gestis
Philippi Augusti,* ap. Bouquet, T.
XVII. p. 82 (cf. p. 395).

there admitted into the 'fellowship of the elect Masters [1].'
The Abbot died 'full of days' in 1214. He may, therefore, be assumed to have become a Master not much later
than 1170 or 1175 A. D. At about that date then the
Society of Masters had some kind of existence, however
indefinite, inchoate, and rudimentary. The complete silence
of John of Salisbury, whose works are full of reminiscences
of student life at Paris, and the whole account which he
gives of his own career as student and teacher, forbid us to
place the first beginnings of the University earlier than the
middle of the century. It is therefore a fairly safe inference that the period 1150–1170—probably the latter years
of that period—saw the birth of the University of Paris.
We must beware, however, of exaggerating the extent and
definiteness of the association implied by the use of such
expressions as Society or University. They prove little
more than the fact that it was customary for a Master, after
being licensed by the Chancellor, to be formally initiated
into the society of his fellow Masters. They point to the
existence of meetings of the Masters for the celebration of
these Inceptions, and probably also for disputation and
perhaps upon rare emergencies to concert measures for the
vindication of an injured colleague or student, for the
punishment by expulsion or professional excommunication
of a breach of professional etiquette, or for the pursuit of some
similar common object. But two facts are a sufficient indication of the amorphous and merely customary character
of the bond which held together the guild into which the
Masters of Paris were spontaneously, and perhaps almost
unconsciously, constituting themselves. Till *circa* 1208 A. D.
the University had no written statutes, and till a considerably later period no Head or presiding officer [2].

[1] 'Hic in juventute scolarum Parisiensium frequentator assiduus ad
electorum consortium magistrorum
meruit attingere.' *Gesta Abbatum
Mon. S. Alb.* ed. Riley, London,
1867, I. p. 217. Bulæus, indeed,
(II. pp. 489, 490) represents the

University as sending a legate to the
Pope in 1192, but his authority does
not necessarily imply corporate or
official action. Cf. Stephanus Torna-
censis, *Ep.* 185 (Migne, T. 211. c. 471).

[2] Innocent IV, on the authority
of the Civil Law, lays it down that

The evidence for these assertions will appear in the sequel. For the present it will be enough to clear the ground for its reception. The two great problems connected with the early history of the University are the origin of the Four Nations and the origin of the Rectorship. The solution of these problems has been hitherto impeded by a gross misinterpretation of two important pieces of documentary evidence. In the first place, an episode in the history of Thomas Becket's quarrel with Henry II has been, by all the historians of the University before Denifle, relied upon as proving the existence of the 'nations' at that time. Henry offered to submit his quarrel to the arbitration of 'scholars of different provinces, examining the matter with equal scales [1],' or (as the Archbishop himself says) of 'Parisian scholars [2].' It is natural enough that to minds preoccupied with the antiquity of

'adesse collegii non exigitur, quod ibi sit prælatus.' Decret. 3. De præbend. *Cum non* (Venet. 1578, p. 147). To say with Denifle (I. 129) that the Chancellor was to some extent ('gewissermassen') *caput generale* of the University seems to me essentially misleading. He may have been *caput* of the *Studium*, but he was not even *ex officio* member of the *Universitas*. A most important piece of evidence would have to be added to the above if one could be sure of the right reading in the following statement of Giraldus Cambrensis, who completed his Arts' course at Paris before 1172: 'Quod nos quidem et coætanei nostri tempore sereniori pariter et feliciori; donec non solum in trivio, verum etiam in auctoribus et philosophis, necnon et metricis ac dictaminum studiis magistrati plenius essemus et consummati xx annorum.' *Speculum Ecclesiæ*, ed. Brewer, IV. p. 3. Such is the editor's reading, but the solitary and mutilated MS. has 'magis sati.' If Wood's account of the contents of the following paragraphs (which he saw before the fire in the Cotton Library) could be implicitly trusted, the allusions to the system of graduation would be more definite than the existing text enables us to affirm them to be. The expression 'magistrari' also occurs in the life of a pupil of Abelard, written after his death in 1166. Bouquet, XIV. p. 443 D. It may be added that Innocent III speaks of himself as 'in minoribus constitutum, magisterii honore insignitum.' This must have been before 1190. See *Gesta* (Migne, T. 214, p. xvii. *note*).

[1] 'Scholaribus diversarum provinciarum æqua lance negotium examinantibus.' Radulphus de Diceto, *Op. Hist.* ed. Stubbs, 1876, I. 337, and Matt. Paris, *Chron. Maj.* ed. Luard, II. 1874, p. 263.

[2] 'Paratum esse stare dicto curiæ Domini sui Regis Francorum vel judicio Ecclesiæ Gallicanæ aut Scholarium Parisiensium.' *Materials for the Hist. of Thomas Becket*, ed. Robertson, VII. p. 164: *Chartul.* T. I. pt. i. No. 21.

their Alma Mater the former passage, when interpreted by
the latter, should have appeared incontrovertible proof of
the existence of the 'nations,' and even of the practice of
voting by nations in or about 1169 A.D. But in reality the
words imply no more than a proposal to submit the matter
to the arbitration of learned men from the Parisian Schools,
chosen from different nationalities to secure impartiality.
With equally little ground an allusion has been found to
the Rectorship in the celebrated charter granted to the
Scholars of Paris by Philip Augustus in 1200 A.D.

Riot of
1200 A.D.
The occasion of this first extant charter of Privileges was
the fatal issue of the first recorded 'town and gown' disturbance at Paris. The riot began in a tavern. The
servant of a noble German student (a Bishop-elect of
Liège[1]) was assaulted, whereupon a concourse of his fellow-
countrymen took place ; the host was severely beaten, and
(according to the usual formula of medieval chroniclers on
such occasions) 'left half-dead.' The Provost of Paris at
the head of an armed band of citizens in return attacked a
Hall or Hostel (*hospitium*) of students of the same nation-
ality. In the fight which thereupon ensued, several students
were killed, including the Elect of Liège himself. The
Masters appealed to the King for redress, which—from fear,
it is said, lest the Masters should withdraw from the city
altogether—was granted with no niggard hand. The Provost was sentenced by the King to perpetual imprisonment,
subject however to a curious proviso. The accused was to be
allowed if he pleased to go through the ordeal by water or
by fire : if convicted by the ordeal, his punishment was to
be aggravated to hanging ; if acquitted, it was to be com-
muted to banishment from Paris. The houses of the
offenders who had fled from justice were destroyed ; those
who were caught were sentenced to the same fate as the
Provost, unless they could prevail upon the injured scholars
to intercede for them. The scholars relented so far as to ask
to be allowed, in lieu of all other satisfaction, to flog them

[1] Henricus de Jacea, Archdeacon of Liège. Hoveden, *Chronica*, ed.
Stubbs, IV. (1871) 120, 121 *and note.*

'after the manner of scholars,' in their Schools [1]. But this
request was refused as detrimental to the royal prerogative.
The charter now granted secured that any scholars arrested
by the royal officers should forthwith be handed over to the
ecclesiastical judge. The Burghers of Paris were required
to swear to respect the privileges of scholars, and to give
information unsolicited against anyone whom they might
see maltreating a scholar. The Provost was also on admission to his office to swear to respect the scholastic
privileges in presence of the assembled Masters in one of
the Churches of Paris. This was the origin of the position
of the Provost of Paris as 'Conservator of the royal
Privileges of the University.' Cases in which the defendant
was accused of violating any privileges granted to them by
the King, came to be tried in the Court over which the
Provost presided, the Châtelet. For the further protection
of the clerks, it was ordered that trial by battel or ordeal
should be refused to prisoners charged with assault on a
Scholar. Then follows a clause which protects from arrest
by the hands of secular justice the *capitale Parisiensium
scholarium* [2]. Bulæus and his followers (including even

[1] 'Ut præpositus ille et complices
sui more scholarium in scholis flagel-
lati, essent quieti et facultatibus suis
restituti,' *l. c.* The Provost escaped
the grim alternative by breaking his
neck in an attempt to escape from
prison.

[2] The clause runs as follows : ' In
capitale Parisiensium scholarium pro
nullo forifacto justitia nostra manum
mittet ; sed si visum fuerit illud esse
arrestandum per justitiam ecclesias-
ticam arrestabitur et arrestatum custo-
dietur, ut de illo capitali fiat quod
per Ecclesiam fuerit legitimè judi-
catum.' (Bulæus, III. 2, text corrected by Denifle, I. p. 7 ; *Chartularium*, T. I. pt. i. No. 1.) Hemeræus
(p. 95) understands the Chancellor
to be meant. I had already conjectured from the meaning of cognate
words in Du Cange that *capitale*

must mean ' chattels,' when I came
upon the French translation of the
Provost's oath, in which the provisions of each of the clauses in
the charter are given in succession.
It runs, ' Vous jurerez qu'en chastel
des écoliers ne ferez mettre main '
(Jourdain, p. 66).

I may add the following remarks :
(1) The use of *capitale* either for
' head ' or ' regent master' is unex-
ampled. (2) The continued use of
the neuter for a person would be
unparalleled. (3) The clause would
be mere surplusage, since masters as
well as scholars have been already
privileged from arrest. (4) For the
quite common use of *arrestare* of the
sequestration of property, cf. Jourdain, Nos. 371, 551 (*arrestari bona*),
Bulæus, III. 469. (5) Provision is
made for the case where the *jus-*

Savigny) have interpreted these words of the Rector,
whose office the former at least believed to date from the

titia ecclesiastica cannot be found in the case of a scholar, not in the case of the arrest of the *capitale*. The reason on my view is obvious. The case could not be so urgent where only property was concerned as to require a temporary detention by the secular arm. According to the other interpretations a privilege is conferred on the ‘scholar’ which is withheld from the rector or master.

M. Jourdain’s own view is that ‘hæc verba non ipsum rectorem sed aliquem e magistris aperte declarant’ (p. 66, *note*), and to this view Denifle, though not without hesitation, subscribes. M. Jourdain (No. 274, p. 47) relies upon a passage contained in the pleadings of the University against the Chancellor. A doctor of medicine had upset the water in which he had been steeping his herbs upon the watch in the street below. The officers entered the house, and after nearly killing him by their violence carried him off to the King’s prison. The University contended that its privileges had been violated by the arrest and imprisonment in two distinct ways: ‘quod de quocumque esset scholari non debuisset fieri, sicut in privilegio regis continetur,’ and because ‘justitia laycalis in capitale scholarium, quantum ad illam injuriam, manum imposuit, quod tamen per privilegium regale fieri non debuit similiter.’ According to M. Jourdain’s interpretation there is hardly any distinction between the two breaches of privilege complained of. It is easy to suppose that the Doctor’s property had been seized by the guard even if the forcible entry was not construed as an attachment of property

by lay justice, or the clause may be mere surplusage added by a careless scribe. Even if *capitale* is here understood of a Master, it must be a misinterpretation.

Denifle now replies *ex cathedra* that ‘arrestare capitale, letzteres im Sinne von “Vermögen” genommen, kennt das Mittelalter nicht.’ (*Hist. Jahrbuch*, X. 2. Heft, 1889, p. 372, *note*). With all deference I submit that it is enough to show that each word can bear the sense assigned. If we may have ‘arrestare bona’ (which is habitual), why not ‘arrestare capitale,’ since ‘capitale’ undoubtedly has the same meaning as the commoner ‘catallum’? At all events it is clear that this meaning was assigned to ‘capitale’ by the medieval translator, who presumably knew medieval Latin as well as Denifle himself. The argument from usage is the less valuable since ‘capitale’ was obviously a comparatively rare form which suggested different interpretations within a century after the date. It should be stated that the thirteenth century Phillipps MS. (No. 76. f. 54 *b*) translates: ‘Vous jurrès que en le chevetaine des escoliers de Paris pour nul forfait vous ne mettrès main, ne ne ferès mettre’: and this reading has been adopted by Denifle (*Chartularium*, pt. i. No. 67). But over ‘chevetaine’ is written in an early hand ‘chateils’ (as also in the copy followed by Bulæus, *Recueil des priv. de l’Un. de P.* p. 277)—a fact which Denifle omits to chronicle; and (as he tells us) the Vatican codex renders: ‘qu’en l’enqueste des escoliers ne ferés mettre main.’ I must observe that the Cheltenham reading can give no support to Denifle: if it is worth

times of Alcuin and Erigena. Recent writers have strangely understood the *capitale* to mean 'a regent master,' but without offering any explanation of so strange a mode of expression. Even Denifle has here missed or rather rejected the true explanation. The word *capitale* merely means ' chattels ' or property, which, like the persons of the scholars, was protected from sequestration except by process of the ecclesiastical court. It is obvious that the correction of these two blunders involves a rewriting of the whole constitutional history of the University during the first half-century of its existence. As the charter of Philip Augustus has sometimes been treated as a kind of deed of foundation, or at least as the first official recognition of the University, it may be added that the privileges which it bestows are bestowed upon Masters or scholars simply as such. There is no official recognition of the University, its officers or members : except in so far as it recognizes the existence of the Assemblies of the Masters by requiring the Provost's oath to be taken before them. The conferment of privileges upon Masters and scholars no more implies the existence of a University than the exemption of chemists or dissenting ministers from jury service by act of parliament implies the existence of Guilds or corporations composed of members of those classes of the community.

anything, it makes for the old view which interprets it of the Rector. But Denifle knows that in 1200 there was no Rector : and he himself thinks that the translation was made *circa* 1231, i. e. just when the Rectorship was rising into importance, when a scholar of Paris would have been as eager to see additional tribute to the dignity and antiquity of the office as Bulæus was 400 years later. Under these circumstances it cannot be doubted that ' chateils ' or ' chastel' represents the wording of the oath which the Provost actually took. My view of the matter has been accepted by Kaufmann.

II. *Development of the University from 1210–1249:*
Origin of the Four Nations.

CHAP. V,
§ 1.
—+—
The Uni-
versity a
corpora-
tion in
germ.

We have seen that the bare existence of a University of Masters can be traced from about the year 1170. It was not, however, till some years after the beginning of the thirteenth Century that the Society assumed anything like the form of a legal corporation or obtained in its corporate capacity recognition and privilege from the civil and ecclesiastical authorities.

Advance
in organ-
ization.

Four steps would seem to have been preeminently necessary to give to mere customary meetings of Masters for the initiation of new members or similar purposes the character of a definite and legally-recognized corporation : (1) The reduction of their unwritten customs to the form of written statutes or bye-laws, (2) the recognition or (if authoritative recognition was unnecessary) the exercise of the right to sue and be sued as a corporation, (3) the appointment of permanent common officers, (4) the use of a common seal. We must now briefly investigate the date at which each of these stages in the development of the University was reached.

First
Statutes,
c. 1210.

The first two steps were taken considerably before the two latter and at about the same period, i. e. about the year 1210. The actual text of the earliest Statutes is lost : but there is a Bull of Innocent III of about the last mentioned date which sanctions the restitution to the Society of a Master who had been expelled for a breach of them. From this document it appears that they were three in number[1]. The first dealt with the dress of Masters, no

---

[1] 'Ex litteris vestre devotionis accepimus, quod cum quidam moderni doctores liberalium artium a majorum suorum vestigiis in tribus presertim articulis deviarent; habitu videlicet inhonesto, in lectionum et

doubt prescribing the 'round black cope reaching to the heels at least when new,' mentioned in one of the earliest extant statutes[1]; the second enforced the observance of 'the accustomed order in lectures and disputations'; the third required 'attendance at the funerals of deceased Masters.' From the extreme simplicity of these regulations, and the fact that their enactment is spoken of as something new, it is sufficiently evident that they were the first ever formally made by the society—the first reduction to a written form of the established but hitherto unwritten customs of the profession. They are also interesting on account of their close analogy with the Statutes of the ordinary Guilds or religious confraternities of the Middle Ages, with which attendance at funerals and the obtaining of prayers for deceased members was likewise a primary object[2]. Sometimes too their members wore a common livery. This first step towards the consolidation

disputationum ordine non servato, et pio usu in celebrandis exequiis decedentium clericorum jam quasi penitus negligenter omisso, vos cupientes vestre consulere honestati octo ex vobis juratos ad hoc unanimiter elegistis, ut super dictis articulis de prudentium virorum consilio bona fide statuerent, quod foret expediens et honestum ad illud imposterum observandum vos juramento interposito communiter astringendo, excepto dumtaxat magistro G., qui jurare renuens et formidans fidejussoriam pro se tantum optulit cautionem. Fuit insuper ad cautelam a vobis fide prestita protinus constitutum, ut si quisquam magistrorum adversus alios duceret resistendum et primo, secundo tertiove commonitus infra triduum universitati parere contempneret magistrorum, ex tunc beneficio societatis eorum in magistralibus privaretur.' Bulæus, III. p 60: *Chartul.* T. I. pt. i. No. 8. The bull is undated, but appears in the Vatican Register

between the years 1210 and 1211. Denifle dates it 1208-9. At about this date the University took some kind of corporate part in the condemnation of Almaric. See Guillelmus Armoricus, ap. Bouquet, XVII. 83, but the words 'compellitur ab Universitate confiteri,' &c., are suspicious, since *ab Universitate* is omitted by Vincentius Bellovacensis, who reproduces the rest almost *verbatim* (*Bibliotheca Mundi*, Duaci, 1624, IV. 1221).

[1] 'Nullus Magistrorum legentium in Artibus habeat capam nisi rotundam, nigram et talarem, saltem dum nova est. Pallio autem bene potest uti.' Bulæus, III. 82: *Chartul.* I. pt. i. No. 20. The 'Confirmatio Statutorum' which Bulæus (III. p. 52) ascribes to Innocent III really belongs to Innocent IV, and the date is 124⅘. See Jourdain, p. 116 *Chartul.* I. i. No. 169.

[2] See Toulmin Smith, *English Gilds,* 1870, *passim.*

CHAP. V,
§ I.

or crystallization of the hitherto fluid organization must therefore have been taken in the year 1209 or not much later. A modern mind, accustomed to look for very definite expressions of corporate existence, might indeed be disposed to assign the 'foundation' of the University to the decade 1200–1210 rather than to the years 1160–1170 : such a conception would, however, be thoroughly anachronistic.

Recognised
as a
Corporation.

At about the same date the University acquired a definite recognition of its existence as a legal corporation. A Bull of Innocent III (himself a Parisian Master) empowers the Society to elect a proctor, i. e. a syndic or common *procurator ad litem*, to represent it in the Papal Court[1]. By this permission the Society acquired, in modern legal phraseology, the right 'to sue and be sued' as a corporation. It must not, however, be supposed that according to the ideas of the thirteenth century any Charter from either Pope or King was conceived to be indispensable

No Charter
necessary.

to enable a private Society to acquire a legal corporate existence. Whether owing to the predominance of ideas ultimately derived from the Roman Law[2], or simply from the mere absence of a clearly defined conception of a cor-

---

[1] Bulæus, III. p. 23, *sub anno* 1203. Denifle, no doubt rightly, connects the bull with the suit of 1210-11 (I. p. 86) : but in his *Chartularium*, T. I. pt. i. No. 24, places it vaguely between 1210–1216.

[2] For the ideas of medieval Civilians as to freedom of Association, see Denifle, I. pp. 191, 192, 169-75. They would seem to be to a certain extent inconsistent with the true interpretation of the Roman Law in Imperial times (see Mommsen, *De Collegiis et Sodaliciis Romanorum*, Kiliæ, 1843, p. 72 *sq.*). But still the idea seems always to have been that unauthorized *Collegia* were forbidden, not that *a priori* special legislation was necessary to create artificial or fictitious persons. It must be remembered that the Roman

Law had everywhere some recognition in relation to the clergy (see Savigny, *Gesch. des Röm. Rechts im Mittelalter*, cap. 15). Thus we find Bishops incorporating Colleges of Priest-Vicars (see e. g. Freeman, *Cathedral Church of Wells*, 1870, p. 137 *sq.*). So in 1347 the Chancellor of Oxford incorporates the Barber-Surgeons (Wood, *Hist. and Antiq. of Oxford*, ed. Gutch, I. pp. 443, 444), who enjoyed the privilege of the University. But there is no necessity to appeal to the conceptions of the Roman Law. As to the spontaneous origin of English Guilds and Boroughs, see the excellent treatment of the subject in Gross, *The Gild Merchant*, Oxford, 1890, I. p. 33 *sq.*

poration as a distinct legal personality, we find that the growth of corporations of all kinds was at this period gradual and spontaneous. The Borough, the Guild-Merchant, the ordinary social or religious Guild, all came into existence, held corporate property, and exercised other attributes of corporate personality without any formal Charter or legal incorporation. Charters and formal Privileges were for the most part granted to confirm or extend a corporate existence already *de facto* established. A Sovereign or other superior authority might and often did deny to a particular class or community the right to form a particular kind of corporation or to claim particular corporate privileges; but there was no idea that for the mere holding of common property a definite act of legal incorporation was necessary. That notion is an invention of later Jurists, and is responsible for a great deal of bad history [1].

Thus Innocent expressly recognizes the inherent right

---

[1] The best account of the origin of the University as a voluntary society is that given by the Masters themselves in their letter to the Prelates of Christendom in 1253¾ (Bulæus, III. pt. i. No. 230): 'Magistri reverendi vita et doctrina clarissimi, mente religiosi, omnes tamen degentes in habitu seculari, qui processu temporis crescente numero auditorum, sicut oportuit, ampliati, ut liberius et tranquillius vacare possent studio litterali, si quodam essent juris specialis vinculo sociati, corpus collegii sive universitatis cum multis privilegiis et indultis ab utroque principe sunt adepti.' In the controversy with the Mendicants they even denied the right of the Pope to meddle with the University, *qua* University, at all: 'I. Quia secundum juris civilis ordinationem nullus ad societatem compelli debet, cum societas voluntate firmetur. 2. Authoritas Apostolica non se extendit nisi ad

ea quæ ad Cathedram pertinent. Ad Cathedram autem non pertinet studentium societas, sed collatio Beneficiorum, administratio sacramentorum et alia hujusmodi.' (Abstract in Bulæus, III. p. 649.) When the University attempted, in later times, to subject the Chancellor to its regulations in the conferment of the License, it was by virtue of his personal oath of obedience as a member of the University. A curious illustration of the medieval view of freedom of Association is quoted by Sarti from Manni, *Degli antichi Sigilli*, T. XII. (Firenze, 1742) p. 117. When the Pisans were defeated by Genoa in 1284, a large body of Pisan captives were kept in prison for eighteen years, and assumed the right of using a common seal which bore the legend, 'SIGILLUM UNIVERSITATIS CARCERATORUM JANUÆ DETENTORUM.' State-authorization is here of course out of the question.

of the Masters to a corporate existence, both in the Bull authorizing them to appoint a proctor[1] and in the Bull sanctioning the readmission of the expelled Master. In the latter case the Pope was called upon to dispense with the obligation of the oath which the Masters had taken to refuse their *consortium* to all offenders against the statutes. In the former the necessity for appointing a proctor arose from the suit with which the Society was engaged against the Chancellor and Church of Paris, to whom the claims of the new organization seemed inconsistent with the allegiance of the individual Masters to the Chancellor. Hence to secure from the Pope the recognition of their proctors was to win half their case.

Influence of Bologna.

In taking the momentous step—for such it proved in its ultimate consequence—of passing written statutes, it is not impossible that the nascent Society was influenced by the example of the Student-universities of Bologna[2]. It is true that the existence of the Parisian Society of Masters becomes traceable in a rudimentary form considerably before we have express evidence of the existence of the earliest Student-university at Bologna. But in the more congenial atmosphere of Italian city-life, these Societies rapidly attained a higher stage of development and organization than the looser association of Masters which had grown up

---

[1] 'Innocentius, &c. Scholaribus Parisiensibus. Quia in causis que contra vos et pro vobis moventur interdum vestra Universitas ad agendum et respondendum commode interesse non potest, postulastis a nobis ut procuratorem instituere super hoc vobis de nostra permissione liceret. Licet igitur de jure communi hoc facere valeatis, instituendi tamen procuratorem super his auctoritate presentium vobis concedimus facultatem.' Bulæus, III. p. 23 : *Chartul.* T. I. pt. i. No. 24.

[2] The Statutes were made by a Committee of *eight*, which suggests the eight *Statutarii* of Bologna. See

above, p. 191. The Statutes of 1215 required that a Master should be at least twenty (see below, p. 453), and it is probable that the regulation was not uncalled for. Cf. the complaints of Stephen of Tournay a quarter of a century earlier : 'Facultates quas liberales appellant, amissa libertate pristina, in tantam servitutem devocantur, ut comatuli adulescentes earum magisteria impudenter usurpent, et in cathedra seniorum sedeant imberbes, et qui nondum norunt esse discipuli laborant ut nominentur magistri.' *Ep.* ccli (Migne, 211. c. 517); *Chartul.* Introd. No. 48.

around the Cloister-school of Paris. Though the Italian
Universities were Universities of students, the Parisian
Masters formed a body numerous enough to imitate their
organization. It must be remembered that the great mass
of the Masters at Paris were Masters of Arts—men not
much older than the Italian Law-students, and many of
them actually students in the higher Faculties as well as
Masters in the lower. When we come to deal with the
formation of the Nations and the appointment of their
officers, the influence of the institutions of Bologna on
those of Paris will be still more obvious.

Both these steps towards a legal incorporation of the Development of
University
due to
struggle
with the
Chancellor.
University are unmistakably connected with the great
struggle which was now beginning against the Chancellor
of the Cathedral Church of Paris [1]. It was perhaps some
invasion of the unwritten customs of their order by a
Licentiate forced upon them by the Chancellor that suggested their reduction to writing and the exaction of the
oath to observe them. It was still more certainly the
appeal of the Masters to Rome against the tyranny of
that official which called for the appointment of a common
proctor. It was in fact the necessity of mutual support
and united opposition to the Chancellor which called into
existence the University-organization if not the University
itself. A clear understanding of the original relations between the Chancellor and the Masters is essential to any
intelligent appreciation either of the process of the University's growth or of the complex constitutional system
in which that process finally resulted.

The control which the Chancellor exercised over the

---

[1] As to its earlier stages, we only
know that in 1208 the Cardinal-
legate Guala ordered that scholars
should not be excommunicated till
after two admonitions, ' (1) generaliter . . . per magistros, (2) nomina-
tim . . . in scholis.' Since the injunction begins ' volentes . . . magistris
et scholaribus deferre, eatenus erga
ipsos rigorem, si quis est, nostre
constitutionis duximus temperan-
dum,' it is clear that an earlier
Legatine decree has been lost. *Chartul.* T. I. pt. i. No. 7. (In Hemeræus,
p. 93, the Ordinance is mistakenly
attributed to Walo Bp. of Paris in
1108.)

Masters before the rise of the University and in the first few decades after its emergence, was not limited, as in later times, to the conferring of the License. He could not only grant or refuse the License at his own discretion in the first instance: he could deprive a Master of his License or a scholar of his 'scholarity,' with its attendant ecclesiastical privileges, for adequate cause. He was an ecclesiastical Judge as well as the Head of the Schools. He claimed to be the *judex ordinarius* of scholars, though his jurisdiction was not exclusive of that of the ordinary Bishop's Court[1]. He enforced his judgments by excommunication and possessed a special prison for the confinement of refractory clerks. Besides enforcing the ordinary ecclesiastical law, he claimed, at least with the concurrence of the Bishop and Chapter, the right of issuing Ordinances or regulations for the government and discipline of the

The
Chancellor
not an
officer of
the Uni-
versity.

Masters and scholars. But in spite of the large extent of his powers over the Masters as individuals, or rather just because of those powers, the Chancellor had no position whatever in the University as such. As Chancellor, he was not even member of it[2]. Though it was probably from an early period customary for the Chancellor to ascertain from the Masters the qualifications of a candidate for the Mastership, the Masters could not force the Chancellor to grant a License, nor could the Chancellor compel the Masters to admit to their Association one whom he had licensed, but who had not complied with the regulations or customs of the Society. In their power of recognizing or refusing to recognize the Inception of a new member[3] and of requiring a new Master to swear to obey

[1] It should be remembered that in the Middle Ages the Chapter or Capitular officers everywhere exercised actual spiritual jurisdiction, enforced by Excommunication, over the inferior members of the Cathedral body. The Cantor was the ordinary superior of the singers, the Chancellor of the scholars. A document bearing on a dispute between the Subdean and the Chancellor as to jurisdiction over the scholars at Salisbury is quoted by Caius, *De Antiq. Cantabrigiensis Acad.* p. 110.

[2] So in 1381 the University alleges 'que comme chancelier il n'est pas membre de l'université, mais comme maistre en arts.' Bulæus, IV. 609.

[3] This is well illustrated by a

the rules of their Society as a condition of his admission
to professional Association, the Masters possessed an equivalent to the Chancellor's control over the License. This
right, which in its essence was nothing more or less than
the power wielded by all professional Associations, of refusing to associate with professional brethren guilty of
unprofessional conduct, served as the *point d'appui* for
their resistance to the Chancellor. Originally formed for
the purpose of self-protection rather than of aggression,
the University soon aimed like other Trades-unions at
acquiring a monopoly. The University could not prevent
a Licentiate from teaching, but they could refuse to dispute
with a Licentiate who would not submit to their regulations, and they could refuse to present for the License or
to admit to their own Guild a Scholar who persisted in
attending the lectures of a Master whom they had deprived
of their *consortium*[1]. By these means the admission to
the University by Inception was rendered practically as
essential to the teacher as the Chancellor's License. The
Licentiate was not reckoned a full Master till he had been
received into the Society by a public and duly authorized
Inception.

Originally the Chancellor and the University were thus
quite independent of one another. Each party tried by
the use of its unquestionable prerogative to nullify in practice the equally unquestionable prerogative of the other.
Had the parties been left to fight the matter out without

Emancipation by 'boycotting' helped by Papal authority.

Statute of the Faculty of Medicine
in 1270 enacting that 'quicumque
Bachelarius recipiet licentiam contra
consuetudinem Facultatis, vel Magister qui hoc procuraret, ipso facto
esset privatus in sempiternum societate Magistrorum et omni actu Scho-
lastico predicte Facultatis.' Bulæus,
III. p. 398 ; *Chartul.* T. I. pt. i. No.
433.
[1] Thus in the Statute of the
Faculty of Theology against the
Dominicans, the Masters declare
'Quod si aliquis contra dictas eorum

ordinationes venire presumpserit, ei
societatem suam tam in principiis
quam aliis penitus denegabunt'
(Bulæus, III. p. 245 ; *Chartul.* T. I.
pt. i. No. 200) : and in 1253 the
University resolves that no Master
shall hold or be present at the
Inception of a Bachelor who has
not taken the oath to the Statutes,
adding 'Nec idem bachelarius si
alio modo inceperit, magister a
nobis aliquatenus habeatur.' Bulæus,
III. pp. 252, 253 ; *Chartul.* T. I. pt. i.
No. 219.

CHAP. V,
§ 1.

interference, the legal weapons at the disposal of the Chancellor might have strangled the rising Society in its birth or reduced it to dependence upon himself. Coercion might have proved a match for 'boycotting.' As it was, the interference of the Papal authority turned the scale. Except where the claims of the still more favoured orders of Friars introduced a new factor into the dispute, the University gained in the end, though not without temporary rebuffs, by every appeal to the Roman Court. But in so doing, it naturally lost to a great extent its own autonomy. It entered into the ecclesiastical system (as the Merchant-guilds entered into the political system by their acquisition of a share in the Town-government[1]), and became as completely subject to ecclesiastical regulation as the Monasteries or the Chapters.

Illustrations.

The relation of the Chancellor to the University may thus be compared with that of the Crown to the extinct Serjeant's Inn. The Crown alone could make a man a Serjeant-at-law just as the Chancellor alone could make a Licentiate: but, though the appointment by the Crown in the one case and the Chancellor's license in the other was the condition of eligibility, it was by the free election of his professional brethren that the new-comer entered the professional Society. The presentation of rings by the newly admitted Serjeant to his colleagues[2] was one of the last relics of those customary presents of hats, gloves, gowns and the like by the new member of a Guild in which the more prosaic degree-fees of modern Universities have their origin.

The 'Circuit Mess' at the English bar illustrates the enormous power which may be wielded by a Society which has no legal or corporate existence. A barrister expelled therefrom for breach of professional etiquette retains his

---

[1] It must not, indeed, be supposed that the Guild Merchant was identical with, or in any way superseded, the Municipality proper. For the true relation between them, see Gross, *The Gild Merchant*, I. pp. 61–105.

[2] Pulling, *The Order of the Coif*, p. 245.

legal position, but he is effectually incapacitated from CHAP. V,
practice, since no member of the Mess will hold a brief § 1.
with him, even if a Solicitor should be found bold enough
to give him one.

A Bull of the year 1212 makes it evident that a suit Suit
between the Chancellor and the University had been pro- between
Chancellor
ceeding for some time past. It was addressed by Innocent and Uni-
III to the Bishop, Dean, and Archdeacon of Troyes and versity
ante 1212.
required them to compel the Chancellor by ecclesiastical
censure to redress the grievances of the Masters [1]. The
matters in dispute were referred to arbitration and the
decision of the arbitrators enforced by the Apostolical
delegates in a formal sentence [2] which is of capital importance for the light which it throws upon the beginnings of
the University. The Chancellor had, it appears, required
the Masters to take an oath of obedience to himself. Had
he succeeded in the attempt, either the University could
not have continued to exist or the Chancellor's position in
it would have become even more powerful than that of the
Chancellor of Oxford in the days when he was really the
Bishop's officer and before the Masters had succeeded in
making him merely the executor of their own decrees.
He would have become himself (like our Oxford Chancellor) the Head of the Masters' Guild: and there would
have been no room for the growth of the Rectorship. As Papal
it was, the Papacy, with that unerring instinct which marks restrictions
on the
its earlier history, sided with the power of the future, the Chancellor.
University of Masters, and against the efforts of a local
hierarchy to keep education in leading-strings. The obligations of the oaths already taken were relaxed and the
exaction of such oaths in future forbidden [3]. The Chancellor was required to grant the License gratuitously: and
further he was enjoined (without prejudice to his right of

---

[1] Jourdain, No. 13; *Chartul.* T. I.
pt. i. No. 14. Jourdain wrongly dates
this and the next-mentioned document 1210.

[2] Jourdain, No. 15; *Chartul.* T. I.
pt. i. No. 16.

[3] 'Quod Cancellarius sacramenta
fidelitatis vel obedientie vel aliam
obligationem aliquam pro licentia
legendi danda non exiget ab aliquo
lecturo Parisius, et etiam relaxa-
buntur prestita juramenta.'

licensing at his own discretion) to grant the License to all candidates recommended by a majority of the Masters in any of the superior Faculties of Theology, Civil or Canon Law, or Medicine, or by six selected Masters in the Faculty of Arts: the six examining Masters being chosen three by the Faculty and three by the Chancellor[1]. Moreover, the Chancellor had grossly abused his judicial power. He had imprisoned scholars for very trifling offences and had exacted fines by way of penance which were appropriated to his own benefit—a mode of ecclesiastical discipline which was in universal employment where the sins of the laity were concerned, but which was unusual in dealing with the privileged clerical order. Henceforth the Chancellor was not to imprison pending trial when the offence charged was a slight one; in any case he was to allow the accused to be discharged on finding sufficient bail, and he was not to impose a pecuniary penance on a scholar under any circumstances whatever, though he might award damages to the injured party.

De Courçon's Statutes 1215.
Two years later, most of these provisions were embodied in a permanent Code of Statutes imposed upon the University by the Cardinal, Robert de Courçon. At the same time the right of the University to make Statutes for its own government and to administer oaths of obedience to them was recognized, but only in the following cases—'on occasion of the murder or mutilation of a scholar or of grievous injury to a scholar, if justice is refused, for taxing the rents of Hospitia, concerning dress, concerning burial, concerning lectures and disputations,' and with the proviso 'that the Studium be not thereby dissolved or destroyed[2]'. The

---

[1] This regulation was, however, only of temporary force, 'quamdiu videlicet predictus cancellarius cancellariam tenebit.' A curious difference is noticeable as to the way in which the Masters of the different Faculties were to bear testimony to the fitness of candidates. The Doctors of Law and Theology were to give it 'in verbo veritatis': the Physici were required 'dare fidem': the Masters of Arts were only to be believed 'fide corporaliter prestita.'

[2] Bulæus, III. 81, 82; *Chartul.* T. I. pt. i. No. 20. Note how the threat of migration, here as at Bologna, is the great instrument of academic warfare.

clause relating to the 'taxation' of Hospitia no doubt shows that the custom of fixing the rents of houses in the occupation of scholars by a joint board of scholars and burghers was already in existence.

The support of the Holy See was, however, unable to prevent the renewal of the attempts of the Bishop and Chancellor to stifle the newly-born University. The old grievances remained unredressed—the grant or refusal of the license without consultation of the Masters, the vexatious imprisonments, the pecuniary penances and so on: and fresh subjects of dispute were added to them. The oppression of the Chancellor called forth fresh efforts after corporate autonomy, and these efforts in turn became offences which called down upon the Masters fresh measures of ecclesiastical vengeance, necessitating renewed appeals to Rome. *The conflict continues.*

It was in the conduct of this continued litigation that the University first experienced the want of the two important attributes of corporate existence which were still lacking to it. The support of its legal representatives at the Roman Court compelled the University to borrow money, and a seal was wanted to affix to the bond for its repayment [1]: while officers were required to collect the money and direct the legal proceedings. From Bulls of the years 1219 [2] and 1222 [3] it is evident that the Bishop and Chancellor were straining every nerve to suppress the formidable organization which threatened to destroy the authority of the ancient Church of Paris over the Masters and scholars who were multiplying beneath her shadow. An old ordinance or proclamation against 'conspiracies' was furbished up, and the University was excommunicated *en masse* *The struggle necessitates common seal and officers.* *Effort of Chancellor and Cathedral to crush the University, 1219–1222.*

---

[1] See the Bull of Alexander IV in 1259 ordering payment of a debt incurred 'thirty years and more before' to certain Florentine merchants 'prout in litteris compositionis ejusdem Universitatis sigillo sigillatis plenius continetur.' Jourdain, No. 184 ; *Chartul.* T. I. pt. i. No. 330.

[2] Bulæus, III. p. 93 ; Bouquet, T. XIX. pp. 679, 685 ; *Chartul.* T. I. pt. i. Nos. 30, 31.

[3] Bouquet, T. XIX. p. 724 ; *Chartul.* T. I. pt. i. No. 45. Stephen Langton, Cardinal and Archbishop of Canterbury, and others had been appointed delegates by a bull now printed by Denifle, *Chartul.* T. I. pt. i. No. 41.

for disobedience to it. To the mind of a Canon of Paris the very existence of the University was nothing more or less than a conspiracy—an unlawful secret society formed by a certain class of inferior ecclesiastics (men whom he would look upon very much in the light of Priest Vicars or Singing-men) for the purpose of resisting their canonical superiors. The language of the Bulls[1] makes it quite plain that the acts of the conspiracy were simply the passing of Statutes by the Masters for the government of themselves and their scholars and the administration of oaths to observe them. The Church of Paris claimed that no such 'constitutions' should be passed without the consent of the Bishop, Chapter, or Chancellor. When the University respectfully enquired whether the prohibition applied to all constitutions or only to unlawful constitutions, they were expressly told that it applied to all constitutions, 'lawful or unlawful, good or bad'[2]. It is obvious that the very existence of the University was at stake.

Papal decisions.

The definitive sentence of the Holy See upon the points at issue has not come down to us[3], but there can be no doubt from the sequel that Honorius III and Gregory IX

---

[1] 'Dilecti filii magistri et scholares Parisienses nobis graviter sunt conquesti, quod venerabilis frater noster . . . Parisiensis episcopus excommunicationis sententiam ab O. bonæ memoriæ, prædecessore suo, et O. Hostiensi episcopo quondam apostolice sedis legato latam de conspirationibus et conjurationibus scholarium minime faciendis jam dudum innovans eos qui, circa statum scolarium sine consensu ipsius vel capituli seu cancellarii Parisiensis, conspirationem, conjurationem, constitutionem, seu aliquam obligationem, juramento fide vel pena vallatam, facere attemptarent, pro sue voluntatis arbitrio, simili vinculo innodavit, et ipsorum insuper pedibus laqueos excommunicationis expandens, in illos qui noverint scholares

arma portantes ac de nocte incedentes, nisi eos infra certum tempus ipsi vel ejus officiali, seu Cancellario nunciarent, similem sententiam fulminavit, &c.' Bouquet, XIX. p. 679; *Chartul.* T. I. pt. i. No. 30.

[2] 'Quesierunt interpretationem ... utrum videlicet intelligerent generaliter tam de constitutione licita utili et honesta, quam de illicita erronea et injusta, quibus respondentibus, quod intelligebant generaliter de omni licita vel illicita, bona vel mala,' &c. *Chartul.* T. I. pt. i. No. 31.

[3] If the document of 1219 in *Chartul.* T. I. pt. i. No. 33 refer to this matter, the dispute must have broken out again before 1222. Cf. Bulæus, III. 130; *Chartul.* T. I. pt. i. No. 58.

continued in the main the policy initiated by Innocent III CHAP. V,
§ 1.
of supporting the claims of the new Society. The Bulls of
1219 and 1222 are of an interlocutory character, though
the first of them decides an important point in favour of
the Scholars by ordering the instant abolition of the Chancellor's prison, and forbidding the wholesale excommunication of the University without the special license of the
Holy See [1]. It is in these Bulls that we find the first traces Nations
and their
Proctors.
of the existence of Nations and their officers. It appears
that the University had elected certain officers 'according to
their Nations' 'for the avenging of injuries' and especially,
it would appear, for the conduct of the pending suits at
Rome against the Chancellor and the collection of money
for that purpose [2]. We also hear of the levying of fines by
the University [3] in a way which suggests that these officers
had authority to impose such fines for offences against the
University regulations.

In the year 1222 the election of such officials is prohibited Rectors or
Proctors.
pendente lite. We hear no more of them again till 1231 or

---

[1] See the bull of 1219 in Bulæus,
III. p. 93; *Chartul.* T. I. pt. i. No. 31.
The immunity of the University as
a whole from excommunication without the special license of the Holy
See is re-enacted in 1222 (Bouquet,
T. XIX. p. 724; *Chartul.* T. I. pt. i.
No. 45). M. Thurot (p. 12) makes the
astounding assertion that Honorius
III forbade the excommunication of
'*aucun membre* de l'université sans
l'autorisation du St.-Siège.' So Malden (p. 30), and others.

[2] 'Porro, cum ad prosecutionem
appellationis predicte foret nuntius
ad sedem apostolicam destinandus,
et sine collecta universitas [*sc.* a
corporation] non haberet expensas,
magistri liberalium artium fide inter-
posita se ac suos discipulos astrincxe-
runt ad servandum quod super hoc
a suis procuratoribus contingeret
ordinari' (Bulæus, III. p. 94; *Chartul.*
T. I. pt. i. No. 31). From the bull

of 1260 (Jourdain, No. 134) it appears that these *procuratores* were
four in number. We have possibly
an earlier trace of the custom of
appointing four representatives upon
such occasions, and so perhaps of
the Nations, in Innocent III's bull
of 1208–9. The Master who had
been expelled for breach of the
statutes 'in quatuor vestrum juramento interposito compromisit, illorum dictum pro bono pacis se
gratum et ratum pariter habiturum.'
Bulæus, III. p. 60; *Chartul.* T. I. pt.
i. No. 8.

[3] 'Magistri etiam a magistro vel
scholari penam pecuniariam per
tempus non exigent supradictum,
nec scholares interim secundum nationes suas sibi quemquam preficient
ad injurias ulciscendas.' Bouquet,
T. XIX. p. 725; *Chartul.* T. I. pt. i.
No. 45.

(since the text is there doubtful) 1237, when the institution appears thoroughly established. A Bull issued in the latter year forbids the unauthorized excommunication not merely of the Masters and scholars, but of their ' Rector or Proctor,') when acting officially on their behalf [1]. It is possible that Rector and Proctor are here alternative titles for the same official [2]. But whether this was so or not, it is quite clear that when the first appointment of these officials took place, there was only one official to each Nation and no general head of the whole body. At a later date the term Proctor was appropriated to the Heads of the several Nations : while a common Head of all four

---

[1] The injunction was repeated in 1237, each time for a term of twelve years : ' Ut nullus contra universitatem magistrorum vel scholarium seu rectorem vel procuratorem eorum aut quemquam alium pro Universitatis vel facto vel occasione, &c.' Such is the reading of Jourdain, No. 49, for the document of 1237. Denifle, in his *Entstehung d. Univ.* I. p. 112, gave ' rectorum'; (upon the unsatisfactoriness of which Kaufmann has commented in his *Gesch. d. Deutsch. Univ.* I. p. 270). Denifle has since accepted ' rectorem' as the true reading in 1237 (*Archiv*, III. p. 627 and *Chartul.* T. I. pt. i. No. 113); in the doc. of 1231, printed for the first time in *Chartul.* T. I. pt. i. No. 95, he gives ' rectorum' as the reading of his MS. (the Vatican Register). If this is the true reading, ' rectorum' must of course = ' Regentium.' There is much uncertainty about the text of these successive renewals ; see Jourdain, pp. 11 *b*, 14 *a* ; Denifle, I. pp. 113, 114 ; *Chartul.* T. I. pt. i. No. 162 *note*.

[2] There are some slight indications of such a use of terms : (1) William of S. Amour referring to the year 1256 says that he was not then (as he had been earlier) ' pro-
curator scholarium vel rector de collegio eorum.' (*Opera*, Constantiæ, 1632, p. 94.) The two titles here seem to be alternative titles for the same office, though it is just possible (with Denifle) to take Rector in the sense of Regent : (2) In 1264 we hear of the Seal-Chest being opened ' presentibus Rectoribus et Procuratoribus.' *Chartul.* T. I. pt. i. No. 405. But cf. below, *note* 5. (3) In 1254, the Pope, retaining the older phraseology, clearly uses the term ' rectores artistarum' to include the four Proctors as well as *the* Rector. *Chartul.* T. I. pt. i. Nos. 338, 342. (4) At Vercelli, in 1228, when the heads of three Nations are spoken of respectively as *rector*, *procurator*, and *provincialis*, but at other times collectively as *Rectores* (see below, vol. II. cap. ii. §§ 4, 5). (5) At Oxford and Cambridge the Proctors were called ' Rectores sive Procuratores.' Whence could such a usage be derived except from Paris ? But see below, vol. II. cap. xii. § 2. The term Procurator was commonly used of any legal agent or attorney, but especially of a financial agent. In continental Colleges it is the common equivalent of our ' Bursar.' It is the ordinary Latin of our ' churchwarden.'

Nations was elected with the style of Rector. We may CHAP. V, conjecture that the term *procurator* was first employed in § 1. view of the temporary, representative, and financial character The Rector. of the official[1]: while the analogy of the four Bologna Rectors may have suggested that of Rector as a name for the National officers, as they passed from temporary into permanent delegates, until the election of a common Head by the united Nations required a distinction between the two titles. At the same time, a trace of their original character remained in the short tenure of both offices, which were at first held for periods of only a month or six weeks and afterwards for three months[2].

The first document in which the Rector and Proctors are Rector and Proctors in 1245. clearly distinguished from one another is a Statute of the Faculty of Arts in 1245[3], which visits offenders with expulsion till 'satisfaction shall have been made to the Rector and Proctors on behalf of the University' (sc. *universitas artistarum*) 'to the full and at their pleasure.' In the same year a Statute of the whole University orders that Scholars who take a house which has been interdicted to Scholars by the University are to be expelled after monition by the Rector or a servant sent by him, or in like manner by the Proctors or a messenger sent by them[4]. It is now clear that the term Rector has come to be reserved for the head of the whole body of Artists, the term Proctor alone being applied to the heads of the Nations, while in 1249 we meet with an agreement between the four Nations as to the mode in which

---

[1] From the Town-statutes at Bologna it appears that a Guild, the 'Homines artis lanæ,' were governed by 'Castaldi et *procuratores*.' (Frati, ii. p. 72.) So the 'Company of Merchants of Alnwick' was governed by an Alderman and Proctors. Gross, *Gild Merchant*, i. p. 130. Rector was also a name for Guild-officers. See above, p. 164.

[2] From 1279. Bulæus, III. 444; *Chartul.* T. i. pt. i. No. 492.

[3] 'Quousque pro qualitate et quantitate delicti vel transgressionis mandati Universitatis Rectori et Procuratoribus pro Universitate fuerit ad plenum et pro ipsorum voluntate satisfactum' [Feb. 124⅘]. Bulæus, III. p. 195; *Chartul.* T. I. pt. i. No. 137.

[4] 'Per Rectorem vel servientem ab eo missum, vel Procuratores similiter.' Bulæus, III. 195; *Chartul.* T. I. pt. i. No. 136.

[5] Bulæus, III. 222; *Chartul.* T. I. pt. i. No. 187. It appears that at

this new officer—the common head of the four Nations—should be elected by the four Proctors. It should be added that the Bedels or 'common servants of the Scholars,' i. e. of the University or Nations, make their appearance at about the same time as the Proctorships in their earliest form [1].

The Nations composed only of Masters of Arts.

We see, then, that the Nation-organisation came into existence at some time between 1219 and 1221, that it was for a time suspended by papal authority, but that by 1231 it seems to have obtained a fully recognised legal existence; while at some time between 1222 and 1249 [2] the common Rectorship was instituted by the united Nations. Like the formation of Statutes, the appointment of the common proctor, and the use of the common seal, the new organisation is clearly connected with the great war against the Chancellor. But in one respect the step differs from the preceding efforts after corporate autonomy; they were taken by the University of Masters in all faculties, while in the first mention of the Nations we find that it is the 'Masters of the Liberal Arts' who are forbidden to elect an officer 'to avenge their injuries.' This circumstance may at first sight seem to negative the theory which I have put forth as to the origin of the Proctorships. It is true that the suit against the Chancellor was instituted in the name of the whole University, but the Masters of Arts formed by far the most numerous body of Masters; the

this time there were two Rectors, one presiding over the French nation only, the other over the remaining three nations. Whether this arrangement, closely parallel to the later Bologna constitution, had lasted some time, or whether the Agreement was merely designed to settle a disputed election, cannot be determined; but it seems to be treated as irregular and exceptional. The one thing that comes out clearly is that the *single* Rectorship is much later than the four National Headships, by whatever name called. It is

worth noticing that Gregory IX in 1231 gave the administration of the goods of intestate scholars to 'episcopus et unus de Magistris quem ad hoc Universitas ordinavit.' (*Chartul.* T. I. pt. i. No. 79.) This suggests that a single representative of the Masters was already appointed for some purposes. This very enactment may have had something to do with the growth of the single Rectorship.

[1] *Chartul.* T. I. pt. i. No. 28 (dated by Denifle *circa* 1218).

[2] Probably after 1237. See above, p. 314, *note* 1.

Masters of the superior Faculties who were left outside the new organisation were in fact a mere handful [1]. And it is probable that it was the Masters of Arts and their pupils who were particularly interested in resisting the oppression of the ecclesiastical authorities. It was not the elderly and dignified Doctor of Divinity, but the young Master of Arts and his still younger pupils who would be most in danger of having their heads broken in a tavern brawl, or being lodged in the Chancellor's prison for breaking other people's heads, and who would have needed the assistance of powerful organisation for the 'avenging of injuries.' It is probable, therefore, that the suit at Rome was practically carried on mainly by the Faculty of Arts and at their expense.

The peculiar relation which must at this time have existed between the legal corporation of Masters of all Faculties and the more popular and informal Nation-organisation which had grown up within it is well illustrated by a Papal Bull of 1260 [2] ordering the payment of debts contracted by the Society 'thirty years and more before.' The suit is distinctly spoken of as the suit of the whole University; the bond for the repayment of the money was sealed with the University seal; the Bull itself is directed to the whole body of Masters [3]. But it appears that the money had been borrowed by four Proctors whom we can hardly avoid identifying with the Proctors of the Nations; and the order for the repayment is in a special manner addressed to the Rector, though it was not till

---

[1] In 1207 Innocent III limited the theological chairs to eight. (Bulæus, III. 36; *Chartul.* I. pt. i. No. 5.) In 1289 there were about 120 Regent Masters of Arts (Jourdain, No. cclxxiv. p. 45*a*; *Chartul.* T. I. pt. i. No. 515).

[2] Jourdain, No. 84; *Chartul.* T. I. pt. i. No. 330.

[3] Moreover in 1218 it appears that though only Masters of Arts and their scholars had been excommunicated, 'in omni Facultate silet Parisius vox Doctrine.' (*Chartul.*, T. I. pt. i. No. 31; Bulæus, III. p. 94.) When John of S. Victor says 'tota universitas quatuor Nationum decrevit quod a lectionibus cessarent' (Bulæus, III. 564), there is no reason with Denifle (I. p. 83) to make the expression an anachronism. It is quite probable that the Nations of Arts took the lead in all these movements.

much later that it became the habitual practice to address official communications to the 'Rector, Masters, and Scholars.' The small proportion which the Masters of the superior Faculties bore to the whole body, together with the fact that but for the Rector the University was still an acephalous corporation, is almost a sufficient explanation of the curious circumstance that the Rector of the inferior Faculty of Arts rapidly became the real head of the whole society. The probable history of the relations between the University and the Faculty of Arts during this transition period is that, in consequence of its superior numbers, organisation, and activity, the affairs of the University were passing more and more into the hands of the Faculty of Arts. The Doctors of the superior Faculties were called in to give their assent to what had been already settled upon by the Masters of Arts. Since the superior Faculties had as yet perhaps no heads of their own, the position of the Rector in such 'general congregations' must have been from the first virtually that of a presiding officer.

The common seal broken c. 1225.

It is impossible to fix the exact date at which the practice of voting by Faculties in the University and by Nations in the Faculty of Arts came into vogue, but a circumstance in the anti-chancellor movement which has hitherto been passed over helps to explain its origin. In one only of the main issues between Chancellor and University does the papacy seem to have failed to support its protégé. The Bull addressed to Archbishop Langton and his colleagues in 1221, while referring the other points at issue to the discretion of the delegates, contains a peremptory order to break a seal which the Masters had recently made for themselves [1]. How far this order was obeyed, we know not : but in 1225 a University seal—the same or a successor—was, upon the complaint of the Chapter, solemnly

[1] *Chartul.* T. I. pt. i. No. 41. The Chapter had also complained of the Masters unreasonably 'juramentum non solum super observatione factarum (constitutionum) sed etiam faciendarum decetero exigentes penis gravibus constitutis'; and on this point also the Pope here seems to decide against the Masters in advance.

broken by the Papal Legate, Romano Cardinal of S. Angelo, and the University peremptorily forbidden to make another. The sentence provoked an attack by a mob of Masters and Scholars armed with swords and sticks upon the Legate's house: the doors had been already broken when the Cardinal was preserved from further outrage by the timely arrival of the soldiers of S. Louis[1]. It was not till 1246 that the right of common seal was conceded[2]: but meanwhile it is very possible that the prohibition had already been evaded by the formation of four separate seals for the four Nations, which were used to signify the assent of the Faculty of Arts whether to its own deeds or those of the whole University[3]. It is obvious that this measure, necessitated by the action of the Legate, would have the effect of consolidating the Nations and emphasizing the fourfold division of the Faculty of Arts. Henceforth, in fact, the Faculty of Arts ceased to exist except as a federation of the four independent Nations: and since the seals could not be used without the consent of the Nations to which they severally belonged, separate deliberations would be necessary whenever a document had to be sealed[4].

It remains to state the actual constitution of these Nations. They were named from the nationalities which predominated in each of them at the time of their formation, namely the French, the Normans, the Picards, and the English[5]. Picardy was held to include the whole of the

Composition of four Nations.

---

[1] *Chron. Turonense,* ap. Martène, *Ampliss. Collectio,* V. c. 1067. At the ensuing Council of Bourges, some eighty Masters appeared and received absolution for this assault.

[2] *Chartul.* T. I. pt. i. No. 165.

[3] The first extant document which bore these seals is the agreement as to the election of Rector in 1249 (see above, p. 315). That the seals were made to evade the prohibition of a University seal is supported by the fact that as late as 1283-4 the Chancellor ' asserit se a Facultate gravatum esse, inserendo ibi quedam

de sigillis quibus utuntur Nationes Facultatis predicte.' (Jourdain, No. 274 ; *Chartul.* T. I. pt. i. No. 515.)

[4] It was distinctly ordered in 1266 by the Papal Legate that ' fiant in licitis casibus ipsius facultatis statuta . . . communi et expresso cujuslibet nationis interveniente consensu.' *Chartul.* T. I. pt. i. No. 409.

[5] It is not easy to indicate briefly the differences between my view of the origin of the Nations and Denifle's. 1. He holds (following the *Anon. Refut.,* p. 325 *sq.*) that the Nations were an organisation of

Low Countries[1]. The more distant regions were divided between the English and French Nations, the French embracing all the Latin races, the English including the Germans and all inhabitants of the North and East of Europe. It is clear that the classification is to a certain extent arbitrary[2], and in later times constituted a very unequal division of the academic population, the French Nation often outnumbering the other three. But at the beginning of the thirteenth century it is quite possible that it represented as fair a division of the countries from which the bulk of Parisian students came as could be effected consistently with the preservation of the number four. This number was in all probability adopted in imitation of the practice of the early Italian Universities. If it gave the strictly French members of the University somewhat less influence than the rest, that also was in accordance with Bolognese ideas.

Frequency
of Schism.

The French Nation was, however, far from submitting

scholars, in which the Masters of Arts were included as scholars of the superior Faculties (I. pp. 84, 88, 97); but, as he admits that those below M.A. had no voice in the assemblies (p. 102), and as the University itself is constantly spoken of as a body of *scholares,* the distinction seems to rest on a somewhat slender basis. I admit that the Nations were formed for a different purpose from the Faculties, though I see no reason to believe that after the Nations were once formed any distinction was in practice maintained between the Faculty of Arts and the collective Nations, or that when once the Rectorship was established, the Rector did not preside in all meetings of the Masters of Arts for whatever purpose assembled. 2. He holds that the Nations were formed for purposes of discipline among the scholars (i. p. 104). This view seems to me unfounded and anachronistic. The discipline

of scholars, in so far as such a thing existed, was left to their own Masters. I believe that the primary purpose of the organisation was (*a*) 'ad injurias ulciscendas' by legal process and otherwise, (*b*) to elect officers for this purpose and for collecting and administering funds with the same object. See above, p. 313. In 1251 we find the English Nation prescribing the studies of candidates for 'determination' (*Chartul.* T. I. pt. i. No. 201). Both the Nations and their Officers are found performing precisely the same functions as were discharged by the other Faculties in relation to their own studies.

[1] In 1358 the Meuse was fixed upon as the boundary between 'Picardy' and France. Bulæus, IV. 346.

[2] If this is his meaning, Denifle (I. 95) rightly contrasts the 'artificial' Nations of Paris with the 'natural' Nations of Bologna.

unquestioningly to this preponderance of the foreign element in the Faculty. More than once we find the Faculty of Arts temporarily splitting up into two bodies — the French electing a Rector of their own and the other three Nations another Rector[1]. In the year 1266 the liability of the University to such schisms had been so signally manifested that, upon an appeal to the Papal Legate, a dissentient Nation was accorded a constitutional right to secede from the other Nations and elect a Rector of its own, provided that it succeeded in satisfying a Board of arbitrators consisting of the three senior Theologians and the four senior Canonists in the University of the reasonableness of its grievances[2].

At a much later period these Nations were subdivided into Provinces or Tribes, which had regular Deans at their head, and in some cases the officers of the Nation were chosen from the Provinces or Tribes in regular succession and the votes of the National Congregations were taken by Provinces[3].

Provinces.

---

[1] This was the case when the Statute of 1249, prescribing the mode of electing a Rector, was introduced. Bulæus, III. p. 222; *Chartul.* T. I. pt. i. No. 187.

[2] Cf. the Statute in *Chartul.*, T. I. pt. i. No. 409; Bulæus, III. 375. The fact that there were often two Rectors at Paris is not without importance in suggesting a possible source of two ' Rectores sive Procuratores ' at Oxford and Cambridge. See below, vol. II. cap. xii. § ii.

[3] Thus the French Nation was divided into five ' Provinces ' corresponding with the five ecclesiastical Provinces of France which were subdivided into ' Dioceses.' We hear of ' magistri de quinque provinciis consuetis nostre nationis ' in 1327. Bulæus, IV. p. 213; *Chartul.* T. II. No. 871. The German Nation (as the English was usually called after about 1440) was divided at first into an English and a non-English Province, afterwards into three ' tribes,' viz. (1) *Altorum Almanorum*, (2) *Bassorum Almanorum*, (3) *Insularium* or *Scotorum*. Picardy was also at one time divided into two sections of five dioceses each. Bulæus, III. p. 558 *sq.*; Thurot, pp. 19, 20. The Norman Nation seems to have been divided into seven ' Episcopatus ' as early as 1275. Bulæus, III. 413 *sq.*; *Chartul.* T. I. pt. i. No. 460. The internal arrangements of the Nations as to the mode of voting and election to National offices varied considerably in different Nations and at different periods. It does not seem worth while to enter into further detail. Sometimes we find elaborate processes of indirect election, in which the first Nominator was elected by lot (' per inventionem nigre fabe '). *Chartul.* T. II. No. 997. The Provinces had at times separate funds, meetings, and festivals.

III. *The Faculties and the Rectorship.*

CHAP. V,
§ I.
—◆—
The
Superior
Faculties
left out-
side the
Nations.

Such an account as our data permit has now been given of the origin of the celebrated four Nations at Paris. We have seen that a new organization has arisen within the University, composed not of all its members, but of the most numerous section of it—the Masters of Arts. We have seen how from the first the officers of the federated Nations had begun to act as the officers and representatives not only of the Faculty of Arts but of the whole University of Masters. The Faculty of Arts had thus attained the full attributes of a corporation or group of corporations with seals, officers, and common funds, at a time when the University proper was still in an acephalous and half-organized condition, and when the Doctors of the Superior Faculties, who were left outside the Nations, possessed hardly any separate organization at all. The eventual predominance of the Faculty of Arts and of its Head, the Rector, in the whole University, was rendered almost inevitable by this state of things. In order, however, to trace in detail the complicated history of the relations between the Faculties, it will be necessary to go back to the origin of the distinction between the different classes of teachers in the Schools of the Middle Ages.

We have seen how clearly the distinction between two main branches of study—Theology and Arts—was recognized in the time of Abelard. The teaching of the Civil Law was introduced into Paris soon after the revival of that study under Irnerius at Bologna; and the study of
the Canon Law was fully established when Giraldus Cambrensis studied and taught in the Parisian Schools about 1177[1]. Indeed, although the legal fame of Paris was

---

[1] *Opera*, I. ed. Brewer, p. 44 *sq.*

never comparable with that of Bologna, Daniel de Merlac, Chap. V, § 1.
who visited its Schools at about this period, speaks of Law
as the most prominent study of the place[1]. Medicine was Medicine.
certainly taught in Paris at about the same time. A Medical School in a great capital could not be without a
certain importance, but the Parisian School of Medicine
always stood far below those of Salerno and Montpellier.
Alexander Neckam, who studied at Paris (it is said) between
1180 and 1186, thus sums up the studies of his time :—

Hic florent artes, cœlestis pagina regnat,
Stant leges, lucet jus : medicina viget[2].

The four
Faculties.

Such were the four 'Faculties' recognized by the me- Civil Law
forbidden,
1219.
dieval Universities. It should be added that the study of
the Civil Law was forbidden in 1219 by Honorius III[3], not
(as is sometimes represented) in a narrow spirit of hostility
to legal or to secular studies in general, but because it
threatened to extinguish the study of Theology in the one
great theological School of Europe[4]. It is probable that
the Pope's zeal for the theological fame of Paris was

---

[1] Daniel of Merlac or Morley (in Norfolk) visited Paris, *c.* 1170–1190, and gives an amusing account of seeing 'quosdam bestiales in scholis gravi authoritate sedes occupare, habentes coram se scamna duo vel tria, et desuper codices importabiles aureis litteris Ulpiani traditiones represen-tantes, necnon et tenentes stilos plumbeos in manibus, cum quibus asteriscos et obelos in libris suis quadam reverentia depingebant.' Printed by Prof. Holland in *Collec-tanea* (Oxf. Hist. Soc.), II. p. 171.

[2] *De laudibus divinae sapientiae,* ed. Wright, 1863, p. 452.

[3] Bulæus, III. p. 96 ; *Chartularium,* T. I. pt. i. No. 32. At the same time its study was forbidden to Priests, Regulars, and beneficed clerks. It was afterwards explained that the last restriction did not extend to mere parochial cures ; while Univer-sities and whole orders frequently

obtained dispensations. No general dispensation appears to have been given for Paris.

[4] There can be no doubt that the Civil Law continued to be studied and quoted by the Canonists of Paris : and the education of a Pari-sian Canonist usually included a study of the Civil Law at another University. The evidence collected by Péries (pp. 99–108) fails to prove that formal and avowed lectures in Civil Law were ever given at Paris after 1219, still less that degrees were ever taken in that Faculty. The only exception is an allusion to 'Baccalarii Decretales et leges le-gentes' in 1251 (*Chartul.* T. I. pt. i. No.197), which need not imply more than that a certain instruction in Civil Law was mixed with that of Canon Law in Extraordinary lectures. Much of the later evidence produced by Péries tends the other way.

Y 2

seconded by the French King's suspicion of a legal system
which endangered the supremacy of the customary Law of
his country in the Courts of his capital. After this change
the four Faculties of Paris were Theology, Canon Law or
Decrees, Medicine, and Arts[1]—the three former being
styled the superior Faculties as contra-distinguished to the
inferior Faculty of Arts whose course was regarded more
or less as a preparation for the other three. In what relation did the Professors of these four Faculties stand to
one another in the earliest days of the Parisian Guild of
Masters?

*Theology
always dis-
tinguished
from Arts.*
From the beginning of the thirteenth century the documents show that the Society or University included Masters
of three Faculties, Theology, Law, and Arts; the Masters
of Medicine are not yet mentioned as a distinct element[2].
And in the earliest corporate act on the part of the University itself which is preserved to us—the deed by which
in 1221 that body transfers its rights over the Place S.
Jacques to the newly arrived Dominican order as a site
for their Convent—it appears distinctly that the members
of all these Faculties were included in the same Magisterial
corporation. The consideration for which the University
sold its property was to be a right of burial for Masters 'of
whatever Faculty[3]' in the Church of the Order together
with certain Masses and 'whole Psalters,' and it is added
that, if the deceased is a Theologian, he is to be buried in

---

[1] Jourdain, No. 15; *Chartul.* T. I.
pt. i. No. 16. Denifle (I. 70) well remarks that 'die Promotionsfrage
war in Paris der erste Schritt zur
Facultätsbildung.'

[2] 'Universis doctoribus sacre pa-
gine Decretorum et Liberalium
Artium Magistris Parisius commorantibus.' (*Chartul.* T. I. pt. i. No. 8;
Bulæus, III. 60, reads Rectoribus
which here, of course, would mean
Regent Masters). This was the
usual order of precedence, though
at Oxford the Medical Doctors
have now acquired equality with

the Lawyers. Where there was
a Faculty of Civil Law, its Doctors ranked between the Decretists
and the Medicals. The Licentiates
and Bachelors of Superior Faculties
ranked among themselves in the
same order; Bachelors of Theology
(at least *Baccalaurei formati*) ranked
above Regent Masters of Arts, but
not so Bachelors of the other superior
Faculties.

[3] 'Pro quolibet Magistro cuius-
cunque Facultatis fuerit de nostris.'
Bulæus III. 106; *Chartul.* T. I. pt. i.
No. 42.

the Chapter-house, if 'of another Faculty[1]' in the Cloister. The document bears the seals of the individual Doctors of Theology and of them alone: the Theologians are not merely members but representatives of the University[2].

As soon as the Masters of Theology and Canon Law became at all numerous, they must have held meetings of their own apart from those of the Masters of Arts. The Artists could not have taken part in the Inception of a Theological Master, in a Theological disputation, or in the discussion of a case of heresy submitted to them by the Bishop of the diocese. The agreement of 1213 recognizes the right of each Faculty—including the Medical Doctors (who are here for the first time mentioned in connexion with the University)—to testify to the qualifications of candidates to the License in its own department, and this right practically involved the regulation of the studies and the discipline of the students.

The Superior Faculties always distinct corporations within the University.

At the same time it does not follow that, when the united University of Masters met in General Congregation, they voted by Faculties in the manner which afterwards obtained. It is, however, probable that in so far as anything like 'voting' took place in these primitive Assemblies, the consent of all Faculties would have been practically necessary to make a resolution or Statute binding upon all. It would have been a matter of little importance to the Theologian to be denied the fellowship or *consortium* of the Artists, if he were still admitted to the disputations, discussions, and Inceptions of his theological brethren. But we really know nothing of the procedure of University Congregations before the growth of the Rectorship.

Voting by Faculties.

---

[1] 'Alterius Facultatis.' The distinction between 'alter' and 'alius' was habitually neglected in the Middle Ages.

[2] According to Denifle (I. p. 71) the *word* Faculty is first found in the sense of a distinct branch of learning in connection with Paris in a Bull of Honorius III addressed to the scholars of Paris in 1219. But Giraldus Cambrensis († *c.* 1220 A. D.), in his celebrated description of Oxford, speaks of 'doctores diversarum facultatum' as early as *circa* 1184 (see *Opera,* ed. Brewer, I. p. 73). Its use for a body of teachers in a particular subject grew out of the earlier usage by imperceptible stages. Cf. the use of 'Facultas nostra' in Bulæus, III. p. 280; *Chartul.* T. I. pt. i. No. 246.

CHAP. V,
§ 1.

Import-
ance of
Rector
founded on
power of
the purse.

We have already traced the process by which the Nations of Artists and their officers grew up within the University, and to a large extent superseded it in the conduct of what was strictly speaking the business of the whole body. We have seen that though the Rector was technically the Rector of the Artists only, he was from the first employed in the collection of money for University purposes, in the conduct of University litigation, and in the execution of University decrees. He was from the first the representative or agent of the whole University: he rapidly rose to the position of its *Head*, though still elected only by the Faculty of Arts. This predominance of the 'inferior' Faculty of Arts in the University of Paris is explained in exactly the same way as the predominance of the 'lower' House in the British Parliament. The Licentiates, Bachelors and students of the superior Faculties remained subject to the authority of the Nations[1] (though their studies and exercises were regulated by the several Colleges of Doctors); so that the power of the purse lay almost exclusively with the Rector and Masters of the Faculty of Arts[2].

His posi-
tion in
General
Congrega-
tions.

If it should still appear strange that when the four Faculties met together they should have been presided

---

[1] If M.A. they had votes as Regent or Non-Regent Masters. If B.A. they were 'jurati Facultatis Artium.' The authority of the Masters of Arts over the Bachelors of the Superior Faculties who were not B.A. or M.A. is rather a constitutional anomaly, but, when once established, would be sanctioned by the oath to obey the customs of the University.

[2] The old theory—that of Du Boulay and Crevier—was that the Masters of the Superior Faculties were originally included in the Nations, and that the Faculties did not, so to speak, emerge out of them till after the Mendicant controversy. This view is inconsistent with all the facts: and with it goes the boast

that the University was 'founded in Arts.' It is possible, however, that though the Theologians and Canonists were from the first members of the University, they were considered to be so as ex-Masters of Arts, and that admission to the University was originally obtained only by Inception in Arts. Filesacus, the historian of the Theological Faculty, declares that in the time of Philip Augustus there were no Inceptions in the Theological Faculty (ap. Conringius, V. p. 455). If this was so, it would go far to explain the confusion introduced into the whole system by the Mendicant Doctors, who had not graduated in Arts.

over by the head of the lowest of them, it must be remembered that (if we may infer the earliest mode of
proceeding from the later practice) there was no actual
debate in the meetings of the whole University. When
the affair had been laid before the Congregation by the
Rector, the matter was debated by the respective Faculties
and Nations, and the assent of each Faculty and Nation
signified by the respective presiding officers. The proceedings thus resolved themselves into a sort of conference
between these officials, which could be conducted without
any of them asserting a formal superiority over the rest.
But it is clear that in such conferences the representative of
the great mass of the University must have been from the
first the most conspicuous and important figure. The
internal organization of the superior Faculties developed
itself much more slowly than that of the Artists. As soon
as there were separate meetings of these Faculties, the
senior Doctor must have enjoyed the right of convoking
them and presiding in them, but it is not till 1264 that we
actually hear of ' Deans ' of the superior Faculties [1]. It is Deans.
not till 1252 that we hear of one of the superior Faculties Statutes
making written Statutes of its own [2]; nor till about 1270 and Seals
that the Faculties of Law and Medicine acquired corporate Faculties.
seals [3]. At first the Deans appear to act rather side by The Rector
side with the Rector than in obedience to his authority: Deans.

---

[1] In 1265 there is a dispute between the Chancellor, who claims to
be the sole head of the Faculty, and
the Theologians, who claim that
' hactenus pacifice observata consuetudine Parisius sit obtentum ut antiquior ex eisdem magistris in actu
regendi nomen decani habeat et in-
dicat festa per nuntium proprium, et
alia faciat que ad suum noscuntur
officium pertinere.' *Chartul.* T. I. pt. i.
No. 399. In 1267 we find Deans of
the other two superior Faculties.
Jourdain, No. 216; *Chartul.* T. I. pt. i.
No. 416. There is a serious error in
the text of Bulæus (III. p. 387). Cf.

Jourdain, No. 327. The Deanship
of Medicine had become elective by
1338 (*Chartul.* T. II. No. 1017.)
The Deanship of Canon Law was
also elective; that of Theology was
always held by the Senior Secular
Doctor.

[2] Bulæus, III. 245; *Chartul.* T. I.
pt. i. No. 200.

[3] The step is complained of as an
innovation by the ever-jealous Chancellor, *circa* 1271 in the case of Law,
in 1274 in the case of Medicine,
Chartul. T. I. pt. i. Nos. 446, 451.
The Faculty of Theology continued
sealless.

though from the first the initiative and superior importance of the Rector is plain enough. During the heat of the great conflict with the Mendicants (1250–1260) which contributed so much to develope the importance of the Rectorship, we hear of no disputes on this head. When the tie of a common enmity was removed, the Superior Faculties seem to have awaked to the fact that they were falling under the authority of an official not elected by themselves. Hence perhaps the attempts to increase their own corporate solidarity by separate Statutes, seals and officers. At about the same time (1279) we find a dispute arising between the Faculty of Arts on the one hand and the Faculties of Canon Law and Medicine on the other as to the manner in which the latter should be summoned to General Congregations[1]. The superior Faculties contended that the Rector was bound to wait in person upon the Deans, who would in turn summon their respective Socie-ties. The Rector on the other hand maintained that he was at liberty to send a Bedel with the summons. A little later (1283–4) we find the Theologians contending that the Rector could only summon them through their Dean 'by way of supplication and request[2].' In both cases the Rector eventually carried the day. The Dean of Theology continued for some time longer to maintain a claim to be consulted before the day was fixed for a General Con-gregation; but both incidents testify to the fact that the Rector's right to summon all the Faculties was by this time practically undisputed. They no doubt point back to a time when 'General Congregations' were summoned rather by arrangement between the Rector and Deans than by the previous summons of the former.

Gradual
emergence
of Rector
into Head
of the
University. We have seen that as early as 1244—that is to say, as early as we have any certain evidence of the existence of a single Rector—he is employed in the execution of the University decrees. In 1255 he is styled by the secular

---

[1] Bulæus, III. 445; *Chartul.* T. I. pt. i. Nos. 490, 493.

[2] 'Supplicando et rogando.' Jour- dain, No. 274 (p. 49 *b*); *Chartul.* T. I. pt. i. No. 515.

Masters of all Faculties 'Rector of our University[1].' In 1259 he is addressed by the Pope as 'Rector of the University' and required to enforce payment of a debt incurred in the name of the whole University[2]. In 1276 a deed runs in the name of the Deans of Canon Law and Medicine and the Rector and Proctors of the Nations (mentioned in that order) 'by the assent and consent of all the Masters Regent at Paris in the aforesaid Faculties and in Arts[3].' The eight Masters of Theology assent as individuals, their names being recited at the end of the deed. In 1289 we find the Rector mentioned before the 'Deans of Faculties, the Proctors of the Nations and the Masters of the four Faculties[4].' It has seemed worth while to enumerate these facts because they will enable the reader to observe for himself the gradual steps by which the Rector emerged from an undefined initiative or presidency to an acknowledged Headship of the whole University. It is really impossible to say at what exact date the Rector may be considered to have attained this position. He was from the first the executive officer, and the only executive officer, of the whole University. By about the decade 1280–1290 he had unquestionably attained the Presidency if not the formal Headship of the whole Society, and the Faculty of Arts was already endeavouring to convert that Presidency into a formal and acknowledged Headship. It was not, as we shall see, until the middle of the following century that these efforts were crowned with entire success. One of the means by which the Faculty endeavoured to effect their object is of especial interest and constitutional importance.

The oath administered to a Bachelor of the Faculty of Arts upon his Determination had at first bound him to obey the Rector only ' as long as he should profess the Faculty

The oath *ad quem-cumque statum,* c. 1280.

---

[1] Bulæus, III. p. 257; *Chartul.* T. I. pt. i. No. 230.

[2] Jourdain, No. 184; *Chartul.* T. I. pt. i. No. 330.

[3] Jourdain, No. 216; *Chartul.* T. I. pt. i. No. 416.

[4] *Chartul.* T. II. No. 559.

of Arts[1].' About the year 1256 or earlier it would seem
that this last clause was omitted; and the oath to 'obey the
liberties and honest customs of the Faculty' was supplemented by the words 'to whatever state you shall come[2].'
Sooner or later similar words were added to an explicit
oath of obedience to the Rector, thus making the subjection of every member of the Faculty of Arts to that official
permanent and unalterable[3]. As at least the vast majority
of the Secular Masters of all Faculties had taken the oath[4],
the ingenious change practically secured the supremacy of
the Rector over the whole University. If in a certain
technical sense the Rector was still the Head of the Artists
only, the members of the superior faculties were henceforth
extraordinary or Non-Regent members of the Faculty
of Arts. Hence there could be no question about the
Rector's right to summon them to Congregations, to enforce
against them the decrees of the whole University, and to
declare them 'perjured and rebels' if they disobeyed. The
new oath supplied a much-needed connecting link between
the four Faculties. In time it even made possible the
establishment of the principle that a majority of the
Faculties had the right to override the opposition of one
of them. The Rector, after hearing the decision of the
several Faculties, pronounced in accordance with the
decision of the majority: in other words, he commanded
every individual member of the University to obey the
decision of the whole body. Hence the almost superstitious importance attached to his Rectorial 'conclusion,'

---

[1] 'Item eidem injungatur, quod
per totam quadragesimam et dein-
ceps, quamdiu facultatem arcium
profitebitur in illis studendo vel
regendo, mandato rectoris et procuratoris pareat in licitis et honestis.'
[A. D. 1252.] *Chartul.* T. I. pt. i. No.
201.

[2] 'Item jurabitis, quod libertates
singulas facultatis et consuetudines
facultatis honestas et tocius univer-

sitatis privilegia deffendetis ad quemcunque statum deveneritis.' *Chartul.*
T. I. pt. i. No. 501. This document is
of *circa* 1280.

[3] *Chartul.* T. II. App. No. 1675,
p. 674.

[4] It was by no means the habitual
practice of Canonists to take the
M.A., but most of them would
probably have studied Arts up to
B.A.

which was deemed essential to the legal validity of any CHAP. V,
resolution of the University [1]. The oath of obedience to §1.

[1] A very curious light is thrown upon the nature of the bond which connected the Superior Faculties with the parent body, of which, as I have endeavoured to show, they were offshoots, by a deed of composition between the Faculty of Arts and the Theologians in 1341. The Rector having on one occasion sent a written summons to Congregation to the Dean of Theology by a deputy, the latter refused to summon his Faculty. Thereupon the Faculty of Arts—not the University—expelled the Dean from their Society on the ground that he had acted ' contra jura et libertates Rectorie et per consequens facultatis Artium predicte, contra etiam juramentum ab ipso magistro Simone dicte Facultati Artium olim prestitum temere veniendo.' And the Dean on his part expressly admitted ' quia a magnis temporibus et per magna tempora fuerat et erat juratus dicte Facultatis Artium '; and supplicated the Faculty ' si injuste esset privatus, facere sibi justitiam, et in casu dubii, facere sibi gratiam, et ipsum dicte facultati artium reunire ' (Bulæus, IV. p. 268; *Chartul.* T. II. No. 1051). So in 1451 at a Congregation of the Faculty of Arts, we read that ' vocati fuerunt et comparuerunt multi Magistri de singulis Facultatibus superiorum singularum Facultatum *ad consulendum* ' (Bulæus, V. 560). So on another occasion when a difficulty was experienced in getting a representative of the Theological Faculty to go on an embassy to the King, the University ' volebat in crastino Facultatem Artium Præclaram congregari apud S. Julianum Pauperem solemniter per D. Rectorem, processuram contra eosdem

Magistros nostros [a technical name for Doctors of Divinity], quorum uterque erat Magister Artium, omnibus viis et modis possibilibus, etiam usque ad privationem inclusive ipsorum Magistrorum nostrorum tanquam periurorum, si prædictam Ambassiatam recusarent accipere.' Bulæus, V. p. 583.

Denifle holds that the Rector was not recognized as the head of the Faculty of Arts till 1274 (pp. 110, 119, 120), or as the Head of the University till the middle of the fourteenth century. I have not space to examine his arguments in detail, but the contention rests mainly on the fact that the Rector's name is not mentioned in the enacting clause of the Statutes of the Faculty till 1274, or in those of the University till 1338 (pp. 109, 110). Denifle relies upon the analogy of Oxford and other Universities; but, though there was never any doubt as to the Chancellor being Head of the University of Oxford, the Statutes, &c., by no means uniformly run in the name of the Chancellor and University. Besides, in 1309 Clement V. does speak of a suit as being the suit of the Rector and University. Jourdain, No. 385: and in 1327 a Statute is ' facta per venerabilem et discretum virum M. Joannem Buridam Rectorem Vniversitatis supradicte.' (Bulæus, IV. p. 212; *Chartul.* T. II. No. 870.) Denifle further alleges (p. 121) that the Rector cannot have been considered Head of the University in 1283 or 1284, since the Faculty of Arts at that time declares that the Pope was Head of the University. This is inaccurate. What the Faculty says is that ' Parisiensis universitas non

CHAP. V,
§ 1.
——◆——
His
Headship
generally
if not
universally
admitted.

the Rector was the key-stone of the Academic constitution[1].

From this time at least, there could be no doubt about the
Rector's position as virtual Head of the whole corporation.
As a constitutional technicality it might be maintained, and
no doubt was maintained by the Theological Faculty and
especially by the sworn enemies of the Faculty of Arts,
the Dominican Theologians, that the Rector was not the
Head of the University, as is still maintained with much
earnestness by the learned Dominican who has thrown so
much light upon the history of the medieval Universities.
The fact that the precedence of the Rector at ecclesiastical
functions was till the middle of the following century dis-

credit nec confitetur *secundum
suum rectorem* habere caput aliud
a Vestra Sanctitate' (Jourdain, No.
274), or according to Denifle's reading, ' supra rectorem suum' (*Chartul.*
T. I. pt. i. No. 515). The words
distinctly imply that the Rector
was Head of the University. What
they deny is the Headship of the
Chancellor. Moreover, it is useless
for Denifle to explain that in 1261
'rector universitatis' means 'rector
universitatis artistarum,' when as
early as 1255 we find the secular
Masters of all Faculties speaking of the Rector as 'rectorem
universitatis nostre.' Another good
instance of his recognition occurs in
1278, when the King enjoined that
the candidate selected by the University for a Chaplaincy in its gift
should be presented by the Rector
(*Chartul.* T. I. pt. i. No. 482). Father
Denifle hardly realises that the question whether the Rector was or was
not ' Head' of the University is one
which might have been answered
differently by different persons at
the same time. I admit that the
Rector's Headship was not formally placed beyond dispute till the
middle of the fourteenth century.

But Denifle's treatment of the subject obscures the fact that his *virtual*
Headship was established, and his
formal Headship persistently asserted by the Faculty of Arts, at a
much earlier date.

Denifle's contention that the
Rector was not Head of the
Faculty of Arts, but only of the
Nations, till 1274, rests on the
same inadequate ground as his contention with respect to the University—i. e. that his name does not
appear in the Acts of the Faculty.
The fact that, when the University
proclaimed its own dissolution in
1255, it sealed the deed with the
seals of the four Nations, 'utpote
ab universitatis Collegio separati,'
at most goes to establish a distinction between the Nations and the
University, not between the Nations
and the Faculty of Arts (below,
p. 381).

[1] It was probably on this account
that we find it alleged that the
Faculty of Arts can expel from the
University, while the Superior Faculties cannot expel even from their
own 'consortium' without the consent of the University. *Chartul.* T. II.
No. 930.

puted by the Dean of Theology—often, it must be remembered, a Bishop or Archbishop—proves little against his virtual Headship. An officer who summons the meetings of a Society, whom every member of the Society is bound to obey, and who executes its decrees, is for practical purposes the Head or at least the President of that Society. In the English House of Lords the Royal Dukes and the Archbishop of Canterbury take precedence of the Lord Chancellor; but he is the unquestioned President of that House, though his very limited powers in that capacity supply but an incomplete analogy to the Rector's importance in the University Congregations.

Another circumstance which tends to explain the facility with which the Faculty of Arts managed to thrust their Rector into the position of Head of the whole University is the peculiarly close relation in which the most important and, in a sense, most ancient of the superior Faculties stood to the Chancellor. As late as 1264 the Chancellor is found claiming to be *ex officio* Dean of the Theological Faculty[1]; and, though this claim is denied by the Masters, it is certain that there must have been a time when they had no Head other than the Chancellor. The Chancellor was himself originally chief Theological teacher of the Cathedral School; and not only the Chancellor but the Canons of Paris long retained the right of teaching Theology and Canon Law without any authorisation from the Faculties[2]. The Chancellor was thus the natural Head of the Theological Faculty in its relations to the Bishop of the Diocese and to the Church at large. The earliest recorded instances of the corporate action of the Theo-

Dependence of Theological Faculties on the Chancellor.

---

[1] *Chartul.* T. I. pt. i. No. 399.

[2] Thus the Canons of Paris are specially exempted from the privileges conferred upon other Masters and Scholars by the Charter of Philip Augustus in 1200, on the ground that they have special privileges of their own as Canons. Bulæus, III. p. 3 (who has a 'volumus'

for 'nolumus'); *Chartul.* I. pt. i. No. 1. Their position as Canons of course originally gave them no rights in the University; but in 1384 Canons teaching Theology or Decrees were granted the rights of 'Regency' by the Avignon Pope, Clement VII (Bulæus, I. 280).

logical Faculty are occasions on which it was formally asked for its decision on a theological question, or when its members were called upon to meet as the Assessors of the Bishop in a trial for heresy[1]. On such occasions, even after the University had completely shaken off the yoke of the capitular official, and the Theological Faculty had acquired a Dean of its own, the Chancellor continued to preside over the deliberations of the Theological Doctors. But it was clearly impossible for the Chancellor to act as the Head and representative of the Faculty in its relations with the Masters of the other Faculties. Of the Guild of Masters, the Chancellor was not necessarily even a member; much of the early corporate activity of both Faculty and University directly grew out of resistance to his pretensions. Thus the Faculty was for a time left without a Head at all in its relations to the other Masters: and even when a Dean of Theology was appointed his position was weakened by the rival claims of the Chancellor.

The extra-Academical Chancellorship explains anomalous position.

It was this extra-Academical position of the Chancellor which prevented him becoming, like the Chancellor of Oxford, the Head of the Magisterial Guild[2]. At the same time the close connexion between the Chancellor and the Theological Faculty long prevented the latter acquiring a Head who might have taken that position in the University organization which would naturally have been accorded to the Head of what always ranked as the first among the Faculties of Paris. The position in which that Faculty was placed by its peculiar relations with the extra-Academic Chancellor thus explains that singular and otherwise unintelligible feature of the Parisian constitution by which the Headship of the whole University was vested in an officer elected exclusively by and from the 'inferior' Faculty of Arts.

---

[1] For early instances, see Bulæus, II. p. 411 (1174 A.D.); III. p. 249; *Chartul.* T. I. pt. i. No. 216. We find the Theological Doctors acting as the assessors of the Bishop in a case of heresy in 124$\frac{6}{7}$. (Jourdain, No. 59; *Chartul.* T. I. pt. i. No. 128.)

[2] In 1385 the University resolved 'quod ipse Cancellarius Parisiensis nec est caput Universitatis *nec alicuius Facultatis*.' Bulæus, *Remarques sur la dignité, &c., du Recteur*, pp. 7, 8.

IV. *The Great Dispersion and the Papal Privileges.*

The University, as we have already seen and we shall have frequent occasion to observe, lived upon its misfortunes. The 'Town and Gown' disturbance of 1200 procured its first Charter from the Crown: the oppression of the Chancellor produced its first batch of Papal privileges. The third era in the growth of its privileges is introduced like the first by a tavern brawl: but this time the quarrel brought it into collision not merely with the citizens or the Chapter, but with the Monarchy itself. Its eventual triumph over Court and Capital united shows that a new force had been introduced into the political system of Europe—that a new order had arisen who were to share the influence hitherto monopolized by nobles and Priests.

Chap. V, § 1.
Profit- able mis- fortunes.

During the Carnival of $122\frac{8}{9}$ some students were taking the air in a suburban region known as the Bourg of S. Marcel, when they entered a tavern and 'by chance found good and sweet wine there[1].' A dispute arose with the landlord over the reckoning. From words the disputants rapidly proceeded to blows—to pulling of ears and tearing of hair[2]. The worsted inn-keeper called in his neighbours, who compelled the clerks to retire severely beaten. The next day they returned with strong reinforcements of gownsmen armed with swords and sticks, who broke into the tavern, avenged their comrades on the host and his neighbours, set the taps running, and then 'flown with insolence and wine' sallied forth into the streets to amuse themselves at the expense of peaceable citizens, men and women alike, in the fashion now in favour only with the lowest roughs in

Carnival Riot of $122\frac{8}{9}$.

---

[1] 'Invenerunt ibi casu vinum optimum in taberna quadam et ad bibendum suave.' Matt. Paris, *Hist. Maj.* ed. Luard, III. 166.

[2] 'Alapas dare et capillos laniare.' Matt. Paris, *l. c.*

CHAP. V,
§ I.

the lowest quarters of London and Liverpool. So the ecclesiastics continued to disport themselves until the tables were once more turned in favour of ' Town' by the appearance on the scene of the Provost and his satellites—the savage police of a savage city. The Prior of S. Marcel had complained to the Papal Legate and to the Bishop, who had urged upon the Queen, Blanche of Castille, the instant suppression of the riot. The Queen 'with female impulsiveness' (as Matthew Paris has it) rashly ordered the Provost and the mercenary body-guard (*Ruptarii*) to punish the authors of the outrages. The soldiers fell upon the offenders or (if we may trust our historian) a party of perfectly innocent students engaged in their holiday games outside the walls ; and several of them were killed in the ensuing *mêlée*.

Suspension
of Lectures.

The Masters, availing themselves of the singular mode of protest expressly conceded to them by Royal authority, suspended their Lectures. But complaints to the Bishop and Legate were alike in vain. We may judge of the strength of the feeling against the University on the part of the Bishop and Church of Paris by the fact that in an age when under ordinary circumstances the slightest insult to a 'clerk' was thought adequate cause for wholesale excommunication or interdict, the murder of a number of students by a brutal soldiery was welcomed by their official superiors as tending to the humiliation of the upstart University. The Court was much under clerical influence, and was particularly attached to the special enemies of the University, the Canons of Paris. And in this one instance the Legate took the same side : it was but four years since he had been mobbed on account of his conduct in the matter of the University seal[1].

---

[1] The fullest account of the affair is given by Matt. Paris, *Hist. Maj.* III. pp. 166–8. Bernardus, *Chron.* (ap. Raynaldus, T. XIII. p. 401), says: 'Anno Domini . . MCCXXIX facta fuit Parisius inter Scholares dissensio, quam mox secuta est ad tempus multifaria dispersio, alii quidem Rhemis, alii Andegauis, alii Aurelianis, alii in Angliam, alii in Italiam, vel in Hispaniam . . . multi quoque Magistri et Scholares Tolosam venerunt et rexerunt ibidem.' So Albricus, *Chron.* (ap. Pertz, *SS.* XXIII. p. 923) : 'Guerra pessima nimis et crudelis orta est Parisiis intrante quadragesima inter

Finding the 'Cessation' ineffectual, the Masters on the Easter Monday following [1] proceeded to a more extreme remedy. They resolved that, if justice were not done them within a month, they would dissolve the University for a period of six years, and would not return even at the expiration of that period unless satisfactory redress had been granted in the interval [2]. And the Masters were as good as their word. The great mass of the Masters and scholars left Paris. Many of them no doubt accepted the pressing invitation of Henry III of England, crossed the channel, and reinforced the rising Universities of Oxford and Cambridge [3]. Others retired to the smaller Studia Generalia or Cathedral Schools of France—Toulouse, Orleans, Reims, and especially Angers which perhaps dates its existence as a University from this dispersion. Here they could pursue their studies at their own discretion, without interference from either civil or ecclesiastical authority. The prestige of the Paris Masters was so high that at Angers they could even venture to grant licenses on their own authority, without the sanction of Bishop or Chancellor [4].

Though the individual Legate was hostile to the University, his master, Pope Gregory IX, showed no signs of

clericos et laycos satis pro nichilo... Paucis remanentibus in civitate, exierunt omnes alii, maxime eminentiores magistri.' Cf. also *Chron. Simonis Montisfortis*, ap. Duchesne, *Hist. Franc. SS.* V. p. 778; *Annales Monast.* (Dunstable) ed. Luard, III. p. 117; *Chronicon Fiscamnense* (Migne, T. 147. cc. 482, 483) Guill. de Nangis, *Chron.* ap. Bouquet, T. XX. p. 546; John de Oxenedes, *Chronica*, ed. Ellis, 1859, p. 157. It would appear from the *Annales Stadenses*, ap. Pertz, *SS.* XVI. p. 360, that the chief migration was to Angers: 'ita ut studium in Andegaviam transferretur.' So Matt. Paris, *l. c.*: 'Quorum tamen maxima pars civitatem Andegavensium metropolitanam ad doctrinam elegit universalem:' and below,

p. 372 *n.* According to Ralph of Coggeshall, 320 clerks were thrown into the Seine (ed. Stevenson, London, 1875, p. 192). Cf. also Bouquet, T. XXI, pp. 3, 214, 599, 695, 764.

[1] March 27, 1229.

[2] Jourdain, No. 30; *Chartul.* T. I. pt. i. No. 62.

[3] Bulæus, III. p. 133; *Chartul.* T. I. pt. i. No. 64 (original in Public Record Office, 13 Hen. III. m. t.). An invitation was also received from the Duke of Brittany to transfer the Studium to Nantes. John of S. Victor, ap. Bulæum, III. p. 555.

[4] The Licenses afterwards received an *ex post facto* validation by Papal Bull. Bulæus, III. p. 146; *Chartul.* T. I. pt. i. No. 89.

CHAP. V, abandoning his *protégé*; he peremptorily required the King
§ 1. and the Queen-mother to punish the offenders, and recalled
the obnoxious legate, Romano Cardinal of S. Angelo [1].
What redress exactly was granted to the Masters, or when,
we are not able precisely to say [2]. At last, however, the
Court was seriously alarmed at the loss of the prestige and
of the commercial prosperity which the capital derived from
its scholastic population. It would appear that the dispersion continued throughout the years 1229 and 1230.
During the whole of this interval, and for some time afterwards, the agents of the University were busily engaged at
the Roman Court extracting Bulls and privileges on behalf
The Re- of their clients [3]. It is not till the beginning of 1231 that
turn, 1231. we find the Masters and scholars at work again in their old
quarters. The heroic remedy of a dispersion had not been
applied in vain. Not only the particular grievance which
had immediately provoked it, but others which had no
doubt contributed to the disaster now met with effectual
redress. To the month of April 1231 belong Bulls for the
punishment of the outrages at S. Marcel, Bulls requiring
the King to enforce the privilege of Philip Augustus and to
allow the rents of the Scholars' Halls or Hostels to be
'taxed' (as at Bologna) by two Masters and two burghers;
Bulls to the Abbot of S. Germain-des-Prés and to the Bishop
requiring respect for the University privileges within their
secular jurisdictions [4]; most important of all, the great

[1] Bulæus, III. 135; *Chartul.* T. I.
pt. i. No. 71.

[2] 'Tandem procurantibus discretis
personis, elaboratum est, ut factis
quibusdam pro tempore exigentibus
utrobique culpis, pax est clero et
civibus reformata, et scolarium universitas revocata.' Matt. Paris, *Hist.
Maj.* III. p. 169. The date is given
more exactly by Albricus (*l. c.*):
'tandem infra triennium reversi sunt
quicumque voluerunt, omnibus sedi-
tionibus pacificatis.'

[3] It appears that one Master, Wil-

liam of Auxerre, was accredited by
the King (*Chartul.* T. I. pt. i. No. 74)
at the command of the Pope; Alexander, and afterwards Geoffrey of
Poitou, were despatched by the Masters at Angers (*ib.* Nos. 75, 88, 90).
The various privileges to be mentioned are marked with the name of
the Masters at whose instance they
were granted: many of them bear
the name of William, the King's
envoy.

[4] Bulæus, III. 144 *sq.*; *Chartul.* T.
I. pt. i. Nos. 81–88.

Charter of Privilege which Father Denifle has justly called the *Magna Charta* of the University. By the Bull *Parens Scientiarum* the University received Apostolical sanction for its great engine of warfare, the right of suspending lectures, in case satisfaction for an outrage were refused after fifteen days' notice, and for its authority to make Statutes and punish the breach of them by exclusion from the Society[1]. At the same time a new set of shackles was forged for the Chancellor, and even on some points for the Bishop himself. Every new Chancellor is to be required before installation to swear to be impartial in the conduct of Examinations, and not to reveal the votes of the examining Masters. The Bishop is required to be moderate in the exercise of his jurisdiction over scholars; he is forbidden to have innocent scholars arrested instead of the guilty (a significant indication of the way in which godly discipline had heretofore been administered at Paris), to imprison for debt or to impose pecuniary penances. The Chancellor is forbidden to have a prison at all; scholars are to be imprisoned in the Bishop's prison only, and bail is to be allowed in all cases[2]. The effect of this measure would seem to be to destroy the Chancellor's criminal jurisdiction altogether. How far he still retained a civil and spiritual jurisdiction would appear to have remained a matter of dispute till late in the century[3],

---

[1] Bulæus, III. 140; *Chartul.* T. I. pt. i. No. 79. Denifle (i. p. 73) declares that this Bull recognizes the power of *each Faculty* to make Statutes. But of this I see no trace: the power is conferred 'vobis,' i.e. on the Masters generally. Cf. also *Chartul.* T. I. pt. i. No. 61.

[2] 'Quod si forte tale crimen commiserit quod incarceratione sit opus, Episcopus culpabilem in carcere detinebit, Cancellario habere proprium carcerem penitus interdicto.'

[3] From the long indictment against the Chancellor, Philip de Thori, in 1283-4 (Jourdain, No. 274; *Chartul.* T. I. pt. i. No. 515), it appears that scholars were still in the habit of citing one another before the Chancellor, but that the University had forbidden the practice. They deny his jurisdiction, and contend that 'Cancellarius Parisiensis non est judex ordinarius scholarium, nec delegatus; et ideo unus de ipsis non debebat facere alterum convenire coram cancellario, nec conveniri coram eodem.' Among the almost equally formidable array of grievances presented against another Chancellor in 1290 (Jourdain, No. 302; *Chartul.* T. II. No. 569) we find no allegation of judicial usurpation or oppression. Hence we may perhaps assume that the Chancellor's jurisdiction began to fall into desuetude at about this time.

after which almost all traces of his strictly judicial authority disappear except in so far as is implied by the exercise of certain faculties entrusted to him from time to time by special delegation from the Holy See[1]. Of these the most important was the power of absolving scholars who had incurred *ipso facto* excommunication for violence upon clerks. This being a *casus papalis*, it would otherwise have been necessary for every boy who inflicted a scratch upon another in the course of his academical career, to undertake a journey to Rome before he could get absolution. The disciplinary power of depriving a Master of his license would seem to have remained in theory but to have gradually become obsolete, though the Chancellor retained the right of depriving scholars of 'Scholarity' with its attendant privileges for carrying arms or the like, and of excommunicating 'vagabond, truant and incorrigible scholars[2].'

The License.

In regard to the most important of all the matters in dispute between the Masters and the Chancellor, the conferment of the License, the Bull of Gregory IX seems somewhat less favourable to the Masters than the Statutes already in force. The Chancellor is merely bound to consult the Masters before conferring a License, and to swear upon admission to his office to exercise his powers 'in good faith according to his conscience,' whereas formerly he was bound to grant a License whenever it was demanded by a majority of the Faculty or Examiners[3]. The previous Statutes are

[1] E. g. by Innocent IV in 1252 (Bulæus, III. 244; *Chartul.* T. I. pt. i. No. 215). So he is required to enforce the Papal regulations as to the taxation of Halls by Innocent IV in 1244 (Bulæus, III. 196; *Chartul.* I. pt. i. No. 138); and 1252 (Jourdain, No. 92; *Chartul.* T. I. pt. i. No. 203). But this power was of course derived entirely from the special delegation of the Holy See, and was conferred only for a term of years. At other times we find other ecclesiastics not specially connected with the University entrusted with similar powers,

e. g. the Abbot of S. Victor in 1212 (Bulæus, III. 63; *Chartul.* T. I. pt. i. No. 15), or the Prior of the Cistercian House at Paris in 126⅔ (Bulæus, III. 370; *Chartul.* T. I. pt. i. No. 379, &c.).

[2] Goulet, f. viii. *b.* He is silent as to the power to unlicense Masters.

[3] Jourdain, No. 15 ; *Chartul.* T. I. pt. i. No. 16. It is true that this restriction was only laid upon the Chancellor then in office. In 1331-3 there was a great quarrel between the Chancellor and the Faculty of Medicine, in the course of which

neither expressly confirmed nor expressly repealed : and
the ambiguity in which the matter was left naturally gave
ample scope for misconception and litigation. The issue
between the Chancellor and the University was not finally
fought out till towards the close of the century.

It was a fact of immense importance to the University in
these struggles with the Chancellor of Paris that there was
another source from which the Masters could obtain their
licentia docendi. Whether or not any continuity can be
established with the Schools of the 'Mount' which were
so flourishing in the days of Abelard and his successors, is
a somewhat doubtful point. There can, however, be no
doubt that at the end of the twelfth century the Schools of
the Masters were for the most part situated in the narrow
and overcrowded Island round the Cathedral[1], and (even
if there were Masters teaching at Ste. Geneviève) there is no
trace of any other License than that of the Cathedral Chancellor. Early in the thirteenth century, however, Masters
began to recross the river, and to open schools in the southern
suburb recently enclosed within the City-walls by Philip
Augustus and only now beginning to be built over. By
this measure they placed themselves outside the jurisdiction
of the Cathedral Chancellor, who accordingly attempted to
bind the Masters by oath to teach only 'between the two
bridges[2].' This imposition was forbidden in 1227 by Gregory IX, who recognized the right of the Abbot and
Canons of Ste. Geneviève to license Masters of Theology,

The Chancellor of Ste. Geneviève.

the Chancellor's Official excommunicated the Masters. *Chartul.* T. II.
Nos. 930, 930 *a*, &c. This was evidently at that time an unwonted exercise of authority. The Masters do
not categorically deny his jurisdiction, but contend that if he has any,
he has it 'tanquam subdictus . . .
Parisiensi [episcopo],' to whom
they appeal. On the other side it
is alleged that the punishment of
offences 'circa actum scolasticum'
belongs to him, 'tam de jure quam
de usu, stilo *et privilegiis sedis apos-*

tolice.' (*l. c.* No. 931.) It appears
that he still demanded an oath to
respect the privileges of his office
(No. 937), though the Faculty deny
his right to do so. No permanent
settlement of the matters in dispute
seems to have been arrived at.

[1] See above, p. 279.

[2] 'Ad regendum inter duos Pon-
tes.' Bulæus, III. 124–5 ; *Chartul.*
T. I. pt. i. No. 55. Denifle identifies
this oath with the oath of obedience
to the Chancellor, of which we hear
so much from 1210 onwards.

Canon Law and Arts to teach within their jurisdiction [1]. As a matter of fact, however, the permission was never taken advantage of except by the Faculty of Arts [2]. The Arts Schools gradually transferred themselves to the *Rue du Fouarre* (*Vicus Stramineus*), so called from the straw-strewn floors of the Schools—in the region which is still known as the *Quartier Latin*, and is still the haunt of Parisian students. Candidates for the License in Arts could now obtain it either at the Cathedral or at the Abbey. If attempts at extortion were made by the Cathedral, they had the remedy in their own hands. The Faculty could even (in the event of a dispute with the Chancellor of Paris), direct all its students to apply for Licenses only at Ste. Geneviève [3]. At first the Licenses at Ste. Geneviève were granted by the Abbot; in 1255 we find an Abbey Chancellorship established [4], in imitation of the office so called at Notre Dame, the Chancellor being a Canon nominated by the Abbot with the approval of the Faculty. The existence of *two* Chancellors ought by itself to have prevented English writers from identifying the position of the Cathedral Chancellor (whom they persist, in defiance of medieval usage, in styling 'Chancellor of the University') [5] with that of the Chancellor of Oxford or Cambridge.

[1] Bulæus, I. 274; *Chartul.* T. I. pt. i. No. 55. The Pope had already recognized *pendente lite* the rights of licentiates of Ste. Geneviève in 1222 : ' nec episcopus et officialis ac cancellarius memorati licentiatos ab . . . abbate Sancte Genovefe quin ubi consueverint libere incipere valeant interim molestabunt.' Bouquet, T. XIX. p. 725; *Chartul.* T. I. pt. i. No. 45.

[2] Bulæus (III. 464) declares that Licenses in the Superior Faculties were granted by Ste. Geneviève during the quarrel with the Parisian Chancellor in 1281-4, but seems to be unsupported by the documents. The Cathedral Chancellor's jealousy of Ste. Geneviève is illustrated by the mutual recriminations in the suit of 1283-4 (Jourdain, p. 44 *b*, 45 *a*; *Chartul.* T. I. pt. i. No. 515). The Chancellor of Paris alleges ' quod vix potest aliquis obtinere licentiam ex parte Sancte Genovephe, nisi pecunia mediante '—a libel for which the Faculty of Arts lay the damages at 1000 golden marks.

[3] Bulæus, III. 501; *Chartul.* T. II. No. 579.

[4] Bulæus, III. 293; *Chartul.* T. I. pt. i. No. 260.

[5] In the Middle Ages he is always ' Cancellarius Ecclesiæ Parisiensis ' or ' Cancellarius B. Mariæ ' or ' Cancellarius Parisiensis.' *Chartul.* I. pt. i. No. 142.

We have already several times noticed by anticipation the influence of the great dispute with the Mendicants upon the development and consolidation of the University constitution. The history of this conflict is of so much importance in itself and throws so much light upon the real nature and constitutional theory of the University that it demands a section to itself. But before we leave this period of our history it may be well to mention the grant of a privilege which became henceforth *the* characteristic University privilege, not only of Paris but of all Universities which were in any degree influenced by Parisian usage— the *jus non trahi extra* or *privilegium fori* by which (in order to prevent the interruption of studies) students were exempted from citation to Courts at a distance from Paris[1]. This privilege the University obtained in 1245 from Innocent IV in so far as regards ecclesiastical jurisdiction[2]: and it was afterwards granted by the King in respect of civil matters[3].

Jus non trahi extra.

A year later the Pope entrusted to the Archbishop of Reims and the Bishop and Dean of Senlis a general power of protecting the University from molestation and securing respect for privilege by ecclesiastical censure[4]. In these Bulls of Innocent IV must be sought the origin of the very extensive jurisdiction rapidly accumulated by the Apostolic Conservator. Though in form a temporary and extraordinary Commission (like the *conservatorium* commonly attached to all Papal Bulls of privilege), the business which the exemption of the University from other tribunals and the protection of its extensive privileges brought before the Conservator was so great that a regular 'Court of Conservation' sat periodically in the Mathurine Convent, which ere long developed such a host of extortionate officials that

The Conservator Apostolic.

---

[1] I. e. by Papal delegates under Apostolic letters, 'nisi expressam de indulgentia huiusmodi fecerint mentionem.' *Chartul.* T. I. pt. i. No. 142.

[2] *Chartul.* T. I. pt. i. No. 142.

[3] See below, p. 412.

[4] *Chartul.* T. I. pt. i. No. 163. The Bull ran only for seven years, but was renewed from time to time. For the growth of the jurisdiction, cf. *ib.* Nos. 377, 391.

the University was forced to seek protection against its own protectors and procure Bulls from Rome to rectify the abuses of this tribunal[1]. The University, or rather the Faculty of Arts, early obtained the right of electing the Conservator, though by law or custom obliged to elect the Bishop of one of three Sees in the neighbourhood of Paris —Meaux, Senlis, and Beauvais[2].

[1] Bulæus, IV. 206; *Chartul.* T. II. No. 841.

[2] There is an allusion to the election of a Conservator by the Nations in 1266 (Bulæus, III. p. 378; *Chartul.* T. I. pt. i. No. 407). Clement V, in 1308, made the Bishops of Meaux, Senlis, and Beauvais Conservators (Bulæus, IV. p. 113, but there must be reasons for its omission from the Chartularium); but later we find the University electing one or other of these prelates. *Ib.* V. pp. 653, 654, 778; *Remarques sur la dignité du Recteur,* p. 17.

§ 2. The Mendicants and the University.

An interesting Monograph on *Les Dominicaines dans l'Université de Paris* has been written by the Abbé Eugène Bernard (Paris, 1883), which, however, throws no special light on the constitutional growth of the University. The *Scriptores Ordinis Predicatorum* (Lutetiae Parisiorum, 1719) of Quétif and Echard, is here of great value; also *Chronica Fr. Salimbene Parmensis*, Parma, 1857 (in *Mon. Hist. ad prov. Parmensem et Placentinam pertinentia*). Great light has been thrown upon the subject, and indeed upon many other points of University history, by the publication of the *Lettres de B. Jourdain de Saxe*, 1865, ed. Bayonne. The writings of Gulielmus de Sancto Amore I have consulted in the edition printed at Constance in 1632. The case of the Mendicants is stated by Thomas Aquinas, *Contra impugnantes religionem* (*Opera*, Antverpiæ, 1612, T. XVII. p. 127), and Bonaventura (*Opera*, Romæ, 1688, VII. p. 373 *sq.*). The edition of Albertus Magnus which I have cited is that printed at Lyons in 1657. For modern writers on the philosophical aspects of the subject, see above, pp. 21, 22.

I. *The Intellectual Revolution.*

In the age which preceded the rise of the Universities the Monks were the great educators of Europe. A revival of monastic life—a return to some nearer approach to the old Benedictine ideal—was one of the signs of that great revival of ecclesiastical activity which the twelfth century ushered in. But it was in the nature of things that every revival of Monasticism should carry in itself the seeds of renewed corruption. A revival of monastic life meant an increase of wealth, of influence and of ecclesiastical independence for the great Convents. By the twelfth century the old Benedictine and Cluniac Monasteries had for the most part sunk into rich corporations of celibate landed proprietors, whose highest ambition was the aggrandisement of the House to which they belonged. Even the reforms initiated by Bernard and Norbert were transitory : the new orders of Cîteaux and Pré-

montré[1], though they professed a stricter asceticism and
more primitive simplicity than the ordinary Benedictine
Houses, had no prominent intellectual or educational aims.
On the contrary the tendency of the monastic reformers of
the twelfth century was distinctly hostile to the more intellectual side of the old monastic ideal. The 'external'
Schools which the Carolingian age had introduced were
found to interfere with the discipline of the cloister: and in
the course of the twelfth century the Monasteries ceased to
be, to any considerable extent, places of higher education
for the secular clergy. Anselm of Bec was the last of the
great monastic teachers[2]. Among the many educational
changes of the century none is more important than the
transference of educational activity from the regular to the
secular clergy. It was, as we have seen, the Cathedral
Schools which formed in Northern Europe the germ of the
Universities. To those who are fond of speculating on the
'might have beens' of History, it were an interesting question to ask what would have been the consequences to the
intellectual development of Europe, had the University
Faculties of Theology remained as exclusively in the hands
of the secular clergy as was the case at the beginning of the
thirteenth century.

New
monastic
Ideal of
Francis and
Dominic.
　　　Just at this crisis in the intellectual history of Europe,
two great minds, S. Francis and S. Dominic, conceived
almost independently and almost simultaneously a wholly
new ideal of monastic perfection[3]. The educational and
social usefulness of the older Orders had been, it may be
said, almost accidental. Study or labour were enjoined

---

[1] Technically the Premonstra-
tensians were Canons Regular,
not Monks, but the Canon
Regular, as much as the Monks,
belonged to the old class of Religious grouped together as *posses-
sionati.*

[2] Unless, indeed, we except the
School of S. Victor. But the Canons
Regular of S. Victor did not (after

this period) teach Seculars. See
above, p. 278.

[3] S. Dominic was himself a Pre-
monstratensian, and his brethren
were long regarded as Canons Regular; but this does not much affect
his originality. See Denifle, *Archiv,* I.
p. 169. Still the Regular Canons
were a link between the Monks and
the Friars.

upon the monk rather as a means of fighting against the
evil passions of his own heart than as a means of bringing
the world into subjection to the Gospel or to the Church.
Monks had become teachers only because there were no
other teachers to be had : Monasteries had become houses
of learning only because learning had become impossible
outside them : it was inevitable that the intellectual light
which the Monasteries communicated should wane with
the diffusion of intellectual light in the outside world.
Every advance of civilization diminished the value of the
Monasteries as civilizing agencies. The ideal of the new
monastic orders in the twelfth century was a still more
emphatically non-social ideal than that of their predecessors. The spiritual benefit of the surrounding population may have been no part of the Benedictine Founder's
aim, though it often happened that the foundation of a
Monastery was the foundation of a town. The Cistercians
deliberately turned their backs upon the towns and villages
in search of more absolute seclusion from the world which
they professed to forsake. To the Friars Preachers and the
Friars Minors on the other hand was assigned not a wilder-
ness to be turned by patient labour into a retreat in which
some foretaste of the repose and the worship of Heaven
might be enjoyed by souls weary of earth, but a world to
be Christianized. To the Mendicants the calm, monotonous
round of solemn service was but a subordinate object : the Attitude
end of their existence was the salvation of souls. Like the towards
Education.
great modern order which, when their methods had in
their turn become antiquated, succeeded to their influence
by a still further departure from the old Monastic routine,
the Mendicant Orders early perceived the necessity of
getting a hold upon the centres of education. With the
Dominicans, indeed, this was a primary object : the immediate purpose of their foundation was resistance to the
Albigensian heresy : they aimed at obtaining influence
upon the more educated and more powerful classes.
Hence it was natural that Dominic should have looked
to the Universities as the most suitable recruiting-ground

Chap. V,
§ 2.
The Domi-
nicans
have their
head-
quarters in
Universi-
ties.

for his order: to secure for his Preachers the highest theological training that the age afforded was an essential element of the new monastic ideal. Hence the head-quarters of the Dominicans in Italy were fixed at Bologna[1], in France at Paris, where a colony was established from their first foundation in 1217[2]: in England their first convent was at Oxford. These central houses from the first assumed the form of Colleges[3]: and a Dominican convent was ere long established in every important University town. Jordan of Saxony, the third master of the Order, passed his Lent alternately at Bologna and Paris, preaching to students[4]; at other times he travelled from one University to another, holding missions and enrolling new members. He is never so happy as when he can report the 'capture' of 'famous Masters' or 'good Bachelors.' To get into their own hands the theological teaching of the Universities themselves formed, indeed, no part of their original design, but, when circumstances suggested the attempt, the Dominicans were not slow to avail themselves of the opportunity.

The Franciscan ideal was a less intellectual one. Their Founder was a simple and unintellectual layman: he would have been content that his disciples should have been the same. To him secular if not even theological learning was one of the vanities upon which the fisher of men must turn his back. But, though the Franciscans laboured largely among the neglected poor of crowded and pestilential cities, they too found it practically necessary to go to the Universities for recruits and to secure some theological education for their members. In 1230 the first Franciscan convent was established at Paris, and rivalry with the Dominicans

---

[1] Echard, I. pp. 18, 20, &c.

[2] Echard, I. p. 16; Bernard, p. 89.

[3] Thus in 1220 Honorius III speaks of 'dilectos filios Fratres Prædicatores, in sacra pagina studentes apud Parisius.' *Chartul.* T. I. pt. i. No. 36.

[4] 'Frequentabat ... civitates in quibus vigebat studium; unde Quadragesi mam uno anno Parisius, alio Bononiæ faciebat.' *A. S.* Feb. T. II. p. 726. So again 'totum se dabat ad trahendas bonas personas ad ordinem, et ideo morabatur quasi semper in locis in quibus erant Scholares, et præcipue Parisius.' *Chron. Humberti,* ap. Echard, I. p. 97.

soon made the Minorite friends of the poor almost as conspicuous for intellectual activity as the Dominican champions of the Faith. Other mendicant Orders—Carmelites,
Austin Friars, and some others of less importance—likewise
established convents at Paris and sent their novices to the
Theological Schools, but they played a comparatively small
part in the life of the University[1]; on the other hand the
intellectual history of Europe for the next two hundred
years is intimately bound up with the divergent theological
tendencies of the two great Orders of S. Dominic and S.
Francis.

In spite of their general similarity in aim and constitution, the two orders preserved in a marvellous degree the
stamp impressed upon them by the genius and character of
their respective founders. The Dominican mind and the
Franciscan mind were each of them as clearly marked, as
clearly distinguished from all other ecclesiastical types and
as clearly the reflexion of a founder's individuality as the
Jesuit mind has been for the last three hundred years.
With the Dominican love of souls there was always mingled
a fiery zeal for conservative orthodoxy—an orthodoxy which
the more emotional temper and more democratic sympathies of the Franciscan constantly threatened. The main
lines of Dominican orthodoxy in Philosophy and Theology
were laid down early in their history, and the Order has
remained to this day faithful, as far as external pressure has
permitted, to the teaching of its great Doctors[2]. Fran-
ciscanism all through the Middle Ages was the fruitful
parent of new philosophies and new social movements, of

---

[1] The four Orders above mentioned
had Convents in all scholastic centres, but the two last were always of
secondary importance. The Augus-
tinians were, indeed, more important
in the history of Scholasticism in
Italy, their great theological luminary
being Ægidius Romanus, who,
however, taught at Paris. The
Carmelites possessed considerable
influence in England, which pro-

duced their *Doctor Ordinis*, John
Baconthorp.

[2] Repeated Statutes were passed
by the Chapters General, enforcing
the strictest adherence to Thomist
principles. In 1315 a Bachelor at
Florence was silenced for two years
and given ten days' bread and water
for 'determining' against the Thomist doctrine. *Chartul. Univ. Paris,* T.
II. No. 717 *note.* Cf. No. 676, &c.

new orthodoxies and of new heresies.   At the beginning of
the thirteenth century, however, we find the two Orders
united in the effort to crush or rather to control the prevalent Rationalism.   We have seen the alarm which the
Abelardian spirit of enquiry and discussion inspired in men
like S. Bernard.   But by the time at which we have now
arrived the relations between Theology and Philosophy
were very different from what they had been in the time of
Bernard.   The movement which is associated with the
name of Abelard was of purely Western, purely Latin,
purely Christian origin.   Aristotle had contributed nothing
to the contest but the dialectical weapons with which it was
fought.   In the time of Abelard few, if any, of the writings
of Aristotle were known but the *Categories*[1] and the *De
Interpretatione*, which had been regularly taught in the
Church's Schools since the time of Charles the Great.   In
the generation after Abelard, the whole of the *Organon*,
long since translated by Boethius, came again into general
use in new translations by James of Venice[2] and others :
but there was nothing in the *Organon* to excite the alarm
of Churchmen who did not disapprove of Dialectic altogether.   The heresies which alarmed S. Bernard and the
mystics of S. Victor's were the outgrowth of a spontaneous
revival of intellectual activity within the bosom of the
Church herself.   But the most daring heretics of the twelfth
century never dreamed of assailing the essential truths of
Christianity or even the authority of the Bible or the
formulæ of the Church.   If in Abelard himself there is at
times a suggestion of Protestantism, his pupils did not take
it up; they became the orthodox Prelates and Scholastics
of the next generation.   John of Salisbury, the best representative of the twelfth century Classicism, was the sturdiest
of Churchmen, the counsellor and apologist of Becket
himself.   By the end of the century indeed, the alarm with

---

[1] For a time only the abridgment.
See above, p. 33.

[2] *Circa* 1128; Jourdain, *Recherches*,
p. 58.   Gilbert de la Porrée (†1154)

cites the Prior Analytics : John of
Salisbury had the whole Organon
before him.

which the mere application of Dialectic to Theology had CHAP. V,
been at first regarded had pretty well subsided. On the § 2.
whole the Church had adopted and absorbed into herself
the intellectual movement of the age; the Scholastic
method in the treatment of Theology had triumphed.   Introduc-

At the beginning of the thirteenth century an entirely tion of
new intellectual influence was introduced into the Schools Aristotle.
of the West. In order to understand the nature of that
influence and the channel by which it reached the Schools
of Paris, we must recall for a moment the strange fortunes Aristotle in
of Greek culture in the far East. At the decline of the the East.
Eastern Empire the proverb 'Græcia capta ferum vic-
torem cepit' received a fresh illustration. The despised and
persecuted Nestorians formed the connecting link by which
Hellenic Science and Hellenic Philosophy were transmitted
from the conquerors to the conquered. When the Caliphate was usurped by the Ommiades, the fugitive Abbasid
princes, Abbas and Ali, sojourned among the Nestorians of
Arabia, Mesopotamia, and Western Persia, and from them
acquired a knowledge and a love of Greek Science and
Philosophy. Upon the accession of the Abbasid dynasty
to the Caliphate in 750 A. D., learned Nestorians were summoned to Court. By them Greek books were translated
into Arabic from the original or from Syriac translations[1],
and the foundations laid of Arabic Science and Philosophy.
In the ninth century the School of Bagdad began to flourish,
just when the Schools of Christendom were falling into
decay in the West, and into decrepitude in the East. The
newly-awakened Moslem intellect busied itself at first
chiefly with Mathematics and Medical Science; afterwards
Aristotle threw his spell upon it, and an immense system of
orientalized Aristotelianism was the result. From the East
Moslem learning was carried to Spain; and from Spain
Aristotle re-entered Northern Europe once more, and
revolutionized the intellectual life of Christendom far more

---

[1] Usually direct. Jourdain, *Re-* Averroës were based on the Syriac.
cherches, p. 86. Renan, however, (*Averroès*, p. 51.)
declares that the translations used by

CHAP. V, completely than he had revolutionized the intellectual life
§ 2.   of Islam.

The Arabic   During the course of the twelfth century a struggle had
Philo-   been going on in the bosom of Islam between the Philosophy.
sophers and the Theologians (*Mutakallemin*).   It was just
at the moment when, through the favour of the Caliph
Almansur, the Theologians had succeeded in crushing the
Philosophers, that the torch of Aristotelian thought was
handed on to Christendom.   The history of Arabic Philosophy, which had never succeeded in touching the religious
life of the people, or leaving a permanent stamp upon the
Religion of Mohammed, ends with the death of Averroës in
1198.   The history of Christian Aristotelianism and of the
new Scholastic Theology which was based upon it, begins
just when the history of Arabic Aristotelianism comes
abruptly to a close.   At a much earlier date the Peripatetic
Philosophy in its orientalized form had spread from the
Mosque to the Synagogue, and with far more profound and
Jewish   lasting results; the fact is of importance for our present
Philosophy. enquiry inasmuch as the Jews played a large part in the
transmission of the Græco-Arabic philosophy from Islam
to Christendom.   Among the Arabs Averroës was persecuted as a heretic during his life-time, and was remembered
only as a Physician or a Jurist after his death.   With a
large section of the Jewish community Moses Maimonides
obtained an authority second only to that of his namesake,
the founder of Judaism ; in the Synagogue the Philosophers
on the whole succeeded in holding their own against the
Theologians[1].   The intellectual life of medieval Judaism
was long based upon a Philosophy, the natural tendencies of
which were as frankly opposed to orthodox Theism as those

[1] Renan's (*Averroès*, p. 173 *sq.*)
account of the prevalence of Averroism in the Synagogue may be
balanced by reference to Dr. Neu-
bauer's contribution to the *Hist. Litt.*
XXVII. p. 647 *sq.*   He remarks : ' Il
semble que la pensée de Maïmonide
resta toujours contradictoire, que

Maïmonide théologien et Maïmonide
philosophe furent deux personnes
étrangères l'une à l'autre et qui ne se
mirent jamais d'accord ' (*l. c.* p. 648).
The attempt to introduce Averroism
into Theology by mysticizing the
Old Testament does not seem to
have been made till the fourteenth

of its Arabian sources[1], though here much greater conces-
sions were made to effect a harmony between the philosophical and the religious creed[2]. The destiny of the
orientalized Aristotle in the Christian Church was to be a
very different one alike from his triumph among the Jews
and from his extinction among the Arabs[3].

Soon after the beginning of the thirteenth century
the new Aristotle began to make its appearance in the
Schools of Paris. Before the middle of the same century
Avicenna's († 1111 A.D.) paraphrases or adaptations of the
various Aristotelian treatises—works composed on the same
subjects, with the same titles, preserving the same order
of treatment, and embodying the doctrine of Aristotle
interpreted in accordance with the views of the author
—had been translated into Latin at Toledo by a band
of translators, headed by the Archdeacon Dominic Gondi-
salvi, in the employment of Raymund, Archbishop of

century, when a keen controversy broke out between the Philosophers and the Theologians in Southern France, in which neither party gained a decisive victory.

[1] I have here corrected the somewhat exaggerated impression which Renan (*Averroès,* 173 *sq.,* 191 *sq.*) gives of the unorthodoxy of Maimonides by Ueberweg, I. p. 427, and the E. T. of his chief work, *The Guide of the Perplexed,* by Friedländer (London, 1881). Later Jewish philosophers, such as Levi ben Gerson, were perhaps Averroists pure and simple; but Maimonides himself expressly disclaims belief in the Eternity of the World: he believes creation *ex nihilo* to be unprovable but also unassailable, and accepts it upon the authority of 'the Prophets,' for which he provides a philosophical basis. (Friedländer, I. 285; II. 76, &c.) M. Renan is too prone to assume that theological Liberalism (such as we undoubtedly find in Maimonides and his disciples) must

consciously or unconsciously be Pantheistic or Naturalistic. See also the chapters on Maimonides and his followers in Graetz, *Gesch. d. Juden,* VI (Leipzig, 1871), p. 287 *sq.*: E.T. ed. Löwy, vol. III. p. 460.

[2] It will be unnecessary to remind the student of Philosophy that the Averroistic tendency derived by Jewish Philosophy from the Arabs did not end with the Middle Ages. Spinoza was no philosophical Melchizedek—nor was Hegel.

[3] The Council which condemned Almaric (below, p. 355) speaks of 'libri Aristotelis de naturali philosophia' and the 'Commentaries' thereon (Martène, *Thes. Nov. Anecdot.* T. IV. c. 166). M. Jourdain's opinion (*Recherches,* p. 197) that the works of Avicenna and Algazel are meant is based upon the character of the doctrines ascribed to Almaric and David de Dinant. He even thinks that the study of the true Aristotle was pursued largely with a view to find weapons to combat the

CHAP. V,
§ 2.

Seville. And it has been maintained, though without sufficient ground, that the first works bearing the name of
Aristotle which reached the Schools of Paris were these
translated Paraphrases of Avicenna, and not actual Translations. But in any case the earliest translations of
Aristotle were made from the Arabic. Aristotle thus came
to Paris in an orientalized dress; and that was not all. He
was accompanied or followed by Arabic commentators
and by independent works of Arabian philosophers, some
of which at first claimed the sanction of Aristotle's name.
Now the Arabic intrepretation of Aristotle as exhibited by
Avicenna and more decidedly by Averroës, taking the
direction first imparted to Peripatetic thought by the commentator Alexander of Aphrodisias, emphasized and developed precisely the most anti-Christian elements in the
teaching of the philosopher—the eternity of matter, the
unity of the 'active intellect,' the negation of individual immortality. The Neo-Platonic element is still more explicit
in the *Theologia* and the more famous Arabic or Jewish compilation known as the *Liber de Causis*[1], both of which at the

pseudo-Aristotelian philosophy of
the Arabs. Roger Bacon, however
(*Op. Tertium*, ed. Brewer, p. 28),
distinctly says that the Council
'damnaverunt et excommunicaverunt
libros Naturalis et Metaphysicæ Aristotelis qui nunc ab omnibus recipi-
untur pro sana et utili doctrina.' In
any case, there was clearly much
confusion between the genuine Aristotle and the interpretations and
even writings fathered on him by
the Arabs As late as *c.* 1220 Giraldus Cambrensis speaks of an intellectual revolution created by
'Libri quidam, *tanquam Aristotelis*
intitulati, Toletanis Hispaniæ finibus
nuper inventi et translati' (*Opera*,
ed. Brewer, IV. p. 9). So Robert of
Auxerre (Pertz, *SS.* I. 26. p. 276),
who adds that the prohibition to read
the works of Aristotle was for three

years only. William the Breton
says that in 1209 'legebantur Parisiis
libelli quidam de Aristotele, ut dice-
bantur, compositi, qui docebant Metaphysicam, delati de novo a Constan-
tinopoli et a græco in latinum translati' (Bouquet, T. XVII. p. 84).
Denifle (*Chartul.* T. I. pt. i. No. 11
note) appears to have no doubt that
the actual works of Aristotle were
meant by the Paris Council of 1210.

[1] Albert the Great tells us that
the book was compiled by David
the Jew from the (pseudo-)Aristo-
telian epistle, *De Principio Universi*,
'multa adjungens de dictis Avicennæ
et Alpharabii' (*Opp.* V. p. 563 *sq.*).
Thomas Aquinas rightly regards it
as a compilation from the Neo-Pla-
tonist Proclus. (In lib. de Causis,
Opera, T. IV. p. 1; Ueberweg, I.
p. 426).

beginning of the thirteenth century passed in Latin versions CHÁP. V,
under the name of Aristotle. § 2.

The result of these importations was an outbreak of Scepticism
speculation of a much bolder character than any that had at Paris.
been known in the twelfth century. To about this period
belongs the celebrated story of the Parisian Master, Simon
de Tournai. Intoxicated with the applause which greeted
his dialectical defence of the doctrine of the Trinity—conducted 'so lucidly, so elegantly, so catholicly'—the Doctor
announced that if he pleased he could demolish with equal
plausibility the faith which he had that day maintained.
His audacity is said to have been rebuked by an immediate
stroke of paralysis, which deprived him at once of speech
and of memory. With difficulty did the famous Doctor in
time relearn from his own child his *Credo* and his *Pater-
noster*[1]. In the earlier years of the thirteenth century Paris
was, indeed, the scene of an outburst of free-thought, which
at one time threatened to pass far beyond the limits of the
Schools. About the year 1207 Almaric of Bena, a theo- Almaric
logical Doctor of Paris, died of chagrin at an enforced of Bena,
c. 1207.
retractation, though (according to some accounts) he was
burned to death 'with his adherents.' He was accused
of teaching a doctrine which sounds innocent enough to
modern ears—the doctrine that every believer should regard
himself as a member of Christ. But the Pantheistic
character of his teaching, and the still more unorthodox and anti-sacerdotal interpretation given to it by
his followers, did not come to light till after his death[2]. At

---

[1] The story is told by Matt. Paris, *sub anno* 1201 (*Chron Maj.* ed. Luard, II. pp. 476, 477), who says he heard of the miracle from an eye-witness, Nicholas (of Farnham), afterwards Bishop of Durham. Another story of the same type illustrates the antagonism which existed at the time between the religious and the scholastic spirit of the age—an antagonism not yet bridged over by the work of the An-

gelical Doctor. A Master of Arts named Silo is said to have promised in life to appear to his favourite pupil after his death. He appeared ' cum cappa de purgamento, tota de sophismatibus descripta et flammâ ignis tota confecta.' He declared that this was given him ' pro gloria quam in sophismatibus habui.' The Scholar became a Cistercian (Bulæus, II. p. 393).

[2] This is the account of the sect given by Cæsarius Heisterbachensis

a Synod held in Paris in 1210, in which the Masters of the University took part, the works of one David de Dinant were condemned to the flames[1]. At the same time the body of Almaric was ordered to be dug up and buried in unconsecrated ground, and a posthumous excommunication launched against him. A batch of persons infected with the heresy—Priests and clerks from the Schools, as well as a goldsmith from the neighbouring Grand-pont[2]—were handed over to the secular arm, some for the stake, others for perpetual imprisonment. At the same time the 'books of Aristotle upon Natural Philosophy, and his Commen-

The New
Aristotle
forbidden.

(*Mirac. et Hist. Mem.* Lib. V. Antverpiæ, 1605, p. 292): 'Dicebant non aliter esse corpus Christi in pane altaris, quam in alio pane et in qualibet re, sicque Deum locutum fuisse in Ouidio, sicut in Augustino : negabant resurrectionem corporum, dicentes nihil esse paradisum, neque infernum, sed qui haberet cognitionem Dei in se, quam ipsi habebant, haberet in se paradisum : qui vero mortale peccatum, haberet infernum in se sicut dentem putridum in ore.' But, according to this monastic scribbler, there was another and less edifying side to this Spiritualism. ' Si aliquis est in Spiritu sancto, aiebant, et faciat fornicationem aut aliqua alia pollutione polluatur, non est ei peccatum ' As, however, the Sentence of the Council is silent as to any such doctrine, it must be regarded as a libel. There can be no doubt, however, that the movement had a naturalistic as well as a religious side. In the present century we have seen a very parallel instance of a highly speculative and essentially naturalistic philosophy clothing itself in the phrases of a high-flown spiritualism or even of orthodox piety, and not revealing its true character till the second generation. We are beginning to understand the real drift of Hegelianism even in England.

[1] Guill. Armoricus, *De gestis Philippi Augusti* (Bouquet, T. XVII. pp. 83, 84) ; Gaguinus, *Hist. Francorum* (Francofurti, 1696), p. 100; Vincentius Bellovacensis, *Spec. Hist.* l.xxix. c. 107 (Ven. 1691), p. 424, l.xxx. c. 63, p. 437; *Chron. de Mailros* (Bannatyne Club, Edinb. 1835), pp. 109, 110. The identity of his doctrine with that of Johannes Scotus comes out much more clearly in Martinus Oppaviensis, ap. Pertz, *SS.* T. XXII. p. 438; Trivet, *Annales* (ed. Hog) 1845), pp. 193, 194. The Acts of the Council are given in Martène and Durand, *Thes. Nov.* IV. cc. 163, 164, 165, and in *Chartul.* T. I. pt. i. Nos. 11, 12. See the interesting monograph of Ch. Jourdain in *Mém. de l'Ac. des Inscriptions,* &c. T. 26 (1867), p. 467, and a detailed account of the Council by Hauréau in *Comtes-rendus de l'Ac. des Ins.* T. VIII. p. 291. Denifle (*l. c. note*) prints another account of Almaric's heresies. The tenets of David de Dinant are explained by Albert the Great (in whose time he still had disciples), *Opera,* T. V. p. 563 ; T. XVIII. pp. 62, 63. The condemnation of Almaric was repeated at the Fourth Lateran Council. Mansi, xxii. 986; *Chartul.* T. I. pt. i. No. 22.

[2] The later accounts increase the number of lay adherents, including even women.

taries' were forbidden to be read at Paris publicly or
privately for a period of three years. It is not certain (as
has been said) whether the work aimed at was the actual
Physics of Aristotle or one of the Arabic adaptations or commentaries. It is difficult to define with precision the part
which was played in the generation of the Almarician
heresy by the new Aristotle. M. Renan is inclined to see
in this Parisian heresy in the main a wave of the great
popular Catharistic movement[1], which was rapidly under-
mining Catholicism in Provence and the neighbouring
countries. And in so far as the movement was philosophical
as well as mystical, it seems generally agreed that the
revived influence of Johannes Scotus is more clearly dis-
cernible than that of the *Liber de Causis* and other pseudo-
Aristotelian writings[2]. In the works of David de Dinant,
however, the only Almarician who seems to have been
important from a strictly philosophical point of view, the
influence of Alexander of Aphrodisias is the predominant
one[3]. The thought of the time exhibits a strange fusion of
popular mysticism of a more or less Christian character with
a speculative Averroism which showed a tendency to assume
Pantheistic or even Materialistic forms which would have
been repudiated by the Arabian Master himself. But though
the Almarician heresy may have derived its most direct
inspiration from other sources, the outbreak of that heresy
goes far to explain the alarm with which the advent of the
Arabic Aristotle was at first regarded. The rapidity with
which Aristotle and even his Arabic commentators lived
down these suspicions is one of the most remarkable facts
in the intellectual history of the Middle Ages.

In 1215 a body of Statutes was drawn up for the
guidance of the Masters of Paris by the Papal legate de
Courçon. The reading of the Physical and Metaphysical

---

[1] Renan, *Averroès*, p. 223.

[2] See especially the Bull in
Chartul. T. I. pt. i. No. 50, ordering.
search for the *perifisis* (περὶ φύσεως, i. e.
περὶ φυσέων μερισμοῦ); and Denifle's
important note.

[3] David seems to have had before
him Alexander's comment on the
De Anima and his *De Intelligentia
et Intelligibili.* Jourdain, *Mém. de
l'Acad. d'Ins.* T. 26 (1867), pp. 493,
497.

CHAP. V,
§ 2.

books of Aristotle (the latter now mentioned for the first time) was again forbidden, and an oath not to read the works of David and certain other heretics was enforced on all candidates for the license in arts. Among these was one Mauritius Hispanus who is plausibly identified with Averroës himself [1]. The prohibition of the books condemned by the Council of Paris was renewed by Gregory IX in 1231 with the significant reservation 'until they shall have been examined and purged from all heresy [2].' The Theologians seem quickly to have satisfied themselves as to the innocuous character of the suspected work or to have learned the art of distinguishing the genuine Aristotle from spurious imitations. William of Auvergne, a Parisian Doctor who became Bishop of Paris in 1228 and was still writing in 1248, makes free use of the suspected books, and labours to refute the heresies which had been deduced from them: and in 1254 we find nearly the whole range of the Aristotelian writings prescribed by a statute of the Faculty of Arts as text-books for the lectures of its Masters [3].

Toleration of Aristotle.

Early Arab-Latin Translations.

The Physical books of Aristotle were in the first instance known only through Arab-Latin commentaries or translations. The earliest translators from the Arabic were Hermann the German, Gerard of Cremona, and Michael Scot [4], whose half-magical reputation still testifies to the

---

[1] Bulæus, III. p. 82; *Chartul.* T. I. pt. i. No. 20. M. Renan remarks: ' Ce n'est là toutefois qu'une conjecture à laquelle il ne faudrait pas attribuer une trop grande probabilité' (*Averroès*, p. 222). The reserve turns out to be not misplaced. Denifle shows that Albert the Great distinguishes Mauritius and Averroës (*Chartul.* T. I. pt. i. No. 20 *note*). Perhaps after all this is not absolutely decisive.

[2] Bulæus, III. p. 142; *Chartul.* T. I. pt. i. No. 79. If it was only the Physics that were condemned by the Council the Metaphysics may now have been tolerated (so Martin, *Hist. de France*, T. I. 1856, p. 163).

At this time Gregory IX directs the absolution of offenders against the decree of the Council and appoints a commission for the examination of the books (*Chartul.* T. I. pt. i. Nos. 86, 87).

[3] Bulæus, III. p. 280; *Chartul* T. I. pt. i. No. 246.

[4] Michael Scot's translations made at Toledo appeared in Northern Europe shortly before 1230. Jourdain (*Recherches*, pp. 128–30) ascribes to him an Arab-Latin translation of the *De Cœlo et Mundo* (cf. Denifle, *Chartul.* T. I. pt. i. No. 87 *note*), the *De Anima*, and the *Historia Animalium*. M. Renan (*l. c.* pp. 205–6) ascribes to him a translation of the Commen-

air of mystery and dark suspicion which surrounded the CHAP. V,
§ 2. labours of these pioneers of the later Scholasticism. In this way the eight books of the *Physics*, the nineteen books of the *De Historia Animalium*, the *De Cælo et Mundo*, the spurious *De Plantis*, and the *Meteorica* became known in Northern Europe by about 1232 A.D. But while the Arabic Aristotle was thus re-entering Northern Europe from the South, another chain of events was bringing him back from the East in his original Greek. The Direct Translations from Latin conquest of Constantinople in 1204 threw open the Greek. the original home of Greek Philosophy to Latin scholars. Latin ecclesiastics accompanied the crusading host : others were settled in Greek towns as Bishops of the Latinized Sees. Some of these men made good use of their opportunities as translators, or collectors of MSS. which were afterwards translated by others [1]. In this way the *De Anima* had already become known to William of Auvergne in Græco-Latin translations before the Arab-Latin version of Michael Scot reached the Schools of Paris. The *Rhetoric* and the collection of small treatises known as the *Parva Naturalia*, the *De Coloribus*, the *De Lineis Inse-*

---

taries of Averroës on the two first-mentioned books, and (probably) of his Commentary on the *De Generatione et Conceptione* and the *Meteorics*, paraphrases of the *Parva Naturalia*, and the original work *De Substantia Orbis*. M. Jourdain brings Michael Scot to Oxford (*Recherches*, p. 125), but his name seems to have escaped most of the patriotic inventors of Oxford *Alumni*. At about this time Frederick II is said to have despatched his famous letter to the Masters of Bologna and of Paris (ap. Jourdain, *Recherches*, p. 156), sending them some rare translations of Aristotle and other Greek writers, composed under his orders ; but since these were logical and mathematical books, their introduction has not much bearing upon the history of Aristotle at Paris. It should be observed that some of the MSS. of the above letter have the name Manfred instead of Frederick. Jourdain decides for Frederick (*l. c.* p. 164) ; but cf. Roger Bacon, *Opus Tertium* (*Opera*, ed. Brewer, p. 91), and *Chartul.* T. I. pt. i. No. 394, with Denifle's note.

[1] The best known of them is perhaps John of Basingstoke, who was taught Greek by a learned daughter of the Archbishop of Athens (who predicted pestilences and eclipses) and assisted Robert Grosseteste in his efforts to procure MSS. and translations (Matt. Paris, *Hist.Maj.*v. pp. 284,286 *sq.*; Jourdain, *Recherches*, p. 63). The latter can hardly be looked upon as the actual author of the translations which he caused to be made (cf. Roger Bacon, *l. c.* p. 91).

cabilibus, part at least of the *Metaphysics*, and the first four books of the *Nicomachean Ethics*, together with the *Politics* and the *Magna Moralia* were known from the first in translations from the original Greek [1] ; though the earliest complete versions of the *Metaphysics* and *Ethics* were Arab-Latin. In the case of many of the Aristotelian treatises the direct and indirect versions were long current side by side. The earliest Græco-Latin translations were slavishly literal word for word reproductions of the original Greek : but they were less unintelligible than translations which at times bristled with Arabic words in Latin letters ; for the medieval translators (like the authors of the Septuagint), when unable to construe a word in the original, cut the knot by simply transliterating it. It is true that the Græco-Latin translators not unfrequently resorted to a similar expedient, but some at least of the Arab-Latin versions laboured under the further defect of having passed through even more than one language in the process of translation [2]. The paraphrase of Avicenna and the commentaries of Averroës were alike made not from the original Greek but from the Syriac : and the nominal translator—the Latin ecclesiastic who gave his name to the work—was commonly as ignorant of the Arabic as he was of the original Greek. The version was produced by the collaboration of a Western who knew no Arabic and a Saracen or a converted Jew who knew no Greek, the Spanish or other vernacular language serving as the medium of communication between the translator and his animate Dictionary. Under these circumstances it was natural that the Arab-Latin versions

[1] Only ten books of the Metaphysics were known to Northern Europe in 1271, and those with some hiatus ; only twelve to S. Thomas. (Charles, *Roger Bacon*, Paris, 1861, p. 316 ; Roger Bacon, *Opera*, ed. Brewer, p. 473.) The Politics is said not to have been known at all till after 1292 (Charles, *l. c.*). If so, the Commentary attributed to Albert the Great must be spurious.

[2] See above, p. 251. As to Averroës himself, M. Renan declares that the printed editions of Averroës ' n'offrent qu'une traduction latine d'une traduction hébraïque d'un commentaire fait sur une traduction arabe d'une traduction syriaque d'un texte grec.' *Averroës*, p. 52. But this is denied by Leclerc, *Hist. de la Méd. Ar.* I. p. 133.

should have been gradually supplanted by the versions direct from the Greek: and the later Graeco-Latin versions were somewhat superior to the earlier. Thomas Aquinas endeavoured to procure better translations from the original Greek, and his efforts were seconded by Pope Urban IV. Special translations or special revisions of the existing Graeco-Latin translations were prepared for his use by a Dominican Friar of Greek birth, variously known as Wilhelmus de Brabantia or Wilhelmus de Moerbeka. To him at least the common tradition of the Middle Ages ascribes the 'translatio nova' of the books of Natural and Moral Philosophy, which, in spite of many imperfections, held its place in the Schools as a kind of authorized version of Aristotle till the dawn of the New learning [1].

To a large extent no doubt the suppression of independent speculation was due to the vigorous exertions of the ecclesiastical and civil authorities. The burning of the Almaricians in 1210, and the ruthless suppression of the not wholly unconnected though much more popular and more distinctly religious movements in the South of France, taught the daring speculators of the Schools a lesson which could not easily be forgotten. Above all, the establishment of the Inquisition, wherever it got a firm hold, placed medieval Orthodoxy beyond the reach of open attack for another three centuries. Averroistic free-thought smouldered on in a more disguised and more purely speculative form, occasionally bursting forth into a short-lived flame which called for ecclesiastical extinction. The favourite device of disputants in the Arts Schools was to take refuge under cover of the convenient distinction (very prominent in Averroës himself) between philosophical and theological truth: what was true in Philosophy might be false in Theology and *vice versa*. At times this distinction no doubt represented a really divided state of the thinker's mind: but an examination of the heretical doctrines con-

Suppression of Heresy.

Pantheistic errors of 1270 and 1277.

[1] Jourdain, p. 67 *sq.*; Denifle, *Archiv*, II. pp. 226, 227.

demned in 1270[1] and of the still more explicit errors
enumerated in 1277[2] leaves no doubt that the introduction
of the new Philosophy into the medieval Schools was
attended by a real outburst of Pantheistic thought, at times
bordering (as Pantheism always will border) on pure
Materialism, and even to a recrudescence of Paganism in
Ethics[3]. After this date, however, the heresies condemned
at Paris become less and less destructive. This result was
due (as has been said) partly to the steadily continued
pressure of a vigilant authority, partly to the natural
evaporation of the excitement and unsettlement which
attended the first introduction of the new ideas. But the
most effectual counteractive of the dangerous influence of
Averroistic Aristotelianism was supplied by the development of a great system of orthodox Aristotelianism. The
work had been begun by the cautious Alexander of Hales,
the first Doctor of the Franciscan Order. In the domain
of Logic he began what may be called the rehabilitation of
Realism, the cruder forms of which had been discredited by
the criticism of Roscellinus and Abelard. But he was in

Heresy counter-acted by Orthodox Aristotelianism.

Alexander of Hales.

[1] Among these errors were the following (Bulæus, III. p. 397; *Chartul.* T. I. pt. i. No. 432) :—

'Quod omnia que hic in inferiori-bus aguntur subsunt necessitati corporum celestium (a clear indica-tion of the source of the distinctly theological errors which follow).

Quod mundus est eternus.

Quod nunquam fuit primus homo.

Quod anima post mortem separata non patitur ab igne corporeo.

Quod Deus non cognoscit alia a se.'

[2] 'Dicunt enim,' complains the Bishop of Paris in 1277 (Bulæus, III. 433; *Chartul.* T. I. pt. i. No. 473), 'ea esse vera secundum Philoso-phiam, sed non secundum fidem Catholicam, quasi sint due contrarie veritates, et quasi contra veritatem Sacre Scripture sit veritas in dictis Gentilium dampnatorum.' Among the errors condemned on this occasion were the denial of the Trinity, of the Immortality of the Soul, and of the Creation, &c. These 219 proposi-tions exhibit a curious mixture of Aristotelian and Platonic notions with the Oriental Astrology which had been infused into the ancient philosophies by the media through which they had reached the Pa-risian thinker. Among the Masters who held them occurs the name of Sugerius de Brabantia, assumed (without evidence) to have been Dante's Master. It would be curious to know the source of the heresy, 'quod lex naturalis prohibet interfectionem irrationabilium sicut rationabilium licet non tantum.'

[3] See the 'errores de vitiis et virtutibus' in Bulæus, III. 442; *Chartul.* T. I. pt. i. No. 473, p. 553.

the main a Theologian, not a Philosopher[1]. He was the first great medieval Theologian who was free to use the whole of the newly imported Aristotelian writings, and who set the example of employing them in the defence and exposition of the Catholic Faith. But in the main the construction of a Catholic Philosophy and an Aristotelian Theology was the work not of the Franciscans but of the Dominicans. Although on the actual question of Universals a very moderate Realistic position was now taken up, the general tendency of Franciscan Philosophy as seen in the writings of Alexander of Hales, of his successor Jean de la Rochelle, and still more markedly of the mystic Bonaventura (1221–1274) was towards a Platonic or Arabic interpretation of the Master whom all medieval Schools alike acknow-ledged : the Franciscan School from the first maintained within its bosom the germs which were to attain their most luxuriant growth in the multiplied 'entities' of Scotism. The most unquestionably orthodox and at the same time most genuinely Aristotelian system of the Middle Ages was the creation of the two Dominicans, Albert the Great (1193–1280) and his more famous if not greater pupil Thomas of Aquino (1225 or 1227–1274), who successively taught in the Convent of their Order at Paris between 1245 or 1248 and 1257. If the larger part of their literary labours were carried on elsewhere, the Dominican Convent at Paris was the most influential centre from which their teaching diffused itself through Europe. It was Paris that made the Theology of S. Thomas the Theology of the Catholic Church. Just as the Jesuits in later times turned the universal desire for the new Learning, hitherto associated with the new Religion, into an instrument for attaching men to their Order and their Creed, the Dominicans conceived and executed the idea of pressing not merely (as of old) the Aristotelian Logic but the whole Aristotelian Philosophy into the service of the Church.

---

[1] His ponderous *Summa Theo-logiæ* ('quæ est plus quam pondus unius equi,' as Roger Bacon has it, *Opp. Ined.* ed. Brewer, I. p. 326) was completed after his death in 1245.

Albert continued the system of loose paraphrase or adaptation adopted by Avicenna[1]. In this way the whole of the Aristotelian Philosophy was for the first time presented to the world in a Christian dress. This mode of presentation gave opportunity for the discussion, criticism, or modification of the principles of his author as well as of other writers on the same subjects: the twenty-one folio volumes of Albert are a perfect Encyclopædia both of the knowledge and of the polemics of his time. Aquinas in his purely philosophical treatises adopted Averroës' method of comment on the actual text of Aristotle: while, as a Theologian, he composed independent treatises so superior in form, method, and relative good sense, that they have nearly doomed to oblivion the more cumbrous and discursive works of the predecessor from whom, nevertheless, the basis of his doctrine was derived. The Italian imparted form, system, even style (if the term may be applied to a language which had now become as technical as the language of Law or of Physical Science), to the rough masses of thought heaped up by the ruder genius of the Teuton. The unimpeachable orthodoxy of the two Dominicans finally dissipated alike the prejudice against the Scholastic method which had filled the minds of strict churchmen in the days of S. Bernard or Walter of S. Victor, and the better-founded alarm excited by the introduction of the Arabian and Aristotelian Philosophy at the beginning of the thirteenth century. It was from this time and from this time only (though the change had been prepared in the region of pure Theology by Peter the Lombard) that the Scholastic Philosophy became distinguished by that servile deference to authority with which it has been in modern times too indiscriminately reproached. And the discovery of the new Aristotle was by itself calculated to check the originality and speculative freedom which, in the paucity of books, had characterised the active minds of the twelfth century. The tendency of the sceptics was to

---

[1] Except the work attributed to him on the Politics, which is a regular Commentary.

transfer to Aristotle or Averroës the authority which the orthodox had attributed to the Bible and the Fathers of the Church. The Dominican Theologians made peace between the contending factions by placing Aristotle and the Fathers side by side, and deferring as reverentially to the one as to the other, except on the few fundamental points upon which the former could not be interpreted into harmony with the latter. The Scholastic form of argument which attained its full development in Aquinas—a chain of authorities and syllogisms in defence of one thesis, another series for the opposite view, a conclusion in harmony with Augustine or Aristotle as the case might be, and a reply to the opposing arguments by means of ingenious distinction or reconciliation—afforded exceptional facilities for the harmonious combination of orthodoxy and intellectuality. The Dominicans showed the Latin Churchman how to be ingenious, startling, brilliant, even destructive, without suspicion of heresy. Bernard would have been shocked at the idea of inventing or even of fairly stating objections to the Catholic Faith. By the time of Aquinas it was felt that the better the imaginary opponent's case could be stated, the more credit there was in refuting it. The scholar's intellectual enjoyment of thirty ingenious arguments against the Immortality of the Soul was not diminished by the thirty-six equally ingenious arguments with which the attack would immediately be met [1]. In scholastic disputation — now as freely practised in the cloister of the ascetic Mendicants as in the Arts-Schools of the profane and audacious Seculars—restless intellectual activity found an innocent outlet, love of controversy and speculation an innocent gratification ; and into love of controversy and speculation the real ardour for truth and knowledge which distinguished the age of Berengar and the age of Abelard had for the most part degenerated.

In Logic Albert and his greater pupil were moderate Realists—the latter so moderate that it is possible for a

---

[1] This is the mode of argument adopted by Albert the Great in his *De Unitate Intellectus* (*Opp.* Vol. V, p. 218).

Chap. V,
§ 2.
--+--
The Tho-
mistic
Philo-
sophy.

Nominalistic admirer like Hauréau to contend with some
plausibility that he may be called Nominalist with as
much truth as Realist. With Aquinas the reality of the
Universal *ante rem* was acknowledged, but only as an idea
in the Divine Mind : the Universal *post rem* was admitted
to be an abstraction from the particulars ; the Universal
in re became as with Aristotle, as with Gilbert de la
Porrée in the preceding century, a Form inseparably im-
manent in Matter. Enough of Realistic doctrine was preserved to harmonize with the teaching of the Platonically-
minded Fathers, and with the recognition of the substantial
existence of the body and blood of Christ beneath the
species of bread and wine : on the other hand good sense
was no longer shocked by the idea of Universals with a
real existence apart from and before the particulars, nor
were Theism or Morality endangered by positions which
tended to reduce all realities to one. But in the age of
Aquinas the old quarrel of Realism *versus* Nominalism
which had absorbed the speculative energies of the preceding century was thrown into the shade, or rather it was
merged in wider and more fundamental issues, by the discovery of the Aristotelian writings. Logic had now become
merely the basis of a vast Encyclopædia of Science.
Albert and Aquinas wrote upon Psychology, Metaphysics,
Physics, Physiology, Natural History, Morals. These
subjects had to be treated directly from a purely scientific
point of view ; while their theological applications opened
a wholly new region of thought to the Theologian proper.
The Dominicans neither maintained, with the Obscurantists
and the Mystics, that religious truth lay entirely beyond
the domain of Logic and of Reason, nor, with Rationalists
like Erigena or Abelard, did they attempt either to establish or to criticise the most mysterious doctrines of the
Church by *a priori* reasoning. By Albert and Aquinas
a clear line was—perhaps for the first time—drawn between the provinces of Natural and of Revealed Religion,
between the truths which Reason could establish for herself
and the region in which she could only examine the

credentials and demonstrate the self-consistency or ration-
ality or at most probability of what is placed before it by
authority.   It is hardly too much to say that the lines laid
down by S. Thomas as to the attitude of Reason towards
Revelation are, amid all change of belief as to the actual
content of Revelation, the lines in which, as much in the
Protestant as in the medieval or modern Roman Churches,
the main current of religious thought has moved ever
since.   Hitherto Philosophy had been either an avowed
foe to Theology or a dangerous and suspected ally.   By
the genius of the great Dominicans all that was Christian
or not unchristian in Aristotle was woven into the very
substance and texture of what was henceforth more and
more to grow into the accredited Theology of the Catholic
Church.   The contents of whole treatises of the pagan
Philosopher—including even his great treatise on Ethics—
are embodied in the *Summa Theologiæ* of Aquinas, still the
great classic of the Seminaries.   To that marvellous structure—strangely compounded of solid thought, massive
reasoning, baseless subtlety, childish credulity, lightest
fancy—Aristotle has contributed assuredly not less than
S. Augustine.

Chap. V,
§ 2.

Attitude
towards
Reason.

The work which Aquinas did for the Church of his day
—the fusion of the highest speculative thought of the time
with its profoundest spiritual convictions, the reconciliation
of the new truths of the present with the kernel of truth
embodied in the traditional creed—is a task which will have
to be done again and again as long as the human mind continues progressive and Religion remains a vital force with
it.   It will have to be done in a different spirit, by different
methods, and with very different results from those of the
Summa.   But in one respect the work of Aquinas is built
on the solid foundation upon which all such efforts must
repose—the grand conviction that Religion is rational and
that Reason is divine, that all knowledge and all truth,
from whatever source derived, must be capable of harmonious adjustment.   Of that conviction—not often so
intensely held as by the best minds of the thirteenth

Concilia-
tion of
Religion
and Philo-
sophy.

century — the *Summa Theologiæ* remains a magnificent
monument, still on some points not wholly useless as a help
to the rationalization of Christian belief.

It is a striking fact that the authority which his
Dominican advocates thus secured for the great pagan
Philosopher extended itself also in a measure to the
Moslem disciples by whom he had been first introduced
to Latin Christendom. Though Averroism was still practically a synonym for free-thought, a distinction was drawn
between Averroës the thinker and Averroës the commentator. Averroës became almost as much the authoritative commentator as Aristotle was the authoritative
Philosopher. The oath not to read the works of 'Mauritius'
continued to be administered to Inceptors in Arts : but
when about the middle of the fourteenth century Nominalism, the defiant foe alike of Aristotle and of Averroës,
began to rear its head again, the University, in sublime
ignorance of its inconsistency (if Mauritius was indeed
identical with Averroës), required the candidate almost in
the same breath to abjure Mauritius and to swear to teach
no doctrine inconsistent with that of 'Aristotle and his
commentator Averroës[1].' Under cover of this commenta-
torial fame, Averroës had still a great part to play in the
Schools of medieval Christendom. Repudiated by the
Dominicans of Paris, an orthodox Averroism found a
welcome among the Franciscans of Oxford and, in a very
different form and with very different consequences, among
the sceptical Physicians of Italy. We have already glanced
at one of these contrasted though closely connected movements[2]; of the other we shall have something to say hereafter.

[1] Bulæus, IV. p. 273; *Chartul.* T.
II. App. p. 680. So a Statute of
Heidelberg requires the Inceptor to
swear 'quod textum Aristotelis et
sui commentatoris . . . firmiter et
tamquam authenticum observabit.'
Hautz. *Gesch.* II. p. 352, where the
extraordinary explanation is given,
'wahrscheinlich Porphyrius.'

[2] See above, chap. iii. § 7.

II. *The Constitutional Struggle.*

SUCH were the effects which followed the introduction into the Parisian Schools, nearly at the same time, of a new Philosophy of non-Christian origin and of a new Order pledged to the defence of the Christian Faith. We must now go back to the early days of the movement whose progress has been sketched, and trace the relations between the new Orders and the great educational organization of secular clerks which was just beginning to be known as the University of Paris. The influence which the coming of the Friars exercised upon the constitutional development of the University was not less important than its effects upon the intellectual life of the University and of the world which looked to that University as to its intellectual centre.

CHAP. V, § 2.

The training of theologically educated Preachers was (as we have seen) an essential part of Dominic's original design. At first the Friars were sent to the ordinary theological Schools to study under secular Doctors: and there was some scruple about seeking promotion to the Doctorate for men who were supposed to have renounced all ideas of ecclesiastical as well as of worldly promotion [1]. The lectures of the public Schools were, however, supplemented by private lectures in the Convent given by members of the Order, probably those who had already been admitted to the degree of Bachelor of Theology before entering it [2]. On their first advent, not the slightest

The early Schools of the Friars.

---

[1] The 'Evangelical Counsel,' *Ne Vocemini Magistri*, was appealed to on this head.

[2] Echard I. p. 17. To become a Bachelor of Theology, it is probable that at this time no more was required than five years' study and the permission of the student's own Master. See below, p. 462 *sq.*

hostility was shown by the University as a body to the new Order : it was from the University in part that the Friars obtained, in exchange for certain Masses and funeral services, the site of their famous convent, hitherto occupied by the Hospital of Saint Jacques [1]. The great dispersion of 1229, however, entirely changed the relations between the Friars and the University. Whatever truth there may be in the accusation that the Friars had contributed to that event by poisoning the minds of the Court against the secular Masters [2], it is certain that they were not disposed to relinquish their studies and incur the hostility of their Royal patrons in a quarrel that was none of theirs. On the contrary they availed themselves of the opportunity to start an independent theological School of their own, or rather to throw open to secular scholars a School which they had long possessed, and which was now taught by the distinguished Italian Canonist, Roland of Cremona, who had become a Friar of the Order. Upon the return of the University, there seems to have been at first no disposition on the part of their secular rivals to disturb the *status quo*, whatever irregularity there may have been in the mode by which the Dominican Doctor had ascended the magisterial chair. But an unexpected event tempted the Friars to venture on a still further innovation. The eminent English Theologian, John of S. Giles, was invited

Dominican Schools at Dispersion of 1229.

A second Dominican Doctor.

---

[1] The Hospital was given them by the secular Doctor, Jean de Barastre, Dean of S. Quentin, who had attached himself to them as their theological teacher ; but the University surrendered in favour of the Preachers certain rights over the ground. Thus one of the witnesses at S. Dominic's process of canonization says : 'data fuit ei et sociis suis a magistro Joanne decano S. Quintini tunc regente in theologia Parisius et ab universitate magistrorum et scholarium Parisiensium ecclesia S. Jacobi posita in porta Aurelianensi, ubi steterunt et fecerunt conventum.' Echard, I. p. 50. (Cf. *Chartul.* T. I. pt. ii. No. 43.) The University's deed of gift is printed in Bulæus, III. p. 105, *Chartul.* T. I. pt. i. No. 42. For other documents, see Echard, I. p. 17 *sq.*; Bernard, p. 35 *sq.*; *Chartul.* T. I. pt. i. No. 34 *sq.*

[2] As to their influence with the Queen, Jordanus says in 1227, 'ipsa regina tenerrime diligit fratres, que mecum ore proprio satis familiariter loquebatur.' Ep. No. 17 (ed. Bayonne) ; *Chartul.* T. I. pt. i. No. 52.

to preach *ad clerum* in the Dominican Church[1]. He preached on the beauty of voluntary poverty. In the midst of his discourse he stopped, and, 'that he might confirm his words by his own example, descended from the pulpit, received the habit of the Friars, and therein returned and finished his discourse.' The scholars were eager for the famous Doctor to continue his lectures: but the Order was not inclined to silence Roland in his favour. Henceforth two regular Schools were opened in the Convent of S. Jacques.

At about the same time another Englishman, Alexander of Hales, entered the Franciscan convent, and continued there the lectures which he had begun as a Secular[2]. The example was followed by other religious Orders[3], and the University now began to awake to the irregularity of the whole proceeding; particular exception was taken to the erection of the second Dominican chair. It is, indeed, difficult to say how far the Mendicant Doctors had been admitted to their degrees with the usual formalities. The first Dominican Doctor had certainly been licensed by the Chancellor and had incepted under John of S. Giles, apparently before that Doctor's entrance into the Order: but, as the majority of the secular Doctors had dispersed, he could hardly have been regularly admitted to their 'consortium.' The second Dominican Doctor had graduated as a Secular, but his continued teaching in the Convent of the Order is expressly said to have been 'without the consent of the Chancellor.' Other Mendicant graduates appear to have 'incepted' under Mendicant Doctors, prob-

Constitutional position of Friar-doctors.

---

[1] Trivet (ed. Hog, p. 211), Echard (I. p. 100) and Bernard (p. 267) make this incident occur at the General Chapter of the Dominican Order held in 1228. But this view appears to be inconsistent with the chronology, unless indeed John of S. Giles entered the Order then but did not begin to teach till 1231.

[2] Trivet, l. c.; Echard, I. p. 101.

[3] By 1254 the 'Clarevallenses,' Præmonstratensians, the Order 'De Valle Scholarium,' and the Trinitarians or Mathurines had regular Colleges and theological cathedræ at Paris, besides unattached Mendicant Doctors. Bulæus, III. p. 255; *Chartul.* T. I. pt. i. No. 230. The Carmelites and Austin Friars acquired Houses in Paris about 1260. *Ib.* pt. i. Nos. 358, 358 *a*, 360.

ably without the License of the Chancellor, and certainly without any regular incorporation into the magisterial Guild of Masters[1]. It must be remembered that at this time the organization of the Theological Faculty and its connexion with the more elaborately organized Faculty of Arts was of a very loose and irregular description. This anomalous state of things continued for twenty years after the great Dispersion. During this period we are not able positively to determine how far the Mendicant Doctors were regularly licensed by the Chancellor, or whether, if so licensed, they were admitted to the Congregations, disputations and other privileges of the

[1] Such appears to be the meaning of the Letter to the prelates of Christendom (Bulæus, III. 255 ; *Chartul.* T. I. pt. i. No. 230.) : 'translata majori parte studii Parisiensis Andegavis, in illa paucitate Scholarium que remansit Parisius ... conniventibus episcopo et cancellario Parisiensibus qui tunc erant, in absentia magistrorum sollempne magisterium et unam magistralem cathedram sunt adepti. Deinde . . . *per eandem cathedram multiplicatis sibi doctoribus* successive preter voluntatem cancellarii, qui tunc erat, majoribus nostris qui nondum aliis regularium scholasticorum conventibus arctabantur dissimulantibus, per seipsos secundam cathedram erexerunt.' It is thus interpreted by the Catalogue of Dominican *Lectores* at Paris (ap. Echard, I. p. 100): 'n. 1. F. Rolandus Lombardus Cremonensis fuit primus licentiatus Parisius de ordine Prædicatorum. n. 2. F. Joannes de Sancto Ægidio Anglicus, qui intravit ordinem Prædicatorum magister existens. Sub eo incepit F. Rolandus.' Trivet (p. 212) in speaking of John of S. Giles says : 'Occasione ejus habuerunt Fratres duas scholas infra septa sua, resumente eo lectiones suas post ordinis ingres-

sum ad importunam instantiam auditorum.' So the *Chronicon Humberti* : ' Sub eo etiam fuerunt prius licentiati Fratres Parisius ad legendum, et habuerunt duas scholas' (Echard, I. p. 97). Cf. Bulæus, III. p. 138 ; Echard, I. p. 100; Denifle, *Archiv*, II. p. 204. In the further history of the conflict the documents are our best authorities ; they may be supplemented by the following : Nangis, ap. Bouquet, T. XX. pp. 384 *sq.*, 390 *sq.*, 554 *sq.*; Matt. Paris, *Chron. Maj.* (ed. Luard), VII. pp. 416, 417, 506, 528, 645 ; *Hist. Anglorum*, III. pp. 148, 330 ; Cantipratanus, *Bonum universale de Apibus* (Duaci, 1627), II. c. 10. p. 173 *sq.*; Richerius, *Chron. Senonense*, ap. Pertz, T. XXV. p. 327 *sq.* ; *Chron. Normanniæ*, ap. Duchesne, *Gesta Normannorum in Francia*, p. 1009; Salimbene, *Chronica*, pp. 101 *sq.*, 129 *sq.*, 233 *sq.*; Wadding, *Ann. Minorum* (Romæ, 1732), III. p. 371 *sq.* Several of the poems of the *trouveur* Rutebeuf (*Œuvres*, ed. Tubinal, Paris, 1839, I. p. 151 *sq.*) relate to this conflict ; they side strongly with the Scholars, and testify to the strength of the feeling in their favour and the importance of William of S. Amour.

University. A good deal of friction there must no doubt have been before matters came to an open breach[1]: but there is not sufficient evidence of any official resistance of the University to the Mendicant claims before 1250[2]. The difficulty which arose in that year was one of the Friars' own making, though it was no doubt eagerly seized upon by the jealous Seculars as a pretext for refusing to increase the number of the Regular Doctors. While the desire for promotion to the magisterial chair was not thought incompatible with the humility and unworldliness professed by the Orders, it was considered inconsistent with their Rule to ask for such an honour : and hitherto it had not been the practice of the Chancellor to confer the License upon those who did not apply for it. This delicacy made it necessary for the Friars to procure a Bull from Rome enjoining the Chancellor to confer the License upon as many Religious as, after examination, he should 'according to his conscience' consider qualified, even if they had scrupled to ask for the honour[3]. The rights of the other theological Doctors were entirely ignored. The Bull arrived in 1250. It now became necessary for the Society to assert its right to refuse to recognize the Inception of a Doctor who had been licensed without its consent. The Theologians accordingly, in 125½ passed a formal Statute against the Mendicants—the first formal statute (so far as we know) ever enacted by the Theologians or any other of the

---

[1] Richerius (*l.c.*), thus states a side of the controversy which is not very distinctly indicated by the official documents : 'de difinicione questionum et magistrorum legentium approbatione . . . nam predicatores dicebant ab eis questionum diffiniciones debere proferri, quia potior sciencia in personis Ordinis ipsorum vigeret . . . Clerici vero e contra asserebant se antiquitus Magistros et difinitores habuisse, qui scholarum et scholarium Rectores extiterant.'

[2] Wadding (III. p. 371) speaks of Papal injunctions *c.* 1244 to admit

the Regulars to the full rights enjoyed by the secular Doctors ; and the previous historians of the University have accepted the statement. But, as the researches of Denifle have failed to discover any trace of Bulls on this subject of the date specified, we may safely accept his suggestion (*Chartul.* T. I. pt. i. No. 191 *note*) that the Bull of 1250 has been mistakenly referred to an earlier date. Cf. *Mém. de la Soc. de l'hist. de Paris et de l'Ile de France*, X. 246.

[3] Bulæus, III. 223 ; *Chartul.* T. I. pt. i. No. 191.

superior Faculties. It was ordered that 'no Religious not having a College at Paris' should be admitted to the Society of Masters [1], that each Religious College should in future be content with one Master and one School and that no Bachelor should be promoted to a chair unless he had already lectured in the Schools of an actually Regent Master, i. e. a Master recognized as such by the Faculty. Any Master refusing to assent to this Statute was 'deprived of the society of the Masters.'

We know nothing of the progress of events for more than a year [2]. It seems clear that, the decree of the Theological Faculty notwithstanding, the Mendicants, even the second Dominican Doctor, were admitted to General Congregations of the University [3]. But in the year 125⅔ an event occurred which gave the Seculars the opportunity of renewing the contest. The affair was very much like the incident which produced the Dispersion of 1229. Lent in the Middle Ages, whether through an unseemly prolongation of Carnival disorder or through the reaction of youthful spirits against enforced abstinence, was as fruitful a source of crime as the Ramadan in Turkey : nearly all the great University riots took place at this season. In the present year a scholar was killed by the Provost's

---

[1] 'Ut de cetero religiosus aliquis non habens collegium et cui est a jure publice docere prohibitum, ad eorum societatem nullatenus admittatur,' Bulæus, III. p. 245 ; *Chartularium*. T. I. pt. i. No. 200. The Bull of 1255 in reciting this prohibition inserts the word ' Parisius' after ' collegium.' Bulæus, III. p. 283; *Chartul.* T. I. pt. i. No. 247. To appreciate the situation, it should be remembered that the Mendicant system was to change their *Lectores* frequently. Thus if Roland's ' Inception ' was regarded as regular, he was in 1230 succeeded by Hugh of S. Cher (Denifle, *Archiv*, II. pp. 173, 174), who may not have had the Chancellor's License.

[2] The matter is the more puzzling inasmuch as, though the Theological Statute of 125½ removed at least one Dominican from the College of Doctors, the Pope in Aug. 1253 (*Chartul.* T. I. pt. i. No. 225) requires that ' in ea libertate ac quiete sistere permittatis eosdem in qua a duobus annis retro extitisse noscuntur.'

[3] Otherwise they could hardly have been subsequently expelled. It is clear that they attended the Congregations at some period later than the publication of ' The Perils of the Last Times' from the complaint of the Masters that they had libelled its author as well as the Pope ' in Congregationibus nostris.' (Bulæus, III. p. 290 ; *Chartul.* T. I. pt. i. No. 256.)

officers in a street-brawl: others had been outrageously illtreated and imprisoned in defiance of the scholastic privilege. The University decreed a 'Cessation of Lectures'; the two Dominican Doctors and the one Franciscan refused to obey it, and, since obedience to duly ordered Cessations was enjoined under ecclesiastical penalties, appealed to Rome against the decision of the University. The Cessation proving ineffectual, the University agreed that all its Masters should take an oath to insist on obtaining justice. Again the three Friars refused compliance: whereupon they were expelled from the 'consortium' or company of the Masters, and the scholars forbidden to go to their lectures. A tardy redress for the outrage was at length obtained through the intervention of the King's brother, Alfonse, Count of Poitiers and Toulouse. Two of the offenders were convicted, dragged through the streets at the heels of horses, and finally hung. But, though the immediate cause of complaint was removed, the Friars—or at least the two Dominicans—were not readmitted.

CHAP. V, § 2.

Friars refuse to obey the Cessation.

The affair had brought out more clearly than ever the fact that the Friars were claiming to enjoy the privileges of membership of the Masters' College while they refused to submit to its authority. The University accordingly determined to bring matters to a head. A Statute was passed by the whole University enacting that henceforth no Master of any Faculty should be admitted to the 'College of Masters or fellowship of the University,' unless he should first have sworn in full Congregation, or at least in the presence of three Masters of his own Faculty specially deputed for the purpose, to obey the Statutes of the University, to keep its secrets, and further to observe a 'cessation' when ordered by the University[1]. The secular Masters of the superior Faculties would have taken such an oath to the Statutes on Inception in the Faculty of Arts: but the Friar-Doctors, having never graduated in Arts, would have hitherto escaped it. The erection of the

The University demands an oath of obedience.

[1] Bulæus, III. 250; *Chartul.* T. I. pt. i. No. 219.

second chair, however, and the attitude taken up by the two Dominicans and the Franciscan in the matter of the Cessation determined the secular Masters to insist on their rights, and to compel the intruders to acknowledge the authority of the University if they wished to enjoy its rights and privileges. The exact extent of the authority claimed by the University should be clearly understood. No one denied the right of a Friar duly licensed by the Chancellor to teach Theology to members of his own Order or to others. What the Masters asserted was the hitherto unquestioned right of the University to impose its own regulations upon its own members, to refuse professional association to Masters who did not choose to comply with them, and to exclude from their Society the pupils of such unrecognized extra-University Masters[1]. The question which was thus really at stake was the autonomy of the Society. It had in truth already parted with its voluntary character too far by its acceptance of Papal Statutes and privileges to claim to be treated purely as a private club. And by the issue of the present controversy it was placed beyond dispute that henceforth the University was as much a part of the ecclesiastical system, as much subject to Papal regulation, as the older capitular body whose authority it had by Papal favour nearly succeeded in shaking off.

Importance of the Oath.

The oath of obedience to the Statutes was, to an extent which it is hard for us to realise, a matter of vital importance to the Universities. Their whole power over their

---

[1] Cf. the words of the Bull of 1255, ‘ eos beneficio Societatis in Magistralibus privavistis, ipsosque privatos publice nuntiantes, injunxistis districte ut Scholares lectiones eorum de cetero non audirent.’ (Bulæus, III. p. 282 ; *Chartul.* T. I. pt. i. No. 247.) In the letter of 1255 (Bulæus, III. p. 290 ; *Chartul.*T. I. pt. i. No. 256) the Masters expressly declare that they do not want to prevent them ‘ quominus tot scolas habeant et Scolares, sive de Secularibus sive de Regularibus, quot habere volunt et possunt, nec quominus Privilegiis nostris omnibus tam ipsi quam eorum Auditores gaudeant.’ They only demand ‘ ut nos ex una parte Civitatis patiantur pacifice et quiete, nec ad domos aut Scholas nostras, seu etiam ad Conventus nostros, in quibus Magistri non nisi rogati conveniunt, sicut nec consuetum extitit, invitis se ingerant violenter.’

members, their very existence depended upon the sanction
of this oath. The obligation of such oaths, according to
the notions of the time, could not be neutralized by the
claims of conflicting duties or obligations. They were
(subject to the Papal power of dispensation) absolute,
irrevocable, eternal. An oath, according to medieval
notions, was no mere appeal to the conscience, no mere
solemn recognition of an already existing duty. Whatever
the nature of the act to which the oath pledged the
deponent, the violation of it placed him in a state of mortal
sin, and doomed him to eternal perdition should he die
unabsolved. A good illustration of the unbounded claims
which the Academical oath was supposed to give the
University over its members is afforded by an incident
which occurred about a century after the period with which
we are dealing. The Bishop of Paris had, with a severity
very unusual in dealing with the sins of the clergy,
imprisoned as well as excommunicated a scholar convicted
of rape, and imposed upon him a fine of 500 livres as a
condition of absolution. The University asserted, though
the Bishop denied, that the privileges of the University
forbade the imposition of a pecuniary penance upon a
scholar under any circumstances whatever, and the Bishop
had sworn to maintain these privileges upon his admission
to the degree of Doctor in Canon Law. They accordingly
placarded the walls of the Bishop's Cathedral city with
broad-sheets proclaiming him a perjurer. The Bishop was
powerless to resent the insult, and was forced to go to
Avignon for a Papal Bull absolving him from the obligation
of his oath so far as it affected the discharge of his episcopal
duties[1]. A century later still, we find the University affecting, on the strength of the same all-powerful oath, to dictate
to its graduates in the King's Privy Council the advice which
they should give to the King on matters of public policy[2].

But we must return to the events of the thirteenth century.
The Statute of the University requiring the oath under

---

[1] Bulæus, IV. 226; *Chartul.* T. II. Nos. 899, 903.　　[2] Monstrelet, *Chronique*, Paris, 1857. T. II. p. 106.

penalty of expulsion was ~~drawn up~~ shortly before Easter, 1253—the Easter immediately following the Cessation. Though not finally sealed till September, its contents appear to have been at once published and acted upon.

Expulsion of Friars.

The Friars were solemnly expelled and proclaimed excommunicate as having disobeyed Statutes to which Papal authority had been annexed. The Order promptly procured Papal Bulls requiring the University to readmit them to 'fellowship' (*consortium*) and to suspend all Statutes against them pending the decision of their appeal to the Holy See [1]. The Bulls were entrusted for execution to two Bishops, who in the heat of summer had doubtless no inclination for a visit to Paris and appointed as their sub-delegate one of the traditional enemies of the University

Suspension of Masters.

—the Chapter of Paris, who with indecent alacrity (as the University complained), without admonition, citation, or other formality, had the whole body of Masters and Scholars solemnly ' suspended from their office or privilege one Sunday morning during Mass in all the churches, in the presence of all the laity to the grave scandal of us and of all the clergy [1].' The Bull and the ecclesiastical censures notwithstanding, the University persisted in its course, and, that the unwary freshmen might be warned against attending the Schools or Sermons of the expelled and excommunicated Brethren, once more at the beginning of the October term the Bedels were sent round the Schools to proclaim the Academical ban. They even made an attempt to publish the edict in the Schools of the Friars themselves, when the University officers were attacked and maltreated ' even to the effusion of blood ' by the sturdy young Friars, who seldom had such a chance of letting off their somewhat pent-up spirits in so holy a cause. The Bedels reported what had happened to the Rector, who came to publish the edict in person but met with no better reception. The Papal legate vainly endeavoured to mediate. The Masters paid no more respect to the

---

[1] *Chartul.* T. I. pt. i. Nos. 222, 223, 225, 226; Bulæus, III. 254.

'suspension' than was implied in appealing against it.
The Friars remained expelled, the Seculars impenitent[1].

At the beginning of the following year ($125\frac{3}{4}$) the
Masters unfolded their grievances in a letter to the Prelates
of Christendom[2], which throws much light upon the real
grounds of the quarrel. There were, it appears, at the time
fifteen Doctors of Divinity at Paris. Of these, three were
Canons of Notre Dame, and taught (in accordance with
the ancient privileges of the Chapter) without any authorization from the University. Of the rest, nine were Regulars
of various orders. The Masters naturally complained that
secular students were virtually deprived of the principal
inducement to study—the hope of themselves occupying
the Professorial chair. Even apart from the limitation of
the number of the theological Doctors to eight which had
been enacted by Innocent III[3], the theological students were
not numerous enough to supply fees, or even audiences,
for an unlimited number of teachers. And the Mendicant
Doctors, being maintained in part or entirely by the contributions of the charitable, must have competed at an
advantage with the Seculars, even had not such teachers
as Albert the Great and S. Thomas Aquinas been among
the number of the former[4].

The enemies of the University were powerful. The
Court was much under the influence of the Friars. The
party of the Seculars had the disadvantage, like the

---

[1] The above narrative is chiefly
from the University circular letter
mentioned in the next paragraph.

[2] Bulæus, III. 255-258; *Chartul.*
T. I. pt. i. No. 230.

[3] Bulæus, III. p. 36; *Chartul.* T. I.
pt. i. No. 5. The regulation had
been relaxed in favour of the Mendicants.

[4] The Friar Cantipratanus puts
the inferior teaching powers of the
secular Masters down to heavy feed-
ing and the excessive vacations which
their luxurious habits compelled them
to give. 'Videbant enim scholares

quod magistri seculares, sicut viri
diuitiarum, dormierunt somnum
suum, ducebantque in bonis dies suos.
Et cum vespere multiplicitate fercu-
lorum obtuerentur et potuum, et
postea vigilare non possent, nec studere, et per hoc nihil inuenire in
manibus quod proferrent, sequenti
mane solemnem diem constituebant
auditoribus in condensis (*sic*) et sic
per ineptas vacationes, quibus sua
clerici inaniter expendere se dole-
bant, optato priuabantur studio.'
De Apibus, II. c. 10. p. 181.

Jansenists of a later day, of fighting the King's Confessor, who was invariably chosen from the ranks of their opponents. At first, indeed, there was some hope of obtaining at all events a compromise through the favour of Innocent IV, who had, except in this matter, shown himself disposed to favour the Seculars and to repress the usurpations of the Friars. The death of Innocent IV in 1254, just after issuing a Bull withdrawing the extraordinary privileges of the Mendicants [1], destroyed the last hope of a settlement favourable to the University. Alexander IV at once reversed the policy of his predecessor. The Bulls which Innocent had issued to restrain Mendicant encroachments upon the rights of Ordinaries and Curates were promptly revoked [2]: and a few months later, in April 1255,

Bull *Quasi lignum vitæ* decides for Friars, 1255.

appeared the celebrated Bull *Quasi lignum vitæ*, which decided the matters in dispute, on almost every point, in favour of the Mendicants [3]. The expulsion of the Dominicans was annulled. The Chancellor was directed to grant the License to as many duly qualified candidates as after examination (by himself alone) he should think fit, thus implicitly conceding the second Dominican chair. The Friars were indeed to obey a cessation, but only when voted by a two-thirds majority of the Masters in each Faculty. This put it in the power of the Mendicant Theologians to stop a cessation whenever they pleased, as more than a third of the Theological Faculty at any one time were sure to be Friars. Finally all sentences of expulsion or deprivation were quashed by Apostolical authority, and the University required peremptorily to readmit the two Dominican Doctors [4] into full membership. The execution of the Bull

---

[1] Bulæus, III. 270; *Chartul.* T. I. pt. i. No. 240.

[2] Bulæus, III. p. 273; *Chartul.* T. I. pt. i. No. 244.

[3] Bulæus, III. 282; *Chartul.* T. I. pt. i. No. 247.

[4] In 1253 the University is directed to readmit both Minorites and Preachers (Bulæus, III. p. 254; *Chartul.* T. I. pt. i. No. 222). In 1255

(Bulæus, III. 286; *Chartul.* T. I. pt. i. No. 249) only the two Dominicans, Bonushomo and Helias, are mentioned. We should naturally infer (cf. *Chartul.* p. 258 *note*) that the Minorites had made their peace with the University: but in 1256, in the first of the series of submissions to the *Quasi lignum*, we find the penitents promise to receive the Franciscan Bona-

was entrusted to the Bishops of Orleans and Auxerre [1] ; CHAP. V, and upon the refusal of the University to obey, its §2. members were excommunicated *en masse* by the two ~~Wholesale~~ Excommunication.
prelates.

The Masters now resolved upon a very curious manœuvre, which illustrates with great clearness the real nature of the University dissolves itself. institution whose very existence was attacked by the Mendicant privileges. In spite of the Papal recognition, in spite of Statutes and the privileges bestowed upon it by both the Crown and Holy See, the Society was still, like the English Inns of Court, which enjoy nevertheless legal privileges at least as extensive as those of the Paris Society of Masters, ostensibly a ' voluntary Society,' and, unlike the Inns of Court, a voluntary Society almost unencumbered with property. The Masters contended that the Society could be dissolved in the way in which it was originally formed. They accordingly sought to evade the Papal restrictions upon their liberty of association as well as the excommunication launched against its members by proclaiming the dissolution of their Society. At the end of the long Vacation the individual Masters and Scholars who returned to Paris addressed a letter to the Pope, formally declaring the dissolution of the University, and renouncing all Papal and other corporate privileges and immunities whatsoever. The existence of the Nations was, however, considered to be unaffected by the dissolution of the University itself and the document bore the seals of these four bodies [2]. The Masters did not want, they declared, to

---

ventura as well as the Dominican Thomas Aquinas (Bulæus, III. p. 315; *Chartul.* T. I. pt. i. No. 293).

[1] Bulæus, III. p. 286; *Chartul.* T. I. pt. i. No. 248.

[2] The Letter is headed ' Singuli Magistri et Scolares omnium Facultatum, Reliquie dispersionis Parisiensis studii, preter Universitatis Collegium Parisius commorantes.' It concludes, ' Nos autem Magistri et auditores omnium Facultatum, Magis-

tris fratribus et eorum auditoribus duntaxat exceptis, quoniam sigillum commune non habemus utpote ab Universitatis Collegio separati, sigillis quatuor Nationum ab antiquo Parisius distinctarum in hac littera usi sumus.' (Bulæus, III. 288-292; *Chartul.* T. I. pt. i. No. 256.) The Dominican General Humbert adds that ' novam quamdam societatem, nomine universitatis verbotenus extincto, pariter inierunt ad sedem apostolicam appel-

prevent the Friars from having as many Schools and as many scholars, whether secular or regular, as they pleased. All that they wanted was the right to exclude these unwelcome intruders from the Schools which they held in their own hired houses and the Congregations conducted in convents lent by friendly bodies. The Friars, it was suggested, had already shown that they were quite capable of getting on without the enforced association of the Seculars, since they had of late been holding their own Inceptions apart from the rest of the University under the protection of an armed guard placed at their service by their Royal patron. Such were the circumstances under which the Prince of the Schoolmen, Thomas Aquinas, was admitted to his degree in the University of which he was for ever afterwards regarded by Dominican and Secular alike as the most distinguished ornament[1].

'The Perils of the Last Times' and the 'Introduction to the Eternal Gospel.'

An important underplot had been going on by the side of the main action. The Seculars were trying to procure the condemnation of a work emanating from the fanatical section of the Franciscan Order, among which the Apocalyptic speculations put forth by the Abbot Joachim had taken a new and more startling form. This work, styled an 'Introduction to the Eternal Gospel,' was selling in large numbers (it would appear in a French translation) under the very eyes of the Masters of Paris on the 'Parvis' of Notre Dame[2]. The Friars retaliated by getting up an agitation against a work entitled 'The Perils of the Last Times,' attributed to William of S. Amour, the leading spirit among the secular Masters—a violent attack upon religious Mendicancy which sought to represent the Friars

lantes' (*Chartul.* I. pt. i. No. 273)—an evasion to which the Pope replies by declaring that by the name of 'University' is meant 'omnes magistros et scolares commorantes Parisius cujuscunque societatis seu congregationis existant.' (*Chartul.* T. I. pt. i. No. 262.)

[1] *Chartul.* T. I. pt. i. Nos. 270, 280.
[2] See the *Roman de la Rose*, ed.

Francisque-Michel, Paris, 1864, II. p. 35 *sq.* Cf. Richerius, *Chron. Sen.* ap. Pertz, *SS.* T. XXV. p. 328. The *Introductorium* and the *Pericula novissimorum temporum* both appeared in 1254, Gul. de S. Amore, *Opp.* pp. 37, 38; *Chartul.* T. I. pt. i. No. 243. In the *Roman* the date of the former is wrongly given as 1255.

as the 'ungodly men' whose advent the Apostle had fore-
told as the immediate sign of the coming of Antichrist and
of the end of the world[1].

The Franciscan brochure seemed to erect S. Francis into
a position as much superior to Christ's as the position of
Christ was to that of Abraham : it attacked the Pope
and hierarchy with prophetic vehemence, if also with prophetic vagueness, and announced the speedy advent of a
reign of universal poverty, wherein the true ideal of the
Gospel should be for the first time realised, and the secular
clergy superseded by bare-footed Mendicants. Such a
work was naturally not likely to find much favour with
Popes and Cardinals. But, though the majority even of
the Franciscans had no sympathy with these ideas, the
orthodoxy of the whole Order and even of the other
Mendicant Orders was undoubtedly compromised by the
book, especially as it was believed to represent the views of
the Franciscan General, John of Parma. The consequence
was that the book was condemned, but with all the leniency
possible under the circumstances, the burning being conducted privately and without *éclat*[2].

Very different was the fate of 'The Perils of the Last
Times.' The first accusations of heresy against William of

---

[1] Special emphasis was laid upon
the obvious applicability of the texts,
Ex iis sunt qui penetrant domos,
and *Coaceruant sibi magistros.* The
writer's general conclusion is : 'Ergo
nos sumus in ultima ætate huius
mundi ; et ista ætas iam plus durauit
quam aliæ, quæ currunt per mille-
narium annorum ; quia ista durauit
per 1255 annos ; verisimile ergo est,
quod nos sumus prope finem mundi ;
ergo propinquiores sumus periculis
nouissimorum temporum ; quæ futura
sunt ante aduentum Antichristi.'
Opera, p. 37. It is interesting to
observe that the two parties were
agreed as to the mysterious significance of the year 1260. (See Apoc.
xi. 3, xii. 6.) Denifle points out

that Christian of Beauvais (another
of the representatives of the University) also indulged in Chiliastic
speculations. (*Chartul.* T. I. pt. i.
No. 280 *note.*)

[2] The errors found or alleged to
be found in the *Introductorium* are
given in *Chartul.* T. I. pt. i. No. 243 ;
the condemnation, *ib.* Nos. 257, 258,
277 ; Bulæus, III. pp. 292, 293, 302.
The second of these Bulls enjoins
the Bishop of Paris ' quod sic pru-
denter, sic caute, sic provide in apo-
stolici super hoc mandati executione
procedas, quod dicti fratres nullum
ex hoc opprobrium nullamque im-
famiam incurrere valeant sive notam.'
On the history of the *Everlasting
Gospel,* see Appendix X.

S. Amour seem to have been based not upon the contents of this book but upon pulpit utterances against the Mendicants. He was cited to appear before the Bishop of Paris by a Papal Chaplain. But on the day appointed for the hearing, intimidated by the storm which the attack upon their champion had awakened among the secular clergy, the promoter did not venture to appear : and the Bishop of Paris, no friend to the scholars but still a secular, was obliged to admit the accused to canonical purgation in the presence of a great assemblage of four thousand clerks [1]. After the final breach with the Mendicants, William of S. Amour was cited to answer charges of heresy contained in 'The Perils of the Last Times' before an assembly of prelates belonging to the Provinces of Sens and Rouen. The accused availed himself of the thin veil of anonymity which he had thrown over the objects of his attack. They had been assailed in general terms as 'false prophets' and the like, so that he was able to plead that the libel was not meant for the Dominicans. The Prelates and the University were in favour of a Council [2]. But the Friars distrusted a tribunal composed mainly or entirely of secular prelates and members of the old religious Orders. The pious but Friar-ridden King was persuaded to send the book to Rome with a request for the decision of the Holy Father upon its orthodoxy. With splendid audacity the University resolved to send as its proctors to the Roman Court the accused himself, whose excommunication, banishment, imprisonment, had already been commanded by the Pope [3], together with three other Theologians, accompanied by the Rector of the University [4] and another Master of Arts to represent the inferior Faculty. For once the proceedings of the Roman tribunals were not dilatory. The proctors did not leave Paris before August 1256. By the beginning of October the affair had been committed to the decision of a

---

[1] Bulæus, III. 290; *Chartul.* T. I. pt. i. No. 255.

[2] Bulæus, III. 309; *Chartul.* T. I. pt. i. No. 287.

[3] Bulæus, III. 306; *Chartul.* T. I. pt. i. No. 282.

[4] So Matt. Paris styles him. *Chron. Maj.* ed. Luard, V. 599.

Commission including the Dominican Cardinal Hugh of S. Cher[1], their report had been accepted, and the Bull of condemnation issued. The language of the book about religious mendicancy and its implied though unavowed contempt for the authority of the sovereign Pontiff were condemned as scandalous and pernicious, but not (the historians of the University are careful to remark) as heretical : even Alexander IV could not venture to burn a priest for saying what wellnigh every French secular clergyman in France was thinking. But, as might have been anticipated, obstacles were placed in the way of the return of the ringleaders in the anti-Mendicant conspiracy to the scene of their crime and their influence. The other envoys of the University soon gave in their submission[2] : it is a curious indication of the hold which Mendicancy had got over the religious feelings of the time, that one of these stalwart champions of the secular clergy on his death-bed desired that he might be buried in the Church of the Dominican Convent at Paris[3]. William of S. Amour, a man endowed with more than the pugnacity if with less than the piety of a Wyclif or a Huss, alone remained firm, and refused at all costs to associate with the Friars. With difficulty was he allowed to leave Anagni, and then only on condition of banishment from France and perpetual suspension from preaching and teaching[4]. S. Louis was at last reluctantly compelled to supplicate the Pope that he might be allowed the Papal permission to recall a French subject to his own dominions[5]. But the Pope was inflexible : and the darling of the University retired impenitent to his native soil in Franche-Comté, safe under the protection of the Anti-papal Empire[6], until the death of Alexander IV allowed him once more to revisit Paris.

It is difficult to construct from our documents a consecu- The struggle in Paris.

---

[1] Author or at least beginner of the first great Biblical Concordance.

[2] Bulæus, III. 308, 315, 316, 344 ; *Chartul.* T. I. pt. i. Nos. 293, 317, 320.

[3] Cantipratanus, p. 179.

[4] Bulæus, III. 342, 343 ; *Chartul.*

T. I. pt. i. Nos. 314, 315, 318.

[5] Jourdain, Nos. 166, 168; *Chartul.* T. I. pt. i. Nos. 355, 356, 357.

[6] *Hist. Litt.* XX. p. 752; *Opp.*, Ep. Introd. p. 63 ; this was apparently in 1260.

tive narrative of events at Paris during these troubled years.
It must be remembered that what the Pope enjoined was
not merely an official recognition of the Friars' Doctorate
but a cordial and friendly reception of the unwelcome
intruders by every individual Master and scholar. ' Boycotting' is notoriously an offence with which it is difficult
for the most resolute authority to deal: it was only by
slow degrees that the implacable Pontiff could secure
respect for his commands. We have seen that the decree
of Dissolution was finally promulgated in October 1255;
the general Excommunication already mentioned followed
in December of the same year ; and deprivation was
threatened against the ringleaders if they refused to receive
the Friars within fifteen days[1]. A reiterated appeal to
Rome and an abortive attempt at compromise suspended
the execution of the sentences for some months longer[2].
Meanwhile a pathetic letter of the Dominican General,
Humbert[3], gives us a lively picture of the kind of treatment
the Friars of Paris had had to put up with during that
winter of strife. The Masters had forbidden their pupils
to approach the Mendicant convents for any cause whatever, to receive a Friar into their own houses, to confess
to him, to give him alms, or to attend his Sermons. And
in practice the 'boycotting' passed, as is its wont, into
intimidation and violence. The Friars were victorious in
the battle of the law-courts, but they still had to face the
rough battle of the streets. They were treated as 'black-
legs' are treated in a great strike. It was dangerous for a
Friar to be seen abroad: it was not only the clerks they
had to fear, but a section, at all events, of the lay mob was
equally hostile. No sooner was a Friar caught sight of
(Humbert complained), than he was surrounded by the
human swarms that poured forth from every house and
hostel in the narrow street, ' hurrying as if to a spectacle.'
Instantly the air was full of ' the tumult of shoutings, the

---

[1] Bulæus, III. 294; *Chartul*. T. I. pt. i. No. 262.
[2] Bulæus, III. 296; *Chartul*. T. I. pt. i. Nos. 268, 280, 284.
[3] *Chartul*. T. I. pt. i. No. 273.

barking of dogs, the roaring of bears, the hissing of ser-
pents,' and every sort of insulting exclamation. Filthy
rushes and straw off the floors of those unsavoury dwellings
were poured upon the cowled heads from above; mud,
stones, sometimes blows greeted them from below. Arrows
had even been shot against the Convent, which had henceforth to be guarded night and day by Royal troops. When
every allowance is made for the exuberance of medieval
rhetoric and the tendency of a Friar, with the evangelical
blessing on the persecuted ever in his ears, to make the most
of his own or his brethren's sufferings, there can be no
doubt that the Friars whose lot it was to beg their bread
from door to door in the Quartier Latin during the winter
of 1255–6 must have had a decidedly hard time [1].

Bulls commanding the re-admission of the Mendicants
and denouncing every possible penalty upon transgressors
now follow one another in bewildering profusion. From
the way in which these Bulls succeed one another it is
evident that, entrusted as they were to secular prelates who
secretly sympathized with the University, they must have
been very tardily and partially executed, and such execution as they obtained must have been attended with very
partial success. In December 1256 the two Chancellors
were forbidden to license candidates without exacting a
formal acceptance of the *Quasi lignum* [2] : so that from this
date onwards there must have existed an official University (so to speak) which admitted the Mendicants to their
company on formal occasions, though the majority of the
Masters may have long held aloof and adhered to the
schismatical Society which they had set up in place of the
old and professedly dissolved University of the Papal
privileges. In all probability the neck of the rebellion
was broken after the discomfiture of S. Amour and his

---

[1] Humbert's narrative is supported
by *Chartul.* T. I. pt. i. Nos. 272,
275.

[2] Bulæus, III. p. 334; *Chartul.* T.
I. pt. i. Nos. 298, 299; repeated in
March, 1257, *ib.* Nos. 303, 304. In
Dec. 1255 the Chancellors had been
ordered not to admit any who would
not observe the *Quasi lignum*, but
without apparently requiring a formal pledge. *Chartul.* T. I. pt. i. Nos.
259, 260.

colleagues on their last journey to Italy in the summer of 1257. But the surrender of the Seculars, so far as we can judge, did not take place at any one definite moment ; their opposition was broken down by slow degrees, as individual after individual, with his eyes fixed on preferment, deserted the strikers, joined the official University, and obtained absolution. But, even after formal and official resistance had ceased, the opposition to the Mendicants was long kept up by private annoyance and unofficial exclusiveness [1]. It was not till September 1257, two years after the solemn expulsion of the Friars, that the Bishop of Paris received powers from the Holy See to absolve those who had submitted to the Apostolic injunctions [2] : it was not till the April of the following year that the Pope is able to declare that something like peace was established [3], though in that very Bull he is still obliged to denounce those who attempted to keep alive the feud by private avoidance. It is followed by a succession of fulminations against those who still refused to treat the Mendicants with the cordiality exacted by Apostolical authority [4] and persisted in hiding

[1] See e. g. a Bull of 1259 (*Chartul.* T. I. pt. i. No. 342), in which the Pope denounces a Bedel of the University who had circulated a ' libellus famosus' among the congregation when Thomas Aquinas was preaching. Verily the treatment of Thomas Aquinas by the University of Paris is a notable example of building the sepulchres of the prophets! (See the petition of the Faculty of Arts that his body might be buried among them. *Chartul.* T. I. pt. i. No. 447.) Another Bull of the same year enables us to see the ' ingeniose adinventiones ' that the Masters resorted to in order to repel the ' consortium' of the Friars. Since the Friars could not for fear of spiritual penalties (' spirituales plage') take any part in the movement for the recall of William of S. Amour, they were accustomed to bring the matter on at

every Congregation, so that the Friars had to retire. *Chartul.* T. I. pt. i. No. 343.

[2] Cf. *Chartul.* T. I. pt. i. No. 319.

[3] *Chartul.* T. I. pt. i. No. 331.

[4] It even seems as if, in consequence of the Artists refusing to hold any *consortium* with the Mendicants, they were still afraid to attend General Congregations. In the document of 1276 already mentioned (p. 329), the Secular Masters of Theology give in their assent to the Acts of the other Faculties before the Rector, the Regulars before a Notary. Bulæus (III. p. 356) prints an act readmitting the Dominicans, but degrading them to the lowest place among the Theological Doctors, which he and all subsequent enquirers have referred to the year 1259. But Denifle (I. p. 67) has

their treasured copy of that storehouse of anti-Mendicant libel, 'The Perils of the Last Times,' or in singing and circulating 'indecent songs' against the Friars, while at the same time the numerous submissions of individual Masters and faculties for the absolution of less prominent penitents attest the gradual victory of the Friars.

With the accession of the Parisian Canonist Urban IV in 1261, documents of this kind come suddenly to an end and Bulls of privilege and protection take their place. It is therefore reasonable to conclude that the Dominicans, now that they had lost their great patron, quietly submitted to some of the restrictions which we find practically imposed upon them at a later date. These restrictions were as follows :—

(1) While the University as such had received the Mendicants, the Faculty of Arts still refused to admit them or their pupils to membership in spite of the repeated injunctions of Alexander IV [1]. Here the Faculty of Arts succeeded in maintaining its ground : the exclusion of all Regulars from its ranks remained a permanent feature of the Academic constitution [2].

(2) No Religious College was allowed to have more than *one*, or in the case of the Dominicans *two*, Doctors acting as Regents and sitting at the same time in the General Congregation of the University [3].

(3) Though as a matter of Canonical or University Law, there was no objection to a Secular attending the theological lectures of the Friar-Doctors, it seems probable that in

conclusively proved that it really belongs to the quarrel in the time of Johannes de Montesono. This is ignored by Kaufmann (I. p. 286).

[1] Bulæus, III. p. 351 ; *Chartul.* T. I. pt. i. Nos. 342, 501. The Friars were at first forbidden to study Arts at all. (*Chartul.* T. I. pt. i. No. 57.) In 1259 there was an order for the establishment of a Studium Artium in each province (*ib.* No. 335), perhaps in consequence of failure to get

admission to the Arts Schools of the University.

[2] Regulars were also excluded from the Faculty of Medicine. The older Orders were admitted to the Faculty of Canon Law in 1337–1339. Bulæus, IV. pp. 253, 315 ; *Chartul.* T. II. Nos. 1002, 1018.

[3] A larger number were often summoned to Congregations of the Faculty of Theology for the discussion of theological questions.

CHAP. V,   practice their lecture-rooms were henceforth attended chiefly
§ 2.   by members of their respective orders[1].   At all events the
most valuable privilege of the Doctorate was secured by the
custom that secular students should incept only ' under '
secular Doctors.   The oath[2] now administered to every
Master of Arts at his ' Inception ' may perhaps have been
held to prevent his attendance at Friars' lectures ; since it
pledged him to ' stand with the secular Masters to whatever
state he should come.'

Friars'   Technically the Mendicants had triumphed : practically
victory   the University had by stolid persistence, by the tremendous
partial and
short-lived.   power of organized combination and by the death of its
great Pontifical enemy, secured for ever a large part of
what it had all along been contending for.   By 1318 the
University had grown strong enough to impose once more
upon the Friars the oath of obedience to the Statutes, and
this time they had quietly to submit to the demand which
had created such a storm of opposition sixty years before[3].

Constitu-   The controversy left permanent effects upon the sub-
tional   sequent organization, and still more upon the tone and
Results.   temper of the University.   We may trace its influence in
three main directions :—

(1) We have already said something about the effect
of the *Quasi lignum* upon the separate organization of
the Faculties.   It is no doubt a mistake to suppose (with
du Boulay) that the theological Doctors were before this
date included in the Nations.   There were meetings of
the theological Faculty almost as early as there were
formal meetings of the whole University ; and even the
practice of voting by Faculties had perhaps grown up

---

[1] This aspect of the question lost
its importance as Doctors ceased to
lecture. For Biblical Lectures seculars certainly resorted to Friar-
Bachelors, but for Lectures on the
Sentences they probably as a rule
went to a secular : but on this point
I have come across no definite information.

[2] ' Item stabitis cum magistris

secularibus . . . toto tempore vite
vestre ad quemcunque statum deveneritis.' *Chartul.* T. I. pt. i. No.
501.

[3] Bulæus, IV. 181 ; *Chartul.* T. II.
No. 776. Non-regent Mendicants
might of course be specially summoned by the Theological Faculty.
Bulæus, V. p. 387.

by a process of spontaneous development[1]. But, however this may be, the *Quasi lignum*, by requiring a two-thirds majority in each Faculty to legalize a ' Cessation,' sanctioned and stereotyped the practice[2]. In the earlier part of the thirteenth century the Theological Faculty appears rather as a separate organization whose members were also members of the University than as a distinct member of a Federal Body. The necessities of the anti-Mendicant campaign, however, compelled the Theologians at once to reduce their customs to the form of written Statutes and closely to ally themselves with the rest of the University, especially with its most powerful factor, the Faculty of Arts. It is in the course of this controversy that the University for the first time distinctly claims to legislate, not merely for the Theologians as individual members of the larger society, but for the theological Faculty as such. The process of welding the Faculties into the University-system was completed in 1281, when a University Statute formally lays down the principle that the acts (*facta*) of the Faculties are the acts of the University[3].

(2) In yet another way the Mendicant affair contributed to the consolidation of the University. The University was first compelled to borrow money for the purposes of its litigation with the Chancellor, and we have seen reason to believe that it was this financial necessity which more than anything else contributed to the growth of the Rectorate and the four Proctorships. The expenses of the Mendicant suit must have been much heavier[4]. It

---

[1] In 1277 we find a Statute passed 'per totam Universitatem, quatuor Facultatibus hoc volentibus.' Bulæus, III. p. 432; *Chartul.* T. I. pt. i. No. 478.

[2] The Dominican Friars of Oxford contended that the two-thirds majority was required not only for a Cessation, but for every other purpose. *Collectanea* (Oxf. Hist. Soc.), II. p. 221. Of this I find no other trace.

[3] Bulæus, III. p. 456; *Chartul.* T. I. pt. i. No. 505.

[4] The collection is thus described by the Friar Cantipratanus: ' Nequitiæ primordialis actores [*leg.* auctores], simplices Uniuersitatis scholares sibi velut unum corpus miris astutiis adunarunt, ut in multis librarum milibus eos roderent placitantes; ut sic in dictos ordines crudelius deseuirent, et id quod per se

was now that the financial system of the University may be supposed to have grown up—the system of levies of one or more *bursæ* (i. e. the sworn amount of his weekly board) upon each member of it, by means of which a system of proportionate taxation was secured. Regular payments were exacted at Determination[1] and Inception[2], while special calls were made on all students when circumstances required, and the payment of such contributions was enforced by Papal privilege[3]. The constitutional importance of this financial system has already been explained.

Seeds of
Gallican-
ism.

(3) But still more important than its constitutional results were the effects of the controversy upon the theological tone and temper of the University. Till now there had been no reason whatever for any hostile feeling against the Papacy on the part of the University. The University in so far as it was anything more than a private Society was as much the privileged creature of the Holy See as the Mendicant Orders themselves: so far from the University having any special tenderness for the rights of Bishops and secular prelates, we have seen that it was in its origin an organized rebellion against episcopal authority. The alliance between the Holy See and the Mendicants sowed the seeds of Gallicanism in the University which was to be its stronghold[4].

non poterant, non sufficiente pecunia, in euacuatione bursarum innocentiæ puerilis, multorum copiis obtinerent.' *De Apibus*, II. c. 10. p. 182.

[1] i. e. the B.A. degree. See below, p. 443 *sq.*

[2] 'Item antequam bursam unam talem vel tantam, quam ponit fide corporali prestita super hoc, ad opus Universitatis persolverit et ad opus nascionis alium, eidem determinandi licentia non largiatur.' *Chartul.* T. I. pt. i. No. 201. On Inception: 'Dabit tres bursas unam Universitati, aliam nascioni, tertiam bedellis, quas solvet procuratori sue nascionis.' *Ib.* No. 202 (*c.* 1252 A.D.).

[3] *Chartul.* T. I. pt. i. Nos. 352,376,&c.

[4] To complete our account of the relations between the University and the Friars, it should be mentioned that Friars who had studied elsewhere were constantly admitted at once to the reading of the Sentences, or had their course otherwise expedited by Papal Bulls. (See *Chartul. passim.*) In 1376 Gregory XI conferred on the Minister General of the Franciscans the power to confer the Licenses in Chapter-General after examination by their own Doctors; in 1429 this privilege was withdrawn by Martin V. Bulæus, IV. 448; V. 389. See also App. XII.

§ 3. The Constitution and Privileges of the University.

By the end of the thirteenth century the University constitution had attained the form which in its main features
lasted till the close of our period.   The penultimate decade Comple-
of the century is marked by the last important conflict in tion of the
that long struggle with the Chancellor to which the Uni- tional de-
versity corporation owes, if not its very existence, at least velopment.
much of its importance and many features of its organization.   From the mutual recriminations of the parties in the
Papal Court [1] it appears that the Chancellor, Philip de Conflict
Thori, had renewed the illegal demand of an oath to re- with the Chancel-
spect the liberties of the Church of Paris.   He had licensed lor, Philip
a princely candidate (the brother of the King of Aragon) de Thori,
without the consent of the Masters.   In some cases he had 1280–1290.
dispensed with the conditions, in respect of time, age, and
study, required by the University; in others he had arbitrarily rejected Bachelors who presented themselves for the
License.   Moreover he had disobeyed the Papal Bulls relating to the appointment of Examiners.   When the Chancellor was required to examine with the assistance of six
Masters of the University, it was intended (the University
alleged) that they should be Regent Masters : instead of
which the Chancellor had appointed old Non-regents who
'are ignorant of modern opinions and have forgotten the
old ones [2].'   The Chancellor replied by contending that the
Masters had in a variety of ways exceeded their powers,
and infringed upon those of his office.   There is a general
accusation of making statutes to the prejudice of the Bishop

---

[1] Jourdain, Nos. 266, 274; *Chartul.*   [2] ' Nesciunt modernas opiniones et
T. I. pt. i. Nos. 503, 515.   amiserunt antiquas.'

CHAP. V,   and Church of Paris.   More specifically the Chancellor
§ 3.   contended that the Masters had resisted his judicial authority by forbidding scholars to cite one another before him :
they had compelled students to go to Ste. Geneviève to be
examined instead of to the 'Examination of S. Mary,' and
they had enforced Determination as a condition of the
License.   But most presumptuous of all, they had dared
to cite him through the Bedel—him, the 'Head of the
University' (as he contended but the Masters denied)—to
attend Congregation not (as he alleged was the custom)
'by way of supplication and request' (*supplicando et rogando*)
but peremptorily and *sub pœna* in his quality of a Doctor
of Theology, and upon his refusal had actually suspended
him from lecturing, and forbidden scholars to attend his
Sermons.   In the course of the conflict the University
even advanced to a pitch of audacity beyond this.   On
this one occasion and this only, in the whole course of its
history [1], the University presumed altogether to dispense
with the aid of the Chancellor of Paris, and to elect a
Chancellor of their own to bestow the License.   We do
not possess the final judgment of the Holy See upon all
the points at issue, but on these two last points the rights
of the Chancellor were peremptorily vindicated.   He was
exempted from compulsory attendance at Congregation,
and the Licenses granted by the University were quashed
or invalidated [2].

Suit
against
Chancellor
Bertrand of
S. Denys.

In 1290 we have a fresh batch of complaints against
Philip de Thori's successor, Bertrand of S. Denys.   He
had persisted in rejecting duly qualified candidates in the

---

[1] 'Scholares Parisienses institue-
runt quemdam Cancellarium propria
authoritate, contra libertatem Ecclesiæ Parisiensis.' *Chron. Rothomagen.*
ap. Hemeræum, p. 79.   In 1482 the
Theological Faculty, incensed at the
appointment of a Canonist instead
of a Theologian to the Chancellor's
stall, conducted the *Birettatio* of certain Licentiates without the Chan-

cellor, but did not, it would seem,
attempt to license.   Bulæus, V. p.
749 *sq.* ; Hemeræus, p. 84.   A B.D.
had been appointed Chancellor in
1387 and a Licentiate of Decrees
in 1433.   Hemeræus, pp. 134, 136.
With these exceptions the Chancellor had always been D.D.

[2] Bulæus, III. p. 464 : *Chartul.*
T. I. pt. i. Nos. 516, 528.

teeth of the Examiners' verdict. Before the unfortunate candidates could get the answer to the first question out of their mouths [1], the Chancellor, 'carried away by the whirlwind of his impatience and captiousness,' had driven them from his presence with insult and abuse, 'vilely and irrationally expelling them from the Examination.' At other times when Bachelors had presented themselves to him in the Church or Cloister requesting admission to the examination, he had refused to examine them at all, and had so far forgotten himself as to call them 'stinking asses.' Amid a host of minor irregularities, he had carried on an extensive traffic in Licenses, allowing passes in the Chancellor's Examination to be sold by laymen, women, actors, or servants of his household. In some cases the License had been given without the Examiners even having the opportunity of setting eyes on the candidates. Here again there is at present an hiatus in our documents. We possess neither the Chancellor's reply nor the judgment of the Holy See. On the majority of the questions at issue between the University and the Chancellor, there can be no doubt that in the long run, whether by virtue of Papal decision or by the irresistible growth of custom, the University gained the day. From this time the strictly judicial authority of the Chancellor fell into desuetude : he ceased to be, if he had ever been, the *judex ordinarius* of scholars [2]. He even ceased to have any real control over the grant or refusal of Licenses, except in so far as he retained the nomination of the Examiners in Arts [3]. His position remained one of great dignity, though more and more overshadowed by the growing pretensions of the Rector : but its sub-

Loss of the Chancellor's Judicial Power.

---

[1] 'Antequam possent in unius argumenti repetitione vel solutione a vobis audiri.' Jourdain, No. 302 ; *Chartul.* T. I. pt. i. No. 569.

[2] But see above, p. 340.

[3] There was an occasional attempt of the Chancellor to shake off the fetters imposed upon him by the Examiners. The last attempt which I have noticed to license against the opinion of the Examiners occurred in 1385. Bulæus, IV. p. 605. The illegal fees were, however, persisted in, the Chancellor pleading the poverty of his prebendless stall and the expenses he was at in the way of 'Vinum et species' for the Masters and others. Bulæus, IV. p. 606 *sq.*

stantial power was gone.   Only his mysterious prerogative
of conferring the License was left him, and that remained
henceforth almost as sacred and incommunicable as the
Bishop's power of conferring Orders: though, as already
explained, his powers were as regards the Faculty of Arts
shared by his upstart rival, the Chancellor of Ste. Geneviève [1].

The *Jus
ubique
docendi.*
In order to appreciate the peculiar sanctity which attached to the Chancellor's barren prerogative, it is necessary to bear in mind the change which we have already
noticed as taking place in the course of the thirteenth century with respect to what may be called the constitutional
theory of University institutions.   We have seen that in
its origin the University was nothing more than a private
Society: the Schools in connexion with which it grew up
were nothing more than a development of the episcopal
School of Paris: the 'License' no more than an episcopal
permission to teach in a particular city or diocese.   The
extraordinary prestige of Paris and Bologna—and in a
subordinate degree a few other *Studia,* most of which had
imitated more or less closely the organization of Paris
or Bologna—had practically given to their Licenses an
ecumenical prestige and validity.   It was little more than
a recognition of an accomplished fact when in 1292 Nicolas
IV conferred on the licentiates of Paris the prerogative of
teaching in all other Schools and Universities throughout
the world, without any additional examination [2].   Henceforth the Chancellor conferred the License in the name not
of the Bishop but of the Pope,—a circumstance which has
largely contributed to blind historians to the recognition
of his original position as Head of the Episcopal School.

Increasing
importance
of Rector-
ship:
In proportion as the practical importance of the Chancellorship declined, that of the Rectorship increased.   The
Rector, as has been already said, was elected by represen-

---

[1] The Chancellorship of Paris was
in the gift of the Bishop but was
often 'reserved.' *Chartul.* T. II. No.
592, &c.

[2] *Chartul.* T. II. No. 578.   The
Bull is wrongly ascribed by Bulæus
(III. p. 449), Jourdain, &c., to Nico-
las III.

tatives or 'Intrants'[1] of the four Nations, who were shut up after the manner of the Sacred College at Papal elections in a 'Conclave' after the solemn singing of the *Veni Creator*. They were required to complete the election before a lighted taper had burnt itself out[2]. Though a peculiar sanctity was supposed to attach itself to this method of election, known as the 'way of the Holy Spirit,' the solemnity of the proceeding was not always sufficient to prevent the 'Intrants' coming to blows in their seclusion[3]. If an election had not been made by the expiration of the time, fresh Intrants were elected: and if a majority were not secured in this way, the ex-Rector was called in to give a casting vote[4].

Mode of Election.

By the end of the thirteenth century we have seen that the Rector has attained a virtual presidency but not an acknowledged Headship of the whole University of four Faculties: another half a century secured his triumph over all rivals. The dispute as to the mode of summoning the Dean and Faculty of Theology was settled in 1341 by a compromise: it was ordered that the Rector or a Master of Arts deputed by him should personally wait upon the Dean, but if the Dean were not at home, a written summons might be left for him[5]. In 1339 and 1347 there were disputes between the two officials for precedence in Church: here victory was secured for the Rector by the superior numbers and athletic prowess of the young Masters of Arts and their younger pupils. On the last occasion the Dean of Theology, though an Archbishop and Papal Legate, was forcibly expelled from the Rector's chair of state in the Choir of S. Germain-des-Prés[6]. Even after this (in 1353)

Conflicts with the Dean of Theology.

---

[1] Originally the Proctors were themselves the first Intrants: the practice in this respect seems to have varied at different times and in different Nations. Cf. Bulæus, IV. 246 (*Chartul. T. II*. No. 989), V. 530, 877, &c.

[2] Bulæus, III. p. 451 (cf. V. pp. 530, 554); *Chartul. T. II*. No. 554.

[3] Bulæus, V. p. 550; *Remarques sur la dignité du Recteur*, p. 11.

[4] Bulæus, III. p. 451; *Chartul. T. II*. No. 554.

[5] Bulæus, IV. 267 *sq.*; *Chartul. T. II*. No. 1051.

[6] Crevier, II. 386, 389; Jourdain, No. 613; *Chartul. T. II*. No. 1145; cf. No. 1143.

the Faculties of Theology and Canon Law opposed the despatch of a letter in the name of the 'Rector and University[1]': but in 1358 the innovation received the sanction of the Pope, who addressed a Bull to the 'Rector and Masters of the University[2].'

The Rector's precedence.

His position in the University itself being secured, the Rector entered upon a series of disputes with the highest ecclesiastical dignitaries for precedence at Royal funerals and other public processions. For a time the difficulty was met by allowing an academical and a capitular dignitary to walk side by side, while the Bishop of Paris brought up the rear in solitary grandeur. This arrangement brought the Rector to the side of the Dean of Notre Dame ; but ere long we find the ambitious functionary backing his way to the side of the Bishop, and, after a riot or two, he succeeded in securing that position[3]. The ex-Rector, du Boulay, records with a glow of official and antiquarian pride the numerous occasions on which some plebeian and moneyless Rector of the Artists took precedence of Bishops, Cardinals, Archbishops, Papal Nuncios, Ambassadors, and Peers of France[4].

Dignity of the Rectorship representative

A very mistaken impression will, however, be given of the real importance of the office if it is compared to the Oxford or Cambridge Chancellorship. Its dignity was

[1] Bulæus, IV. p. 329; *Chartul.* T. II. No. 1143.

[2] Bulæus, IV. p. 359. An instrument of the Theological Faculty cited by the Anon. Refut. (p. 356) says that the Faculty of Arts elects a Rector 'non ut regat Universitatem, nec præferatur, sed Rectorem, id est, rerum Actorem aut procuratorem negotiorum Universitatis, cuius mandata et deliberata per eam idem Rector vel Actor et procurator ac etiam merus exequutor et minister habet et debet exequi etiam per proprium juramentum.' This would have been denied by the Artists who long required Bachelors to swear

'quod Decretum factum et ordinatum per Facultatem Artium de præpositione Rectoris in Actibus communibus Universitatis inviolabiliter observabitis, ad quemcunque statum deveneritis.' Bulæus, *Remarques sur la dignité du R.* p. 40.

[3] Bulæus, VI. 402. It should be observed, however, that in purely University processions the Rector still walked with the Dean of Theology. Goulet, f. xiii. ; Bulæus, *Remarques sur la dignité du R.* pp. 67–88.

[4] Bulæus, I. 269, 270; IV. 585; V. 543; *Remarques sur la dignité du R.* p. 41.

mainly symbolic and representative. It was held at first
only for a month or six weeks, afterwards for three months[1].
The Rector, while appearing in state with his eight Bedels[2]
at the head of the University, rarely spoke in its name—a
function usually entrusted to some eloquent 'Orator' chosen
for the occasion from the Theological Doctors, just as a
municipal deputation is headed by the Mayor, but finds
its mouthpiece in the more intellectually qualified Re-
corder. Moreover, unlike the Chancellor of Oxford, the
Rector had scarcely any judicial powers, except those
which he derived from the Statutes. Consequently, his
jurisdiction extended only to members or 'clients' of the
University[3]. His punishments (except in so far as he could
indirectly call in the aid of spiritual terrors by pronouncing
a contumacious Master to be a 'perjured' person) were
purely academical,—fine, suspension, and expulsion.

No continuous records of proceedings before the Rector's
Court appear to be preserved, and we are therefore left
somewhat in the dark as to the exact sphere of its
jurisdiction. Its ordinary business, we may suppose,
consisted in the hearing of disputes about the rent of
hostels[4], and of complaints against members of the trades
carried on under the supervision of the University, in the
granting of certificates of scholarity, the initiation of
measures for procuring the release of an imprisoned or the
satisfaction of an injured scholar, the settlement of disputes
and the trial of strictly personal actions between Masters
and scholars, the administration of deceased scholars'
estates[5], and above all the punishment of offences against

---

[1] From 1266; *Chartul.* I. pt. i. No.
409. The Proctorship remained a
monthly office, but a Proctor was
more often than not re-elected for
another month or more. Bulæus,
V. 631, and Registers, *passim.*

[2] We are told by Bulæus (III. 561)
that each Nation elected two Bedels
who walked before its Proctor with
silver maces, but these appear to
have also attended the Rector. The
Superior Faculties had Bedels of

their own.

[3] In the seventeenth century it
would appear, from the *Recueil des
Priviléges de l'Un. de P.*, pp. 1–9,
that the 'greater part' of personal
actions were triable by the Rector's
tribunal, while 'real' causes went
to the Royal Conservator.

[4] Jourdain, No. 551; *Chartul.* T.
II. No. 803.

[5] Jourdain, No. 373; *Chartul.* T.
II. No. 663; Bulæus, V. 382.

the Statutes. In the exercise of this jurisdiction, the Rector was assisted by the Proctors who formed the permanent 'deputies' or (as they were afterwards called) 'Tribunal' of the Faculty of Arts[1]. From the decision of a Nation

Appeals.

or its Proctor there was an appeal to the whole Faculty of Arts or its officers. From the decision of the Rector and Proctors, or from one of the Superior Faculties, there was an appeal to the whole University, which heard the case by means of specially appointed deputies[2]. In the post-medieval period the Rector, Proctors, and Deans formed a permanent board of deputies or 'Tribunal' of the whole University, which eventually succeeded to a large extent in ousting the popular Congregation from the government of the University. From about the middle of the seventeenth century the 'Tribunal' of the University at Paris, though more popular in its constitution, passed into something like the position of the old, oligarchic 'Hebdomadal Board' of Oxford[3].

No University Buildings.

Each of the Faculties and Nations constituting the University had some Church or convent which was usually borrowed for its meetings: but the place of meeting was not invariable, and neither the University nor its constituent bodies assembled in a building of its

---

[1] Bulæus, IV. 128, 211, 218; *Chartul.* T. II. Nos. 803, 870, 881. Crivier (II. p. 309) attempts to find the Tribunal of the University in this last document; I see no express evidence that when the deputies of the University are mentioned in medieval times, the Rector, Proctors, and Deans are invariably meant.

[2] Bulæus, III. 594–6, IV. 172; *Sur la Dign. du R.*, pp. 98 *sq.*, 119 *sq.*; *Chartul.* T. II. No. 721; Jourdain, No. 741. The legality of any appeal to the University was not beyond dispute. See Bulæus, VI. 22 *sq.* It was a moot point whether the Rector and Proctors ought to be present with the 'deputies' in hearing appeals from themselves. Thus

in 1365 we hear of the Dean of Decrees wanting to retire because they refused to withdraw on such an occasion. The Rector ordered him to sit down 'primo simpliciter, secundario sub juramento.' The lawyer replied with true medieval boyishness, 'Non curo de Præceptis vestris plusquam de uno obolo.' Upon the matter being referred to the University the Dean apologized, but three Nations and the Faculty of Medicine ('quibus accessit Rector') against the two remaining Faculties and one Nation held that the Proctors should sit: 'Et fuerat eatenus indecisa controversia.' Bulæus, IV. pp. 387, 388.

[3] Bulæus, III. 577, 578; Dubarle, I. 352.

own. The great medieval Universities (as distinct from their Colleges) were poor corporations. Neither Paris nor Oxford possessed any endowments whatever, except a few legacies devoted to special purposes, such as a bene-faction for poor scholars, or the patronage of a few chap-laincies or other Benefices[1]. In this poverty lay the real strength of the Universities, upon occasions of collision with the spiritual and temporal authorities : just as their wealth was the weakness of the great ecclesiastics in their struggles with the secular arm. If a University 'seceded' or 'dispersed,' there were no temporalities which could be sequestrated ; it took all its property—the fees of its students—with it. Wherever there were rooms to be hired for Schools, and Churches and convents to be borrowed for Congregations, a University could soon make itself at home. At Paris it is not till the beginning of the four-teenth century that it becomes clear that the Nations even undertook to rent the Schools in their corporate capacity[2] : and it was still later that the Nations and Faculties began to acquire Schools of their own[3]. The only property which in the early part of our period belonged to the Univer-sity or rather to the Faculty of Arts as a whole was the Pré-aux-clercs—a sort of University play-ground out-side the walls, the freehold of which it had acquired by custom, or by usurpation from the neighbouring monks of S. Germain, with whom the Masters and scholars were engaged in incessant litigations and a succession of

[1] The Benefices (other than Chap-laincies) to which the University presented were (1) SS. Cosmas and Damianus, (2) S. Andreas de arcubus, (3) S. Germanus Vetus ; all in Paris. Bulæus, III. 612 *sq.*

[2] Bulæus, IV. pp. 100, 187, 213, 224; *Chartul.* T. II. Nos. 655, 793, 897. It is at about this time (1329) that we find the first certain evidence of the concentration of the Arts Schools in the Rue du Fouarre.

[3] A School was bought by the Nation of France in 1372. Crevier,

II. p. 483. In 1415 the Faculty of Decrees built two large Schools in the region long appropriated to the Schools of the Faculty—the Clos Bruneau. The Musée de Cluny still preserves a block of stone in-scribed ' Scole secūde facultatis Decretorum.' Péries, pp. 50, 51. The old Schools of Medicine in the ' Rue des Rats ' date from 1369; but not having found materials for a com-plete history of these buildings, I shall not attempt to enter further on the subject.

murderous affrays. Each Nation borrowed a Church for its National Mass. The University sermons took place in the Churches of the Franciscans and Dominicans, or at times in the Chapel of the College of Navarre[1]. To the last-mentioned Chapel was transferred in the course of the fourteenth century the chest containing the Archives of the University, hitherto kept at the Mathurine convent, and the seal-chest, which had previously been deposited at the Abbey of Ste. Geneviève. In the early days of the University General Congregations were commonly held in the Church of S. Julien-le-Pauvre. Later on, that Church came to be appropriated to the Congregations of the Faculty of Arts[2]: and the University itself met sometimes at the Dominican or Franciscan Convent, sometimes (on occasions of special importance when a large attendance was expected) in the more ample Chapter-house of the Bernardines or Cistercians, but most commonly in the mean little refectory of the Mathurine or Trinitarian Convent[3].

Composition of the General Congregation.

Before explaining the procedure of these 'General Congregations,' it may be well to recapitulate what has already been said as to their constitution. The University consisted of four Faculties—the three superior Faculties of The-

---

[1] 'Sermones in Scholis' appear among the writings of the twelfth century. Bulæus, II. p. 374. In the fourteenth century there was a sermon in the morning and a *collatio* or 'conference' in the afternoon of every Sunday or holiday. The preacher in the afternoon (at least if a Regular) was required to take the same subject as that of the morning sermon whether he himself or another had preached it. Bulæus, IV. pp. 181, 278, 427 (*Chartul.* T. II. Nos. 774, 1057). Statutes relating to the conduct of Students, e. g. the Statute against bullying freshmen (Bulæus, IV. p. 267; *Chartul.* T. II. No. 1057), and notices of many kinds were published at

University sermons. On one occasion we find that a decayed and deserted College was ordered to be put up to public auction (*subhastari*) from the University pulpit, 'secundum morem et consuetudinem in casu simili hactenus observatos.' Bulæus, IV. 368. (Possibly only the announcement of the sale was so made.)

[2] Held at least once a week. Bulæus, III. 420; *Chartul.* T. I. pt. ii. No. 460.

[3] Bulæus, III. 486, IV. 223-4, V. 696; *Chartul.* T. II. App. p. 692. The full title of the last-mentioned Order was the 'Ordo fratrum SS. Trinitatis de redemptione captivorum,' founded during the Crusades by John de Mathu.

ology, Decrees, and Medicine, and the inferior Faculty
of Arts. The Faculty of Arts was subdivided into four
'Nations'—France, Picardy, Normandy, and England.
Each Faculty was presided over by a Dean: each Nation
by a Proctor. The Rector had come, at least by the middle
of the fourteenth century, to be the incontestable Head
of the University, as well as of the united Faculty of Arts.
Each of these sections of the University was a corporation
in itself, with its own Head, Receiver, Bedels, common
seal[1], Congregations, Statutes, &c. But all scholars and
graduates of the superior Faculties except the Masters
remained under the jurisdiction of the Nations and their
officers[2]. The General Congregation was composed of the
united Masters of all the Faculties. The University was
originally composed exclusively of Regents, i.e. Masters
actually engaged in teaching in the Schools; and, in the
Faculties of Arts and Medicine, every Master upon his
Inception was required to swear to complete a period of
'necessary Regency,' i.e. to lecture for two years[3], unless
dispensed by the University. This system must be borne in
mind in order to realize how large, youthful, and fluctuating
a body the Masters of Arts really were, and in order to appreciate the resemblances in spite of diversity between the
Master-University of Paris and the Student-Universities of
Bologna. At the end of his necessary Regency, the Master
was at liberty to continue his lectures as long as he pleased;
but only so long as he continued to give an 'ordinary'
lecture every 'legible' day in one of the Schools in or
near the Rue du Fouarre throughout the 'Grand ordinary'
of each year (i.e. from Oct. 1, the Feast of S. Remigius,

Regents and Non-regents.

---

[1] Except the Faculty of Theology
which long used the Chancellor's
seal.

[2] Crevier says (II. p. 56), 'Les
trois Facultés dites supérieures ne
renferment que des docteurs. Leurs
bacheliers sont restés dans les Nations,' but, since it appears that none
but M.A.s voted in the Nations, the

remark must mean that only such
Bachelors of the superior Faculties
who were also M.A. could have
possessed votes, though they would
all be subject to the Statutes and
officers of the Nations.

[3] *Chartul.* I. pt. i. Nos. 501, 937.
In practice the period appears to
have been usually one year.

to Easter) or the greater part of it, did he retain his rights to take part in the deliberations of his Nation or Faculty or of the whole University[1]. His rights ceased on becoming a Non-Regent: but not so his obligations. The oath of obedience to the Rector was of perpetual validity, and hence, when summoned by the Rector, he was as much bound as the Regent to attend a Congregation and give his late colleagues the benefit of his advice and support. At first the summoning of the Non-Regents was a rare and extraordinary event. But, as the Non-Regents would always include a large number of persons highly placed in Church and State, their presence was naturally desired when anything like a demonstration was to be made. After the middle of the fourteenth century the attendance of Non-Regents seems to have become increasingly frequent, and eventually they were summoned on all occasions of importance except elections[2]. But they voted as members of their respective Nations or Faculties; and it is not clear whether their presence ever became legally necessary to the acts of the University, as at Oxford or Cambridge[3].

Procedure in General Congregations.

At these Congregations the mode of proceeding was as follows. The Rector notified the time and place of the meeting and the matters to be discussed at it, to the Dean of Theology by calling at his house in person or through a Master of Arts, and to the other Deans and the Proctors

[1] Bulæus, IV. 164 (*Chartul.* T. II. No. 697), V. 71.

[2] Yet in 1349 we find Non-Regents joining in electing a Proctor. Bulæus, IV. 314. But this was in the English Nation which was possibly at this time small. In the Superior Faculties Non-Regents had the right of voting in Examinations. *Chartul.* T. I. pt. i. No. 465.

[3] A Statute of 1312 directs the Bedels 'nullum intrare vel accedere permittent, nisi magistros actu Regentes vel illos qui per Rectorem fuerint evocati.' Bulæus, IV. 164; *Chartul.* T. II. No. 697. In 1456 the privileges of Regency were extended

to 'Magistri et Pædagogi qui per longa tempora rexerint in vico straminis,' except participation in the 'distributiones pro Missis et Vesperis,' i. e. payments from the funds of the Nation or University to all Masters who had attended the weekly University Vespers and Mass, sums which were spent in potations at a tavern immediately after the service. Intruders on these occasions were to be expelled, or if they had eaten or drunk anything before detection to be compelled 'ad solvendam cotam suam de propriis pecuniis.' Bulæus, V. p. 617.

by sending them a *schedula* containing these particulars [1]. These officers in turn summoned the Masters of their respective Faculties or Nations by sending a Bedel round the Schools during morning lecture. In most cases the business to be discussed would have originated with one of the component bodies, who would either have arrived at a resolution and ordered its Head to demand the 'adjunction' of the other Faculties and Nations, or simply referred the matter for further deliberation to the whole University [2]. When the University was assembled, the Rector laid the question before it. In every Church or Convent where the University was in the habit of meeting, each Faculty and Nation had its accustomed place for separate deliberation. In the Church of S. Julien for instance there were chairs for the Four Proctors in the four corners of the Nave. To these four corners upon a division the Nations retired and held their separate Congregations. The three smaller bodies—the Doctors of the three superior Faculties—repaired to other parts of the Church. Debate took place only in these separate Assemblies. On the re-assembling of the Congregation the vote or opinion of each Nation [3] was reported by its Proctor, the vote of each Faculty by its Dean. The Rector then summed up the collective sense

[1] If due notice of the agenda were not given, the proceedings might be annulled (Bulæus, V. 527). In the fifteenth century the Senior or French Proctor, with the concurrence of the other Proctors, claimed the right of summoning a Congregation of the Faculty of Arts if the Rector refused to do so. Bulæus, V. p. 718-720.

[2] At times the proceedings were spread over several Congregations. Thus in 13$\frac{68}{69}$ 'cum idem rector alias tradidisset, in quadam congregacione generali, magistris trium facultatum videlicet medicorum, decretorum et theologorum, tres cedulas papireas, in quibus cedulis continentur articuli et modus per quem

detrahentes, malefactores et detractatores scolarium bejaunorum corrigerentur, ut dicti magistri predictarum facultatum dictas cedulas corrigerent,' &c. Jourdain, No. 567; *Chartul.* T. II. No. 1032. This document gives a very clear and detailed account of a General Congregation.

[3] It was taken by show of hands and shouting combined, ' et cuicunque placeret illud, levaret manum et diceret : ita.' *Chartul.* T. II. No. 1072 ; but elsewhere—presumably when a poll was demanded or perhaps on personal ' graces '—we find allusions to secret voting. *Chartul.* T. II. App. p. 672.

Voting by
Faculties.

of the House, and pronounced the 'conclusion' of the whole University [1].

At first, as we have seen, the principle was that a majority was required in each Faculty. The earliest instance of decision by a majority of Faculties which occurs is an exception exactly of the kind which is said to prove the rule. It occurs in 1303 when only a majority of the Faculties could be induced to support the appeal of the Prelates of France against Boniface VIII's excommunication of the adherents of Philip the Fair in his struggle against the Papacy. The language used in the Act of Adherence implies that the step was exceptional : it was rather a declaration of opinion by the majority to which they were emboldened or compelled by Royal pressure to give the sanction of the University seal than a constitutional decision of the University itself [2]. The document to which the seal was appended was a mere academic protest or manifesto, not a Statute claiming the obedience of individual Masters. The precedent was no doubt not without its influence in the development of the new constitutional theory : at all events it illustrates the way in which the

Growth of
majority-
voting.

[1] An attempt of the Dean of Theology to 'conclude' in default of the Rector was violently resented by the Artists. Bulæus, V. 589. The act of Conclusion was made the more indispensable and the more difficult since no actual 'motion' or 'question' was commonly put before the retirement of the Nations and Faculties. Hence the Rector's function was not merely to count or declare votes, but to sum up the collective sense of resolutions which might be variously worded. Where no majority appeared for any one resolution, the Rector 'nihil conclusit.' He had no casting vote.

[2] 'Ad notitiam singulorum volumus peruenire quod nuper nonnullis ex vobis majorem partem Facultatum nostrarum [et] totius Parisiensis studii facientibus pro certis causis et nego-

tiis accedentibus ad presentiam excellentissimi Principis D. Philippi . . . recitatum fuit,' &c. Bulæus, IV. 47. The original text appears to have no *et* (*Chartul.* T. II. No. 634), but the passage can hardly be construed without it. The precautions taken in 131⅔ against abuse of the University seal (Bulæus, IV, p. 163 *Chartul.* T. II. No. 698) suggest the kind of way in which a majority might forcibly attempt to override the minority: it is provided 'cuiuslibet Facultatis teneatur unus Magister cum clavi in loco sigillationis personaliter interesse.' All previous writers (Denifle does not touch on the question) have assumed (1) that voting by a majority of bodies dates from the earliest days of the University (2) that on a division, a Nation was equal to a Faculty.

majority may have introduced the theory of majority-voting by the forcible creation of successive precedents. But as late as 1313 the Dominicans of Oxford allege in their pleadings against that University that at Paris the consent of the whole four Faculties was requisite to the making of a Statute, though from the same document it appears that the practice of majority-voting existed *de facto* in the University of Oxford[1]. But it is not till the year 13$\frac{39}{40}$ that we get a decisive instance of an attempt to carry a Statute by a majority of the Faculties only[2]. Even now, however, the principle is only struggling for recognition. A Statute or Decree against the bullying of freshmen was carried in spite of the dissent of the Faculty of Law from a particular clause of it. But since the dissent of the Faculty from this part is specified in the official record, it is not clear how far it was intended that the Lawyers should be bound by those parts of the Statute to which they had not consented. In the very same year, however, the Theologians refused their consent to a contribution or levy voted by the other Faculties for the expenses of an embassy to the Holy See. Though the majority were determined to override the opposition of the Theologians, it was considered necessary to obtain their formal consent, and they were accordingly forced to yield by the threat of being suspended from six ordinary lectures in the event of

---

[1] See above, p. 391, n. 2, and below, Vol. II. chap. xii. § 2.

[2] ' Quatuor Facultates seu magistri earumdem dixerunt, ac etiam concorditer pronunciaverunt, quod volebant et concordabant, quod omnia, in predicta cedula contenta, per modum ordinacionis de cetero tenerentur, hoc tantum excepto, quod vir venerabilis et discretus magister Nicholaus de Hamello, doctor in decretis, qui non fuerat in correctione predicte cedule, ut dicebat, nomine sue Facultatis decretorum, sic dixit, quod non erat bonum, quod magistri regentes tenerentur, injurias minas vel violencias bejaunis illatas, prout in cedula continebatur, alicui revelare, quia non videbatur Facultati sue decretorum justum nec consonum rationi.' Jourdain, No. 567; *Chartul.* T. II. No. 1032. There are traces of the practice before this. In 1318 a document was sealed, though an amendment had been suggested by the Theologians, but it does not appear whether the amendment was accepted. Bulæus, IV. p. 181; *Chartul.* T. II. No. 774. Cf. also Bulæus, IV. 208 *sq.*; *Chartul.* T. II. No. 845.

CHAP. V,
§ 3.

continued recusancy[1]. Long before the end of the century, however, the right of the majority of Faculties to bind the minority had ceased to be disputed[2]. The historians of the University have indeed pretended that the vote of the University was determined by the majority of the seven corporations, each Nation being thus placed on an equality with one of the superior Faculties[3] : but such a contention is contrary to the most explicit statements in the medieval documents which have come down to us[4]. The Faculty of Arts did sometimes attempt, not unsuccessfully, to overcome the opposition of the superior Faculties by virtue of the Rector's authority over its individual members; but the constitutional principle was that the vote of the Faculty of

---

[1] Bulæus, IV. p. 261; *Archiv.*V. 246.

[2] In 1347 the majority claims that a resolution (not a Statute) has been passed 'per dictam Universitatem seu majorem et saniorem partem ipsius,' though the Faculty of Decrees and two Nations protested against it. (*Chartul.* T. II. No. 1129.) But its validity is apparently undisputed. See a clearer case in 1348 (*ib.* No. 1152). The principle is fully established by the year 1377, when the University resolved that no judgment in respect of the Schism question should be binding without the unanimous consent of the Faculties (Bulæus, IV. pp. 565, 566). It would even appear that the principle had been sanctioned by some Statute which is not extant, since the University enacts ' quod D. Rector in colligendo vota quando determinandum erit et concludendo non concludat pro tribus Facultatibus aliquando secundum quod potest per statutum, quando materia non est tam gravis et ponderosa, sed . . . faciat consentire aliquod omnes Facultates et Nationes.' The clearest possible evidence of the continuance of the same practice is supplied among other places by Bulæus, V. pp.

725, 807, 831–2. The last reference brings us to the year 1499. In explanation of the Bulæan misrepresentation, it must be remembered that the Faculty of Arts voted by Nations, so that three Nations could carry the day against one Nation with the aid of two other Faculties, or with one Faculty could prevent a conclusion. The only exception to the above generalizations which I have come across is an occasion on which, in a dispute between the Superior Faculties and the Faculty of Arts, the Rector ' requisitus sæpius ab illis tribus [Facultatibus] ut concluderet pro illis, conclusit ad conclusionem Facultatis Artium' (Bulæus, *Remarques sur la dignité du R.* p. 88), but this appears to have been an arbitrary stretch of authority, not based on any constitutional theory as to the Nations counting as a Faculty.

[3] Crevier, III. 29 ; Thurot, pp. 24, 25.

[4] The principle was usually observed in the appointment of delegates to award Benefices or *legati* to represent the University (Bulæus, V. pp. 347, 348, 583 ; Jourdain, No. 1385), but not in voting on a Statute or Decree.

Arts was determined by the majority of Nations, the vote of the University by the majority of Faculties. The whole history of the voting arrangement in the University of Paris supplies an interesting illustration (to borrow Mr. Bryce's happy expression) of constitutional development by usage.

Long before the principle of majority - voting finally triumphed in the University itself, we find it well-established as between the Nations in the Faculty of Arts : though here the minority-nation had the remedy of an appeal to the whole University. But even after the establishment of the principle, it did not by any means follow that a dissentient Faculty or Nation would submit unhesitatingly or unquestioningly to the decision of the majority. It is indeed extremely difficult to give the modern reader any adequate idea of the turbulence, the boisterousness, the quarrelsomeness of these Academic assemblies, or of the chaotic condition of the constitutional principles by which they were supposed to be regulated. Here as in other departments of medieval life we constantly see side by side the strongest passion for legal chicane or constitutional subtlety and the most reckless defiance of all rule. Hardly any principle is so well established that it cannot be disputed. Not only corporations but even individuals at times put forth a claim to veto or at least delay the decision of the majority [1].

There was one quasi-legal means of obstruction by which a dissentient Faculty or Nation might prevent the acts of the majority taking effect. The University seal was kept in a chest to which each Faculty and Nation possessed a separate key. When party feeling ran high, a dissentient Faculty or Nation would direct its Dean or Proctor to attend the Rector's summons without his key, and obsti-

---

[1] Thus in the Register of the large Nation of France we read, 'et quia unus nostrum, ut dictum est, reclamaverat, dictum statutum non fuit sigillatum.' Bulæus, IV. 225 (cf. V. 387, 423); *Chartul.* T. II. No. 897.

Yet it is abundantly clear, that under ordinary circumstances a majority-vote was considered sufficient : ' Conclusi a pluritate vocum in vigore statuti antiqui.' Bulæus, V. 532.

nately to refuse to produce it. Under such circumstances there was no remedy but to direct the chest to be broken open[1]. A still more constitutional method of resisting the decision of the majority was by lodging an appeal to the Holy See, a threat, which even when not seriously meant, created delay, and meanwhile relieved the conscience and character of those who refused to obey from the imputation of perjury[2].

Drinking
of surplus.

The origin of the University in a voluntary society of teachers bound together at first merely by a body of unwritten customs or class-law is eminently illustrated by the sources of its revenue and the way in which it was spent. The fees and expenses on taking degrees were really nothing more than the money exacted by the Masters from a new-comer on plea of making him pay his footing, precisely on the level with the demand of 'Bejaunia' by the students from freshmen so often condemned by the Masters themselves[3]. Every favour that the Masters conferred had likewise to be paid for. Thus we find that the first time a Master was appointed Proctor and Receiver of his Nation, he was expected to pay down a sum of money which that august body immediately proceeded to spend in drink at a neighbouring tavern[4]. Surplus revenues seem to have been habitually disposed of in the same jovial fashion[5].

---

[1] Bulæus, IV. 163; V. 555, 776. In some cases this manœuvre seems adopted to compel an appeal ' ad Universitatem ipsam melius congregandam.' Cf. also Bulæus, IV. 579, 580. Sometimes this kind of opposition compelled the majority to agree to a compromise. Bulæus, V. 555–6.

[2] In some cases when this threat of ' Appeal' is made, it is not clear to whom the appeal was made. Bulæus, V. pp. 633, 664.

[3] See below, vol. II. chap. xiv.

[4] The books of the Nations contain such entries as the following:

' M. Nicolaus solvit Nationi unum scutum pro Procuratoria et statim perpotatum fuit illud scutum per Magistros in taberna ad imaginem nostre Domine in vico S. Jacobi.'

[5] These drinkings were abolished in the German or English Nation in 1391 except the accustomed celebration of the Feast of S. Edmund. The statute provides ' quod de cætero nullæ fient potationes nec simplices nec generales ... de pecuniis recipiendis a Magistris pro prima Procuratoria et pro jocundo introitu et pro mensibus distribuendis in examine S. Genovefæ.' The money was hence-

It has been already pointed out that neither the Rector nor the Cathedral Chancellor held the position at Paris which the Chancellors of Oxford and Cambridge occupied in those Universities. The jurisdiction in causes which concerned scholars—at Oxford and Cambridge merged in the Chancellor's Court—was divided between three tribunals (the Rector's court being put aside as wielding in the main a merely academical or disciplinary and consensual jurisdiction, extending only to cases where both parties were members or clients of the University or owners of University Hostels):—(1) The Bishop's Court, (2) The Châtelet, (3) The Court of the Conservator of the Apostolic Privileges of the University.

To understand the distinction between these different jurisdictions, it is necessary to bear in mind that prior to any privileges from King or Pope, the Masters and scholars of Paris were presumed to be clerks, and as such entitled to all the ordinary immunities of ecclesiastics. This was the foundation of their exemption from the ordinary Tribunals, though they managed to retain many of their privileges after other ecclesiastics had partially lost them.

(1) The Bishop's Official heard all ordinary criminal or ecclesiastical prosecutions against a scholar, and might hear civil cases in which he was engaged either as plaintiff or defendant [1]. A scholar might also appeal to the Bishop's Court, where he was himself injured, but, if the defendant was a layman, the Court could in that case only impose spiritual penalties, i.e. excommunication and penance as the condition of absolution.

(2) The Châtelet as the Court of the Provost of Paris, the 'Conservator of the Royal Privileges of the University,' tried all civil actions in which a member of the University was engaged, wherever the cause of action arose, which

---

forth to be applied 'pro bono communi totius Nationis.' Bulæus, IV. 674.

[1] There were of course changes in the extent of these various jurisdictions. Without attempting to trace them in detail, we may say that by the close of our period, the trial of Civil Causes had probably passed from the Bishop to the Rector and the Royal Conservator.

lay out of the jurisdiction of the ecclesiastical Courts (e. g.
actions affecting real property), and which (but for the
royal privilege) would be heard by some other secular
Court in or out of Paris. Criminal cases in which a scholar
was prosecutor, and in which he did not elect to be satisfied with such penalties as the ecclesiastical Court could
inflict, would also be tried by the Provost or his lieutenant.
A general power to protect scholars was, as has been mentioned, entrusted to the Provost of Paris by the Charter of
Philip Augustus in 1200 [1]: but the right to bring up cases
from secular courts in all parts of France seems to have
been first conferred by a Royal Charter in $13\frac{40}{41}$ [2]. This
jurisdiction was of course merely an extension of the ordinary civil and criminal jurisdiction which the Châtelet
exercised over all inhabitants of Paris.

The Con-
servator
Apostolic.
(3) Cases affecting a scholar in which the jurisdiction in
the ordinary course belonged to the Holy See or to some
Apostolic delegate out of Paris, were transferred to the
Court of the Conservator Apostolic in Paris [3]—subject to
the reservation that a defendant might not be cited further
than four days' journey beyond his own diocese [4]. To
this Court belonged also the right of interfering to protect
either the University itself, or any member of it, from the
violation of any of its Papal privileges [5].

---

[1] See above, p. 297 *sq.*

[2] Bulæus, IV. 264; *Chartul.* T. II.
No. 1044. As an example, we may
take a tithe-case affecting a Curé in
the Duchy of Normandy transferred
from one of the Civil Courts of the
Duchy. Bulæus, IV. 682. Power to
protect Scholars against violence in
all parts of the Kingdom was given
in 1306. *Chartul.* T. II. No. 657.

[3] The right of citing a defendant
before the Conservator is often called
the ' droit de *Committimus.*'

[4] From 1317 the previous permission of the Rector and University, or
its deputies, was necessary before
application could be made by an in-

dividual student to the Court of Conservation. Bulæus, IV. 178; *Chartul.*
T. II. No. 736.

[5] A specimen of the kind of monition or prohibition which the Conservator addressed to persons attempting to cite a scholar out of the
city is given in *Chartul.* T. I. pt. i.
No. 529. In explanation of the fact
that the Privilege is limited to citation before Papal delegates out of
Paris, it must be remembered that
by ordinary Canon Law a person
must be cited in the diocese where
he *resides,* so that the scholars were
already protected from being cited
before all other ecclesiastical tri-

To define the limits of these several jurisdictions with greater precision would involve a treatise on a difficult and complicated branch of medieval Law. It is clear that in many cases several ways of proceeding were open to a scholar or a layman involved in a dispute with a scholar. But, whatever difficulty there may be in distinguishing the cases which fell to these different Courts, the difference in the penalties imposed by them is quite clear. The distinction between academical, ecclesiastical, and secular jurisdiction was always maintained, and never merged as it was at Oxford and Cambridge in the Chancellor's Court. The *ultimum supplicium* of the Rector or the University was expulsion ; that of the Conservator Apostolic and the Bishop, in the case of laymen, excommunication followed by penance. The Bishop's Official could only imprison his own subjects, i. e. clerks, whether scholars or otherwise : he could only touch the goods or person of a layman by invoking the aid of the secular arm[1]. One class of cases of course formed an exception to the general exemption of scholars as of other ecclesiastics from lay Tribunals. In the height of their power, the ecclesiastical Courts were never allowed to take cognizance of a cause involving the right to a lay fee[2].

---

bunals out of Paris—even in respect of an offence committed in some other diocese.

[1] In 1347 a difficulty arose as to the powers of the Conservator Apostolic to imprison for contempt. It was decided that he was to imprison only in the Bishop's prison, but without prejudice to his right 'eos questionibus subicere et torquere' (*Chartul.* T. II. No. 1137). The case in which the difficulty arose was in connexion with a scholar who had counterfeited the Conservator's Seal (*ib.* No. 1129). I presume that the Court could not have proceeded in this way against a layman. As to the attempts of the ecclesiastical Courts to directly touch property,

see Paul Fournier, *Officialités du Moyen Age,* pp. 228, 229, and as to the whole question of the competence of these Courts in France, *l. c.* p. 64 *sq.*

[2] Other exceptions might no doubt be adduced, especially in the later Middle Ages, when the benefit of Clergy was everywhere greatly curtailed. Thus in 1427 (Bulæus, V. p. 381) a M.D. 'clerc non marié' was imprisoned by the Châtelet for contempt in falsifying a document under the Seal of the Court. The Bishop claimed his surrender, which was decreed by the Parlement, subject to the condition that he should not be discharged from custody and that 'seront deux des dits Conseillers de

We have already noticed some of the privileges which scholars enjoyed over and above the ordinary privileges of the ecclesiastical order in the ecclesiastical Courts themselves, such as the requirement of two warnings before they could be excommunicated, and the prohibition of pecuniary penances for moral delinquencies. In addition to these privileges, for which the University could undoubtedly produce Papal Bulls, it seems eventually to have claimed a right to demand that the Bishop's Official should in all cases liberate a scholar committed to his custody by the secular Courts until trial upon his mere oath to appear [1].

The officials of the University (even when not Masters or scholars) enjoyed the full privileges of scholars. Of these the most important were (1) the Bedels whose duties were much the same as those of the Bedels at Bologna ; (2) the common *Procurator ad litem* or *Syndicus*, afterwards styled the *Promotor Universitatis*, who was the chief permanent official of the University, combining the functions of a University Counsel or Solicitor with some of those which would now be discharged by a Registrar. (3) At a later date a *Scribe* or Secretary was appointed distinct from the Syndic [2]. The duties of Registrar had in early days of the University been discharged by the Rector, who was also the collector and treasurer of the common funds. (4) These last duties were afterwards delegated to a Receiver (*Receptor* or *Quæstor Ærarii*). The last two offices are not mentioned till the beginning of the fifteenth century. The Nations and Faculties had also by that time Receivers of their own [3].

---

la Cour presens, avec l'Evesque ou son Official à faire le procez du dit M. Bernard.' This led to a great dispute between the University and the Parlement, but the decision of the Court was ultimately upheld.

[1] 'Ad cautionem juratoriam, secundum formam Privilegii Universitatis' (Bulæus, V. 533). The University or rather the Nation of France

declares, 'quod de ejusmodi re habebat declarationem a summo Pontifice.'

[2] Bulæus, III. 583, 585 ; *Remarques sur l'élection des Officiers*, p. 9 *sq.*

[3] *Remarques*, p. 92 n. The Receiver of the Faculty of Arts was also Receiver of the University. *Ib.* p. 93.

Another office which calls for a passing mention is that CHAP. V, of University Messenger (*Nuntius*). The transmission of § 3. money and goods to scholars must have been a business of The considerable importance from an early period. Eventually *Nuntii.* it became a regular University office, the scholars of each diocese electing their own Nuntii. Of these there were two classes. The *Nuntii majores* would seem to have been merchants or bankers who undertook to pay to scholars money advanced by their parents in distant regions, and lent money to scholars on their own account[1]; while the 'petty,' 'flying,' or 'ordinary' messengers[2] actually travelled backwards and forwards with consignments of goods or money to scholars, and even took charge of the scholars themselves[3].

Besides the actual members or scholars[4] (*suppositi*) of Clients the University, and the officers, there was a numerous of the body of 'Clients' who enjoyed the full privileges of mem- University. bership, or at least a considerable portion of them.

The most important classes of Clients were the *Sta-* Book- *tionarii* and *Librarii*, or Booksellers, over whom the Uni- sellers, &c. versity established the same kind of control that existed at Bologna. The trade of the *Librarius* consisted largely, if not entirely, in the sale of books for private individuals, the tradesman being remunerated by a percentage on the price obtained, while the *Stationarius* employed the writers who actually produced new books which were either sold or much more often lent for a fixed sum on security for their value being deposited by the borrower[5]. The *Sta-*

---

[1] Crevier, VII. p. 158. Cf. de Lens, *Univ. d'Angers*, I. p. 108.

[2] 'Parvi, volantes, Ordinarii.' Bulæus, V. 787–791 *sq.*

[3] Bulæus, V. p. 807. So at Oxford, where the common carriers continued to be licensed by the University down to quite recent times.

[4] Strictly speaking non-graduate scholars were not members of the University (*jurati Universitatis*) but only *suppositi* or subjects. The last

term is often extended to the Clients.

[5] The system is in the main established by 1275 (Bulæus, III. p. 419; *Chartul.* pt. i. No. 462). This document shows that the power claimed by the University rested solely on its right to forbid its own members from dealing with a recalcitrant trader. Other particulars are gathered from the more elaborate Statutes of 1323 and 1342 (Bulæus, IV. pp. 202, 278; *Chartul.* T. II. Nos. 733, 1064. Cf.

tionarius in fact combined the functions of publisher, book-seller, and circulating library-keeper. No book might be sold or let out on hire (whether for reading or for copying) till the correctness of the copy had been examined and the price or rate of hire fixed by a joint-board, composed of four Masters and four Principal Booksellers annually nominated by the University [1]. The Stationer was forbidden to sell a book to a stranger till he had informed the University assembled in General Congregation of the intended bargain, in order that they might take measures to prevent it going out of their reach [2]. In order to check collusion between the Librarii to the injury of those who had entrusted them with books, they were forbidden to sell a book (without the owner's express consent) to another person in the trade till it had been exposed for sale on four days at the Blackfriars' Convent during sermon-time [3].

Extent of Book-trade.

As an illustration of the extent of the book-trade in medieval Paris, it may be mentioned that in 1323 there

also *l. c.* T. II. No. 628, 642, 724, 825, 1064). In 1275 we hear of 'Stationarii qui vulgo Librarii appellantur': in 1323 we have the names of twenty-eight 'Stationarii et Librarii,' but the context seems to establish the distinction given in the text between the two terms, though both branches of the trade were no doubt followed by the same persons. M. Delalain, however, in his interesting Monograph (*Étude sur le Libraire Parisien du XIIIᵉ au XVᵉ siècle*, p. xviii *sq.*) makes the Librarius as well as the Stationarius let books out on hire, while the characteristic of the Stationarius is that he produces new books. The allusions to the 'correction' of books by the University would seem to imply the existence of Officials resembling the 'correctores peciarum' at Bologna. All Stationers and Booksellers were sworn to obey the University and were required to give security. The control of the University passed into

a legal monopoly. Delalain, pp. 48 *sq.*, 55 *sq.* For the very similar Oxford regulations, see *Mun. Acad. Oxon.* ed. Anstey, pp. 383–7.

[1] As far as appears the Taxations were for loans, but possibly also for sale. It is curious that we nowhere find the period to which the taxed rate applied, mentioned. Cf. *Hist. Litt.* T. XXIV. p. 294 *sq.* It is there suggested that the term Stationarius was restricted to the mere 'étalagistes,' which must be wrong.

[2] 'Item quod nullus Stationarius exemplar aliquod alienabit, sine eo quod prius notificet Universitati in Congregatione Generali ut Universitas ordinet viam per quam ipse Stationarius a profectu suo non impediatur et Universitas exemplaris usu non defraudetur' (*Chartul.* T. II. No. 733).

[3] So at Cologne, there were book-stalls on Festivals 'in ambitu Ecclesiæ majoris.' Bianco, I. *Anl.* p. 22.

were twenty-eight sworn booksellers besides keepers of book-stalls in the open air, who were restricted to the sale and loan of books of small value. Books were no doubt bought and borrowed more extensively by Masters than by scholars ; but the Statutes required every Theologian to bring a copy of the Bible or Sentences, as the case might be, to lecture with him, at least during the first four years of his attendance. Many College Statutes required the student attending Logic or Philosophy lectures to have a copy of the text [1]. So at Vienna, a scholar attending lecture without his book lost his term [2]. The importance of oral teaching was no doubt greatly increased by the scarcity of books ; but facts such as these warn us against the exaggerated and indeed absurd statements often made as to the booklessness of the medieval student. The difficulty arising from the expense of books was met by the system of lending-libraries ; and the expense even of purchase has been greatly exaggerated. The enormous prices often quoted in illustration of the dearness of books, relate (so far as the University period is concerned) to the gorgeous illuminated works of art prepared for great personages or rich Monasteries.

The Parchment-makers, Illuminators, Binders, and (later) the Paper-merchants and Paper-makers of Corbeil and Essones [3], were also under academical superintendence as

Parchment-makers, &c.

---

[1] At Harcourt College for instance, we find ' Cæterum pro Artistis statuimus quod quilibet librum de quo audierit, sibi a principio ordinar procuret et illum principali domus ostendat.' Bulæus, IV. 159.

[2] 'Statuimus quod Scolaris non habens librum in Scolis . . . non recipiat tempus suum.' Kink, *Wien*, II. p. 132. So in most German Statutes : but at Ingolstadt ' looking over' is recognised, it being permissible ' tres habere unum textum in qualibet eorum lectione, quod ita se complevisse jurabit quisque in congregatione facultatis ante admissionem ad examen.' Prantl, *Gesch. d.*

Ludwig-Maximilians Univ. II. p. 74. The first business of a student, in coming up, was to provide himself with books. Odofredus quotes, apparently as a sort of typical piece of Undergraduate extravagance, the case of a man who on coming up with an allowance of 100 *libræ* from his father, 'fecit libros suos babuinare (*sic*) de literis aureis' (ap. Sarti, 1888, I. pt. i. p. 167).

[3] A doc. of 1414 (Bulæus, V. p. 279) shows that these mills were set up about sixty years before that date. Before that time, what paper was used at Paris is said to have been imported from Lombardy.

Clients of the University. The Parchment-makers were obliged to bring the bales of parchment on their arrival in Paris to the Hall of the Mathurines to be 'taxed' or valued by the 'four sworn Parchmenters' of the University under the supervision of the Rector, who also visited the great Fair of S. Denys for the like purpose. The parchment had to remain at the Mathurines for twenty-four hours, during which it might only be sold at the appointed rate to members of the University. By some means or other—probably by sheer imposition afterwards sanctioned by Law—the Rector succeeded in levying a tax upon all parchment sold in Paris, which formed the most important perquisite of the Rectorial office [1].

The Chirurgeons.

Another body of Clients were the Surgeons. In Northern Europe the learned Physicians [2] looked down upon the Chirurgeons as mere manual operators, who were, according to strict professional theory, only allowed to practise under the supervision of a Doctor [3]. From the

[1] Bulæus, III. p. 499 *sq.*: VI. p. 478: *Chartul.* T. II. No. 574, 575: Crevier, II. pp. 130–132: V. p. 419. This duty consisted of 16 *denarii Parisienses* on each '*botte*' of parchment. The Rector also received a 'Cappa' from each Nation and a 'bursa' from each 'Licentiandus' or 'Magistrandus' (Bulæus, V. 304). He also received an allowance of 40 *solidi Parisienses* 'pro stipendiis suæ receptæ' (III. 589). This entertainment consisted, it appears, in *vinum et species* provided at his house for the Masters who accompanied him home after his election. Du Boulay tells us that in his day the Feast had fallen into desuetude, though the 'deductio' of the new Rector was kept up (III. 573). (A similar ceremonial is still observed after the admission of the Vice-Chancellor and of the Proctors at Oxford. The Masters have however lost their 'wine and spices,' which at the Vice-Chancellor's admission have been superseded by a lunch for the 'Heads' and other magnates.) Further provision might be made by the Nation for a Rector chosen from the number of its own Masters. Cf. Bulæus, IV. 377.

[2] Besides the Doctors, other Physicians might be licensed to practise by the Bishop upon the recommendation of the Faculty: all other practitioners were suppressed by the Ecclesiastical Courts. *Chartul.* T. II. Nos. 900, 933. It is curious to see the 'medical woman' question fought out in a prosecution directed by the Medical Faculty at Paris against a woman who had cured the Royal Chancellor, and many others for whom the Physicians could do nothing. She alleges *inter alia* that 'mulier antea permitteret se mori quam secreta infirmitatis sue homini revelare' &c. *Chartul.* T. II. No. 814.

[3] Bulæus, III. pp. 400, 401: *Chartul.* T. I. i. No. 434. By an Edict of Philip le Bel in the year 1311 'nullus

year 1436 the Chirurgeons, hitherto merely Clients, were admitted as actual 'scholars' in the Faculty of Medicine, and were thus allowed to attend lectures though not to proceed to degrees[1]. In 1491, however, elated by their newly acquired academical learning, the Chirurgeons rebelled against the subordinate position to which the pride of the full-blown 'Doctors' condemned them. The Faculty retaliated by throwing open its lectures to the inferior class of Barber-surgeons. To this the Chirurgeons objected as an infringement of the Statutes, since to be intelligible to these unlearned practitioners the lectures had to be given in the vernacular. The difficulty was got over by delivering the lectures first in Latin for the avoidance of perjury, and then in French for the edification of the audience. This expedient brought the Chirurgeons to their knees, and in 1506 they again acknowledged themselves the humble 'disciples' of the Doctors and were readmitted to the favour of the Faculty[2]. The Apothecaries were also under the supervision of the Medical Faculty, which was carried to the point of forbidding the sale of a 'laxative medicine' without a Physician's order[3].

During the earlier part of its history, the University had been subject to constant interference on the part of the Holy See. In the event of a dispute between different Nations or Faculties, the aggrieved party could always have recourse to the Pope or his Legate, who would dispose of the matter almost independently of the King's consent. In the fourteenth century, the Royal prerogative began to assert itself in academical as in other matters. Papal injunctions were not invariably obeyed, and never

Interference of Papal Legates.

---

chirurgicus, nulla chirurgica' was allowed to practise without being examined by the 'magistri chirurgici jurati,' under the presidency of the King's Chirurgeon, and licensed in the Châtelet. *Ordonnances des roys de France*, I. p. 491. This arrangement is, however, said to date from Louis IX. Félibien, I. p. 438.

[1] Pasquier, *Recherches de la France*, L. IX. ch. 30 (Paris, 1621, p. 865). The Surgeons had a Guild of their own and were admitted to the Mastership by *birettatio* in much the same way as University Graduates.

[2] *Ib.* cap. 31, pp. 868, 869.

[3] See the Apothecary's Oath, *Chartul.* T. II. No. 817.

The Uni-
versity and
the Par-
lement.

without the Royal concurrence. Hence, occasionally in the fourteenth century, and frequently in the fifteenth, we find the Parlement interfering in the affairs of the University. The University, however, claimed as the 'eldest daughter' (a very spoiled child) of the King of France, the right of pleading as a corporation before no secular Judge but the King himself[1]. On more than one occasion it refused to obey a citation before the Parlement, or appeared only under protest. For a time the preposterous claim was, it would seem, admitted or rejected according to the humour of the Court. But as taxation in France became heavier, and the wealth of the academic ecclesiastics attracted the attention of the fiscal officials, the Court began to look unfavourably upon the exemptions enjoyed by Regents and scholars. Whenever an attempt was made to tax a member or sworn Client of the University, the matter was declared to be one of 'privilege'; the University appeared as an 'intervening party' and demanded audience of the King. These occasions at length became so frequent that in 1445 a Royal edict put a stop to the nuisance, and definitively proclaimed the jurisdiction of the Parlement in the suits of the University[2].

Arrogant
abuse and
consequent
loss of
Privileges.

This was only the beginning of its downfall from the proud position once held by the University in the days when it could use the language of menace to Kings and Parlements, and when rival princes or statesmen had thought it worth while to court its favour. Under Charles VII, indeed, the University still continued to be treated with great indulgence. Though it had to admit the jurisdiction of the Parlement when a matter was once brought before it, it still ventured to exercise the terrible penalty of *privatio* against individual members of its own body who carried their complaints from the University tribunals to the supreme Court of the realm[3]. Never were its privileges more jealously, more factiously asserted. Not content with

---

[1] 'Cum sola Regia Majestas præsentialiter sui corporis causas solita sit tractare tanquam filiæ primogenitæ et perpetuæ.' Bulæus, V. 537–8.

[2] Bulæus, V. 539.

[3] Bulæus, V. 588, 595.

the 'privation' or expulsion of members who had violated its privileges, the children of the offenders to the fourth generation were made incapable of taking a degree, and the University sometimes persisted in executing such a decree in spite of an order of Parlement [1]. The spiritual thunders of the Conservator Apostolic were in constant requisition against violators of privileges, and appear at this time to have been launched as a matter of course, without the exercise of any judicial discretion, against any offender whom Congregation had ordered to be delated [2]. On one occasion the University even directed the Conservator to disregard the interim injunction of Parlement to raise an excommunication pending an appeal to that Court [3]. The old remedy of a 'Cessation from Sermons and Lectures' was exercised upon the slightest provocation with an alacrity which does little credit to the zeal of the Masters either for the instruction of their pupils or for the edification of the public. Since there could have been few preachers in Paris who were not connected with the University [4], a cessation of sermons must have meant the almost complete silencing of the pulpits throughout the capital. And since a large proportion of the Judges and other Government officials were also graduates of Paris, the power of *privatio*—which involved the publication of notices in all public places denouncing the offender as perjured and excommunicated, or as 'an arid, rotten, and infamous member' [5]—gave the University an amount of power which it is surprising to find tolerated so long in the capital of the most despotic Sovereign in Europe. One of the most serious of the disputes in which the University was engaged at this period, was its collision with the *Générales des Aides*, a Commission appointed for the collection of a special war-tax ordered by the King in 1459. There appears to have been no avowed attempt to interfere with

---

[1] Bulæus, V. 596–7; cf. 641.

[2] Bulæus, V. 600, 635.

[3] Bulæus, V. 597.

[4] It probably had to be obeyed by all the Regular Orders who were connected with the University through

any of their members.

[5] 'Quod affigeretur privatus per Quadrivia et valvas tanquam membrum Universitatis aridum, putridum, et infame.' Bulæus, V. 713.

the exemption of the University from this imposition : but
it is obvious that there would often be a difficulty in ascer-
taining the *bona fide* character of a claim to exemption ;
and the *Générales* claimed to take cognisance of such disputed claims. The University contended that they ought
to go before the Royal Conservator. Those of the *Générales*
who were University men—including a Bishop—were deprived, and all were excommunicated and compelled to
leave their parish churches on Easter Day before the Priests
would begin Mass [1]. Even a Royal Ordinance does not
appear to have immediately put a stop to these proceedings:
and, though in the result the jurisdiction of the Court was
upheld, so much consideration was shown to the wounded
amour propre of the sensitive corporation that the President was appointed ' Conservator of the exemption of the
University from the *Aides*,' and ordered to take oath, like
the Provost of Paris, to respect and enforce the privileges
of which he was constituted the guardian [2].

Taste for
University
business.
　　In the latter part of the fifteenth century the whole
energy of the University was absorbed in constant conflicts
with all manner of civil and ecclesiastical authorities on
questions of privilege. Many of these privileges were
getting out of harmony with the temper of the age. But
the University might probably have retained more of them
than it did, had it been a little less outrageous and pre-
cipitate in the use of its formidable but antiquated weapons
of self-defence. The 'idle and thankless pursuit which they
call doing University business ' (to borrow the phrase of a
great censor of our own University [3]) had become a mania
with the Masters of that day. During the Conciliar period
the academical dignitaries had really become politicians of
importance: the decisions of the University Congregation
had been a matter of European interest. Now the age of
academical politics was over : but the taste for 'University
business' remained [4]. The consequence was that matter

[1] Bulæus, V. 634–8.
[2] Bulæus, V. 644.
[3] Mark Pattison, *Memoirs*, 1885,
p. 331.

[4] As early as 1346 a Pope had
found it necessary to remonstrate
with the University on account of
the number of Congregations, in

for agitation had to be made out of every trumpery collision with the police or the tax-gatherers, and every election to a University office.

The reign of Louis XI saw the extinction of the last relics of the old independence and influence of the University, as of so many other ancient liberties. For a moment, in the stress of the first outbreak of the War of the Public Weal, the King had sought to conciliate the capital by adding six Burgesses, six Councillors of Parlement, and six Masters of the University to his own Privy Council[1]; but two years later, in 1467, the King, alleging that some members of the University were caballing with his enemies, forbade the University to meddle with politics, 'even in letters to their relations,' and demanded the revival of an old statute requiring that a Royal officer should be present at the Rectorial elections[2]. It was with difficulty that the University succeeded in protecting its students from compulsory military service upon the walls of Paris[3]. By a succession of minute interferences with its internal affairs the way was prepared for an absolutely unparalleled exertion of prerogative. For some two centuries the University had behaved as if it owed its rights and privileges to some *jus divinum* underived from any earthly authority, civil or ecclesiastical. It was now to be rudely reminded that privileges which the King gave, the King could take away. In 1474 the King ordered that the Rector should always be a subject of his own; the order being disobeyed, the alien Rector was compelled to resign his office, and all the privileges of the University were summarily suspended. They were restored as soon as a new election had been made[4]. But the measure had the desired effect. The spirit of the once haughty corporation was completely broken. It is most instructive to compare the tone which the

---

consequence of which 'perduntur et impediuntur lectiones, disputationes et alii actus scolastici, ac illi, qui deberent proficere, infructuose ut plurimum transeunt tempus suum.' *Chartul.* T. II. No. 1125.

[1] Gaguin, *Rer. Gall. Ann.* (Francofurt., 1577), p. 248.
[2] Bulæus, V. 681.
[3] Bulæus, V. 682–4: Gaguin, p. 246.
[4] Bulæus, V. 716–7.

University adopts in its dealings with King and Parlement at the beginning and at the end of this single reign. Hardly a Rectorial election now passed without a dispute as to its validity, and a schism of more or less duration. Appeals to Parlement in such cases became more and more frequent. The interference which the University had once resisted with so much vehemence, she now seems positively to court, and we find Congregation passing hearty votes of thanks to the Judges for the trouble they had taken in adjusting University squabbles[1]. The University now tamely submits to the orders of a body which the 'eldest daughter of the King' had once insisted on regarding as its 'younger sister,' on such matters as the censorship of plays acted in College and the repression of wandering and froward (*discholi*) scholars[2].

Loss of
the right
of Cessation, 1499.
The University enjoyed somewhat more favour under Charles VIII, and was gratified by the degradation and punishment of his predecessor's barber, who had instigated most of the late outrages upon academic privilege[3]. But on the accession of Louis XII a final blow was struck at its old prerogatives. It lost the right of Cessation[4]—the great instrument of academic aggression. This punishment was provoked by the opposition which it offered to an edict limiting its privileges and guarding against their abuse. These privileges—including extensive exemptions from taxation[5]—had hitherto been claimed by all members of the University, even Non-Regent graduates, that is, practically by the greater number of the lawyers, doctors, higher clergy, and higher government officials residing in the capital, to say nothing of the fraudulent use of scholars' names by traders and other private individuals[6]. It was

[1] Bulæus, V. 745 *sq.*
[2] *Ib.* V. 761, 811–2.
[3] Bulæus, V. p. 762: Gaguin, p. 282.
[4] Already limited by Pius II. Bulæus, V. 832.
[5] It is difficult to define the exact extent of these exemptions, which were matters of incessant dispute. The members of the University seem

as a rule to have been exempt from all ordinary secular taxation; while they often gained special exemption from contributing to aids voted by the clergy. See *e. g.* Bulæus, IV. 361.

[6] Real or nominal members of the University abused their exemption from the tax on imported wine to carry on a trade in that commodity.

now very reasonably enacted that these privileges should
extend only to *bona fide* students and Regent Masters.
The University notwithstanding ordered a Cessation. The
Parlement cited the Rector, Deans and Proctors to appear
before it. These officers refused to obey, and in their
absence the Court proceeded to order the withdrawal of
the Cessation. The order was not immediately complied
with : and a deputation was sent to the King. They met
him at Corbeil on his way back to Paris, and found that
he had been informed (with whatever truth) that seditious
placards had been stuck upon the walls of the capital by
the scholars, and that he had been denounced from the
pulpit by some of the indignant Doctors. The deputation
consequently found the King in such a humour that they
at once returned to Paris, and advised their colleagues to
propitiate the angry monarch by a speedy and unconditional
surrender. The Cessation was revoked[1] ; and from this
time forth the University never again ventured to have
recourse to such a measure. Thus, just at the epoch which
has been adopted for the purposes of this work as the limit
of the Middle Age, the subjection of the University to the
Crown and the Royal Court was completed, and there
passed away for ever one of the last relics of those privileged
licenses and uncouth, lawless liberties which so strangely
tempered the iron régime of medieval Feudalism. In the
sixteenth century, governments were everywhere setting
themselves to abolish the local immunities and class-
privileges of the medieval system[2]. However much we may
regret the temporary extinction of the spirit of Liberty,
there can be no doubt that a vigorous assertion of the
principle of Order was called for, and nowhere more so
than in the streets of University towns.

Bulæus, V. 656, 686. There are incessant allusions to similar abuses.

[1] Bulæus, V. 830–832. According to
Richer (I. f. 131), the University tried
to extend this Cessation or compulsory strike not only to teachers and
preachers but to physicians who were
members of the University.

[2] Exactly the same tightening of
discipline was going on all over Europe. Riccobonus (f. 132) dates the
cessation of student-riots at Padua
from the execution of a scholar for
the murder of a police-officer during
an attempted secession to Ferrara in
1580.

§ 4. THE STUDIES OF PARIS.

IN the regulations prescribing the courses of lectures which must be heard by the student at different stages of his career, we shall constantly be met by a distinction between 'ordinary' and 'cursory' lectures. The discussions which have taken place as to the meaning of this distinction would have been much simplified, had the comparative method been more frequently employed in the exploration of University antiquities.

Distinction between Ordinary and Cursory Lectures.

The 'cursory' lectures of Paris are the 'extraordinary' lectures of Bologna. The Bologna distinction between 'ordinary' and 'extraordinary' *books* was, as we have seen, confined to the Faculty of Law. In the Faculty of Canon Law this distinction lasted at Paris in its oldest form even after it had been modified at Bologna. Ordinary lectures were confined to the Decretum[1]; lectures on all the other books were extraordinary or cursory. In the other Faculties the same books might be the subject of both ordinary and extraordinary lectures. The distinction between them was mainly one of *time*: the ordinary lectures were those delivered by Masters during certain hours of the morning on 'legible' days. In the Faculty of Arts the earliest hour was reserved for the Masters: the time for ordinary lectures ending in winter usually at tierce, in summer going on till dinner-time[2]. In

---

[1] See above, p. 209. At Paris, the Doctors lectured as a rule only on the Decretum. The refusal of Paris to put the Decretals on a level with the Decretum is not without significance in relation to the development of Gallicanism. Cf. Péries, pp. 39, 72; Thurot, p. 181. So at Oxford (*Mun. Acad.* p. 398), it is ordered that Lectures on the Decretals shall henceforth be given in the morning *quasi ordinarie.*

[2] The regulations were exceedingly complicated, varying with the season and according as the day was 'legible' or 'non-legible'. *Chartul.* T. I. pt. i. No. 137: Bulæus, III. 194.

the Vacation (when ordinary lectures were suspended) cursory lectures might be given at any time of day. The lectures of the Masters of Theology and Canon Law were also in the morning, though (in the case of Theology) after tierce—later than the ordinary hours of the Faculty of Arts, so as to enable them to be attended by Masters of Arts after giving their own lectures [1]. But in the course of time the actual teaching in this Faculty came to be almost entirely abandoned to the Bachelors : and then even ordinary lectures were delivered by Bachelors and in the afternoon [2]. But still the distinction continued to be primarily one of time : ordinary lectures were those delivered at the hours reserved originally for Masters and always for the authorised teachers of the Faculty : extraordinary or cursory lectures might be delivered (except on certain holidays) at any time at which no ordinary lectures were going on, by either Master or Bachelor [3]. Moreover, cursory lectures might be delivered anywhere, while ordinary lectures (at least in Canon Law and Arts) had to be delivered in the recognised Schools of the Nation or Faculty. But though an 'extraordinary' lecture meant originally nothing more than a lecture delivered out of the close time reserved for the more formal lectures prescribed by the Faculty, it is probable that the term 'cursory' came in time to suggest also the more rapid and less formal *manner* of going over a book usually adopted at these times as opposed to the more elaborate and exhaustive analysis and exposition, characteristic of the ordinary lectures [4].

[1] Bulæus, IV. 412, 413.

[2] Bulæus, IV. 428.

[3] Mr. Mullinger (*Cambridge*, I. p. 358, *sq.*) is mistaken in supposing that cursory lectures were *only* given by Bachelors, and ignoring the fundamental distinction of time.

[4] Bulæus explains the term *cursor* 'quia cursum peragebant ad Licentiam.' So in a Statute of Perpignan we read ' Nemo censeatur dignus ad cursandum legendo Sententias pro gradu,' etc. (*Chartul.* T. II. Appendix p. 704.) But that the term also implied a difference of manner appears from the following indications : (1) Robert de Sorbonne (Bulæus, III. p. 231) says : 'Non reputabitur aliquis Scholaris propter lectiones *transitorias*, nisi audiat ordinarias.' (2) So at Oxford : 'In disputatione solemni (i. e. ordinaria)

Theology
and Arts
the most
important
studies.

A comparison of the 'Reforms' from time to time imposed upon the University by papal authority supplies us with tolerably full information as to the nature of the University *curriculum* and the changes which it underwent in the course of one period. In summarising the results obtained from such a comparison, we shall confine ourselves for the most part to the characteristic studies of Paris, Theology and Arts. But a few words must first be said as to Medicine and Canon Law.

Medicine.

Medicine.

A School of Medicine situated in a great capital could not fail to acquire considerable importance; and the Medical Doctors of Paris were a wealthy and influential body of men. But as a School of Medicine, Paris never attained anything like the European reputation of Montpellier and Salerno: it did not attract students from distant lands. The standard of its Examinations for Bachelors cannot have been high if M. Thurot is right in inferring from the silence of the Registers that no candidate failed to satisfy the Examiners during a period of more than a century[1]. The earliest Statute of the Faculty (*circa* 1270–1274) requires thirty-two months of study for the Bachelorship, and five and a half years of study for the License in the case of one who has already been licensed in Arts,

The
Medical
Curri-
culum.

---

non cursorie, solemniter et non furtive, respondeat.' *Mun. Acad.* p. 390. So at Oxford 'festine' is a synonym for 'cursorie' or 'extraordinarie.' Mr. Anstey (*Mun. Acad.* pp. cxxxix, 371) mistakenly explains the expression 'Le. fe.' in the Calendar as a 'day on which lectures were shortened.' (3) The expression in the Paris Statute of 1215 that certain books are to be read 'ordinarie et non ad cursum,' can hardly refer only to the time of the lectures. Bulæus, III. 82: *Chartul.* T. I. pt. i.

No. 20. (4) Again, in a Statute of 1460 we read: 'desides, ignavi, *cursores* et discholi omni penitus Scholasticâ disciplinâ carentes' (Bulæus, V. 646) which seems to indicate that the word carried with it the idea of rapid, superficial treatment; cf. the familiar English 'coach.' (5) So the 'Cursor' at Heidelberg swore '*non extense* sed *cursorie* legere litteram dividendo et exponendo.' Hautz, *Gesch. d. Un. Heid.* II. p. 335.

[1] From 1395 to 1500. Thurot, p. 189.

otherwise six years [1]. The books prescribed are the *Liber Tegni* of Galen, and works of Theophilus [2], of the Jewish Physician Isaac [3] and his disciples (translated from the Arabic by Constantinus Africanus), of the Salerno Physician Nicholas and of Ægidius, the celebrated Parisian Physician of the time of Philip Augustus [4]. To these are added 'one book of Theoretica and another of Practica.' It will be observed that Galen is represented by only a single work, and that, though Salerno influences are traceable, Hippocrates is altogether absent. There appears to be no later Statute from which we can ascertain how far this meagre course was afterwards improved and expanded. But we shall be tolerably safe in assuming that the Statute on the subject at Cologne [5] represents the Paris tradition of the

---

[1] *Chartul.* T. I. pt. i. Nos. 452, 453. Elsewhere fifty-six months for the M.A., otherwise sixty months. *Chartul.* T. II. No. 921.

[2] Theophilus (Protospatharius) was a Byzantine Physician, said to have lived in the seventh century A. D.

[3] He wrote a *Liber dietarum universalium, Liber dietarum particularium, Liber urinarum, Liber febrium.* The *Viaticum* alluded to in the Statute was the work of a disciple, Abu Djàfar Almuad.

[4] ' Debet audivisse bis artem medicine ordinarie et semel cursorie exceptis *urinis Theophili,* quas sufficit semel audivisse ordinarie vel cursorie: *Viaticum bis* ordinarie, alios *libros Ysaac* semel ordinarie, bis cursorie, exceptis *dietis particularibus,* quas sufficit audivisse cursorie vel ordinarie ; *Antidotarium Nicholai* semel. *Versus Egidii* non sunt de forma. Item debet unum librum de *theorica* legisse, et alium de *practica.*' By the last expression Denifle (*l. c.,* note) understands that the *Opus Pantegni* of Ali ben Abbâs is meant. But though this may have been the usual text-book, the expression ' unum librum de

theorica,' can hardly be intended as the title of a particular book. I am indebted to Denifle for most of the information given in the text, but I cannot plead his authority for identifying the 'ars medicine' with the 'Liber Tegni' or Τέχνη of Galen.

[5] At Cologne a Bachelor was required to have lectured on some of the following books :—(1) 'Ysagoge Johannicii, et libri tegni Galieni cum commentario Haly,' (2) 'Libri aphorismorum Ypocratis cum commentario Galieni,' (3) 'Libri Theophili de urinis et Philareti de pulsibus, et prognosticorum Ypocratis cum commentario Galieni,' (4) 'Versus Egidii de urinis et pulsibus cum suis commentariis,' (5) 'Viaticus Constantini,' (6) ' Nonus et decimus Almonsorum,' (7) 'Liber de morbo et accidente,' (8) 'Liber de ingenio sanitatis' (Bianco, *Die alte Univ. Köln,* I. *Anl.* p. 29). Before License the Bachelor was required to swear ' quod non sit excommunicatus nec infamis nec homicida, nec publicus cyurgicus operans cum ferro et igne, nec transgressor statutorum, nec uxoratus.'(*l.c.*) These Statutes contain quite a code of medieval professional eti-

medieval period. If so, it would appear that Hippocrates was now included together with the works of such writers as Johannicius [1], Philaretus [2] and the others already mentioned ; but that Avicenna and the Arabs, though certainly known and studied [3], were not placed on a level with the great classical physicians by Paris and its daughter Universities [4].

Scholasti-
cism in
Medicine.

Although the exclusion of the Arabic physicians and their astrological Medicine may have been by no means an unmixed loss, it is evident that little real progress was ever made in Medicine at the Northern Universities. In the great centres of Scholasticism, Medicine also became Scholastic. The importance attached to disputations in the Medical Curriculum of Oxford and Paris is by itself sufficient to show the spirit in which Medicine was here studied: on the other hand we hear nothing even of the very occasional dissections which were usual in the Southern Schools of Medicine. To the Parisian physician theory was everything. The great Montpellier Surgeon, Arnauld of Villeneuve, complains that he knew of an excellent Northern Professor of Natural Science and Medical Theory in general, who could not apply a clyster or effect the cure of the most ordinary disease in particular [5].

---

quette, e. g. the M.D. may not attend a patient who has not paid his bill to another physician (p. 31) ; nor ' conversetur in practica cum judeis practicantibus, aut cum illiteratis viris, aut mulieribus practicantibus ' (*l. c.*).

[1] The Jew Honain ben Isaac.

[2] His *de pulsibus* is an epitome of Galen. The author is usually identified with Theophilus. See Gwilt, *Bibliograph. Lex. d. hervorragenden Aerzte*, ed. Hirsch, *ad voc.* Theophilus.

[3] See the Catalogue of the meagre Library possessed by the Faculty in 1395. Corlieu, *L'Anc. Fac. de Méd. de Paris*, p. 148.

[4] This conclusion is supported by a comparison of the Statutes of Oxford (which adds the ' liber Febrium '

of Isaac the Jew and the ' Antidotarium Nicholai ') in *Mun. Acad.* pp. 406, 409, and of Caen (avowedly based on Paris) in *Bull. de la Soc. des Ant. de Normandie*, XII. p. 498.

[5] ' Et propter hoc Parisienses et ultramontani medici plurimum student, ut habeant scientiam de Universali, non curantes habere particulares cognitiones et experimenta. Memini enim vidisse quendam maximum in artibus, naturalem, logicum, et theoricum optimum. In medicina tamen unum clysterem seu aliquam particularem curationem non novit ordinare, et vix ephemeram [i.e. a fever recurring daily at a certain hour] sciebat curare.' *Breviar.*, IV. 10. Quoted by Haeser, *Gesch. der Medicin*, 1875, p. 653.

Canon Law.

Law at the University of Paris was never studied in the
scientific spirit which characterised the early School of
Bologna, and in a lower degree the other Universities of
the Bologna type. As a School of Law, Paris always
stood below Orleans, Angers, and Toulouse. The prohibition of Honorius III confined its students to the Canon
Law, and the scientific study of the Canon Law was not
likely to flourish where the Civil Law was not taught.
The course of study and method of teaching were of course
derived from Bologna : the formalities of graduation were
the same as in the other Faculties of Paris. Hence it is
unnecessary to dwell upon them in detail. As in the other
Faculties, the exact period of study required for degrees
varied from time to time. At the middle of the fourteenth
century, forty-eight months, extending over a period of six
years, was required for the Bachelorship and another forty
months for the License[1]. For those who had studied Civil
Law the period was shorter.

Too many students of Canon Law at Paris were, however, men with whom the attractions of the capital and the
ecclesiastical influence of its University were recommendations which far outweighed the scientific superiority of the
great provincial schools. It was to the Faculty of Decrees that the great mass of the well-born, well-beneficed
or wealthy idlers of the University belonged, whether their
object was to get on in the world and attain high preferment in the Church or merely to pass their time pleasantly
in a University town. The cadet of a noble house, the
wealthy merchant's son, or the capitular dignitary who had
got leave of absence from his benefice for five years on
pretext of study, enrolled himself as a matter of course
in the Faculty of Decrees[2]. Hence it is especially with

---

[1] Bulæus, IV. 428, 429. In the
prominence of teaching by Bachelors,
the Faculty imitated the Paris Theo-

logians rather than the Jurists of
Bologna.

[2] Study was a recognized ground

reference to this Faculty that we meet with constant legislation—sometimes initiated by the Faculty itself, more often
imposed upon it from without—against sham or 'froward'
(*discholi*) students and against bribery and corruption in
the purchase of degrees or dispensations from the statutable
conditions for obtaining them. Cardinal Estouteville for
instance in 1452 enacted that no one should be accounted
a student of the Faculty who did not attend morning
lecture three times or at least twice a week, and fixed a
limit to the sum which might be paid by wealthy men as
the amount of their 'bursa' or weekly expenses by which
the dues payable to the Faculty were regulated. The in-
tentional over-estimation of the 'bursa' supplied an easy
and frequent means of corruption[1]. In short, it is pretty
clear that it was almost as easy to buy a Paris Degree in
Canon Law as it is, or was till very lately, to buy the title
of Doctor from certain American Universities, though the
tariff was much higher and the forms of residence, study
and examination less sweepingly dispensed with[2]. The
presents and fees paid by candidates made the position of
Regent in this Faculty a lucrative privilege, which its
possessors naturally sought to convert into a monopoly.
Hence admission to the Doctorate ceased to confer the
rights of Regency, and the Regents became a coopting
Professoriate something after the manner of the Bologna
'College of Promotion'[3].

---

for non-residence as early as the
time of Stephen of Tournay. See
Epp. xiii, ciii (Migne, T. 211, cc. 321,
393). The right of absence for purposes of study was granted to
students of Paris and most other
Universities by Papal Bulls. *Chartul.*
T. I. pt. i. Nos. 32, 134, 242: T. II.
No. 1068, &c.

[1] Bulæus, V. 568. In the sixteenth
century we hear that this Faculty 'spe
maioris utilitatis et corradendæ atque
emungendæ undique pecuniæ, infra
privatos parietes, imo sæpe inter
pocula suos Baccalareos promoveret.'

Bulæus, *De la Prés. du R.* p. 117.

[2] In 1466 a Statute was made requiring Licentiates to swear that they
would not incept ' nisi habueritis in
reditibus octuoginta (*sic*) libras parisienses in portatis, sive in patrimonio,
sive in beneficiis.' Another Statute of
this aristocratic Faculty required an
oath 'quod non sit mercenarius seu ca-
pellanus alicujus collegii vel Domini,
ut per hoc magis servetur honor
Facultatis et gradus doctoralis.' Doc.
ap. Péries, p. 36.

[3] Péries, pp. 39–41. It is evident
from the complaints made in the six-

Arts.

The first complete account of the studies required for a Master's degree in Arts is contained in the Statutes drawn up by the Papal legate, Robert de Courçon, in 1215[1]. If the conclusions at which we have already arrived as to the unformed condition of the University at the beginning of the century are well founded, nothing approaching what we understand by a 'curriculum' can well have existed at any much earlier period. It is not improbable that the Bolognese Examinations in Law—a subject wherein any Examination is necessarily an Examination in set books— may have helped to suggest the idea of prescribing a fixed cycle of books as the subjects of Examination in Arts: though the medieval reverence for the *littera scripta* makes such a hypothesis not absolutely necessary. The medieval idea of knowledge, or rather of its ultimate foundations, rarely went beyond knowing what somebody had said about something. At all events it is hardly possible to exaggerate the importance of this innovation in the history of education: the very idea of a 'curriculum' in the sphere of liberal education (so far as our evidence goes) originates with the University legislation of the Englishman de Courçon[2]. It would perhaps be fanciful to see in the circumstance the early exhibition of a national characteristic of what has now become *par excellence* the country of Examinations.

The entire omission of the poets, historians, and orators of ancient Rome from the course now prescribed has been already noticed. Instruction in the Latin language is limited to 'Grammar,' which is to be studied in the 'two

CHAP. V, § 4.

Statutes of De Courçon, 1215.

The curriculum of 1215.

---

teenth century, that there was a great deal of corruption in the bestowal of these chairs, though ostensibly they were awarded after the 'concours' or competitive trial lecture. The students, moreover, had frequently to bring actions against the Professors to compel them to lecture. Péries, pp. 150, *sq.*, 185, 190 *sq.*

[1] Bulæus, III. 81: *Chartul.* T. I. pt. i. No. 20.

[2] Such he is said to have been, though the evidence is not conclusive.

Priscians'[1] or at least one of them. Logic forms the main subject of instruction. The Old and New Dialectic of Aristotle, *i.e.* the whole Organon together with the *Isagoge* of Porphyry, are to be read *ordinarie* : Rhetoric and Philosophy are reserved by way of a treat for Festivals[2]. In Rhetoric the only books specified are the Barbarismus (i. e. the third book of the Ars Major) of Donatus and the Topics of Boethius: Philosophy apparently includes the Nicomachean Ethics of Aristotle and the subjects embraced in the Quadrivium, *i.e.* Arithmetic, Geometry, Music, and Astrology, for which no particular books are prescribed. The newly recovered Metaphysics of Aristotle and his works on Natural Philosophy are peremptorily forbidden together with 'the doctrine' of Master David de Dinant, Almaric the heretic, and Maurice of Spain[3].

B.A.
Course
of 1252.

We have already seen reason for believing that this prohibition of the new Aristotle was removed about the year 1235[4]. A Statute of the English Nation in 125½[5] shows the effect of this revolution (it was no less) upon the University course. Unfortunately the document does not give us a complete curriculum, as it only relates to

[1] According to Denifle (*Chartul.* T. I. pt. i. No. 201, *note*) the first sixteen books were called *Priscianus magnus* or *major*, the last two *Priscianus minor*.

[2] 'Non legant in festivis diebus nisi Philosophos et Rhetoricas et Quadrivialia et Barbarismum et Ethicam si placet et quartum Topicorum.' It is thus clear that at this time there were extraordinary books (as well as extraordinary times), which afterwards disappeared. (The expression *libri ordinarii* in Bulæus, V. p. 617 apparently means all the regular books of the Faculty except those on Grammar.) In the fifteenth century the Ethics was still reserved for holidays, but was read 'ordinarie' (Bulæus, V. p. 726). Thurot is in error on this point (p. 78). At Oxford there were always 'libri ad

lectiones extraordinarias specialiter reservatas' (*Mun. Acad.* p. 371). At Vienna, Mathematics were thought specially suitable for holiday afternoons : there is a curious Statute beginning ' Quamvis Divinum officium sicut non debemus, ita nolumus perturbare, tamen sanius reputamus quod nostri scolares simul et Baccalarii eciam diebus festiuis visitent Scolas quam Tabernas, dimicent disputando lingua quam gladio, Ergo,' &c. Kink, *Gesch. d. Univ. Wien*, II. 196.

[3] See above p. 356.

[4] See above, p. 358.

[5] This very important document (with others) exists only in a MS. of C.C.C.,Oxon : and is printed for the first time by Denifle, *Chartul.* I. pt. i. No. 201.

the studies required before 'Determination,' *i. e.* the degree of B.A. The *de Anima* is the only one of the prohibited books prescribed at this stage. The other books are the same as those of 1215, except that the *Sex principia* of the great Parisian Schoolman Gilbert de la Porrée is now included in the Old Logic[1], and that the *Divisiones* of Boethius appears as well as the Topics. But the most remarkable feature of this course is the large number of times which the student was required to have 'heard' each of these books; in most cases they are required to have attended one or two courses of ordinary and one of cursory lectures on each book. Under the circumstances one is not surprised to find that there soon grew up a regular system of wholesale dispensations[2].

The next Statute bearing on the subject belongs to the year 1254, and enables us to reproduce the whole curriculum of a student in Arts at that date. The Aristotelian treatises mentioned in this Statute in addition to the 'old[3] and new Logic' and the Ethics are the following—*Physica*,

---

[1] 'Insuper quod audiverit libros Aristotelis de *Veteri logica*, videlicet librum *predicamentorum* et librum *periarmenias* bis ad minus ordinarie, et semel cursorie; librum *sex principiorum* semel ordinarie ad minus et semel cursorie; libros videlicet tres primos *topicorum* et *librum divisionum* semel ordinarie vel ad minus cursorie; libros *topicorum* Aristotilis et *elencorum* bis ordinarie et semel ad minus cursorie, vel si non cursorie, ad minus ter ordinarie; librum *priorum* semel ordinarie et semel cursorie, vel sit in audiendo ... librum *posteriorum* semel ordinarie complete. Item quod audiverit *Prissianum minorem* et *barbarismum* bis ordinarie, et ad minus cursorie; *Prissianum magnum* semel cursorie semel (*sic*). [One 'semel' should follow 'et,' two lines above.] Item librum *de anima* semel audiverit vel sit in audiendo' (*l. c.*).

Porphyry is not mentioned, but is probably not deliberately excluded.

[2] Cf. the oaths in *Chartul.* T. II. App. p. 673. A number of rubrics indicate the portions of the old regulations 'dispensed' or 'interpreted' away by the Faculty. Boethius *de Consolatione* appears in the list, but is dispensed. The document is of date anterior to the Reform of 1366. Among these dispensations, it is interesting to notice that the necessary portion of the Ethics was reduced to the first four books now taken up for 'Pass Greats' at Oxford.

[3] Which here includes the *Isagoge* of Porphyry, the *Prædicamenta* and *de Interpretatione* of Aristotle and the Divisions and Topics of Boethius. Bulæus, III. p. 280: *Chartul.* T. I. pt. i. No. 246. As to this distinction, cf. above, pp. 37, 61.

Metaphysica, de Anima, de Animalibus, de Cælo et Mundo, Meteorica, de Generatione, de Sensu et Sensato, de Somno et Vigilia, de Memoria et Reminiscentia, de Morte et Vita. To these are added the *de Plantis* still included in editions of Aristotle though believed to be spurious, and (it is surprising to find) the extremely sceptical *Liber de Causis.* This work at first passed under the name of Aristotle, though it never had a Greek original, and was recognized by Thomas Aquinas to be a translation from the Arabic. Another translation from the Arabic occurs under the title *de differentia Spiritus et Animæ*[1]. The grammatical or rhetorical treatises specified are the *Sex principia* of Gilbertus Porretanus, the *Barbarismus* of Donatus, the Priscians, and the Divisions and Topics of Boethius. Such are the books which were sufficiently in use at Paris to be included in a Statute prescribing the length of time which the Lecturer was required to spend over each book.

Legatine
Reform of
1366.

In 1366 a body of Statutes was imposed upon the University by the Papal Legates, Giles de Montaigu, Cardinal of St. Martin, and John de Blandy, Cardinal of St. Mark. The list contained in this 'Reform' represents, not (like the last) the whole range of the lectures, or, at all events, of the ordinary lectures usually given at Paris, but the books actually 'taken up' at each stage of the student's career. For the 'two Priscians' were now substituted the new Grammar or 'Doctrinale' of Alexander de Villa Dei, written in verse or doggerel, which retained its place as the universal School Grammar till the sixteenth century[2]. The whole of the Old and New Logic (including the Topics of Boethius) was taken up as before, and part or the whole of the *de Anima.* For the License were further required the following Aristotelian books — the

[1] The work of Costa ben Luca, sæc. ix–x. See Denifle's note. (*Chartul.* I. pt. i. No. 246.) The authors of the various books are in most cases not specified.

[2] Over one hundred editions of or comments upon the whole or parts of this work are enumerated by Hain (*Repertor. Bibliograph.* 1826, *sub voce*) as printed before 1500. It continued to be reprinted till much later.

Physica, the *de Generatione et Corruptione,* the *de Cælo et Mundo,* the group of minor treatises known as the *Parva Naturalia* (viz. : the books *de Sensu et Sensato, de Somno et Vigilia, de Memoria et Reminiscentia, de Longitudine et Brevitate Vitæ*), the *Liber Mechanicæ,* and certain mathematical books not further specified [1]. Moreover, the candidate for the License was required to have attended disputations at least throughout one 'grand Ordinary' and to have himself responded in at least two disputations. The Ethics (the greater part of it) and at least three books of the Meteorics were reserved for the period between the reception of the License and Inception [2]. This distribution is somewhat more systematic than in the earlier lists; the course of instruction may now be said to have been divided into three stages, which may be thus characterized :—

For B.A.—Grammar, Logic, and Psychology.

For the License in Arts—Natural Philosophy.

For M.A.—Moral Philosophy, and completion of the course of Natural Philosophy.

The Reform of Cardinal Estouteville in 1452 makes no important change in the curriculum : his insistence on verse-making may perhaps be taken as a sign of the times, but it was probably always supposed to be taught under the head of Grammar [3]. His Statutes are chiefly interesting on account of the light which they throw upon the discipline and mode of teaching in vogue at the time. These regu-

Reform of Cardinal Estouteville, 1452.

---

[1] 'Librum Mechanicæ, vel qui actu audiat eundem, et quod aliquos libros Mathematicos audiverit.' Bulæus, IV. 388. A notice in the book of the Chancellor of Ste Geneviève prescribes 'centum lectiones de Mathematica,' which was interpreted by the Faculty to mean the hearing of Johannes de Sacrobosco (*i. e.* Holywood, sometimes identified with Halifax in Yorkshire, but probably Holywood in Dumfrieshire, † 1252) *de Sphæra* and one other book. This must have been introduced at some time before 1366. *Chartul.* T. II. App. p. 678.

[2] 'Libros morales, specialiter librum Ethicorum pro majori parte, et librum Metheororum.' This arrangement probably did not supersede the Ethical lecture on Festivals for students before License.

[3] 'In arte metrificandi fuerint competenter edocti.' Bulæus, V. 573. This stage was to be got over before Logic was begun.

lations exhibit a laudable disposition, sometimes wanting in University Reformers, not to insist on the impracticable. He follows indeed the Reformers of 1366 in sternly repressing the laxity which allowed boys in the Art Schools to sit on benches, and requires the old custom of making them sit on the ground to be strictly enforced 'that all occasion of pride may be taken away from the young [1].' But the uselessness of attempting to forbid by legislative enactment modes of lecturing which were equally in favour with the Regents and their auditors was at length perceived. A succession of Statutes had peremptorily required the Master to lecture *ex tempore* instead of reading or 'dictating' his lecture. They had even gone so far as to prescribe the exact pace or rapidity with which the words were to flow from the teacher's lips : he was to lecture not 'drawlingly' (*tractim*) but 'rapidly' (*raptim*), that is to say, 'bringing out the words as rapidly as if nobody was writing before him [2].' And the eagerness of the medieval Undergraduate to take full notes was so intense that it was considered necessary to accompany this anti-dictation Statute with penalties against persons resisting its execution by 'shouting, hissing, groaning, or throwing stones by themselves or by their servants or confederates [3].' Estou-

Dictation.

---

[1] 'Ut occasio superbiæ a juvenibus secludatur.' Bulæus, V. 573.

[2] 'Sic scilicet proferendo, ac si nullus scriberet coram eis. Secundum quem modum fiunt sermones in Universitate et recommendationes : et quem Lectores in cœteris Facultatibus insequuntur.' Bulæus, IV. 332. This practice was even more ancient than the University itself. 'Cahiers' evidently dictated by Masters are extant which belong to the first half of the twelfth century. *Hist. Lit.* T. IX. p. 72.

[3] 'Auditores vero hujusce nostri Statuti executioni obviantes clamore, sibilo, strepitu, jactu lapidum per se aut per suos famulos, vel complices, seu quovis alio modo privamus et

resecamus a nostro consortio usque ad unum annum,' *l. c.* The Statute, however, permits the 'Nominationem ad pennam alicujus determinationis notabilis Tractatus vel Expositionis quam in vico straminis scribunt quandoque juvenes in diebus Festivis.' Ramus lays down the following rules on the subject :

Philosophiam continua voce et perpetua raptione prælegito.

Ne tractim nominato et dictato.

Discipulus Magistri verba mente capito.

Manu et penna ne exarato.

Notabilis tamen sententiæ dictandæ et excipiendæ facultas esto.

Scholæ in Liberales Artes, Basileæ, 1578, c. 1063.

teville contented himself with the moderate requirement
that the teacher should take the trouble to read the lecture himself instead of handing his MS. to a scholar who
dictated it to the rest [1]. In the same way he allowed the
Theological Bachelors to read their lectures or exercises
for degrees, requiring only that they should not read word
for word the *quæstiones* of another [2]. It may be observed
that the discussion of *quæstiones* had by this time largely
replaced—at least in the higher Faculties—the older method
of exhaustive analysis and textual comment. In the same
practical spirit, the regulations on the subject of academical dress were relaxed. The enforcement of the 'Cappa'
was now limited to Masters. Equal common sense is exhibited in the abolition of enforced celibacy for Doctors of
Medicine, as a condition of continuing to enjoy the privileges of Regency. Nobody seems to have thought of extending this relaxation to the other Faculties. In several
trifling points an effort was made to reduce the enormous
amount of conventional perjury involved by that reckless
multiplication of oaths which characterized all medieval
University legislation [3]. Of about forty oaths required

---

[1] Bulæus, V. pp. 572, 573, 'Specialiter autem et sub poena excommunicationis, inhibemus ne quasdam
quæstiones, quamvis bene compilatæ
existant, tradant uni de Scholaribus
suis ad legendum et nominandum
cæteris studentibus ; quod, ut accepimus, quidam facere non erubescunt
in damnum Scholarium et grave
scandalum Facultatis Artium.'

[2] In the same way candidates for
Theological degrees were allowed to
read their 'Principium' or 'Sentences,'
but provided they were written by
themselves, ' cum memoria hominum labilis maxime circa subtiles
Theologiae materias plerumque de-
ficiat.' *Ib.* p. 565. On the other
hand in the Faculty of Decrees,
Baccalariandi were still required to
perform their exercises and deliver
their lectures ' corde tenus' and

' absque ullo (*sic*) quaternione, sive
codicello legendo, sive expediendo.'
Ib. p. 567. At Greifswald lecturing
or disputing 'ad pennam' is still
forbidden ; note-taking is allowed
' dummodo fiat sine pronuntiatura'
(Kosegarten, *Greifswald*, II. p. 301).
At Ingolstadt special lectures seem
to have been established to enable
poor scholars to provide themselves
with books ; ' Conclusum fuit . . .
quod statuantur duo magistri lectores textuum ad beneficium calami.'
Prantl, II. p. 73. An Edict against
' Dictation,' still popular with the
students, was issued at Padua by
the Doge and Senate of Venice in
1596. Riccobonus, *De Gymn. Patav.*
p. 100.

[3] The ' Volumus' of du Boulay's
text (V. p. 576) is, as the context
shows, a misprint for ' Nolumus.'

from Inceptors by the Reformers of 1360, Estouteville abolished some half-dozen, probably those whose obligations were most systematically neglected—such as the duty of attending the funerals of Scholars, of saying a 'whole Psalter' on the occasion of every death among the Regents, of incepting in a 'new cope not borrowed or hired [1],' of lecturing for two years [2], and the requirement that each Master should have a black cope of his own.

Other Text-books in use at Paris.

This sketch of the principal reforms introduced from time to time by the Cardinal-legates, will give the reader a fair notion of the general character of Parisian teaching and of the more important modifications which took place in the University curriculum during our period. He must, however, be warned that the picture is by no means complete. The Statutes of the German Universities, which we know to have been in the main based upon Parisian usage, mention a considerable number of minor books which do not appear in any of the above-cited lists. It follows that in the periods intermediate between these University Commissions various changes took place of which no account has reached us, or more probably that lectures were given upon a certain number of books not actually 'taken up for the Schools [3].' The most important of the books excluded from the above lists which may thus be presumed to have been studied at Paris are the Politics, Economics, and Rhetoric of Aristotle [4] : as to the first two we have posi-

[1] 'Item juramentum de incipiendo in cappa nova non accommodata, non conducta.'

[2] Du Boulay prints 'sex,' but from other evidence it appears that the true reading must be ' duos ' (ii for vi). Cf. *Chartul.* T. II. App. p. 680.

[3] Thus at Heidelberg we find a ' Pastus (table of fees) librorum quos non oportet scolares formaliter in Scolis ratione alicuius gradus audivisse' (in 1443), including the ' Parva logicalia Marsilii,' the Politics, Petrus Hispanus, the Economics, ' de perspectiva, de Algorisimo, de

bona fortuna, de proportionibus.' Alexander [de Villa Dei] pt. i. and ii, Donatus, ' de Theorica planetarum.' Hautz, II. p. 355.

[4] A Statute of Caen prescribes the Politics and Economics ' prout est solitum fieri Parisius' (*Bull. de la Soc. de Normandie*, XII. p. 497). All three appear at Prague (*Mon. Univ. Prag.* I. i. pp. 56, 76), where also the *de Vegetalibus* is mentioned : at Leipsic the Politics and Economics, and in 1499 the Rhetoric (Zarncke, *Statutenbücher d. Univ. Leipzig*, pp. 399, 465). Tradition makes Dante attend

tive evidence that such was the case. The rest are smaller
and slighter books. They include the more popular treatises of Boethius such as the *de Consolatione Philosophiæ*,
and occasionally even the spurious *de Disciplina Scholarium* [1]. Then there are the short logical treatises or text-
books composed by the leaders of the various medieval
schools of thought. At this period the logical studies of every
young student began probably with one of these school-
books, even where they are not specified in the official
curriculum. The most important were the *Summulæ* of
Petrus Hispanus (Pope John XXI) [2] and the *Parva Logicalia* of Marsilius of Inghen [3]. Other medieval treatises
used as philosophical text-books were the *Tractatus* of the
Realist Albert of Saxony [4] and the *Quæstiones* of Buridan [5].
The *Labyrinthus* and *Grecismus* of Eberhard [6] are fre-

Siger's lectures on the Politics while
at Paris. *Hist. Lit.* XXI. p. 106.

[1] *Mon. Univ. Prag.* I. i. pp. 76, 77.

[2] At Prague for M.A., *Mon. Univ.
Prag.* I. i. p. 48. The first and fourth
books of Petrus Hispanus were also
called 'Parva Logicalia.' Prantl,
Ingolstadt, II. p. 89. Goulet (f. xix *b*)
observes that *Summulæ* were usually
read at the smaller Universities by
students who afterwards came to
Paris. But we also find a class of
Summulistæ in the Paris Colleges.
See Launoi, *Navarræ Gymn. Hist.*
1677, I. p. 174. So in the Cistercian College (1493) : 'Similiterque
ad logicam nullus accedat, nisi qui
ordinarie sub magistro summularum
glosas audiverit, et textum ex corde
reddiderit.' Félibien, III. p. 174.
It is obvious to any one acquainted
with the contents of the Organon
and the youth of the medieval
student that any real knowledge of
it must have been acquired by the
aid of abridgements of some kind.

[3] See above, p. 440, n. 3. At Heidelberg we find in addition to those
which usually appear, lectures 'de

textibus suppositionum, Amplifica-
tionum et Appellacionum, De con-
sequenciis, De obligatoriis, De in-
solubilibus' (Hautz, II. p. 353) ; also
on 'textum cum glosa Bnn. (Bottonis
s. Bernardi Parmensis) cum suis ad-
ditionibus' (*l. c.* p. 339). The 'Parva
logicalia Marsilii obligatoria et in-
solubilia' were lectured on at Freiburg in 1465 as well as '*Controversæ
Marsilii et theoreticæ*' (Schreiber,
Gesch. d. Stadt u. Univ. Freib., 1857,
II. i. p. 51).

[4] *e. g.* at Freiburg, *l. c.* II. i.
p. 45.

[5] The *Quæstiones Buridani* were
read at Prague *circa* 1370 (*Mon.
Univ. Prag.* I. i. p. 82). So at
Cologne Bachelors were admitted
'ad legendum Summulas Petri His-
pani et Buridani et parva logicalia
[?Marsilii]' (Bianco,I.*Anl.*pp.66,67).
Leipsic used the 'Parva Logicalia' of
Maulfelt or of Greffinstein or of Marsilius. Zarncke, *Statutenbücher*, p.
311; where also appears 'Logica
Hesbri' (i.e. Heytisbury. See above,
p. 249 *n.*).

[6] *Mon. Univ. Prag.* I. i. p. 77.

CHAP. V,
§ 4.

quently added to the more classical treatises on Grammar or Rhetoric [1]. Moreover these German lists enable us to supply the names of the 'Mathematical books' vaguely required by the legatine Statutes. Such books were Euclid (the first six books), the *Almagestum* of Ptolemy, the *de Sphæra* of the Englishman Johannes de Sacrobosco [2], the *Perspectiva Communis* (*i.e.* Optics) of another Englishman, John of Pisa [3] (written in 1280). Instruction in Algebra and Arithmetic is also mentioned in general terms. At the same time the mere fact that the Mathematical books are passed over with such scant courtesy by the reforming Cardinals seems to show what there are other grounds for supposing, namely, that Mathematics were more seriously

The *Grecismus* (written? 1124 A.D.) is a hexameter poem on the figures and parts of speech, printed with comments by Jo. Micentius Mehilinus, Regent at Poitou [no date] and with Alexander de Villa Dei at Lyons in 1490 and recently edited by Wrobel (*Eberhardi Bethuniensis Græcismus,* Uratislauiæ, 1887) : the *Labyrinthus* is an elegiac poem *de Miseriis Rectorum Scholarium* (ed. Leyser, *Hist. Poetarum Med. Ævi,* Halæ Magdeb. 1721, p. 796 *sq.*), consisting partly of advice to Schoolmasters, partly of rules relating to figures of Speech and Versification.

[1] In *Mon. Univ. Prag.* I. i. p. 77 the *Poetria Nova* of Galfridus de Vino (an Englishman, fl. 1198–1216 A.D. ed. Leyser, *op. cit.* p. 861). At Ingolstadt a *libellus de arte epistolandi* is prescribed. Prantl, *Gesch. d. Un. Ingolst.* II. p. 76.

[2] In 1340 a Swede is specially authorised to lecture on this book at Paris. In 1427 a Finlander lectures on the *Theorica planetarum* of Campanus de Novara : but even a lecture on Geometry seems to be an extraordinary thing at Paris. About 1378 Charles V founded two Bursarships in the College of Maître Gervais as

Mathematical Lectureships. Thurot, pp. 81, 82.

[3] Prague in 1390 required for M.A. 'sex libros Euclidis, sphæram, theoricam, aliquid in musica et arithmetica, perspectivam communem' (*Mon. Univ. Prag.* I. i. p. 56). The works referred to are the *de Sphæra* of Johannes de Sacrobosco, the *Theoria Planetarum* of Campanus de Novara, and the *Perspectiva Communis* of John of Pisa, written in 1280, better known to Englishmen as John Peckham, Archbishop of Canterbury. See an interesting account of the MSS. of this work in *Reg. Epist. Jo. Peckham,* ed. Martin, vol. III. p. lviii *sq.* At Freiburg, the Mathematical subjects include 'Latitudines' and 'Proportiones' [of the English Archbishop Bradwardine or its abridgement by Albert of Saxony]. Schreiber, *Gesch. d. Stadt u. Univ. Freiburg,* vol. II. i. p. 51. We find lectures on 'Algorismus' and 'Almanachus' (presumably the method of finding Easter) at Prague (*Mon. Univ. Prag.* I. p. 77), and again on 'Arithmetica accurata' (*ib.* p. 83): cf. *ib.* p. 91 'algorismus de integris.' On the meaning of the last see above, p. 243.

cultivated in Oxford and some of the German Universities
than at Paris[1]. Oxford and the German Universities seem
to have agreed also in requiring Boethius *de re Musica*, or
some other Musical work[2], so as to keep up the theory that
the Arts course consisted of the complete Trivium and
Quadrivium. At Paris we hear nothing of Music, and less
importance seems to have attached to the theory of the
Trivium and Quadrivium.

We have already seen that the student's course was
divided into two clearly marked periods, during the first of
which he was a scholar pure and simple, while during the
second he was allowed or required to undertake a certain
amount of teaching himself, though still continuing his studies
under a Master. The Baccalaureate perhaps originated in
the superior Faculties. We have seen that it existed from
an early period in the Law-schools of Bologna, though
there the teaching by Bachelors never became much more
than an academical exercise. By the Statutes of Robert de
Courçon students of Theology were allowed to deliver
'private lectures' after five years' study, though the word
Bachelor does not occur. In the Faculty of Arts the Baccalaureate does not appear till rather later : neither the name
nor the thing occurs in Robert de Courçon's Statutes, though
it is probable that the custom of employing the assistance
of pupil-teachers was of great antiquity in the medieval
Schools. There is, however, a provision that no banquets
should be allowed at the 'responsions or oppositions of
boys or youths.' These disputations, a kind of imitation
of the Inceptions and other disputations of the Masters,
took place during Carnival-tide and Lent every year,
and came to be technically known as 'Determinations[3].'

---

[1] The Astronomical tables of the
Prague Master, Johann Schmidel,
were of use to Tycho Brahe. Tomek,
p. 132.

[2] At Prague the '*Musica* Muri'
(*i. e.* Joannes de Muris, an Englishman who fl. 1330 A.D.) : *Mon. Univ.
Prag.* I. i. pp. 82, 83. So at Leipsic,

Zarncke, *Statutenbücher*, p. 311. The
book is printed by Gerbert in *Scriptores Eccles. de Musica*, III p. 189 *sq.*

[3] In 1476 we hear of Determinations taking place between Martin-
mas and Christmas (Bulæus, V. p.
722), but this is so contrary to the
usual practice that it seems probable

To 'determine' meant to maintain a thesis against an opponent[1]. On these occasions the 'determiner' was a student entering upon the Bachelor-stage of his career, and the opponent a student of somewhat lower standing. This rehearsal of the part which the student aspired eventually to play as a Master was at first quite voluntary. It originated perhaps with the scholars rather than with the Masters[2]. At about the middle of the thirteenth century, however, it became at first a customary and then a compulsory part of the training of every student in Arts who wanted to become a Master. In 1279 it was made obligatory for students in Arts to 'determine' before presenting themselves as candidates for the Chancellor's License[3], though it had already been enforced for some time by particular Nations[4].

that the preliminary Responsions must be meant or that the occurrence was exceptional.

[1] Mr. Boase's explanation (*Reg. of the Univ. of Oxford*, I. p. viii) 'instead of disputing himself, he presided over disputations, and gave out his determination or decision on the questions discussed,' is incomplete. The determiner was the leading disputant, though after debating the question with an opponent, he would appear to have wound up with certain 'conclusions' (*Chartul.* T. II. App. p. 673, *note*). Mr. Clark (*Reg. Univ. Oxf.* II. Pt. i. p. 50 *sq.*) gives a detailed and interesting account of the Determination and its attendant ceremonies in the sixteenth century at Oxford. The last relic of Determination was abolished (alas!) in 1855. 'Up to that time on Ash-Wednesday the Deans of the several colleges attended at a special Congregation and ... read over a supplicat for all those of their College who had been admitted to B. A. during the year. These were then held to have lawfully determined,

though they were no longer present in person, and though no exercises were performed' (Clark, *l. c.* p. 63).

[2] A curious relic of this state of things survived till recently at Oxford. The *Collectores Baccalaureorum* were B.A.'s supposed to manage these disputations under the Proctors. They wore the full Proctorial robes, *i.e.* the M.A. full dress. Cox, *Recollections of Oxford*, London, 1870, p. 242.

[3] The Statute enacts that an oath to this effect should be taken before the candidate was admitted to the Examination at Ste Geneviève, and before Inception in the case of a Bachelor who elected to be licensed at Notre Dame. The Faculty does not venture to impose its regulations on the Cathedral Chancellor: it can only refuse to admit to its membership a Licentiate who had disobeyed them. (Bulæus, III. p. 447: *Chartul.* I. i. No. 485.)

[4] See the Statute of the English Nation in 1252. *Chartul.* T. I. pt. i. Nos. 201, 202. It is of course quite possible that it was already enforced by the whole Faculty.

In 1275, if not earlier[1], a preliminary test or 'Responsions' CHAP. V,
was instituted to ascertain the fitness of those who wanted § 4.
to take part in the public performance [2]. At these 'Respon- Responsions,' which took place in the December before the Lent sions.
in which the candidate was to determine, he had to dispute
in Grammar and Logic with a Master. If this test was
passed in a satisfactory manner[3], the candidate was admitted
to the *Examen Baccalariandorum* which was conducted by Examina-
a board of Examiners appointed by each Nation for its tion for
own candidates. The duty of the Examiners was twofold, B.A.
firstly to ascertain by inspecting the *schedulæ* given by

---

[1] The Statute of the English Nation in 1252 runs: 'Item det fidem [before Determination] quod per duos annos diligenter disputaciones magistrorum .. frequentaverit, et per idem tempus de sophismatibus in scolis requisitus responderit.' (*Chartul.* T. I. pt. i. No. 201.) The obligation of 'sitting in the Schools' during the *viva voce* examination of other candidates which lasted at Oxford till a generation ago was the last relic of the obligation to attend disputations.

[2] 'Statuimus quod nullus decetero nisi prius in Scholis publice Magistro Regenti actu, de Questione responderit ante Natale, ad examen Determinantium admittatur.' Bulæus, III. 420: *Chartul.* I. pt. i. No. 461. In Oxford, in the sixteenth century, the Examination seems to have assumed the form of a disputation between the Examinee and a senior scholar, before the 'Magistri Scholarum.' The disputations were in Grammar and Logic, and took place in the ninth term. The retention of the term 'Magistri Scholarum' and the *Testamur*, which (till abolished in 1893) stated that the candidate 'quæstionibus Magistrorum Scholarum in *parviso* pro forma respondit' (see below, chap. xii. § 5) testify to the identity of the modern

Examination known as Responsions or 'Smalls' with this ancient institution. The *four* Masters of the Schools at Oxford were possibly an inheritance from the four Nations of Paris. At Oxford a hood of plain black stuff (*simplex caputium*) was conferred with some ceremony after the disputation, by which the student became '*sophista generalis.*' This hood was worn in the Final Schools till some thirty years ago. See Clark, *Reg. Univ. Oxf.*, II. pt. i. pp. 21, 22.

[3] The same regulation was adopted at Oxford in 1267. *Mun. Acad.* p. 34. The Examination is described in Bulæus, V. p. 647 (1460): 'Item circa Baccalariandorum examen statuimus et ordinamus quod maturius graviusque de coetero ipsi Baccalariandi examinentur; videlicet in grammaticalibus quilibet ab unoquoque Examinatorum. Similiter in Parvis Logicalibus ab unoquoque examinetur. In aliis vero libris Porphyrii et Aristotelis examinentur per ordinem; ita tamen quod quilibet in unoquoque librorum unam ad minus habeat quæstionem.' The Examiners are at the same time required to draw up a list of those who have passed immediately after the Examination, for fear of there being moved 'multorum precibus importunis.'

his Masters that the candidate had completed the necessary residence and attended Lectures in the prescribed subjects, and secondly to examine him in the contents of his books. If he passed this Examination, he was admitted to determine. It was perhaps at about the period when Determination was made a necessary preliminary to the Mastership that the word Bachelor, borrowed from the terminology of the Guilds and hitherto applied vaguely to any student allowed by his Master to teach in his school or to a student who was a candidate for the Mastership [1], came to be technically restricted in the Faculty of Arts to candidates who had, after passing the prescribed Examination, been duly admitted to determine and permitted to give 'cursory' lectures [2]. The Baccalaureate became in fact an inferior 'degree' to which the candidate was regularly admitted by the Proctor of his Nation, after taking the oath of obedience to the Rector and Faculty, and to his Proctor and Nation. Determination thus played the same part in the admission to this new degree that Inception played at the final stage of his career. Part of the ceremony consisted in the Determiner's putting on his Bachelor's *cappa* and taking his seat for the first time among the Bachelors [3]. It is important to remember that at Paris and in most continental Universities the Chancellor had nothing to do with the conferring of the Bachelor's Degree.

---

[1] 'Mesme en Massonerie et tout autre mestier de France où il y a maistrise, l'on appelle Bacheliers ceux qui sont passez Maistres en l'Art, mais qui ne sont pas Iurez, et lesquels pour amander le rapport fait par les Docteurs Iurez doiuent estre deux fois autant.' Claudius Falcetus, *De Origine Equitum*, c. 1. ap. Bulæum, II. p. 680.

[2] Thus at Oxford the form of admission to B.A. was 'Domine A. B. ego admitto te ad lectionem cujuslibet libri Logices Aristotelis et in-super earum artium quas et quatenus per statuta audivisse teneris ; insuper auctoritate mea et totius Universitatis do tibi potestatem intrandi scolas, legendi, et disputandi et reliqua omnia faciendi quæ ad gradum Baccalaurei in artibus spectant.' Clark, *Reg. Univ. Oxf.*, II. i. p. 48.

[3] So at least at Prague in 1371, (*Mon. Univ. Prag.* I. i. p. 52), and elsewhere. At Oxford the disputation had to be performed twice by each Bachelor in the course of Lent. Clark, *l. c.*, II. i. p. 58.

Determination was a great day in the student's University life. The ceremony took place in one of the Schools of the Vicus Stramineus (*Rue du Fouarre*). The Determiner had to pay his Master—the Master under whom (as the phrase ran) he was determining—for the use of his School : and the Master expected to get back the greater part of his year's rent by the fees which he received from his determining Bachelors. Even after an official character had been given to Determination by the recognition of the Faculty, it retained much of its primitive character of a students' festivity. It was not, it would seem, till the middle of the fifteenth century that the student's Master was required to be officially present at it[1]. The Speech-day of a Public School if combined with considerably more than the license of the Oxford Encænia would perhaps be the nearest modern equivalent of these medieval exhibitions of rising talent. Every effort was made to attract to the Schools as large an audience as possible not merely of Masters or fellow-students but if possible of ecclesiastical dignitaries and other distinguished persons. The friends of a Determiner who was not successful in drawing a more distinguished audience would run out into the streets and forcibly drag chance passers-by into the School. Sometimes the Halls were invaded by eager partisans for the same purpose[2]. Wine was provided at the Determiner's expense in the Schools : and the day ended in a feast given in imitation of the Master's Inception-banquets, even if dancing or torch-light processions were forborne in deference to authority[3].

---

[1] 'De qualibet Domo, seu de quolibet Pædagogio unus assistat Magister Regens, qui non permittat in dictis Disputationibus aut eundo aut redeundo aliquas insolentias fieri.' Bulæus, V. 574. There was always no doubt a certain supervision by the Proctor.

[2] *Mun. Acad.* p. 411 : Bulæus, V. p. 574.

[3] Bulæus, III. 420 : V. 575. Among the exuberances of spirits condemned (III. p 420) is the election of a 'capitaneum quocumque nomine censeatur; sed regimine Rectoris et Procuratorum sint contenti.' It is interesting to observe the Masters of Paris repressing movements among the students exactly similar to those which led to the formation of the Student-Universities at Bologna.

A very interesting document has fortunately been preserved which shows us that a Bachelor who cut a good
figure in these boyish word-tournaments might win something more than applause or complimentary speeches. The
document contains the pleadings on the part of the University in the great suit of 1283 against the Chancellor.
That official had complained of the requirement of Determination from intending Masters as an infringement of
his prerogatives: he was acute enough to discern in the
innovation the establishment of a new degree over the
conferring of which he had no control. The Faculty replies
that 'since great men of every Faculty come to their
Determination, Magnates, such as Archdeacons, Chanters,
and Provosts of Cathedrals and many others, they acquire
that boldness of speech which is necessary to an Artist,
as well as acquaintance with the Magnates, by which they
used to obtain promotion to ecclesiastical benefices [1].'

After Determination, a student resumed his attendance
at Masters' lectures. He was moreover required to take
part in a certain number of disputations and to give a
course of 'cursory' lectures himself, usually on one of
the books of the Organon [2]. When he had completed
five or six years of study from his Matriculation, had
'heard' all the books prescribed by the Faculty and had
attained the age of twenty, he was free to present himself
for the Chancellor's Examination.

Enough has been said as to the contests between the
Chancellor and the University with regard to the conduct
of these Examinations [3]. We have already traced the steps

---

[1] Jourdain, No. 274: *Chartul.* T.
I. pt. i. No. 515. Much discussion
has arisen as to the meaning of determining 'sub alio' (Bulæus, III.
p. 487: IV. p. 993). I believe it
meant to have one's expenses paid
by a richer Determiner, who was
said at Oxford to determine 'pro
alio.' See *Mun. Acad.* pp. 242, 243,
and below, Vol. II. chap. xii. § 5.

[2] In 1252 the Incepting Bachelor

is required to swear that 'intererit
lectionibus bachellariorum si magistri
eorum sint actualiter regentes'; and
not to present (for License) a Bachelor 'qui nec in disputationibus
nec in lectionibus visitaverit aliquem
magistrorum.' (*Chartul.* T. I. pt. i.
No. 202.) Cf. Thurot, p. 52 ff.

[3] In the agreement of 1213 (Jourdain, No. 15; *Chartul.* I. pt. i. No. 18),
the Artists are required to give their

by which the Chancellor lost all real control over the License which he conferred. It appears, however, clear that in the case of the Faculty of Arts there always was an actual Examination—at one time a serious Examination—by the Chancellor and four Examiners in the books taken up, before the actual ceremony of conferring the License, while at the ceremony itself some at least of the candidates were required to give expositions or lectures (known as *Collations*) after the manner of Masters lecturing in the Schools upon various portions of the texts, after which the Chancellor himself took part in the discussion of ' questions ' arising therefrom.

In the superior Faculties the Examination before the Previous Chancellor seems to have first been reduced to the barest Examina-tion by the formality, and then to have disappeared altogether [1] : the Faculties. fate of the candidate was really determined beforehand at a meeting of the Faculty in the absence of the Chancellor.

testimony as to the qualifications of candidates upon oath, the Physicians ' dare fidem,' the Theologians and Canonists merely ' dicere in verbo veritatis.' So far there is nothing to show that an actual Examination in the modern sense took place. The Sermon of Robert de Sorbonne, how-ever (*circa* 1270), makes it plain that this was the case. ' Item si Cancel-larius Parisiensis examinet aliquem Clericum in aliquo libro, sufficit quod reddat ei septem vel octo lectiones . . . Item si aliquis respondeat coram Cancellario de quatuor quæstionibus, ad tres bene transit et licentiatur' (Bulæus, III. 228, 230). It appears, however, that ' Cancellarius non audit omnes qui licentiantur in pro-pria persona, sed facit eos audiri ab aliquibus aliis magistris' (*l. c.*). In the great suit of 1283 (Jourdain, No. 274 : *Chartul.* I. pt. i. No. 515) the Masters relied upon a passage in the bull of 1231 which they cited as ordering that ' De fisicis et artistis cancellarius bonâ fide *pe*rmittat ex-aminare magistros' (*ib.*); but it ap-pears that the true text is ' *p*romit-tat' (Denifle, I. 89). Bulæus (IV. 280) tells us that in his own day the Chancellor no longer examined the Theologians, but that the formal Ex-amination of the Bachelors of Arts was still kept up.

[1] This was certainly the case in the Faculty of Medicine, in which the Chancellor would naturally have been an inefficient Examiner. See the long series of newly published documents relating to a great liti-gation between the Chancellor and the Faculty in 1330–1332. *Chartul.* T. II. Nos. 918–943. The Chancellor had licensed a Bachelor not pre-sented by the Faculty, which claims that it is customary for the Bachelor ' ire per singulos magistros regentes Parisius in facultate predicta, ante-quam presentetur cancellario Pari-siensi, et petere ab eisdem quod ipsi audiant de una questione sc-lempni' (No. 921). The custom re-ceived the Royal confirmation in 1331 (*ib.* No. 934).

Eventually the Faculty of Arts claimed the same right for itself, though only as regards the Licenses given at Ste Geneviève. Four *Temptatores* were appointed by the Faculty itself to conduct an independent Examination (*Temptatores in cameris* or *in propriis*) which took place between the Examination before the Chancellor [1] (*in communibus*) and the *Collations* at the actual bestowal of the License [2]. The first Examination, conducted by the Chancellor and four *Temptatores* named by him but accepted by the Faculty, included an inquiry into the candidate's residence, attendance at lectures, and performance of exercises, as well as some Examination in the prescribed books ; at its conclusion, the Chancellor, guided by the votes of the Examiners, admitted those who were judged worthy to the Examination before the Faculty, which was perhaps the more important Examination in the modern sense of the word. The Faculty appears never to have ventured on imposing an additional Examination on the candidates at the 'Inferior' or Cathedral Examination. There the only *Temptamen* was conducted by the four Examiners chosen from the Faculty by the Chancellor,

---

[1] Or his Sub-Chancellor. The Chancellor of Ste Geneviève, if not M.A., was obliged to appoint a D.D. as Sub-Chancellor. The Chancellor of Notre Dame also had a Sub-Chancellor who was a B.D. *Chartul.* T. II. App. p. 676, *note.*

[2] Bulæus (V. p. 858) distinctly states that this Examination by the Faculty applied to all Bachelors, to whichever Chancellor they applied for the License. And Du Boulay lived while some of the institutions he described were still living, and others must at least have been known by tradition. If he is right, the bulls allowing the Faculty to name the Examiners at the Examination of Ste Geneviève must apply to his own Examination (*Chartul.* T. I. pt. i. Nos. 333, 346, 363: Bulæus,

III. pp. 346, 361 ; but cf. pp. 735–6), though these are elsewhere spoken of as nominated by the Chancellor. In *Chartul.* T. I. pt. i. No. 363 the Faculty distinctly claims to elect both sets of Examiners ; the appointment of Examiners *in communibus* was evidently matter of dispute between Faculty and Chancellor, though they certainly had to be formally admitted by the latter. The above account in the main follows Thurot's (p. 53 *sq.*), which is, however, criticised by Feret (*L'Abbaye de Ste Geneviève*, I. p. 286), whose book is based upon the older work of Molinet. See also *Chartul.* T. II. App. p. 675 *sq.* (with Denifle's notes), and below, Appendix xiii. I have made an independent study of the Registers.

together with the purely formal public Examination or Collations on the day of the License-ceremonial.

The candidates who had passed their Examination or Examinations were sent to the Chancellor to be licensed in batches of eight or more at a time, the names being arranged in order of merit. This order, which the Chancellor was expected to follow in actually conferring the License, was the only approach to a competitive Examination which the Parisian University system admitted. The only 'honour' which a student could win in taking his degree was a good place in his *Camera* or *Auditio* [1]. The 'honours' of the University were, however, no more above suspicion than the degree itself. In 1384 a Chancellor of Paris, defending himself against a charge of exacting illegal fees for the License, numbers the supplications and entreaties which he received from great persons on behalf of their relatives for precedence in their *Auditio* among the most serious and oppressive burdens of his ill-remunerated office. The right of determining the order of precedence was, it may be observed, still claimed by the Chancellor, though the Masters treated this last relic of his ancient independence as a usurpation [2]. Between the 'private Examination' and the License, the *Licentiandi* were required to maintain a thesis chosen by themselves in S. Julian's Church, the ceremony being known as the *Quodlibetica*, i. e. disputation on a subject chosen by the candidate himself.

On the day appointed for the conferment of the License, the successful candidates [3] in full academical dress (*cappati*)

The License.

[1] Goulet, f. viii *b*. At Prague we find the candidates in the Bachelor's Examination arranged in order of merit, and after the sixteenth century in *three classes. Mon. Univ. Prag.* I. pt. i. pp. 43, 44 : pt. ii. p. 341.

[2] Bulæus, IV. p. 606. Gerson indulges in a similar vein of self-commiseration, *Opera* (Parisiis, 1606), II. c. 825. The above evidence shows with what small reason the authors of the *Hist. Litt.* (T. XXIV. p. 271), little enough disposed to idealise the

medieval Universities, still praise them as homes of absolute 'égalité,' and for 'la plus stricte justice dans les examens, dans la collation des grades,' &c.

[3] In some Universities the result of the Degree Examination was announced to the candidates by the Examiners sending them a candle, either an allusion to the parable of the light not to be set under a bushel, or to be offered in a church. At Leipsic a curious mode of voting

CHAP. V, proceeded in state from the Mathurine Convent to the Epi-
§ 4. scopal Palace or the Abbey of Ste Geneviève, as the case
might be, accompanied by the Rector and Proctors, and
preceded by the Bedels of the Faculty. They were then presented to the Chancellor, and, after the formal 'Collations'
already mentioned, received kneeling before him the solemn
License in the name of the Trinity, to incept or begin to
teach in the Faculty of Arts, together with the Apostolical
benediction[1]. This ceremony was in fact the same as that
which is now inaccurately termed taking a Master's degree
at Oxford or Cambridge. The Licentiate, as has been fully
explained already, did not become a full Master until he
had actually entered upon the duties of his office and been
incorporated into the society of his new colleagues. An
interval of half a year commonly elapsed between License
Inception. and Inception. Before the actual ceremony of the *birettatio*
the Licentiate had to appear before a Congregation of his
Nation and obtain its *placet* for his promotion. This being
granted, he was immediately sworn to obey the Rector and
his Faculty and Nation, and to do or abstain from doing
some scores of things which had, from time to time, been enjoined or forbidden by University, Faculty, or Nation[2]. The
evening of the day before the Inception he took part in a
peculiarly solemn disputation known as his 'Vespers[3]'.
He was then free to give his formal inaugural lecture or

was in use. The caps of the candidates were spread out on the table :
each Examiner passed down the
table and put a pea [*pisum*] in the
cap of the candidate for whose passing he voted, a pebble in the caps of
those whom he rejected. The candidate's fate was decided by the predominance of peas or pebbles.
(Zarncke, *Statutenbücher*, p. 319.)

[1] The formula in Bulæus is as follows: 'Ego N. auctoritate Apostolica
qua fungor in hac parte do tibi potestatem docendi, regendi, interpre-
tandi, omnesque actus scholasticos
exercendi hic et ubique terrarum,'
concluding no doubt ' in nomine

Patris, Filii, et Spiritus Sancti ' (Bulæus, I. 278). But in the book of the
Chancellor of Ste Geneviève (*Chartul.*
T. II. App. p. 679) it runs : ' Et ego
auctoritate apostolorum Petri et Pauli
in hac parte mihi commissa do vobis
licentiam legendi, regendi, disputandi
et determinandi ceterosque actus
scholasticos seu magistrales exercendi in facultate artium Parisius et
ubique terrarum, in nomine, etc.
Amen.'

[2] The oaths occupy two folio pages
in Bulæus (IV. 273–5).

[3] Already alluded to, though not
by that name, in 1252. *Chartul.* I.
pt. i. No. 202.

rather disputation in the presence of the Faculty, to receive the Magisterial *biretta* and the book from the hands of the presiding Regent, to receive the kiss of fellowship, and to take his seat upon the magisterial Cathedra [1].

The evening concluded with a banquet given at the expense of the Inceptor or a party of Inceptors to the Masters and others, at which it is probable that the prohibitions which we find in some Universities against dancing or the introduction of actors and trumpeters were not always strictly complied with [2]. There were others in which the latter form of jubilation was recognised by Statute [3].

The time occupied by the course in Arts varied considerably at different periods. Robert de Courçon fixed it at six years, requiring twenty years of age for the License [4]. In 1275 the same age was required for the Mastership, but only fourteen for Determination [5], so that a student who came up young would spend most of his time as a Bachelor, and would have to reside somewhat longer than the minimum period. On the other hand, the Statutes of the English Nation in 1252 require the Determiner to have passed five or at least four years in the study of Arts, and to be at least nineteen years of age, so that the Bachelor's degree would come late in his career [6]. It is, impossible to say how far this regulation was a peculiarity of the English Nation. It is, however, certain that at

---

[1] Bulæus, V. 858.

[2] 'Quod tripudiare vel choreare nullo modo audeant publice vel occulte.' (Devic et Vaissette, *Hist. Gén. de Languedoc*, VII. 1879, Docs. c.536). So at Caen, 'mimi seu bucinatores' are forbidden. Comte de Bourmont, *Bulletin de la Soc. des Antiq. de Normandie*, T. XII (1884), p. 405.

[3] *E. g.* Toulouse : Devic, *l. c.*, c. 537.

[4] *Chartul.* T. I. pt. i. No. 20 : 'Nullus legat Parisius de artibus citra vicesimum primum etatis sue annum;' *i. e.* 20, not 21 as commonly stated. The age 12 given in Du Boulay's transcript of the Statute of 1215 (III. p. 81), upon which

Malden, Prof. Laurie and others have based grave reflexions, is an obvious misprint for 21.

[5] *Chartul.* T. I. pt. i. No. 201. It is observable that the residence must be kept 'continue' : the abuse of completing residence by scraps of a few weeks at a time, which has been permitted by some modern Universities, is thus guarded against.

[6] It may, or may not, be more than a coincidence, that the English Universities continued to place the Bachelor's degree later in the course than Paris, and (consequently perhaps) to attach more importance to it.

Paris the tendency was towards shortening the course in Arts, and towards an early Baccalaureate. In the course of the fourteenth century the minimum period for the M.A. degree was reduced to five years and (after 1366) to four years and a half; yet even before this date we find the Book of the Chancellor of Ste Geneviève requiring only three years' study at Paris, with the reservation that the Faculty interpreted the three years as two complete years and part of a third [1]. There was probably at all times so much discrepancy between the letter of the Statutes and the liberal interpretation put upon them by the Faculty as to add considerably to the difficulties of the University historian. Two years' residence in another Studium Generale which had at least six Regents was reckoned as equivalent to one year's study at Paris [2]. Many students passed the earlier half of their University course in some minor University nearer home, and then came to Paris after taking their Bachelor's degree, and thus avoided the Examination for that degree at Paris, an Examination which, if not severe, was something more than a form of which the substance consisted in the payment of fees. The time of those who kept their full residence of four years and a half at Paris appears usually to have been divided thus—they went up in October, took their B.A. in the spring of their second year, the License two years after that, and 'incepted' towards the end of the same year. It is, however,

---

[1] *Chartul.* T. II. App. p. 678. It is possible that this applied only to those who had kept some residence at another University.

[2] In the fifteenth century students from other Universities were frequently allowed to pass the Examinations for the Baccalaureate, the License and the Mastership in the same year, even though ' neque Parisius, neque in aliquo studio solemni seu generali, libros audiverant requisitos ad hujusmodi gradus, neque studuerant per tempus requisitum.' Moved by jealousy of the new University of Caen, the Nation of France provided against this abuse in 1444. (Bulæus, V. 529-30.) Examples of similar laxity as to all manner of University regulations might be multiplied indefinitely. The case of each student who supplicated for this or that step, was more or less considered on its own merits : and neither statutes nor oaths could really prevent a great deal of ' dispensation.'

certain that in the fifteenth century a man frequently took his Bachelor's degree within a year after his coming into residence [1]. The tendency to an earlier Baccalaureate and a still further curtailment of the Arts course is observable after the medieval period. By the sixteenth century it had been reduced to three years and a half [2]. On the continent the Baccalaureate has eventually disappeared altogether or become practically equivalent to Matriculation. In England the curtailment of residence made inevitable by the improvement of Grammar Schools and the later age for commencing the University course has been effected by dispensing with residence after admission to the Bachelor's degree and reducing the final degree to an expensive formality [3].

The obligations of a scholar to his University did not end with taking his degree. In the first place, he was (in the early period) bound to dispute or 'determine questions' for forty days continuously [4]. Then he was required after taking

Necessary Regency.

---

[1] See the Statute of the German Nation in 1460 (Bulæus, V. p. 646). In the German Universities the usual period before the Bachelor's degree seems to have been a year and a half (so at Leipsic, Zarncke, *Statutenbücher*, p. 374) and two years more for the Mastership. The Statutes of Cornouaille College at Paris allow five years for the License (Félibien, III. p. 497) probably as a *maximum*.

[2] Bulæus, V. p. 858: Launoi, *Regii Navarræ Gym. Hist.* Parisiis, 1677, I. p. 272. At this time scholars in Colleges were usually divided into four classses, each of them taught by one Regent (*Summulista, Logicus, Physicus, Intrans*) in the manner of a form at a Public School. This arrangement is still preserved in Scotland, where the Bachelor's degree has likewise disappeared, though one of the classes was long called the Bachelor-class. The same Regent took his pupils through the whole course, changing his class every year. Ramus, *Prœmium Reformandæ Parisiensis Academiæ* in *Scholæ in Liberales Artes*, c. 1116. Cf. below, chap. xi. The arrangement is probably much older than the time of Ramus.

[3] M. Thurot's statement that 'le baccalauréat n'était pas un *grade*, mais un état' (p. 137), seems to imply a somewhat transcendental conception of the nature of a 'degree.' The fact is the term *gradus* was originally used *only* of the Baccalaureate and perhaps the License: they were so many *steps* to the Mastership. Thus *circa* 1284 the Faculty of Arts declares that 'determinatio est unus honorabilis gradus attingendi magisterium.' Jourdain, No. 274 : *Chartul.* T. I. pt. i. No. 515.

[4] So at least in the English Nation in 1252 : 'Disputabit hora determinata, et questiones suas determinabit per quadraginta dies continue post

his degree to stay up and teach in Paris for a certain number of years. An oath to teach for two years, unless previously dispensed, continued to be enforced upon Inceptors [1] till it was abolished by Estouteville in 1452, though it had probably long since ceased to be strictly enforced. So long as the Schools were merely rooms hired in the houses of the Rue du Fouarre by individual Masters, there was no necessary limitation to the number of Regents. If Schools could not be obtained in the street thus consecrated to scholastic uses, Schools in the immediate neighbourhood were recognised by the Faculty as entitling the Masters who occupied them to the privileges of Regency [2]. But when the Nations came to possess or at least to rent Schools of their own, the Regent was required to teach in these Schools. After 1452 it would seem no obstacle was placed in the way of those who wanted to 'go down' immediately after taking their degree, while those who wished to teach had to supplicate *pro regentia et scholis*, and if the petition was granted, to wait for their turn to succeed to the use of a vacant School [3].

Value of a medieval Degree in Arts.　At this point it seems desirable to discuss one of the most important and yet most difficult questions which is suggested by our review of these Parisian Exercises and Examinations—the question ' What was the real difficulty of a medieval Examination ? What was the real value of a medieval degree ? ' With regard to the earliest part of our period, we are left to mere inferences from isolated expressions of contemporary writers. In the third quarter of the thirteenth century it would seem that the Examination before the Chancellor must have been a *bona fide* though by

---

inceptionem.' (*Chartul.* I. pt. i. No. 202.) This requirement, which seems to have early become obsolete at Paris, left a curious trace behind it at Oxford. Every Inceptor was bound to wear his full Academical dress for forty days, which included, in the case of theologians, boots (' *botys* '), while Inceptors of other Faculties were bound to go ' cum sotularibus quodam-

modo conatis vulgariter nuncupatis Pynsons.' (*Mun. Acad.* p. 450.)

[1] See above, p. 440, n. 2.

[2] Bulæus, IV. 212: *Chartul.* T. II. No. 872. By this time (1327) it would seem that the Determiners paid directly to the Nation, who provided Schools for the Masters.

[3] Bulæus, V. 858, 9.

no means a strict or inexorable Examination. A very amusing sermon or treatise, addressed by Robert de Sorbonne possibly to the scholars of the College which he had just founded at Paris, consists of an elaborately drawn out parallel between the Examination before the Chancellor and the Last Judgment. Indefinitely more severe as the latter Examination was represented to be, the illustration could hardly have been used at all had the Chancellor's Examination been a mere farce. The writer distinctly contemplates the possibility of a candidate's rejection, though he points out that in the earthly Examination, unlike its celestial antitype, the Chancellor or his assistants were amenable to personal or pecuniary influences: even if a candidate were discomfited, he could still by tears and entreaties and presents to the Chancellor's assistants induce him to reconsider the matter [1]. Moreover, he tells us that many magnates were licensed without any Examination at all [2]. It is probable that in this passage the writer had chiefly in view the Faculty of Arts, in which his hearers had already graduated. For at this time the number of Theological chairs at Paris was usually fixed by Papal authority, so that admission to the Theological Doctorate really amounted to selection for a Professorship, for which there must have been many applicants: when this limitation was removed, we get complaints both of the admission of unworthy and of the rejection of worthy candidates [3]. But still the whole tone of the allusions to

---

[1] 'Si refutetur aliquis Parisius a Cancellario, hoc non est nisi per annum: qui si post annum redeat, si bene respondet, licentiatur. Item data sententia per preces aliquorum vel per dona vel per servitia aliquando data vel facta collateralibus Cancellarii vel examinatoribus aliis,' &c. . . . 'Item, si quis habet confusionem animi quando refutatur a Cancellario, delebilis est et traditur oblivioni per processum temporis.' Bulæus, III. pp. 226, 227. The discourse is more correctly printed in the *Bibliotheca*

Veterum Patrum, T. XIII. Coloniæ Agrippinæ, 1618.

[2] 'Multis enim magnatibus fit aliquando gratia et licentiantur sine examinatione,' *l. c.*

[3] Innocent III in 1207 limited the Theological Chairs to eight (Bulæus, III. 36: *Chartul*. T. I. pt. i. No. 5): but from a document of 1218 (*Chartul*. T. I. pt. i. No. 27) it appears that this regulation was not strictly observed. In 1221 Honorius III enjoins Archbishop Langton and his brother commissary to reimpose some

the Mastership in the Faculty of Theology at this time is such as to imply that it was not every student, not even the average student, who could look forward to obtaining it as a matter of right, at least unless he were supported by exceptional favour or direct bribery [1]. Incorruptibility in the Examination room is as much a late product of modern civilization as incorruptibility upon the judicial Bench. How much the value of a theological degree sank in the course of the next two centuries, we shall see hereafter. With regard to the Faculty of Arts, the mere number of Masters is sufficient to show that the standard of learning expected in the candidates—and perhaps of impartiality in the Examiners—was very much lower, though taking a degree is spoken of as not quite a matter of course [2]. In the litigation which took place between the Chancellor and the Faculty of Arts in the last quarter of the century, the Masters accuse the Chancellor of appointing incompetent Examiners at Notre Dame while the Chancellor retorts with an accusation of venality against the Examiners at Ste Geneviève [3]. This document and many Statutes directed against venality and corruption tend to show that, however lax the Examination, and however dubious the means adopted for passing it, there really was an Examination to be passed [4]. The Examiner's fangs still retained

---

limitation, since ' ad docendum non solum in aliis facultatibus set etiam in theologia interdum repulsis dignis admittuntur indigni et adeo excrescit numerus magistrorum ut tum pro numerositate tum pro insufficientia eorumdem vilescat auctoritas magistralis.' *Chartul.* T. I. pt. i. No. 41.

[1] See for instance the Statute of the College of Rouen (or de Saana) in 1268, which provides that Fellowships shall terminate after six years ' nisi aliquis illorum in tanta prerogativa scientie emineat, quod possit in scolis alicujus magistri theologie publicas legere lectiones ; et tunc dimittatur ibidem, si voluerit, donec

ad cathedram valeat ascendere magistralem.' *Chartul.* I. pt. i. No. 423. Later College Statutes simply provide that Fellows shall take their degree as a matter of course.

[2] In 1261-1268 the Pope complains that ' Magistri [no particular Faculty is mentioned] creantur subito, non quos juvant morum scientieque suffragia, sed quibus favor et preces ne pretium dixerimus suffragantur ;' as a consequence of which ' ingeritur convocationum necessitas,' pointing to frequent dispensations. *Chartul.* T. I. pt. i. No. 425.

[3] See above, p. 393 *sq.*

[4] At Freiburg (in the sixteenth

sufficient keenness to make it worth while to draw them. When we turn to the latter half of our period, the case is by no means equally clear: but the evidence obtainable both from the registers of Paris and from the records of the German imitations of Paris make it tolerably certain that the actual rejection of a candidate must have been a matter of the rarest possible occurrence. At Paris we do occasionally get allusions to the rejection of a candidate, but the exceptions are of the kind which prove the rule; since we hear of such rejections only in connexion with appeals to the Faculty against the decision of the Examiners [1], and it was a frequent practice in such cases to give the rejected a fresh chance before a special board of Examiners. In one of the German Universities we get actual records of the number examined and the number passed, and the figures are identical year after year for long periods [2]. It does not follow that the degrees did not imply a certain irreducible minimum of attainment. The candidate really had to go through a certain number of disputations, to hear a certain number of lectures, and to

century) ' ultra quinque tentamina observari non debent, neque etiam durabit aliquod ex his ultra duas horas.' Schreiber, II. p. 47. At Greifswald there were thirty ' Sessiones pro baccalariatus gradu' (presumably for all the candidates together or at least an *auditio*) of two hours each, 'quia nullius aut minimi fructus est disputationem adire et statim recedere ab eadem.' Kosegarten, II. p. 307.

[1] ' Supplicaverunt aliqui magistri pro aliquibus scolaribus refutatis ut eis fieret gracia et per facultatem admitterentur.' MS. *Reg. Nat. Angl.* (No. 3) f. 94 *a, et passim.*

[2] At Greifswald, where it appears that from 1456 to 1478 no candidate failed to satisfy the Examiners (Kosegarten, II. p. 232, *sq.*). On the other hand such an occurrence must have been not unknown at Ingolstadt,

where a new Statute was passed enacting ' ut nullus ad gradum baccalariatus rite reiectus proxima suae reiectioni sequente angaria [Ember season] per facultatem rursus ad examen pro eodem gradu admittatur.' Prantl, II. p. 51. A Statute of Caen allows the Examiners ' differre licentiam et imponere illis lecturam certorum librorum,' (*Bull. de la Soc. des Ant. de Normandie*, XII. p. 496). Other Statutes forbid such conditional passes (*approbatio cum cauda*). No refusal of a degree is recorded in the fragmentary fifteenth-century Register which we possess at Oxford, except one in 1455 when ' frater Philippus Herford ordinis predicatorum repulsus fuit a susceptione gradus bachellariatus in sacra theologia.' (Archives Aa. f. 90 *a*.) Friars stood in an exceptional position. See below, chap. xii. § 2.

get a Master to present him for his degree. From the Registers of such Universities as present us with detailed statistics on this head, it is evident that as a matter of fact only a certain proportion—at the outside half—of the students who matriculated in the Faculty of Arts proceeded even to the B.A. degree, and of these again much less than half went on to the M.A.[1] It is probable that incompetent students were more often prevented from entering at all by laziness or conscious incapacity or a hint from their Masters than actually rejected at the Examination itself[2]. On the whole it may be inferred that a student who was notoriously ignorant of the merest elements of Latin or Logic would scarcely have found a Master to present him for a degree, and the Examinations, as may be presumed from the length of time which they occupied, were considerably less of a farce than the Pass Examinations of Oxford and Cambridge have been almost within the memory of persons now living[3].

Degrees
of Laxity.
It is clear, however, that there were degrees of laxity in the different Universities and at different times, though complaints of extreme laxity are universal, especially in the fifteenth century[4]. We frequently find the Universities

---

[1] Paulsen computes that at Leipsic only one-fourth to one-third of those who matriculated proceeded to B.A., one-twentieth to one-sixteenth to M.A. But see below, Vol. II. chap. xiii.

[2] Thus in the S. Andrew's Register (MS. *Acta Fac. Art.* f. 24), which contains no instance of actual rejection, we find under the year 1441 that ' decanus facultatis ut moris est secundum formam statutorum inquisivit a regentibus an nouerint aliquos bacalarios ydoneos ad examen anno presente, ad quod respondetur negative.' In the Colleges students were not allowed to enter the Examination without leave of the College. So at Angers : ' Item, quod hujusmodi pædagogi non permittant ali-

quem scholarium suorum subire examen alicujus gradus, nisi ipsi crediderint esse sufficientem et idoneum, quoad gradum obtinendum, sed ipsum exhortentur et moneant, ut non se subjiciat hujusmodi examini, ne contingat ipsum reprobari et inde diffamari.' *Statuts des quatre Facs. de l'Un. d'A.*, p. 70 (1494).

[3] For an amusing account of an Examination at Oxford in 1781, see *Letters of Radcliffe and James*, ed. Evans (Ox. Hist. Soc., 1888) pp. 160-1.

[4] One of D'Ailly's demands in his treatise *De Reformatione Ecclesiæ* is ' Ut gradus distribuerentur sine favore aut acceptione personarum, et cum rigore examinis in scientia et moribus.' *Fascic. Rer. Expetend.*, I.

themselves taking measures to check the growing uncon-
scientiousness of Examiners : and in one instance—at
Leipsic in 1444—we find the Chancellor arbitrarily suspending the Examinations in consequence of the scandalous
extent to which abuses had recently been carried. A little
later in the same University it became necessary to pass
a Statute to forbid the Dean and Vice-Chancellor giving
the Candidates private information as to the questions
which would be asked [1]. All this goes to show that the 'Art
of Pluck,' though little practised, was not quite unknown in
the medieval University.   From the frequent insistence
on secrecy of voting and the oaths against taking vengeance
upon the Examiners it is evident that its practice was not
unattended by personal risk [2].

It may be laid down as a general principle in all spheres
of medieval life that rich and noble persons enjoyed in
practice exceptional privileges. But it is not certain whether
Toulouse borrowed from Paris the unblushing provision by
which the Chancellor of Toulouse was allowed to dispense
with the public Examination in the case of nobles who support companions in livery [3]. The University of Cambridge
was probably the last University in the world to abolish the
privilege which excused an Examination to sons of nobles [4].

Privileges of Nobility.

It should be added that the Examination included an
enquiry into the legitimacy, conduct and character of the
candidates, and 'ploughing' for moral or disciplinary
reasons appears to have been less infrequent than for intellectual incompetence.   It must be remembered that the
degree was not a mere certificate of having passed an Ex-

Moral and other Qualifications.

Cf. Von der Hardt, *Concil. Constant.*
I. pt. iv. c. 427.

[1] Zarncke, *Statutenbücher*, pp. 367,
446. The Faculty had shortly before
ordered that Examiners should be
chosen by lot. *Ib.* p. 363.

[2] E. g. at Caen candidates are to
swear that ' si contingat ipsos re-
futari post examen, nullum malum vel
dampnum occasione sue repulse
cuicumque magistro examinatori vel

alteri per se vel per alium fieri pro-
curabunt.' *Bull. de la Soc. des Ant. de
Normandie,* XII. p. 498.

[3] ' Nobilibus tenentibus socios de
raupis ' (*i. e.* robis). Devic et Vaissette, *Hist. de Languedoc,* VII. Docs.
c. 591.

[4] The *jus natalium* which excused
the ' General' Examination and a
year's residence was abolished in
1884.

amination but the admission to an official position.　Thus at Vienna we find that in 1449 of forty-three Candidates for the License seventeen were rejected, one for having spoken uncivilly to a Master, another for irregularities in the matter of academical dress, another for going out to see an execution in the middle of the Examination, another for going about disguised and for the heinous offence of ' wandering by the Danube [1],' another for gambling, another for taking part in a knife-fight with certain tailors—none, apparently, for failure in the literary part of the Examination.

Theology.

Increasing length of the course.
　We have seen that in the Faculty of Arts the course had by the close of the medieval period come to be very much shorter than that prescribed by Robert de Courçon in 1215.　In the Faculty of Theology an opposite tendency was at work.　M. Thurot attributes this to the influence of the Colleges, whose bursarships were held only till the attainment of the Doctor's degree, while in some cases a longer period of study was allowed than the minimum prescribed by the Faculty [2].　More weight ought perhaps to be ascribed to the desire to limit the number and keep up the prestige of the Theological Doctors and maintain the value of their lucrative perquisites, at a time when other restrictions on their multiplication were removed.　Robert de Courçon required five years' study as the qualification for ' publicly

---

[1] ' Quia infra examen exiverunt ad locum, in quo plures fuerunt puniti crucis supplicio ... quia etiam notatus fuit de mutatione habitus et de spaciamento ad Danubium ' (Kink, I. pt. i. p. 35). Moral, political, and theological considerations were frequent grounds for refusing a degree at Oxford in the sixteenth century. Cf. Clark, *Reg. Univ. Oxf.* II. i. p. 37, *sq.* So at Padua a candidate was objected to because he had called one of the doctors ' ihhus ignorans et lavator scutelarum '; and told

another who had threatened not to present him for his degree ' quod nesciebat unam literam.' Gloria, *Mon. di Padova* (1318–1405), I. p. 271.

[2] *De l'organisation de l'enseignement,* p. 133. Paulsen (*Hist. Zeitschr.* T. 45, p. 393) suggests that it was considered simoniacal to take fees for Lectures on Theology and Canon Law. If so, this would account for the desire to thrust the teaching on to Bachelors, but I know of no evidence for this.

giving private lectures' after tierce on days on which
Masters lectured. For the Doctorate eight years of Theological study were prescribed, so that the student who took
his final degree in the minimum period would spend three
years as a 'Bachelor[1].' Moreover the Doctor was required
to have reached the thirty-fifth year of his age.

We have not materials for tracing the gradual extension
of the period of Bachelorhood and the gradual increase in
the number and complication of the exercises required for
the attainment of the high dignity of the Theological
Doctorate. By the Reform of 1366 the complete course is
made to extend over a period of sixteen years, and this
was reduced by only one year under the Statutes of
Estouteville in 1452. Though the exact number and
character of the disputations, sermons, acts, and exercises
of one kind or another demanded of the candidate varied
slightly from time to time, the following account will be
applicable to the greater part of the fifteenth century[2]. It
should be added, however, that this inordinately protracted

---

[1] Such appears to me to be the
plain meaning of the clause which
runs as follows : ' Circa statum Theologorum statuimus, quod nullus Parisius legat citra 35 etatis sue annum,
et nisi studuerit per octo annos ad
minus, et libros fideliter et in scolis
audiverit, et quinque annis audiat
Theologiam antequam privatas lectiones legat publice, et illorum nullus
legat ante tertiam in diebus quando
Magistri legunt.' (Bulæus, III. p.
82 : *Chartul.* T. I. pt. ii. No. 20.)
Denifle, however (I. pp. 100, 101),
strangely understands by these
words that the candidate must have
studied eight years in all before becoming a 'Lehrer' (i. e. presumably
Doctor), *i. e.* three in Arts and five
in Theology. But then there will be
no time allowed for the cursory lectures which it is clear were to be
delivered by persons who were not

Masters in Theology. It is evident
that 'legat' in the first sentence
means to lecture *as a Master*, and
the advanced age required for the
Mastership makes it improbable that
the minimum course was so short as
five years.

[2] Two collections of Statutes are
extant, the earlier one belonging to
the end of the fourteenth or beginning of the fifteenth century in
D'Achéry, *Spicilegium* (1723), III. 735
sq., Bulæus, IV. 426 : a later one in
D'Argentré, *Collectio Judiciorum*, vol.
II. p. 462 *sq.*, now more accurately
printed in *Chartul.* T. II. App. No.
1189. They may be compared with
the Statutes of Vienna (Kollar,
*Analecta monumentorum Vindobonen-
sia*, I. p. 127 *sq.*), which are based on
the Statutes or customs of Paris. I
am here much indebted to Thurot,
p. 109 *sq.*

CHAP V,
§ 4.

Teaching
left to
Bachelors.

course of study was constantly curtailed by a liberal employment of the Faculty's powers of dispensation[1].

As the time of study lengthened, the teaching more and more devolved upon Bachelors. The distinction between 'ordinary' and 'extraordinary' lectures became in the Faculty of Theology purely one of time, even 'ordinary' lectures being given by Bachelors. By the sixteenth century it appears that Doctors of Theology merely lectured once a year by way of maintaining their Regency[2]. The Doctors had developed or degenerated into mere dignitaries (like the Oxford Professors of a past generation or the 'Heads' of the present), who officiated at Disputations, Examinations, and other meetings of the Faculty, while the only real teachers were the Bachelors. It may be observed that abuses of this kind prevailed more or less in the higher Faculties of all Universities in which the Masters possessed supreme and irresponsible authority. They were unknown in the Student-Universities, in which there can be little doubt that the most efficient teaching of the Middle Ages was to be found.

The Theologian's
Career.

The theological student passed the first six years of his course as a simple *auditor*. For four years he attended lectures on the Bible, for two years on the Sentences of Peter the Lombard, these being the only text-books with which the Theological Doctor necessarily became acquainted during the whole of his fifteen or sixteen years of study. How completely the Sentences were placed side by side with the Bible as the very source and fountain-head of all Theology is illustrated by Albert the Great's disquisition on the knowledge possessed by the Mother of Christ.

---

[1] This may be inferred with certainty from the fact that later College Statutes sometimes allow less time for the License or the Doctorate than the University Statutes required, *e. g.* at Coll. le Moine, nine years for the whole course (Félibien, V. p. 610); at Narbonne, 'duodecim annos ad licentiam obtinendam.' (*Ib.* p. 663.) At Plessis, however, ten years are allowed to become *Sententiarius.* (*Ib.* III. p. 376.) It should be added that some Religious Orders had Papal privileges curtailing the period of study for their students (e. g. *Chartul.* T. II. No. 992, 1002), and still more extensive dispensations for their individual members were very common.

[2] Bulæus, VI. p. 133.

After demonstrating in detail that the Jewish peasant-woman must have been acquainted with the *Trivium* and *Quadrivium*, the Doctor proceeds to discuss the extent of her attainments in the Faculties of Medicine, Civil and Canon Law, and Theology; in the latter he holds that she must have had a 'summary' knowledge of the Bible and Sentences[1]. At the end of these six years of study, provided he had attained the age of twenty-five, the student might appear before the Faculty with his certificates (*Cedulæ* or *Schedulæ*) of due attendance on the prescribed lectures and supplicate for his first course (*pro primo cursu*). He was then examined by four Doctors, and, if passed, would be formally admitted by the Dean to the reading of his 'first course,' *i. e.* be made a Bachelor. He entered upon his Baccalaureate by responding in a public lecture called a *principium*, and then began a course of lectures on a book of the Bible, which occupied a year, and in the following year a second course on another book. If the student were a secular, these courses were 'extraordinary,' and the Bachelor was at this stage of his career described as a *Cursor*. The secular Theologian was in practice usually a Master of Arts[2], who would be thirsting for the time when he might once more bring his Logic and his Philosophy into play upon the more congenial questions suggested by the Master of the Sentences. The Bible afforded few materials for metaphysical discussion. The Secular's lectures on the Bible were merely delivered 'in course'—because they were required by the Faculty as a condition of proceeding to the higher degrees. The only serious students of the Bible in the Middle Age were supplied by the regular orders[3]. The 'ordinary' Lectures on the Bible were delivered by 'religious' Bachelors. Each

---

[1] 'Beatissima Virgo Bibliam et sententias in summo habuit.' *Opera* (Lugduni, 1651), T. XX. p. 80.

[2] I do not know of any Paris Statute to this effect, but the Statutes of Vienna, which are based on the customs of Paris, require the B.D. to be M.A., 'uel saltem quomodocumque

ita edoctus, quod sufficienter sciat in Theologycis scolis et opponere et respondere.' Kink, II. 107.

[3] As to the absurdity of medieval exegesis, until its partial reform by the Franciscan Nicholas of Lyra (†1340), see Farrar, *Hist. of Interpretation*, pp. 251 *sq.*, 274 *sq.*

of the Mendicant orders in Paris (as well as the Cistercian College) was required to supply a fresh Lecturer (*Biblicus Ordinarius*) every year[1].

The Tentative.
In the course of his ninth year of study, the Bachelor was required to respond in a disputation known as the *Tentative*[2], at which a Master presided and assigned a question to be disputed upon, while a number of Bachelors awaiting their License (*Baccalarii formati*) opposed the respondent's theses, and afterwards conferred with the Master as to whether the exercise should be accepted by the Faculty. Eventually this like all other academical disputations reduced itself to a farce, and consisted in a succession of complimentary speeches after which the candidate was by acclamation pronounced *ingeniosus et doctissimus*[3]. The Bachelor might now, after nine years' study, be admitted to the ordinary reading of the Sentences, entering upon each of the four books into which the Lombard's work was divided by a solemn *principium* or public discourse upon some difficult theological problem[4],

---

[1] Bulæus, V. 564. Cf. *Chartul.* T. II. App. p. 692 *sq.*

[2] The following Statute of Valladolid, though of late date (approved by the Emperor Charles V), may throw light on the nature of the *Tentative*: 'Statuimus et ordinamus, quod Licentiandus . . . faciat unam publicam et solemnem disputationem quæ tentativa dicitur, sub Regentia Magistri in turno existentis; hoc modo, Magister Regens . . . Cathedram tenens, leget paululum de aliquo textu sacræ Scripturæ, circa quem unus assistentium cui fuerit commissum, movebit quandam Theologalem questionem ad utramque partem singulis mediis ventilatis, quam remittet determinandam tentativam facienti, quis ad locum ante Cathedram determinaturus veniens, ad determinationem dictæ quæstionis aliqua breviter notabit, ponetque pro eius maiori decisione tres conclu-

siones, singulis duo corollaria anectendo quorum ultimum sit responsivum, probabit vero dictas conclusiones, et corollaria ad nutum Regentis, et his breviter peractis, arguat Regens primo duobus, vel tribus mediis, manebitque verbum in ore eius, et deinde arguant volentes, nec cessabit actus ille, quousque nemo sit qui arguat, si tamen copia sit opponentium, transactis horis tribus (si Regenti visum fuerit) arguendi finem imponet.' Here the act did not count unless 'judicio arguentium sustentans per ipsum Regentem fuerit approbatus.' *Estatutos de la insig. Univ. Valladolid*, Valladolid, 1651, p. 43.

[3] Bulæus, VI. 19.

[4] At Vienna the *Principians* 'collacione brevi premissa subjungere habet questionem, in qua conferre . . . debet cum aliis sentencias legentibus.' Kink, II. p. 106.

to which every Doctor of the Faculty was invited by the Bedel while one at least was obliged to be present. Sometimes these occasions were further enlivened by an 'honest and moderate beer-drinking' furnished by the Lecturer[1]. The *Sententiarii* of the year followed one another in these principia in a regular order, and, after each Bachelor's own thesis had been laid down in the first principium, the remaining three were largely occupied with disputing against the positions maintained by others or replying to attacks made upon himself[2].

In the Theological Faculty there were practically three distinct degrees of Bachelorship, to the first two of which there was a regular admission quite as formal as the single admission to read cursory lectures in the other Faculties— the degrees of (i) *Biblicus Ordinarius* or *Cursor* (according as he was regular or secular), (ii) *Sententiarius,* and (iii) *Baccalarius Formatus.* This third term was applied to Bachelors who had completed their course on the Sentences. From this time to the License the candidate was supposed to remain in Paris, attending or taking part in disputations and other 'public acts' of the Faculty. From the frequent renewal of the Statutes requiring these Bachelors to reside continuously at Paris during the three or four years which elapsed between the completion of the Sentences and the License, it may be inferred that the obligation of residence was at times loosely observed. Some probably did little more than put in an appearance now and then when it was their turn to take part in one of the three great disputations in which each Bachelor was required to respond at this period of his career[3]. The *Baccalareus formatus* was also liable to be called upon to preach a University

The three Bachelor-ships.

---

[1] 'Fiant cerivisia honesta et moderata per incipientes primum cursum Biblie et tertium sententiarum.' Stat. in Hemeræus, MS. *Sorbonæ Origines,* f. 298.

[2] The *collationes* or constructive part of these discourses appear to have been privately circulated among the Bachelors of the years before the public disputation.

[3] 'Responsiones de Quolibetis, Sorbonica, ordinarias et aulae.' *Chartul.* T. II. App. p. 701. The 'Ordinaria' took place 'sub magistro incipiente de novo' (Stat. of Caen, *Bull. de la Soc. des Ant. de Norman-*

CHAP. V,
§ 4.
——
Length of
Sermons.

The Sor-
bonic.

sermon, or to give what was called a Conference (*Collatio*) in the afternoon when a Master had preached in the morning[1]. Medieval University sermons were not wont to err on the side of brevity. A Statute of Ingolstadt, *de quantitate Sermonum*, provides that 'with a view to avoid prolixity' these discourses should be limited to an hour and a quarter[2]: at Vienna the preacher might go on for an hour and a half, or at most two hours[3].

One of the disputations in which the Bachelor was required to take part in this last stage of his career is too curious and characteristic an illustration of medieval ideas of scholastic prowess to be passed over. The favourite phrase *militare in scholis* was something more than a figure of speech in those days. A certain amount of animal combativeness and physical endurance was almost as necessary in the 'warfare of the Schools' as in a tilt or a tournament. At this disputation known as the *Sorbonic*, from its taking place in the Hall of the Sorbonne, the respondent was required to reply standing, alone, and without the assistance of any moderator or judge except an audience which occasionally signified its approbation or disapprobation by stamping or clapping, to a succession of opponents who relieved each other at intervals from

---

die, XII. p. 504), the Aulica no doubt with an Inceptor performing the 'Aulica' for his own degree.

[1] In early times it would appear that no degree of Orders was required even for D.D. (Bulæus, III. 601, 602). But when preaching became an essential exercise for the degree, the B.D. must have been at least in Sub-Deacon's Orders. The German University Statutes generally prescribe the Order required at each stage in the Theologian's career, but their exact provisions vary. At Vienna (in 1389) the B.D.s must be 'Acolyti et infra annum aut

biennium Subdiaconi' (Kink, II. p. 104–5). The same Statute informs us that graduates at Paris must be legitimate 'et non turpiter corpore viciati' (cf. *Chartul*. T. II. App. p. 706). At Cologne, the Theologian must be Acolyte before B.D., and Sub-Deacon before License (Bianco, I. *Anl*. p. 37). Hemeræus tells us that at Paris the Dean was required to demand of candidates for the License, 'si sint omnes in sacris ordinibus' (*i.e.* at least Sub-Deacons). MS. *Sorbonæ Origines*, f. 298.

[2] Prantl, II. 58.
[3] Kollar, I. c. 134.

six in the morning till six in the evening, an hour's
relaxation only being allowed for refreshment in the middle
of the day [1].

In the Theological Faculty Licenses were only conferred on or about All Saints' Day in every alternate
year, at which was called the Jubilee. In the case of the
superior Faculties, all the Doctors had a right to be
present and take part in the Examination, and, after the
candidate had withdrawn, to advise the Chancellor as to
granting or withholding the License. In the Faculty of
Canon Law, and still more in that of Medicine, the share
of the Chancellor in the Examination must from the first
have been little more than formal and ceremonial: in conferring the License upon the Lawyers and Physicians, a
Theologian would be obliged to accept the 'depositions'
of the Doctors and confer or refuse the License in accordance with their advice. Under these circumstances it is
probable enough that the Faculties from the first practically
decided upon the fate of the candidate in private, so that
the Examination in the Bishop's Hall had become a mere
formality by 1384; when, roused by an attempt of the then
Chancellor to assert his independence of the Doctors, all
three superior Faculties resolved to hold previous meetings
for the discussion of the merits of candidates, and to present
their recommendations in writing to the Chancellor [2]. In
the Faculty of Theology we know that these meetings
included the non-regent members and that a list of
candidates was drawn up, about whom the Chancellor was
to make private enquiries of the individual Doctors [3]. But

---

[1] Ramus, *Scholæ in Lib. Artes,*
c. 1127: Crevier, II. p. 242 ff.:
Bulæus, IV. 172. The institution
is probably much later than these
writers represent.

[2] 'Quod Magistri dictarum Facultatum ante apertionem tentaminis et
examinis Domini Cancellarii ecclesiæ
Parisiensis seu vocationem et deposi-
tionem Magistrorum ad partem
deliberent inter se et ordinent

de Bachelariis et sufficientia eorun-
dem et de ordine licentiæ sive locorum.' Bulæus, IV. 601. The innovation led to litigation, in which the
Masters allege that the Chancellor
does not question the candidates,
but 'interroge les Maîtres qui facent
leur rapport et il les croid.' *Ib.*
pp. 606–9.

[3] *Chartul.* T. II. App. p. 683.
During this meeting the candidate

neither before the Chancellor nor before the Faculty was there any literary Examination : the only questions were whether he had duly performed all the residence, exercises, and acts required by the Statutes, and whether the reputation he had acquired during this University course for ability, character, and orthodoxy was such as to entitle him to the License.   In practice we may assume that at this stage the enquiry would as a rule limit itself to the question of residence and exercises.   But it must be remembered that there was an Examination for the first Bachelor's degree [1], and that the disputations or at least the more important of them, such as the Tentative, were in themselves Examinations.   The candidate was not considered to have performed the exercise unless he was pronounced by a majority of the *Baccalarei formati* present to

Action by
a rejected
candidate.

have acquitted himself satisfactorily [2].   By 1426, however, failure to 'satisfy the Examiners' had become so unheard of an event that a Bachelor whom the Doctors had refused to present for his License brought an action against the Faculty before the Parlement, and in his pleadings boldly claimed the degree as the right of any candidate who had complied with the proper forms.   In their answer the Doctors maintain their right to exercise a discretion [3], but it is not alleged that any one had actually within the

stood at the door and bowed to the Doctors as they entered.

[1] 'Cum aliquis volens admitti ad legendum cursum suum primum, aut Bibliam, comparuerit in facultate, dabuntur quatuor magistri, a quibus examinabitur in generalibus theologie, et fiet per eos in facultate relatio.' *Chartul.* T. II. App. p. 703. It seems probable that there was also an Examination for *Sententiarius*.

[2] D'Argentré, II. p. 467 : *Chartul.* T. II. App. p. 703.   In the Faculty of Canon Law there were sometimes more rejections than admissions to the Bachelorship. Whether this was, as the Abbé Péries thinks (p. 28), be-

cause 'Les épreuves du baccalauréat étaient très sérieuses,' or because they failed to satisfy the Examiners in another sense, the reader must judge for himself.

[3] Bulæus, V. 377-381 : 'Et ledit serment (i. e. of obedience to the Faculty and its Statutes) fait, ont ensemble deliberation et le examinent se bon leur semble;' after which they allow or refuse to allow him to present himself before the Chancellor.   The plaintiff had alleged that when a candidate had kept his terms and performed the required Sermons and Exercises, 'On ne lui pouvoit ou devoit refuser ou denier

memory of man been rejected for mere incapacity. In this exceptional case, the failure ' to satisfy the Examiners ' was attributed by the candidate to *odium theologicum* [1].

It is clear from the mere fact of such an action being brought—it is hardly necessary to add that it was unsuccessful—that an enormous decline had taken place in the standard of qualification necessary to the attainment of the Theological Doctorate. The only wonder is that the Theological Faculty of Paris should have retained the prestige which it actually enjoyed in the fifteenth century. We may suppose perhaps that though a candidate was never sent back when he was approaching the topmost rungs on the long ladder of promotion, though actual failure at an earlier stage may have been almost equally rare, a process of natural selection was nevertheless brought into play. The Examinations were really held, though no one was refused his *testamur* : the lectures had really to be attended or delivered : the disputations had really to be gone through, and that with great publicity, against opponents and in the presence of an audience who would be by no means delicate in their treatment of an embarrassed or hesitating disputant. This trial by ordeal may have been a rough and barbaric mode of testing intellectual capacity, but it was probably sufficient to shut the door of the Faculty to hopeless incapacity or gross ignorance, except in the case of very aristocratic or wealthy candidates. The hired thesis which serves or served till but yesterday to make a D.D. in modern Oxford (though the institution was probably not altogether unknown at Paris) would hardly have been by itself sufficient to bring the highest degree which a University can bestow within the reach of the meanest capacity. Still when all allowances have been made for the possibility of an indefensible system 'working well,' the low standard of

---

ladite license et Maistrise, ainçois devoit estre presenté ' &c.

[1] Cf. a document in *Chartul.* T. II. App. p. 683 : ' Quemlibet autem de gratiosis (persons dispensed some of the conditions) quilibet magister po-test impedire. Nec unquam visum est quod aliquis rigorosus impediretur nisi propter mores. Et dicitur rigorosus, qui complevit tempus suum pro licencia statutum.'

the degrees must be reckoned as one of the causes which contributed to the utter extinction of real intellectual life in the Universities of the fifteenth century. When a degree which was within the reach of every average man made its recipient a Professor, the teaching of the University must have sunk to a lower depth of inefficiency than at Oxford in the days when every 'close' or 'Founder's kin' Fellow was qualified for a College Tutorship. It is, however, worth noticing that even in the days of Louis XI the University had the spirit to refuse a D.D. which the king requested for a courtier of the King of Castile [1], nor did it ever carry the prostitution of academical grades so far as to confer a Doctorate upon the sons of Kings and Princes for the mere accident of birth.

The ceremony of the License itself has been sufficiently described in connexion with the Faculty of Arts, though graduation in the superior Faculties was naturally attended with ampler pomp and circumstance [2]. On the day before this function, a solemn Assembly of the University was held, at which the Rector received the Paranymphus [3], a messenger of the Chancellor who appeared in a gorgeous scarlet robe and velvet cap, to invite the attendance of the Licentiandi who had passed the Examination. The title recalls the idea that by graduation a student was wedded to Science. The Paranymphus made an oration in praise of Science, and then presented the 'signeta' containing the names of the candidates whom the Chancellor was to license. The occasion, *more medii ævi*, was further improved by a reception at the candidate's house, at which cake and wine were kept going all day for the friends

The Para-nymphus.

---

[1] The University of Cambridge obeys a Royal Mandate to confer a degree, a degradation which Oxford has happily escaped.

[2] The formula ran: 'Auctoritate Dei omnipotentis et apostolorum Petri et Pauli et sedis apostolice do vobis licenciam disputandi, legendi, et predicandi et omnes actus exercendi in theologica facultate qui ad magistrum pertinent. In nomine Patris et Filii et Spiritus Sancti.' After the ceremony, 'licentiati simul vadunt per domos omnium magistrorum ad regraciandum eis, et si aliquos non invenerint non est cura.' *Chartul.* T. II. App. p. 683.

[3] The bridegroom's messenger or attendant at a wedding.

who called to offer their congratulations, and the messenger of the Chancellor returned with divers illegal and simoniacal fees for his Master, himself, and the rest of the Chancellor's 'familia.' Later on the candidates went round in person to invite the attendance of the Lords of Parlement and the Canons of Paris at the graduation ceremonial [1].

The final stage of the Theologian's career—his admission to the Mastership—differed (as we have before noticed) in an important particular from that of the Masters of the other Faculties. The ceremony of *birettatio*, in the case of the other Faculties, took place in one of the Schools and was performed by one of the Regents; the Chancellor took no part in the ceremony of incorporating the duly licensed Master into the Society of his fellow-Masters. In the Faculty of Theology the ceremony took place, like the License, in the Bishop's Hall, and the Chancellor himself, with the words *Incipiatis in nomine Patris, Filii et Spiritus Sancti, Amen,* placed the *birettum doctorale* on the head of the Licentiate, who thereupon mounted his *cathedra* and, after an introductory 'harangue' in praise of Holy Scripture in general, maintained two theses of which due notice had previously been given to the members of the Faculty [2]. A disputation or discussion followed, in which different parts were assigned, in accordance with a rather elaborate ritual, to the Chancellor, the presiding Master, the other Masters present, and a Bachelor whose performance on this occasion was one of the exercises for his own

---

[1] The details are from Goulet, f. xv *b*; *Chartul.* T. II. App. p. 683. I presume that this elaborate ceremonial only applies to the superior Faculties.

[2] Kollar, l. c. 158. The following account of the *Aulatio* is given in the Statutes of Heidelberg, which may be taken as a faithful reflexion of the Parisian custom: after the oaths and *birettatio*, 'novus magister faciat recommendacionem sacre scripture, qua finita aliquis magister in artibus (i. e. a student of Theology) vel alius ad hoc ydoneus surgens proponat questionem cum argumentis disputandam per novum magistrum ad quam unus de senioribus baccalariis respondeat cui et magister novus arguat et post eum magister qui biretum imposuit.' Afterwards other *questiones* were propounded by other Masters. Hautz, *Gesch. d. Univ. Heid.* II. p. 338. The Birettatio does not seem to have been performed by the Chancellor as at

degree.   The Chancellor's interference in the *birettatio* of
the new Theological Master is a curious relic of his ancient
position as himself the principal, originally no doubt the only,
authorised Master of Theology in the Cathedral School.

Vesperiæ
and Re-
sumptio.

The ceremony which has just been described was known
as the *Aulatio* of the new Master, the actual disputation
being known as the *Aulica*.   It was preceded, on the eve
of the Inception, by an equally elaborate and ceremonious
disputation known as his *Vesperiæ*[1], and followed at the
beginning of the ensuing academical year, when he took
possession of his Regency, by a disputation called the *Re-
sumptio*.   These public discourses before the assembled
Faculty naturally presented great opportunities for the dis-
play of ingenuity and subtlety.   Nothing is more difficult
than to combine originality with unimpeachable orthodoxy,
and it is not surprising that the young Theologian, ambitious
of distinguishing himself at these imposing functions (especially the member of a Mendicant order with its pet doctrines
or cherished innovations), not unfrequently overshot the
mark, and had humbly to recant his daring 'positions'
before the Faculty would allow him to proceed to any
further step in his career.

Paris.   At Cologne it is performed
by 'Cancellarius, vel ex commissione
Cancellarii magister sub quo ves-
periatus incipit.'   Bianco, *d. alte
Univ. Köln*, II. Anl. p. 47.

[1] The following description of Vespers is found in the Theol. Statutes
of Heidelberg : 'Vesperie fiant post
prandium hoc modo : Magister tenens
vesperias disputet unam questionem
ad quam respondebit unus de Baccalariis cui presidens arguat et breviter
post hoc arguant omnes Baccalarii
per ordinem et post argumenta Baccalariorum proposita soli seniori re-
spondeatur.   Item post hoc unus de
magistris senioribus proponat questionem cum expositione terminorum
et argumentis pro utraque parte, qua

per vesperiandum determinata sequens Magister proponens questionem arguat contra dicta aliqua et
postea sequens magister contra alia,
contra que per precedentem non
est argutum : hoc facto fiat recom-
mendatio vesperiandi per magistrum
vesperias tenentem.' Hautz, *Gesch. d.
Univ. Heid.* II. p. 338.   At Ingolstadt
in 1475 (Prantl, II. p. 70) the earlier
part of the ritual is much the same,
but the latter part is more elaborate.
Detailed accounts both of *Vesperiæ*
and *Aulatio* are given from the Statutes of Bologna in *Chartul.* T. II.
App. p. 693.   From the MS. Matri-
logium at Caen, written in 1515
(f. 24 *a*), it appears that this disputation had already become an elaborate

We have already alluded to the method of taxation
adopted by the University—the demand (when occasion
required) of so many *bursæ* from each Master, Bachelor,
or student. The same method was adopted in fixing the
fees payable to the respective Faculties on taking the
Bachelor's degree, on admission to the License, and at
Inception. These fees constituted the most important part
of the ordinary revenue of the University or its constituent
bodies. A large part of them were, however, especially in
the case of the superior Faculties paid to the individual
Doctors who took part in the graduation-ceremonies. In
the Colleges it is clear that there could not be an indefinite
variety in the scales of living which were open to the
paying boarders who lived with the foundationers. These
'pensioners' or 'commoners' were eventually divided into
two classes—'commensales magnæ portionis' and 'commensales parvæ portionis,' corresponding roughly to the
Fellow-Commoners and Pensioners of Cambridge and the
Gentlemen-Commoners and 'Commoners' of most Oxford
Colleges [1]. In the fifteenth century this classification was
adopted by the University: the 'bursa' of the former was
estimated at eight *solidi Parisienses,* that of the latter at six.
Besides these were three classes of very poor scholars, the
Martinets, the Camerists, and the Servitors, who paid only
four. Noblemen and ecclesiastical dignitaries remained
outside this classification and were specially taxed according to their means [2]. No complete table of fees and other
expenses of a degree at Paris is before us ; it is obvious
that a considerable part of the expense, which consisted in
the Inception banquet, could not be precisely regulated. In
the superior Faculties there were also presents of robes to
all the Doctors and of caps to other dignitaries present.

---

burlesque : ' Presidens tentando pati-
entiam doctorizandi sibi multa vel
puerilia facta dicta gesta ridiculosa
dicit et in medium propalat quibus
assistentes in risum prouocat.'

[1] Bulæus, V. 748, 825. Nothing is
said here of the Servitors (no doubt

including College *Beneficiarii*), who
are, however, usually associated with
the *Martinetæ, Cameristæ,* or *Cameristæ Pauperes.* The *Cameristæ* exactly answer to the Oxford Batteller
(see below, chap. xiv.).

[2] Péries, p. 34.

CHAP. V,
§ 4.

Ramus estimates the expense of a Master's degree at Paris in 1562 as 56 *livres* 13 *sols* in Arts (together with a mysterious 60 *livres* for 'locus nominationis in licentiatu'), 881 *livres* 5 *sols* in Medicine, 1002 *livres* in Theology. It must be remembered that this estimate includes only the cost of the License and Inception, and not the smaller fees paid at earlier stages: but it is not clear for what class of students the expenses are thus calculated[1]. At Oxford we find the Prior of a religious College paying £10 as a commutation for the Inception banquet[2]. The Prior's position and the honour of his House must have demanded more than a minimum scale of expenditure: but still the amount can hardly have exceeded what would have been expected in an ecclesiastic of good position. The entertainments given by great noblemen on such occasions were on the scale of the festivities which would take place on the coming of age of the heir to a great title. George Neville, of Balliol, brother of the Earl of Warwick, took his M.A. in 1452, when 'on the first day there were 600 messes of meat, and on the second 300 for the entertainment only of scholars and certain of the proceeder's relations and acquaintances,' in addition to 'provisions for the poor and other ordinary sort of people of the University.' Any one who reads the varied *menu* given in full by Savage and Wood will not be surprised to read that the popularity of the young nobleman was such that he was 'the next year Chancellor of the University, and three years after that, though still only twenty-three years of age, Bishop of Exeter[3].' The Council of Vienne in 1311 had limited the expenses of Inceptors to 3000 *livres tournoises* and required every Licentiate to take an oath that he would not exceed that limit: but on such occasions as the above the University of Oxford was gracious enough to dispense with the provisions of the Pope

---

[1] *Procem. reform. Par. Acad.* (*Scholæ in lib. Artes,* c. 1110 *sq.*).

[2] *Munimenta Academica,* ed. Anstey, p. 565. Cf. Bulæus, V. p. 864.

[3] Savage, *Balliofergus,* p. 105:

Wood, *Hist. and Antiquities of the Univ. of Oxford,* ed. Gutch, I. 598–9. Cf. Hearne's note in Walteri Hemingford [*i.e.* Hemingburgh], *Hist.,* Oxon. 1731, II. p. 515. He was not consecrated till 27.

and General Council in a way which says much for the Chap. V, spiritual independence of the Anglican Church in the fifteenth century [1].

The length of the Vacations gradually increased during the medieval period. In 1261 Gregory IX ordained that the summer Vacation should not exceed one month [2], but Papal thunders failed to check the rapid elongation of the 'Great Vacation.' We find from a Calendar belonging to the end of the fourteenth century that the long Vacation then began at tierce on the Vigil of S. Peter and S. Paul (June 28) and lasted in the Faculty of Arts to the morrow of St. Louis (Aug. 25) or to the morrow of the Exaltation of the Holy Cross (Sept. 15) in the case of Theology and Canon Law. But it appears that this beginning of term was of a more or less formal character: it was at this time that ordinary lectures *might* be recommenced. We always find the Feast of S. Remigius (Oct. 1) treated as the real inauguration of the winter term [3], when the courses of the year were usually begun. The period from Oct. 1 till Easter was styled the 'grand Ordinary,' the period from Easter till the end of June constituting the 'little Ordinary.' Only a few days' holiday is officially recognised at Christmas and Easter, and even in the Long Vacation cursory lectures might be delivered except upon certain festivals. Numerous festivals in term-time were observed by a total suspension of Lectures, or by a suspension of ordinary Lectures only.

§ 4.

Vacations.

---

[1] 'Non teneatur .. ad stratitudinem statuti de tribus millibus turonensium grossorum.' Oxford Archives. Aa. f. 66 *a*.

[2] Bulæus, III. 141: *Chartul.* I. pt. i. No. 79, and the Calendar, *ib.* T. II. App. p. 709.

[3] Crevier, II. p. 141. At Heidelberg the period from Aug. 25 to Oct. 9 is styled a 'Parvus Ordinarius in Cappis Nigris.' Toepke, *Matrikel d. Un. Heid.* I. 629 *sq.*; and by the Statute of 124⅘ at Paris, 'a festo . . .

B. Johannis Baptiste usque ad festum B. Remigii quilibet suas lectiones ordinet, prout melius sibi et auditoribus suis viderit expedire.' Bulæus, III. p. 280: *Chartul.* I. pt. i. No. 246. M. Thurot (p. 66) is thus wrong in confining ordinary Lectures to the 'Grand ordinary.' At Oxford the terms corresponded roughly with the existing Statute-terms, except that there was a Vacation of eleven days at Whitsuntide. See Calendar in *Mun. Acad.* p. cxxxiv *sq.*

§ 5. The Colleges of Paris.

A large quantity of documentary material for the Colleges, not contained in Bulæus, is to be found in Félibien, *Histoire de la ville de Paris*, Paris, 1725, to which Jourdain (*Index Chartarum*, &c.) makes large additions.

For the Sorbonne, I have consulted the MS. *Sorbonæ Origines*, by Hemeræus, in the Bibliothèque Nationale at Paris Cod. Lat. 5493 : and the MS. Register (*ib.* 5494 A). Many of the documents contained in it (including the Statutes of 1274) are now printed in the *Chartul. Univ. Paris.* Franklin, *La Sorbonne*, Paris, 1875, contains a short account of the foundation, but is chiefly a history of the Library. Gréard, *Nos adieux à la vieille Sorbonne* (Paris, 1893) is a more elaborate, and an eloquently written work, but more valuable for later periods than for ours. The *Histoire de la Sorbonne* by Duvernet (Paris, 1790), is really an account of the Theological Faculty of Paris. A somewhat detailed account of the College and its Founder is given in *Hist. Litt.* XIX. 291 *sq.*

For the College of Navarre, there is a very full history by Launoi, *Reg. Navarræ Gymnasii Historia*, Parisiis, 1677. Sauval, *Hist. et Recherches des Antiquités de la ville de Paris* (Paris, 1724) gives a list of Colleges (T. II. p. 372) and some documents in T. III. See also Lebeuf, *Hist. de la ville de Paris*, ed. Cocheris, Paris, 1890, and Berty, *Topographie de Paris*.

There are also the following monographs : Marquis de Belbeuf, *Notice sur le C. du Trésorier*; Geffroy, *Les Étudiants Suédois à Paris* (*Rev. des Soc. Savantes*, 1858, T. IV. p. 659); Quicherat, *Hist. de Sainte-Barbe*, Paris, 1860; Rolland, *Recueil des délibérations du C. Louis-le-Grand*, *Mémoire donne par le bureau d'administration du C. Louis-le-grand*; Chapotin, *Le Coll. de Dormans-Beauvais*, Paris, 1870; Jourdain, *Le Coll. du Cardinal Lemoine* (*Mém. de la Soc. de l'hist. de Paris*, T. III. 1877); Bouquet, *L'Ancien Collége d'Harcourt*, Paris, 1891. Cf. also *Mém. de la Soc. de l'hist. de Paris*, T. I. (1875), p. 93 *sq.* In compiling the list at the end of the section I am specially indebted to Jourdain's Catalogue, with its indications of other authorities. I have been obliged to insert several Colleges on the authority of Félibien or others, without having seen the original authority for their existence or date. Two or three are due to the *Hist. Litt.*

Paris the home of the Collegiate system.

Even learned historians have sometimes allowed themselves to speak of Colleges as institutions peculiar to the English Universities[1]. The reader of the present work will by this time be aware that Colleges are not even peculiar to the class or family of Universities to which Oxford and Cambridge belong. Few of the Italian and other Student-Universities continued long without Colleges or endowed

[1] *e.g.* Malden, p. 109.

residences for poor students being provided by pious foun- CHAP. V,
§ 5.
ders.   The earliest of them, however, arose somewhat later
than was the case at Paris.   They were, with a few exceptions, small foundations, and exercised comparatively little
influence over the educational system and constitutional
development of the Universities in connexion with which
they were established.   The true home of the collegiate
system is Paris: from Paris it passed to those Universities
upon which it has obtained its longest and firmest hold.

To understand what the Colleges were, it is necessary in The
Hospicia.
the first place to appreciate the social conditions of the
Universities wherein they arose.   It has been usual to trace
back the system of boarding in Masters' houses, which was
nearly universal at Paris before the close of the medieval
period, to the earliest days of the University ; and, when
the extreme youth of the Parisian Arts-student is considered, it is no doubt difficult for persons familiar with
modern ideas of education to believe that he was allowed
to live in a great city without some kind of domestic supervision.   It is, however, quite certain that in the thirteenth
century the Parisian Arts-student of fourteen was, so far
as the University was concerned, as free to live where and
how he pleased as the Canon or Rector of twenty-five or
thirty who had left his benefice in the country to read
Canon Law at Paris or Bologna.   Nor is it clear that the
earliest Hospicia or Houses of residence hired by parties of
students at a rent fixed by a joint University and City
board[1] differed fundamentally, even when occupied by
Arts-students, from the Hospicia of the Bologna Law-
students.   Where, however, a large number of boys and
young men were packed together into a very narrow space,
the necessities of the case must inevitably have evolved
some kind of government, whether democratic or aristo-

---

[1] By de Courçon's Statute of 1215
(Bulæus, III. 82 ; *Chartul.* T. I. pt. i.
No. 20) the Scholars are authorized
to make Statutes ' pro taxandis pretiis
hospiciorum.'   By the Bull of Gregory IX in 1231, the taxation is to
be by two Masters and two Burghers,
' sive, si burgenses non curaverunt
interesse, per duos magistros, *sicut
fieri consuevit.*' (Bulæus, III. 143 ;
Chartul. I. i. No. 82.   Cf. Nos. 429,
511.)

cratic. It became usual for the House to be governed and managed by one of the community, styled a Principal, who appears to have made himself responsible for the rent to the landlord, and charged the other inmates their share of the rent, board, and other domestic expenses [1]. But the Principal was by no means necessarily a Master. The ordinary custom was no doubt that he should be at least a senior student or Bachelor; ultimately it became first usual, and then compulsory, that he should be a graduate if not a Master. But there was at first nothing to compel him to be even a member of the University [2]. The student was, in fact, left to take care of himself like the often equally youthful Scotch undergraduate of to-day or yesterday. The usual practice from the first was no doubt to live with a party of other students in a Hospicium; and gradually residence in a house presided over by a Master became universal except for two classes of students—the richest, who lived in their own houses with a private tutor, and the poorest, who could not afford the expense of the Hospicium, and lodged or boarded in some miserable garret of a townsman's house. Eventually the University attempted to suppress this last class altogether.

[1] Some early but undated Statutes at Oxford contain the first allusions to the office of Principalis. We hear of a ' Principalitas Scholarum' as well as of ' Hospicii' or ' Domus.' Neither kind of ' Principalitas' is to be bought or sold (*Mun. Acad.* p. 14). The ' Principalis' is here primarily the person responsible for the rent ('solvens pro domo vel Scholis,' *ib.* p. 15). Cf. the ' qui domum princi-paliter conduxit' of the Cambridge Statutes (*Camb. Documents*, I. p. 351). In 1313 (*Mun. Acad.* p. 93) the ' principalis inhabitator sive ejus vicem gerens, tam Aularum quam Came-rarum' (it thus appears that the com-munity might occupy only a single room between them) is required to swear to delate grave offenders to the Chancellor, but nothing is said of his personal authority. At Paris also the scholar responsible for the rent was called a Principalis (Jour-dain, No. 551 : *Chartul.* T. II. No. 1007) or ' principalis inhabitans,' and it is only reasonable to infere that the Principal grew into the Pædagogus of later times. Cf. 'the Principalis magis-ter pedagogii,' at Nantes. Fournier, *Stat. des Univ. franç.* III. No. 1595.

[2] An undated Oxford Statute (*Mun. Acad.* pp. 468, 469) finds it neces-sary to enact ' quod nullum man-cipium vel famulus Scholaribus de-serviens, etiam etsi Scholaris fuerit, principalitatem, seu inhabitationem domus ... quoquo modo habere pos-sit.' At Paris no legislation about the authority of Principals or the internal management of Halls occurs till the fifteenth century.

As to the internal government of these communities, we CHAP. V,
§ 5. have in regard to Paris hardly any direct evidence before the period when the Head was usually a Master and when his authority over his fellows (*socii*) was more or less backed up by the University as a whole. Even for that period the evidence is very scanty. We may, however, safely transfer to Paris the conclusions to which we are led by a study of similar institutions in other Universities, and especially at Oxford. Reserving the details of this evidence for the chapter on Student-life in the Middle Ages, it will be enough for me here to say that it establishes the somewhat startling thesis that the original Hospicium or Hall (as it was usually called at Oxford) was a democratic, self-governing Society, that its Head— the Principal or, as he was more commonly called at Paris, Regent—owed his authority to the free election of his fellows and to the formal Statutes or traditional customs accepted by the Community, and that the Community always participated in the management of the common funds and the general government of the House[1]. It was only very gradually that this highly democratic *régime* was transformed first into a limited and then into an absolute monarchy. At Paris the transformation is fitly symbolized by the eventual adoption of the term Pædagogium for the institution and Pædagogus for the Head.

Self-government of Hospicia.

The importance of this conclusion for a correct appreciation of Collegiate institutions is obvious. The College was,

Origin of Colleges.

---

[1] In some cases it would appear that the community acquired property, which passed from one Head to another, thus bringing the institution still closer to the collegiate type. Thus a Statute of Rostock (Westphalen, *Diplomatarium*, c. 1027) orders that ' omnia Clenodia et Utensilia Regentiæ comparata per Rectorem domus de communi collecta scolarium debent manere in dicta regentia mutato Rectore et alio succedente.' This was, of course, the case at Oxford. For the Oxford evidence, see below, chaps. xii. § 6, and xiv. So at Cracow we find (in a 'Bursa' governed by an elected 'Senior' and four 'Conciliarii') the consent of the Community required for the purchase of furniture. Cf. *Regestrum Bursæ Cracoviensis Hungariorum* (Budae, 1821), pp. 1–5, 51, 61, 68, &c. (In this case, however, the building at least appears to have been provided by endowment.) The democratic character of the ancient Halls has never been properly appreciated.

CHAP. V,
§ 5.

in its origin, nothing but an endowed Hospicium or Hall. The authority of the Master placed at its head by the Founder was naturally better supported than that of a Principal selected by the free choice of the students: but in both cases the Community was admitted to more or less participation in the management of the House. If that share was (as we shall see) somewhat less extensive at Paris than at Oxford, it is quite possible that this corresponded with some difference in the traditional customs of the free Hospicia or Halls in the two places. But substantially the principle of constitutional government was admitted in both. It was only when the students were mere Grammar-boys that they were governed like schoolboys. That students at the Universities should live together in Societies was established by custom before the first College arose. But for this circumstance there was no reason why endowments for the benefit of poor students should have assumed the form of Colleges. The object of the earliest College-founders was simply to secure board and lodging for poor scholars who could not pay for it themselves. At Paris the endowed Scholars' home always had a Master at its head: but the instruction which he was supposed to give was entirely subordinate to that of the public Schools. The Colleges introduced no innovation into the educational system of the Universities: nor were their founders primarily influenced by the enlightened and far-reaching design which has sometimes been attributed to them, of correcting by a system of domestic instruction and supervision the dangerous license allowed by the earlier form of the University life, though of course they took precautions to secure that their bounty was not thrown away upon idle or ill-conducted students. Eventually the College-system did, as we shall see, exercise a most important and on the whole salutary influence both upon the education and upon the morals of the Universities in which it took root. But originally the College was nothing more than an endowed Hospicium.

The earliest Parisian College-foundation was one of

the very humblest description. At right angles to the
West front of the Cathedral of Notre Dame, there
stood already in the twelfth century (and still stands
under a strangely altered *régime*) the 'Hospital of the
Blessed Mary of Paris,' commonly known as the Hôtel-
Dieu. In this Hospital a single room was customarily
set apart for 'poor clerks.' Many, perhaps most, of
these must have been scholars, but there was no express
limitation to this particular class of clerks. In the year
1180, however, a visit was paid to the Hospital by
'dominus Jocius of London,' just returned from a pilgrimage or crusade to Jerusalem. As the result of this
visit, the pious Londoner, after taking counsel with the
Dean and the Chancellor, determined to buy the room from
the Hospital and appropriate it for ever to the support
of 'eighteen scholar-clerks,' the Proctors of the House
agreeing with the benefactor to supply the eighteen with
'sufficient beds' (how many beds is left doubtful), and to
pay them twelve *nummi* a month out of the alms collected
in the Hospital Chest[1]. The College (if such it can
be called) was obviously a very simple affair—intended
for the very poorest class of clerks. It does not even
appear that they were a permanent body : it may have
been intended merely for the relief of casual distress. At
all events, the scholars were under no special rule or
government except that under which other inmates of the
Hospital were placed : their sole statutable obligation was
to take turns in bearing the Cross and holy water at the
funerals of those who died in the House, and nightly to
say the seven penitential Psalms and other customary
prayers. By the year 1231, however, we find the Community established in a house of its own near the Church

---

[1] 'Tali facta conditione, quod
ejusdem domus procuratores decem
et octo scolaribus clericis lectos suf-
ficientes et singulis mensibus duodecim nummos de confraria que
colligitur in archa, perpetuo ad-
ministrabunt.' (From the deed of
the Dean and Chapter accepting
the endowment, first printed from a
MS. copy in the National Archives
by Denifle). *Chartul.* T. I. Introd.
No. 50.

of S. Christopher[1]. It was henceforth known as the 'Collége des Dix-huit.'

The next College-foundation or attempt at a College-foundation is perhaps the College of S. Thomas of the Louvre. About the year 1186, Count Robert of Clermont, with the approval of King Philip Augustus and of Urban III[2], established a Hospital in some houses of his own near the Palace of the Louvre. The House was designed for the benefit of 'poor clerks.' It does not, however, appear distinctly whether these clerks were scholars, and the foundation was perhaps originally of the nature of a Hospital for aged and sick persons[3], under a Community of Brethren, who are described as 'religious persons,' *i.e.* (as was usual in Hospitals) Canons Regular. At what date (if not from the first) scholars were admitted to the foundation cannot be precisely determined: but in 1210 the Community is described in a Bull as the 'Provisor and Brethren of the Religious House of the poor scholars of S. Thomas the Martyr at Paris[4]'; and in 1228 abuses had sprung up in this scholastic community which called for the peremptory interference of the Bishop of the diocese. 'We have found,' says that Prelate, 'that certain scholars who had long since lived of the goods of the same House, have been carried to such a pitch of insolence that they have attempted to break the doors of the House of the Brethren by night and violently to effect an entrance; others, as though secure of their victuals through having unduly long eaten the bread provided for students, making

[1] Doc. in Brièle, *Cartulaire de l'Hôtel-Dieu*, No. 260. Félibien, however (I. p. 419), gives the date 1269 for the foundation of the College. Perhaps this was the time at which it acquired its separate habitation before the gate of the Hôtel-Dieu, from whence it removed to a building near the Sorbonne. This was destroyed to make room for the Church of the Sorbonne.

[2] The Bull of Urban III alone survives (without date). Bulæus, II. pp. 463–4: Dubois, II. p. 184: *Chartul.* T. I. Introd. No. 14: cf. No. 18.

[3] The object of the Bull is to authorize the benediction of a cemetery 'ad opus fratrum et familie ipsius atque infirmorum decumbentium.' *Ib.* No. 14.

[4] Bulæus, II. p. 465; *Chartul.* I. i. No. 10.

little progress and unwilling to study, burdensome to the
real students, were molesting in various ways the quiet
and studies of others[1].' Evidently the College is by this
time an established institution : already its 'burses' have
degenerated into 'idle fellowships,' and the Bishop is
obliged to make them terminable at the end of the year,
unless specially prolonged by delegates appointed by
himself.

Of much the same type is the College of the 'Good
Children of S. Honoré,' founded in 1208–9 by a citizen of
Paris, Étienne Belot or Berot and his wife[2], to contain thir-
teen beds, whether to be used singly or otherwise does not
appear. The only difference is that, instead of being
attached to a Religious Hospital, the boys were placed
under the government of the secular Chapter of the Church
of S. Honoré; the 'Provisor' was to be one of the Canons,
appointed, after the death of the Founders, by the Bishop
of Paris. As to the educational character of the House of
S. Honoré we are completely in the dark. We do not
know whether its Scholars studied Grammar or Arts, or
whether they were taught in the House or out of it.
But in all probability they were merely Grammar-boys.
It is not clear whether they originally lived under the
supervision of a Master : though they certainly did so
at a later date[3]. Thus two of the earliest foundations of
Paris are to be regarded rather as among the first
endowed Grammar or Charity Schools than as Colleges
for University students. Both of them were mere adjuncts
of ecclesiastical corporations which existed for other pur-

'The Good
Children of
S. Honoré,'
1208–9.

---

[1] Guérard, *Cart. de Notre Dame
de Paris* I. 350 : *Chartul.* T. I. pt. i.
No. 60. Colleges were not peculiar
to Universities. A 'Collegium Bo-
norum Puerorum' was founded in
connexion with the Cathedral
Schools of Reims before 1245.
Varin, *Archives administratives de
la ville de Reims*, I. 663 *sq.* If we
may trust Hemeræus, a College with

a similar title, in connexion with
the Church of S. Quentin, dates
from 843. See his *De Scholis pub-
licis pro regali ecclesia S. Quintini*,
Lut. Par. 1633, p. 161.

[2] Bulæus, III. p. 45 : *Chartul.* T. I.
pt. i. No. 9 (where the text is corrected).

[3] Sauval, III. p. 119 : Jourdain, No.
711 : Félibien, I. p. 246 *sq.*

poses. One of the earliest independent foundations at Paris was the ' College of the Good Children of S. Victor,' about the origin of which we know nothing except that it existed in 1248, when Innocent IV allowed them a Chapel of their own[1], and that it was placed under the supervision of the Chancellor of Paris[2]. From its designation we may assume that this, too, was a College for Grammarians.

College of Constanti- nople.

The first College at Paris which was more than a Grammar-school was perhaps the College of Constantinople. It is supposed that the foundation of this College was connected with the Latin conquest of Constantinople in 1204, and the consequent projects of Innocent III for the reunion of Christendom. A host of Parisian ecclesiastics, armed with Missal and Breviary, was to be despatched into the East[3] : while Greek youths were to be sent to Paris to be indoctrinated with the Theology of the West. That such a project was formed is an historical fact : its connexion with the foundation of the College of Constantinople appears to be no more than a conjecture, though a very probable one. Of the subsequent history of the College little is known till the year 1363, when the single ' bursar ' or foundationer who was found quartered in its ruined and dilapidated buildings was persuaded to make over its property to the founders of the Collége de la Marche[4].

S. Nicholas de Lupara.

According to Félibien, the historian of the City of Paris, the Scholars of S. Thomas of the Louvre were in 1217 removed from the Hospital and established as a separate community under the title of ' The Scholars of S. Nicholas in the Louvre[5].' The identity of the two Houses,

---

[1] Dubois, II. 511.

[2] Bulæus, III. 217 : *Chartul.* T. I. pt. i. Nos. 184, 323.

[3] In 1205 Innocent IV issued a Bull to invite Parisian ecclesiastics to go on this mission. Bouquet, T. XIX. p. 475 : Bulæus, III. 10: *Chartul.* T. I. pt. i. No. 3.

[4] Bulæus, IV. 366-7.

[5] Tom. I. p. 211. The foundation for this statement appears to be the

Bulls printed in Dubois, II. p. 184. The first of these, a Bull of 1212, effects a separation between certain property which the Brethren and the Canons of S. Thomas had hitherto used in common; the second, an episcopal brief of 1217, authorizes a cemetery and chapel for S. Nicholas, but there is nothing to identify the two Hospitals. The ' hospitale pauperum scolarium Sancti Nicolai de

is however, improbable, since we continue to hear of
the Scholars of S. Thomas in the Louvre long after that
date [1]. The Hospital or (as it was afterwards called)
College of S. Nicholas in the Louvre was, in any case, a
House of much the same type as that of S. Thomas, being
a Religious House of Brethren governed by a Master. Its
origin must remain obscure: all that we can say is that
some of its endowments are as old as 1241, a fact which
appears from a Royal Charter of protection granted in
1293 [2]. We have no information as to the original nature
of this foundation; but, if we may assume that the Statutes
of 1316 are a safe guide to its earliest condition, it is clear
that here at least we have a College for Artists attending
the Schools of the University [3].

The secular College would never perhaps have developed
into the important institution which it actually became
but for the example set by the Colleges of the Mendicants. We have already noticed the formation of the
Mendicant Convents in Paris, beginning with the establishment of the Dominicans in 1217 [4]. A little later some
at least among the older monastic orders, which had
hitherto stood aloof from the new Academical learning,
became anxious to remove the reproach of ignorance

Influence of the Regular Colleges.

Lupara' is mentioned in *Chartul.* I.
pt. i. No. 168 (1247 A.D.). The
identity of the two is denied by
Bournon, *Rectifications et additions à
Lebeuf* (Paris, 1890) I. 27. It appears that they were really united
in the eighteenth century.

[1] In the Episcopal Ordinance of
1228 (above, p. 484), and in the will
of S. Louis (12$\frac{6}{9}\frac{9}{8}$), by which they
were left 15 *libræ* (Bulæus, III. 393:
Chartul. T. I. pt. i. No. 430 *a*. Cf. also
No. 83). An identity is, however,
supported by a document of 1419
(Bulæus, V. 345), in which the
College of S. Nicholas de Lupara is
spoken of as the oldest in Paris.

[2] Bulæus, III. 508. A Bull ascribed

by Bulæus (III. 370) to Urban IV
in 1263 is addressed 'Magistro et
Fratribus Hospitalis Pauperum Scholarium S. Nicolai de Lupara,' but
it does not appear in the *Chartularium.*

[3] Bulæus, IV. p. 139. These
Statutes make no allusion to Brethren — had the College by this time
been separated from the Hospital?
They are governed by a Master and
Procurator, after the manner of later
Colleges of Artists. On the other
hand, the Statutes are of a more
ecclesiastical character than usual.
The Scholars are required 'interesse
qualibet nocte matutinis' (*l.c.* p. 140).

[4] Above, p. 350.

freely hurled against them by the more ambitious and progressive Friars. In 1246 a Cistercian College, known as the Collége du Chardonnet, was founded by the Englishman Stephen of Lexington, Abbot of Clairvaux, for students of his House[1]. Subsequently, however, he was deprived of its management by the Chapter General of the Cistercians, and the College thrown open to the whole order. The students in this and other monastic Colleges were supported by pensions derived from their respective Monasteries. In these Parisian Houses of the Monks and Friars the monastic life was adapted to academical needs. A Convent inhabited by students necessarily assumed the form of a College[2]: and the ' regular ' College may have done much to suggest the idea of the more elaborate secular foundations which began to come into existence about the middle of the thirteenth century. In particular it is to these regular Colleges that we must look for the origination of the idea of a College of Theologians. The earlier foundations were, as we have seen, mere eleemosynary institutions for poor boys. The College founded about the year 1257[3] by S. Louis' Chaplain, Robert de Sorbonne (Canon of Cambray and afterwards of Paris), was a College for men who had already taken the degree

[1] Brother of Robert and John of Lexington, Judges in England, and Henry, Bishop of Lincoln. Bulæus, III. p. 184. The Pope's approval was given in 1244. *Chartul.* T. I. pt. i. No. 133. Cf. Nos. 146, 148, 157, 166, &c. See also Félibien, I. p. 309 *sq.*; III. p. 160 *sq.* The Cistercians petitioned for a Dominican Doctor of Theology; a significant indication of the standard of learning in the old Orders and the new. *Chartul.* I. pt. i. No. 151.

[2] The ordinary Monasteries also received students of their Order. According to Péries (p. 18), students from all parts were received at S. Germain-des-Prés.

[3] S. Louis' gift of adjoining houses and stables ' ad opus scholarium qui inibi moraturi sunt,' is dated 1250 by Hemeræus (MS. Hist. f. 9) and Bulæus (III. p. 224). But its true date seems to be Feb. 125⅔ (see Jourdain, No. 150, and *Chartul.* T. I. pt. i. No. 302). According to Richer (I. f. 411 *b*) the traditional date of foundation, preserved in an inscription in the Library, was 1252. But it is evident that the arrangements for the purchase were spread over a considerable period. The House is still spoken of as future in 1258 (*Chartul.* I. pt. i. No. 325), and the formal donation of the property did not take place till 1270 (Jourdain, No. 222: *Chartul.* T. I. pt. i. No. 431);

of Master of Arts and were desirous of entering upon the CHAP. V,
long and laborious career which led to the Theological § 5.
Doctorate. In face of the attractions offered to the pious The
by the Mendicant Orders and to the worldly by the lucra- Sorbonne,
c. 1257.
tive profession of a Canonist, some such institution was
absolutely needed if the class of secular Theologians was
to be kept from entire extinction. From this point of view
the establishment of the 'Sorbonne' was an event of European importance.

'The House of Sorbonne' was originally designed for six- The
teen students of Theology, four from each Nation. This ab- Sorbonne,
1258–70.
sence of narrow local restrictions is an unusual feature in Parisian College-constitutions, and perhaps laid the foundations
of the future greatness of the College. Its numbers were
soon increased by supplementary benefactions to thirty-six[1].
Indeed, a large number of purses contributed to the erection of this illustrious House. S. Louis gave part of the
site, close to the ancient Palace of Julian (the *Palatium
Thermarum*), south of the Seine, and otherwise contributed
to its endowment[2]. One of many early benefactors was
Robert Geoffrey of Bar, one of the four champions of the
secular clerks in their battles with the Mendicants[3], all
remembrance of whose former heresies was now extinguished beneath a Cardinal's hat. He was also the Founder's
executor for the completion of the undertaking[4]. Collections on behalf of the pious object were even made in the
Churches by the aid of Papal and Episcopal indulgences[5].
Besides the full Bursars, a certain number of *Beneficiarii*
were supported by the broken meats of the Hall dinner
and supper, in return for which they performed some menial
services to the Fellows. At a later date each Fellow had
a 'poor clerk' as his personal attendant, sharing the cham-

but the College no doubt existed, its founder being the first Provisor—a fact which goes a long way to explain the position of that official.

[1] Franklin, p. 19.

[2] *Chartul.* T. I. pt. i. Nos. 302, 329, 347.

[3] Franklin, p. 17.

[4] Franklin, p. 19: *Chartul.* T. I. pt. i. Nos. 515, 519.

[5] Jourdain, Nos. 180, 189: *Chartul.* T. I. pt. i. Nos. 348, 378.

ber in which he lived and slept [1]. Though the 'Bursars'
were associated in the government of the House, they hardly
possessed the independence of an Oxford or Cambridge
College. The supreme government of the foundation and
the filling up of its 'burses' was entrusted to a body of
external Governors—the Archdeacon and Chancellor of
Paris, the Doctors of Theology, the Deans of the other two
Superior Faculties, and the Rector and Proctors of the
University [2]. The ordinary administration of the House
and the management of its property was vested in a Provisor, appointed by the Governors, in conjunction with the
Sorbonnists themselves. The position of the Provisor was
apparently something between that of an Oxford Visitor
and that of an Oxford Head. He was not a member of the
Community, but some important ecclesiastic who governed
it from the outside ; on the other hand he possessed,
though he rarely exercised, disciplinary powers more
like those of the medieval Master or Warden at Oxford.
The internal presiding officer of the Society was an annually
elected Prior or *lator rotuli* [3], the financial administration
being entrusted to two greater and two lesser Proctors [4].

Later
position of
Sorbonne.

A word must be said as to the later history of this
illustrious Society, though it hardly falls within our period.
Originally, as we have seen, the 'Sorbonne' was nothing
more than a College of Theologians like University or
Oriel College in Oxford. In the sixteenth and seventeenth
centuries, however, the title came to be popularly applied
to the whole Theological Faculty of Paris. This usage
was, it would appear, due to two causes. In the first place,

---

[1] Hemeræus, MS. Hist. f. 31;
Richer, MS. I. f. 448. It would
seem that the *beneficiarii*, who originally lived in a separate but adjoining
House (Hemeræus, f. 37), passed
into the *clerici convictores* of a later
date.

[2] In practice it would appear that
the Provisor was usually left to act
by himself, and he rarely interfered

with the College, unless appealed to.
MS. Reg. *passim.*

[3] Franklin, p. 19: *Chartul.* T. I.
pt. i. No. 421. For the identification,
see Hemeræus, MS. f. 241 *b* : Richer,
MS. I. f. 432 *a*.

[4] Hemeræus, f. 239. The Statutes
of the Sorbonne (1274) are now
printed in *Chartul.* T. I. pt. i.
No. 448.

the College early took to receiving as *Hospites* students or rather Bachelors of Theology who had passed their 'Tentative,' to live with the foundation-members. Others became full members without endowment (*socii sine bursa*); and time the value of the burses fell off to such an extent that their possession ceased to carry with it any considerable pecuniary advantage. Membership of the Sorbonne thus became an honorary distinction which was usually sought by most of the Theological Doctors of the University [1]. And, secondly, the Hall or Schools of the Sorbonne became the scene of disputations and other public acts of the Theological Faculty, especially of its meetings to discuss and pronounce judgment upon heresies or Theological novelties. This circumstance especially led to the habit of speaking of the judgments of the Theological Faculty upon matters of Faith as judgments of the Sorbonne [2].

A far more extensive and splendid foundation than the subsequently more famous Sorbonne was the College of Navarre, founded in 1304 by Joanna, Queen of Navarre, the Consort of Philip the Fair. The foundation of this College forms the same kind of epoch in the history of Paris College-building that the foundation of New College (suggested perhaps by its Parisian prototype) constitutes in our Oxford history. Its organization illustrates more markedly than the Sorbonne the points of resemblance and of contrast between the Parisian and the English College.

College of Navarre, 1304.

[1] Hemeræus, ff. 40–48 *b*. The election was by ballot among the members, after a 'probatio morum et doctrinæ' (Hemeræus, f. 52 *b*). It should be observed that whereas the 'bursarii' were compelled to retire from the College after graduation, the honorary membership of the Sorbonne could be granted for life (*ib*. f. 54). A peculiarity of the domestic economy of the Sorbonne, likewise due to the insufficiency of the original bursa of 5 *solidi*, 6 *den*., was that the common life had eventually to be abandoned in favour of a system of dining (as we should say) by 'commonses' (i. e. *à la carte*), which continued down to Hemeræus' time (*ib*. ff. 39, 44 *b*). But this usage is post-medieval.

[2] Launoi (I. p. 452) dates this usage from the time of Francis I. According to Richer (f. 423), all Doctors of Theology in his time styled themselves Doctors of the Sorbonne, 'propter illum actum Sorbonnicum qui die Veneris a sexta matutina ad sextam serotinam æstivo tempore absque ulla intermissione continuat.'

The object of College-founders in both countries was to help poor students, and to ensure a supply of educated secular clergy to the Church. The lucrative professions of Medicine and Law needed no artificial encouragement. Comparatively few Fellowships or Bursarships either in England or at Paris were founded for Canonists, fewer still for students of Medicine. The Grammarians at Paris, however, formed a more important element in the Parisian Colleges than was the case at Oxford. The only representative of this youngest class of students in the Oxford and Cambridge Colleges, are the Choristers of New and other Colleges : since the full foundationers were generally admitted only after entrance upon the Arts Course, and usually when already Bachelors. At Paris some of the Colleges were (as we have seen) founded entirely for Grammar boys. Thus the founder of the little College of Ave Maria (1339 A.D.) for a Master, Chaplain, and six 'young and poor boys,' provided that they should be admitted at the age of eight or nine and superannuated on the completion of their sixteenth year, the age at which, according to the Founder's melancholy experience, boys ' commonly begin to incline to evil [1].' Most Colleges, however, had burses for Artists as well as Grammarians, or for Artists and Theologians, and the larger ones for all three classes of students. At Navarre there were to be twenty students in Grammar with a weekly allowance of four *solidi*, thirty in Arts with six *solidi* a week, twenty in Theology with eight *solidi*. Each class of students was presided over by a Master, whose salary was fixed at double the allowance of a Scholar of his Faculty [2]. The Master of the Theologians was Rector or 'Grand Master' of the whole College. Each class of students had its separate Hall, kitchen and dormitory [3] : they met only in the Chapel, for the services of which four Chaplains and four clerks were appointed [4].

The most characteristic differences between the Colleges

---

[1] Bulæus, IV. 261.

[2] Launoi, I. p. 8.

[3] Launoi, I. p. 11.

[4] Originally two of each. Launoi, I. pp. 9, 11, 17, 25.

of Paris and those of Oxford were constituted by (1) the
entire separation between the Faculties prevalent at Paris,
(2) the totally different position of the Head, (3) a difference in the mode of filling up vacancies. At Paris the
Colleges were essentially Colleges for students : the burse
usually expired as soon as the candidate had finished his
course of study and (in the case of the two higher classes of
students) taken his degree. If he wanted to proceed to a
higher Faculty, a fresh election was necessary, though the
existing members of the College had a preferential claim to
succeed to vacancies in the higher divisions[1]. Where
students from more than one Faculty were embraced in the
same College, each division had a Master of its own,
though the Master of the highest Faculty governed the
whole College : and these Masters were actual teachers who
presided over the studies and disputations, and supplemented by their private instruction the public lectures of the
Schools. At Oxford the Head was primarily a governor
and administrator of the property of the House ; at no
period had he any direct concern with the studies of the
Scholars. The different position of the Paris Head was
connected with the rather inferior degree of autonomy enjoyed by the Colleges of that University. The details
varied at different Colleges : but it would appear that, at
least in many cases, the property of the Paris College was
far less the common property of the Head and Fellows
than was the case at Oxford and Cambridge : the powers
of the external Visitors or Governors were usually much
greater than those of the Oxford ' Visitor.' Nearly always
the patronage of the College—the appointment to the
Masterships and the Bursarships or Scholarships—rested
either with the Bishop or other ecclesiastical dignitaries in
the province or diocese to which the burses were reserved,
or with some dignitary in the immediate vicinity of Paris[2].
These patrons might or might not be identical with the
external governing or visiting body. At Navarre the body

---

[1] Launoi, I. 28.

[2] Or in some cases to the Founders'

heirs, *e.g.* at Tréguier. Félibien,
I. 540.

entrusted by the Founder both with the government and
the patronage of the College was the Theological Faculty
of Paris [1]. Afterwards their powers were transferred to the
Bishop of Melun together with the Chancellor of Paris, the
Dean of the Theological Faculty, and the Grand Master [2].
But after numerous changes the government and patronage
were arbitrarily assigned by the King to his Confessor [3].
The management of the property would seem to have
remained with the Royal *Gentes Computorum* or Masters of
the Exchequer, who paid over the annual revenues to a
Provisor [4] appointed by the external Governors. Even
where a College had the management of its own property,
it usually had to account for its administration of the
revenues at the end of the year. At Navarre and elsewhere the Theologians were to a certain extent associated
with the Master in the government of the House [5] : but the
Artists usually seem to occupy a position more like that of
the later 'Scholars' of Oxford Colleges, when there came to
be a body of Scholars distinct from the Fellows. The ideal

[1] Launoi, I. 8, 9.

[2] Launoi, I. 28, 29, 54, 152, 183.
At Narbonne, the 'Procurator domus' merely received his weekly
supply of funds 'a mercatore qui
tenebit pecunias domus.' Félibien,V.
p. 674. At the College of Plessis,
the consent of the Abbot of Mar-
moutier at Tours is required for all
important transactions relating to
property. (*Ib.* III. p. 386.) At the
College of Boncour, it seems contemplated that the external 'Provi-
sores' may interfere with the details
of internal discipline. (*Ib.* p. 442.)
Occasionally we find the Master
elected by the College, *e.g.* at Laon.
(Jourdain, No. 500.)

[3] Launoi, I. 56, 112 *sq.*

[4] In Launoi, I. 22, we read 'Provisor seu Magister,' but from later
documents it would appear that the
Master was the Head, and that the
Provisor occupied the position of

an Oxford 'Bursar,' ranking second
in the College. In the eighteenth
century the ordinary administration
was in the hands of the Officers (*i.e.*
Grand Master, Provisor, and the two
Principals) and a body of elected
deputies. But the whole College
was summoned on rare occasions.
Register in Archives Nationales
(MM. 469).

[5] From Launoi, I. 159, it appears that the consent of the Theologians was usually asked to the
admission of non-foundation Theologians, and so with the Artists: but
in general the Artists were admitted
to less active participation in the
College affairs than at Oxford, where
the Artists who were full *socii* were
usually B.A. before admission. The
absence of all allusion to a College
seal in the Navarre Statutes is significant.

of the Parisian Founder was a body of Students governed by a Master[1], though the character of his rule naturally varied with the age and status of those students. The idea of an Oxford College was rather a self-governing corporation whose ordinary administration, like that of a Monastery, was in the hands of its elected Head with the assistance of a certain number of the Seniors, while the consent of all was required for the more important legal acts. Even the youngest full member of the foundation took part in the election of the Master or Warden.

The internal arrangements of the Colleges at Paris were, however, as might be expected, very similar to those of Oxford and Cambridge Colleges, of which we shall have more to say hereafter. The most notable differences arose from that sharp separation between the Faculties which has been already noticed. In our own Colleges the younger members of the Society—whether full 'Fellows' or inferior members of the foundation like the Demies of Magdalen—instead of being placed under the government of a Master of the Artists, lived under the general supervision and, at a later date, instruction of the older students of Theology. The usual arrangement at Oxford was to put three, four, or more students in a room with one senior in each. At the College of Navarre, however, and some other Parisian Colleges, the students slept in large dormitories, one for each Faculty, though elsewhere we hear of students living two in a room or even enjoying the luxury of single apartments[2]. The 'Beneficiarii' of the Parisian College always remained mere servitors like the medieval 'Choristers' of New and other Colleges[3], and never developed into an important class of inferior foundationers like the 'Scholars' of our present

---

[1] This was not the case with the Sorbonne. See above, p. 490.

[2] ' Bini et bini habeant suas cameras in quibus studeant et jaceant.' (Félibien, III. p. 442.) At Narbonne College, only 'in casu necessitatis . . . poterit una camera duobus juvenibus bursariis assignari ad tempus.' (*Ib.* V. p. 671.)

[3] The duty of waiting on the Fellows was usually combined with that of singing in chapel. See the Statutes of New College, p. 78. At Winchester the 'choristers' still wait at table.

system. How important an influence these two distinctions exercised over the subsequent development of the two
University systems, the sequel will show.

Commoners or
Pensioners.

The Statutes of the College of Harcourt are dated a few
years later than those of Navarre, though the foundation
itself belongs to the year 1280. Here we find a provision
which became of great importance at a later date[1]. The
Master is allowed to receive into the House ' any suitable
scholar of whatever country who may wish to dwell with
the said Scholars ' of the foundation, upon his paying the
amount of his keep (*bursa*), the rent of his rooms and such
a contribution toward the expenses of the establishment as
shall be determined on by the Master and Fellows. At
first the reception of such ' Commoners ' or ' Pensioners,'
or as they were usually called at Paris ' Guests,' was no
doubt an exceptional thing—confined for the most part
either to students in the Superior Faculties as at the Sorbonne, or, among the students of Arts, to the richer class.
The Collegian, however, evidently possessed many advantages over the pupil of a private Hall and still more
over the 'Martinet,' as the student was called who lodged
with townsmen instead of in a regular Hospicium. He was
under stricter discipline than the young Master anxious

---

[1] ' Item statuimus quod si aliquis
scholaris idoneus undecumque fuerit
oriundus, desideret cum dictis scholaribus habitare, recipiatur a nobis,
vel a deputato a nobis quamdiu
vixerimus, et post decessum nostrum a magistro dictæ domus secundum quod loca domus ad hoc
se potuerint extendere, ponendo
bursam suam, ac conducendo cameram suam, ac emendo tantum de
munitionibus, quantum reperietur
tempore receptionis suæ propor-
tione cujuslibet scholaris juxta æsti-
mationem magistri et sociorum.'
(Bulæus, IV. 154.) In the Statutes
of 1317 for the College of Narbonne,
a similar provision is made (Félibien,
V. p. 674), while in 1379 we find a

Statute against keeping horses by
any student ' nisi socius commen-
salis,' as if the institution was quite
established. (*Ib.* V. p. 670.) So in
1380 the Statutes of the College of
Cornouaille forbid injuries ' alteri
conscholari suo, nec etiam hospiti
suo intraneo qui debito modo fuit
ad manendum et convivendum inter
ipsos receptus.' (*Ib.* III. p. 500.)
So the Statutes of Dainville College
in the same year provide for the
lodging of 'foranei scholares ... sicut
in aliis collegiis Parisiensibus est
aliquando fieri consuetum,' but here
only Decretists in Priest's orders are
to be received, though the College
includes Artists and Grammarians.
(*Ib.* III. p. 511.)

above all things to fill his Hall would have the inclination
or the power to enforce. He enjoyed the advantage of a
private Tutor besides the public Regent selected for him
by the Head of his College[1]. At Navarre, the Master,
or, as he was usually called, Principal of the Artists, was
required 'diligently to hear the lessons of the Scholars
studying in the Faculty of Arts and faithfully to instruct
them alike in life and in doctrine[2].' He was also to
answer their questions and to read with them some
'Logical, Mathematical or Grammatical book' agreed upon
by the majority of the Scholars in addition to the Lectures
of the public Schools. Then there were advantages in the
greater numbers of the larger Colleges. Thus at Navarre
those who attended the same lecture were upon their return
to College 'to meet together and peaceably go over it,' and
he who could best repeat it was to be listened to by the
rest[3]. There was more chance of the rule requiring
scholars 'commonly to speak Latin' being enforced than
in the private Hospice. The Colleges too had libraries,
the want of which had long been felt as putting the secular
Masters at a disadvantage compared with their rivals, the
Regulars[4]. Then there were disputations on winter even-

---

[1] By the 'Reformatio' of S.
Nicholas de Lupara in 1310, the
Master is 'assignare libros quos
audiant.' (Bulæus, IV. 139.)

[2] Bulæus, IV. 93.

[3] Launoi, I. pp. 33, 34. So in the
College of Dainville (1380): 'Quod
statim finita lectione ad domum
redeant, et in uno loco pariter conveniant ad suam lectionem repeten-
dam; ita quod unus post alium
totiens lectionem repetat, quod
ipsam eorum quilibet bene sciat, et
quod minus provecti magis provectis
lectiones quotidie reddere teneantur.'
(Félibien, III. p. 512.) We hear of
the custom of *repetitio* as early as
c. 1284, when the Masters, in their
suit against the Chancellor, say that
if two lectures are given one after

another 'pueri doctrinam recipientes
in una materia, antequam habituati
sint in eadem, ex repetitione sequente, suam doctrinam omittunt.'
(Jourdain, No. 274: *Chartul.* T. I.
pt. i. No. 515, p. 607.)

[4] The advantage which the Regulars enjoyed in this respect was a
sore point with their secular critics.
Bonaventura in his reply to their
advocate (*Opera* VII. p. 384) says:
'Videntur tibi fratres in hoc Regulæ
contraire, cum tibi videantur pecuniam per interpositam personam recipere, libros habere et domos, cum non
possint harum rerum quas habent
Dominos assignare. In labore etiam
manuum sibi injuncto, ut videtur,
sub praecepto culpabiles tibi videntur, cum nec Laici laborent in operi-

ings or (in some cases) during dinner or supper. These advantages might naturally induce parents who wanted their sons to be kept out of mischief and to make the most of their time in the University to send them into the Colleges as 'Pensioners' or 'Commoners.'

Growth of College Teaching.

The tendency was connected, partly perhaps as cause and partly as effect, with a change which came over the educational system of the University in the course of the fifteenth century. The Theological Masters at the Sorbonne and at Navarre [1] appear from the first to have lectured in the College, and it is possible that these lectures were open to outsiders. At all events they counted as regular lectures of the Faculty. The Grammarians, not having begun to keep terms in the Arts Schools, were, it would appear, taught exclusively by their own Master

bus mechanicis, nec Clerici manu propria in libris scribendis, quin potius cum magnis sumptibus faciunt eos scribi, ac si per se haberent numismatum percussores.'

S. Louis divided the large library (consisting of about 1200 volumes, Hauréau, P. ii. T. I. p. 186), which he had been incited by the example of the Saracen Sultan to form in the Library of the Royal Chapel, between the Dominicans, the Minorites, and the Cistercian House (of Rogaumont) of his own foundation (Bulæus, III. 658).

Similar complaints were made at Oxford. Richard of Armagh tells us 'quod non reperitur in Studiis communibus de Facultate Arcium, sacre Theologie et Juris Canonici aut etiam, ut fertur a pluribus, de Facultate Medicine atque Juris Civilis, nisi raro, aliquis utilis multum liber venalis, set omnes emuntur a Fratribus, ita ut in singulis Conventibus sit una grandis ac nobilis Libraria et ut singuli fratres habentes statum in studiis . . . nobilem etiam habeant Librariam.' Two or

three Rectors of his diocese whom he sent to Oxford returned because they could not find a decent copy of the Bible or other theological books for sale. *Defensorium Curatorum* in Brown's *Appendix ad Fasciculum Rerum Expetendarum.* Londini, 1690, p. 474. (The text is corrected from MS. Bodley 144 f. 261; but 'nobilem' ought no doubt to be 'notabilem' as in Bulæus, IV. 339.)

At Paris the difficulty was largely met by the College Libraries. The Library of the Sorbonne was partly formed by its original benefactors, and by 1338 amounted to 1700 volumes. (Franklin, p. 56.) At Navarre the surplus revenue was to be spent in books. (Launoi, I. p. 37.) The Library is mentioned in many other College Statutes. While some of the books were chained in the Library, others could be taken out by the Fellows and retained for long periods, so that they were dispensed from the necessity of buying even text-books for lecture.

[1] 'Qui in domo prædicta legere teneatur.' Launoi, I. 44.

in the College. The students of Arts were, however, bound to complete the courses of 'ordinary' lectures required by the Faculty in the public Schools in or near the Rue du Fouarre[1]; and it is quite clear from the Statutes of the earlier Colleges that it was contemplated that they would have to go outside the house for lectures like the members of Halls or Pædagogies[2]. The College instruction was merely supplementary to that of the public Schools. Gradually, however, the lectures and still more the catechetical lessons or 'Repetitions' given in the College or Hall became more and more important, and the lectures out of it more and more formal and perfunctory. To assist the Master of the College or the Master of the Artists other 'Regents' were taken into the College: and the Masters of the Pædagogies also employed assistant Regents to teach their students. It is difficult to give exact dates for the beginning or the completion of this educational revolution. It is certain that many boarders were received by the Colleges in the fourteenth century. But it was in the course of the fifteenth century[3], and especially towards the middle of that century, that the pensioner-system and the new educational methods which accompanied it, attained their fullest development. In 1445 we find[4] the University

[1] Thus a Statute of 1276 forbids lectures 'in locis privatis' except 'in grammaticalibus et logicalibus.' Bulæus, III. 430: *Chartul.* T. I. pt. i. No. 468.

[2] It is impossible to say how often the *Pædagogus*, or Master of the College, himself acted as *Proprius Magister* to the boys in his own House, though obliged to go to the Rue du Fouarre to give them their lectures. A Statute of 1456 forbids a Master to participate in the banquets of the Nation: 'nisi fuerit verus actualis et continuus Regens habens proprios Scholares *quos continue ducat ad vicum Straminis* et quibus legat libros Logicales,' &c. Bulæus, V. 616–7. On the other hand at the

College of Dainville (in 1380) the Master is to choose the Regents whom his scholars are to hear. Félibien, V. 512.

[3] The reception of Pensioners (and also of non-boarders for instruction) is mentioned as common in other Colleges by the Statutes of the College of Beauvais *c.* 1370 (Chapotin, p. 77). The appointment of a Sub-Magister in Arts at Navarre in 1404 suggests that College-teaching was increasing in quantity and importance (Launoi, I. p. 103). In 1428, however, it is still contemplated that scholars in the Coll. de Séez will have to go to the Rue du Fouarre. Félibien, V. 691.

[4] 'Item praecipue aperiatur quo-

declaring in a petition to the King that 'almost the whole University resides in the Colleges.' In 1459 the excessive multiplication of non-bursarial students in the College of Navarre led to disorders which called for the appointment of a Royal Commission[1]. The growth of the system is the more remarkable if (as du Boulay states) it had only been introduced into that College some ten years before[2]. From the report of the Commission it appears that many dined and attended lectures in the College without sleeping in it: and it was now ordered that none should dine in College except those who lodged in it or in an adjoining house. By the beginning of the sixteenth century it seems to have been possible to obtain a degree without attending any but College lectures[3]. Eventually the Schools of the Rue du Fouarre were deserted except for formal Acts such as Determinations and Inceptions. Ramus, the great assailant of the Aristotelian traditions of medieval Paris,

modo ipsa Universitas Parisiensis in suis Collegiis maxime fundata est in quibus quasi tota residet, immo et durantibus guerrarum dissidiis jam ipsa perisset, si ipsis Collegiis non esset conservata' Bulæus, V. 536. The war with England leading to the desertion of the Halls, which must then have passed to other hands, may have contributed to the growth of the pensioner-system when the University began to fill again. So in England the depopulation of the Universities, consequent upon the Reformation, led to the extinction of all the Cambridge, and most of the Oxford, Halls.

[1] The Commission issued in 1459 (*ap.* Launoi, II. p. 165); the Edict of Louis XI enforcing its recommendations appeared in 1464 (*ib.* II. p. 170 *sq.*). The following extract illustrates the spontaneous way in which the system had grown up: 'Item, ad tollendam excessivam Scholarium non Bursariorum multitudinem quæ confusionem parit et magna

affert incommoda, usque etiam ad destructionem morum, scientiæ et ædificiorum dicti Collegii, obstruetur infra festum beati Remigii proxime venturum ille ingressus seu illa muri apertio, quam Magister Grammaticorum fieri fecit citra viginti aut sexdecim annos, ut de suis privatis et acquisitis domibus ad Domum collegialem Scholares non Bursarii transire possent, quatenus Collegium predictum ad modum et statum quos, dum maxime floreret, habuit, ponatur et reducatur' (*ib.* p. 171). It will be observed that here the Pensioners are the private boarders of the Master, rather than of the College, like the non-foundation boarders received by the Head Master of a foundation-school.

[2] 'Convictores nobiles tum primum accepit, Scholares extraneos et professores.' Bulæus, IV. 97.

[3] None but College lectures seem contemplated by the Statutes drawn up for the College of Montaigu in 1501. Félibien, V. 727 *sq.*

lived to see the death of the last Regent who had taught in
the Schools of the Vicus Stramineus[1]. The assault on the old
scholastic ideas and the metamorphosis of the educational
system by which they had been kept alive, were connected
by something more than an accidental synchronism. It was,
in part at least, the revival of Classical studies, and the new
and more individual method of instruction which that revival
brought with it, that led to the substitution of College
teaching for the old University lectures. Perhaps, indeed,
the earliest phase of their revival was not itself due to the
better discipline and elementary instruction of the Colleges.

The stricter discipline of the Colleges gradually reacted Influence of the Colleges upon the University.
upon the discipline of the University generally. The
University was in its origin a voluntary Association of
individual Masters rather than a single educational institution conducted by an organised staff. The University
prescribed the studies which were to lead to the Master's
chair; but it did not attempt to interfere with the discipline of the scholars. In a sense all scholars were
regarded as members, though not as governing members,
of the 'University of Masters and Scholars'; but, as
primitive society recognised only heads of families, so the
primitive University recognised only Masters. The discipline of the streets was left to the ordinary police and
the ecclesiastical tribunals. The discipline of the Schools
and the Hospices (in so far as such a thing existed) was left
to their respective Masters or Principals and the autonomous
Societies over which the latter presided. When a dispute
arose as to whether a captured clerk was entitled to the
University privileges, the sole question was whether any
of the Masters would claim him as a pupil. It was not till

---

[1] Ramus, *Procem. reform. Par.
Acad. (Scholæ in lib. Artes* c. 1116).
The only survival of the University
Lectures in the Faculty of Arts was
the Ethics Lecture which passed into
a sort of Professorship filled by annual
election of the Nations in turn. We
hear that a new Rector in 1458 'sup-
plicavit Nationi cujus vices erant pro
lectura Ethicæ' (Bulæus, V. p. 630.
Cf. p. 726). The Moral Philosophy
Professorship, long held at Oxford
by the Senior Proctor for the time
being, seems to have been a survival
of much the same kind.

1289 that the University required the names of all students together with an inventory of their property to be inscribed on the list or *Matricula* of some Master as a condition of enjoying those privileges [1]. There was no University *Matricula* as in the Italian or German Universities. As late as 1460 we find one of the Nations providing, apparently for the first time, that students wishing to begin the course in Arts shall appear before the Congregation of the Nation on the first day of the Grand Ordinary—or, as we should say, of the October term—and have their names inscribed in the Register of the Nation by the Proctor [2].

Improved
Discipline.　In the fifteenth century, however, the University, or rather the Faculty of Arts, began, as it had never done before, to make in its corporate capacity a serious effort to put down the violent encounters between armed student-mobs or between students and townsmen which had hitherto been affairs of almost every-day occurrence in the streets of Paris. On these occasions neither College nor Pædagogy afforded that sanctuary against the pursuit of Proctorial justice which are supplied by the walls of an Oxford or Cambridge College [3]. The Rector and Proctors were empowered by the University to enter the College or Hospice and there superintend the enforced chastisement of the offenders [4]: while Masters who had participated in these exuberances of youthful spirits were deprived of their Regency.

Authority
of the
University
over the
Colleges.　One of the most remarkable features of the Parisian as compared with the English College-system is the extent to which at Paris the University or its constituent Faculties and Nations managed to acquire complete control over the Colleges, to enforce regulations for their internal government [5], and to remove their officers or foundationers, some-

---

[1] Bulæus, III. 449 ; *Chartul.*, T. II. No. 561. (Date wrong in Bulæus.) In 1341 the Inceptor is further to swear, ' Non dabitis testimonium de aliquo Scholari, nisi vobis juraverit, quod intendit esse verus scholaris vester.' Bulæus, IV. p. 275.

[2] Bulæus, V. 646-7.

[3] By custom, perhaps not by Law.

[4] Bulæus, V. 704, 713, 726.

[5] The Faculty of Arts for instance forbids the celebration of ' festa ... cum minis [? mimis] seu instrumentis altis [? aliis] cum tapetis et brevibus seu quibusvis dissolutis habitibus animum scholarium distrahentibus

times even without consulting the Visitors named by the CHAP. V,
§ 5. Founder [1]. On one occasion the University actually sold the property of a College which had fallen into decay [2]. The right of visiting the Colleges thus acquired by the University rested upon sheer usurpation—a usurpation which was made possible by its undoubted authority over the individual officers and members of the College [3]. It is obvious that such claims had only to be asserted to be irresistible, since expulsion from the University would have prevented the accomplishment of the purpose for which students entered the College.

a profectu et inducentibus ad lasciviam.' Bulæus, V. p. 560. The Bedels are directed to read the Statute in the presence of the Principal and the assembled Scholars.

[1] *E.g.* in 1466 when the French Nation appointed a Master of the Collége de la Marche. Bulæus, V. 679-80. In one case, indeed, the Nation in asserting its right to fill a vacant Headship inserts the qualification 'maxime in absentia Collatorum seu Provisorum.' Bulæus, V. 385. Cf. Jourdain, No. 1202.

[2] The College of Constantinople, in which in 1362 a single Bursar survived, who assents to the transaction as ' Scholaris unicus Constantinopolitanus ac gubernator solus.' Bulæus, IV. p. 366.

[3] Thus the Nation of France in 1419 resolved that ' Collegium illud [de Lupara] erat Nationis, quia major pars Scholarium debent esse de Natione,' and further, ' quod Universitas et Nationes habent reformare sua Collegia' (Bulæus, V. 345). The confusion into which the Colleges had fallen during the Civil Wars, and the consequent ruin of their estates, probably contributed to enable the University to strengthen its hold upon them. Thus in 1421 the Nation of France decreed a

' Reformatio' of a number of Colleges which had fallen into ruin. This ' Reform' was inaugurated by an enquiry, carried out with all the thoroughness of a modern University Commission, into the state of the College revenues. It required a return (' codicillos') as to the statutes and property of the Colleges, respecting, however, the 'secreta ipsorum Collegiorum, sicut vasa argentea, Iocalia Capellarum, thesaurus sive pecuniæ eorum.' In some cases deeds of foundation and title-deeds had been lost and were recovered by the enquiries of the Commission. The Nation also ordered ' quod omnes viri Practici tam Magistri quam Scholares similiter et Officiarii Regii qui non studii gratia loca occupant Collegiorum, a dictis Collegiis expellantur' (Bulæus, V. 350-352). How different might not the history of Oxford have been had there been medieval precedents for a similar interference by the University with College abuses. For other instances of such University Visitation, see Bulæus, V. 384-386. Even where the Visitor or ' Collator' had appointed, his nominee came to the Nation to obtain its authorization for his installation as Master. *Ib.*, V. 385-6.

In the Reform of 1452 the internal discipline of the Colleges is thoroughly dealt with ; and the duty of ' Pædagogues ' with reference to the moral well-being of their boarders is enforced in a manner which is in marked contrast with the absolute silence of the Legates who had legislated for the University at previous Visitations. The Reformers descended to such details as the price, quality, and equal distribution of provisions [1]. At the same time the Commission ordered an annual Visitation of the Colleges and Pædagogies by a permanent board of four Censors who were to be senior Masters of Arts and also graduates in the superior Faculties [2].

If the Visitatorial claims of the University constituted a violation of the older College autonomy, the state of matters revealed by one of the first of its Visitations shows that some such usurpation was not uncalled for. A student in the College of Boissi had been in the habit of leaving the College by day and by night without permission of the Master ; at times he had come accompanied by a party of boon companions armed with great swords and had assailed the College gates, which he found closed against him, with heavy stones [3]. Excommunicated for an assault upon one of his fellow-scholars, he had refused to seek absolution and had tried to enter the Chapel. Upon being forcibly ejected, he retired to his chamber while the others were engaged at Mass, and set fire to his bed, so that the College narrowly escaped being burnt to the ground. On another occasion he had thrown big stones on to the roof of the Hall during supper with so much force that the food was covered with dust [4]. Similar annoyances had compelled the students to give up attending their lecture-

---

[1] ' Quodque justum et moderatum pretium pro victu secundum rerum et temporum qualitatem a Scholaribus exigant ; victualia munda, sana atque salubria Scholaribus subministrent et ex illis, honestâ fragilitate [*leg.* frugalitate] servatâ, præstent cuique congruam portionem.' Bulæus, V. 572.

[2] Bulæus, V. 571.
[3] Bulæus, V. 93.
[4] ' Et dictis Scholaribus in prandio existentibus plancherium [ceiling] desuper cum grossis lapidibus percutiebat, pulveres super eorum cibaria cadere faciebat.' *Ib.* p. 94.

rooms. Finally, being summoned before the Rector to answer for these enormities, he had stationed his brother and a party of eight or ten armed men[1] between the Bernardine convent, where the University Court assembled, and the Rector's house,—a measure which had the desired effect of preventing that official from attending the Court. Even this catalogue of offences was not visited with deprivation till it was ascertained by examination that he was of 'rude intellect, not fitted or apt for acquiring proficiency[2]': and even then the sentence was merely deprivation of his Bursar's place in the College, not expulsion from the University—a further punishment which was held over his head *in terrorem* in case he should refuse to quit the College within four days.

There was one great difficulty in the way of the University reformers who were trying to bring up the general discipline of the University to the stricter standard aimed at in the best Colleges : and that was the absolute liberty of migration enjoyed by the students in the Hospices or Pædagogies. The imagination declines to picture to itself the state of a public School in which a boy who found his House Master's régime too exacting and restrictive should be perfectly free to transfer himself to the boarding-house of a more easy-going pedagogue. Yet such was the state of things which prevailed in the University of Paris with students of the same age as the modern Fourth-form boy up to the year 1452. In that year Cardinal Estouteville, whose regulations for the internal conduct of Hospicia have already been referred to, enacted that no Pædagogue should receive into his house a student who had left his former Master 'to avoid correction[3].' One

---

[1] 'Magnis ensibus et aliis armis invasivis munitos.'

[2] 'Rudis intellectus, non idoneus, nec habilis ad proficiendum.' *Ib.*, p. 93.

[3] 'Quatenus correctiones et disciplinas scholasticas faciant erga scholares secundum exigentiam culparum, ... sed non liceat scholari juste ob culpam negligentiamve correcto ad evitandam disciplinam ac correctionem ad alium transire pædagogum, inhibentes ne talis ab alio pædagogo recipiatur in domo sua, qui propter correctionem debitam prioris Magistri domum exierit.' Bulæus,

CHAP. V,
§ 5.

Suppres-
sion of
'Martinets.'
1457.

more step was wanted to complete the triumph within the University of order over anarchy, and that was the enforcement of residence either in a College or a Pædagogy. This step was taken in 1457 [1]. It seems probable that by this time the Pædagogies had already become so far an essential part of the University-system that even the Martinets went to some College or Pædagogy for lectures and other exercises, though their own masters out of school [2]. It was now ordered that the Martinets 'should be bound to live in the Pædagogy or adjoining places [3].' At the same time the migration from one Master's house to another was forbidden in all cases except with the leave of the scholar's Nation or Faculty. Moreover the Mastership of a Pædagogy was for the first time recognised as a University office by the provision that no one should open a new Pædagogy without the permission of the Faculty. In 1463 actual residence within the Pædagogy or College was explicitly required, except in the cases of those who lived in the house of relatives or of some 'notable person' himself a Regent or student of the University [4].

Parallels
at Oxford,
&c. It is instructive to notice that Oxford purged itself or attempted to purge itself of its 'Chamberdekyns' twenty years before the suppression of the corresponding class of Martinets at Paris; while the history of every German University of which we possess any detailed record exhibits, through the whole of the fifteenth century, a

V. 572. A Principal thus bereft of his pupil was to reclaim him, 'coram Cancellario vel ejus Officiali.'

[1] Bulæus, V. 622. The resolution is one of the Nation of France, but was intended for adoption by the Faculty of Arts.

[2] As much seems to be implied in the name, which is derived from their habit of roosting under the eaves of the Pædagogy instead of inside, or, (according to others) from their flitting from one house to another.

[3] 'Voluit insuper Martinetos adstringi Pædagogia aut loca vicina in-

habitare.' Bulæus, V. 622.

[4] 'Quod nulli de cætero in ipsa Artium Facultate tempus acquirent, neque eisdem sigillum Rectoris, aut Procuratoris, aut signeta Pædagogorum et Regentium pro examinandis ad gradum Baccalaureatus aut licentiæ expedientur, nisi per tempus sufficiens ad gradum obtinendum moram traxerint in Collegio, Pædagogio aut domo suorum parentum, aut alicuius notabilis viri in aliqua 4 Facultatum Regentis aut studentis, gratis serviendo.' Bulæus, V. 658.

similar course of increasingly severe legislation for the enforcement of College discipline or its equivalent upon all students of the Faculty of Arts[1]. It should be observed that at Paris, as at Oxford and elsewhere, these Statutes had constantly to be renewed; so that it was only by slow degrees that this lowest, idlest, and most lawless class of students were improved away[2].

There was, however, one most important feature in which the Parisian system of College education differed from the system which was growing up at the same time in the English Universities. That difference was a necessary outcome of the difference in the original constitution of the two kinds of College. At Paris, as has been said,

---

[1] As to Oxford, see *Mun. Acad.* p. 320. At Vienna, in 1410 (Kink, II. p. 236), scholars not residing in a Master's house are deprived of the privileges of the University in the event of arrest or imprisonment, except 'honestæ personæ notæ tamen in suis Statibus, quibus in priuatis domibus stare solitarie sua cum familia aut cum aliis habitare placuerit,' who are required to obtain the license of the Rector. The Rector is given the power of deposing or depriving 'negligentes hospites,' whether Masters or not. A scholar expelled from one 'Bursa aut habitatio Studentium' is not to be received into another without leave of Rector and Dean. An elaborate Statute of 1413 regulates the discipline of these 'Bursæ.' The punishments are fines, and, in the last resort, expulsion from the House. The mildness of the discipline now imposed is a sufficient illustration of its previous absence, *e.g.* for laying violent hands upon the 'Conventor Bursæ' (*i. e.* the Master) 'absque tamen sanguinis effusione aut alias notabili corporis læsione,' the penalty is expulsion and a fine of 24 grossi (p. 249):

'si quis Bursalium cum muliere suspecta in Bursa occulte deprehensus fuerit,' 3 grossi (p. 253), &c. It is satisfactory to find, however, that a student who 'invasit suum conventorem cum cultello et fugavit eum ad tertiam domum' was actually imprisoned (*ib.* I. pt. i. p. 38). The Stat. of 1413 further orders 'quod non stent plures simul quam quatuor sine Magistro, Baccalaureo aut alio, cui tanquam Rectori obediant' (II. p. 255). Provisions were made for enforcing some decency of behaviour on those who lived 'cum hospite' or 'in domibus pauperum'; in these cases alone is corporal punishment contemplated (they were probably the poorest scholars). They may be punished 'vel in pecunia, vel in corpore, vel in carceratione, seu in promotionibus, prout Rectori' etc. The Visitors of the University appointed by the Council of Bâle in 1436 made further provisions for domestic discipline, *e.g.* Bachelors of Arts were not allowed to preside over a Hall (p. 281): and in 1509 (p. 316) every student was placed under the supervision of a Tutor (*Præceptor*).

[2] See Bulæus, V. pp. 810, 812.

the original constitution provided the Arts-students of a College with one Master and only one. Even if the College had other Masters of Arts on its foundation as students of Theology, these had nothing to do with the discipline or instruction of the Artists; and many Paris Colleges were Colleges of Artists only, some of them very small ones. It is obvious that the single Master could not supply the whole of the instruction needed by all his pupils through the whole of their course. At Oxford the instruction of the junior members of the foundation and of non-foundationers (in so far as it was conducted within College walls) was entrusted to the numerous M.A. Fellows, who had always been closely associated with the students in Arts. The system of University teaching was gradually supplanted by the Tutorial system which has lasted down to our own day [1]. At Paris the bigger Colleges—especially no doubt those who had succeeded in attracting a large number of paying students—hired additional Regents to lecture to their men in College, and these Regents gradually took the place of the Regents in the Rue du Fouarre with less change of educational method than was ultimately necessitated at Oxford by the responsibility of the single Tutor for almost the whole work of his pupils. Meanwhile the smaller Colleges and the Pædagogies were glad to send their members for lectures to the larger and better equipped establishments. And the number of Colleges which supplied a full course of instruction to their members continually diminished till, before the end of the fifteenth century, the 'Colléges de pleine exercise' (as those which provided a full educational course were called) had reduced themselves to eighteen, though the whole number of Colleges was considerably over fifty. In the Faculty of Theology lecturing had likewise become confined within the walls of two secular Colleges—the Sorbonne and the College of Navarre—together with the Houses of the

---

[1] It was, however, only gradually that instruction passed into the hands of the pupil's single Tutor. In the 16th and 17th centuries there was often a well-organized system of *Prælectors*.

Regulars[1]. Thus, in place of the system of College
isolation which prevailed in Oxford down to our own
times, the system of education in the University of Paris
resolved itself (so far as the Faculty of Arts was concerned)
into a system of inter-collegiate lectures—a system which
has quite recently reproduced itself in Oxford as the best
practicable means of combining the advantages of College-
teaching with that of a purely Professorial or University
system. Of course no comparison is intended between
the details of the two systems. At Paris the larger
Colleges came in the sixteenth Century to be organised
very much after the manner of large Schools divided into
classes, each of them comprising the students of one year
and taught by a separate Regent, while the smaller
Colleges and Pædagogies reduced themselves to boarding-
houses dependent on the 'Colléges de pleine exercise.'

While the system of College-teaching had many advantages from the point of view of the student or at least from
that of his parents or guardians, it was no less attractive
from the point of view of the Master: and these advantages
no doubt contributed largely to its growth and also to the
eventual concentration of teaching in the larger Colleges.
Originally, the Schools or lecture-rooms of the University
were merely rooms hired from private individuals. The
Master depended for his support (if not beneficed) upon
the fees of his students, while for the payment of the
rent he depended mainly upon the fees of his Bachelors
at Determination[2]. When the Nations acquired Schools of
their own near the Church of S. Julien[3], the situation was
not materially altered, except that the Master was responsible for the rent to the Nation instead of to the landlord.

---

[1] Goulet, f. xiiii.; Bulæus, V. 827,
857; Launoi, I. 263, 265.

[2] In 130⅚ the French Nation provided that if a Master's Determining
Bachelors were insufficient to pay
the rent, the deficiency should be
supplied 'de bursis Determinantium
vel de aliis obventibus.' Bulæus,

IV. 100: *Chartul.* T. II. No. 655.

[3] Towards the end of the 14th
century we find the various Nations
beginning to buy or build schools of
their own. The movement in favour
of University buildings appears to
have begun at about this time, or
a little later, all through Europe.

The Colleges at least freed the Regent from anxiety as to his rent; while, as the practice of boarding in Colleges began with the richer scholars, it is probable that they were able to offer larger as well as less precarious incomes to competent teachers. The superior ability and experience of the more permanent College Regents no doubt enabled them to compete at an advantage with the young Master who was teaching for a year in the Rue du Fouarre to satisfy the Statutes of the University, and even with the keeper of the private-adventure Pædagogy.

Position
of the
College-
Regent
in the
University.

By accepting a College appointment of this kind and giving up his School in the Rue du Fouarre, the Regent lost the rights of Regency. It appears, however, that considerable laxity prevailed in the enforcement of this regulation. For, though every duly incepted Master had a right to the position of Regent, he had to supplicate for 'Regency and Schools,' and, since the number of Schools at the disposal of the Faculty was limited, the *supplicat* could not invariably be granted, and Masters who were thus kept waiting for Schools were provisionally admitted to all the rights of Regency[1]. There were thus a considerable number of Regent Masters not actually teaching in the Rue du Fouarre : hence it is easy to understand that, under cover of this exception, many College Regents may have continued to enjoy their University privileges, though they had no intention of ever teaching in the Schools of their Faculty. This state of things no doubt contributed to the growth of the College-system. In 1456, however, an attempt was made to check these growing irregularities by enacting that no Regent who did not 'continuously conduct pupils to the Rue du Fouarre' and lecture to them there, should enjoy the privileges of Regency[2]. An exception is, however, made in respect of

[1] Bulæus, V. 858, 859.

[2] Bulæus, V. p. 617. (See above, p. 404 *note* 3.) The regulation was renewed in 1474, *ib.* pp. 711, 712. The resolutions are silent as to the power of voting in Congregation, but it would seem that College Regents must be excluded since their position must have been different from that of the Honorary Regents who were likewise excluded from distributions, and complaints were

the 'Masters and Pædagogues' who had long lectured in Chap. V,
§ 5. the Rue du Fouarre. These were to enjoy all the privileges of Regency except a share in the weekly distributions at the National Vespers and Mass, and were henceforth called Honorary Regents. The resolution is interesting as an indication of the growth of College-teaching. The College Regents are now a numerous body, but presumably not in a large majority, though it is of course conceivable that they may have taken a less active part in the affairs of the University than the more constitutional, but less employed and more needy, Regents of the Rue du Fouarre. Nothing, however, is said as to the exclusion of the pupils of the College Regents from the University degree: hence we may conclude that by this time College lectures have acquired a tacit recognition as 'ordinary lectures' of the University.

In 1486 the constitutional position of the Regents again Dismissal
of
Regents. attracted the attention of the University. *De facto* the status of the Regents was simply that of the Assistant-master in a modern English Public school. Under these circumstances it is not surprising that the Principal of the College of Lisieux should have thought he had a right to dismiss his Regent. The deprived Regent, however, appealed to the Faculty of Arts, which, conformably with its general claim to supervise the Colleges, determined that in future Regents in Colleges, though nominated by the Principal, should receive their appointment from the Faculty and be removable only by that body. It was further enacted that none should be allowed to teach Arts in the Colleges who were not actual members of the Faculty [1]. Hence the system of College-teaching at Paris was further differentiated from the College-system of Oxford by being subject

---

made that Collegians suffered through being examined by 'Pædagogi suos baccalarios habentes domesticos et commensales.' *Ib.* p. 575. It is implied that College Regents could not be Examiners, presumably because not full Regents in the University sense.

[1] Bulæus, V. pp. 771–4. The Superior Faculties, however, asserted the right of their graduates to preside over Colleges or Pædagogies of Artists. Crevier, IV. p. 424.

CHAP. V,
§ 5.

Number
and vicissi-
tudes of
the Paris
Colleges.

to University supervision [1], which extended at times even to the actual inspection of College-lectures [2].

A more detailed account of these extinct Parisian Colleges would not be interesting to the English reader. A list of the Colleges with their founders and dates of foundation is appended to this chapter. It will at all events serve to impress upon the reader's mind their very large number, and to warn him against exaggerating the peculiarities of the English College-system. It must, however, be added that the list is very probably incomplete. More than one College mentioned in it is revealed to us only by a single accidental allusion. There can be no more interesting illustration of the contrast between English and French history than the fate of the Oxford and of the Paris Colleges respectively. Some of the Parisian Colleges may be said to have enjoyed only an intermittent existence. From time to time war emptied the College-rooms, or prevented the collection of the revenues from the country estates [3]. We constantly hear of Colleges falling into total decay [4]. Sometimes the scanty remains of their property

---

[1] It is true that by the Oxford Statutes a College Tutor (not Lecturer) could not be dismissed without the consent of the Vice-Chancellor, but since it rested with the Head to assign pupils to different Tutors, and as each Tutor was paid solely by the fees of his pupils, the Statute was inoperative. The Provost of Oriel was thus able virtually to deprive Newman of his Tutorship.

[2] In 1498, a Statute of the French Nation reciting that ‘ multi [Regentes] sunt qui dicunt se habere materias qui forte non habent,’ appoints delegates ‘ visitare Lectiones singulorum Collegiorum.’ Bulæus, V. p. 827.

[3] How war affected the Universities is indicated by a Paris College Statute of 1397, which provides that there shall be ‘ unus parvus cofrus catenatus pro pecuniis servandis, qui

ponatur in aliquo loco tuto, quando propter generales guerras, vel alias, essent pauci scolares ydonei in domo.’ Félibien, V. p. 667.

[4] So in 1430 the College of Hubant was so much overwhelmed by debt and dilapidation that all payments to Bursars had to be suspended. (Jourdain, p. 253). The College of Montaigu was in ruins and without revenues in 1483, when Jean Standonc became Master, took rich boarders, and made them support the ‘ Pauperes ’ (*Ib.* p. 301 *note*). In 1463 the Collége de Cocquerel was found to have no Bursar and to be full of workmen and their families who had occupied the empty rooms. (*Ib.* p. 290 *note*.) In 1445 the English had applied the revenues of College estates in Normandy to the support of the rival University of Caen, to which all Norman students were

(occasionally nothing was left but a dilapidated building) were merged in some wealthier foundation. And at the Revolution the collegiate system as a whole fell with the other institutions of medieval France—never (like so much of the Ancien Régime) to reproduce itself under altered forms in modern times. In England — thanks to our insular position and the comparative mildness of our civil wars—no College ever disappeared through a failure of revenue[1]: in most of them the increasing value of their estates has (till very recently) more than kept pace with the rise of prices : a few of them have at times been scandals of corporate opulence. Of all the secular foundations which medieval piety bequeathed to Oxford[2] she has lost not one. During the present century the College-buildings and the College-system alike have silently adapted themselves to the altered needs of the present with that power of spontaneous self-development which is the happy peculiarity of English institutions. It is with a melancholy feeling that the dweller in Oxford quadrangles wanders through the old Quartier Latin of the Mother University and finds scarcely anything left to remind him of the historic Colleges and

---

now compelled to go. Bulæus, V. pp. 536, 537.

The following resolutions of the University may be left to speak for themselves :—

'Tertium Caput rerum ab Universitate hoc anno gestarum fuit lustratio et reformatio Collegiorum, quorum pleraque calamitate temporum aut funditus ruebant, aut Præfectos non habebant, aut reditus non percipiebant, aut prave administrabantur.' Bulæus, V. p. 350. an. 1421.

'Item placuit Nationi quod omnes viri Practici, tam Magistri quam Scholares, similiter et Officiarii Regii qui non studii gratia loca occupant Collegiorum, a dictis Collegiis expellantur.' *l.c.*

'Item placuit Nationi quod Collegiis in quibus nulli vel pauci et antiqui habitant, præficiantur et ordinentur ad eorum regimen et salvationem utensilium, librorum, redituum et litterarum duo vel 3 notabiles Magistri.' *l.c.*

[1] Except the very modern Hertford College (founded 1740) and that only for a time. It is said that during the decay of this College, when there was only one (insane) Fellow left, all sorts of unauthorised persons took up their abode in the ruinous buildings. (Cox, *Recollections of Oxford*, 1870, p. 190.) See below, Vol. II. App. on 'Lost Colleges at Oxford.'

[2] The same might be said of Cambridge but for the merging of older Colleges in Trinity and the extinction of God's House.

Schools and Convents which once occupied the sites now covered by dirty slums or trim boulevards, save the street-names—always the most durable landmarks of urban history. Those silent witnesses of the past will remain there to remind modern students of the rock whence they were hewn and the hole of the pit whence they were digged, until the fertile brain of some municipal councillor is fired with the ambition of replacing them by names less contaminated by clerical associations.

LIST OF THE COLLEGES FOUNDED
BEFORE 1500 A.D.

[* denotes a College for Monks. The Mendicant Colleges are not included in this list.]

Colleges.	Date.	Founders.
Collége des Dix-huit . .	1180	Jocius de Londonio.
S. Thomas du Louvre .	c. 1186	Count Robert of Clermont.
C. de Constantinople .	c. 1204	
C. des bons Enfans de S. Honoré	120$\frac{8}{9}$	Étienne Belot and wife.
S. Nicholas du Louvre .	ante 1217	Robert de Dreux, brother of Louis VII (died 1188).
*Maison de l'Ordre du Val des Escoliers (Austin Canons) . . .	c. 1228	
*C. du Chardonnet . .	1246	Stephen Lexington, Abbot of Clairvaux.
C. des Prémontrés .	c. 1252	John, Abbot of Prémontré.
C. de la Sorbonne . . .	125$\frac{6}{7}$	Robert de Sorbonne, Canon of Paris, Royal Chaplain, &c.
C. de Calvi (or La Petite Sorbonne) . . .	c. 1260(?)	Robert de Sorbonne, Canon of Paris, Royal Chaplain, &c.
*C. de S. Denys . .	ante 1263(?)	
C. du Trésorier (or de Saône, or de Rouen) . .	c. 1268	Guill. de Saône, Treasurer of Rouen.
*C. de Cluny	1269	Yves de Vergi, Abbot of Cluny.
C. d'Abbeville . . .	1271	Gerard d'Abbeville, Archdeacon of Ponthieu.
C. des Daces	1275[1]	

[1] According to *Hist. Litt.* XVI. p. 53, before 1200.

Colleges.	Date.	Founders.
C. d'Harcourt . . .	1280	Raoul d'Harcourt, Doctor of Decrees, Canon of Paris, Archdeacon of Coutances, Chancellor of Bayeux, Chanter of Evreux, Grand Archdeacon of Rouen.
C. des Cholets (*or* de Beauvais)	1295	Jean Cholet, D.U.J., Cardinal and Papal Legate in France.
C. du Cardinal Lemoine	*c.* 1302 (?)	Cardinal Jean Lemoine [1].
C. de Navarre . . .	1304	Joanna, Queen of Navarre and Consort of Philip IV.
C. de Bayeux . . .	1308	Guill. Bonnet, Bishop of Bayeux.
C. de Laon } C. de Prêles }	1314	Gui de Laon, Canon of Paris, Laon, and the Sainte Chapelle. Raoul de Prêles, King's clerk. (Originally these two foundations were a single College, separated in 1323.)
C. des Aicelins, *afterwards* de Montaigu . . .	1314	Giles Aicelin, Archbishop of Rouen; restored in 1388 by Pierre Aicelin deMontaigu, Bishop of Nevers and Laon and Cardinal.
C. de Suède . . .	1315	Andrew, Provost of Upsala.
C. de Narbonne . . .	1317	Bernard de Farges, Archbishop of Narbonne.
C. de Cornouaille (*or* Quimper)	1321	Nicolaus Galeranus, clerk.
C. du Plessis . . .	1322	Geoffroi du Plessis, Notary Apostolic and Secretary of Philip the Long.
C. de Maclou . .	*c.* 1323	Jacques Rousselet, Archdeacon of Reims, executor of Raoul Rousselet, Bishop of Laon.
C. de Tréguier . .	1325	Guill. de Coetmohair, Chanter of Tréguier.
C. des Écossais . .	1326	David, Bishop of Moray.
*C. de Marmoutier (*or* de S. Martin) . . .	*c.* 1329	Geoffroi du Plessis (for the Monks of the Abbey of Marmoutier at Tours).
C. d'Arras . . .	1332	Nicholas le Caudrelier, Abbot of S. Vast.
C. de Bourgogne . .	1332	Joanna of Burgundy, Dowager of Philip the Long.
C. de Tours . . .	133¾	Étienne de Bourgueil, Archbishop of Tours.
C. des Lombards . .	1334	Andrew Ghini (of Florence), clerk of Charles le Bel, Bishop of Arras and Tournay, and Cardinal: François de l'Hôpital (of Modena),

---

[1] Papal Bull in 1308.   Reg. Clem. V. ed. Benedict, No. 3575.

Colleges.	Date.	Founders.
		clerk of the Royal Cross-bowmen (*Albalêtriers*): Renier Jean (of Pistoja), Apothecary: Manuel de Rolland (of Piacenza), Canon of S. Marcel in Paris.
C. de Lisieux (*or* de Torchi) .	1336	Gui d'Harcourt, Bishop of Lisieux: absorbed in the College founded [1414] by Guill. d'Estouteville, Bishop of Lisieux, Estond d'Estouteville, Abbot of Fécamp and their brother, the Seigneur de Torchi.
C. d'Hubant (*or* de l'Ave Maria) . . .	1336 *or* 1339	Maître Jean de Hubant, President of the *Chambre d'Enquêtes.*
C. de Bertrand (*or* d'Autun) .	1341	Pierre Bertrand, Bishop of Nevers and Autun and Cardinal.
C. de S. Michel (*or* de Chanac)	1343 (?)	Guill. de Chanac, Bishop of Paris and Patriarch of Alexandria.
C. des Allemands .	*ante* 1348	(A *Domus Pauperum.*)
C. des trois Evêques (*or* de Cambrai)	1348	Hugues de Pomare, Bishop of Langres. Hugues d'Arci, Bishop of Laon and Archbishop of Reims, Guill. d'Auxonne, Bishop of Cambrai and Autun.
C. de Maître Clément . .	1349	Maître Robert Clément.
C. de Tournai . . *c.*	1350	
C. de Mignon . . *ante*	1353	Maître Jean Mignon.
C. de Boncour (*or* Bécond) .	1353	Pierre Bécond, Chevalier.
C. de Justice	1358	Jean de Justice, Chanter of Bayeux and Canon of Paris.
C. de Boissi	1359	Étienne Vidé de Boissi-le-sec, Canon of Laon.
C. de la Marche . . .	1363	Maître Jean de la Marche (an Ex-Rector). (Absorbing the ruined College of Constantinople.)
C. de Vendôme . . *ante*	1367	
C de Dormans (*or* de Beauvais)	1370	Jean de Dormans, Bishop of Beauvais and Cardinal.
C. de Maître Gervais . .	1370	Gervais Chrestien, First Physician of Charles V.
C. de Dainville . . .	1380	Gerard de Dainville, Bishop of Cambrai, and Jean de Dainville, Knight.
C. de Fortet	1391	Pierre Fortet, M.A., Lic. U.J.
C. de Linkoeping . . .	?	} (Empty in 1392.)
C. de Scara	?	
C. de Tou (*de Tulleio*) . *ante*	1393	
C. de Tonnerre . *ante*	1406	The Abbot (Richard de Tonnerre) and Convent of S. Jean en Vallée.

Colleges.	Date.	Founders.
C. de Reims	1409	Guy de Roye, Archbishop of Reims.
C. de Donjon . . .	1412	Olivier de Donjon.
		(Afterwards united with Tréguier.)
C. de Thori . . *ante*	1421	
C. de Kerambert (*or* de		(United to C. de Tréguier.)
Léon) . . *ante*	1421	
C. de Séez	1428	Grégoire l'Anglais, Bishop of Séez.
C. de Rethel . . *ante*	1443	(In that year united to College of Reims.)
C. de Lorris . . *ante*	1444	
C. d'Aubusson . . .	?	
C. de Sainte-Barbe . .	1460	Geoffroy Lenormant, Master of Grammarians at Coll. of Navarre.
C. de Coquerel . . .	1463	Nicolas de Coquerel, B.D., Canon of Amiens.
C. de Boucard . . .	1484	Jean Boucard, Bishop of Avranches.

Hist. Litt. XXIV. 249 speaks of a College as founded by the will of the Countess of Pembroke in 1356 for a Principal and two Scholars, but adds that there is no evidence to show whether the provision ever took effect. Can there be some confusion with the Countess's foundation of Pembroke College, Cambridge? Pending the publication of the volume in the *Chartul. Univ. Paris.* containing the College documents, any list must be looked upon as merely provisional.

§ 6. The place of the University in European History.

Political influence of the University : due to its situation in a great capital.

Alone among the earliest University towns, Paris was a great capital. It occupied indeed more completely the position of a modern capital than any other city of continental Europe. It is hardly too much to say that the descendants of Hugh Capet eventually succeeded in making themselves the real masters of France, just because, when their power was at its lowest, they were still masters of Paris. The political position of Paris gave its University a place in the political and ecclesiastical world which no other University has ever occupied. Its Masters played as important a part in medieval politics as men of the pen or of the tongue could well play in an age which was governed by the sword. The influence of the University in this direction was most strongly felt after the period of her greatest intellectual brilliancy. In the thirteenth century the University was too cosmopolitan a body to concern itself much with French politics. The French King protected foreign clerks, even when he was at war with their country[1]. In the twelfth and thirteenth centuries scholars were, indeed, to a degree which is hardly intelligible in modern times, citizens of the world. Though almost all the greatest Schoolmen from the time of Abelard onwards taught in Paris at one period or other of their lives, hardly one Parisian Scholastic of the very first rank was a Frenchman by birth[2]. Moreover, just at the period at which the University was growing into a great corporation, the influence of the Friars—at the Court of Rome, at the Louvre, and everywhere else—was at its

Period of this influence.

---

[1] See *e. g. Chartul.* T. II. Nos. 718–720.

[2] Bretons of course being excluded. But cf. below, p. 538, n. 3.

zenith. During the first century of its corporate life the University had enough to do to make good its right to an independent existence. An age of Friars succeeded an age of Monks ; and the age of Doctors was not yet come. But just as the Papacy exercised a really more command- ing and certainly a more elevating influence over European affairs in the days of Hildebrand than in the days of the bolder and more arrogant usurpations of Innocent III, and a more powerful influence under Innocent III than in the days of Boniface VIII or of the Avignon Schism, so the intel- lectual ferment of the Schools of Paris was most vigorous, the genius which inspired its teaching most brilliant, its monopoly of the highest education most complete, almost before a University existed at all. The political influence of the University did not begin till the greatest Parisian Schoolmen were in their graves ; while just as its influence, its privileges, and its pretensions rose to their highest point, the period of intellectual decadence set in.

This organized scholastic democracy became politically important in much the same way that the Corporation of London acquired so much political importance under the Stuart Kings of England. Here under the very Palace of a despotic King, in the midst of subjects almost without municipal privileges, and placed under the arbitrary authority of the Royal Provost, was a body of educated men protected by the sanctity of their order against the hand of secular justice, possessing the right of public meeting, of free debate, and of access to the throne. And the tendency of a body so situated to become a great organ of public opinion, a channel through which the Court might address itself to the Nation and the voice of the Nation might reach the Court, was strengthened by the deliberate policy of the House of Valois—with whose accession this tendency became for the first time distinctly visible—the policy of depressing the nobility and con- ciliating the support of the clerical and lawyer classes. *The Uni- versity an organ of public opinion.*

At all public ceremonials, in those great assemblies of Notables which the French Kings from time to time

Chap. VI,
§ 6.
—◆◆—

'The eldest
daughter
of the
King.'

gathered around them, in the Councils of the National Church, and even in the States General, the Universities were fully represented. We find a symbol of this new position of the University in the title 'eldest daughter of the King,' which was first assumed under Charles V. But it was especially in the paralysis of the Royal authority which ensued upon the death of that monarch in 1380 that the University, emboldened by the Royal favour and widely diffused prestige to which it had become accustomed, most conspicuously asserted itself as a factor in the political forces of the age. To enumerate all the instances between 1380 and the reign of Louis XI in which the University played, or attempted to play—for it is needless to say that it met with some rude rebuffs when its presumption was unwelcome to the ruling powers—a political *rôle*, would involve a review of the whole course of French history. An illustration or two must suffice.

More than once during the Burgher-rising under Étienne Marcel, in 1357–1358, the good offices of the University were sought as mediators between the Court with which its real sympathies lay and the rebellious Provost of the Merchants in whose power it for the moment found itself[1]. In 1382, after the suppression of the Maillotin rising against the tyranny of Anjou, the intercession of the University was implored, together with that of the clergy, on behalf of the convicted rebels. The Rector and the Bishop appeared as the representatives of the two bodies, and pre-audience was given to the 'Orator' of the University. An amnesty was granted to all but the ringleaders[2]. In 1418, when Rouen was besieged by the English and on the point of surrender, the hard-pressed citizens implored the assistance of the University

---

[1] Bulæus, IV. 344. Jourdain in his Article, *L'Univ. de P. à l'époque de la domination anglaise* (*Excursions Historiques*, pp. 339–361) collects other evidence as to the part played by the University at this crisis, and shows that historians are mistaken in attributing to the University an active sympathy with Étienne Marcel.

[2] Bulæus, IV. 585, 586: *Chartul.* T. III, No. 1465 *et not.*

as the one body in all France whose intercession might move their Sovereign to come to their relief[1]. As a rule, of course, the sympathies of the University were with the powers that be, with the nobles and the prelates rather than with the burghers or the peasants, but it must not be supposed that the attitude of the University towards the throne was one of unvarying sycophancy. Medieval Paris was not Royalist after the fashion of seventeenth century Oxford. There were many occasions when the University united with the citizens of the capital in deputations to the Sovereign, and on such occasions its views on the conduct of affairs were expressed with a freedom which frequently excites the unfeigned amazement of Crevier, the courtly academic historian of the age of Louis XV[2].

During the dismal period of conflict between the Armagnac and Burgundian factions, it is commonly alleged that the sympathies of the University were on the Burgundian side. This, to say the very least, has been much too absolutely stated[3]. In the first place, when the sympathies of 'the clergy' are set down as Burgundian, too little account is taken of the never-dying antagonism between the secular clergy and the Regulars. The strength of the Burgundian party lay in the support of the populace of Paris and of the Mendicant Orders[4]: the University

The University exclusively Burgundian.

[1] Bulæus, V. 334.

[2] See the Oration of Jean Courtecuisse, ap. Bulæum, V. 83–93, wrongly referred by Bulæus to 1403. It was really delivered on the occasion mentioned below in 1413. See Coville, *L'Ordonnance Cabochienne*, Paris, 1891, p. iv. For other instances, cf. Lea, *Hist. of the Inquisition in the Middle Ages,* II. p. 135 *sq.* Mr. Lea is, however, mistaken in supposing that the University ever possessed or claimed *for itself* the power of excommunication.

[3] An exception must be made as to the Nation of Picardy, which

was largely composed of the Duke of Burgundy's subjects.

[4] *Censures et Conclusions de la Faculté de Théologie touchant le souveraineté des rois*, Paris, 1720, pp. 247 *sq.*: Gerson, *Opera* (Parisiis, 1606), I. cc. 396 *sq.*, 409 *sq.* : Bulæus, V. p. 257 *sq.* Bishop Creighton, if I may venture to criticise the admirable account of this period in his *History of the Papacy during the period of the Reformation*, London, 1882, I. 372 *sq.* seems to me not to have quite appreciated this element in the party divisions of the time. The advocate of Petit's propositions at Constance

would therefore be inclined to the Orleanist party by the tie of common enmities. The great democratic rising of the Cabochiens in 1413 is known to have been largely inspired or at least aided by the Carmelites, whose convent lay in the butchers' quarter—the head-quarters of the Burgundians. In the Carmelite Doctor Jean de Pavilly the rioters found their mouth-piece. Then it is forgotten that in the University as outside it public opinion was liable to fluctuations. Private individuals were not committed irrevocably to one or the other side, nor were they in all cases prepared to follow the party which they favoured to all lengths. The great crises at which we find the University as a body unmistakably identifying itself with the Burgundian cause occur at moments when the outrageous misgovernment of the Orleanist Princes had driven even the most conservative classes of Paris and of France generally into the arms of the Burgundian faction. This was eminently the case on the occasion of the Cabochien rising. It is true that the University as a corporation backed up the Cabochien demands, and that prominent seculars had a share in the compilation of the famous 'Ordonnances': it does not follow that the University must be looked upon as an assembly of Burgundian partisans. In the very year in which the Ordonnance Cabochienne was published, the theological Faculty, by a large majority, condemned the work of Jean Petit, the Franciscan apologist of the murder

---

defended them 'authoritate Menticantium qui subscripserant illarum veritati' (Bulæus, V. 284): while Gerson declared 'non esse cum eis duos Magistros in Theologia seculares; vel si veniant ad ternarium, totum est' (*ib.* p. 289). Cf. Launoi, *Reg. Navar. Gymn. Hist.* I. 126: Dubarle (1829), I. p. 238 *sq.* Ample materials for the study of the subject are now provided by the very careful study of M. Coville, *Les Cabochiens et l'Ordonnance de 1413,* Paris, 1888, to whom the reader may refer for references to the original authorities. M. Coville has also edited the Ordonnance itself (*L'Ordonnance Cabochienne,* Paris, 1891). Bulæus systematically represents the University as throughout Orleanist and anti-English. (Cf. also *Hist. Litt.* XXIV. p. 60.) This may be an exaggeration on the other side, but it is evident to me that the Burgundian sympathies of the University, even in the earlier part of the conflict, have been greatly overstated.

of the Duke of Orleans, and their judgment was embodied in a formal sentence against the book (its author was now dead) by the Bishop and Inquisitor[1]. At Constance the University exerted itself to procure the condemnation of Petit; but not all the influence of Gerson or of the University of Paris in the height of its power could extract from the Council, which exhibited in so practical a manner its zeal against heresy any proof of its sincerity in condemnation of political assassination[2]. The influence of the Duke of Burgundy and his partisans was strong enough to prevent the Council coming to a definite decision on the matter. It even imposed silence on both parties to the controversy for a period of forty years, and reversed the decision of the Bishop of Paris in so far as the personal honour of the Duke was concerned[3]. The strength of the feeling against Petit at Paris may be measured by the unusual form of manifesto adopted on the occasion; the condemnation was subscribed not only by Doctors, but by the Bachelors of the Theological Faculty to the number (in all) of 141[4]. Nor is there any evidence that, even on occasions when the University sided with the Burgundians, there was anything like unanimity in its ranks. Every party had its representatives among the Masters of Paris: every faction-leader among the Princes and the nobles naturally sought for his tools among the educated clergy. Moreover, it must be remembered that not every formal decision of the University Congregation represents the real opinion of its members. By the fifteenth century the approbation of the University had come to be considered essential to the party in power at any important political crisis; and consequently had to be forcibly extorted when it was not freely forthcoming. Thus in 1418 the Bur-

---

[1] Petit's *Justificatio Ducis Burgundiæ super Cæde Ducis Aurelianensis* is printed in Gerson, *Opera*, Antwerpiæ, 1706, Tom. V. p. 15 *sq.*, where it is followed by the proceedings against Petit in the University and Council of Constance *in extenso*.

[2] Gerson, *Opera*, V. cc. 601, 602.

[3] See the letters of the University in Bulæus, V. Von der Hardt, T. IV. and Gerson, Tom. V. *passim*.

[4] Bulæus, V. p. 294. But cf. Jourdain, Nos. 1078, 1135.

gundian triumph was followed by the arrest or proscription of many leading Masters, while the College of Navarre was pillaged by the Burgundian mob[1]. What was left of the University revoked the edicts against the Duke of Burgundy and Petit, in a document which alleges that they had only been obtained by force and by the whole-sale imprisonment of opponents. There may of course be truth in the allegations of violence on both sides : at all events the facts are quite inconsistent with the idea that the University was unanimous in the matter[2]. So again in 1430, during the English occupation, while the majority of the Masters fled (many of them to Poitiers, where a new University was called into existence to receive them), those who continued teaching in Paris were com-pelled to assent to the infamous proceedings against the Maid of Orleans[3]. On the whole it must be pronounced exceedingly doubtful whether—putting aside the Mendi-cants and the Picard Nation which was largely composed of the Duke of Burgundy's subjects—there is sufficient evidence for attributing to any large majority of the University a strong and definite Burgundian partisanship.

Unique
position of
Paris.
　　　It is its political and ecclesiastical importance as a great corporation that places Paris in a unique position among the Universities of the Middle Ages. Many of the early

---

[1] Rel. de S. Denys, VI. 234.

[2] Bulæus, V. pp. 331, 332, 334. It is alleged that when the Norman Nation attempted to mediate between the parties its Proctor was im-prisoned, and many Principals of Halls 'proscribed.' But it was, it would seem, only the Picard Nation who actually voted against the condemnation, which seems to imply that in the other Nations and Faculties the majority was in favour of it.

[3] Documents in Quicherat, *Procès de Jeanne d'Arc*, Paris, 1841. I. pp. 8 *sq.*, 17, 411 *sq.*: Bulæus, V. p. 395 *sq.* Considerable fees were

paid by the English king to the Parisian Doctors who assisted at the trial (*ib.* V. p. 197 *sq.*). Neither Mr. Lea (*Hist. of Inquisition*, III. p. 357 *sq.*) nor Ch. Jourdain (*Excur-sions Historiques*, p. 311) seems to recognise that 'the University of Paris' was composed of different persons at different times. Not only were the opponents of the dominant portion liable to be silenced, but in 1436, after the expulsion of the English, we read that ' Natio Gall. decrevit ut e libris seu Actis suis eraderentur eorum nomina qui reg-nante Anglo per vim inscripti fuerant.' Bulæus, V. p. 439.

Jurists of Bologna were individually prominent politicians; and at a later time great weight was often attached to the opinion of the College of Doctors on points of Canon or Public Law. But the Doctors were not a numerous body, and the Universities proper were Universities of students. The exclusion of citizens of the towns in which the Italian Universities were situated prevented the exertion of political influence by the Universities as corporations. The strength of Paris lay first in its situation within the walls of the French capital, and secondly in an organization by which the weight attaching to the judgment of the greatest School of Theology in Europe was backed by the weight of numbers—by its hundreds of Masters of Arts and its thousands of students. The importance of the first of these causes is well illustrated by the contrast which the influence of Paris presents to the political insignificance of the English Universities [1]: that of the second by the contrast in this respect with Bologna.

The influence of Paris, considerable in secular and domestic affairs, was naturally greatest in the sphere of ecclesiastical politics. General councils were extraordinary remedies for extraordinary evils. Even National Councils met but rarely, and then not without the 'commandment and will of princes.' When no Council was sitting, the University of Paris was able to act as a sort of standing Committee of the French, or even of the Universal, Church.

Ecclesiastical influence.

That it was able so to act, and to act with effect, is a proof of the revolution which had taken place since the thirteenth century in the relations between the Church and the Schools. We have seen with what suspicion the disputations of the Parisian Schools were watched by the ecclesiastical authorities after the first great outburst of Averroistic speculation. For a moment it looked almost as if the revolt of the human mind against the intellectual despotism of the Church had come already. Ere long,

'The first School of the Church.'

---

[1] It is true that at such a crisis as the Barons' War the students of Oxford might take a side. What I have said applies to corporate and official influence.

however, persecution, bribery (in the shape of patronage), the natural tendency of any unusual stimulation of intellectual activity to wear itself out, and above all the genius of the great orthodox Schoolmen prevailed over a purely speculative movement rarely backed by much moral or religious earnestness, and almost entirely unconnected with the main currents of intellectual and religious life in the nation at large. The new Scholastic Theology triumphed alike over the sceptics and over the mystical reactionaries : and Paris became 'the first School of the Church'—the theological arbiter of Europe. However much the theological dictatorship assumed by the University may have blasted the fair prospects of the twelfth century 'illumination,' it is by means of this theological dictatorship that Paris conferred on France—and indeed on all northern Europe— one of the most memorable services which she rendered to the cause of enlightenment, of civilization, and of humanity. It was largely to the influence of the University that northern France owed her comparative immunity from the ravages of the Holy Inquisition [1]. The Inquisition was, indeed, in existence at Paris, but it was never very powerful: its work was largely done for it in far milder fashion by the University. In that age a theological dictatorship of some kind was inevitable. It was something that such a dictatorship should be vested in a large and popularly constituted body of secular Theologians, eminently amenable to the influences of public opinion and always favourable within certain limits to free discussion and theological ingenuity, and without motive for unnecessary or malignant persecution. Paris—and in a measure that Northern world of which Paris was the centre—suffered little from the most cunning instrument that has ever been devised for the suppression of religious and intellectual life and for the gratification not merely of theological passion but of personal

---

[1] This is well pointed out by Mr. Lea, *History of the Inquisition in the Middle Ages* (1888). I must take the opportunity of expressing my profound admiration (in spite of occasional lapses in matters of ecclesiastical technicality) for this truly learned and valuable work.

malice, of unhallowed greed and of that terrible blood-lust Chap. VI, which sometimes gets possession of the human soul under § 6. the guise of religious zeal.

In matters of ecclesiastical polity and discipline, indeed, Its Theo-the Mendicants were often too strong for the University: logical Dictator-she could only keep alive a kind of constitutional opposi- ship. tion against the dominant impulse towards autocracy and centralization. But in matters of pure Theology the conflicting tendencies of the great Mendicant Orders neutralized the influence which they might have had if united. There it was left to the Theological Faculty of Paris to hold the balance between them, and on such questions her will was almost supreme. Again and again Paris led the way and Rome followed [1]. In the main it was no doubt the Theology of the great Dominican Doctor S. Thomas which became the accredited Theology of the Church. In one matter, however, Franciscan teaching was too completely in harmony with the tendencies of popular Religionism to be extinguished beneath the inquisitorial frown of the Dominican. In the The Im-great controversy on the doctrine of the Immaculate Con- maculate Concep-ception which began to rage during the latter part of the tion. fourteenth century, Paris declared herself against that absolute negation of the popular opinion on which the conservative Dominicans insisted (1387)[2]. In this as in similar cases we find the Faculty of Theology taking upon itself the theological police of the Church[3]. For once, the In-

---

[1] Thus a controversialist of the Conciliar epoch says 'dum inde trahitur causa fidei per appellationem ad Curiam Romanam, solet remitti ad Universitatem Parisiensem, sicut visum est pluries temporibus nostris' (Launoi, *De Scholis celebrioribus*, p. 231). And Gerson goes further, ' Nec Papa nec Doctores Juris Canonici, si non sint Theologi, circa ea quæ sunt fidei, aliquid canonice discutiunt, vel authentice determinant sine Theologorum doctrinali determinatione prævia, cum Papa in hæresum condemnatione

consueverit reddere Theologicam rationem' (Bulæus, IV. 900). Cf. also a passage in the Edict of Charles VI against the doctrines of Jean Petit: ' Cognovit etiam ipsa quandoque Romana sedes, dum olim et nuper, si quid apud eos ambiguum in doctrina Christianæ Religionis obtigerat, certitudinem ab ipso consilio fidei Parisius causa existente postulare, nec puduit, nec piguit' (*ib.* V. p. 259).

[2] Bulæus, IV. 618 *sq.*; d'Argentré, *Coll. Judic.* I. ii. 61 *sq.*

[3] On this same occasion the following position which had been

quisitor as a Dominican sympathized with the accused, but the Faculty proceeded against John de Monson, the Friar who had taken the lead in the recent preachings against the rising Mariolatry[1], before the Bishop and procured his condemnation. An appeal to Avignon, where the University was represented by Peter d'Ailly, went against the Dominican Doctor[2]; he was excommunicated, fled to his native Aragon, and afterwards found protection with the rival Pontiff. His brethren refused to subscribe the judgment of the Faculty and were expelled the University. For sixteen years the Black Friars as a body clung to their unpopular orthodoxy, and during that time something like a persecution raged against them throughout the length and breadth of France[3]. But at last, in 1403, as was the wont sooner or later of beaten theological parties in the Middle Ages, they surrendered, and their Doctors were re-admitted by the University. Their recantation was conducted with every circumstance of ignominious publicity; the Order was degraded to the lowest place in University processions, and the triumph of the University was enhanced by the fact that the King's Confessor and a Dominican Bishop were among the penitents[4]. Opinion at Paris soon abandoned the merely negative attitude which it hitherto professed to take, and insisted upon positive adhesion to the doctrine of the Immaculate Conception. Less than a century afterwards, three centuries and a half before the Immaculate Conception became a dogma of the Roman Catholic

maintained by a Dominican, was condemned: 'Asserere aliquod verum quod est contra sacram scripturam est expressissime contra fidem.' It was condemned 'tanquam falsa et injuriosa Sanctis et Doctoribus si eam intelligit universaliter' (Bulæus, IV. 620). This is a good illustration of the conservative character of Dominican orthodoxy.

[1] One of the Dominican Doctors had declared in a Sermon that to hold that the Virgin was not conceived in original sin was a heresy and mortal sin, adding 'en volés-vous faire une Deesse?' (Bulæus, IV. 644).

[2] Bulæus, IV. p. 623 *sq.*, 627 *sq.* Rel. de S. Denys, I. 490 *sq.*, 512 *sq.*, 576 *sq.*

[3] Bulæus, IV. p. 619. Gerson in urging their readmission speaks of the 'vexationes, opprobria, et carceres ab illis quos loquimur perlatas.'

[4] Bulæus, V. pp. 82, 83. Individual submissions occur earlier. Many new documents are now printed in *Chartul.* T. III. N. 1557 *sq.*

Church, an oath to defend it was exacted from all candidates for theological degrees at Paris [1].

More often it was against extreme developments of Franciscan tendencies that the University was called upon to defend the dominant Creed of the Church. We have seen how the Theologians of Paris compelled Alexander IV to condemn the Franciscan ' Everlasting Gospel [2].' But the leaven of Joachimism went on working in the Franciscan body: and it was necessary for the University to procure from John XXII the condemnation as a heresy of the doctrine of the absolute poverty of our Lord and his Apostles—a measure which drove the extreme party among the Franciscans into open schism, into the avowed advocacy of the most violently anti-papal and anti-hier-archical, though not anti-sacerdotal, Theology—a Theo-logy (if the chaotic body of ideas which emanated from the Franciscan interpretation of the dreams of Joachim deserve that name) which, in spite of all suppressions, went on working like a mighty undercurrent beneath the smooth surface of medieval orthodoxy, occasionally coming to the surface in the teaching of the Fraticelli, the Beghards, and Beguines, the Brethren of the Free Spirit, and the like [3].

It required but little pressure to procure the condemna-
tion of the ultra-Franciscan dreams of universal brotherhood and a pauper clergy from the monarch of that Babylon against which much of the prophetic wrath of the visionaries had been launched. A more striking instance of the power of the University to force the hand of the supreme Pontiff is afforded by the fate of the curious Franciscan doctrine [4]

[1] In 1497. Bulæus, V. p. 815. Again the controversy was aroused by the preaching of a Dominican.

[2] See above, vol. I. p. 382 *sq.*

[3] As to the relations between the earlier Spiritual Franciscans and the Fraticelli—i. e. the rebels against John XXII's condemnation of the doctrine of the absolute poverty of Christ—the reader may be referred to the important researches of Ehrle in the *Archiv für Litt.- u. Kirchengesch. des Mittelalt.* B. III., IV. Cf. Lea, *Hist. of Inquis.* III. pp. 1–180.

[4] It is interesting to find the usual state of things reversed by the im-prisonment of a Dominican, Thomas Walleis or 'Anglicus,' by Franciscan Inquisitors at Avignon. The Pope alleges that he was imprisoned for

of the 'retardation of the heavenly vision.' The popular view was that the Saints and all who had no need of purgatorial purification, passed at once—without waiting (like ordinary souls) for the day of judgment—into the full enjoyment of the beatific vision of the Blessed Trinity, a doctrine which was supposed to have incurred the peculiar displeasure of the reigning Pontiff, John XXII. The Pope himself originated the controversy by attacking the received opinion in a sermon at Avignon. From Avignon the controversy passed to Paris. The Franciscan General, Gerald Otho, excited the popular indignation by preaching a doctrine which appeared derogatory to the honour due to the saints; while he moved the wrath of the Theologians of Paris by calling in question the view for which their Faculty had (by implication) pronounced as long ago as 1241[1]. The General was believed to have been sent to Paris for the express purpose of inculcating the theological crotchet of this cruel and avaricious Pontiff. The question was debated with so much fury as to call for the interference of the civil government. In 133⅔ Philip of Valois summoned the theological Faculty to Vincennes, and called upon them to settle the matter among themselves once for all, one way or the other[2]. The Faculty reaffirmed the judgment of their predecessors, and thirty Doctors signed the condemnation of the retardation theory, which the King despatched to Avignon with the peremptory request that the Pope would endorse their decision, and punish those who dared to maintain the contrary[3]. The Doctors of Paris, he told his Holiness, knew what ought to be believed in matters of faith

---

[1] It had condemned the proposition 'Quod anime glorificate non sunt in celo empireo cum angelis, nec corpora glorificata erunt ibi, sed in celo aqueo vel crystallino quod supra firmamentum est, quod et de beata Virgine presumitur.' *Chartul.*T.I. pt. i. No. 128.

other heresies, but it was generally believed that his denial of the Papal tenet was his real offence. *Chartul.* T. II. No. 973 *sq.*

[2] Peter d'Ailly boasted at Constance that the King had caused an intimation to be made to the Pope 'qu'il se revoquast, ou qu'il le feroit ordre.' (Bulæus, V. p. 238.)

[3] Bulæus, IV. pp. 235–238. A number of additional documents relating to the affair are now published in *Chartularium,* T. II. Nos. 970-987.

much better than the lawyers and other clerks about the Pope, who knew little or no Theology. The reply of John XXII is as humble and apologetic as if he were a young student at Paris in danger of losing his Bachelor's degree for heresy. He apologizes for venturing to express an opinion upon a theological question when he was not a Doctor of Divinity [1], denies that the Franciscan General's utterances were inspired by him, and declares that he had in his sermon only explained the two views taken on the subject by different Fathers without positively committing himself to either side of the question. He refused, however, to condemn the opinion to which he personally leaned. But in the following year it is said that, being on his death-bed, he published an express recantation of all that he might have said in favour of the Retardation hypothesis [2]. This document, however, was not published till the accession of his successor, who pronounced decidedly against his predecessor's view, and is of somewhat doubtful authenticity. The combination of King and University against John XXII already seems like a shadow of the coming events which culminated in the deposition of John XXIII at Constance. It is a significant indication of the change which had taken place in the mutual relations of the University and the Holy See that John's successor, Benedict XII, a D.D. of the Cistercian College at Paris, began the

---

[1] 'Et quia, fili dilectissime, forsan tibi dicitur, quod nos non sumus in theologia magister, audi quid unus sapiens dicat: "Non quis, inquit, sed quid dicat, intendite."' *Chartul.* T. II. No. 978.

[2] The retreat is a little masked by the position that the 'anime purgate separate a corporibus sunt in celo... et vident Deum ... ac divinam essentiam facie ad faciem clare in quantum status et conditio compatitur anime separate'; but the document proceeds, 'si qua alia sermocinando, conferendo, *dogmatizando*, *docendo* seu alio quovis modo diximus

. . . in quantum essent a premissis fide catholica, determinatione ecclesie, sacra Scriptura vel bonis moribus aut aliquo ipsorum dissonantia, reprobamus' (*Chartul.* T. II. No. 987). The genuineness of the document has been denied, and the older printed copies represent the interpolated edition in Benedict XII's Register. The existence of such copies is an argument for the genuineness (which is defended by Denifle) of the original in John XXII's Register, though it is admitted not to have been sealed till after his death.

custom of officially notifying his election to the University, which was thus recognized as one of the great powers of Europe [1].

The University a champion of the secular clergy.

Divided in matters of speculative Theology, the Mendicant Orders were (as has been said) equally obnoxious to the secular clergy by reason of those exemptions and privileges which carried confusion into the discipline of every diocese and parish in the Kingdom. In the long struggle of the prelates and parochial clergy against the Papal Bulls enabling the Mendicants to hear confessions, to preach, and to give burial without the consent of Diocesan or Curate, the University formed the rallying-point for the opposition of the Seculars. The Bishops and Curates of the future naturally sympathised with the Bishops and Curates of the present. It was, as has been suggested elsewhere, the support given to the Mendicants by the Papacy in their quarrel with the University which for the first time brought the Masters of Paris into antagonism with the authority to which they owed a large part of their own privileges—nay, their legal existence—as much as the religious Orders themselves. It was, indeed, the continual growth of Mendicant pretensions, together with the steadily increasing drain upon the revenues of French benefices involved in the Papal system of Annats, Provisions, Expectatives, Tenths, and the like, which produced between the age of S. Louis and the close of the fifteenth century a complete revolution in the attitude of the Gallican Church towards the See of S. Peter.

The Rotulus Beneficiandorum.

We have seen, in the affair of the Heavenly Vision, how completely all reverence for the theological judgment of the Pope had vanished from the minds of the Parisian Theologians. But the opposition of the University to those ecclesiastical usurpations of the Papacy which went on increasing in exact porportion to the decline in its political power was long bought off by an ingenious system of patronage. When the seat of the Papacy was transferred to Avignon, its moral prestige was destroyed, but the French

[1] Bulæus, IV. p. 242.

Universities were allowed to profit by its abuses. The
Papal power of 'provision' was largely exercised in favour
of Parisian graduates by John XXII, and on the accession
of Clement VI (if not before) the custom began of sending
to the Papal Court a *rotulus nominandorum* or roll containing the names of graduates to whom the Pope was
invited to give provisions or expectative graces to benefices
in ecclesiastical collation. The roll eventually became
an annual affair[1]. The names of the applicants were
placed on the roll in order of seniority, but with a preference for Regents over Non-Regents and for residents
over non-residents[2]. A special petition was presented on

---

[1] It is disputed whether the custom began under John XXII or
under Clement VI. See the dissertation in Bulæus, IV. 901. In
1322 we find Oxford petitioning
John XXII that he would bestow
on Oxford graduates the same
favours which had been conferred
upon 'doctores tam philosophos
quam theologos' at Paris. (*Chartul.*
T. II. No.818), and there is a general
injunction to prelates to promote
graduates (*ib.* No. 729); but the
first actual benefice-roll sent by the
University belongs to the Pontificate
of Clement VI. (*Chartul.* T. II. No.
1062 *et not.*) Several Oxford rolls
sent to Clement VI are among the
Roman transcripts sent to the Public
Record Office by Mr. Bliss.

[2] Of the petitions prefixed to the
roll specimens are given in Bulæus
(IV. pp. 901-911 and V. pp. 366-373).
It seems that every name sent in
was placed upon the roll, the only
duty of the Deputies being to determine the precedence due to the
applicant and that the order of precedence determined who should have
the benefice when more than one
had applied for it. This was certainly the plan followed in drawing
up a Roll to be sent to the French
Bishops in 1421, when 'voluit Natio

(Gallicana) quod quilibet Magister
offerret suam supplicationem Procuratori Nationis et eas Procurator
in uno Rotulo scriberet.' (Bulæus,
V. 349.) A usual request in these
Rolls (e. g. 1424) is the petition that
every Master whose name is inscribed
therein may have the power of
choosing a Confessor 'qui possit eos
et eorum singulos absolvere ab omnibus peccatis suis et etiam plenam
indulgentiam saltem semel in mortis
articulo eisdem concedere' (*ib.* p.
370). Another clause of the earlier
roll of 1414 is interesting as an indication of the number of Gram-
mar-schools throughout the country
(Bulæus, IV. 909) : —

'Item cum in nonnullis partibus
iam inoleuerit consuetudo, imo potius abusus intolerabilis, quod scholæ
magis danti licet tamen ignoranti
distribuantur, vel potius vendantur in
graue Doctorum, Doctrinæ, Juuenum
et Reipub. et totius Ecclesiasticæ po-
liticæ (*sic*) detrimentum, dignetur S.V.
tale remedium apponere quod amplius non ita distribuantur, sed pauperibus Magistris scientificis mere
gratis conferantur.' It is clear that
this cannot refer to the Schools of
the University, which were entirely
under the authority of the Masters
themselves.

behalf of the Rector for the time being[1]. A deputation of
Masters was appointed to carry the roll to the Papal
Court, and to occupy themselves for two months amidst
the swarm of greedy and simoniacal benefice-hunters in
pressing the claims of the absent Masters on the Pope and
Cardinals. That these claims should really have been
attended to is no small evidence of the extraordinary influence which the University had acquired[2]. From the
complaints which began to be made immediately after the
withdrawal of obedience[3], it is evident that the most
corrupt Popes were much better patrons of learning than

---

[1] At first the exact amount and
nature of the Papal benevolence was
left to the donor: but later rolls
often specify the patron to whose
benefices they aspired or the Church
in which they wanted a prebend.
Sometimes even at Paris the roll
includes non-graduate students
(*Chartul.* T. III. No. 1378), and this
was habitually the case in the
Student Universities. Thus in a roll
from Florence in 1404 we find the
Scholars asking for ' one, two, three
or more benefices,' in one or more
specified dioceses up to a certain
value, which varies in different
cases. Thus the Rector specified
300 florins as the goal of his ambition, though he already enjoyed
a prebend and parochial cure which
brought in between them some 120
florins. The most modest limit their
expectations to 150 florins. (*Stat.
Fiorent.* p. 383.)

[2] I have not come across any
distinct evidence as to any feeing or
bidding practised by the Masters.
At all events, it is clear that they
must have been preferred to much
higher bidders.

[3] Among other indications of this
feeling we find the University in
1399 decreeing a cessation of Lectures, which lasted till Lent, because
a Royal edict had restored the col-

lation of benefices to the Ordinaries
(Bulæus, IV. 884 ; Rel. de S. Denys,
II. p. 746). So in 1411, when a
discussion arose as to whether a
roll should be sent to John XXII,
the majority determined in favour
of the proposal 'aientes Pontificum
Gratias et favores certiores esse quam
Prælatorum : quippe Universitatem
experientia propria didicisse, spretis
suis suppositis, Episcopos aliosque
Beneficiorum Collatores et Patronos
conferre solitos famulis suis et illiteratis hominibus' (Bulæus, V. 221.
Cf. also *ib.* pp. 186–188). After the
deposition of John XXII, in 1417, a
Royal Ordinance again restored the
collation to the Ordinaries ; when the
University appealed to the Pope.
The Rector and deputies of the University were summoned before the
Parlement to answer for their conduct, and were, by the orders of the
Dauphin, who was present, arrested
for high treason ; they were only released on abandoning the appeal
(Bulæus, V. p. 307 *sq.*; Pasquier, *Recherches de la France*, 1596, L. III.
chap. 20. f. 152 *b, sq.*). And this from
the University which was the great
champion of the rights of the Gallican
Church against Curialist usurpations :
and which had just succeeded in
getting a Pope deposed by a
Council !

the Gallican Bishops. The Bishops had between them more
nephews and dependents than the Pope, and fewer personal
or political ends to serve by the promotion of able men
and the propitiation of the most powerful corporation
in the Gallican Church. That the *carrière ouverte aux
talens* should have been secured by the system of Provisions is a striking illustration of the indirect utilities which
were often bound up with the most indefensible and most
corruptly intended of Papal usurpations.

The Schism made the Avignon Popes more than ever
dependent upon the support of the King and Church of
France. On the arrival of the news of Clement VII's
election, much difference of opinion was expressed among
the Doctors of Paris. A paper warfare immediately broke
out between the partisans of the rival Pontiffs. Sufficient
indications of the existence of an Urbanist party were given
to elicit from the Roman Pope a letter of warm thanks
to the University for not having joined the schismatics [1].
The academic body seems at once to have appreciated
the importance of the position in which it was placed by the
Schism. It resolved to petition the Court, which had very
decidedly taken the side of the Avignon claimant, not to
insist upon a hasty conclusion. It determined, moreover,
as if with the express view of lengthening the period of its
neutrality and adding to the weight of its eventual judgment,
that the Rector should not 'conclude' for either side without
the unanimous vote of all the Faculties and Nations [2]. The
proposal to adhere to Clement VII encountered strenuous
opposition from the two Nations, Picardy and England, which
were chiefly composed of the subjects of Urbanist Sovereigns.
In spite of the eagerness of the Court, whose policy
required a close alliance between France and Avignon,
more than six months elapsed before a very peremptory

---

[1] Bulæus (IV. 565) says, 'Universitas quandiu non est de Urbani
electione dubitatum, *ei quoque ad-
hæsit;* deinde ut dubitari cœpit, nec
statim ei adhærere destitit.' But this
was before the election of Clement.
Cf. *Chartul.* T. III. Nos. 1605–
1616.

[2] Bulæus, IV. 565. *Chartul.* T. III.
No. 1616.

CHAP. VI.
§ 6.

letter from the King compelled the University to declare by a majority consisting of the three superior Faculties with the Nations of France and Normandy, in favour of Clement VII[1]. And it was not till September or October, 1379 that the University, as a whole, committed itself to the Clementine faction so far as to send a roll of petitioners for benefices to Avignon[2].

Growth of Anti-Papal feeling.

But, in spite of this forced adhesion, there can be no doubt that there was a strong feeling in the University against the Avignon Cardinals and their nominees, and that this feeling deepened enormously the growing indignation against the now doubly onerous exactions of the Papal Court. As the Schism went on, this indignation found ever louder expression in the discussions of the Parisian Schools and the writings of Parisian Doctors. In accordance with the traditional policy of the French Kings towards the foreign students in their capital, the scruples of the foreign students were respected. The English Nation eventually consented to send a roll to Clement, but till the year 1382 it continued in its corporate capacity neutral, while its members were allowed as individuals to acknowledge and send rolls to Urban VI[3]. After that date it adopted a wavering and uncertain attitude. The existence of this Urbanist minority within the University itself must have had an important influence in keeping the existence of the Schism and its attendant evils con-

[1] *Chartul.* T. III. Nos. 1616-1627. In accordance with the previous resolution, or because the Rector was a German, there was no technical ' conclusion,' but the King was informed that what was done by the three Faculties and two Nations was considered the act of the University.

[2] The King declared his adherence to Clement VII on Nov. 16th, 1378. The declaration of temporary neutrality by the University was voted Jan. 8, 137⅞ (*Chartul.* T. III. No.

1616): the adhesion to Clement VII was handed in to the King at Vincennes on May 30, 1379 (Nos. 1427, 1627). The Nation of France and some members of the Faculty of Medicine had already sent a roll to Clement VII (*ib.* No. 1622). Denifle points out that the revulsion of feeling in the University against Clement was due to his consent to the King's imposition of a tax upon the clergy, including the University (*ib.* No. 1636). Cf. below, p. 557 *note.*

[3] Bulæus, IV. 591 592, V. 65.

stantly before the minds of the Parisian Theologians, and in
stimulating discussion as to the best means of terminating it.

The Schism, indeed, by the reaction which it induced
against the intolerable scandals and abuses of the ecclesiastical system in which men had hitherto tacitly acquiesced,
exercised a stimulating effect upon the intellectual, if not
upon the educational, life of the University. We have seen
how, with the complete enslavement of the academic mind
to the dogmatic system, the freshness and vigour of its intellectual life began to decline ; and in the first half of the fourteenth century, though the privileges and apparent splendour
of the University never stood higher, this decline appears to
have been very rapid indeed. Throughout the fourteenth
century, Oxford, not Paris, was the head-quarters of Scholastic activity. Richard of Bury[1], for instance, an Oxford
man, it is true, but one who speaks with the utmost enthusiasm of his earlier visits to Paris, describes in the most
forcible language the utter extinction of intellectual life and
original thought which had taken place there within his own
memory. Its lectures and disputations, he tells us, had
degenerated into sterile logomachies or else into a dull and
unacknowledged reproduction of contemporary English
speculation. Minerva had forsaken Paris as completely as
she had forsaken Egypt and Athens[2]. Towards the
end of the century, however, a marked improvement is
noticeable. Several distinct influences combined to produce
a certain revival of intellectual life. The first of these was
the growth of Nominalism. Nominalism was, no doubt,
one of the Oxford importations which Richard of Bury

---

[1] Or Robert Holcot, if (as seems to be the better opinion) he was the real author of the *Philobiblon*.

[2] 'Isto, pro dolor ! paroxysmo, quem plangimus, Parisiense palla-dium .nostris mæstis temporibus cernimus iam sublatum : ubi tepuit, immo fere friguit zelus scholæ tam nobilis, cuius olim radii lucem dabant universis angulis orbis terræ. Quies-cit ibidem iam calamus omnis scribæ, nec librorum generatio propagatur ulterius, nec est qui incipiat novus auctor haberi. Involvunt sententias sermonibus imperitis et omnis logicæ proprietate privantur, nisi quod Anglicanas subtilitates, quibus pa-lam detrahunt, vigiliis furtivis ad-discunt.' (*Philobiblon*, ed. Thomas, p. 89.)

recognized on his later visits to Paris: and it is always in the English, or, as it was afterwards called, the German, Nation, that we find Nominalism most prevalent[1]. In the rest of the University the Realists were at present in a majority. In 1339 the exposition either in public lectures or 'private conventicles' of the writings of William of Ockham was forbidden[2]; and in 1346 Nicholas de Ultri-curia, who, with a much more brilliant metaphysical genius than Ockham, anticipated the system of Berkeley, was compelled to retract his extremely enlightened errors[3]. But, in spite of all repression, Ockhamism seems to have made way; and, at the beginning of the fifteenth century, many of the leading spirits in the University, notably d'Ailly and Gerson, were avowed Nominalists. Possibly the growing anti-Papal feeling may have helped to procure toleration for the anti-Papal and Imperialist Friar. Thus, for the second time in her history, Nominalism infused new

---

[1] It is significant that the oath 'contra scientiam Okamicam' which appears in the British Museum *Liber Rectoris* is omitted in the English Master's book. *Chartul.* T. II. p. 680.

[2] Bulæus, IV. p. 257. *Chartul.* T. II. No. 1023.

[3] Bulæus, IV. p. 308, *Chartul.* T. II. No. 1124 (only a fragment appears in Bulæus). Antrecourt is in the diocese of Verdun. Among the retracted positions are the follow-ing : 'quod de rebus per apparentia naturalia quasi nulla certitudo potest hab[eri; illa tamen] modica potest in brevi tempore haberi, si homines convertant in[tellectum suu]m ad res, et non ad intellectum Aristotilis et Commentato[ris] . . .' 'Quod de substantia materiali alia ab anima nostra non habemus certitudinem evidentie . . .' 'Quod nescimus evi-denter quod aliqua causa causet efficienter que non sit Deus,' and a number of other propositions tending to the denial of the 'necessary con-nexion' between phenomenal cause and effect. At times his scepticism seems to have been carried further, e. g. in the proposition 'Deus est, Deus non est, penitus idem significant, licet [alio modo].' He also divined that light has velocity, in which he was anticipated by Roger Bacon (*Op. Maj.* ed. Jebb, pp. 248, 300), to whom he is not likely to have been indebted. Some of his views are ascribed by Denifle to the influence of Bradwardine. Nicholas was de-prived of his Mastership in Arts by Papal authority, his books burned in the Pré-aux-clercs, and a solemn recantation took place thereon be-fore the assembled University. It is a notable instance of the success of persecution that the name of this brilliant metaphysical genius is not mentioned in histories of Philosophy or even in works specially devoted to the Scholastic Philosophy.

light and new life into the torpid traditionalism of the
Parisian Schools.

It is interesting to notice that as soon as the impetus imparted to the intellectual activity of Paris by the discussion of the really important questions of ecclesiastical polity and discipline raised by the Schism and the Councils died away, we find Ockhamism again proscribed as a heresy, now not merely by the University, but by the King, who was under the influence of a Realist Confessor, and the Parlement. This association of the rise and fall of Nominalism with the rise and fall of intellectual activity, may be supposed to lend some colour to the theory put forward by the late Mr. Pattison as to the intrinsic connexion between Nominalism and intellectual progress on the one hand and between Realism and religious or political reaction on the other[1]. But if in the annals of medieval

---

[1] Bulæus, V. pp. 678, 679, 706–710, Dubarle, I. p. 310. By the edict of Louis XI, published in 1473, Masters are enjoined to teach the doctrine of Aristotle ' and his Commentator Averroes, Albertus Magnus, Thomas Aquinas, Ægidius Romanus, Alexander of Hales, Scotus, and Bonaventura, and other Realist Doctors,' instead of that of William of Ockham, ' Monachus Cisterciensis,' de Arimino, Buridan, Peter d'Ailly, Marsilius, Adam Dorp, Albert of Saxony, and other ' Nominalists or Terminists.' The teaching of the latter is strictly forbidden under pain of perpetual banishment and other ' arbitrary penalties ' : and all Nominalistic books are to be surrendered to the officers of Parliament and chained up so that they cannot be used. (Bulæus, V. 708, 9.) All Regents were required to swear obedience to the Statute; which they did 'exceptis paucis (Theologis) qui sustinent Nominales qui nihilominus conditionaliter iuraverunt.' The Faculty of Arts, however, protested against the ' Excatenatio ' of the books; and ordered that only one volume should be surrendered from each Library, and at last the king was persuaded to be satisfied with this merely symbolical muzzling of the offensive writers. (Bulæus, V. 711, 712.) The decree was procured by the influence of the King's Confessor, the Bishop of Avranches. It was, however, revoked in 1481, and the imprisoned books restored. (Bulæus, V. 739, 740, 747.) The German Proctor goes into raptures in recording the joy of his nation ' doctrinam illam salubrem, Christianam, Universitatis fulgorem, totiusque machinæ mundi lucernam super candelabrum poni,' &c. (*ib.* p. 740). We find measures spontaneously taken against Nominalism by the University before the edict of 1473 (Bulæus, V. 678, 679), which shows that the majority, then as always, except in the German Nation, were Realists, though no doubt some of the ablest men were on the other side.

Paris the prevalence of Nominalism may to some extent be taken as an index of intellectual vitality, that is simply because opposition to an established Philosophy, whatever be its character, is a sign of intellectual vigour; but the heresy tends to lose its vitality as soon as it becomes an orthodoxy. At Prague we shall find an established Nominalism associated with the narrowest and most intolerant ecclesiasticism, while Realism (though its religious earnestness might have destroyed for some minds its claim to any association with progress) was certainly the creed of some of the ablest men and the most fearless reformers that ever made their appearance in a medieval University. Ockham no doubt possesses an importance in the history of Philosophy which cannot be accorded to John Hus or even to his master Wycliffe, but this importance does not extend to the nominalist opponents of Wycliffe at Oxford or the nominalist burners of Hus at Constance.

The New Classicism.
Moreover, at this time a first faint breath of that Renaissance which was already an accomplished fact in Italy reached the Schools of Paris. We have already noticed the decline of Latin style and the extinction of classical education under the influence of the wider Scholasticism which followed the introduction of the new Aristotle into the Schools of Paris. Now—perhaps through the mere rumour of the new enthusiasm for Cicero and Virgil which was springing up beyond the Alps, but more probably through an independent operation of the same Renaissance spirit [1]—Paris could once again boast, in Nicolas of Clemangis, of a scholar whose style, though of course not critically faultless, bore the classical ring more decidedly than the style of Abelard's Letters or even John of Salisbury's 'Metalogicus [2].' Though Clemangis' scholar-

[1] There is no trace of *direct* contact with Italian Scholarship.

[2] Sismondi appears to attribute the increase of classical study and the growth of a school of classical historians, who took Livy as their model, to the influence of the Colleges. 'Une génération nouvelle commençoit à se former dans les colléges; le nombre de ceux qui étudioient les Classiques, qui admiroient l'antiquité, alloit croissant. La brillante carrière qu'avoient parcourue quelques érudits, à la

ship exerted, so far as appears, very little influence on the ordinary education of the Schools [1], it contributed towards a great improvement in the theological writing of the period. The Wycliffite heresy had aroused in all reflecting men some consciousness of the scandal arising from the prevalence of simony, from the avarice and extortion of the Papal Collectors, and from the flagrant immorality of the clergy; and in men like Clemangis and his more earnest pupil Gerson this consciousness inspired a real desire for reunion and reform. In the presence of such problems, the more earnest minds began to turn away in contempt or disgust from aimless and incessant disputations over the serious questions of a bygone age, and from the increasingly subtle and increasingly frivolous discussions which amused the Schoolmen of the present. Gerson deplores the 'useless speculation without fruit or solidity,' and the increasing subtlety and technicality of the Theologians of the day, whom he goes so far as to call 'verbose and fantastic sophists [2].' In his own treatises he inaugurated a new school of theological writing which occupied itself not with debating in dry logical and syllogistic form the speculative questions of the Schools, but with the discussion in a more popular style and a more practical spirit of the ecclesiastical questions of the day and the principles of Church government upon which their solution was to be based. By the time of Gerson the knell of Scholasticism was already sounded; an age of controversial but literary Theology was setting in.

---

tête desquels il falloit mettre le pape regnant, mettoit les lettres latines en honneur.' (*Hist. des Français*, T. XIII. Paris, 1831, p. 607.)

[1] D'Ailly at the Council of Constance urged the appointment of 'institutores Rhetoricæ et linguarum Græcæ et Latinæ.' (Von der Hardt, I. pt. iv. c. 427.)

[2] Gerson asks: ' Cur non ob aliud appellantur Theologi nostri temporis Sophistæ verbosi, immo et Phan-tastici, nisi quia relictis utilibus et intelligilibus pro auditorum qualitate transferunt se ad nudam Logicam vel Metaphysicam, aut etiam Mathematicam, ubi et quando non oportet, nunc de intensione formarum, nunc de divisione continui, nunc detegentes sophismata theologicis terminis obumbrata.' (*Opera*, Parisiis, 1606, I. c. 502.) He speaks of this evil as specially rife in England. For similar complaints of Clemangis, see Bulæus IV. 889.

Chap. VI,
§ 6.
—◆◆—
Growth of
Gallican-
ism since
the reign
of Philip
IV.

A favourable political situation was, of course, necessary to enable the views of the little group of reforming Gallican Theologians to pass out of the region of speculation into that of action.   But a comparison between the part which the University played at this time with its attitude in an earlier quarrel between France and the Papacy will show the enormous change which a century had effected in the position of the great corporation and in the theological temper of its Masters.   During Philip IV's quarrel with Boniface VIII the University had merely joined, by a majority[1] and with considerable reluctance, in the King's 'subtraction of obedience' and appeal to a General Council, 'and to a future true and legitimate Supreme Pontiff.'   The step was forced on the University as upon the clergy at large by the policy of the King and his lawyer advisers.   The University took no part whatever in leading opinion on the subject.   But at the end of the fifteenth century the views of the University were far in

advance of those of the Court.   The idea of forcing a termination of the Schism on the reluctant Pope of Avignon may be said to have originated in the University, or at all events to have been kept alive only in the University after the death of Charles V.   The Duke of Anjou, the first of the Regents by whom the government was carried on during the unhappy reign of Charles VI, was a Clementine who was anxious to perpetuate the alliance between Avignon and the French crown for the plunder of the French Church.   The first 'Orator' who ventured to appear before the Regent with a resolution of the Uni-

---

[1] 'Nonnullis ex nobis majorem partem Facultatum nostrarum tocius Parisiensis studii facientibus pro certis causis et negociis accedentibus ad presentiam excellentissimi Principis D. Philippi,' &c. (Bulæus, IV. 147, *Chartul.* T. II. No. 634.) We are not told which Faculties dissented: the words might mean a majority in each Faculty.

Bulæus, as usual, asserts that the University took a more promin-
ent part in these proceedings than is warranted by the documents which he produces. The tractate printed in Bulæus, IV. p. 935 *sq.*, cannot be assumed to represent the opinion of the University as a whole. The Doctors who wrote in defence of the King took the ground that Boniface's election was invalid, as his predecessor could not canonically resign. See Denifle's note in *Chartul.* T. II. No. 604.

versity in favour of a General Council—one John Rousse or Ruysche—was the next night dragged from his bed in the Collége Lemoine, and lodged in prison by order of the Regent. He was only released on promising to recognise the claims of Clement: and the Rector was threatened with the same penalty for having received a letter from Urban and read it before the assembled University[1]. Both the Rector and de Rousse eventually took refuge in the Court of Urban VI. The Schism, however, and the method to be adopted in healing it continued to be the one absorbing subject of thought and discussion in academic circles, and gradually the chaotic body of opinion shaped itself into certain definite schemes for its immediate termination; so that, when early in 1394 the University was at length allowed openly to discuss the subject, the question was ripe for settlement[2]. In order to allow of greater freedom in the expression of individual judgment, a novel expedient was adopted. A chest was placed in the Mathurine convent, into which members of the University—even, it would appear, mere students—were invited to place their written opinions[3]. The deputies appointed to examine these papers reported that the expedients recommended fell for the most part under three heads: (1) The way of 'Cession,' or concerted abdication by both Pontiffs; (2) The way of Arbitration; (3) The way of a General Council. A letter, setting forth these three methods, and adding that if the Pope refused to adopt one of them he ought to be held a schismatic, was immediately drawn up in the name of the University by Clemangis, and presented to the King[4]. The presentation of a similar

---

[1] Bulæus, IV. 583; Rel. de S. Denys, I. 86; *Chartul.* T. III. Nos. 1637, 1640.

[2] The University had met with another rebuff in 1390 or 1391. Rel. de S. Denys, I. 692, 694.

[3] 'Cedulas repertas, que decem mille numerum excedebant.' Such is the printed text of the *Chronique du Religieux de Saint-Denys*, ed. Bellaguet (*Docs. inédits sur l'hist.*

de France), T. II. p. 100: but Bulæus (IV. 683) prints ' quæ . . . numerum excedebant': hence it seems possible that the text may have been somehow tampered with by some scribe desirous of illustrating the numbers of the University.

[4] Bulæus, IV. 683, 687; *Chartul.* T. III. Nos. 1678–1686. The order of the method above given expresses the order of preference.

letter to Clement himself, coupled with the news that the College of Cardinals had all but unanimously assented to the action of the University, produced an explosion of wrath which contributed to hasten the end of the unfortunate Pontiff, and so, as it seemed for the moment, to give practical effect to the views of the remonstrants[1]. But the hurried election of Benedict XIII by the Avignon Cardinals speedily dashed to the ground the hopes which began to be entertained of a peaceful solution of the difficulty, and compelled the University to renew its efforts for the extinction of the Schism.

Declares for the Via Cessionis, 1395.
In 1395 the Via Cessionis was definitely adopted as the best of the three methods already laid before the Pope, first by a Council of the National Church, and then by the University[2]. At present the project of a General Council did not find much favour with the academical divines; for, if precedent was to be followed, such a Council would be composed exclusively of Bishops, or at most of Bishops and Abbots, and no theory of conciliar infallibility seems to have blinded French Churchmen to the probability that, if it came to a counting of heads, the Italian 'Bishoplings' would inevitably outnumber the rulers of the larger dioceses of Northern Europe. Moreover, it never seems to have occurred to the strongest Churchmen of that day that episcopal consecration could prove a substitute for theological or legal training; and the Masters of Paris did not relish the prospect of handing over the decision of the momentous question to an assembly which would have been largely composed of uneducated or half-educated men[3]. As soon as this decision taken at Paris became

[1] Bulæus, IV. 699, 703; *Chartul.* T. III. No. 1690; Rel. de S. Denys, II. p. 184.

[2] Bulæus, IV. 729, 732, 747, 773, Rel. de S. Denys, II. 218 *sq.*

[3] Thus, in its first Appeal of the University from Benedict XIII, the writer dwells upon the difficulties involved in the summons of a General Council. There would be no agreement as to where it was to meet, who was to summon it, or who were to sit. A Council composed of Bishops must include 'Episcopellos Italicos Juris ignaros quorum infinitus est numerus, Bellacores (*sic*), Alemannos cæterosque de Mævii promotione puerulos Gallicanos': (Bulæus, IV. pp. 817, 818.) We should read perhaps 'Bellatores Alemannos.'

known, Benedict began to initiate proceedings against CHAP. VI,
§ 6. the members of the University, with a view to deprivation of their benefices ; whereupon the University in 1396 *Appeal* appealed to the 'next sole, true, orthodox, and universal *against* *Benedict* Pope.' The University thus openly declared war against *XIII, 1396.* the Avignon claimant of the Papacy[1].

To record the successive efforts of the University, *The Uni-* first to force a simultaneous resignation upon the rival *versity a* *European* Pontiffs, and then, as experience proved the hopelessness of *power.* bringing about any scheme which required the co-operation of the two—or, after Pisa, three—claimants, to bring about the convocation of a General Council, would lead us further than our limits would allow into the general history of the period. During the twenty years which preceded the meeting of the Council of Constance, the history of Europe centres round the debates of the Parisian Congregations. In the work of preparing for the Reformation of the Church 'in its head and members,' the University played the part of a European potentate. Her ambassadors travelled to all parts of Europe—at one time they are found as far north as Scotland—with despatches or missions to Emperor, Pope, or King, to Princes, Prelates, and Universities, in the hope of establishing a European concert. And that such a concert was ultimately established is due in very large measure to the peculiar and unique prestige of the University, and the excellent use which for once was made of that prestige under the guidance of men like Clemangis and d'Ailly, and later of Gerson and Jean de Courtecuisse. In the main, the subtraction of obedience by the Gallican Church from Benedict XIII in 1398 was *The great* directly the work of the University, while the assembling *Councils* *the work* of the Council of Pisa and more decidedly of the Councils *of the* of Constance[2] and Bâle were results, partly of the actual *University.*

---

[1] Another of the Letters of the University had, however, already suggested that an equal number of Doctors of Theology and Law, should sit with the Prelates, 'quia

plures eorum, proh pudor ! hodie satis illiterati sunt.' *Ib.* IV. 690.

[2] For what follows as to the Council, the most important authorities are Von der Hardt, *Magnum*

diplomacy of the University, and still more largely of the ideas which had gradually shaped themselves into something like a new theory of ecclesiastical polity in the minds and the writings of the Parisian Theologians. Of course there were more powerful political forces working in the same direction, and above all due credit must be given to the determination of the Emperor Sigismund[1]. But the Council of Pisa did not spring out of the discontent of a few Cardinals; nor was the Council of Constance the result of the mere *fiat* of Sovereign Princes. The Councils were emphatically the work of public opinion. But a mere floating mass of unarmed opinion can never become operative unless it finds definite and concentrated expression through recognized organs. At this crisis in the history of Europe the Universities performed the function which is discharged at the present day by the press, by the platform, and even by the polling-booths. Two conditions had to be fulfilled by any body or institution which aspired to constitute itself the mouth-piece which the growing discontent against the protracted Schism demanded. It must be more than a merely national institution, and it must be to some extent an ecclesiastical body.

An international institution. The University of Paris with its four Nations, the common mother of all northern Universities, the recognised fountainhead (as it was constantly styled in official rhetoric) of ' the streams of knowledge' which watered the whole Christian world, could claim something of that international character which medieval theory accorded to the Papacy and the Empire. Never indeed did the University more completely justify the position so often assigned to her by medieval panegyrists as the third of the great powers or organs of the European system—France's equivalent for the Italian Papacy and the German Empire[2]. Now, in the paralysis

---

Œcumenicum Constantiense Concilium, Helmestadt, 1700: L'Enfant, *Histoire du Concile de Constance*, Amsterdam, 1727 (Eng. Trans. London, 1730).

[1] Strictly King of the Romans.

[2] Cf. Budinszky (p. 25), 'Darf es uns nach dem Gesagten Wunder nehmen, wenn der Nimbus, der unsere Universität umgab, sie gera-

of one member of the mysterious triad, it seemed the
natural office of the other two to unite in restoring health
to the disordered European system. And the second
condition of success was no less happily satisfied by the
peculiar relations of the University to the ecclesiastical
system. Its theological Faculty of scarlet-robed Priests, the
clerical status of all and the high ecclesiastical rank of
many of its members sufficiently guarded against the danger of wounding clerical susceptibilities or rousing genuine
scruples in devout minds as to the lawfulness of disregarding
Papal censure and setting up the authority of a General
Council—long considered a mere adviser of the Papacy—
against the Vicar of Christ. In the Middle Ages intellect,
learning, common sense, were not forces strong enough
to demand a hearing in their own right. They had to
clothe themselves with some semblance of sacerdotal
sanctity, and to speak with some tone of spiritual authority
before they could command the reverence of the world.
It is curious to observe the extent to which this mere
semblance of traditional and ecclesiastical authority, which
had gathered about an institution not three centuries old,
succeeded in blinding the clerical mind to the partly secular,
partly Papal origin of the Universities whose voice was
now raised against the system of ecclesiastical government
which had been dominant in Europe at least since the
time of Hildebrand. The hand of secular power which
first attempted to force the rival Pontiffs into abdicating,
and which then compelled John XXIII to convoke a
General Council of Constance, wore a glove of quasi-spiritual
authority. Probably no theory of ecclesiastical polity
that ever was expressly formulated found a place for
Universities in its system of divinely authorised Councils
and Synods, or elevated Doctors as an order of its divinely
commissioned Ministry to the side of Bishops and Presbyters. Yet when the scheme of 'Cession' broke down

dezu als genügende Entschädigung   andern Nationen des Reiches Karls
für Papstthum und Kaiserkrone   des Grossen als Erbtheil zugefallen
auffassen liess, welche den beiden   waren.'

and all thoughts were turned to the plan of a General Council, so subtly had the Universities insinuated themselves into the ecclesiastical system of Western Europe that no serious opposition seems to have been offered to the Parisian suggestion that their representatives must take their seats in the supreme tribunal of the Church beside the older hierarchy of Bishops and Abbots[1].

The University at Constance, 1415.

The most important part which was played by the great University and the other Universities associated in the movement lay in preparing the public mind for the ecclesiastical revolution implied in the convocation of a Council by the College of Cardinals and in the deposition of a Pope on other grounds than heresy[2]. When the Councils were once assembled, the Universities had no doubt called into existence forces which they could not completely control; and it would be too much to say that the leading part in the deliberations of the Councils was always taken by the actual delegates of the existing body of Masters. Still, even at Pisa, the Council which was less directly the work of the University than Constance, we are told that out of 123 Theologians present eighty were French subjects[3]. At Pisa and in the earlier sessions of Constance the moving spirit was Cardinal d'Ailly. This ambitious politician had been to some extent estranged from the Parisian Reformers by the offer of a Cardinal's hat. Their left wing had, indeed, advanced beyond the theological position, not only of d'Ailly, but of Clemangis and Gerson[4]. Still d'Ailly could never have

---

[1] See the Letters to and from the University in Bulæus (esp. T. III. No. 1680), the *Chartul.* and *Correspondence of Thomas Bekynton*, ed. Williams, London, 1872.

[2] It was thought advisable, however, to invent the doctrine that obstinate Schism amounts to Heresy.

[3] So Bulæus, V. 193. The idea that the Cardinals of both obediences might without the consent of the Pope summon a General Council

is said to have been first suggested by the Parisian Theologian, Henry of Hesse (Crévier, III. 76): though this has been disputed.

[4] Peter Plaoul, for instance, in 1406 contended 'Diœcesim Romanam non aliter esse Diœcesim quam Parisiensem et eum qui Episcopatum obtinet Romanum, toti ecclesiæ presidere,' and that the King could summon Councils 'in negotiis etiam fidei.' (Bulæus, V. p. 132.)

played his part as an intermediary between the Curialist
Cardinals and the conciliar party but for his Gallican
education and his early relations with the Gallican leaders.
And in the later sessions it was the actual delegates of the
University who took the lead.   In particular, there was
one critical moment when the University was able to
interpose with decisive effect.   The right of presiding in
a General Council was conceded by moderate Gallicans,
as it is still theoretically conceded by some Anglicans, to
the occupant of St. Peter's Chair: and it was only the
firm attitude of the academical delegates, together with
the strenuous efforts of Sigismund, which prevented the
dissolution of the Council after the flight of John XXIII[1].

But there was one matter in which the University was 'Voting by
able by the mere accidents of its constitution to exercise Nations'
at Constance a more powerful effect on the moulding of by the
the destinies of Europe than it exercised by any express University
utterance of its delegates.   We have already seen how long tion.
the convocation of the Council was prevented by the fear
that the enormous number of petty Italian sees would give
to the Curialist party a representation out of all proportion
to its real strength.   It is difficult to divine by what means
this catastrophe could have been evaded, had not the expedient of imitating the system of voting by Nations, which
had been copied from Paris in almost all her daughter-
Universities, suggested itself to that assembly of graduates.
The division into four Nations, likened by the medieval
imagination to the four streams which watered the Garden
of Eden, seemed by this time so completely a part of the
eternal constitution of things, that it was without difficulty
assumed that the voice of the Universal Church—nay, the
voice of the Holy Spirit Himself—would be heard un-
erringly through an organ of similar constitution.   The
anomalies of the Parisian system of voting were faithfully
reproduced at Constance.   A quarter of a century later,
for instance, the English, or, as it was then called, the

---

[1] Von der Hardt, II. c. 165 *sq.* IV. p. 75 *sq.*

German, Nation at Paris had dwindled to a single Master;
yet he was allowed to elect himself Proctor and to vote on
behalf of his Nation on a level with the representative of
a hundred or more French Masters in a Rectorial election[1].
At Constance, the seven representatives of the English
Nation enjoyed a voting power scarcely less out of proportion to its numerical strength. The adhesion of England
to the Council was secured, as it could hardly have been
secured otherwise in the hey-day of English ascendancy on
the Continent, by an arrangement which thus neutralized
the disadvantage it would otherwise have been under
owing to its distance from the place of meeting.

Revolu-
tionary
character
of the
conciliar
movement.
To sketch even in briefest outline the position of the
Council of Constance (including its continuation at Bâle)
as a turning-point in the history of the Western Church,
would lead us far beyond the limits of the present work.
It will be enough to indicate how these Councils form the
turning-point in the history of the University to whose
activity they in so large a measure owed their existence.
The Council of Constance represents the fleeting triumph
of Gallicanism. By the time that Council met, the Theology of Paris and the Parisian Universities, the Theology
which had grown up in the secular Faculties of Theology,
had become the Theology of the clergy—at least of the
secular clergy—everywhere beyond the immediate en-
tourage of the Papal Court. At Constance the German
ecclesiastics were louder even than the French in their
opposition to Papal abuses and their demands for reform.
That the effort would fail, that the clergy would never
reform themselves, might have been predicted by anyone
acquainted with the state of morals and religion among
the clergy of that age. Had there been any doubt about

---

[1] See the very amusing account
of the incident in the German Proctor's Book for 1439 (Jourdain, No.
772). A German Master coming into
residence found that the only Master
of his Nation who had lately been
resident had gone out of town for
some time. He had left the book,
key, &c. of the Nation with a Priest,
with instructions that they were
not to be surrendered to any one
Master but himself. The new comer's
claim was, however, recognised by
the Faculty of Arts.

the matter before, the hopelessness of expecting serious results from such assemblies became apparent enough when it was discovered that the mere presence of so many reforming ecclesiastics had bred a moral pestilence in the place of their assembly [1]. The conciliar movement was at bottom a merely clerical movement, the outcome of no deep convictions, supported by no widely-spread religious fervour, entirely without root in popular sympathy. Nor were even its leaders (with the exception of Gerson and a very few others) actuated by any passionate zeal for those objects for which Churches are supposed to exist. They were for the most part at best respectable ecclesiastical politicians and pamphleteers, who had little or no regard for the spiritual destitution of the people. D'Ailly for instance held more than fourteen benefices, and Peter Plaoul was accused of scandalous corruption in University Examinations [2]. The real reformers of the age were more harshly treated at Constance in all probability than they would have been treated at Rome or Avignon. The most conspicuous achievement of this vast assemblage of clergymen, beyond the termination of the Schism, was the burning of two heretics, one of whom had come to the place with the Emperor's safe-conduct, which the Council had taught him to violate [3]. The refusal of the Council to condemn Petit shows how little the divines so eager for orthodoxy cared for morality in comparison with the political interests of their order. With too many of its members all this talk about reform meant little more than a desire to protect the pockets of the clergy against Papal extortion. The most respectable feeling by which the mass

[1] The 'meretrices' attracted by the Council were variously estimated at from 450 to 1500. See authorities in Robertson, *Hist. of the Christ. Ch.* (1875) VII. 345.

[2] *Chartul.* T. III. No. 1511. Cf. note, *ib.* p. 340.

[3] Mansi, *Concilia* (1784), XXVII. 799. The much more explicit sanction to perjury in the interests of dogma given by L'Enfant (E. T. I. p. 514) does not appear in the printed Acts, and there seems to be no evidence that it was actually passed. But even the first-mentioned decree assumes that the secular arm is to carry out a temporal sentence in spite of having given a safe-conduct.

of the Fathers were actuated was a professional dislike of irregularities which (as they phrased it) generated scandal against the clergy.

Nor were the Councils much more successful in their merely political action against Papal usurpation. The Council of Constance found itself powerless as soon as it had elected Martin V. The Council of Bâle was defeated by the policy of Eugenius IV. The fact is that a Council could not diplomatise. Already at Constance Martin V succeeded in breaking the opposition against him by creating division in its ranks and entering into a separate Concordat with the German Nation. And the Council of Bâle ceased to be a serious business from the moment (1440) when Charles VII of France adopted the policy of semi-neutrality, recognising the already-made decrees of the Council, but adhering to Eugenius IV against the Conciliar Anti-Pope Felix V [1]. The University of Paris was compelled to acquiesce in his decision, and withdraw its envoys from the Council. From this time forth it became apparent that no great measure of Church reform was to be looked for from the united action of the clergy of Christendom. The real religious reform of the Roman Church had to wait till a schismatical Reformation movement had awakened a religious reaction. For the mere protection of the national Churches against pillage by the Pope and Cardinals, the clergy had to look henceforward to their respective Sovereigns. The Popes more and more degenerated into Italian princes. With the secular Sovereigns of Europe the awe of their spiritual thunders was a thing of the past; but as an Italian prince and as the head of the ecclesiastical order throughout Europe, the Pope could still do much to aid or thwart political designs of rival monarchs. At the same time, within their respective Kingdoms, the control of the secular princes over their own clergy was becoming stricter. Hence diplomatic agreement between King and Pope for the settlement of the ecclesiastical relations of the national Churches with

---

[1] *Ordonnances des roys de France*, XIII. pp. 321, 324: Bulæus, V. p. 449.

the Papacy took the place of independent movements on CHAP. VI,
the part of the clergy. The age of Councils was succeeded § 6.
by an age of Concordats.

This nationalization of the Catholic Church throughout Policy of
Europe—this breaking down, so to speak, of the solidarity Louis XI.
of the ecclesiastical order—almost involved the destruction
of the ecumenical character of the University of Paris.
And the nationalization of the University was completed
by the deliberate policy of Louis XI. Previous Sovereigns
had used every endeavour to protect the foreign students in
their capital even when at war with the countries from which
they came. In 1470, Louis XI, with the morbid suspicion
which was one of his strongest characteristics, compelled
all the subjects of the Duke of Burgundy to take the
oath of obedience to himself as the condition of remaining
in Paris. Some four hundred Burgundian scholars who
declined the oath were allowed to leave the country, but,
with extraordinary meanness, their modest goods were con-
fiscated[2]. Not long afterwards the edict which has been
referred to in another chapter required that no alien should
be elected to the Rectorship or any other University
office[3]. The multiplication of Universities throughout
Europe in the course of the fifteenth century tended in
the same direction—towards the nationalization of Paris as
of all other Universities.

The effect of this nationalization, combined with the The Uni-
growth of centralization and absolutism, was completely versity
to destroy the influence of the University beyond the loses its
borders of the French Church. Within those limits, the tional
Theological Faculty—though, like every other part of the character.
ecclesiastical system, henceforth completely subservient to
the Crown—retained at least as much importance as
formerly. The University itself, indeed, the great scholastic democracy of the Middle Ages, could not live in
the France of Henry IV or Louis XIV. The functions
of its Congregations were more and more transferred to

<hr>

[1] Bulæus, V. 692.   [2] Bulæus, V. 716.

what was called the Tribunal of the University—a Court composed of the Rector, the four Proctors, and the three Deans. Its constitution thus became practically almost as oligarchic as that of Oxford under the Laudian Hebdomadal Board. More completely even than at Oxford the University passed into an aggregate of Colleges; and the Colleges of Artists sank, as the Colleges of Oxford with their perpetual Fellowships never could sink, into mere boarding-schools for boys. Even as schools, they were eclipsed in scholastic fame and in social estimation by the schools of the Jesuits. But the Theological Faculty—now centred in the restored College of the Sorbonne—continued for the French Church to give oracles which often emboldened King and people to defy the thunders of the Vatican. 'The Sorbonne' was a less dangerous, more manageable, and even more venerable authority to pit against the autocracy of Rome, than the resolutions of prelates too feudal and of Councils too popular to find favour in the eyes of absolutist monarchs.

The University becomes the home of Gallicanism.

We have seen how after the break-up of the Council of Bâle a European concert on the great Roman question became impossible. The attitude of the French Kings for a time wavered, like that of other princes, with the political exigencies of the moment. The Pragmatic Sanction of 1438, with the maintenance of which the newly developed Gallicanism became practically identified, was alternately withdrawn and reinforced. But in the main the tendency of political requirements outside France was in the direction of alliance with the Vatican: and as a consequence the tendency of Catholicism outside France was to become more and more completely Roman or Ultramontane[1]. In France, equally from political considerations, the tendency was in favour of resistance to Papal encroachments. It was in the main political causes that determined this bifurcation of the

---

[1] Thus at Vienna, graduates were required to swear: 'Item abnego et reuoco illas propositiones indistincte positas, videlicet quod concilium est supra papam; item quod papa non potest reuocare per concilium generale conclusum' (Kink, I. Pt. ii. p. 26).

theological tendencies of Europe. At the end of the fifteenth
century the Theology of the secular clergy throughout
northern Europe was almost everywhere as anti-Roman
as that of France. But the prestige of the University and
its Theological Faculty enormously facilitated the opposition of the French Kings to Roman encroachments. The
Sorbonne became the home of a distinctively national
School of Theology. The Gallicanism of earlier ages had,
indeed, to undergo a change; the older ecclesiastical
liberties—the free elections to Bishoprics and Abbacies,
the frequent Councils and Synods, and the right of free
debate in them—were as offensive to the Kings of the
sixteenth and seventeenth centuries as Papal interference.
The Gallicanism which the great name of Paris and the
cherished traditions of the Gerson epoch still kept alive
was an erastianised Gallicanism. But in the preservation
of this Gallicanism the most potent spiritual force was 'the
Sorbonne,' as the most potent material instrument was its
younger, but now more powerful sister, the Parlement of
Paris[1].

One of the last occasions on which we find the University
still standing forth, at least in the imagination of men, as
the theological oracle of Europe, was in the course of
Luther's controversy with the Papal Legate. Luther
pitted the authority of Paris against Rome[2]; and at one
time he seems to have entertained hopes of finding support
for the Reformation movement in the old adversary of
Benedict XIII and John XXIII. But of this there was
never any real probability. The very virtues of the
University, the very services which she had performed

---

[1] As an illustration of the growth
of Gallicanism, see Bulæus, V. p. 807,
where the University (in 1491) resolves, in accordance with the decision of the Faculties of Theology
and Canon Law, that an excommunication threatened by the Pope should
not be feared or obeyed. In 1502
the resolution was repeated, when

Alexander VI had actually excommunicated the French Clergy for
refusing a Tenth. (D'Argentré, T. I.
ii. 346.)

[2] On account of its recent appeal
in 1517 against the Pope's condemnation of the Pragmatic Sanction
to a General Council. (Bulæus, VI.
p. 88.)

for the French Church, tended to check the progress of the Reformation in France. While throughout Southern Europe theological education and theological study were practically abandoned to the Mendicant Orders, the theological Schools of Paris kept alive some knowledge of the Theology and discipline of earlier ages, while her Colleges secured theological training for large numbers of the higher clergy, a class which in Italy, for instance, was mainly given up to the demoralising education of the Canonist. The academic conflicts with the Mendicants and their incessant cabals against the rights of the secular clergy filled the Parisian scholar with an instinctive dislike for a Friar, and consequently with a traditional suspicion of the great source of Mendicant immunities.

Popularity of the University.

Paris was proud of her University. We have seen with what effect upon occasion that curious device, the cessation of sermons, was employed as a lever to move public opinion. From the eagerness sometimes exhibited by a parish struck with this peculiar interdict to be readmitted to the favour of the University [1], it would seem as if the greater frequency of sermons, their superior quality, and the fact that they were not all delivered by Mendicants— all three advantages secured by the presence of the University—had done something to diminish in Paris the popular hatred of the clergy at the time so prevalent in the great towns, notably in London, and to indoctrinate minds elsewhere deprived altogether of spiritual nutriment with the Theology of which the University was the accredited guardian. It is sometimes said that the ineradicable Catholicism of Paris was the decisive weight which turned the scale against the Reformation in France. At all events the

---

[1] Bulæus, V. 598. The cessation usually extended to the whole city : but on this occasion it was limited to the parishes in which certain outrages on scholars had been perpetrated. The representatives of these parishes were twice refused audience, but on the third application they were admitted and the cessation relaxed on condition that a tablet with a sculptured or pictorial representation of the penance ('unum epitaphium imaginibus et scriptura descriptum') should be set up in one of the parishes.

national feeling, which was elsewhere such a powerful ally of the Reformation movement, was in France satisfied with resolutely maintaining the attitude which the University had taken up at Constance and at Bâle, and nowhere did the support of the University tend to identify itself with patriotism so closely as in Paris itself. Of course, many of the circumstances just enumerated might have told in the opposite direction, had there arisen in the University itself a strong party in sympathy with the Reform movement outside. For the absence of such a movement no reason perhaps can be given but the non-appearance of the men to lead it. However the fact be accounted for, the University of Paris never did see within its College walls the growth of a really religious movement at all comparable to the Wycliffite movement at Oxford, to the movement of which Hus was the product rather than the author at Prague, or even to the quieter religious revival inaugurated in the sixteenth century by men like our Oxford Tyndale and the Cambridge Reformers. The complete isolation of the intellectual life of Paris from contact with the stronger currents of popular religious feeling outside is one of the strangest facts of her history [1].

---

[1] The University's attitude during the Schism might have been dealt with in more detail had the third volume of Denifle and Chatelain's *Chartularium* (with an *Auctarium*) reached me before these sheets were in pages. As it is, I have only been able to add a few references. For the fluctuations of the English Nation (determined chiefly by changes in the proportion of Urbanist Germans to Clementine Scotsmen) see *Chartul. Auctarium*, I. lxv. *sq.* The difficult position in which the Schism placed the Germans at Paris contributed to the growth of Universities in Germany.

ADDITIONAL NOTES.

[These Notes are chiefly based on documents in the third volume of the *Chartularium Universitatis Parisiensis*, which appeared after the sheets to which they relate had gone to press.]

p. 297. My argument as to *Capitale* might be strengthened by the Provost's oath of 1364-6: 'Comme ils aient de privilege royal que votre justice pour nul forfait d'escolier ne mecte main es biens de l'escolier, mes seulement soient arrestés et gardés par la justice de l'eglise.' (*Chartul.* T. III. No. 1324.)

p. 321. In note 3, add to the statement about the English Nation: 'In the middle of the fourteenth century we hear also of a "Provincia Sueciae et Daciae"; and the German Nation appears undivided under a "Provisor."'—*Chartul. Auctarium*, I. pp. xviii, xix, &c.

p. 327. In note 3, for 'continued sealless' read 'long continued sealless.' The Faculty had a seal by 1359. *Chartul.* T. III. No. 1246.

p. 333. Note 2. Some documents relating to the suit between the Chapter and the University in 1384 are now printed in *Chartul.* T. III. (Nos. 1486-1489). It should have been said that the permission conceded by Clement VII to retain Regency by lecturing in the cloister of Notre Dame instead of the 'Clo Brunel' was limited to one Canon who must be a Doctor.

p. 395. A mass of pleadings, depositions of witnesses, &c. in the suit alluded to in note 3, are now printed in *Chartul.* T. III. Nos. 1504-1522. It is alleged on behalf of the University that the Chancellor took money-bribes of all amounts up to 100 *franci aurei* and presents of silver cups, 'jocalia,' furred garments, knives, fowls, wine, dinners, and the like. On one occasion certain nobles had positively been refused the License because they had not sent the Chancellor 'vestes cum furraturis more nobilium.' On another when the candidate had already paid eight francs, the Chancellor observing that one remained in his purse, exclaimed 'adhuc illum! adhuc illum!' Other candidates had been compelled to give pledges which were to be redeemed after License—an obligation which in one case was escaped by an 'egregious beating' inflicted on the Sub-Chancellor. The evidence of the witnesses is largely hearsay; but the Chancellor himself pleads that by custom he was entitled to a 'denarius aureus' from every Decretist, two from each M.D., and ten from each Theologian, while the Artists gave presents to his 'famuli.' He represents that these sums were given 'libera et spontanea voluntate, sine exaccione quacumque,' but from the admissions of his own witnesses it is clear that degrees were not to be had without payment (in spite of the Papal prohibition), the only dispute being as to the amount of the bribe and as to the degree of compulsion exercised. There appear to have been various opinions as to the Chancellor's power to license without the assent of the Masters: one witness held that he was bound to accept the 'depositions' as to 'scientia,' but might use his own judgment as to 'mores.' It is clear that the suit was promoted by the Faculty of Arts—largely at the instigation of d'Ailly, who (as Denifle suggests, wanted the Chancellorship himself) in consequence of a renewal of the dispute with the Rector for precedence at the Inception-banquet, and that the Chancellor's irregularities might otherwise have been winked at. Still, though there may have been exaggeration, the case against the Chancellor is a fairly strong one. The matter was terminated by the resignation of the then Chancellor, John Blanchart, at Rome—no doubt by some arrangement satisfactory both to the Holy See and himself (1386). I have perhaps exaggerated the unimportance of the Chancellor at this period; but it is clear from the admission of Blanchart's own witnesses that he was attempting to revive prerogatives which had long lain comparatively dormant. The attempt to demand certain oaths objected to by the University (i. e. probably of obedience to the Chancellor or respect for his rights) and to extort fees or promises was renewed by the next Chancellor, Jean de Guignecourt, in 1389. *Ib.* Nos. 1550-1555, but we hear no more of interference with the Examiners.

p. 398. Even after the Bull of 1358 we find the Faculty of Theology still contending for the supremacy of their Dean. See the newly published document in *Chartul.* T. III. No. 1246. Among other interesting particulars, it shows that the Rector could be, and had on one occasion been removed by the University.

p. 399. From *Chartul.* T. III. No. 1246 (A.D. 1359) it appears that the goods of a scholar were then distributed ' ab episcopo Parisiensi et per alium ab ipsa Universitate deputatum . . . ipso rectore non requisito.'

p. 414. The individual Doctors of the Superior Faculties had Bedels of their own, as at Bologna. *Chartul.* T. III. No. 1702.

p. 432. Much light is thrown upon the teaching arrangements of the Decretists by the pleadings in an action brought in the Parlement by Aymé Dubrueil against the Faculty in 1386. (*Chartul.* T. III. Nos. 1528–1531.) Dubrueil was a Doctor but attempted to read as a Bachelor at 'matins' and also as a Doctor at prime. The rights of Regency had not yet been restricted to a close corporation, but it appears that the Doctors lectured only on the Decretum, and that the lecture was a mere form lasting only a quarter of an hour. One of the points urged by the Faculty against the appellant was that he lectured by candle-light, whereas 'le lecteur du matin doit lire senz chandelle tout par cuer, mesmement en yver, jusques à heure que on puet veoir en son livre.' (The object of this was apparently to enforce an *ex tempore* lecture. Cf. *ib.* p. 642.) It is incidentally mentioned that he had a hundred scholars, and that his lectures (as a Bachelor) brought him in from 200 to 250 francs. The Faculty refused to regard him as a Regent, partly because he had not begun at the right time and partly because he was also lecturing as a Bachelor, and its conduct was upheld by the Court. In 1388, Dubrueil renewed his attempt to lecture, and this time the Faculty refused to recognize him even as a Bachelor. (*Ib.* No. 1546.) His action again failed. It appears that he now had more than 300 scholars, from each of whom he would, but for the action of the Faculty, have received at least a franc.

p. 438. In 1387 the University had petitioned the Pope for a relaxation of Urban IV's Statute requiring Artists to sit on the ground, alleging that ' plures tam nobiles quam alii religiosi et honesti viri ex verecundia moti, quia sedere habent ad terram, dimittunt audire propter defectum scannorum et bancarum, qui nondum sunt sufficienter fundati ut proficiant in aliis facultatibus, quod redundavit hactenus et redundat in prejudicium multorum et totius Universitatis.' (*Chartul.* T. III. No. 1537.)

p. 450. At the second Examination (*in propriis*) at Ste Geneviève, each individual was examined by four Examiners appointed by and from his own Nation. *Chartul.* T. III. No. 1468. Cf. *Auctarium*, I. p. xxxi.

p. 460. There are many allusions to a practice of passing a Candidate conditionally on his subsequently hearing certain lectures. The practice is forbidden at Aix: 'Quod Baccalareus non approbetur cum cauda.' (Fournier, III. No. 1582.)

p. 464. From a document of 1386, printed in *Chartul.* III. (No. 1528), it appears that the lectures of the Doctors in Theology were always on the Bible.

p. 471, note 1. Still earlier at Nantes, in 1461, the Vespers have become a comic entertainment: 'Et teneat omnino ne aliquid turpe vel quod in infamiam possit vergere de ipso vesperisando dicat, sed pro risu modico et alleviatione audientium dicere possint aliqua de eo prosa levia et sine scandalo cujuscumque risu digna.' (Fournier, III. No. 1595.)

p. 473. Add to note 1: 'This is proved by *Chartul.* T. III. No. 1520.'

p. 477. A student of Nantes gives us the rationale of the Long Vacation: 'Cum opportunitas temporis in omnibus sit querenda, et post collationem messium ceterorumque victualium sit ad studium exercendum tempus congruum.' (Fournier, III. No. 1595.)

p. 487. The facts given on p. 486, note 5, show that the College of S. Nicholas in the Louvre must have been founded before 1217.

END OF VOL. I.

Date Due

AUG 2 8 1961		
DEPARTMENT		
DEC 1 1 '61		
NO 20'65		
JA 7'64		
JAN 7 1964 CARREL		
AP 2		
DEPT. FEB 7 1967		
AP 14 '67		
MY 12'67		
MY 23'67		
My 30		
MR 4 '70		
JUN 0 2 1996		
🄶🄱	PRINTED IN U. S. A.	

J. S. WESBY & SONS
JAN 1961
Worcester